# The Reluctant Welfare State

## Other Titles of Related Interest in Social Welfare

Marion L. Beaver/Don Miller: *Clinical Social Work,* Second Edition

Ira Colby: *Social Welfare Policy: Perspectives, Patterns, and Insights*

Beulah R. Compton/Burt Galaway: *Social Work Processes,* Fourth Edition

Donald Critchlow/Ellis Hawley: *Poverty and Public Policy in Modern America*

Danya Glaser/Stephen Frosh: *Child Sexual Abuse*

Dean H. Hepworth/Jo Ann Larsen: *Direct Social Work Practice: Theory and Skills,* Fourth Edition

Bruce S. Jansson: *Social Welfare Policy: From Theory to Practice*

Christine Marlow: *Research Methods for Generalist Social Work*

Paula Nurius/Walter Hudson: *Practice, Evaluation and Computers: A Practical Guide for Today and Beyond*

Albert R. Roberts: *Crisis Intervention Handbook: Assessment, Treatment, and Research*

Albert R. Roberts: *Juvenile Justice: Policies, Programs, and Services*

Allen Rubin/Earl Babbie: *Research Methods for Social Work,* Second Edition

Myron E. Weiner: *Human Services Management,* Second Edition

Charles Zastrow: *The Practice of Social Work,* Fourth Edition

SECOND EDITION

# The Reluctant Welfare State

## A History of American Social Welfare Policies

**BRUCE S. JANSSON**
*University of Southern California*

**BROOKS/COLE PUBLISHING COMPANY**
*Pacific Grove, California*

Brooks/Cole Publishing Company
A Division of Wadsworth, Inc.

© 1993 by Wadsworth, Inc. All rights reserved. No part of this book may be
reproduced, stored in a retrieval system, or transcribed, in any form or by
any means, without the prior written permission of the publisher, Brooks/
Cole Publishing Company, Pacific Grove, California 93950 a division of
Wadsworth, Inc.

Printed in the United States of America

1 2 3 4 5 6 7 8 9 10 — 97 96 95 94 93

*Library of Congress Cataloging in Publication Data*

Jansson, Bruce S.
    The reluctant welfare state : a history of American social welfare
policies / Bruce S. Jansson. — 2nd ed.
        p.·   cm.
    Includes bibliographical references and index.
    ISBN (invalid) 0-534-16388-6
    1. United States — Social policy.   2. United States — Social
conditions.   3. Public welfare — United States — History.   I. Title.
HN57. J25   1993
361.6′1′0973 — dc20                                                    92-25567

ISBN: 0-534-16388-6

Senior Editor: Peggy Adams
Editorial Assistant: Dorothy Zinky
Production Editor: Angela Mann
Managing Designer: Carolyn Deacy
Print Buyer: Barbara Britton
Permissions Editor: Peggy Meehan
Copy Editor: Robert Fiske
Designer: Adrian Bosworth
Cover Designer: Carolyn Deacy
Cover Photograph: Hebrew Orphan Asylum, Amsterdam Ave, New York
                (Bettmann Archive)
Compositor: T·H Typecast
Printer: R. R. Donnelley, Crawfordsville

TO BETTY ANN

# Contents

CHAPTER 5    **Lost Opportunities: The Frontier, The Civil War, and Industrialization    85**

**CHAPTER 8**  **Institutionalizing The New Deal    169**

CHAPTER 9  **The Era of Federal Social Services in the New Frontier and Great Society  200**

# Preface

I made numerous changes in this new second edition. Many of them are relatively small changes of fact and interpretation, but others are major revisions that build upon and accentuate distinctive characteristics of the first edition.

I chose to give "multicultural diversity" even more emphasis in this edition. I greatly expanded materials in virtually every chapter on women, African Americans, Latinos, Asian Americans, gays and lesbians, Native Americans, children, aging persons, and the "differently abled." I added a specific section to each chapter, from the medieval period onward, that focuses on these "outgroups," a term that I use throughout the book to refer to groups that have encountered significant prejudice from the dominant society. I emphasize patterns of prejudice as expressed in social policies of different eras, as well as the determined efforts of leaders of these outgroups, and their allies, to secure policy reforms.

While it was implicit in the first edition, I made the political-economic perspective explicit in this edition. My recent work in many presidential libraries on research that examines factors that have diminished funding for certain kinds of programs in the American welfare state during the past four decades made me even more aware of the political and economic context of the American welfare state. A political-economic framework that provides an overview of policy development is introduced in the first chapter—and used at numerous points in succeeding chapters to analyze cultural, political, economic, and social factors that shaped the American response (or nonresponse) to social problems. This political-economic perspective encourages readers to place social welfare policies in a broader and societal context and strongly suggests that improvements in the American welfare state must be accomplished through political activism. I enlarged an integrative chapter (chapter 12) that pulls together materials from the book into a comprehensive discussion of reasons why the American welfare state is a "reluctant" one.

A distinguishing feature of the first edition was its inclusion of considerable materials on the decades extending from the New Deal to the present. I continued this emphasis by including considerable information about the development of policy during the Presidency of George Bush, including the experiences of outgroups, legal decisions, the Los

Angeles riots, and the waning of the Cold War. I also expanded my discussion of the 1950s and the Reagan period. I added materials about national budget priorities, particularly in the period from 1946 onward by noting implications of Cold War spending *and* relatively low rates of federal taxes (by international standards) for social spending.

This history does not pretend to provide a comprehensive discussion of legal rulings, but I have expanded my discussion of the Warren, Burger, and Rehnquist Courts, because the decisions of these courts profoundly shaped contemporary social welfare policy.

The first edition hardly discussed the historical evolution of the social work profession. I remedied this defect in this second edition by including considerable materials about the profession in the progressive era, the New Deal, the Great Society, and the contemporary period.

Some readers will emerge from this book believing that some specific topic was slighted or some source not consulted. I can only hope that such persons realize that any book that covers more than four centuries of developments provides only a window onto a broader landscape. I will consider this book a resounding success if I have written about policies during this time span in a way that encourages some readers to see the subject in a new light, underscores the truth of the adage "two steps forward and one step back," and prompts some people to be more emboldened to enter the political fray in the contemporary period.

Peggy Adams, Senior Editor at Wadsworth Publishing Company, first suggested revising this book. My interactions with my students, as well as my colleagues, prompted me to make "diversity" a central theme of this new edition. I received extended analyses of the first edition from Professor Charles Atherton and from Professor Richard Steinman that helped me correct some errors or omissions in the book. Reviewers of the book, who included Professors Jim Flanagan, Providence College, Rhode Island; David Humphers, California State University, Sacramento; John Morrison, Aurora University, Illinois; Ann Nicols-Casebolt, Arizona State University; and Thomas D. Watts, University of Texas at Arlington, provided many helpful suggestions. Angela Mann, Production Editor at Wadsworth, skillfully shepherded the book through production. Robert Fiske made many good editing suggestions. Staff at the Library of Congress and the Anthropology Division of the Smithsonian Institution helped me navigate their photographic collections. All errors of omission or commission rest on my shoulders alone.

Betty Ann, as usual, provided a supportive presence as I labored on this revision.

# CHAPTER 1

# The Evolution of American Social Policy in a Multicultural Context

Like other societies, America has experienced social problems from the origins of the nation to the present. Released indentured servants in the colonial period often experienced poverty as they tried to eke out an existence on the American frontier. Poor immigrants encountered poverty, discrimination, and disease in the rough American cities of the nineteenth and early twentieth centuries. Native Americans, African Americans, and Spanish-speaking persons encountered hostility from the broader society as they endeavored to improve their economic conditions or merely to retain their traditional lands and customs. Homeless persons in the twentieth century had their counterparts in the nineteenth century, who were commonly called vagabonds. The victims of AIDS in the 1980s and 1990s, who encountered unfavorable health and social policies that compounded their desperate medical condition, had predecessors in various dread diseases of prior eras, such as the victims of malaria, typhoid fever, cholera, and syphilis.

Whether in prior eras or contemporary times, the victims of social problems depended in considerable measure not only on their personal and familial tenacity and resources but also on the policies of communities (including public and nonpublic agencies), local governments, state governments, and the federal government. If the victims were (and are) fortunate, these policies, singly and in tandem, provided ameliorative assistance. Were they not so fortunate, they received no or scant assistance—or even were subjected to policies that worsened their plight.

This is a book about social problems and the social policies that Americans constructed in different eras to deal with them. It is also a book that discusses specific populations within the broader population who experienced particular hardship in American society, that is, whose members experienced a disproportionate number of social problems. These groups variously included African Americans, women, Native Americans, Latinos, gays and lesbians, persons with chronic physical disabilities, mentally ill persons, and persons who have been accused of violating laws. Moreover, we often discuss problems of persons in the lower economic strata of society who have often experienced a disproportionate burden of social problems.

But this book is not *only* about the social problems of specific subgroups within the larger population since many social problems and needs afflict most Americans at one or another time in their life. In the absence of national health insurance, for example, middle-class and white Americans may experience catastrophic illnesses that can bankrupt them. Moreover, the nation itself has vested interests in maintaining the health, literacy, and well-being of its people—not merely for moral reasons but to be able to compete in the global economy of the twenty-first century.

 ## A RELUCTANT WELFARE STATE

Profound ambivalence toward the victims of social problems has existed in American society since the colonial period. On one hand, Americans have often exhibited compassion toward hungry, destitute, ill, and transient Americans, as illustrated by a host of ameliorative public policies as well as a rich tradition of private philanthropy. But they have also demonstrated a callous disregard for persons who suffered deprivation, as demonstrated by the late development of federal programs, oppressive treatment of racial and other groups, and coupling of assistance with punitive and demeaning regulations. The term *reluctant welfare state* expresses this paradox of punitiveness and generosity.

In the nineteenth century, the nation developed a set of poorhouses, mental and children's institutions, and many sectarian agencies, but these policies were grievously insufficient to deal with the serious economic and social problems of immigrants, factory workers, displaced Native Americans and Spanish-speaking persons, and urban residents. A federal welfare state was fashioned belatedly in the twentieth century during the New Deal to provide assistance to many persons, but it was a limited and harsh welfare state compared to many welfare states in Western Europe. However benevolent or punitive the American social policy response was, by 1993 the total budget expenditures had reached approximately $500 billion. Even most conservatives now agree that the welfare state has become a permanent feature of American society, particularly after the failure of the Reagan administration to achieve many of its budget-cutting objectives. The social policies that have been enacted were often associated with considerable political controversy and conflict between people who opposed reform, sought relatively incremental reforms, and sought sweeping or radical reforms. Some people (we often label them conservatives today) opposed the development of policy initiatives to address the social needs of citizens in specific eras, whether the use of federal funds to build mental institutions in the 1840s, the development of civil rights legislation in the 1960s, or the development of major initiatives to help homeless people in the 1990s. A long succession of social reformers (today, we often label persons who seek incremental reforms liberals), including Dorothea Dix, Jane Addams, Franklin Roosevelt, and Lyndon Johnson, obtained enactment of an array of policy reforms despite the concerted opposition of conservatives and many interest groups. Nor should the efforts of American radicals—persons who seek drastic expansion of social welfare roles of government—be ignored even if they have usually possessed only marginal power in American society. Union organizers, socialists, and communists have periodically pressured liberals and conservatives to consider major expansions of the welfare state, just as various social movements have sought reforms for specific causes.

In light of its importance and size, surprisingly few Americans have studied the emergence of this welfare state and the various political, economic, cultural, and social forces that have shaped it. Traditional history courses and texts emphasize high-level diplomatic, international, and political matters. Social historians, though expanding historical study to include social customs and specific social problems, have not usually analyzed how Americans developed social policy responses to such social problems as hunger, poverty, homelessness, and mental illness. Many courses in social welfare policy in schools of social work emphasize description of laws and programs rather than historical analyses of the emergence of the welfare state, and some schools have withdrawn social welfare history from their curricula altogether.

Yet an understanding of history is crucial to the ongoing debate over moral and policy issues that are posed by the welfare state. Should the United States, like many European nations, devote more resources to social programs? Which kinds of social problems merit public expenditures, and which do not? Which claimants "deserve" social assistance, and which do not? Should social spending receive greater or less priority than defense spending? What policy roles should be granted to the federal government in social welfare?

Many Americans need to be conversant with the evolution of American social welfare policies and associated issues. Voters must decide whether to support politicians who seek drastic cuts in social spending or those who want to increase the size and scope of the welfare state. Taxpayers must decide whether they favor policies to increase or decrease levels of taxation—a decision that influences the resources available for social spending. Members of many professions who deliver to consumers the services and resources of the welfare state must grapple with various policy issues in their daily work and in their professional associations. Social workers, for example, must decide how to implement specific policies in their work settings, whether to contest or change existing policies, and whether to define their professional mission to include advocacy for the needs of powerless populations such as homeless persons.

## INSTRUMENTS OF PUBLIC POLICY

In its broadest social sense, social welfare policy represents a collective strategy to address social problems. Collective strategy is fashioned by laws, rules, regulations, and budgets of government, that is, enactments that affect or bind the actions of citizens, government officials, professions, and the staff of social agencies. To understand how Americans have addressed social problems in the past, various social welfare policy responses need to be identified.

The *constitutions* of American governments are important policy documents because they define the social policy powers of government. By not enumerating specific social welfare functions of the federal government, for example, the federal Constitution retarded the development of social welfare policies since many people believed that it left social welfare functions to state and local governments.

Some social welfare strategies involve *public policies*, laws enacted in local, state, or federal legislatures. The Chinese Exclusion Act of 1882, the Social Security Act of 1935, the Adoption Assistance and Child Welfare Act of 1980, and the Americans with Disabilities Act of 1991 are examples of public laws, as are state and local laws that established poorhouses and mental institutions in the nineteenth century.

*Court decisions* play important roles in American social policy. By overruling, upholding, and interpreting statutes of legislatures, courts establish policies that significantly influence the

American response to social needs. For example, in the 1980s, the courts required the Reagan administration to award disability benefits to many disabled persons even though many administration officials opposed this policy.

*Budget and spending programs* are a kind of policy as well since it is difficult for society to respond to specific social problems if resources are not allocated to social programs and institutions. In understanding the response of Americans to social needs, for example, it is important to know that Americans chose not to expend a major share of their gross national product on social spending prior to the 1930s but greatly increased levels of spending in the Great Depression and succeeding decades. Despite the large increases in spending on social programs in the 1960s, 1970s, and (even) 1980s, however, the nation chose to devote a significant portion of its federal budget to military spending during the cold war as well as to make successive tax cuts — policies that much reduced the spending on an array of social programs.

*Stated or implied objectives* also constitute a form of policy. Many pieces of social legislation, for example, contain preambles as well as titles that suggest broad purposes or goals. Thus, the Family Support Act of 1988 emphasized the provision of services and training to poor Americans (as the title suggests) rather than the provision of economic resources or food. Public pronouncements of presidents and other politicians often suggest their broad strategies for addressing social needs, as can be illustrated by comparing state of the union messages of relatively liberal presidents to those of conservative presidents.

*Rules, procedures, and regulations* define the way policies are to be implemented. Legislation often prescribes, for example, the rules or procedures to be used by agency staff in determining the eligibility for specific programs. Courts often prescribe safeguards that the staff of social agencies must employ to safeguard the rights of clients, patients, and consumers — as illustrated by protections that are afforded people involuntar-ily committed to mental institutions. Government agencies issue administrative regulations to guide the implementation of policies.

The various policies that we have discussed to this point are enunciated by various levels of governments and courts, as well as by nongovernmental entities like social agencies. Every social agency develops policies of its own that are not dictated to it by outside funders or legislation but that supplement these external sources of policy. Staff within an agency determine, for example, their distinctive approaches to providing services. Social welfare historians try to determine how poorhouses and mental institutions shaped their eligibility policies in the nineteenth century. In similar fashion, contemporary policy analysts gauge how different social agencies implement specific policies — variations of which are caused in part by the way they interpret the policies of the agencies that fund them. Some policies of agencies are determined without reference to external funders; one agency may decide, for example, to hire a heterogeneous staff that speaks an array of languages, whereas another may employ only English-speaking staff.

When identifying the policy responses of American society to specific social problems, the discerning analyst is as interested in neglected options and inactivity as in identifying policies that were formally selected. Americans have often chosen to take no action or to ignore serious social problems in their midst. Indeed, the absence of major social spending prior to the New Deal suggests that Americans chose not to address major social problems far more often than they decided to develop social interventions. Furthermore, Americans have often been reluctant to use certain kinds of strategies to address such social problems as unemployment and poverty. Except for the decades of the 1930s and the 1970s, Americans have refrained from developing large public works or public employment programs, even when rates of unemployment have exceeded 10 percent during recessions (or 20 percent for members of racial minorities or 40 percent for minority teenagers).

## THE POLITICAL ECONOMY OF SOCIAL WELFARE POLICY·

We use the term *political economy* to describe an approach to studying social welfare history. Our interest lies not merely in describing those social policies that were selected by Americans in specific eras but in analyzing *why* Americans chose certain policies while ignoring other policies. We cannot determine why certain policies were selected, however, without broadening our inquiry to include those cultural, political, economic, and other contextual factors that shaped the actions and choices of Americans in specific eras. If attention were devoted only to the enumeration of various kinds of policies that have been chosen by Americans, social welfare history would be a rather boring enterprise. Why did Americans develop their welfare state so belatedly, as compared with many European societies? Why are Americans willing to tolerate higher rates of economic inequality, unemployment, and poverty than many Europeans are? Why do Americans often emphasize opportunity-enhancing policies, like education, while deemphasizing policies that redistribute resources from affluent to impoverished persons?

As illustrated in Figure 1.1, a systems framework that identifies an array of contextual factors can facilitate our ability to understand the causes of social policies. Contextual factors,

which include various cultural, political, and economic ones, serve to guide the actions and choices of decision makers, such as legislators, agency officials, and justices of various courts. Their actions and choices in decision-making arenas lead, in turn, to the articulation of an array of policies, such as legislation, budgets, agency policies, and court rulings. These policies influence the work of the staff of social agencies who must implement them in their work. And they have important consequences for those persons who experience various kinds of social problems and needs. (As discussed later, we often evaluate specific policies to determine their relative merit.)

The analysis of the causes of policies is not an easy task, but considerable emphasis must be given to the combined influence of cultural factors, political factors, economic factors, institutional factors, and traditions. In each of the succeeding chapters, which discuss various eras in the evolution of social welfare policies, we discuss these factors.

1. *Cultural factors* include the way Americans perceived the importance and causes of specific social problems, the extent they believed that victims of problems caused

**FIGURE 1.1** • *A systems approach to policy making*

| CONTEXTUAL FACTORS | PROCESSES OF DECISION MAKING | POLICY CHOICES | EFFECTS AND OUTCOMES |
|---|---|---|---|
| Cultural factors | Deliberations in courts | Court rulings | Extent that specific policies help victims of special social problems |
| Political factors → | Deliberations in | → Specific legislation | → |
| Economic factors → | boards and staff of social agencies | → Agency policies | Ethical evaluations |
| Institutional factors | | Budget priorities | |
| Social factors → | Deliberations in legislatures | → Administrative regulations | → |
| Traditions | | | |

their own demise, and the extent they thought that society has an obligation to assist victims with ameliorative programs. We discuss how perceptions of various subgroups within the population, such as women and racial minorities, shaped the way Americans developed their social policies.

2. *Political factors* include the extent specific interests are organized and possess resources to pressure legislators to promote their interests; the extent victims of social problems are organized; and the preferences of incumbent presidents, governors, and other highly placed officials.

3. *Economic factors* include the extent the government possesses resources, such as tax revenues, to fund social programs; the extent corporations provide social benefits to employees; and the budgetary priorities of governments.

4. *Institutional factors* include the extent governments possess administrative capabilities to develop and implement social programs and the balance between federal, state, and local jurisdictions in social welfare.

5. *Social factors* include wars, migrations of populations, demographic changes, industrialization, global economic competition, and urbanization, that is, changes in the social environment that shape the selection of policies.

6. *Traditions* of society, such as those social policies that exist at any point in time, influence the future course of policy development. Since America lacked a strong central government until well into the 1930s, for example, the nation was less likely than European nations to develop national programs until relatively late in its history.

 ## EVALUATING SOCIAL POLICIES IN THE PAST AND THE PRESENT

When examining the policies of prior eras, we ask whether a specific policy choice was well or ill advised given the nature of social problems of that era. Could officials have chosen alternative policies? Did practical resource and technical realities preclude a different policy response?

When asking these kinds of questions, we sometimes want to know if a specific policy *effectively* addressed a social problem of that era. We argue in Chapter 4, for example, that the use of poorhouses (sometimes called workhouses) to incarcerate impoverished persons probably had little or no effect in addressing their basic problem of lack of employment, education, or other abilities. Indeed, the use of a deterrent and punitive strategy probably made many people disinclined to seek assistance from

local governments even when such avoidance endangered their well-being. Conversely, the Food Stamps Program that was enacted in the 1960s and greatly expanded in succeeding decades helped millions of Americans improve their diets, thus helping many of them avert malnutrition.

In other cases, we make *value-based*, moral evaluations of specific policies. The case of single heads of households illustrates moral reasoning in social welfare history. Considerable research during the past several decades suggests that many women who are single heads of household possess scant formal education or job skills and that minimum-wage employment, often their best option, fails to provide resources to allow them and their families to survive.

Rather than addressing the problem directly by giving these women resources, training, and services until they can obtain sufficient wages to support their families, Americans have often given them resources that condemn them to poverty while imposing on them deterrent and harsh policies that do not address their employment, training, and service needs.

Five moral issues frequently recur in policy deliberations, whether in prior eras or today (see Table 1.1).

When assessing the morality of providing social welfare services (issue 1 from Table 1.1), Americans decide whether specific or potential claimants deserve access to social programs; such terms as *deserving* and *undeserving* are used by protagonists in this controversy. Furthermore, Americans decide what conditions are attached to the receipt of social benefits or services when discussing the morality of services; thus, someone may favor granting assistance but only if recipients accept a work test, a means test, frequent reinvestigations of their needs, or extremely low payments.

Policy debates about the size and scope of the American welfare state reflect alternative positions regarding the nature of social obligation (issue 2). When social reformers have demanded that government develop social policies to help victims of social and economic forces, they have usually encountered fierce opposition from persons and groups insisting that the policies are not needed or that nongovernmental philanthropy is better suited. In some cases, opponents have argued that specific social problems fall under the purview of local governments rather than the federal government. Most fundamental, debates about social obligation in contemporary society concern national priorities: What should be the size of domestic spending? What sums should be spent on social welfare programs when contrasted with defense spending? Which kinds of social programs should receive the most resources?

A variety of interventions can be chosen to

**TABLE 1.1** • *Five moral issues in social welfare policy*

1. Morality of Social Services—Who should receive services and on what terms?
2. Nature of Social Obligation—For what needs and problems is society responsible, and which should receive priority?
3. Preferred Interventions—What kinds of policy remedies should be chosen to address specific social problems?
4. Compensatory Strategies—Should society give preferential assistance to members of specific groups that lag behind the rest of the population in economic or other conditions?
5. Magnitude of Federal Policy Roles—What policy powers should federal authorities possess, and what should be the magnitude of federal social spending?

address specific social problems (issue 3). Since social reformers have often contended that unemployment and poverty are caused by economic and social forces such as recessions, discrimination, inadequate job markets for specific workers, low wages, and absence of adequate training, they have sought policies not only to provide the victims of these forces with economic resources but to offset or diminish the environmental causes. Thus, reformers in the 1930s and 1960s developed various public welfare, employment, minimum wage, and job-training policies. By contrast, many Americans have argued that specific social problems are caused by moral character—laziness, lack of motivation, or inclination to accept welfare benefits rather than to seek work. Not surprisingly, such persons have often advocated deterrent strategies that seek to force destitute persons into employment by making social programs unattractive or punitive.

Debates about the causes of social problems pose important choices. If problems are perceived to be caused by defects of character, little support is likely to exist for programs to help destitute or needy persons, and those interventions that are developed will likely be deterrent in nature. Indeed, in later chapters, we note that social reform periods in American history occurred when many Americans became convinced that economic and social forces were responsible for poverty and other social ills.

The burden of many social problems has fallen disproportionately on certain groups; thus, large numbers of African Americans and Latinos suffered grinding poverty and discrimination prior to and during the New Deal. Although a substantial middle class developed with remarkable speed in both groups in the wake of World War II, a massive underclass exists in major cities and rural areas. Despite recent gains, female workers tend to receive far lower remuneration than males and to be underrepresented in many levels of occupation. Throughout history, Americans have had to decide whether to tolerate the concentration of certain problems within specific groups or to develop compensatory policies, such as affirmative action, to equalize their conditions and opportunities (issue 4). Opponents of such policies have insisted that compensatory policies are unfair because they give preference in jobs and resources to members of disadvantaged groups; supporters contend they are needed to help equalize social conditions, particularly when social discrimination assumed a major role in causing inequality in the first instance. If special resources are not directed to the black underclass, for example, how can its members advance their social and economic status sufficiently to decrease the gaps that exist between them and the white population?

In the twentieth century, controversy about the magnitude of the policy roles of the federal government has often polarized Americans (issue 5). When conservatives argued that the Constitution delegates social welfare roles to the states and that states could better develop and implement social policies because they were more responsive to citizens than federal authorities, social reformers retorted that national problems require national solutions and that local governments lacked the resources or the will to redress social problems.

One cannot take a position on a major social issue, then, without taking positions on the five moral issues. Although exceptions exist, conservatives, liberals, and radicals often differ with respect to these moral issues. Conservatives tend to be disinclined to emphasize broad definitions of social obligation, are reluctant to vest the federal government with expansive social welfare roles, and do not like compensatory programs. Liberals have sought various additions to the welfare state though these sometimes represent incremental changes rather than sweeping reforms. And so far as they even exist in American society, radicals often want a truly expansive welfare state that, when coupled with the tax system, promotes equality. (We note in Chapter 12 that radicals have occupied a more marginal position in American society than in many other nations.)

As we read history, then, we often make moral judgments about the choices and actions of specific people or factions. Did conservative opposition to social reforms represent principled opposition or merely a self-interested defense of vested interests? Were the positions of liberal reformers meritorious or flawed in specific historical eras? Did radicals, such as communists and socialists in the New Deal, propose ill-advised or sensible policies? Are the centrist or conservative policies of contemporary American leaders sufficient to address the social and economic needs of the nation?

Positions on contemporary debates about national health insurance, national welfare reforms, revisions of the tax code to redistribute resources to the poor, development of national programs to assist homeless persons, or the expansion of civil rights legislation for specific groups are strongly influenced by moral positions. Indeed, service strategies of professionals such as social workers are influenced as well by moral positions, as we discuss in more detail in Chapter 13; thus, social workers have to devise preferred interventions in their agencies in the context of their definitions of the causes of social problems as well as those of their funders. (When they disagree with the policies of funders, they encounter difficult moral dilemmas.)

The five issues are *moral* because persons are forced to examine the relative merits of competing policies in value-based terms—with respect to concepts like fairness, freedom, and equality. In the broadest sense, we ask what kind of society we favor. What importance do we attach to helping destitute persons, to equalizing conditions between groups in the population, to better balancing domestic and military spending, and to developing national solutions to major social problems?

The preceding discussion suggests that value clarification lies at the heart of social welfare policy. Studying the evolution of American policies provides an opportunity for developing personal positions on the five moral issues by critically analyzing arguments and policies of prior eras. We argue in Chapter 4, for example, that the policy in the nineteenth century that poor persons had to enter poorhouses to obtain assistance was a flawed strategy that rested on punitive orientations toward the poor and the mistaken notion that character defects, rather than lack of jobs, caused poverty. Indeed, our discussion in the ensuing chapters occurs on three levels: (1) We describe policy enactments; (2) we place the enactments in their societal context with emphasis on cultural, political, economic, institutional, and other factors that led Americans to favor certain policies in specific eras; and (3) we discuss the relative merits of specific policies in the context of their effectiveness in redressing specific social problems and value judgments that are posed by the five moral issues.

Critical analysis of policies in prior eras is useful as well because analogous situations and problems that Americans have encountered in prior eras exist in contemporary society, including transiency (vagabonds in the 1870s, transient youth in the Great Depression, and homeless persons in the 1980s and 1990s), immigration (policy issues posed by immigrants from Eastern and Southern Europe and from Asia in the early part of this century and from Mexico and Central America in the 1980s and 1990s), problems of substance abuse (temperance crusades of the nineteenth century and the 1920s and efforts in the 1980s and 1990s to combat cocaine use), and illness (cholera and typhoid epidemics in the nineteenth century and Acquired Immune Deficiency Syndrome in the 1980s and 1990s). Such comparisons need to be done with care because the nature and causes of a specific social problem may change over time. Yet surprising similarities exist in both the nature of the social problems in different eras amd the nature of the policy response by American society.

When we evaluate the merits of the actions and choices of people in prior eras, we must, of course, beware of ignoring differences between the contemporary period and those eras. Governmental institutions were more primitive and the nation lacked a federal income tax in the nineteenth century, for example, so citizens and officials of that era could not contemplate, much less finance and implement, the kinds of major social programs that we take for granted today. Indeed, we have to approach distant eras in somewhat the way that anthropologists analyze different societies and culture, that is, suspend judgments in an effort to understand the way that people perceived their world and the problems in it. Even with these caveats, however, we can and should make evaluative judgments about the actions and choices of people in distant eras. For example, we can note that the founding fathers were convinced they *had* to legitimize slavery by mentioning it many times in the Constitution while nonetheless making the moral judgment that they were insensitive to the brutality and inhumanity of the institution of slavery.

## "OUTGROUPS" AND SOCIAL WELFARE HISTORY

When we analyze the social policies of prior eras, as well as the contemporary period, we often evaluate them with respect to specific groups in the population, such as African Americans, Latinos, women, gays and lesbians, Native Americans, low-income persons, persons with chronic mental conditions, and persons with chronic physical problems. Moreover, certain populations that are relatively prosperous in contemporary society, such as Japanese Americans, Irish Americans, and Jewish Americans, did not always enjoy this good fortune; many members of these groups experienced abject poverty, for example, in the latter part of the nineteenth century. We must include poverty-stricken populations among our outgroups because poverty in contemporary America carries with it stigma as well as hardship.

The prominence of these kinds of groups in specific historical periods stems from the unpleasant fact that social problems are not distributed randomly in the population but are often concentrated in specific subgroups of the population. Thus, many unmarried women in the nineteenth century (whether young women who had not married or women who had become widowed) experienced financial hardship that derived partly from their exclusion from those trades, occupations, and professions that males commonly entered. Moreover, women were denied the right to own property when married, to serve on juries, to vote, and to sign contracts in many jurisdictions in the nineteenth century. In similar fashion, African Americans, Latinos, and Native Americans have experienced disproportionate levels of poverty in the urban areas of the United States in the past several decades, prompting extraordinary controversy about the causes, nature, and solutions of their economic and other problems.

It is useful to call these various groups "outgroups" since they often experienced discrimination that reflected prejudice based on stereotyping (such as racism, sexism, or homophobia). Indeed, a vicious circle often developed; as societal discrimination restricted opportunities for members of specific outgroups, they were less able to compete for jobs and resources—and their relative poverty made it easier for the dominant society to insist that they caused their own demise because of character faults, such as laziness.

We can usefully distinguish among varieties of outgroups. The lower echelons of society constitute an *economic* outgroup whose members are subject to prejudice that stems from "classism." African Americans, Latinos, and Native Americans are examples of *racial* outgroups whose members have often been subject to racial prejudice. Certain groups, notably women and the elderly, have often been perceived as occupying specialized roles that preempt them from entering the economic and social mainstream—we can call these groups *sociological* outgroups. As one example, women were traditionally expected to limit themselves to child-rearing and homemaking functions; indeed, middle-class married women did not enter the labor force in large numbers until World War II. *Nonconformist* outgroups include persons widely perceived to have different lifestyle preferences such as gays and lesbians, to have violated social norms such as criminal offenders and juvenile delinquents, or to possess stigmatizing social problems such as mental illness. As people who have been widely perceived to be outside prevailing norms, members of these groups have often experienced discrimination. The members of some groups, such as Asian Americans, Jewish Americans, and some white ethnic groups, have sometimes

**FIGURE 1.2** • *Boy working in a glass-making factory about 1900*

*Source:* Library of Congress

found it difficult to persuade policy makers to assist their groups because they are widely perceived to be problem-free, *model* outgroups. We discuss how many members of these groups made remarkable progress in entering the economic mainstream, but their progress has often impeded awareness of major social problems that many of their members still experience, such as the lack of health insurance by many members of white ethnic groups. Finally, we can identify *dependent* outgroups, such as children, who occupy an unusual status. Usually lacking political clout, children depend on the goodwill of adults for requisite services, housing, and resources (see Figure 1.2).

Since their members experienced many social problems, much controversy often enveloped members of various outgroups in specific historical periods, as well as those persons who sought to be their advocates. Did *they* cause their own problems and thus not "deserve" the assistance of society, or were their problems caused by the discrimination that they experienced from the broader society? What strategies would have best improved their economic and social condition? To what extent *should* society have sought to raise them to a more equal standing with others? Should they have been encouraged to use self-help strategies, or was governmental assistance needed?

If some outgroups found themselves engulfed in controversy, others found themselves to be the subject of indifference by the broader population. Until the abolitionists succeeded in publicizing their needs, for example, the slaves in the South suffered from benign neglect from government officials, including the founding fathers who legitimized slavery in the Constitution. Although some courageous feminists championed the needs of women in the nineteenth century, most Americans were indifferent to their economic and social needs. Gay and lesbian persons, who were subject to extraordinary discrimination, found few advocates in American history until the last several decades. Children in the 1990s experience high rates of poverty and often lack access to medical care.

In evaluating the policies of any era, then, we often make our judgments with reference to one of these outgroups. We argue in many of the succeeding chapters that Americans often did not develop those kinds of far-reaching reforms that were needed to assist specific outgroups because of the force of tradition as well as deeply seated prejudice against their members.

## POLICY ERAS IN AMERICAN HISTORY

The history of American social policy can be divided into a series of policy eras, specific periods that have an identifiable policy direction, substance, and intensity. *Policy direction* describes the general nature of policy enactments in an era. In relatively conservative periods, emphasis is given to maintaining the status quo, eliminating reforms established in a preceding era, or making major amendments of prior enactments. In relatively liberal eras, major new reforms are enacted that redistribute services and resources or that increase the role of the federal government. The *substance* of policy refers to the general strategies favored by decision makers in a specific era when addressing the five moral issues discussed in this chapter. For example, reformers in the period between roughly 1905 and 1917 enacted a variety of regulatory reforms that established minimum public health, housing, and work-safety standards. Decision makers in the 1930s placed far more emphasis on legislation that redistributed resources and jobs to unemployed and poor persons. The *intensity* of reform describes the rate of policy activity. Relatively few policy changes occurred in the 1920s and 1950s, for example, but many changes were initiated in the 1930s, 1960s, and 1980s.

American social welfare policy has evolved in a series of phases (see Table 1.2). Some eras are sufficiently similar to others that they can be grouped together; in Table 1.2, various conservative eras are presented together because each of them is characterized by lack of interest in social reforms.

During the seventeenth and eighteenth centuries, American colonists brought with them from Europe a cultural inheritance that powerfully influenced the early development of American social welfare policy. As we discuss in Chapter 3, these early Americans were children of sweeping religious, political, and cultural

movements in Europe, such as the Protestant Reformation and the Enlightenment. The ideas of these original settlers influenced the course of American social policy development in the nineteenth and twentieth centuries, and many of their assumptions and beliefs persist in contemporary America.

Social welfare institutions were developed during the nineteenth century that were consonant with the realities of an agricultural, dispersed, and entrepreneurial nation. Social welfare policy was dominated by municipal and county programs and by local philanthropic efforts. (States begin to assume significant welfare functions only in the latter part of the nineteenth century.) The inability of Americans to develop major social welfare programs in this period is illustrated by their failure to assist the freed slaves in the aftermath of the Civil War or to regulate the emerging industrial order.

Americans developed their first sustained urban reform movement between 1905 and 1917

**TABLE 1.2** • *Social welfare policy eras in U.S. history*

| | |
|---|---|
| Era of the Initial Policy Inheritance | Medieval and colonial eras |
| Americanizing of the Policy Inheritance | 1800–1902 |
| First Urban Reform Movement | 1902–1917 |
| Development of Initial Federal Programs | 1932–1941 |
| Development of Federal Roles in Services | 1960–1968 |
| Extension of Federal Economic Security Roles | 1969–1980 |
| Conservative Eras | 1868–1902 |
| | 1917–1932 |
| | 1952–1960 |
| | 1980–1993 |

during the progressive era. Reformers emphasized a regulatory and local response to myriad social problems in the burgeoning cities by enacting regulations to improve working conditions, public health, and housing.

During the Great Depression of the 1930s, or about 150 years after the founding of the republic, Americans developed their first set of national social welfare programs, which assisted victims of poverty and unemployment and culminated in the passage of the Social Security Act in 1935. Programs established during the 1930s represented a remarkable policy breakthrough for the United States, but reforms were still deeply conditioned by traditional American beliefs that limited the size and scope of federal social programs.

Americans enacted many social programs during the administrations of John Kennedy and Lyndon Johnson in the 1960s, when the federal government assumed major roles in medical, educational, mental health, and job training sectors for the first time. Programs were established for specific populations, such as children and the elderly, and civil rights laws and regulations were passed. Emphasis was given to reforms that enlarged national funding of service-oriented programs rather than redistributing economic resources to poverty-stricken citizens.

The period encompassing the presidencies of Richard Nixon, Gerald Ford, and Jimmy Carter from 1968 to 1980 appears at first glance to be profoundly conservative, but this appearance is deceiving because many major reforms were enacted. Unlike the previous era, when emphasis was placed on federal service programs, reforms focused on provision of money and jobs to citizens through expansion of Social Security, food stamps, job training, job placement, and welfare programs.

At various times during the national history, conservative eras interrupted the evolution of social welfare reforms. In the period between the Civil War and 1905, for example, national discourse was dominated by Social Darwinism, which emphasized individualism and deterrent policies. The decade of the 1920s was characterized by preoccupation with material success rather than social reform to address the needs of women, factory workers, and southern blacks. President Dwight Eisenhower presided over the conservative decade of the 1950s, when cold-war rhetoric and suburbanization of the nation drew attention away from the social needs of many urban and rural citizens. A new conservative era was initiated in 1980 with the election of President Ronald Reagan, who cut the funding of many social programs and reduced federal policy and regulatory roles. The presidency of George Bush, from 1989 to 1993, can be viewed as an extension of the Reagan presidency in that Bush's domestic policies mirrored Reagan's. Bush vetoed many social measures that had been enacted by the Democratic Congress.

## THE RECENCY OF THE AMERICAN WELFARE STATE

This book chronicles and analyzes the evolution of American social policies from colonial times to 1993 using a political–economical perspective and emphasizing the particular policy needs of outgroups.

The book also places somewhat greater emphasis on policy developments of the twentieth century than prior eras. Although four chapters (Chapters 2 through 5) discuss the medieval period, the colonial experience, and the nineteenth century, six chapters (Chapters 6 through 11) emphasize developments in the twentieth century. We have chosen to place considerable emphasis on the present century for several reasons.

**FIGURE 1.3** • *Recency of American welfare state*

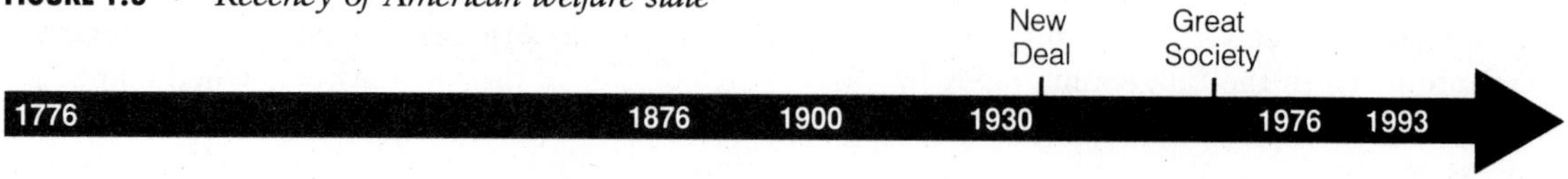

First, we want readers to be able to link contemporary issues with events of prior eras—an objective that would be unachievable if the book failed to bring developments through the 1980s and early part of the 1990s.

Second, the creation of the American welfare state has primarily occurred within the twentieth century, and the vast body of enactments that we typically associate with the welfare state has been created from the 1930s to the present. A time line, which traces developments in American history from colonial times to the present, makes clear how recently Americans have developed major national social programs (see Figure 1.3). It can be seen in Figure 1.3 that the period from 1930 to the present, when the first truly major national social policies were developed, constitutes a relatively brief period in the national experience, which began with the American Revolution (1776). Were we *not* to place somewhat more emphasis on developments in the twentieth century, we could not do justice to the torrent of pol-

icy developments that have occurred from the New Deal to the present.

Of course, this observation about the recency of the American welfare state does not suggest that developments in the colonial period and the nineteenth century are not important to the unfolding of American social welfare policies in the present century. Deeply seated habits of thought, which were established in these periods, have shown extraordinary resilence and have shaped developments of the twentieth century. If many orientations of conservatives like Ronald Reagan and George Bush can be understood only by placing them in the context of developments of distant eras, the proclivities of American liberals have often been shaped by ideas that arose in these earlier periods. Indeed, we discuss in Chapter 12 how a number of cultural, political, and institutional factors that were drawn from earlier segments of the American experience have influenced the course of policy developments in the twentieth century.

# CHAPTER 2

# The European Policy Inheritance

## Selected Orienting Events in the Feudal Era

| | |
|---|---|
| **1100s–1400s** | Peak of feudal society |
| **1492** | Columbus's first voyage to the New World |
| **1500s–1700s** | Policy of mercantilism developed |
| **1517** | Reformation begins when Luther posts his ninety-five theses |
| **1534** | Henry VIII separates Church of England from Roman Catholicism |
| **1600s** | English Enlightenment (see John Locke's publication of *Two Treatises of Government* in 1689) |
| **1601** | English Poor Law Act |
| **1607–1733** | England establishes thirteen permanent colonies on Atlantic Coast |
| **1700s** | Scottish and Continental Enlightenment (see Adam Smith's publication of *The Wealth of Nations* in 1776) |

Americans in the twentieth century are influenced by ideas that had their origin during the nation's formative years. The ideas of the colonists must in turn be understood in their European context. Most of the American colonists were Europeans who were influenced by the ideas of European philosophers and who had strong opinions about issues and leaders in European society. Many colonists came from a segment of English society that rebelled against monarchy, standing armies, aristocracy, and the Catholic Church—and drew inspiration from philosophers and politicians in Europe who hoped to establish a capitalist and democratic social order that would differ markedly from feudal society. We discuss European culture and institutions in this chapter as a prelude to analyzing the perspectives and institutions of American colonists in Chapter 3.

## THE FEUDAL INHERITANCE

With the decline of the Roman Empire after the fourth century, marauding bands of outlaws pillaged local villages and took land from local farmers in England and other European countries. Local populations gradually ceded title of their lands to powerful noblemen, who allowed peasants and serfs to remain on the land but required them to render services in return for protection. By the twelfth century, most of Europe had become splintered into a series of fiefdoms and had developed localistic, hierarchical, communalistic, and traditional social institutions.[1]

Medieval society was hierarchical. Land was held by monarchs, noblemen, and the Catholic Church. Noblemen paid taxes to monarchs and helped obtain recruits for their armies. Serfs worked the land for noblemen and the Church in return for protection, rights, and assistance. Citizens also paid mandatory taxes to the Church in return for its religious, social, and legal assistance.

None of the various groups was homogeneous. Noblemen differed in the size of their landholdings, specific titles, and status. The social status of serfs was determined not only by their rights to land but by their obligations to their noblemen; thus, serfs who were required to give considerable service or shares of their produce to the noblemen or who had rights to work small amounts of land occupied a relatively low social status, as did serfs who worked as tenants for other serfs.[2] All serfs had to give to noblemen some share of the agricultural produce of the land they worked, such as a hen at Christmas and other designated holidays. Most serfs were required to work on their nobleman's personal lands by devoting a certain number of days each year to its cultivation. A variety of statuses and positions existed as well within the villages and towns. Larger villages had an array of tradespeople that included millers, blacksmiths, silversmiths, weavers, barrel makers, and candle makers. A hierarchy of status existed in these various occupations that was partly determined by the amount of skill and training that was needed for the trade.[3]

The glue that was needed to keep this elaborate hierarchical structure in place included deference, mutual obligation, and social control. Obligations were formalized in ceremonies and in elaborate and detailed records. When a serf inherited the right to work specific lands of a nobleman, for example, he had to declare his obedience in a ceremony. The precise rents, services, or crops that he owed to the nobleman were recorded in official documents that were kept in the local court. Noblemen, in turn, declared their homage to their monarch and honored obligations that were recorded in legal documents. The rights of specific serfs to work designated amounts of land were bequeathed to their children. Noblemen honored these inherited rights and in turn expected the descendents of serfs to render the same kinds of services as their ancestors had. The lord was also required to honor traditional commitments to villages, such as providing peasants with certain feasts during the year, storing grain in the event of famine, and offering protection in the event of invasion.[4]

Traditional duties were rigidly enforced in medieval society. A nobleman had the right to grant lands to other families if a serf did not pay rents or provide needed services, but he could not divest a serf of land rights without a hearing in the local court. Duties and obligations were meticulously recorded in official documents. When hearings were held, a jury was elected by the local village, a specified procedure was followed in stating and refuting allegations, and a decision was rendered that was binding on both the serf and the nobleman.[5]

Medieval society was not capitalistic. Commodities were bartered in markets and private transactions. Land was not bought and sold in the modern sense but was transferred through inheritance to successive generations of noblemen so that it remained within specific families for centuries. (Persons were forbidden to sell their property outside their families by prohibitions known as entail, which reflected the prominence of tradition and family.) Land rights of serfs were often defined as rights to certain strips of land, which were fashioned by the furrows as oxen plowed fields. A family might have rights to farm several strips. If a specific field was left fallow, the family would receive rights to a specified number of strips in another field that was under cultivation in that year. (These families did not therefore own their own land but merely had the right to farm certain strips of land held by the nobleman.) Some pastures and woodlands were reserved for the common use of a village so that peasants could graze cattle in them and gather fuel.[6]

Serfs did not live in dispersed housing but within small villages. Villagers elected members to negotiate with the nobleman's representative (the bailiff) to decide which fields would lie fallow, who would tend animals in common pastures, and which members of the villages would serve in the king's armies to meet the monarch's manpower levy.[7]

The work ethic in the modern sense did not exist in this subsistence-oriented society. Serfs worked to meet basic obligations and subsistent needs—and no more. Numerous religious, seasonal, and traditional holidays were observed each year.[8] Noblemen did not expect more than this minimal labor from serfs because they, too, were oriented to a subsistence and bartering economy. Little work was performed in the fall and winter owing to inclement weather.

Though vast amounts of wealth were accumulated by noblemen, crusaders, and traders, there was nonetheless considerable suspicion of the accumulation of wealth by the use of market mechanisms, such as charging interest on loaned money or raising prices of food or commodities. Early merchants who sought to accumulate money—or who tried to withhold grain from the market to realize additional profits—were often persecuted. Some medieval theorists even developed the notion that wealth should be shared since it belonged to the society in which it was developed[9] though this idea was not carried to the logical conclusion that society should take lands or resources from noblemen, the Church, or kings and redistribute them to serfs.

Medieval society emphasized conformity with tradition. People were born into a position or status in society and usually remained within it. Rarely did people move their places of residence. Rights to the use of land as well as attendant obligations to noblemen were inherited. Persons who violated traditions, such as the honoring of obligations and maintenance of deference to social superiors, were subject not only to peer pressure but to various courts. Noblemen who tried to evict serfs from the land and serfs who refused to provide required service to noblemen were subject to sanctions.[10]

The Catholic Church was the only recognized church in the medieval period and was intimately associated with governmental institutions. It collected its own taxes in its local parishes. Many ecclesiastical officials served in government positions and in the inner circle of counselors to the king. Those who wished to establish a separate church—or to urge reforms in the existing one—met with strenuous persecution from Church or governmental officials and were sometimes sentenced to death. The Catholic Church used serfs to farm its vast amounts of land in the same fashion as noblemen.

The Pope in Rome oversaw his Church's domain throughout Europe. A king who threatened to take over Church lands or to urge major Church reforms could be threatened with attack by a king from another country who was loyal to the Catholic Church or by uprisings of Catholics within his own country. Like other social relations in feudal society, religious conformity was maintained by a combination of deference, traditions, and sanctions.[11]

The insistence on a nonpunitive response to social need derived in part from religion, which dominated much of the discourse of medieval times. The Catholic Church was, in effect, a government paralleling secular government with its own taxes, laws, and courts. It was the Church's canon law that established principles about vagrancy and poverty during the Middle Ages, long before secular governments had developed policies. Viewing involuntary poverty as its own deterrent because few people *want* to live in poverty, church leaders saw no need for punitive policies. As Tierney notes, church officials "no more thought of punishing a man for being afflicted with poverty than we would think of punishing a man for being afflicted with tuberculosis."[12] Even by the twelfth century, the Church supervised the care of the poor through the use of tithes, which local parishes collected and used to help fund poor relief. This positive belief about the rights of poor people, and the duty of society to afford relief to the poor, was eventually transferred from the Church to government, as we discuss subsequently, but the initial and primary impetus for poor relief came from the Church.

Church doctrine, as expounded by theologians and theorists like Thomas Aquinas, was explicit on matters of charity. In the midthirteenth century, Aquinas wrote a long treatise titled *On Charity,* that argues that charity is a central human virtue and that discusses its many forms and motivations.[13] Legendary figures, such as Francis of Assisi, led lives of voluntary poverty, befriended and helped poor people and lepers, and sought to prevent wars in a society bedeviled by innumerable conflicts.[14]

Persons in medieval society were circumscribed by innumerable regulations. They worshiped in the established church; donated services and resources to persons above them in the social hierarchy; served in armies of noblemen and kings; and paid a variety of taxes to the Church, local governments, and the king. They were sometimes restricted from moving around the countryside by laws of settlement, which allowed officials in one jurisdiction to return vagabonds or transients to their places of origin.[15]

Those serfs who did not inherit the rights to farm land from their parents, such as younger children, had limited options. Some became nomads in the forests of medieval Europe, some became tenants to other serfs, and some entered the priesthood. Others became apprentices to master tradesmen for a period of years prior to entering trades. Tradesmen were organized into tightly knit guilds that restricted entry into their respective trades. Merchants who wanted to begin a business in a town, such as a trading company, had to receive permission from both the local authorities and the crown.[16] Because some serfs were paid wages for their work by noblemen in certain parts of Europe, they were actually able to buy their freedom from their noblemen and then purchase or rent land.

## SOCIAL WELFARE IN MEDIEVAL SOCIETY

In this localistic, traditional, and hierarchical society, social welfare problems were usually addressed through family and peer relationships and by mutual obligation. Noblemen provided food to serfs in return for labor and maintained stocks of food as reserves for famine. Villagers shared oxen and helped one another plant and harvest crops as they moved together from strip to strip. Families and villagers were expected to assist elderly persons, children, and the mentally ill.[17]

The medieval Church assumed social welfare functions by providing food and lodging to the hungry, the sick, and transients. Such persons approached monasteries and requested food or lodging, which was given without interrogating

**FIGURE 2.1** • *Alms giving in the seventeenth century, an etching by Rembrandt*

*Source:* Rembrandt van Rijn; Dutch, 1606–1669. *Beggars Receiving Alms at the Door of a House,* 1648. Etching, burin, and drypoint, 165 x 128 mm. Gift of the Breeze Family, 1985.1.116. Achenbach Foundation for Graphic Arts. © The Fine Arts Museums of San Francisco

them on the reasons for their destitution (see Figure 2.1). The social welfare functions of monasteries were usually limited in size, however, so that only a small proportion of their resources was expended on aid and services.[18] Unemployment hardly existed because most persons worked the land or engaged in hunting. Massive problems, such as plagues and famines, often overwhelmed local helping institutions and were viewed fatalistically as problems that could not be avoided by society.[19]

The relatively small size of formal social programs should not obscure the fact that medieval society was organized to provide economic and social security. Many persons had rights—which were protected by tradition, courts, and the Church—to farm land, use common pastures and woods, and occupy housing in local villages. There was little unemployment and inflation in a barter economy. Entry into trades was strictly regulated to prevent excessive enrollments and to guarantee life membership to encumbents.[20]

The medieval period contributed certain ideas about social welfare to later societies. First, since social problems such as hunger were seen as inevitable and not caused by personal failings, medieval citizens had a nonpunitive response to social need.[21] Contemporary Europeans' dislike of means tests and other restrictions on use of services stems in part from the tradition of unconditional and nonpunitive assistance to the impoverished in the feudal era.

Second, the concept of mutual obligation was crucial to social welfare. Persons expected both to serve and to be assisted by those who occupied superior status. Many conservative aristocrats in English history subsequently supported social reform, in part because they retained this notion of social obligation.[22] After the dissolution of feudal society, many citizens turned to government to meet their basic needs in return for payment of taxes as they transferred the concept of mutual obligation to a new set of authorities. The strength of mutual obligation in contemporary European society is suggested by the range of social welfare programs that their governments have created as well as by their disinclination to cut them during difficult economic times. For example, national social spending consumes roughly 50 percent of the gross national product in Sweden and includes an extraordinary set of social programs such as nationalized health programs, unemployment and disability insurances that pay benefits virtually equal to the salaries of workers, free daycare services, subsidies to many industries, and six months of subsidized postnatal leave for new mothers or fathers. By comparison, Americans spend less than 25 percent of the gross national product on social programs.

Third, feudal society bequeathed to modern society the notion that rights and obligations of persons should be safeguarded. Manorial and royal courts as well as parish authorities zealously safeguarded these rights and obligations.[23] Fourth, medieval theorists emphasized the notion of a unitary society with common social interests. Persons and rules were not to seek personal interests but were to adhere to a common interest that linked kings, noblemen, merchants, and serfs into an "organic" society.[24] This sense of collective or common interest had profound implications for the development of social welfare policy in Europe in succeeding centuries. It undergirded socialist theory in the nineteenth and twentieth centuries, which promoted development of social programs and policies that addressed collective needs. Finally, medieval society provided a model of a society whose institutions and traditions maximized economic and social security. Persons obtained roles, statuses, and rights, which provided them with subsistence and predictability.[25]

Feudal society should not be glamorized, however. Extraordinary social and economic disparities existed between noblemen and serfs. Serfs were burdened with their obligations, could not hunt without scrutiny of gameskeepers, had no chance for upward mobility, often could not own land, could not migrate, and could be conscripted into armies to fight battles that were often based on petty territorial and religious objectives of monarchs. One other legacy of feudal society, then, was a social and economic conservatism that discouraged basic changes in land ownership and participation in political affairs by ordinary people.[26]

## THE GRADUAL UNRAVELING OF FEUDALISM

The early American settlers immigrated from European societies that were in the throes of transition from feudal institutions to individualistic, democratic, and capitalist societies. These early immigrants tended to identify with the forces of change that were undermining feudal institutions, which they often denigrated in their writings. To understand the perspectives of the early settlers, we need to examine how the roles, sanctions, and controls that existed in feudal society gradually weakened during the sixteenth, seventeenth, and eighteenth centuries as manifested by the emergence of capitalism, the displacement of peasants from the land, the development of new classes, the rise of restrictive notions of the proper roles of government, the Protestant Reformation, changing conceptions of the meaning of human existence, and the Enlightenment.

The barter and subsistence economy of medieval society was gradually replaced by a capitalistic economy in a development that had profound social and political consequences. Paper money, coins, and precious metals were increasingly used as mediums of exchange as bartering diminished. Buyers and sellers of commodities and land, instead of charging or paying a traditional fee, increasingly made economic decisions according to dictates of the market. A merchant might successively raise the price of bread, for example, until demand for it diminished, just as noblemen who wanted to raise cash would sell their land at the highest possible price. People became commodities themselves in labor markets when employers hired laborers at the lowest possible wage. This use of money and markets was complemented by the concepts of saving, investment, and profit. Instead of merely seeking subsistence, increasing numbers of persons hoarded money, which they invested in land or other goods to increase their net worth. Indeed, some persons loaned their assets to others at the highest possible rate of interest.[27]

This gradual conversion to capitalism had many consequences. It created new and powerful classes of merchants and bankers who questioned the authority of the central government to tax and regulate them. It promoted the massive displacement of peasants by giving landowners an incentive to sell their lands and to farm the land with labor-efficient technology. It sometimes led central governments of European nations to develop national economic planning so that their economies would flourish in competitive world markets.[28]

Capitalism fostered widespread economic and social uncertainty among peasants, who could no longer assume a relatively secure position on the land of their ancestors. They found themselves buffeted by the uncertainties of inflation, depressions, unemployment, and displacement. They increasingly had to seek available work even if it paid a miserly wage. Those who had once occupied a secure niche within villages that were affixed to feudal estates often roamed the countryside or sought uncertain lodging in growing cities like London.[29] Europeans had to decide whether to offset the economic and social uncertainty that capitalism brought to peasants, artisans, and workers by enacting ameliorative policies to provide them with economic and other assistance.[30]

Capitalism also promoted (and was itself bolstered by) orientations toward authority and government that were strikingly different from medieval perspectives. Should not market forces operate, some theorists conjectured, without intrusion by government? Should governmental authorities possess the power to oversee the economic decisions of its citizens, or should it instead be confined to relatively restricted police, currency, and military roles? Did not investment and profitmaking imply individualistic and self-seeking behaviors that provide the central meaning to existence?[31] Notions of individualism, limited government, and free markets were not necessarily incompatible with arguments that society should help persons who were buffeted by the economic dislocations that accompanied capitalism, but capitalism implied that persons should control their economic and personal destinies, that government should not intervene in economic affairs even when considerable suffering existed, and that displacement was merely an inevitable consequence of economic forces that would (eventually) further the common good.

Widespread agitation by the serfs in England had diluted their bondage to noblemen even before the emergence of private markets. In many manorial courts, records that specified that tenants had to give services and crops to noblemen in customary patterns that had been prescribed for centuries were destroyed in a series of peasant revolts in the fourteenth and fifteenth centuries. The serfs successfully demanded a status approaching that of the modern tenant farmer, where they worked in exchange for payment of fixed rents and were not required to provide many services to the owner.[32] By the latter half of the fifteenth century, the feudal peasant role had been converted in most parts of England to a tenant status.

The short-term advantages of the tenant relationship were very much negated by subsequent developments. It was widely assumed that noblemen would continue to charge a traditional and fixed rent to the former serfs and that they would grant to their descendants the rights to farm strips. But noblemen's perceptions of their duties to the emancipated serfs gradually changed over many centuries though at different rates of change in different parts of England. When many owners began to raise rents, many angry peasants were driven from the land. Some owners enclosed fields by building fences or hedges around them so that only a single family or several families were needed to cultivate them. Many noblemen also began to convert their fields from crops to livestock, thus reducing the number of peasants who could continue to cultivate the land. Scores of noblemen sold their lands to new owners—to merchants from the city, to other noblemen, or to those peasants who had accumulated sufficient resources to allow them to purchase small holdings.[33] When the population of England more than doubled between 1600 and 1750, many persons could no longer be tenant farmers since insufficient land existed to support them in agriculture. A landless population developed that had to seek wage employment in other agricultural areas or in urban areas.[34]

New names replaced the old ones of *serf* and *nobleman,* a change in terms that reflected the weakening of feudal institutions. *Landed gentry* were persons who owned relatively large amounts of land; *yeomen* were relatively small landowners, who had become numerous in many parts of England; *tenant farmers* worked the land in return for relatively fixed rents; and *common laborers* worked on a wage basis for tenant farmers. These new names suggest, however, that a social hierarchy remained that was linked to the size of landholdings.[35]

The simplicity of feudal society, which facilitated the perpetuation of social power by noblemen, was fractured by the rise of new social classes. Small urban areas began to develop by the fourteenth century as domestic commerce and foreign trade expanded. Merchants increasingly disliked efforts by the royal court and by noblemen to tax and regulate them.

Merchants had been as much an anomaly in feudal society as towns. Early generations of merchants were widely distrusted and persecuted. Even in rural villages, for example, millers who bought and ground grain were distrusted by villagers, who suspected that they took advantage of local citizens by charging excessive prices. Merchants nonetheless became more numerous and wealthier as the bartering and subsistence economy of feudalism was gradually supplanted by a money and trading economy.[36] As more persons in England realized that foreign trade was not a luxury but a necessity in order to create employment in England, merchants became more powerful, demanded a role in decision making in parliamentary settings, sought to enlist government in supporting their economic endeavors, and strenuously objected to regulations placed on

them by the royal court and landed gentry. In similar fashion, bankers and financiers, who became increasingly indispensable to commerce with the eclipse of bartering and the growing importance of currency as the medium of exchange, coexisted uneasily with feudal society.[37]

Usury, the charging of interest on loaned money, was regarded by many persons in medieval society as a sin, but the need to borrow funds for business and agricultural ventures meant that it was increasingly used. Traditional and fixed obligations and relationships in feudal society were further eroded when rates of interest, as with rents and wages, varied according to market forces.

Virulent animosity developed between upper and lower strata in English society by the end of the seventeenth century, which in part was caused by widespread fear of the increasing numbers of vagabonds and unemployed persons. The poor were increasingly referred to by the gentry and merchants as "savages," "beasts," and "incorrigibles." Many persons believed that peasants and the urban poor, who were perceived to be intrinsically lazy, could learn habits of productivity only when subjected to harsh discipline.[38] Landless persons at the bottom of the social order were less likely to respond with deference to social elites and often rioted to protest enclosures of fields, the raising of rents charged to tenant farmers, and the lack of food during famines. Many persons feared, in the seventeenth and eighteenth centuries, that "unruly mobs" would be aroused by demagogues to seek major changes in society—fears that reached fever pitch at the end of the eighteenth century with the French Revolution. Riots, mobs, and scattered incidents of violence, though sporadic, were a decided feature of English life in the long transition from feudal to modern institutions and contributed to the decline of feudal patterns of deference and authority.[39]

The monarch was the ultimate authority in medieval society and was vested both with secular authority and leadership of the state church. From the fourteenth century through the seventeenth century, many monarchs in Europe steadily increased their taxes over the growing class of merchants as well as the landed gentry, placed increasing tax levies on towns, and often insisted that new trading and commercial undertakings be licensed by them. They distributed lands, offices, and official titles in return for support of policies favored by the crown. Royal courts often became bloated with patronage, excessive tax revenues, and corruption.[40]

Many persons in England sought to establish controls or limits on the powers of central government. Many merchants hoped to reduce taxes and regulations. Elected representatives in Parliament, who sought to share decision-making powers with the monarch, had achieved a balance of power by 1700. Parliament obtained the power to veto tax initiatives while ceding trade policy to the crown. Monarchs, who had previously been able to dominate national politics, increasingly had to exercise power by rewarding persons through appointments, granting trade and commercial privileges, and distributing other favors.[41]

Limits on the power of government and monarchs were explicitly developed by a number of theorists in the seventeenth century. John Locke, the seventeenth-century English philosopher, wrote that men did not develop governmental institutions in the original "state of nature" but later constructed institutions to protect citizens from criminal activities. Locke, like other theorists whom American colonialists avidly read, believed government to be a necessary evil that should have its powers limited to police, defense, and record-keeping measures. To avoid the emergence of a despot, for example, he advocated the development of constitutions to define the precise powers of government and to divide its powers among different branches of government. This concept of limited government differed strikingly from medieval notions of governance, which extolled the divine rights and authority of monarchs.[42]

In 1517, Martin Luther, a Catholic priest who had become disenchanted with the corruption and ritualism of the Catholic Church,

posted ninety-five theses on the door of a Catholic church in Wittenberg that stated his opposition to the use of "indulgencies" (which allowed people to contribute money to a worthy cause so as to receive forgiveness for sins) and other church practices. After he was excommunicated in 1521, he founded the Lutheran Church, which became merely one of many sects that were established during the Protestant Reformation. Protestants hoped to increase the personal involvement of parishioners in the church by reducing the use of rituals, by requiring church members to read and study the scriptures, by replacing rituals with sermons, and by giving congregations enhanced roles in church governance. In the several centuries after the Protestant Reformation, an array of sects developed that drew on some of the ideas that Luther, Calvin, and other Protestant leaders had developed in earlier periods; these sects included Anabaptists, Congregationalists, Methodists, Presbyterians, and Quakers. These Protestants often did not object to the concept of an official state church since they hoped to persuade the king to make their faith the established orthodoxy. Others, however, moved inexorably to the notion that all religions should be tolerated in English society, a concept that fundamentally challenged the notion of a single state church.

Partly to enhance his own power as well as to resist foreign encroachments by the Vatican and by Spain, King Henry VIII declared the English branch of the Catholic Church to be a state church in 1534 and wrested control of it from the Vatican. He also assumed control over its land holdings and abolished the monasteries. This English Church replaced the Catholic Church as the official Church of the realm since all citizens were required to contribute tax funds to it and to worship in it.

It is difficult to appreciate today how bold these ecclesiastical challenges were to the religious traditions of European society. Even in the eighteenth century, for example, persons who belonged to Protestant sects were subject to numerous sanctions and regulations in England that strictly limited their ability to worship openly, to read their version of the Bible, and to attend universities.[43] The attack on the established Church was the ecclesiastical equivalent of the questioning of the power of the monarch that had occurred in the secular realm and was another cause as well as symptom of the unraveling of the feudal order.

Many Europeans developed new conceptions of the meaning of human existence. People increasingly sought freedom from the restrictions and regulations that had prevailed in feudal society. Merchants wanted less interference with their businesses by the royal courts and by local authorities. Political representatives believed that they should not be subject to arbitrary decisions of the royal court and believed that elected representatives should be able to frame policies concerning taxation and other domestic issues. Religious dissenters wanted the ability to worship without interference from the state Church. Landowners wanted to be able to enclose or sell their fields without having to honor ancient rights of peasants. In all these cases, a notion of the self-directing and autonomous individual evolved that was strikingly different from the collective notions of the feudal era.[44] Complementing the notion of individual autonomy were economic concepts of personal initiative and risk taking. Many persons, including Protestants, Catholics, and Anglicans, believed that hard work, frugality, and saving of resources were modes of behavior superior to the traditional ideas about subsistence and seasonal labor.[45]

This emphasis on freedom, autonomy, and personal initiative in the secular world complemented the religious beliefs of many Protestants. The major religious purpose in life, many people believed, was to control such evil passions as pride, greed, lust, laziness, and desire for power by cultivating reason and moral virtue, by working hard, and by avidly reading the scriptures. In this emerging religious perspective, each person was charged with developing a personal quest for a moral existence. The Protestants differed among themselves about whether one could actually earn salvation by working hard and suppressing the passions through devotion, but they all emphasized work as a means of controlling the passions.[46]

The emerging emphasis on work and careers fostered attitudes of suspicion toward persons who were poor. Persons who were truly hard working should, after all, have "something to show for it" since God was likely to bestow good fortune on moral persons. This judgmental orientation toward needy persons was reinforced by an emerging class consciousness and resulted in an extraordinarily harsh orientation toward destitute persons, which contrasted markedly with the nonjudgmental relief policies of the monasteries in medieval society.[47]

Peasants in feudal society could usually subsist during famines from their own produce and wood gathering as well as from supplies of grain that had been accumulated. The emergence of private markets subjected them to the uncertainties of markets when recessions swelled the numbers of unemployed persons or when inflation elevated the price of bread. Peasants themselves became labor commodities whose wages fluctuated with economic changes. Urban dwellers could not raise subsistence crops, collect fuel from forests, or raise animals on common pastures. Thus, unemployment and hunger became major social problems that brought a good deal of hardship to many persons and increased social tension within England. Peasants resented their loss of economic security, and many middle- and upper-class persons resented and feared dispossessed persons.[48]

In the seventeenth century, a number of English political theorists, including John Locke, espoused limited government, free speech, secularism, optimism, science, and the use of reason to discover natural laws. They fervently questioned monarchical and religious authorities. Their intellectual assault on traditional and feudal ideas, which has been called the English Enlightenment, was followed by a Scottish and European Enlightenment in the eighteenth century. These thinkers, Adam Smith and Voltaire among them, continued the assault on traditional political and religious institutions and prepared the intellectual climate for the emergence of new capitalist and democratic institutions.[49]

Adam Smith, the Scottish economist, was widely read by American colonists. Locke had argued that the policy roles of government should be restricted to police-keeping functions. Smith further suggested that governments should not assume major roles in overseeing or regulating the economic order because forces of supply and demand, if left to themselves, would maintain market equilibrium. Furthermore, free-market economies would stimulate competition and innovation because entrepreneurs would increase their profits by developing new products. Smith's theories represented a new rationale for sharply restricting the size of government by divesting it of economic roles.[50]

 ## POLICY CHOICES IN THE PERIOD OF TRANSITION

Some English social welfare policies during this period of transition from feudal to postfeudal society advocated assisting unemployed and poverty-stricken persons within the limits of a society that lacked resources and governmental agencies. Other policies reflected a punitive orientation toward impoverished persons, however, that stemmed from the fear and anger of social elites as well as from economic, political, and individualistic ideas that had contributed to the unraveling of feudalism.

In the literature on social welfare policies in this distant era, authors sometimes disagree with one another on the intent and workings of policy. Some authors stress the deterrent and punitive nature of poor relief in the seventeenth and eighteenth centuries, whereas others contend that poor law policies (which we later discuss) were quite benevolent in the South of England, at least until the early part of the nineteenth century.[51] This divergence in opinion stems partly from the local nature of social welfare institutions; punitive approaches in one jurisdiction may have differed from more benevolent approaches in another jurisdiction. Rather than taking sides in this debate, we point to "positive" and "punitive" characteristics of social welfare policy in the unfolding of events as medieval institutions evolved into the capitalistic and democratic institutions that we recognize as bearing affinity to those of today.

Positive policies that developed during this transition period included mercantilism, the Elizabethan Poor Law, the development of welfare roles of the national government, private philanthropy, and policies to address unemployment.

### Positive Policies

Officials in the small towns of feudal Europe had regulated virtually every facet of economic and social affairs during the sixteenth and seventeenth centuries. Entry into trades, decisions about who could set up businesses, the prices of commodities, wage rates, and locations of new construction were strictly regulated by the monarch and by local officials, mainly to protect peasants from economic uncertainties. Local regulations were supplemented by a national policy of the English government to manage the economy to conserve food at home and to facilitate the development of foreign trade. A parliamentary act of 1548, for example, required citizens to eat fish on Fridays and Saturdays to promote the building of ships and to conserve livestock. (Wednesdays were added by an act in 1563!) The English government encouraged immigration of Flemish experts in cotton and weaving to promote the development of a textile industry, provided government subsidies to various industries, and aggressively sought foreign markets.[52]

A policy called mercantilism had evolved by the seventeenth century to develop colonies in the New World so as to obtain raw materials and new markets for England. Mercantilism is a system by which a government regulates its agriculture, industry, and commerce to create a favorable balance of trade. Mercantilism's proponents were convinced that external trade was needed to promote the prosperity of England. The monarch commissioned trading companies to settle lands in the New World, encouraged emigration to these settlements, and hoped that the settlers would both provide markets for English produce and supply England with gold and raw materials. To stimulate the growth of the English navy, the Parliament required trade with these colonies be conducted in English ships.

Mercantilism can be viewed not only as an exercise in economic nationalism but also as a social welfare policy to increase jobs and economic growth in England to help the large number of persons who had been cast off the land by enclosures and population growth. It was supplemented by the establishment of other economic measures that were not narrowly constructed to encourage trade, such as the placing of controls on prices of commodities and foodstuffs so that persons could afford basic necessities like bread and corn. Moreover, the English tried to intervene in job markets by pursuing a policy of employment to accommodate the hundreds of persons flooding the countryside; landed gentry were sometimes asked, for example, to hire servants even when they did not want them and to extend terms of indentured status for servants and apprenticeship for workers.[53]

It will be recalled that the Catholic Church had required its local parishes to collect taxes and to use part of these proceeds to care for the poor. The Church of England inherited this custom, but was often remiss in helping the poor because of the sheer size of the poverty popula-

tion in the wake of enclosures, population growth, and urbanization, not to mention considerable corruption within the church bureaucracy. Government authorities decided to buttress this local system of welfare by requiring the parishes to appoint unpaid overseers, who were charged with collecting taxes and distributing relief to destitute persons. The national government consolidated various laws that had given local parishes these welfare roles in the landmark Elizabethan Poor Law Act of 1601. When parishes could not meet their responsibilities, counties were required to assume relief-giving functions. In effect, then, government became the chief enforcer of poor relief by 1601, thus supplanting the Church of England.

### The Elizabethan Poor Law Act of 1601

Be it enacted . . . that the Churchwardens of every Parish, and foure, three, or two substantial Householders there . . . to bee nominated yeerely . . . under the hande and seale of two or more Justices of the Peace in the same Countie . . . shall be called Overseers of the poore of the same Parish, and they . . . shall take order from time to time . . . for setting to worke of the children of all such whose parents shall not . . . bee thought able to keepe and maintaine their children; and also for setting to worke all such persons maried, or unmaried, having no meanes to maintaine them, use no ordinary and dayly trade of life to get their living by, and also to rayse weekely or otherwise (by taxation of every inhabitant . . . in the said Parish) a convenient stocke of Flaxe, Hempe, Wool, Threed, Iron . . . to set the poore on worke, and also competent summes of money for, and towards the necessary reliefe of the lame, impotent, old, blinde, and such other among them being poore, and not able to worke, and also for the putting out of such children to bee apprentices . . . it shall and may be lawfull for the saide Churchwardens and Overseers . . . to errect, build . . . convenient houses of dwelling for the said impotent poor, and also to place Inmates or more families than one in one cottage, or house.

The Father and Grandfather, and the Mother and Grandmother, and the children of every poore, old, blinde, lame, and impotent person . . . not able to worke, being of sufficient ability, shall at their owne charges relieve and maintaine every such poore person . . .

Local parishes fulfilled their welfare responsibilities in several ways. They could provide "outdoor relief" to persons in their homes, provide "indoor relief" to persons in special institutions that came to be variously known as almshouses, poorhouses, or workhouses, or require persons to become indentured servants or apprentices. These latter two options were more punitive than outdoor relief since they conditioned relief on residence within an institution or assumption of a specific labor status.[54]

The Elizabethan Poor Law represented, on balance, a positive policy even though it required that some able-bodied persons should be made to work in poorhouses. (We note subsequently, however, that it was administered in punitive fashion in many local jurisdictions during the next several centuries.) Recent research on poor law institutions of southern England suggests that poor law officials undertook a range of welfare roles that sometimes approached those of modern welfare states: They provided unemployment relief; initiated public works; regulated local prices to help poor persons; gave such in-kind assistance as food, clothing, and wood; gave health care; removed children from abusive households; and gave legal protections to apprentices.[55] More than 50 percent of the people in the South of England used outdoor relief in specific years.[56] Laws of settlement were not commonly used in punitive fashion but as protections for new agricultural migrants, who used them to claim entitlement to local poor law relief after a year's residence.

Since the poor law did not outline in detail how local overseers were to implement their local programs, considerable local variation ensued. Some overseers placed more emphasis on indoor relief than others. A good deal of controversy developed in the nation about the relative merits of indoor and outdoor relief. In certain periods, advocates of a harsh policy enacted national policies to promote construction of workhouses, yet widespread revulsion against this punitive policy, which sometimes took the form of riots by the poor during times of high unemployment, often surfaced. The Gilbert legislation that was enacted in England in 1782, for example, restricted use of indoor relief to certain groups and required parishes to give paid employment to persons who could not find jobs. In the South of England, a relatively benevolent interpretation of the poor laws was dominant until well into the eighteenth century.[57]

Parliament assumed a major role in orchestrating welfare policies in the seventeenth and eighteenth centuries through the Elizabethan Poor Law Act, its support of mercantilism, and passage of legislation that provided citizens with basic civil rights. In the eighteenth century, Thomas Paine, the Englishman who also agitated for reforms in the American colonies, wanted the English government to enact maternity benefits, progressive taxes, children's allowances, old age pensions for persons over age fifty, and public works to create jobs for the unemployed — an agenda that would appear impressive even in the twentieth century in America, where some of these programs still do not exist. Little support for his innovative suggestions was forthcoming, but they reflect the positive orientations to social welfare that were present in England in the eighteenth century.[58]

Whether motivated by the feudal Catholic tradition of sharing wealth or the Protestant emphasis on giving as a moral duty, affluent persons gave money to many charities, including 800 hospitals in England by the sixteenth century. These hospitals served poverty-stricken persons and were sometimes converted to specialized institutions to serve such groups as orphans. Local governments often shared in the costs of construction and implementation of these institutions, but most charity in seventeenth-century England was provided by private philanthropy.[59] Charitable trusts and bequests were so common that the 1601 Statute of Charitable Uses was enacted to regulate them.

The English economy in the seventeenth century produced an enormous surplus of grain and commodities for export for the first time. An optimistic economic orientation replaced the static and subsistent viewpoint of the feudal era, which led to positive evaluations of former serfs as a national labor resource. The poor law officials in the seventeenth century were urged to develop public works to employ poor persons—not as a punitive policy but to provide them with work and to teach them skills and discipline.[60]

## Punitive Policies

Other policies of the time were relatively punitive, including restrictive interpretations of Elizabethan Poor Law, denial of civil liberties to the poor, and harsh use of laws of settlement. The Elizabethan Poor Law affixed responsibility for the poor to local public officials. The poor could be assisted in their homes, but some poor persons could be placed in poorhouses and set to work on a "stocke of Flaxe, Hempe, Wool, Threed, Iron, and other necessary ware." The distinction between "deserving" and "undeserving" persons led to relatively punitive policies, illustrated by a law that Parliament enacted in 1723 that mandated use of poorhouses by local parishes rather than continuation of the less stigmatizing policy of outdoor relief.[61]

Some theorists were so critical of the poor that they proposed enslaving them in order to teach them discipline and moral virtues—with heavy reliance on corporal punishment. Although later rescinded, Parliament at one point enacted a law requiring indigent persons to wear a sign marked with a P! Many poor persons were exposed to harsh discipline, back-breaking work, and moral teaching in the many workhouses that were constructed in the seventeenth and eighteenth centuries. The harshness of the workhouse strategy was offset, however, by the fact that few counties constructed them until the eighteenth and nineteenth centuries—and by the leniency of some local officials who chose to provide outdoor relief instead.[62]

Laws of settlement, which required persons to remain in their native counties, were enacted during the long transition from feudal to post-feudal society and remained in effect in parts of England as late as the 1870s. In the sixteenth and seventeenth centuries, laws of settlement were sometimes viewed as protections for transient persons since they entitled them to local relief after a year of residence. By the late eighteenth century, however, local officials began to urge local landowners not to hire laborers for more than a year so as to limit the welfare costs of those parishes and counties that experienced a growth in the size of their indigent populations.[63] Vast numbers of peasants found themselves carted home after brief stints of labor.

The poor were sometimes subjected to outright denial of their civil liberties in the seventeenth and eighteenth centuries. A poor person drinking beer in a local alehouse might find himself captured and impressed into the navy or army, or someone might agree to go to the New World as an indentured servant and discover himself imprisoned so that he could not change his mind prior to departure.[64] Criminal penalties were severe, even for minor offenses, as illustrated by the hanging or maiming of persons who were guilty of petty theft. Long delays in litigation were common, so persons were often kept in jail for extended periods before they were tried. Debtors were often imprisoned. Crimes judged to be moral were also subject to harsh punishment. Someone could be hauled into a local court and fined, for example, for swearing at a social superior. Persons judged guilty of adultery or fornication could be asked to stand in public with the offending partner. Because of rioting in the eighteenth century over enclosures and food shortages, a Riot Act was enacted in 1715 that gave local constables the right to arrest persons who were assembled in large groups though they were required to give them one hour to disperse. Various laws outlawed or regulated village merrymaking during holidays since these events sometimes culminated in rioting.[65]

Children were often subjected to harsh treatment by modern standards. Many persons believed that the central task in child rearing was to break the will of children so that they could become right-living persons. Since they were regarded as little adults, they were often apprenticed or indentured at an early age and subjected to harsh working conditions. Free education was not widely available until well into the eighteenth century, and then only for primary school education.

## THE WEAKENING OF SOCIAL OBLIGATION

During the unraveling of feudal society, markedly new and different conceptions of the social order developed. Philosophers such as Locke and Smith favored an individualistic society in which citizens sought to maintain independent economic activity and private property. Many citizens also came to believe that those who could not survive independently were morally flawed and ought to be dealt with in a punitive manner to deter them from seeking further assistance and to encourage them toward independence. Many theorists argued that government should not interfere in the social and economic order.

As citizens were taken from the traditional relationships in feudal society and placed into competitive economic markets, some succeeded in obtaining considerable wealth, but many others found no work or were exploited by industrialists, merchants, and large landowners. These persons found themselves not only stigmatized but also living within a society where mutual obligation had been de-emphasized and where governments were disallowed from interfering in the social and economic order.

The crucial issues of mutual obligation, security, autonomy, and risk taking were posed during the unraveling of feudal society by the enormousness of economic and social needs that emerged as dispossessed serfs and peasants flooded into cities and roamed the countryside as an emergent capitalistic order took hold. Should society structure its social and economic institutions to provide security to its citizens or opt instead to promote autonomy and risk taking? Should citizens expect their governments to help them with a range of social benefits, or should each citizen exist in autonomous fashion, even when stricken with unemployment or illness? Should government assume major economic and social roles to assist persons with problems, or should it provide only residual and punitive programs to needy persons? Even though these questions were not addressed in a debate that contemporary citizens would recognize—after all, the welfare state is largely a creation of the twentieth century—they were posed in rudimentary form as citizens wrestled with issues of social obligation, deterrence, responsibility, and roles of national governments.

## OUTGROUPS IN THE MEDIEVAL ERA

Compared to contemporary society, medieval society was homogeneous. The growth of vast empires by European powers, the movements of persons of color across national boundaries (whether as slaves or by voluntary migration), and the development of cosmopolitan cities had not yet occurred. European societies were almost exclusively Caucasian. We need to inquire, however, what attitudes or predispositions Europeans possessed toward outgroups in the medieval period because the early settlers to the North American continent were émigrés from a Europe that was still profoundly influenced by the culture and institutions of the medieval period.

## Women

Contemporary historians have analyzed the lives of women in medieval society and concluded that, despite notable exceptions such as female royalty, they lived within relatively restrictive boundaries. Virtually without exception, medieval theorists viewed both society and the family as hierarchies—and husbands were seen as the superior member of the family to which women and children were subordinate.[66] Indeed, as Fraser notes, England was governed by feudal law "where a wife passed from the guardianship of her father to her husband (where) her husband also stood in relation to her as a feudal lord."[67] As the subordinate party, women were expected to be obedient, to confine themselves to household duties (or, in pastoral areas, to those farming duties that were most related to the household, such as milking cows, making cheese, and making clothing).

It was widely assumed that women were "weaker vessels," that is, inferior to males not just physically but also morally and in intelligence.[68] Prior to the seventeenth century in England, virtually no women were literate, and educational reformers in that century, who gave some women exposure to education, refrained from allowing them to learn subjects like Latin, a language essential in an era that emphasized classical studies.

The economic roles of women were circumscribed. Guilds and crafts developed to regulate skilled work in the towns and cities, but women were often excluded from them or found them to be dominated by men who made them second-class members. Much of the work that women undertook, as domestic servants, small retailers,

spinsters, or midwives, was not organized into guilds or crafts, thus depriving women of the kinds of security that guilds and crafts gave to their members.[69] Though women often worked alongside their husbands in fields in feudal settings, the rights to farm strips of land were often passed by husbands to their sons so that daughters often lacked land rights.

Women benefited from some protections in this period. The Church of England provided some protections against cruelty, lack of support, and desertion. Divorce was not sanctioned, but women could petition the Church for separations though they often made these petitions only after their husbands had left them.[70]

## Race and the Medieval Mind

As relatively homogenous societies of white persons, most people in medieval society had little or no contact with persons of other races. As Sanders suggests, the idea of race was only "dim and sporadic" for most Europeans during the Middle Ages.[71] But race assumed fateful dimensions in the minds of many Europeans by the late fifteenth century as explorers like Columbus made contact with Indians in the Caribbean, Central and South America—and as Europeans, desperate for labor, sought to import black slaves into these regions.

Although slavery had existed in Roman times and although Christians had long enslaved Moslems, its numbers were relatively small, and slavery had ended in Europe by the end of the fourteenth century.[72] To fill minor labor shortages, Portugal and Spain began using Africans as slaves in their domestic economies in the fifteenth century. Even this minor use of slaves might have ended had Columbus and numerous successors not established colonies in the New World, beginning in the Caribbean and then in Central and South America.[73]

Depicted in older history books as a heroic figure, many modern historians have painted a more somber portrait of Columbus. After a first voyage in 1492 that was primarily a trip of discovery, Columbus set sail on a second voyage—complete with 17 ships and 1,200 men—intending to colonize the New World.[74] When he discovered that a small settlement called Navidad, left from the first voyage, had been burned and its inhabitants murdered, Columbus's dream of concord between the Indians and the Spanish ended. As Dor-Ner suggests, "the Navidad incident would set a pattern of violence and mistrust between Europeans and Native Americans . . . that would be played out in blood as successive waves of Spanish, English, and French colonialists swept through the Americas . . . this poisonous attitude would in time . . . echo at the Little Big Horn, where Sitting Bull took no prisoners (and) would be brutally distilled in the infamous remark of General Philip Sheridan: 'The only good Indians I ever saw were dead.'"[75]

Columbus and his Spanish successors quickly devised a method of controlling the local Indians by placing them in a position akin to serfs of the feudal era. Though Indians in their villages were allowed to keep their property, they were forced to give most of their produce to the conquerors in return for "protection." Moreover, tens of thousands of them were conscripted for forced labor in mining and other endeavors. The Pope as well as Queen Isabella of Spain often tried to place moral constraints on Columbus and other conquistadors, but they had scant success in stopping the brutalization of Indians despite the protests of a handful of courageous priests.[76]

The early forays into the Caribbean were soon followed by the pillaging of Indian settlements in Central and South America. Far more deadly to the Indians than the violence and servitude imposed on them by the conquerers were the diseases that the Europeans brought with them; these Indians had no natural resistance to smallpox, measles, diphtheria, whooping cough, the bubonic plague, typhoid fever, cholera, scarlet fever, and influenza. They died by the millions from these various diseases. The ravages of disease are suggested by the decline of the native population in Central Mexico from 11 million in 1519 to 2.5 million in 1597—a staggering loss repeated throughout Central and South America as well as the Caribbean.[77]

The wholesale deaths of Indians from disease and overwork created an economic dilemma for the Europeans when they introduced the labor-intensive crops of sugar and then tobacco in the Caribbean and South America. To find the laborers for these crops, the Europeans, drawing on experience with slavery, decided to import vast numbers of Africans to the New World. By a quirk of biology, these black slaves proved to be relatively resistant to European diseases, thus allowing them not only to survive but to be a self-replenishing source of labor.[78] Moreover, the huge African population could be regularly raided for a seemingly endless supply of laborers. By 1670, Portuguese Brazil had at least 200,000 slaves, and the English had at least 20,000 slaves in Barbados.

Medieval culture provided the Europeans with orientations that made them ill-disposed to resist efforts to exploit the native populations or to outlaw the use of slaves in the New World. As Christians, for example, the Europeans were prone to define humankind into two groups: Christians and heathens. The Church had long held the notion that heathens could be placed in servitude once they had "rejected" Christianity, as the Crusades, which sought to conquer Moslem peoples in the Middle East, had suggested. Feudalism provided the notion that native villages could be controlled by recreating in the New World the feudal equivalent of serfdom, but these new-world noblemen, far removed from the ancient protections that had provided some assistance to European serfs, could exploit the native population, and then the slaves, with little interference from European courts, the Church, or the Crown.

Nor should we forget racism; when placed in contact with people of different racial background, it was relatively simple for the Europeans to equate blackness (or brownness) with "primitiveness," "heathenness," "savagery," and "laziness." As the native peoples or slaves physically resisted exploitation, the Europeans could seize on their infidelity as proof that they were savages. Nor did the Europeans develop racist ideas only during the conquests of the New World since they had long imagined that cannibalistic and savage people lived in undiscovered territories.[79]

## Homosexuality and Antisemitism

The pioneering work by Boswell on homosexuality from Roman times suggests that relatively little discrimination existed against gays before the fourteenth century. Gay people lived quietly within the general population, did not seek to hide their sexual orientation, and were not regulated by civil laws. Some monarchs were widely known to be gay. Indeed, when referring to the early Middle Ages, that is, before the thirteenth century, Boswell disputes the widely held notion that the Middle Ages were an era of intolerance by citing the general toleration of gays and Jews.[80]

For reasons that historians do not fully understand, Europe became far less tolerant of gays, religious dissenters, and Jews in the thirteenth and fourteenth centuries, as reflected by the Inquisition (efforts by the Roman Catholic Church to investigate and punish religious dissenters) and the Crusades (efforts to capture the

Holy Land where Jesus had lived from the "Muslim infidels"). Moreover, virulent hatred of Jews developed, as is illustrated by the widespread belief that the Jewish population had brought on the Black Death of the fourteenth century, which eradicated between 25 and 50 percent of the population of Europe, by poisoning the water. When a Jewish physician, tortured on the rack, "confessed" that he had poisoned the water with materials provided by a Spanish rabbi, hatred of the Jews spread throughout Europe. Despite efforts by the Crown to protect Jews, they were murdered or forced to leave to the extent that the Jewish population in Spain and Portugal was reduced by 75 percent—and they were eliminated or driven out of large sections of Germany, Belgium, and Switzerland in a manner presaging the Nazi exterminations before and during World War II.[81]

The toleration of gays diminished in this era. Homosexuality passed from being wholly legal to being illegal in many parts of Europe between the years 1250 and 1300—with some local statutes demanding the castration or execution of persons who engaged in sodomy. Moreover, clerical and other theorists variously argued that homosexuals were "unnatural," violated Christian precepts, threatened the normal reproduction of the species, and were subsumed by sexual urges.[82]

## SOME LEGACIES OF THE MEDIEVAL ERA

At first glance, the twelfth through the sixteenth centuries seem scarcely relevant to the American experience, but the medieval period provides a context or backdrop that usefully highlights the distinctive ideas of the American colonists who endeavored to develop a utopia in the New World that would contrast with the Old World. Concepts of individualism, capitalism, punitive treatment of the poor, limited government, and separation of church and state—ideas and insti-

tutions that took hold in the New World— contrast with some of the institutions and ideas of the medieval period, such as the central governments of the monarchs, the nonpunitive treatment of the poor, and the notion of mutual obligation. We argue in Chapter 12 that the *absence* of feudalism in the colonies of the New World may partly explain the greater reluctance of Americans to develop a welfare state compared to Europeans, for whom the feudal tradition was integral to their societies even though they eventually eradicated much of it as they democratized, urbanized, and industrialized over a period of many centuries. If notions of mutual obligation and strong central governments persisted in Europe, they had less strength in the American colonies and (eventually) the United States.

At the same time, the colonists were "part medieval" though they claimed they were not. They inherited the expectation from the medieval period that people ought not to be allowed to starve. The earliest Americans were intensely religious as well though many of them rebelled from Catholicism. Americans, like Catholics of the medieval period, were prompted by their reli-

gion to help the downtrodden, both within their individual parishes or churches and within their specific sects. As we note later in this book, American reformers established an array of sectarian hospitals, schools, institutions for children, and innumerable other philanthropies from the colonial period onward.

Some of the inheritance from the medieval period was not so uplifting. The American settlers replicated the brutal policies of explorers like Christopher Columbus in their dealings with Native Americans. And they drew heavily on the experiences of Europeans in Brazil and the Caribbean when they developed slavery in many of their colonies in the latter part of the seventeenth century.

 **END NOTES**

1. Gerald Handel, *Social Welfare in Western Society* (New York: Random House, 1982), p. 31.

2. See discussion by George Homans, *English Villagers of the Thirteenth Century* (New York: Russell and Russell, 1960), pp. 73–82, 232–252; and Robert Webb, *Modern England: From the Eighteenth Century to the Present* (New York: Dodd, Mead, 1970), p. 7.

3. Homans, *English Villagers,* pp. 285–292.

4. *Ibid.,* pp. 255–284.

5. *Ibid.,* pp. 309–327.

6. K. D. M. Snell, *Annals of the Laboring Poor: Social Change and Agrarian England, 1660–1900* (Cambridge: Cambridge University Press, 1985), pp. 166–194.

7. Homans, *English Villagers,* pp. 319–327, 328–330.

8. Edmund Morgan, *American Slavery, American Freedom: The Ordeal of Colonial America* (New York: Norton, 1975), pp. 64–68; Homans, *English Villagers,* pp. 353–381.

9. Handel, *Social Welfare,* pp. 53–54.

10. Homans, *English Villagers,* pp. 109–116, 133–134, 200–207.

11. George Trevelyan, *England in the Age of Wycliffe* (New York: Longmans, Green, 1925), pp. 268–273.

12. Brian Tierney, *Medieval Poor Law: A Sketch of Canonical Theory and Its Application in England* (Berkeley, Calif.: University of California Press, 1959), p. 12.

13. Lottie Kendzierski, *Saint Thomas Aquinas: On Charity* (Milwaukee, Wis.: Marquette University Press, 1960).

14. Julien Green, *God's Fool: Life and Times of Francis of Assisi* (San Francisco: Harper & Row, 1985).

15. A. L. Rowse, *The England of Elizabeth* (New York: Macmillan, 1951), pp. 318–359.

16. Morgan, *American Slavery,* pp. 64–65; Webb, *Modern England,* p. 28.

17. Homans, *English Villagers,* pp. 353–381.

18. Handel, *Social Welfare,* p. 62.

19. Robert Gottfried, *The Black Death: Natural and Human Disaster in Medieval Europe* (New York: Free Press, 1983).

20. Morgan, *American Slavery*, pp. 65–66.

21. Blanche Coll, *Perspectives in Public Welfare* (Washington, D.C.: U.S. Government Printing Office, 1969), p. 2.

22. Daniel Baugh, "Poverty, Protestantism, and Political Economy: English Attitudes Toward the Poor, 1600–1800." In Stephen Baxter, ed., *England's Rise to Greatness* (Berkeley, Calif.: University of California Press, 1983), p. 83.

23. Homans, *English Villagers*, pp. 309–327.

24. Bernard Bailyn, *The Ideological Origins of the American Revolution* (Cambridge, Mass.: Harvard University Press, 1967), pp. 163, 198–205.

25. Homans, *English Villagers*, pp. 142–143; Snell, *Annals*, pp. 138–227.

26. Joyce Appleby, *Capitalism and a New Social Order: The Republican Vision of the 1790s* (New York: New York University Press, 1984), pp. 1–23.

27. Joyce Appleby, *Economic Thought and Ideology in Seventeenth-Century England* (Princeton, N.J.: Princeton University Press, 1978), pp. 158–198.

28. *Ibid.*, pp. 251–279; Morgan, *American Slavery*, pp. 44–45.

29. Margaret James, *Social Problems and Policy During the Puritan Revolution* (London: George Routledge and Sons, 1930), pp. 78–130; Snell, *Annals*, pp. 228–269.

30. Baugh, "Poverty," pp. 76–84; Morgan, *American Slavery*, pp. 65–68.

31. Baugh, "Poverty," pp. 84–94; Robert Heilbroner, *The Worldly Philosophers* (New York: Simon & Schuster, 1968), pp. 66–69.

32. Rowse, *The England of Elizabeth*, pp. 80–81; Trevelyan, *England*, pp. 183–255.

33. Webb, *Modern England*, pp. 13–14.

34. Morgan, *American Slavery*, pp. 65–68.

35. Webb, *Modern England*, pp. 6–7.

36. *Ibid.*, pp. 15–22.

37. Appleby, *Economic Thought*, pp. 158–198.

38. James, *Social Problems*, pp. 241–302; Morgan, *American Slavery*, p. 326.

39. Charles Tilly, "Collective Action in England and America." In Richard Brown and Don Fehrenbacher, eds., *Tradition, Conflict, and Modernization: Perspectives on the American Revolution* (New York: Academic Press, 1977), pp. 45–50.

40. H. R. Trevor-Roper, *The Crisis of the Seventeenth Century* (New York: Harper & Row, 1968), pp. 61–76.

41. Webb, *Modern England*, pp. 43–46.

42. Bailyn, *The Ideological Origins*, pp. 55–93; John Yolton, *The Locke Reader* (Cambridge: Cambridge University Press, 1977), pp. 296–317.

43. Francis Bremer, *The Puritan Experiment* (New York: St. Martins Press, 1976), pp. 7–17, 43–47.

44. Appleby, *Economic Thought*, pp. 183–184, 190–198.

45. *Ibid.*

46. Morgan, *American Slavery*, pp. 321–325.

47. James, *Social Problems*, pp. 271–283; Morgan, *American Slavery*, pp. 321–325.

48. Resentment by peasants of the loss of their ability to raise crops on common pastures and on strips is discussed by Snell, *Annals*, pp. 209–227; Louise Tilly, "Food Entitlement, Famine, and Conflict." In Robert Rotberg and Theodore Rabb, eds., *Hunger and History* (Cambridge: Cambridge University Press, 1983), pp. 135–151.

49. Arthur Wilson, "The Enlightenment Came First to England." In Baxter, *England's Rise to Greatness*, pp. 1–28.

50. Heilbroner, *The Worldly Philosophers*, pp. 40–72.

51. Appleby, *Economic Thought*, pp. 129–157; Baugh, "Poverty," pp. 66–84; Snell, *Annals*, pp. 104–137.

52. Morgan, *American Slavery*, pp. 196–197.

53. *Ibid.*, p. 67.

54. Snell, *Annals*, pp. 104–137.

55. *Ibid.*

56. Appleby, *Economic Thought*, p. 136.

57. Snell, *Annals*, p. 105.

58. G. D. H. Cole and Raymond Postgate, *The British Common People, 1746–1946* (New York: Barnes & Noble Books, 1961), p. 115.

59. See Baugh's critique of Tawney in "Poverty," pp. 64–75.

60. Appleby, *Economic Thought,* pp. 139–146.

61. Baugh, "Poverty," pp. 84–94; Snell, *Annals,* pp. 108–114.

62. Snell, *Annals,* p. 107.

63. *Ibid.,* pp. 110–114.

64. Morgan, *American Slavery,* p. 98; Webb, *Modern England,* p. 28.

65. Webb, *Modern England,* pp. 29–30.

66. Susan Amussen, *An Ordered Society: Gender and Class in Early Modern England* (Oxford: Basil Blackwell, 1988), p. 133.

67. Antonia Fraser, *The Weaker Vessel* (New York: Knopf, 1984), p. 5.

68. *Ibid.,* pp. 1–4.

69. Maryanne Kowaleski and Judith Bennett, "Crafts, Gilds, and Women in the Middle Ages: Fifty Years After Marian K. Dale." In Judith Bennett, et al., eds., *Sisters and Workers in the Middle Ages* (Chicago: University of Chicago Press, 1989), pp. 11–38.

70. Amussen, *Ordered Society,* pp. 95–133.

71. Ronald Sanders, *Lost Tribes and Promised Lands* (Boston: Little, Brown, 1978), p. 17.

72. Gary Nash, *Red, White, and Black: The Peoples of Early America* (Englewood Cliffs, N.J.: Prentice-Hall, 1974), p. 156.

73. *Ibid.,* p. 160.

74. Zvi Dor-Ner, *Columbus and the Age of Discovery* (New York: William Morrow, 1991), p. 201.

75. *Ibid.,* p. 208.

76. *Ibid.,* pp. 219–220.

77. *Ibid.,* pp. 216–217.

78. *Ibid.,* p. 229.

79. Sanders, *Lost Tribes,* p. 7.

80. John Boswell, *Christianity, Social Tolerance, and Homosexuality* (Chicago: University of Chicago Press, 1980), p. 269.

81. Gottfried, *The Black Death,* pp. 52, 73.

82. Boswell, *Christianity,* pp. 277–302.

# CHAPTER 3

# Social Welfare in the Colonial Era

## Selected Orienting Events in the Colonial Era

| | |
|---|---|
| **1607** | Establishment of Jamestown colony |
| **1620** | Establishment of Plymouth colony |
| **1676** | Bacon's Rebellion in colonial Virginia |
| **Late 1600s** | Establishment of laws in southern colonies reducing blacks to chattel |
| **1680** | House of Burgesses in Virginia recommends every county build a workhouse |
| **1763** | Proclamation Line established to separate settlers' lands from Native American lands |
| **1775–1783** | American Revolution |
| **1787** | Constitutional Convention held in Philadelphia |
| **1788** | Constitution is ratified by the states |
| **1789** | George Washington elected to first of two terms |
| **1791** | Bill of Rights ratified as first ten amendments to Constitution |
| **1800** | Thomas Jefferson elected to first of two terms |

The history of American culture and politics in the colonial era can be viewed as a rapid shedding of feudalistic ideas and institutions inherited from Europe and the emergence of a capitalistic and democratic society. Perhaps because it was a relatively young nation, America cast off feudal institutions faster and more thoroughly than did European nations. Moreover, as we note in the ensuing discussion, many of the early settlers were deeply imbued with the ideas of thinkers like John Locke, whose political and economic ideas (as discussed in Chapter 2) were fraying medieval and feudal institutions in Europe.

The white settlers, who were mostly of English, German, Dutch, and French extraction, had soon developed a triracial society of whites, blacks (whom they imported), and Native Americans. Both in terms of the extent it favored individualism and limited government *and* in the degree it mixed persons of varying racial and ethnic backgrounds, it was a society different from those that had existed in world history.

An overriding question was: Could this heterogenous society evolve humanistic social institutions as well as positive relations among the three races that dominated it? Of course, this new society, which was largely agricultural and possessed limited resources and primitive governmental institutions (compared to modern bureaucracies and industrialized systems of modern societies), would not develop an advanced welfare state, so we seek clues about its likely future directions when we examine the colonial experience. And we derive these clues from the culture, early enactments, and initial political institutions of the emerging society in the New World.

 ## PATTERNS OF CONTINUITY

The earliest American settlers in the early part of the seventeenth century created a communal, hierarchical, and regulated society that conformed to feudal traditions. Settlers in the Massachusetts Bay Colony in the seventeenth century farmed strips, much as their feudal ancestors did, on land given to trading companies by the crown. The farmers were expected to give to the company a large share of their produce in exchange for their rights to work company lands. They lived in villages that were surrounded by company fields rather than in dispersed patterns that typified American agriculture in the eighteenth and nineteenth centuries.[1] Similar patterns were observed in the settlements in Virginia in the early seventeenth century.

The social structure in these earliest colonies was also hierarchical in the feudal sense. A few wealthy investors received rights to large tracts of land and were served by a landless class of indentured servants. A variety of artisans and craftsmen occupied an intermediary position in the social structure. Since participation in the process of governance was conditioned on both holding land and meeting specific religious requirements, many persons were disenfranchised.

Early life was tightly regulated. In Virginia, for example, each settler was required to plant a certain amount of corn to ensure adequate food crops. The colonists decided who could and who could not trap certain kinds of animals, where common pasturage was to be, the maximum levels of wages that could be paid, and the maximum prices that could be charged for specific products. Regulations were also promulgated that established apprenticeship requirements for entry into the various trades.[2] The individual colonies created official churches—Protestant churches in New England and a Church of England in Virginia. They also divided the countryside into parishes and imposed on all citizens, including those who worshiped in different churches, a tax to support the official church. Officials in these early churches, who were accorded extraordinary deference, often assumed roles in secular governance.[3]

## PATTERNS OF CHANGE

The semifeudal nature of some of these colonies in the early seventeenth century soon began to unravel. A market economy emerged rapidly in the New World, almost from the outset, since Europeans wanted agricultural products and other raw materials from the New World in exchange for finished goods from their industries. Unlike many Englishmen, who saw capitalism as an intrusion on traditional arrangements such as entail and primogeniture, Americans tended to believe that capitalism was natural and desirable. By the turn of the nineteenth century, Jefferson and many other leaders had embraced Adam Smith's economic theories and believed that capitalism would bring unprecedented prosperity to the new nation.[4]

Trading companies soon realized that landless persons would settle on open land at the frontier if the companies did not sell it to them, so the purchase and sale of land soon became a massive enterprise throughout the colonies. As the population began to disperse and as significant numbers of settlers acquired their own holdings, it became more difficult to maintain social controls in the early settlements. The new colonies quickly became dispersed agricultural settlements and villages.

Placed on the land, yeomen (small landholders) increasingly expected to participate in the governance of the colony. By 1780, approximately 40 percent of the American settlers owned their own land in plots that averaged between 90 and 160 acres—an extraordinary percentage of the population compared to European societies.[5] Large landholders dominated the politics of Virginia and some other southern colonies through the eighteenth century, but they had to appease growing numbers of small landowners, who were heavily represented in elective bodies.

The conflicts of colonial politics further eroded the communal and hierarchical nature of the early settlements. Settlers in the western sections of the colonies demanded funds for militia to protect them from Native Americans and for construction of roads and other improvements. These demands were often resisted by easterners, and competition for the limited public funds was intense among various localities. Many colonists soon came to oppose the royal governors appointed by the crown, who favored policies of taxation, the exportation to England

of agricultural products even at the risk of food shortages, prohibitions on the establishment of manufacturing, and other policies designed to enrich England.[6]

Conflict also increased because of the absence of a genuine aristocracy that could command deference. An American aristocracy emerged, but it was not very cohesive, and it commanded less respect from Americans than did the English aristocracy from the British. Marked inequality in wealth and land ownership existed in America, too, but the availability of land on the frontier meant that many small landowners were not restrained by traditional politics or deference to social elites.[7]

Maintenance of an official church became increasingly problematic in the various colonies. America soon became a sanctuary for numerous Protestant sects, who, despite various "toleration acts" in England, were still subject to widespread persecution, such as exclusion of their children from English universities, restrictions on suffrage, and enforced tithing to the Church of England. As members of the various sects became representatives in local and colonial government, they urged separation of church and state and termination of the requirement that citizens pay taxes to support the state church. Separation of church and state, which was made explicit in the Constitution, was inevitable in a country with so many religious sects.[8]

The American settlers entered a New World where ancient rights to land, an entrenched aristocracy, and a monarchy did not exist. These settlers were able to fashion a new society, unimpeded by the feudalistic traditions of Europe.[9] They believed they could create a utopia of yeoman farmers by embracing capitalism and democratic institutions. Europeans such as Locke, by contrast, knew that their ideas could be only partially realized in societies that were encumbered by centuries of tradition as well as classes and institutions that resisted change. As Commager put it, the Europeans imagined the Enlightenment while the Americans created it.[10]

In contrast to the English, who assumed that most persons would not own land, Americans believed that land ownership was central to the social order. The importance that colonial leaders attached to land ownership is illustrated by a portion of a letter that Jefferson wrote to James Madison in 1785 from France.

> The property of this country is absolutely co-centered in a very few hands, having revenues of from half a million of guineas a year downwards. These employ the flower of the country as servants, some of them having as many as 200 domestics, not labouring. They employ also a great number of manufacturers, and tradesmen, and lastly the class of labouring husbandmen. But after all these comes the most numerous of all the classes, that is, the poor who cannot find work. I asked myself what could be the reason that so many should be permitted to beg who are willing to work, in a country where there is very considerable proportion of uncultivated lands? . . . The earth is given as common stock for man to labour and live on . . . it is too soon yet in our country to say that every man who cannot find employment but who can find uncultivated land, shall be at liberty to cultivate it, paying a moderate rent. But it is not too soon to provide by every possible means that as few as possible shall be without a little portion of land. The small landowners are the most precious part of a state.[11]

No central government existed in the American colonies until the inception of the republic in 1789. Instead, various trade and defense policies from Parliament were administered by royal governors in the various colonies, and these policies were bitterly resented by many colonists.[12] Furthermore, many colonists revered John Locke and other writers and pamphleteers who championed a limited government, which contrasted sharply with notions of governance that derived from feudalism and the divine rights of kings.[13] Locke wanted government to be restricted largely to police and military roles since he believed government to be an unnatural institution that was needed only because, without it, unprincipled people would take property from others.

When they came to write the Constitution in the 1780s, Americans were so obsessed with the dangers of an oppressive central government that they, to avoid this possibility, created a complex system of checks and balances, including a popularly elected House of Representatives, a Senate elected by an electoral college that was chosen by the public, a president elected by an electoral college rather than by direct election, and an independent judiciary.[14]

The subsequent efforts of many Americans to oppose centralization of power in Washington cannot be understood without understanding this colonial context. Conservatives in contemporary America, as well as some liberals, continue to ally themselves with local prerogatives and to seek diminution of federal social welfare roles. Although they have often been opposed by liberals and radicals who want expanded social welfare roles for central government, a strong defense of social welfare roles of the central government is relatively recent in American history. By contrast, in England and other European countries, extensive central government policy and regulatory roles have existed since (at least) the eighteenth century. Not until the 1930s, or almost 150 years after the founding of the republic, did Americans develop strong social policy roles for the federal government.

The role of government at both national and local levels would be even further restricted, moreover, by American acceptance of the theories of Adam Smith, who maintained that government ought not to interfere in the private market. When Alexander Hamilton suggested in the 1780s and 1790s that the national government ought to follow a mercantilist policy by aggressively subsidizing new industries to enhance American participation in world markets, developing a national bank, and building public works, he was soundly defeated by Thomas Jefferson, who argued that the national government should not assume major economic roles.[15]

Americans were also loath to give state and federal governments considerable power because of fear of favoritism. Since legislatures had limited funds for public improvements, unsuc-cessful claimants, such as people from a specific town or region, accused them of giving preferential treatment to successful applicants. The charge that governmental assistance leads to favoritism is not unusual in the politics of most societies, but this idea was carried to its extreme in the early nineteenth century when some Americans insisted that any governmental assistance to local government or to special projects represented favoritism.[16]

Although the expressed political beliefs of colonial leaders often extolled limited government, their rhetoric often conflicted with reality with respect to *local* governments, which, in townships, emphasized an array of "intrusions" into local economic and social matters. Local governments taxed local citizens and businesses, regulated their affairs (including often establishing prices and wages that they used), required males to work certain numbers of days on roads and other public improvements, and constructed roads and bridges extensively (sometimes with tolls).[17] These patterns of involvement in local economic and social matters, however, established early in the colonial experience the primacy of local government since no central or federal institutions existed. It is no wonder, then, that the American federal government was, in effect, extraordinarily weak when it was finally created in 1789—and it remained weak until well into the twentieth century.

Moreover, even these local governments were weak, partly because Americans prized their individualism and liberty so highly. Greene's depiction of local government is instructive:

> With only a tiny bureaucracy and no police, a localized judiciary system that rarely met more than fifteen to thirty days in any given year, and legislators that in peacetime were rarely in session for more than a month in any given year, government was small, intermittent, and inexpensive. Except during wartime, taxes were low, and the only public activities that engaged most men were infrequent militia or jury service and some more frequent participation in vital public

works such as building and repairing bridges and roads . . . while they wanted enough government to secure peace and to maintain . . . civil order, most Americans were . . . in favor of just so much government as will do justice, protect property, and defend the country.[18]

The work ethic came to assume extraordinary strength in the new society that was predominantly made up of Protestants. Its clearest statement is in *The Autobiography of Benjamin Franklin*, who outlined in detail a regimen of work, persistance, thrift, and self-improvement.[19] Franklin's obsessive preoccupation with industry and other moral habits found wide acceptance since it echoed the popular belief that one could fashion one's own destiny through moral behavior and hard work in the emerging capitalist economy.

The American colonists, in short, had created in the roughly 150 years that elapsed between the earliest settlements and the inauguration of George Washington in 1789 a society that drew heavily on certain ideas of European thinkers while rejecting other elements of European culture. Though there was hardly unanimity, Americans increasingly selected ideas of individualism, limited government, hard work, and capitalism—the very kinds of ideas that had begun to erode feudal traditions in Europe in the seventeenth and eighteenth centuries. The difference between the American colonies and the European society, then, was not in the basic notions that increasingly guided the Americans, for they were largely derivative of ideas that had been developed in Europe. Rather, the Americans were unusual in *the degree* to which they accepted these ideas *and* translated them into their governmental and economic institutions. If the Europeans were "stuck" with their monarchies and large central governments, for example, the Americans were able to fashion a Constitution in the wake of the American Revolution that gave them the kind of limited government that for European thinkers was a theoretical construct.

Nor were many of these American colonists humble about their new society. Writings of

Jefferson, Franklin, and others are frequently punctuated with references to the utopian qualities of the New World, with sarcastic remarks about the evils of the Old World such as its monarchies and urban areas, and with the belief that the Americans had devised institutional and social arrangements that would make other societies around the world wish to emulate their creation. Alas, such hyperbole masked many less savory realities in the cities and on the frontiers of the colonies.

 ## SOCIAL PROBLEMS IN THE NEW WORLD

The widespread belief that America was largely a land of prosperous farmers was unfounded from the outset. Americans were more prosperous than the English because of the abundance of land and the scarcity of labor. Social distinctions were less marked than in Europe, as was noted by a foreign visitor who was amazed to observe ordinary persons talking openly with large landholders.[20] But extraordinary differentials in wealth and landholdings existed in America. Moreover, the American colonies were largely agricultural; only 5 percent of the Americans lived in cities in the eighteenth century, and no American city exceeded 30,000 citizens in 1776.[21]

A wealthy elite, who owned a considerable portion of the land and assets in such colonies as Virginia and such cities as Philadelphia, New York, and Boston, flaunted their wealth in a manner similar to English aristocrats. This American aristocracy, from whom members of the Constitutional Convention were drawn in the 1780s, shared many of the fears of the English aristocracy about the lower class and landless persons. The elite wanted government to be dominated by aristocrats who would be appointed by state legislatures rather than elected by the people.[22] John Adams, who was to become the second American president, even preferred the title of king to president though he wanted him to have limited powers.

Roughly 30 percent of the population in 1780 was farm laborers as opposed to owners of land.[23] Furthermore, more than half the white immigrants to the New World were indentured servants who served a term of four or more years before they became freedmen. (Evidence suggests that many indentured servants left England, Scotland, and Wales because unemployment had increased markedly during the seventeenth century; but a considerable number were also felons who were deported to the colonies as indentured servants.)[24] Local courts provided protection for some indentured servants who were beaten or whose term of service was not honored by their masters, but their legal rights were not so complete as in England. Servants were beholden to their masters because they had paid their transportation costs to this country. Owners could try to extend their service by appealing to local courts if their servants ran away, swore at them, or committed other petty offenses. Female indentured servants were often denied permission to marry by their masters because they feared the women would leave their service.[25]

Indentured servants who had finished their terms often had difficulty in finding an economic niche for themselves. Many of them became tenant farmers who worked at low wages for landowners because they lacked funds to purchase land. Some of them became a relatively poor and landless population in the growing cities of colonial America. Those who purchased land often had to go to relatively cheap land on the frontier, where they encountered danger from Native Americans. Those servants who became apprentices in hopes of entering a trade had to serve an additional seven years of service to tradesmen and were often mistreated by their masters.[26]

Although the early cities were small, the sizable numbers of unskilled and semiskilled persons who came to reside in them were subject to numerous recessions that bedeviled the fragile American economy. Many Americans became overextended, could not pay debts, and were imprisoned in a credit-hungry economy. Produce was often plentiful, but Americans sometimes exported so much grain to Europe that shortages occurred in American cities. Consumer goods were often scarce in a nation that imported most of its manufactured goods.[27] Nash argues that these urban, white, and landless people often became increasingly aware of differences in wealth, thus increasing the likelihood of urban unrest in hard times.[28]

As in England during the same period, mobs sometimes formed that engaged in looting, violence, or angry confrontations. A series of nine major rebellions, which lasted a year or more, erupted in rural areas in the seventeenth and eighteenth centuries. These rebellions were waged by persons with a homestead ethic who believed that their land titles were unfairly seized by trading companies or that their land was excessively taxed by legislatures. Thus, Bacon's Rebellion in seventeenth-century Virginia involved a number of landless freedmen and indentured servants who protested against the monopoly of land by large owners.[29] Riots also occurred in urban areas, where mobs protested high prices of key products such as bread or price fixing by monopolists. These were strictly local protests, but their number suggests that suffering was widespread and that serious social problems existed in the New World.

 ## THE DILEMMA OF OUTGROUPS

Although white indentured servants and tenant farmers often experienced poverty, their lot was enviable compared to Native Americans and black slaves, who were virtually defined as nonpersons in the colonial period. Nor did women enjoy many legal rights in this period.

### The Native Americans

Early estimates by historians placed the Native American population of North America (excluding Mexico) at only one million persons, but recent research suggests that, in fact, this area was "densely populated" by Native Americans, numbering some ten million persons in 1490.[30] Tribes occupied every portion of North America and included coastal tribes on the Pacific and Atlantic, tribes inhabiting the forests east of the Mississippi, the Plains tribes that hunted buffalo, tribes that occupied the Rocky Mountains,

and tribes that lived in the deserts of the southwestern and western portions of the continent.[31] This huge and dispersed population represented a major barrier for the white settlers because they occupied the land—the most valuable resource in the New World.

The early colonists quickly encountered two groups of Native Americans: a string of coastal tribes that occupied coastal areas from New England to Florida and a group of inland tribes that inhabited areas like the Appalachian Mountains. The coastal tribes were immediately vulnerable to the incursion by the white settlers, but the inland tribes, protected by geography, were able to maintain themselves until the mideighteenth century.[32]

Colonists in the earliest settlements in Virginia and Massachusetts viewed Native Americans in the coastal tribes as persons who could be converted to Christianity and who, in the meantime, could help settlers by introducing native crops and hunting techniques to them. "Praying colonies" were established in early settlements in Massachusetts, where converted Native Americans lived as part of the white settlements. The settlers were certain that the Native Americans would opt for Western culture to obtain its technological benefits as well as salvation; how could they, the colonists reasoned, retain their nomadic, un-Christian, and primitive existence when offered the benefits of civilization and Christianity?[33] This expectation was naive on many counts. Native Americans had their own culture, which they prized and which differed markedly from that of the settlers. The Native Americans worshiped their own deities, did not collect or value property, led a nomadic life, and were content with a subsistence existence that required only as much work as was needed for survival.

As the numbers of white settlers increased, it became obvious that Native American culture was endangered. Once they had given up feudal strip farming and communal property, many of the earliest settlers began to develop and enclose fields, much as the English landowners had—a practice that quickly depleted lands of the Native Americans. As Native Americans resisted, their violence was used as evidence that they were savages beyond any hope of conversion to Christianity.[34] If they did *not* resist, the relentless expansion of white settlements continued unabated. The settlers also conducted their share of unprovoked violence—for example, because some group within their settlement enjoyed slaughtering Indians, because they were overcome with fear as they heard of other violence, or because they wished to retaliate for some earlier violence. Petty theft by a Native American led in one case to the massacre of an entire tribe.

As we discussed in Chapter 2 with respect to Spanish migration to the Caribbean, the spreading of diseases, such as smallpox, cholera, and diphtheria, was even more devastating to Native Americans than warfare. Since these diseases were wholly new to the Native Americans, they lacked biological resistance to them. By roughly 1675, the coastal tribes extending from New England to the Carolinas had been virtually eliminated, with remnant survivers pushing inland to join with the still-powerful inland tribes.

The inland tribes that occupied the Appalachian Mountains and their vicinity proved able to resist the white settlers until the mideighteenth century. Their remarkable resilience was possible because of their geographic remoteness from the coastal settlements and because of their ingenuity in developing alliances with the French and adapting their hunting practices for furs to the commercial markets of the white settlers.

The white settlers could have agreed to permanently cede large portions of lands on the frontier to the Native Americans, but they refrained from this for several reasons. Since England and the trading companies established the white settlements in the first instance to provide raw materials and markets for the English mercantile system, they supported continuing migration inland for furs and other commodities that could be used in England. Moreover, the colonists believed that land was created by God to be farmed and that forest and other unfarmed land that was occupied by nonfarming Native Americans was wasted land that should be given to (or taken by) the white settlers.[35]

The settlers attempted to wrest the land from the Native Americans in a manner that would make their exploitation appear to be compatible with moral codes. They successfully used the seemingly legal device of the treaty, which made it appear as if colonists received land that had been voluntarily and legally ceded to them. Native Americans were made to sign under threat of coercion, while intoxicated, or in exchange for money or gifts. When the Native Americans stopped teaching their children to use bows, they could no longer obtain food without obtaining guns, so white settlers could entice them to sign treaties by offering them guns and other commodities. One tribe tried to revive ancient hunting skills in the mideighteenth century so as to decrease their dependence on the settlers, but few of them had the patience to undergo the years of required practice when guns were available.[36]

But the settlers were not so successful in obtaining lands from the inland tribes. Shrewd bargaining by many tribes in an area extending from New York State to the Ohio Valley, who joined in a common negotiating alliance, led the British Crown to draw a line, known as the Proclamation Line of 1763, that separated settlers' lands from Native Americans' lands on the western frontier.[37] (The Crown was willing to make this concession to thwart alliances between the Native Americans and the French, who vigorously contested the English for possession of portions of the New World.) The Crown had difficulty enforcing this line, however, because individual settlers, trading companies, and colonies breeched it as they relentlessly sought lands beyond the Proclamation Line. The Americans displayed far less resolve than the English in enforcing the line when the frontier was ceded to them after the American Revolution.

Inland tribes such as the Iroquois in the North and the Cherokees in the South were doomed, however. They were as subject to the dread diseases as their coastal counterparts were as the frequency of their contact with white settlers increased. As they altered their hunting patterns to collect furs so as to be able to purchase guns and other products, they dispersed their tribal settlements, thus making them more vulnerable to attack. The white settlers soon employed treaties, as well as brute force, to displace them from their traditional lands. The ability of Native Americans to resist the white settlers was diminished, as well, by animosities between tribes, who sometimes fought with one another because of traditional rivalries or over scarce land as the white settlers advanced. As the nineteenth century began, Native Americans were in retreat from large areas immediately beyond the Appalachian Mountains and were being pushed into the inner and western recesses of the North American continent.

## Black Slavery

The New World was a labor-hungry society since land had to be cleared, roads built, and crops raised in a harsh environment. Labor was particularly needed in Virginia and the Carolinas, where the settlers had decided to stake their economic existence on tobacco, a labor-intensive crop. Native Americans were a potential source of labor, but they were not willing to work in the settlers' fields and could not be easily enslaved because they could escape to the wilderness. White indentured servants became the major source of agricultural labor in the early southern colonies, but they also proved unsuitable because many of them objected to the backbreaking work in the intolerable summer heat and had to be replaced when they had fulfilled their prescribed term of indentured service. They posed a political problem as well since the freed indentured servants roamed the American countryside and agitated against oppressive working conditions when they lacked funds to purchase their own land. When the English economy improved in the midseventeenth century, and the harsh working conditions of the tobacco colonies became well known, indentured servants in England were increasingly difficult to recruit.[38]

As we discussed in the last chapter, a precedent existed for the use of black slaves in the sugar colonies of the Caribbean, where they had been used extensively to grow sugar. Massive importation of blacks was delayed, however, because the death rate was so high from malaria and other epidemics that planters would have lost most of their slaves. When the death rate declined, the advantages of slaves as a source of labor became obvious. Slaves were kept for life rather than for brief terms and provided a self-replenishing source of labor that obviated continually importing indentured servants. The political and social problems of accommodating freed servants were obviated since slaves were not released. Slaves could be brutally disciplined without the surveillance of local courts; by contrast, indentured servants could be whipped only with consultation from local courts and could request hearings if they believed they were mistreated.

For slavery to exist, however, the southern plantation owners had to develop laws that circumscribed the rights of blacks and that punished those whites who chose *not* to cooperate in maintaining slavery. They had accomplished this legal task by the beginning of the eighteenth century in the tobacco colonies. Slaves were not allowed to own property; indeed, their property was confiscated in Virginia and given to local parishes for redistribution to poor whites. Whites were forbidden by law to have sexual relations with blacks, and persons who sheltered or assisted runaway slaves were subjected to harsh treatment. The legal status of slaves was thus reduced to chattel.[39]

The new laws cemented the white population, including the poor whites, behind the oppression of the slaves. Although whites were themselves subject to punishment if they assisted runaways or engaged in sexual activity with them, they obtained the right to discipline blacks even without obtaining permission from their owners. By investing even the poor white population with superior rights, the large slaveowners, some historians believe, obtained laws that decreased the likelihood of alliances between low-income whites and slaves.[40] (Before the enactment of these laws, indentured white servants had often worked in the fields alongside blacks and had even intermarried with them.) Indeed, many whites, even those of modest means, saw the owning of slaves as a sign of respectability and upward mobility by the eighteenth century in many southern jurisdictions.

Some slaves reached the New World before 1676, but the torrent of importation began after that date when the Royal African Company's monopoly was shattered and many private slave traders entered the lucrative markets. The slave shipments from Africa rose from 10,000 per year in the 1690s to 40,000 per year in the 1790s.[41] Roughly one million slaves were im-

ported to the colonies or born in the colonies *before* the American Revolution.[42] So many slaves were imported that they constituted almost 20 percent of the population in the New World by the time of the American Revolution—and 40 to 60 percent of the population of many southern jurisdictions.[43]

As with Native Americans, a vicious circle of violence developed. Blacks did not enjoy the harsh working conditions associated with tobacco farming and often refused to work as hard as their masters desired. Their resistance confirmed the beliefs of whites that they were uncivilized and beyond hope of conversion to English values or religion. Racism, the imputation of negative characteristics to entire groups of persons who share similar physiological characteristics, became pervasive in the white community.

The working and social conditions of the slaves were often degrading in the extreme. In the rice-growing areas of the coastal Carolinas, slaves worked in large gangs of fifty or more as they planted, cultivated, and harvested rice. Other slaves were owned by small farmers who used them in smaller numbers to plant corn and other crops. Available evidence suggests that owners made frequent use of whipping; vicious punishment of runaways; "intrusion, inspection, and harassment" of the minutest aspects of their personal lives; sales of "surplus" slaves in a pattern that disrupted familial relationships; imposition of a class system with preferential treatment given to those slaves who worked in the owners' houses; and a conscious pattern of disrupting families by taking children from them at an early age and often placing parents in separate sleeping quarters.[44]

By defining African-Americans and Native Americans as nonpersons, southern whites did not have to feel guilty about their actions or policies. Violence was often rationalized as serving the broader needs of society or even the nonpersons themselves. In killing Native Americans, for example, many colonists believed they were promoting the advance of Christianity and civilization, just as many slaveowners believed they were providing blacks with discipline and good work habits by subjecting them to harsh treatment.

But slavery was not only a southern institution in the colonial period. Slaves were also held in the northern colonies until all of them but New York and New Jersey eradicated it during the period from 1776 to 1783. (New York and New Jersey enacted laws that ended the institution in 1799 and 1804, respectively.) Agitation by Quakers and other religious groups assumed a major role in ending slavery in the North.[45]

Although slavery was largely eliminated in the North, northern representatives at the Constitutional Convention in the 1780s had to decide whether to accede to southerners' wishes to retain the institution. Many of the framers of the Constitution eyed slavery uneasily because they feared that social turmoil from rebellions of slaves would allow England to conquer the South (for its cotton) or might require the federal government to commit troops to restore tranquility. (These pragmatic fears were more prevalent than moral outrage.) Northerners also feared that southerners would bolt the Constitutional Convention—and the new nation—if they mentioned abolition, but they did not want slavery transplanted to the frontier. They also did not want southerners to capture control of the Congress by adding large numbers of slave-favoring congressmen as new states entered the union from frontier areas.[46]

This conflict between northerners and southerners became the most contentious division during the Constitutional Convention and led to a series of compromises. The northerners obtained exclusion of slavery from the frontier north of the Ohio River in the Northwest Ordinance of 1787 and were allowed to place a tax on imported slaves. But southerners won most of the concessions: Slavery was not limited to those states where it existed; slaves were counted as though they were three-fifths of a person for purposes of apportioning congressional representatives; and Congress was not permitted to interfere with the importation of

slaves until 1807. (Legislation to prohibit importation was finally enacted in 1808.)[47] The Constitution legitimized slavery by referring to it in eight places.[48]

In retrospect, both southerners and northerners miscalculated during the Constitutional Convention. Since southerners assumed they would soon control the Congress as new slave states were added to the Union and as the population of southern states increased, they believed no additional interference with the institution would develop. Northerners assumed that slavery would disappear naturally as the economy grew and as yeomen farmers populated the West. Neither side realized that, as both regions obtained new states on the frontier, a political stalemate would culminate in a civil war. Already, in 1787, the two regions disagreed on other issues as well. Southerners wanted a weak central government that could not impose tariffs or supervise interstate commerce, whereas many northerners favored a somewhat stronger central government.[49]

When considering blacks and Native Americans, many colonists were afflicted by racism, the imputation of negative characteristics to people of color. Benjamin Franklin feared blacks would "darken" the people of America, who could, by excluding blacks and Native Americans, increase "the lovely White."[50] And Jefferson advocated the removal of blacks from America so that the New World would be a "sanctuary" for European immigrants and their progeny.[51] Moreover, the Congress in 1790 enacted legislation that restricted citizenship to Caucasians—legislation that was used to deny citizenship to Asian immigrants in the nineteenth century and later.[52]

## The Status of Women

Ultimately, authority in families and in society resided with men in colonial society. Men concerned themselves with farming, business, politics, and professions, whereas women were relegated to domestic matters and the raising of children. Although women might on occasion assume management of a business when their husband died, they generally refrained from seeking expanded economic and social roles.[53]

Feminism, in the modern sense of the word, did not exist in colonial America, even among such articulate women as Abigail Adams, the wife of John Adams. Virtually no one considered the possibility that women might vote. Elaborate codes of etiquette were developed that defined patterns of deference of various members of the family to one another in a hierarchy extending from the husband to the wife to the children. Women could own property and sign contracts when they were unmarried or widowed, but they did not usually retain property or sign contracts when married—though some colonies technically allowed them to sign "marriage settlements" so as to enable them to keep legal possession of property that they brought into a marriage. The children of women were the legal property of husbands after marriages had been officially dissolved, even when the husband had been unfaithful or abusive. Women were not allowed to serve on juries. Except for the Quakers, Protestant sects did not allow women to assume major roles in church governance.[54] Married women were not expected to work although it is likely that women in lower-income groups often had to work to survive. Already in the colonial period, the wages of working women, married or unmarried, were far less than those of men who undertook comparable work—and the segregation of working women into poorly paid work, such as small retailers, seamstresses, laundresses, and domestic servants, suggested that the feminization of poverty, a term used in the contemporary period, had relevance to many women in urban areas in the colonial period.[55] From the professions of law and medicine, women were excluded altogether.[56]

Many colonists believed women to be inferior to men owing to traditions that came from medieval times when Catholic doctrine often stressed that Eve had brought sin into the world by seducing Adam. Though a number of thinkers in the Renaissance criticized the notion that women were, morally or intellectually, inferior to men, the Protestantism of the seventeenth century had strong misogynist (sexist) tendencies, as well, such as the notion that women were seductresses—yet they did support minimal literacy for women so that they could read the Bible and countered the worship of celibacy when they abolished monasteries.[57]

Although limited in their roles, women in the colonial period were probably not so restricted as women in the nineteenth century. The high rate of mortality meant that many women assumed responsibility for the trades or businesses of their deceased husbands. Some women were able to enter some trades because the society desperately needed labor. Midwives delivered many children. Women served a number of economic roles in agriculture by helping their husbands run farms and by producing candles and cloth in a society that lacked manufacturing industries. Much like Gandhi in twentieth-century India, women made homespun cloth during the American Revolution to reduce dependence on imported English cloth.[58] However, we should not exaggerate the economic roles of women in colonial times; as Harris notes, they often assumed economic roles only *after* their husbands had died, and they performed them in a larger context of subordination.[59]

The domestic burdens of women were also less onerous in the eighteenth century than in the nineteenth century since children often entered trades at the age of ten or eleven. By the midnineteenth century, however, children were increasingly seen as needing extended and intensive parenting, which required women to devote a major portion of their lives to parenting and spousal responsibilities.

Some evidence exists that women experienced worsening economic conditions toward the end of the eighteenth century. Increasing numbers of husbands, who often predeceased their wives, left most of their estates to their children rather than to their wives. Although outdoor relief of women who were single heads of households had prevailed in earlier periods, the construction of poorhouses in many jurisdictions meant that women were increasingly forced into the institutions when they could not fend for themselves. Some jurisdictions did allow women, when entering marriages, to construct marriage settlements that kept their rights to the property that they brought into the marriage, but few women availed themselves of these settlements, so they lost control of their property within the marriage and when their husbands predeceased, divorced, or left them.[60]

Women suffered extraordinary hardship because no adequate method of birth control existed; aside from abstinence and coitus interruptus, only herbal and other folk methods were used, and they were of dubious value. Moreover, it was widely believed that the ultimate purpose of marriage was procreation, so few women actively used even these limited forms of birth control aside from the use of abstinence to increase the interval between childbirths. Women tended to marry in their early twenties and to have children every other year, often reaching families of seven or more children. It is estimated that as many as one in five women died during childbirth or from the toll of successive pregnancies. Moreover, many women were pregnant at point of marriage, probably around 20 percent of them in some jurisdictions.[61]

Women received some assistance in the colonial period from the fact that American Protestants strongly favored "peaceable" and intact families—so they favored laws that granted divorces on grounds of desertion (the most common reason women sought divorce) and cruelty. (Most divorce petitions were initiated by men, but they were often rejected by local courts.) Laws existed in many colonies, as well, that forbade physical abuse of women and children and that punished perpetrators of rape though then (as now) many rapists escaped punishment by alleging that the woman had consented.[62]

The colonists developed various codes for punishing fornication and adultery, as well as other kinds of "lewd behavior," partly because they wanted sexual behavior to be confined to procreation within marriages—an orientation that was intensified by the Protestant religions of many settlers. We note later how this regulation of sexual matters, though imperfectly enforced and often flouted, provided a legacy that made it difficult for women in subsequent periods to obtain access to birth control when effective techniques finally emerged.[63]

 ## POSITIVE RESPONSES TO SOCIAL NEED

Americans inherited the same combination of positive and punitive social policies that existed in England in the seventeenth and eighteenth centuries, but they often did not enforce negative policies since they assumed that pauperism and even poverty would not become widespread in their land-owning utopia. Furthermore, most early settlers brought with them the tradition of regulation of local economic affairs that had been so pervasive in Europe. Strange as it seems to contemporary Americans, cities, counties, and colonial assemblies engaged in extensive limiting of wages and prices, granting of business licenses to merchants, controlling of the exportation of grain and other commodities, and regulating of rights and obligations of indentured servants and apprentices. These various regulations did not necessarily benefit poor persons since they could be devised in a manner that assisted the wealthy or those masters who had indentured or apprenticed labor, but colonists nonetheless believed that government should assume a wide range of functions to further economic development and to assist persons in the lower economic strata. The colonists also brought with them the mercantile tradition from England that gave government major roles in promoting the development of jobs and economic growth through the building of roads, bridges, and other capital improvement projects. The development of regulatory policies at the local and state levels must be considered a positive social welfare response to social and economic needs.[64]

A tradition of private philanthropy developed with remarkable rapidity and often led to projects that were jointly funded by government and private donors. Benjamin Franklin participated in many partnerships between the public and private sectors, for example, to develop libraries, fire-fighting services, orphanages, and educational programs.[65] The prevalence of Protestantism in the New World promoted the ethic of charitable giving. Wealth was often perceived by early Protestants as a mixed blessing; although it was the proper reward for a life of hard work, it could also promote laziness, pride, and greed, traits that were viewed by many colonists as sinful. Donation to charity became one method of easing this guilt about material possessions. Many of the earliest Puritan settlers believed that good works were morally correct but could not in themselves influence the Lord to grant salvation; however, by the mideighteenth century, a growing number of clergy and citizens believed that moral living could increase the likelihood of achieving salvation. The sermons of preachers of the Great Awakening, a grassroots movement to revitalize and personalize Protestant religion during the eighteenth century, illustrate this new view of the role of good works in obtaining personal salvation.[66]

Church parishes were a major source of charity, as in England. In the Puritan churches of Massachusetts Bay, for example, officers were elected whose major responsibility was to oversee sick and impoverished members of the congregation. Members of many of the Protestant churches likened church organizations to extended families that cared for their members in times of adversity.[67]

Officials in colonial and local governments also continued the tradition of the English Poor Law by requiring election or appointment of officials in local parishes to collect taxes to pay for poor relief. In assisting persons who had been wounded or disabled in battles with the Native Americans on the frontier, colonial assemblies were particularly generous, often funding assistance to these persons themselves rather than relying on local jurisdictions and without imposing on them punitive policies that characterized other forms of assistance.[68] Thomas Jefferson's portrayal of assistance to the poor in Virginia in the eighteenth century underscores generosity to those persons perceived not to be capable of working even though he notes that vagabonds were sometimes placed in workhouses.

> The poor, unable to support themselves, are maintained by an assessment on the tytheable persons in their parish. This assessment is levied and administered by twelve persons in each parish, called vestrymen, originally chosen by the housekeepers of the parish, but afterwards filling vacancies in their own body by their own choice. These are usually the most discreet farmers, so distributed through their parish, that every part of it may be under the immediate eye of some one of them. They are well acquainted with the details and economy of private life, and they find sufficient inducements to execute their charge well, in their philanthropy, in the approbation of their neighbours, and the distinction which that gives them. The poor who have neither property, friends, nor strength to labour, are boarded in the houses of good farmers, to whom a stipulated sum is annually paid. To those who are able to help themselves a little, or have friends from whom they derive some succours, inadequate however to their full maintenance, supplementary aids are given, which enable them to live comfortably in their own houses, or in the houses of their friends. Vagabonds, without visible property or vocation, are placed in workhouses, where they are well cloathed, fed, lodged, and made to labour. Nearly the same method of providing for the poor prevails through all our states; and from Savannah to Portsmouth you will seldom meet a beggar.[69]

In some jurisdictions, such as Boston, widowed or divorced women with children were able to resist the tendency to place all dependent persons in poorhouses, thus receiving outdoor relief.[70] Of course, these benign interpretations of the workings of poor law institutions need to be balanced by harsher interpretations, which we later note.

Colonial courts also assumed a range of social welfare functions. Many children became orphans in colonial society because of early deaths of many women and men from plagues, accidents, and childbirth. Local courts oversaw the economic affairs of these orphans to ensure that they received funds granted to them by the wills of their deceased parents, which were often given in the form of proceeds over a period of years from the sale of livestock that had been in their estates.[71]

Early Americans often favored the development of policies to equalize opportunity precisely because they favored self-improvement.

Americans emphasized some opportunity-enhancing policies even before the American Revolution, which expanded options for many citizens. Some favored universal and public education though universal education was not developed until the nineteenth century. Suffrage was generally tied to a property qualification, but it was already granted to more persons than in England.[72] Perhaps the largest social welfare program of the colonial period and the early republic, however, was land distribution. Although wealthy people bought large amounts of land in early Virginia, many smaller farmers were able to acquire land from the Crown, trading companies chartered by the Crown, and colonial governments.[73] Americans also developed private philanthropic institutions, which tended to support opportunity-enhancing educational, health, and self-help projects that reflected the preoccupation of the new society with self-improvement.[74]

## THE AMERICAN REVOLUTION

No discussion of the colonial period can avoid the American Revolution, the seminal event that led to the independence of the American Colonies from British control. It is important to ask whether the Revolution led the Americans to build on those positive responses to social problems in their midst by constructing remedies to the emerging social problems of their growing cities, as well as the abuses of Native Americans, African Americans, and women. Was the event a true revolution that, like the French Revolution that followed on its heels, contained substantial components of social reforms? Or was this event mostly a rebellion by angered colonists against the British, with little social reform content?

A host of recent research suggests strongly that the American Revolution, though accompa-

nied by a surge in idealism and sacrifice, had relatively limited effects on social reform. It did not lead to lasting efforts to help women obtain legal parity, to provide just treatment to Native Americans, to end slavery, or to reduce the marked inequality between social classes.[75]

Why was the American Revolution *not* a true revolution but mostly (and merely) a rebellion against the English? The American settlers, with rare exceptions, had developed *prior* to the Revolution a society that emphasized individualism and limited government.[76] Indeed, the Revolution was waged primarily to *preserve* representative government and the freedom of Americans from "unfair taxation" and regulations, rather than from an affirmative notion of creating a more just or equal society that proposed to use the powers of government to create social reforms.

Even casual inspection of the Declaration of Independence underscores the nature of the American Revolution; though it notes that "all men are created equal . . . [and] are endowed by their Creator with certain unalienable rights, that . . . [include] Life, Liberty, and the pursuit of Happiness," it moves quickly to emphasize the way "the present King of Great Britain" specifically overrode the colonists' *political* rights, including overriding laws passed by the colonial legislatures, appointing officials without consent from colonial legislatures, and maintaining "Standing Armies without the Consent of [colonial] legislatures." Our purpose is not to question the legitimacy of the colonial grievances but merely to underscore their limited and focused nature, which did not include the grist of true revolutions: the questioning of social relations *within* a society and between its social classes.

Moreover, the lack of a powerful central government before, during, and after the Revolution meant that the emerging nation lacked institutions to develop, finance, and implement strong social policies, even had its citizens desired them. (Recall that the nation lacked an effective federal government until the Constitution was made final.)

Nor were African Americans, Native Americans, or the "lower orders" within the small American cities effectively organized in this period. African Americans and Native Americans would have required effective advocates from the dominant white population, but such support as existed was miniscule compared to those elements of the population whose self-interest (such as slaveowners and persons who aspired to western lands) led them to oppose reforms to help these groups. Moreover, the extensive racism in the population made reforms for racial minorities unlikely in this period.[77] We note subsequently how the Constitution legitimized slavery. Some Native Americans thought they might benefit from the efforts of some federal authorities in the early years of the new republic to provide assistance to them even if based on the paternalistic notion of converting them to the white man's ways, but these officials were constantly thwarted by the violence and greed of individual white settlers, as well as by the governors of states bordering the frontier, who frequently made assaults on Native Americans and viewed them as mere "savages."[78] Women, who could not vote, found virtually no advocates for themselves among the male population during or after the Revolution.[79]

## OMINOUS SIGNS

If Americans did not believe that pauperism and other social ills would become widespread, ominous signs nonetheless existed that American society would develop a particularly harsh set of policies toward impoverished persons as well as African Americans and Native Americans.

The colonists, who lived in an agrarian society, cannot be blamed for policies or ideas that, when inherited by subsequent generations, proved insufficient to address the social problems of an urbanized and industrialized nation. Many tendencies or themes in colonial thought, however, became dominant or pervasive beliefs in the nineteenth century—extending even into the twentieth century—and served to retard the development of national social programs. In the ensuing discussion, we identify some ideas and policies that profoundly influenced the development of policy both in the colonial era and in the nineteenth century.

## Punitive Policies

Recall that a distinction was made between "deserving" and "undeserving" poor persons in the Elizabethan Poor Law; many Americans viewed unemployed persons as undeserving and, hence, favored punitive treatment of the poor by limiting assistance to indoor relief. In Massachusetts in 1780, vagabonds, paupers, and indentured servants were not granted the vote.[80] The institution of the workhouse gained considerable popularity in colonial America. As early as 1688, for example, the House of Burgesses in Virginia recommended that every county build a workhouse.[81] A frenzied period of construction occurred in New York State in the early and middle eighteenth century.[82] Many jurisdictions lacked the funds to build workhouses, however, so other punitive devices were used. A poor person or family could be auctioned to a low bidder, who would take care of them in return for payments from local officials; a child could be placed as an indentured servant under a willing master; and impoverished persons could find themselves summarily escorted to the boundaries of a jurisdiction since the American colonies had enacted laws of settlement that were similar to those enacted in England.

Americans also took a dim view of "moral crimes." Many jurisdictions enacted laws prohibiting adultery and fornication, swearing, or even malicious gossiping. It was common in colonial Virginia for persons guilty of these crimes to be made to devote a certain number of hours to work on public works, such as construction of a local bridge.[83] Alcoholism was a major problem in the American colonies and sometimes led to imprisonment. Major crimes were similarly met with harsh treatment. Debtors were often imprisoned, even when they had no means of paying debts that had occurred because of disability or health problems. As in England, capital punishment was used extensively, sometimes even for petty theft, and executions were often public events attended by throngs of people.[84]

Assistance of social welfare institutions was not extended to African Americans because they were defined to be outside the social compact and so as to prevent slaveowners from freeing their slaves when they could no longer work or were sick—actions that would have raised poor law costs of local jurisdictions. Laws that made slaves ineligible for assistance from poor law institutions and that forbade their owners from releasing them when they were ill or aged were enacted in various colonies.[85]

The settlers lived in a violent world. Most of them possessed firearms to hunt, to fend off Native Americans, and to obviate the creation of standing armies. They waged several major wars, fought Native Americans, engaged in various sectarian and sectional battles, fought in taverns, participated in various rural and urban riots, and witnessed public executions and lashings.[86]

## Absence of Protections

Feudal society was replete with regulations and traditions that stifled upward mobility, changes in residence, sale of land, and changes in occupation, but it also offered many protections to its citizens precisely because it was so regulated. Courts protected the rights of serfs and their successors, whether tenant farmers, indentured servants, or apprentices. Early Americans brought many feudal regulations from England, but they lacked the rich history of enforcement that existed in England.[87]

The English landed gentry were descendants of the noblemen of feudal times, either in direct family lineage or by accepting their social roles when they purchased large estates. Many of the landed gentry in England in the transition from feudal to postfeudal society resorted to enclosure and other policies that harmed emancipated serfs, but many of them also possessed a sense of obligation to persons in lower social and economic strata, which led them to support policies of job creation and mercantilism, as we discussed in Chapter 2. Conservative philosophers like Edmund Burke contended that English society was an "organic" entity bound together by ancient traditions.

The Americans in the upper social strata had weaker notions of their social obligations than their English counterparts. Few aristocrats and noblemen came to America; most immigrants derived from lower and middle classes. These self-made men—the American version of an aristocracy—sometimes believed, by the nineteenth century, that *everyone* should be able to obtain economic success.[88] An example of the limited sense of social obligation of the elites in American society is provided in colonial Virginia, a part of the country with a landholding aristocracy that appeared to be similar to the English landholding aristocracy. Available evidence suggests that many powerful landowners possessed scant interest in the needs of the lower strata of society since they expanded their holdings through ruthless exploitation of indentured servants, tenant farmers, and slaves.[89]

We noted in the preceding discussion that some colonies had numerous rules that they used to regulate wages, prices, and many other activities. But we also noted that, even with these regulations, the local governments in the colonies were extraordinarily weak and devoted mostly to protecting public order. With the ascendency of an ideology of limited government, which reached its fruition in local, state, and federal jurisdictions in the nineteenth century, the functions of government, limited though they already were, were markedly reduced. In Chapter 6, we note that the progressives, who were reformers in the early part of the twentieth century, devoted much of their time to developing those basic regulations, such as housing codes and public health codes, that American governments *should* have had in place in colonial periods, as well as in the nineteenth century.

## Ambiguous Position of Social Welfare in the Constitution

In no other society has a written constitution assumed such importance as in America. By codifying the functions of federal and local governments and the three branches of the federal government, the founders established rules and procedures that subsequent generations of citizens and courts have used to shape American policies. The founders were motivated by two conflicting objectives. They wanted to create a central government that possessed sufficient power over foreign affairs, the militia, interstate commerce, and currency so as to avoid the confusion that had prevailed in the wake of independence when each of the thirteen colonies fashioned its own foreign, trading, and financial policies. However, they were obsessed with the danger of a despotic central government.[90]

Their ingenious solutions to this tension had profound implications for social policy in succeeding centuries. To limit the federal government, they enumerated its specific powers in a list that included the right to issue currency, to form a militia, and to make treaties, but social welfare functions were noticeably absent from the Constitution since the founders assumed that local and state governments, along with private charity, would suffice. Furthermore, they specifically reserved to the states all powers not given to the federal government. It is not surprising, then, that succeeding generations of Americans opposed the development of federal social programs on the grounds that they were not mentioned in the Constitution.

Because the founders realized that the government needed to evolve to meet the changing needs of the nation, they inserted four provisions that *eventually* provided a legal rationale for the development of federal social policy.[91]

1. They gave the federal government the power to regulate interstate commerce, which was used in the twentieth century to

regulate the work conditions of workers whose companies shipped goods to other states.

2. After enumerating the powers of the government, they included a clause that allowed the federal government to enact laws that furthered the nation's "general welfare." This ill-defined clause was later used by social reformers to justify a range of social interventions.

3. The founders stipulated that the federal government could "make all laws that shall be necessary and proper for carrying into execution the foregoing (enumerated) powers." Like the general welfare clause, this phrase was sufficiently broad to justify a broad range of legislation.

4. By allowing the Constitution to be amended, the founders provided a mechanism for developing amendments that subsequently protected the rights of African Americans and other minorities in the wake of the Civil War.

As originally written, however, the Constitution must nonetheless be viewed as retarding the development of federal social programs because it did not mention social welfare policies and appeared to restrict the federal government to specific and relatively limited enumerated powers. By contrast, the French Constitution, which was written a few years later, outlawed slavery, guaranteed all citizens the right to work, urged humane care of the poor, and declared education to be a public obligation.[92]

## American Social Welfare Mythology

The early Americans hoped to create a utopia of land-owning, hard-working, moral citizens. In the New World, where they could engage in social engineering without the restrictions of feudal traditions, they believed they could create educational, political, and economic institutions to ensure perpetuation of this utopia. Edu-cation would allow children to develop their reason and to learn good work habits. Widespread ownership of land would provide an incentive to work hard so as to improve holdings and increase personal wealth. (Wage earners were believed to lack an incentive to improve their economic and social standing since the fruits of their work went to their employers.) Democratic institutions would provide an incentive to Americans to become informed about policy issues so as to prevent the rise of despots who might try to concentrate property and power in the hands of social elites, cater to the whims of a landless and urban underclass by taking private property from other citizens, or create an urbanized society. Maintenance of an agricultural society would allow Americans to avoid such social problems as unemployment, alienation, crime, and social disorder, which they believed inevitably infested urban areas where wage-earning and poor residents were more prone to social disorder and the appeals of despots. Moreover, the colonists placed extraordinary faith in American families, where moral conduct and the work ethic would be taught and modeled.

The colonists believed that virtuous conduct was systematically fostered in America by education, widespread ownership of land, absence of excessive economic and social inequality, a proper system of governance that prevented the emergence of despots, cohesive families, and an agricultural economy.[93] They were convinced that major social problems could not arise in the New World precisely because they had masterminded a set of political, educational, familial, and economic institutions that would avert them. Thomas Jefferson waxed ecstatic in a letter to John Adams about the utopian nature of this new nation as compared with Europe.

> With respect to aristocracy, we should further consider, that before the establishment of the American States, nothing was known to history but the man of the old world, crowded within limits either small or overcharged, and steeped in the vices which that situation generates. A government adapted to such men would be one

thing; but a very different one, that for the man of these States. Here every one may have land to labor for himself, if he chooses, or, preferring the exercise of any other industry, may exact for it such compensation, as not only to afford a comfortable subsistence, but wherewith to provide for a cessation from labor in old age. Every one, by his property, or by his satisfactory situation, is interested in the support of law and order. And such men may safely and advantageously reserve to themselves a wholesome control over their public affairs, and a degree of freedom, which, in the hands of the *canille* of the cities of Europe, would be instantly perverted to the demolition and destruction of everything public and private. The history of the last twenty-five years of France, and of the last forty years in America, nay of its last two hundred years, proves the truth of both parts of this observation.[94]

The belief that Americans had created a utopian society served to retard the development of social programs by blinding the colonists and succeeding generations of Americans to the existence of social needs in their midst. If America is a utopia, few social programs or regulations are necessary. The utopian image of American society was to act as a denial mechanism, even when the nation began to develop an urban society in the nineteenth century and even when many persons experienced poverty and other social needs. Furthermore, the optimism that social problems could be eradicated was naive and connoted a false expectation. Poverty, disease, mental illness, crime, drug addiction, and many other problems possess a persistence that defies solutions. Oppression of racial minorities and women cannot easily be eliminated even with legislation —something the colonial legislatures did not even attempt. Perhaps the American tendency centuries later to construct programs that would "solve" specific social problems stems from this ancestral optimism. And episodic reform movements were separated by long periods when many citizens, much like their colonial forebears, fantasized that Americans had created a near-utopian society.

## The Notion of an Underclass

Colonial theorists often idealized the yeoman farmer, but wage-earners (whether agricultural workers, tenant farmers, or journeymen) were missing from their conception of society. No place existed in Jefferson's theory of society for such persons, except as a sort of unnatural and feared group that threatened social protest.[95] In England, too, persons without land were often distrusted, but Englishmen were far more aware of a wage-earning class than Americans were since the vast number of serfs who were emancipated in the fourteenth, fifteenth, and sixteenth centuries had become tenant farmers or urban workers. Industrialization did not gather momentum until the Civil War and its aftermath in the United States, but it had already become a major force in English society by the late eighteenth century. Most English theorists, then, were less likely to believe that both rural and urban wage-earners represented a threat to society.[96]

Wage-earners became a sort of phantom "underclass" in America—more so than in England or Europe. This American distrust of wage-earners had crucial implications for the development of social welfare programs since it made many Americans unappreciative of the problems of a group that would experience the brunt of social and economic inequality both in preindustrial America and later in the nineteenth century, when the nation became industrialized. How can a society respond to needs of persons at the bottom of the social hierarchy when it hardly recognizes them—and, indeed, believes they represent a moral and political threat to society? And the widespread belief in America that virtually everyone could become a member of the middle class by dint of hard labor made it unlikely that a cohesive and politically assertive working class movement would arise and seek public policies to address its housing, health, and economic concerns. (We note in later chapters that the American working class and labor movements were weaker than European ones and that this relative lack of pressure

**FIGURE 3.1** • *Bostonians tarring, feathering, and pouring boiling tea into the excise man under the liberty tree*

*Source:* Library of Congress

"from below" delayed the emergence of an American welfare state.)[97]

## Liberty and Not Equality

Americans aimed to achieve freedom in their new society by developing constitutions in various states and in the nation, developing a Bill of Rights, ending taxation without representation, establishing freedom of religion, and expanding suffrage. Few persons would question the importance of liberty as a social objective, but Americans were so enamored with it that they were unable to grapple with the social objective of equality, which would have required them to develop social and economic institutions in order to reduce economic and social discrepancies among various social classes.

The slogan of the French Revolution was lib-erty *and* equality, but Americans emphasized the former objective in their Revolution (see Figure 3.1). Indeed, the American Revolution was more a rebellion than a revolution because it did not seek to create major internal changes within American society that would enhance equality. Issues related to redistribution of land and wealth were hardly discussed during the American Revolution or afterward.[98] The major controversies of the Constitutional Convention concerned tensions between the North and the South, between small and large states, and between the powers of the states and the federal government rather than issues of economic and social equality. When the framers anxiously submitted the document to state conventions for ratification, widespread protests erupted against their work on the grounds that they had not included a Bill of Rights to protect citizens from capricious acts of government, so the first ten amendments were added to the Constitution by the First Congress in 1791.[99]

## Absence of Competing Perspectives

Although the colonists wanted to limit the power of government, they often supported regulation of prices, economic planning, and public improvements. With the American Revolution completed and the Constitution written, however, a remarkable political conflict took place in the 1790s between allies of Jefferson—who formed the Republic party (which later became the Democratic party)—and allies of Washington, Adams, and Hamilton—who formed the Federalist party. The Federalists, who had favored economic planning and a somewhat stronger federal government, were routed, in the election of 1800, by the Jeffersonians, whose beliefs formed an American consensus about drastic reductions in the economic roles of government, reductions in various federal taxes, and a strict interpretation of the Constitution so that the government did not exceed its enumerated powers.[100] The American consensus, which was engineered by Jefferson, had disastrous consequences for social programs since the federal government remained exceedingly weak for generations. Jefferson successfully challenged the hierarchical assumptions of the Federalists by championing the role of the common people rather than the paternalism of an aristocracy, but his preoccupation with liberty and limited government precluded the development of federal programs and regulations to help workers and impoverished farmers.

## THE POLITICAL ECONOMY OF SOCIAL WELFARE POLICY

American social policy in the colonial era cannot be easily characterized because it, like English policy in this period, reflected the transition from feudalism to capitalistic and democratic institutions. On the one hand, policies of mercantilism, local regulations of prices and wages, and the development of poor law institutions represented positive responses to social problems. Indeed, these policies can be viewed as distant ancestors of feudal notions of social obligation, even if they accorded helping roles to governments—roles that during the feudal era had been implemented by the Church and noblemen. On the other hand, many American colonists possessed moralistic (and punitive) orientations toward unemployed persons, believed that government should assist only destitute persons, were extremely fearful of the national government, and believed that social problems like unemployment emanated from moral defects. Americans did not favor the use of compensatory strategies to uplift the social and economic conditions of American slaves or Native Americans, such as guaranteeing them land on the American frontier.

Although considerable ambiguity and local variations existed, we can say that Americans had decidedly tilted toward limited government by the inauguration of George Washington. They had created a society that was strikingly different from European nations that had strong central governments despite the ideology of people like John Locke and Adam Smith. Their governments proceeded to develop in the nineteenth century a variety of public health, housing, and other regulations that can be called forerunners of their expansive welfare states that were developed in the twentieth century. By contrast, Americans had a weak central government and had relegated to local governments, which were also weak, those relatively few social welfare functions that existed, such as poorhouses. Nor did the American government choose in the nineteenth century to develop humanistic policies toward racial minorities and women.

A political-economic perspective suggests that an array of factors shaped American social welfare policies in the colonial era and pointed them in the direction of reliance on local, relatively modest, polices. Cultural factors included the emphasis on individualism and limited government as well as considerable racial prejudice toward Native Americans and African Americans. The politics of the new nation had already suggested by the end of the eighteenth century that the major parties would not be contested by "pressure from below" from the working classes, as already had occurred in Europe before, during, and after the French Revolution when European elites feared uprisings from discontented urban, and even rural, populations. Institutional factors included a weak central government as well as relatively weak local institutions —and Americans were already displaying an aversion to taxation as reflected by their dislike of the British taxes, and a "whiskey rebellion" when federal officials attempted to tax whiskey.

Social welfare policy in the colonial period centered on the local poor law institutions, which included a mixture of institutional relief and outdoor relief. Relatively minor social welfare functions were assumed by local courts with respect to orphans, divorce petitions, and prosecutions of persons accused of rape. Nongovernmental social welfare agencies had already made an appearance in the colonial period, suggesting that the relatively residual governmental welfare institutions might be somewhat supplemented by nongovernmental programs.

We have to condition our evaluations of the relatively primitive social welfare institutions of this era by noting the agricultural nature of the society, the preoccupation of its citizens with clearing the land and establishing commercial and other institutions from scratch, and the lack of strong governmental institutions. The policies of the Americans toward black slaves and Native Americans, however, appear particularly onerous, even when we note that these white settlers sought to create a multiracial society with only the harsh precedent of the Spanish conquests of the Caribbean, Central America, and South America to guide them.

 ## END NOTES

1. Francis Bremer, *The Puritan Experiment* (New York: St. Martin's Press, 1976), pp. 51–52.

2. *Ibid.,* pp. 89–93; Edmund Morgan, *American Slavery, American Freedom: The Ordeal of Colonial America* (New York: Norton, 1975), pp. 133–149.

3. Morgan, *American Slavery,* pp. 149–150; Bremer, *The Puritan Experiment,* pp. 97–105.

4. Joyce Appleby, *Capitalism and a New Social Order: The Republican Vision of the 1790s* (New York: New York University Press, 1984), pp. 25–50.

5. Christopher Collier and James Collier, *Decision in Philadelphia: The Constitutional Convention of 1787* (New York: Random House, 1986), p. 17.

6. Bernard Bailyn, *The Origins of American Politics* (New York: Knopf, 1968), pp. 71–95.

7. Appleby, *Capitalism,* p. 61; Bailyn, *The Origins,* pp. 80–88.

8. See Clinton Rossiter, *Seedtime of the Republic: The Origins of the American Tradition of Political Liberty* (New York: Harcourt Brace Jovanovich, 1953), pp. 36–59.

9. Henry Commager, *The Empire of Reason: How Europe Imagined and America Realized the Enlightenment* (Garden City, N.Y.: Anchor Press, 1977), pp. 176–197; Louis Hartz, *The Liberal Tradition in America: An Interpretation of American Political Thought Since the Revolution* (Cambridge, Mass.: Harvard University Press, 1955), p. 70.

10. Commager, *The Empire of Reason.*

11. Merril Peterson, *Portable Thomas Jefferson* (New York: Viking Press, 1975), pp. 396–397.

12. Bailyn, *The Origins,* pp. 134–161.

13. Bernard Bailyn, *The Ideological Origins of the American Revolution* (Cambridge, Mass.: Harvard University Press, 1967), pp. 22–54.

14. Collier and Collier, *Decision,* pp. 181–194.

15. Appleby, *Capitalism,* pp. 53–61.

16. Discussion of the fear of favoritism is discussed by Louis Hartz, *Economic Policy and Democratic Thought in Pennsylvania* (Cambridge, Mass.: Harvard University Press, 1948), pp. 42–51, 309. Even so, many states maintained economic roles well into the nineteenth century, as discussed by Nathan Miller in *The Enterprise of a Free People: Aspects of Economic Development in New York State* (Ithaca, N.Y.: Cornell University Press, 1962), pp. 258–259.

17. Richard Sheridan, "The Domestic Economy." In Jack Greene and J. R. Pole, eds., *Colonial British America* (Baltimore: John Hopkins University Press, 1984), pp. 70–71.

18. Jack Greene, "The Limits of the American Revolution." In Jack Greene, ed., *The American Revolution:*

*Its Character and Limits* (New York: New York University Press, 1987), pp. 8–9.

19. Benjamin Franklin, *The Autobiography of Benjamin Franklin* (New York: Collier Books, 1962).

20. K. D. M. Snell, *Annals of the Laboring Poor: Social Change and Agrarian England, 1660–1900* (Cambridge: Cambridge University Press, 1985), p. 13.

21. Gary Nash, "Social Development." In Greene and Pole, eds., *Colonial British America*, p. 247.

22. Appleby, *Capitalism*, pp. 51–78; Collier and Collier, *Decision*, p. 17.

23. Collier and Collier, *Decision*, p. 17.

24. Richard Dunn, "Servants and Slaves: The Recruitment and Employment of Labor." In Greene and Pole, eds., *Colonial British America*, p. 160.

25. Morgan, *American Slavery*, pp. 126–128.

26. *Ibid.*, pp. 238–239.

27. Gary Nash, "Social Change and the Growth of Pre-revolutionary Urban Radicalism." In Arthur Young, ed., *The American Revolution: Explorations in the History of American Radicalism* (Dekalb, Ill.: Northern Illinois University Press, 1976), pp. 11–12.

28. Nash, "Social Development," pp. 247–249.

29. Richard Brown, "Backcountry Rebellions and the Homestead Ethic." In Richard Brown and Don Fehrenbacher, eds., *Tradition, Conflict, and Modernization: Perspectives on the American Revolution* (New York: Academic Press, 1977), pp. 73–95; Edward Countryman, "Out of the Bounds of Law: Northern Land Rioters in the Eighteenth Century." In Young, ed., *The American Revolution*, pp. 37–70.

30. Jim Potter, "Demographic Development and Family Structure." In Greene and Pole, eds., *Colonial British America*, p. 133.

31. Angie Debo, *History of the Indians of the United States* (Norman, Okla.: University of Oklahoma Press, 1970), pp. 53ff.

32. Nash, "Social Development," pp. 251–254.

33. Bremer, *The Puritan Experiment*, pp. 198–204; Morgan, *American Slavery*, pp. 22, 47.

34. Gary Nash, *Red, White, and Black: The Peoples of Early America* (Englewood Cliffs, N.J.: Prentice-Hall, 1974), pp. 69–87.

35. Morgan, *American Slavery*, pp. 22–24; John Yolton, *The Locke Reader* (Cambridge: Cambridge University Press, 1977), pp. 289–292.

36. Francis Jennings, "The Indian's Revolution." In Young, ed., *The American Revolution*, p. 334.

37. *Ibid.*, pp. 333–336.

38. Morgan, *American Slavery*, pp. 295–297.

39. Morgan, *American Slavery*, pp. 330–337.

40. Morgan, *American Slavery*, p. 330.

41. Dunn, "Servants and Slaves," pp. 167–168.

42. Nash, "Social Development," p. 254.

43. Collier and Collier, *Decision*, p. 16; Nash, "Social Development," p. 244.

44. Dunn, "Servants and Slaves," pp. 179–180.

45. Sylvia Frey, "Liberty, Equality, and Slavery: The Paradox of the American Revolution." In Greene, ed., *The American Revolution*, pp. 235–236.

46. Collier and Collier, *Decision*, 137–152.

47. *Ibid.*, 166–179.

48. Harold Hyman, *Equal Justice Under Law: Constitutional Development*, 1835–1875 (New York: Harper & Row, 1982), p. 4.

49. Collier and Collier, *Decision*, pp. 174–194.

50. Ronald Takaki, *Strangers from a Different Shore* (Boston: Little, Brown, 1989), p. 16.

51. *Ibid.*, p. 16.

52. *Ibid.*, p. 207.

53. Joan Wilson, "The Illusion of Change: Women and the American Revolution." In Young, ed., *The American Revolution*, pp. 426-431.

54. Nancy Woloch, *Women and the American Experience* (New York: Knopf, 1984), pp. 76–80.

55. Linda Kerber, "I have Don . . . much to Carrey on the Warr": Women and the Shaping of Republican Ideology after the American Revolution." In Harriet Applewhite and Darline Levy, *Women and Politics in the Age of Democratic Revolution* (Ann Arbor, Mich.: University of Michigan Press, 1990), p. 233.

56. Elaine Crane, "Dependence in the Era of Independence: The Role of Women in a Republican Society." In Greene, *The American Revolution*, p. 262.

57. Barbara Harris, *Beyond Her Sphere: Women and the Professions in American History* (Westport, Conn.: Greenwood Press, 1978), pp. 20ff.

58. Wilson, "The Illusion of Change," pp. 426–431.

59. Harris, *Beyond Her Sphere*, p. 20.

60. Crane, "Dependence in the Era of Independence: The Role of Women in a Republican Society," pp. 260–266.

61. John D'Emilio and Estelle Freedman, *Intimate Matters, A History of Sexuality in America* (New York: Harper & Row, 1988), pp. 22–23.

62. *Ibid.,* p. 31.

63. D'Emilio, pp. 15–38.

64. Hartz, *Economic Policy,* p. 4; Morgan, *American Slavery,* pp. 134–136.

65. Robert Bremner, *American Philanthropy* (Chicago: University of Chicago Press, 1970), pp. 5–42.

66. *Ibid.,* pp. 20–24.

67. *Ibid.,* pp. 5–42.

68. June Axinn and Herman Levin, *Social Welfare: A History of the American Response to Need* (New York: Dodd Mead, 1975), p. 39.

69. Peterson, *Portable Jefferson,* pp. 180–181.

70. Alfred Young, "The Women of Boston: 'Persons of Consequence' in the Making of the American Revolution, 1765–76." In Applewhite and Levy, *Women and Politics,* p. 186.

71. Morgan, *American Slavery,* pp. 165–170.

72. Commager, *The Empire of Reason,* pp. 150–153.

73. Jack Sosin, *The Revolutionary Frontier, 1763–1783* (New York: Holt, Rinehart & Winston, 1967), pp. 172–192.

74. Bremner, *American Philanthropy,* pp. 20–41.

75. Greene, "The Limits of the American Revolution," p. 12.

76. *Ibid.,* pp. 7–11.

77. James Merrell, "Declarations of Independence: Indian–White Relations in the New Nation." In Greene, ed., *American Revolution,* pp. 198–199.

78. *Ibid.,* p. 208.

79. Crane, "Dependence in the Era of Independence," pp. 271–272.

80. Commager, *The Empire of Reason,* p. 152.

81. Morgan, *American Slavery,* pp. 326–327.

82. Nash, "Social Change," pp. 8–9.

83. Morgan, *American Slavery,* pp. 150–153.

84. Young, "The Women of Boston," p. 192.

85. *Ibid.,* p. 340.

86. Countryman, *The American Revolution,* p. 74.

87. Stanley Elkins, *Slavery: A Problem in American Institutional and Intellectual Life* (New York: Grosset & Dunlap, 1963), pp. 27–37.

88. For discussion of American aristocrats in the nineteenth century, see Richard Hofstadter, *Social Darwinism in American Thought* (Boston: Beacon Press, 1955), pp. 44–46. More research is needed in orientations of earlier American aristocrats toward social mobility.

89. Morgan, *American Slavery,* p. 235.

90. Collier and Collier, *Decision,* pp. 183–184.

91. *Ibid.,* pp. 183–184.

92. Commager, *The Empire of Reason,* p. 226.

93. See Bailyn, *The Ideological Origins,* pp. 272–319.

94. Peterson, *Portable Jefferson,* p. 538.

95. Henry Smith, *Virgin Land: The American West as Symbol* (New York: Vintage Books, 1950), p. 7.

96. G. D. H. Cole and Raymond Postgate, *The British Common People* (New York: Knopf, 1939), pp. 70–71.

97. Louis Hartz, *The Liberal Tradition in America* (New York: Harcourt, Brace & World, 1955), pp. 228–237.

98. Edmund Morgan, "Conflict and Consensus in the American Revolution." In Stephen Kurtz and James Hutson, eds., *Essays on the American Revolution* (Chapel Hill, N.C.: University of North Carolina Press, 1973), pp. 291–297.

99. Collier and Collier, *Decision,* pp. 249–262.

100. Appleby, *Capitalism,* pp. 53–61.

# CHAPTER 4

# Social Welfare Policy in the Early Republic: 1789–1860

## Selected Orienting Events
## in the Early and Middle Nineteenth Century

| | |
|---|---|
| **1820s** | Speenhamland System used in the South of England |
| **1824** | First House of Refuge founded in New York; Yates Report issued in New York State |
| **1828** | Andrew Jackson elected to first of two terms |
| **1830s** | Zenith of Sunday School movement |
| **1830s–1840s** | Chartist Movement in England; zenith of antebellum temperance movement |
| **1830s–1850s** | Movement to establish public schools |
| **1834** | Report of English Poor Law Commission issued |
| **1843** | New York Association for Improving the Condition of the Poor established in New York |
| **1845** | The term *manifest destiny* coined |
| **1848** | Seneca Falls Convention |
| **1845–1849** | Irish potato famine |
| **1853** | Charles Loring Brace founded Children's Aid Society of New York |
| **1854** | President Pierce vetoed a bill that was initiated by Dorothea Dix to use revenues from land sales to fund construction of mental institutions |

Having established their independence from England and written their Constitution, Americans were free to shape their national destiny both geographically (how would they define the boundaries of a nation with seemingly endless expanses of land on their western frontier?) and institutionally (what political and social institutions would they evolve?). In the many decades from the inception of the republic in 1789 to the Civil War in 1861, Americans devoted vast amounts of energy to addressing problems of poverty, mental illness, crime, illiteracy, and alcoholism in the nineteenth century and developed policies concerning Native Americans, Spanish-speaking persons, and African Americans as the frontier expanded and following the Civil War.

Most of the programs and policies were fashioned in local and state legislatures in this period, with relatively minor involvement of federal authorities aside from the use of federal troops on the frontier.[1] In these local undertakings against social problems and in local skirmishes with native peoples on the frontier, Americans began to evolve a policy identity, that is, a peculiarly American approach to social policy that represented a curious mixture of idealism, simplistic approaches, and punitiveness.

 ## SOCIAL REALITIES IN THE NEW NATION

American society was regionalistic in the early nineteenth century.[2] The Northeast, the Northern frontier extending from Pennsylvania to Kansas and Nebraska, and the South were regions with distinctive social and economic patterns. New Englanders, who had developed some factories and industries by 1860, were concerned with developing their shipping, fishing, and manufacturing industries in the face of efforts by England and other European nations to sabotage the development of American industry. To make Americans dependent on them for such manufactured items as steel, shoes, and textiles, the English dumped cheap manufactured goods to undersell Americans, refused to allow exportation of machines and technology to America, and discouraged the development of an American shipping industry.

The Northern frontier—the contemporary Midwest—produced agricultural staples such as corn, wheat, beef, and pork. Settlers on the Western frontier, who desperately sought cheap land and a ready supply of credit to purchase and develop it, pressured federal authorities and state and territorial legislatures to provide militia to fend off Native Americans. They also sought federal and local funds to build roads and canals to allow them to send their agricultural commodities to the East.

Long before the outbreak of the Civil War, southerners were preoccupied with ensuring the growth and stability of slavery and their agricultural economy based on tobacco and cotton. They obtained passage of federal policies that allowed them to expand slavery into frontier areas such as Texas, and they enacted in southern legislatures, with scant dissent from whites, a series of measures that made it impossible for slaves to marry, to obtain property, or to be educated.

Politicians and political parties often sought to advance the particular economic goals of these regions in battles over tariffs, internal improvements such as canals and roads, and the price of land that was charged by federal authorities to settlers on the frontier. New England wanted relatively high tariffs to protect its growing industry. Frontier areas and the South wanted lower tariffs to minimize the cost of their goods, and they wanted public improvements to allow transportation to and from their areas. Southern and frontier interests also wanted cheap land so that settlers could readily obtain land on the frontier, whereas many New Englanders opposed these policies because they feared depletion of their population to western lands. National politicians catered to these regional issues in national elections that were determined by patterns of regional support. Thomas Jefferson won the presidency in 1800, for example, by obtaining support from frontier and southern regions, Andrew Jackson won the election of 1828 by obtaining similar patterns of support, and Abraham Lincoln became president in 1860 by obtaining support from New England and the Midwest. Preoccupation with local and regional issues in national policy debates meant that little attention was given to issues of social class. Few persons were concerned about barbarous working conditions in the new industries of New England, the plight of tenant farmers on the frontier, or the accumulation of massive quantities of land by speculators and railroads in the West.[3]

Americans in the early and middle nineteenth century were also preoccupied with personal economic issues. Settling the frontier may sound romantic to contemporary Americans, but realities were often harsh. Much like developing countries such as Mexico and Brazil today, the United States was saddled with extraordinary debt as it tried to build its agriculture and industry from scratch. Enormous debts were amassed as Americans borrowed from banks and wealthy individuals in Europe, who financed the speculative American economy. The American banking and currency system was in chaos during much of the century in the context of frequent and sharp recessions, fluctuations between inflation and deflation, unregulated banks that would frequently go bankrupt or charge excessive rates of interest, and the inability of national authorities to develop a national bank that could, like today's Federal Reserve system, promote or discourage economic expansion to avert the twin perils of recession and inflation. Considerable effort was expended in local and national settings in debates about banking and currency policies to foster economic growth and to avert recessions.[4] (Americans were inclined to support a variety of economic panaceas, including abolishing national banking institutions, using hard rather than paper currency, and issuing more paper currency.)

The debates about the economy were fueled by the economic difficulties of countless Americans. The vicissitudes of world markets as well as frequent recessions meant that farmers, merchants, and bankers often could not repay loans from local or foreign creditors, but local laws often allowed imprisonment of debtors even when small sums were involved. (Local courts often practiced leniency.) There was widespread agitation against imprisonment for debt as well as against local banks and speculators who charged excessive rates of interest or profiteered in land speculation prior to the Civil War.[5]

Preoccupation with national and individual economic survival decreased attention to social issues in the emerging society. Furthermore, the scant public resources of the debt-ridden nation were largely devoted to internal improvements, so as to allow transportation within and settlement of this frontier empire, rather than to social needs. American society was predominantly an agricultural nation prior to the Civil War despite the initial appearance of industry in New England. Ninety-one percent of Americans in 1830 lived in towns of less than 2,500 persons. Eastern cities remained small by modern standards—Philadelphia contained only 120,000 persons in 1830 even though it had grown from 40,000 persons in 1785.[6] Many rural Americans were only distantly aware that a growing population of poor persons lived in urban settings. Many rural Americans, who were able to obtain a subsistence living even when they experienced hard times, could not understand that urban Americans lacked this security.[7]

Concern about issues of economic inequality was also blunted by the scope of the American frontier. The settlement of areas extending from Pennsylvania to Nebraska, from the Carolinas to Texas, and from the East Coast to the gold mines of California occurred with unprecedented speed. This speed and range of settlement was possible because of the large number of immigrants from European societies and from large families of nonfrontier communities, favorable soil, favorable weather conditions, and ineffective resistance to the settlers by an outnumbered and technologically inferior indigenous population of Native Americans and Spanish-speaking persons.[8] This enormous frontier brought Jefferson's yeoman republic into existence, diverted attention from serious social problems in the nation, and blunted interest in reforms. Indeed, compassion for persons who lacked physical and financial means to homestead successfully was probably diminished because many Americans assumed that anyone could obtain land and fend for themselves.[9]

## IMMIGRATION AND URBANIZATION

Jefferson's dream of an agricultural utopia seemed partially realized in the early nineteenth century since small landowners, who were often reasonably secure financially, were the dominant social group in the new nation. They were joined by growing numbers of small businessmen, local officials, and government officials to form the American middle class, whose average income was relatively high by English standards. A social and political elite of clergy, businessmen, and large landholders dominated local politics and commanded deference from other citizens.[10]

A youth crisis had developed in the 1840s, when many teenagers, who lacked work opportunities with the end of apprenticeship programs, roamed the streets and countryside, but the crisis was eased by the rise of high school education and increasing numbers of jobs in industry by the end of the century[11] (see Figure 4.1).

America had developed a network of cities even before 1860, particularly on the East Coast, and these cities grew at fantastic rates as the nation industrialized in the wake of the Civil War. Before and after the war, cities were plagued by many problems. They increasingly became repositories for immigrants from Ireland and Germany; indeed, 1.2 million citizens of Ireland descended on the nation in a scant seven years following the disastrous potato famine of 1845 to 1847 that decimated the Irish population.[12] Many English settlers in prior decades had come from middle-class backgrounds, but Irish and German immigrants often derived from lower-class populations and, to the chagrin of many American Protestants, were often Catholic.

Early American cities were rough places. Shanty towns and tenements were hurriedly constructed by speculators in the absence of housing codes. Public health hazards, including open sewers and poor sanitation, abounded and led to epidemics. Prostitution, gambling, street begging, and drinking were rampant in cities.[13] Widespread unemployment occurred in major recessions in 1819, 1833, 1837, and 1857, when as many as one-fifth of the entire populations of large cities such as New York received welfare benefits in almshouses or from outdoor soup kitchens that were maintained by public and private agencies. Persons who were most susceptible to economic straits during recessions were unskilled laborers, such as cartmen, chimneysweeps, woodcutters, and stevedores, who constituted the largest group in the labor force.[14]

Social institutions to address economic and social needs were often lacking or poorly maintained. When Charles Dickens, the noted English author, toured America in the 1840s, he found American prisons and almshouses to be scandalous places even when compared to the inhumane English institutions of that period.[15] Crowded almshouses, which represented the major social strategy to deal with social problems, were often unsanitary and poorly staffed. Orphans, the mentally ill, delinquents, and senile persons were often uneasy coinhabitors of these institutions.

When American industry was still in its infancy, American workers in shoe, textile, and other factories experienced oppressive working conditions; they often worked for an average of twelve hours per day for six days each week, earned subsistence levels of income, and experienced high rates of job-related injuries. Unions maintained a precarious existence due to the newness of American industry, court rulings that were adverse to unions, frequent recessions, and strong-arm tactics of company owners against union organizers.[16]

Census and tax data suggest, contrary to popular belief, that extraordinary differentials in wealth existed in the United States. With the

**FIGURE 4.1** • *Street children about the time of the Civil War*

*"Go out into the highways and hedges and compel them to come in, that my house may be filled."- LUKE XIV 23.*
*"He that hath pity upon the poor, lendeth to the Lord; and that which he hath given will he pay him again."-PROV.*
*XIX 17*
*The above group of children, represents the last class recently gathered in the North Market Hall Mission S. S., and the Superintendents of the school. The street names of the boys will be found in the upper margin, numbering from left to right, commencing with the largest. As a whole, it represents the mission work, in the streets and alleys of our city.*

*Source:* Library of Congress

increase of immigrants and the emergence of agricultural, professional, industrial, merchant, and banking elites, economic inequality increased in the cities of New England between the 1820s, when 1 percent of the population held one-fourth the wealth, and the 1850s, when 1 percent of the population held one-half the wealth. Limited mobility existed between social classes both before and after the Civil War.[17] Residential segregation of social classes existed in all cities. Less information exists about the extent and nature of poverty in agricultural and frontier communities, but a large class of low-paid agricultural laborers helped landowners clear the land and prepare the soil for cultivation. Work on the frontier was often brutally difficult since settlers used hand tools and oxen to clear wooded areas. Immigrants were often conscripted to work for labor-contract companies that skimmed profits from their subsistence wages and intimidated them from seeking private employment.

Most Americans were disturbed not by social and economic inequality but by "willful" violation of the social norms that had characterized village life in earlier periods.[18] Many citizens were troubled by high levels of drinking, vagrancy, begging, and unemployment. They wondered whether the yeoman republic of Jefferson could survive as they viewed the rapid growth in cities. Both the frontier and the city were widely perceived as causing lawlessness, alcoholism, internal discord, prostitution, gambling, and ruination of the morals of American sons and daughters who migrated to them from the tranquility and social order of villages. The

growing legions of Irish and German immigrants, nearly all of whom were Catholic, further exacerbated the fears of the established Protestant population.

Contemporary historians correctly note that many of these fears were unwarranted. Fears of immigrants were partly based on prejudice against Catholics and foreigners.[19] But these attitudes arose in the context of explosive social and economic change. The scale of migration to the frontier is without parallel in world history (except perhaps for the movement of tens of millions of Russians from their western settlements to an eastern frontier to escape the Nazis during World War II). Although most of America remained predominantly agricultural, the large and rapidly expanding eastern cities were new and strange phenomena. As villages expanded into larger towns and towns became cities with heterogenous populations that included immigrants, local leaders were less able to use peer pressure to enforce social norms of deference and religious observation. The social reform policies of the early and middle nineteenth century cannot be understood without placing them in the context of these rapid social changes and the fears they engendered.

## SIMPLISTIC DEFINITIONS OF SOCIAL PROBLEMS

In the early and middle nineteenth century, America had a potpourri of Protestant sects, some Catholic strongholds in eastern cities, and a small number of Jewish settlers. Local clergy assumed major social and political roles in promulgating social norms to the society, in inveighing against such sins as drinking and swearing, and in urging citizens to be industrious.

Partly because of this religious backdrop, social problems were generally seen in moral terms.[20] Many persons believed bankruptcy was caused by profligate spending; crime, by drink-

ing or lack of deference to social superiors; and insanity, by lust. Problems were commonly perceived to be interrelated; thus, persons who ceased to attend church might become alcoholics and then delinquent or insane.

Social theorists, politicians, and citizens believed that alcoholism, crime, insanity, gambling, prostitution, and vagrancy were caused solely by individual and moral defects. They stereotyped paupers as persons who came from families with intergenerational poverty, and they equated common social problems with immigrant populations, whose numbers expanded sharply in the middle and latter part of the century.[21] This preoccupation with morality blinded Americans to alternative explanations of social problems, such as lack of employment, an undisciplined economy that led to frequent recessions, discrimination against immigrants, and lack of adequate social institutions for urban residents.[22] These moral conceptions of social problems furthermore led Americans to embrace equally simplistic solutions, which tended to combine moral, religious, educational, disciplinary, and deterrent policies.[23]

Development of national solutions to social problems was also impeded by the localistic nature of the new society. As we discussed in Chapter 3, the colonists harbored fears that the newly established federal government would interfere with the autonomy of the states. The ratification of the American Constitution in 1788 was nearly sabotaged by a national and grass-roots movement whose leaders believed that it gave the national government excessive authority. Once the republic was established, these fears did not diminish. President George Washington declined to review a state militia at a ceremonial event because he feared it would be seen as an infringement of local rights. Washington's federal taxes on whiskey were met by a rebellion that was suppressed with great difficulty. In the 1790s, Thomas Jefferson fought to stop Alexander Hamilton from instituting policies that would allow the federal government to assume major roles in making internal improvements in the various states or in providing loans and subsidies to American industries.[24]

Localism led not only to attacks on powers of the national government but also to opposition to the economic roles of state governments. Many states provided funds for internal improvements, such as turnpikes and canals, but these were increasingly seen as ill-advised use of governmental power that helped certain sections of states at the expense of others.[25] Many Americans initially resisted assistance to local educational institutions by the states on the

grounds that it represented ill-advised centralization of authority.[26] The major exception to this trend limiting governmental powers was a series of Supreme Court rulings that gave state governments the right to use private land for public purposes (eminent domain), the right to charter monopolies, and the right to interpret the interstate commerce clause in relatively broad fashion.[27]

Jefferson boldly rejected the hierarchical and paternalistic ideology of many of the statesmen who had written the Constitution when he championed participation of people of ordinary means in governance. He also rejected mercantilistic policies when he adopted the tenets of Adam Smith, which he wedded to his predilection for limited government. With the Jeffersonian defeat of the Federalist party in 1800, the nation moved toward an ideological consensus supporting free markets, limited government, and universal suffrage (for white males). To many Europeans, the American consensus appeared revolutionary because it radically departed from traditions that Europeans had inherited from the medieval period. The American consensus also had the unfortunate consequence of so limiting governmental institutions that social programs could not be implemented.[28]

The American presidents in the early and middle nineteenth century, as well as leading statesmen such as Clay and Webster, were unsympathetic to the social needs of citizens because they possessed such restrictive notions of the role of the federal government. Thus, Madison refused in 1817 to fund internal improvements because the power was not mentioned in the Constitution, and Jackson vetoed federal assistance in 1830 to a local turnpike on the grounds it represented favoritism. Indeed, the Jacksonian era (1828–1836) represented a golden age of decentralization and of limited governmental institutions. Critics of this policy believed that this preoccupation with localism and limited government severely impeded the nation's ability to cope with pressing economic problems as Jackson's dismantling of the national bank in 1832 meant that federal authorities could not soften the frequent violent swings in the economy.[29]

Presidents continued to believe that social welfare programs belonged exclusively within the province of local government. Dorothea Dix successfully persuaded the Congress to enact a bill in 1854 to allow the federal government to give the proceeds of some federal land sales to states in order to help them construct mental institutions, but President Franklin Pierce vetoed it with a message that expressed the philosophy of virtually all the presidents of the nineteenth century.[30]

> I can not find any authority in the Constitution for making the Federal Government the great almoner of public charity throughout the United States. To do so would, in my judgment, be contrary to the letter and spirit of the Constitution and subversive of the whole theory upon which the Union of these States is founded. . . . And when the people of the several States had in their State conventions, and thus alone, given force to the Constitution, . . . they ingrafted thereon the explicit declaration that "the powers not delegated to the United States by the Constitution . . . are reserved to the States." . . . Can it be controverted that the great mass of the business of Government—that involved in the social relations . . . the mental and moral culture of men . . . the relief of the needy or otherwise unfortunate members of society—did in practice remain with the States?[31]

 ## SOCIAL REFORM POLICIES

Americans developed three kinds of social policies in the early and middle nineteenth century. Many widely supported policies consisted of "moral treatment" for Americans who had (or might fall into) sinful lifestyles, including crime, alcoholism, mental illness, or neglect of religion. Second, some social policies were initiated to give Americans political, economic, and social opportunities, such as the vote, education, land distribution, and abolition of imprisonment for indebtedness. Finally, a series of policies were devised to control, regulate, and oppress racial minorities, notably, African Americans, Native Americans, and Spanish-speaking persons. (We discuss the latter policies in Chapter 5 in connection with the frontier and the Civil War.)

### Moral Reform

Americans did not separate religion and its related concepts of morality, sin, and salvation from their analysis of social problems in the early and middle nineteenth century. Alcoholics, criminals, and the poor were often described as sinners whose sorry state had been caused by such sinful attitudes as greed, avarice, laziness, and atheism. The use of religious terminology was accompanied by religious indoctrination; residents in public almshouses, prisons, and mental asylums were often made to engage in religious services; and massive outreach projects were organized by religious organizations to proselytize low-income persons, to save their souls, and to teach them moral virtues, such as hard work and sobriety.[32] Reformers sought both personal conversion of sinners to help them obtain moral virtues as well as removal of the environmental conditions that enticed them to develop immoral behavior. Temperance crusaders, for example, simultaneously engaged in personal discussions with alcoholics and tried to reduce the number of taverns and outlaw the sale of beverages.[33]

Social reforms occurred in the context of overt classism since paupers were openly and commonly described as "savages," "beasts," and "sinners." Pauperism was particularly reviled because it was widely assumed that all persons who did not possess serious health problems should be able to support themselves.[34] Classism was also linked with widespread and equally overt racism; African Americans, Native Americans, and Spanish-speaking persons in the Southwest were widely perceived to be innately less intelligent and capable than white Anglo-American citizens.[35]

## Temperance

The Temperance movement, which easily exceeded abolitionism in size and political influence, was the largest social reform movement in the several decades preceding the Civil War. In 1833, the American Temperance Society had 6,000 chapters with a combined membership of one million persons.[36]

The making and selling of alcoholic beverages had been a major business in America since colonial times, when many farmers had derived substantial income from grain sales to distilleries. Alcoholic beverages were sold in a national network of taverns that served local residents in towns and travelers along many stagecoach routes. The tavern was a central social institution in American villages, towns, and cities.

But many Americans perceived even social drinking to represent immoral behavior that had ominous broader implications for individuals and the nation. Temperance reformers believed that someone who sipped alcohol socially moved inexorably toward heavier use, which eventually culminated in alcoholism, crime, insanity, and poverty. They feared the nation would be led to debauchery and decline as large numbers of Americans followed this course. Alcoholism was widespread, and scores of inebriates could be found in cities and in many towns, but this ominous scenario mainly reflected the reformers' own fantasies and fears.

Temperance crusaders sought to restrict licenses for taverns, to tax alcohol heavily, and to limit retail sales of alcohol to consumers in various localities in the 1820s and 1830s. They obtained legislation in some areas that allowed courts to impose fines or prison sentences on sellers and users of alcoholic beverages. Countless pamphlets were written and distributed to warn Americans of the dangers of alcohol, to link drinking with atheism and immoral living, and to warn that "the very first drink is a long step toward Hell."[37]

When these various remedies still had not eradicated the problem, temperance reformers turned to state legislatures to obtain passage of laws modeled after legislation that had first been enacted in Maine. Local and state temperance societies circulated petitions and presented hundreds of signatures to local and state politicians, scrutinized positions of candidates of both major parties as a prelude to supporting or opposing them in local elections, and solicited contributions for acceptable candidates.[38] Thirteen states enacted prohibitions on the sale of alcohol in the 1840s and 1850s that made it possible to seize and confiscate alcoholic beverages. Court cases involving the illegal sales of alcohol were placed in preferred position on court calendars to avoid customary delays in litigation.

The Temperance movement had limited success despite these ambitious efforts. Most states rescinded their prohibition laws by the 1870s because of adverse court rulings that declared that governmental interference with the making and selling of liquor was unconstitutional. Although many white and Protestant citizens supported prohibition, Irish and German immigrants vehemently opposed it—as did substantial numbers of middle- and working-class Americans—on the grounds that drinking and socializing in taverns was integral to their culture. So divisive was the issue in some areas that politicians sought to avoid it by insisting that decisions be made by voters in popular referenda, where restrictive measures were defeated. Local police were often reluctant to enforce prohibition statutes or were so undermanned that enforcement was impractical.[39]

Despite its defeat, efforts to limit consumption of alcohol continued, if ineffectually, in the latter part of the nineteenth century, only to resurface in the early part of this century with passage of national prohibition in the form of the Volstead Act of 1919, which was subsequently repealed by Franklin Roosevelt in 1933.

The temperance crusade illustrates analytic deficiencies that were common to reformers in the antebellum period. Alcoholism is caused by many factors, including culture, the presence of role models in families, genetic predisposition, poverty, psychological and physical factors, advertising, and peer pressure. Temperance reformers took a simplistic approach to a complex problem when they contended that immorality was the primary cause of alcoholism and when they assumed that prohibition would eradicate the problem. Since the use of alcohol is linked to many factors, neither its legal prohibition nor horror stories of ruined lives will suffice as deterrents, as our long history of temperance reform proves.[40]

## Antipauperism Strategies

Americans had always believed that persons could be self-sufficient if they worked hard and adhered to moral principles. Armed with this moral perspective, most Americans were not overfearful in the seventeenth and eighteenth centuries that lack of work would be a major social problem since they believed that virtually all Americans could own land. Although some Americans urged a deterrent approach to welfare, including incarceration of persons in hostile and punitive workhouses, many persons in the colonial era assumed that local poor relief would be largely used by persons who had a legitimate claim to it, such as those disabled from accidents, wars, disease, old age, or death of a spouse.[41]

By the early nineteenth century, and certainly by the 1830s, many Americans feared pauperism as much as alcoholism. They saw numerous paupers for the first time, both within large cities in the East and even in smaller towns. As Americans became part of the world economy, periodic recessions led to massive unemployment, particularly in urban areas. Shortages of food and fuel became so acute during severe winters that large numbers of families risked starvation and death. Disease and work-related accidents left many persons temporarily or permanently disabled, just as high rates of mortality and social dislocation increased the population of orphans, who sometimes became street beggars. Waves of immigrants from Europe, particularly from the 1840s onward, entered eastern cities penniless and without job skills, and many vagabonds roamed the American countryside in search of employment. Children who had lost their parents or who had left their homes in their early teens in search of work often were on the streets or begged work as shoeshiners or sold newspapers.[42] With the demise of indentured service in the nineteenth century, new immigrants were cast into the job market and were free to migrate wherever they wished after their arrival. They could technically be returned to their first residence if they sought relief in a new location, but laws of settlement were difficult to enforce in a society with extensive migration.

To address the problem of pauperism, American reformers devised three major strategies.

1. They sought to vastly increase the number of almshouses that existed in the nation and to modify their internal operations to make them truly deterrent.

2. They tried to establish personal contact with millions of low-income and poverty-stricken youth to prevent pauperism.

3. They tried to establish systems of surveillance so that charity was not given indiscriminately to destitute persons.

(The second and third strategies led to the development of various nongovernmental organizations, which we discuss shortly.)

Many Americans had advocated the construction of workhouses in the colonial era, but they had not been built in many areas because of indifference to the issue of pauperism, the relatively small numbers of public wards, and the absence of economic resources to build and maintain them. Indeed, many localities resorted extensively to outdoor relief, and laws of settlement were often not vigorously implemented. The antipauperism reformers of the 1820s and 1830s sought to breathe new life into the older deterrent ideas and policies that had not been fully implemented. Before 1820, New York State had allowed localities to decide for themselves whether to use almshouses, apprenticing out, or outdoor relief. In 1824, the Yates Report, which was issued by the secretary of the state, recommended the construction of poorhouses by every county in New York State and was followed by an ambitious construction program. Legislation in New York State in succeeding years strengthened laws of settlement and required their vigorous enforcement. New York City, which bore the brunt of the state's welfare costs, succeeded in obtaining state resources to assist it in enlarging its poorhouse and its house of correction.[43]

Policies were also clarified to strengthen the work component of the poorhouse as well as its internal programs. Women and children were often put to work weaving garments and making other articles, whereas able-bodied men were made to engage in various kinds of manual labor such as working on public roads and chopping wood. Some antipauperism advocates even hoped that the poorhouse might actually cover its expenses through the sale of commodities and the labor of its residents. Residents were increasingly placed under a strict regimen that extended beyond work. Staff insisted that they follow a strict schedule that was carefully planned and that included spartan meals, long hours, lectures on morality, and religious observation. Poorhouses truly became "total institutions" that sought the moral regeneration of residents through techniques that their sup-

porters believed could be applied with scientific precision.[44]

As in the instance of temperance reformers, antipauperism advocates soon found that their ambitious plans were foiled by numerous factors. Most persons who sought public relief in many jurisdictions could not be "saved" because the reasons for their pauperism had nothing to do with their moral character. Poorhouses increasingly became places of residence for elderly persons who were sick, senile, or disabled and for mentally disabled or disordered persons. Poorhouse officials had no recourse but to provide outdoor relief when recessions occurred because the number of nearly starving citizens far exceeded available spaces. Epidemics as well as occupational accidents filled workhouses with disabled persons in an era that lacked medical science and work-safety provisions. Many orphans needed assistance because their parents abandoned them or died in epidemics. Immigrants were often forced to seek assistance because they arrived penniless in the new nation.[45]

These crushing realities, which were more significant causes of pauperism than moral character, were generally ignored in an era that was fascinated with personal morality. Antipauperism crusaders joined other crusaders who sought to form nongovernmental organizations to establish personal contact with poor persons so as to elevate them to high moral standards. One of the major crusades to reach the poor was the Sunday School movement, an effort to bring hundreds of thousands of low-income children into Sunday schools. At its zenith around 1835, the American Sunday School Union, which possessed its own administrative staff that was separate from existing denominations, had roughly 400,000 recruits. Thousands of middle-class teachers were recruited, trained, and supervised to provide highly structured religious and moral instruction to low-income youth in order to help them internalize such moral principles as honesty and industry. Teachers avoided physical punishment, relied on a system of rewards and punishments, provided structured lectures and exercises, and used extensive peer pressure to discipline recalcitrant children. (Children who did not take moral instruction seriously were given dunce status and, if necessary, expelled.) Teachers were rigorously trained and supervised in these techniques of moral instruction because leaders in the Sunday School movement were convinced that its success hinged on the instructional skills of the teachers. Massive parades of the various schools were held in cities to increase community recognition of the movement and facilitate recruitment of youth.[46]

As in the case of temperance and antipauperism, however, Sunday school leaders found their hopes dashed by the time of the Civil War. Immigrants were increasingly Catholic and resisted efforts by condescending Protestants to instruct them. The job of instruction, with its high standards and intense supervision, was sufficiently difficult that volunteer teachers became more difficult to find. Since the zeal of reformers diminished as the reform momentum declined, many of them turned to other causes. But as with the temperance crusade, it was the intrinsic weakness of the ideology of Sunday school reformers that led to their demise. Poor immigrants often resisted outreach from reformers as they themselves realized their poverty was caused by labor markets, poor health, and unemployment rather than lack of moral character.[47]

Some reformers believed that the rise in pauperism was due to undisciplined and indiscriminate relief giving by charitable and public organizations. Many nongovernmental charitable groups had arisen in the early nineteenth century, including organizations that helped specific ethnic groups or occupations, widows or single women, and victims of specific problems such as debtors. Local politicians also gave funds to applicants who came to their offices, whether from personal coffers or from the city treasury. Reformers feared that devious applicants could seek aid from multiple sources, feign poverty, or use charity to avoid work.[48]

Their remedy was to tighten the administration of charity institutions, as illustrated by the nongovernmental Association for Improving the Condition of the Poor in New York City during the 1840s and 1850s. The city was divided into many districts where agencies were convened to regularly exchange information about recipients and to tighten their giving procedures. Procedures for carefully interrogating applicants were established so that false stories could be detected. A cadre of middle- and upper-income staff were trained to become skilled interviewers to deny assistance to undeserving persons and to initiate an intensive personal relationship with them so as to teach them moral virtues through instruction and by personal example.[49] (We note in Chapter 6 how charity organization societies developed in a number of cities after the Civil War that were similar to, but larger and more bureaucratic than, the antipauper organizations in the antebellum period.)

## Character-Building Institutions

Many public institutions were constructed in the early and middle nineteenth century, including prisons, mental institutions, houses of correction, and houses of refuge for youth. An institutional strategy was ideally suited to these reformers, who wanted to change moral behavior by modifying the environment and by carefully controlling behavior.

Prisons in colonial societies had been institutions that merely held lawbreakers but did not seek to change their behavior. They contained a wide variety of persons who were indiscriminately mixed together—youth, murderers, burglars, debtors, and the like. Youth who were younger than age seven could not be imprisoned, but some jurisdictions allowed children who were between the ages of seven and fourteen to be imprisoned and even subjected to the death penalty if courts believed they knew the difference between right and wrong. These prisons were often owned by private proprietors, who charged inmates a fee for their residence and would not discharge them until they, or their friends, had paid their bills.[50]

The reformers in the nineteenth century sought to transform prisons from custodial institutions to ones that systematically instructed their residents. Daily regimens of labor, reflection, and instruction were planned as a method of changing the behavior of inmates. Physical punishment was avoided so far as possible since reformers hoped to create an environment where inmates would voluntarily modify their behavior and adopt moral virtues.[51]

Many reformers became convinced that persons with mental problems should be removed from almshouses and placed in separate institutions for the insane. They, too, wanted to use moral treatment to rehabilitate the mentally ill. A cadre of reformers, including many physicians who subsequently became the superintendents of mental institutions, lobbied for the construction of these institutions. The accomplishments of Dorothea Dix were particularly noteworthy. Dix documented problems within states by counting insane persons in almshouses and describing their brutal treatment; then she obtained signatures on petitions that demanded state legislatures build special mental institutions. By the time she had completed her state-by-state lobbying effort and evidence gathering, which included interviewing more than 10,000 mentally disturbed persons in almshouses, thirty-two institutions had been constructed.[52]

These reformers, like many Americans in this era, believed cities to be unwholesome places that created, or at least exacerbated, mental problems. They wanted relatively small institutions to be located in rural areas, where staff could establish a personal and caring relationship with residents and supervise regimens that included meditation, moral and religious instruction, gardening, recreation, and hard work.[53] Like prison reformers, they opposed the use of physical restraints whenever possible because they wanted residents to internalize new moral codes.

Many of these mental institutions probably realized the objectives of their founders and superintendents. Their records show that many residents were discharged after marked improvement. Apart from the moral and religious overlay, their approach to treatment of mental illness had much in common with contemporary efforts to create a supportive and low-stress environment for mental patients. But these institutions, like prisons, were ultimately sabotaged by political and demographic realities. Funds were provided to construct many institutions but not to foster their maintenance or expansion. Their clientele after the Civil War increasingly consisted of low-income, non-English-speaking, Catholic immigrants who resisted the moral regimens that were established by middle-class Protestant reformers. The state mental institutions depended on local boards of overseers for referrals from local poorhouses, but they increasingly referred elderly and senile persons who could not benefit from moral treatment. As low-income and elderly residents moved into the institutions, some middle-class persons began to use private institutions, so the state mental institutions, now perceived as repositories for destitute persons, were even less likely to receive adequate funding from state legislatures.[54]

Houses of refuge were also established for delinquent and neglected children during this period. Colonial laws gave authorities the right to take children from parents when they were neglected or when they were vagabonds though some authorities only reluctantly removed them from their homes. Roughly one-half the children admitted to the houses of refuge came from court orders, and the remainder were voluntarily placed by parents because they lacked the funds or capacity to care for them. Like prisons and mental institutions, houses of refuge combined lecture, study, and physical labor. Reformers believed that these houses were effective in helping many youths, but many residents fled from them, and considerable turmoil existed within them.[55]

These various institutional approaches, including prisons, mental institutions, and houses of refuge, achieved considerable success at first — at least compared to what had preceded them. Children were separated from hardened criminals in houses of refuge, prisons became public institutions that possessed a rehabilitation strategy, and mentally ill persons were rescued from workhouses. Because these institutions existed in a society that was generally indifferent to the fate of criminals, the mentally ill, or incorrigible youth, however, they did not receive sufficient public funding to sustain intensive and ameliorative services. Politicians were unwilling, as well, to divert scarce public resources to institutions when they needed them to fund road construction and other internal improvements in a growing society. Various institutions, particularly workhouses and prisons, were continually engulfed in scandal; superintendents were variously charged with fraud, excessive leniency, or providing contracts to political cronies. Moral reform was often impeded because restrictive funding of the institutions prevented them from hiring enough trained staff.[56]

An articulate if idiosyncratic dissenter from the institutional consensus emerged in the 1850s. Charles Loring Brace founded and then became director of the private Children's Aid Society of New York. Brace believed that street urchins and other vagabond children were intrinsically creative but that their natural virtues became stifled when they were placed in institutions. He believed family life was often as oppressive as institutions. Though the idea was not new, Brace pioneered in placing over 90,000 of these children with families on or near the frontier between 1853 and 1895. Brace believed he was rescuing the children from poverty and from oppressive families, but critics argued that the children were often placed with families that had been inadequately screened and that frequently used the children as a source of unpaid farm labor. Few Americans in this era joined Brace in arguing against the use of institutions that sought to radically reform their residents through a prescribed and rigorous regimen.[57]

The reformers of the early and middle nine-teenth century can be criticized for believing institutions to be a panacea, but they often responded with compassion to the plight of mentally ill persons bound in chains, children begging on the streets, and criminal offenders incarcerated in brutish settings. In considering alternatives, we should not quickly conclude that deinstitutionalization is a panacea, as is illustrated by the plight of mentally ill persons in today's society who are released to the community without adequate housing, income, and medical and social services.

## Opportunity-Enhancing Policies

In the early and middle nineteenth century, America extended suffrage to most white males, developed public schools, and distributed land to many settlers. Americans in the twentieth century take these institutions and policies for granted, but they represented major — even fantastic — reforms to Europeans. During the early and middle nineteenth century, suffrage was extended in Europe only to persons with considerable property, education was restricted to affluent persons who could afford tuition, and land was not widely distributed. Cambridge University refused to fill a position in American studies with an American scholar in the 1840s because its officials feared he would discuss universal suffrage.[58]

No system of public education existed in 1800, but the nation possessed by 1860 a national network of primary and secondary schools. This massive growth in public education, which extended to girls as well, represented a major policy advance in the nineteenth century. Four systems of education existed prior to these reforms — private tutors, boarding schools, day schools that were run by various sects, and charity schools that gave free education to the urban poor. Colonial leaders (such as Thomas Jefferson) who had espoused free public education had been staunchly resisted by those who did not want high taxes and who believed that education should be provided by the family or by religious sects. A rationale for publicly funded education began to be formulated by the 1820s and gathered momentum in succeeding decades. An uneducated citizenry, educational reformers argued, would not be able to participate in American democracy, which could lead to tyranny, mob rule, and other evils. Like other reformers of this era, they believed education to be a moral enterprise that would instill youth with moral rules so as to allow them to avoid poverty, alcoholism, and crime. Some persons also realized that a literate work force was needed if America was to develop an industrial economy.[59]

Crusades to end imprisonment for debt represented one of the major social reform movements of the nineteenth century. Many Americans who could not pay bills because they had to incur large debts to start farms and businesses found themselves threatened with imprisonment. Agitation in various states led to gradual relaxing of these laws and finally to their abolition in most states by the time of the Civil War.[60]

As with public education and land distribution, Europeans were astounded that all white males were granted the vote in most jurisdictions by 1830. Along with suffrage came greater political participation. In presidential contests, for example, opposing candidates were variously called "atheists," "criminals," and "agitators." Interest groups had already assumed prominence in American politics since persons with similar interests found that they could obtain policies by joining with others, lobbying, assisting friendly legislators, and making campaign contributions (or bribes) to politicians.[61]

Political appearances could be deceiving, however. American "interest group" democracy, which seemed to give the common people an unprecedented role in political life, often empowered corporations and privileged persons. Fearing that one faction could dominate American politics, Jefferson and many of the colonial leaders had constructed elaborate checks and balances to prevent this possibility, but these safeguards did not prevent specific interest groups from gaining enormous power. By the latter half of the nineteenth century, industrial tycoons dominated the politics of the nation, just as land speculators and agricultural interests possessed considerable power in the antebellum period.[62]

 ## THE ABSENCE OF POWERFUL RADICAL MOVEMENTS

Although Americans pioneered the enactment of opportunity-enhancing policies, comparisons between England and the United States during the 1830s and 1840s suggest that America provided a hostile environment to social reform. England was hardly kind to its poor and mentally ill, but a relatively strong (by American standards) political mobilization of the lower class known as chartism developed in the 1840s. Its leaders sought a variety of reforms, including repeal of tariffs on corn, termination of workhouses, development of free education, factory regulations, and legislation to strengthen unions.[63] By contrast, despite the presence of local workingmen's associations and scattered union protests, no national or strong local organizations of poor persons emerged in the United States.

Poor persons and laborers were more organized in England than in the United States for several reasons.[64] First, since American workers tended to identify with their ethnic groups, they often did not identify with, or organize around, their social class. Second, partly because the federal government was so weak, Americans focused on such local issues as securing city jobs, garbage collection, and other amenities rather than national economic and social policies. Third, American workers probably regarded poor relief as primarily relevant to an underclass of paupers, whereas English workers viewed poor-law institutions as relevant to working-class interests.[65]

Finally, more dissent and argument existed in England about the causes and nature of poverty. Many Englishmen subscribed to the moralistic and individualistic explanations that were widely accepted by Americans, but many English theorists and citizens emphasized economic and social factors that perpetuated pauperism and poverty.[66] However, the former group, led by Edwin Chadwick, obtained control of an influential commission, whose findings in 1834 recommended that indoor relief and punitive policies replace the relatively generous poor relief that existed in many parts of England. Furthermore, this group adopted the pessimistic conclusions of Reverend T. R. Malthus, who maintained that generous poor relief merely increased the population of poor persons and threatened to ruin England by depleting its food and resources.[67] But these pessimistic conclusions were sharply questioned by many persons who saw industrialization,

recessions, and inflation as causes of dependency. Some reformers even proposed health insurance and old-age pensions for the poor, and liberal reforms of poor relief in the South of England even led to the Speenhamland system of relief in the 1820s, when the wages of working persons were supplemented by poor relief whenever the price of bread rose above a certain amount.[68] Reformers even found assistance from some aristocrats and the English Conservative party, whose leaders, such as Benjamin Disraeli, assumed attitudes befitting the heirs to the feudal nobles who provided assistance to serfs during hard times.[69]

It remained to be seen, then, if Americans could couple their extraordinary interest in facilitating economic, educational, and political opportunity with compassion for persons who were less successful than others. Compassion existed, but it often took the form of relatively harsh or condescending assistance to poor persons, who were incessantly accused of causing their own plight by not being sufficiently industrious or virtuous. Ominously, the working class in the United States was poorly organized, when contrasted with European nations, and so provided uncertain pressure for the development of social welfare programs.

## OUTGROUPS IN THE EARLY REPUBLIC

We noted the American colonists lived in the eighteenth century in a triracial society that included white settlers, African Americans, and Native Americans. As the nineteenth century unfolded, Americans encountered other indigenous populations in the southwestern part of the continent, such as Spanish-speaking people who lived in areas that came to be owned by Mexico when it obtained its independence from Spain in 1821. Moreover, Americans imported significant numbers of Asians from China, Japan, Korea, and the Philippines to work in agriculture and construc-

tion projects of various kinds in the latter part of the nineteenth century. We also need to discuss white, ethnic minorities, particularly the Irish, whose Catholicism, as well as sheer numbers and poverty, exposed them to the ire of the white, Protestant population even before the Civil War. And we must continue our analysis of the policies, laws, and culture that affected women in the colonial period to the first seven decades of the new republic.

We discuss Irish immigrants and women in this chapter, as well as some emerging policies toward sexual matters that had important implications for women and persons who deviated from commonly accepted sexual norms. (We save discussion of the plight of black slaves, Native Americans, Asian immigrants, and Spanish-speaking persons for Chapter 5.)

## Irish Immigrants

Contemporary writers sometimes erroneously imply that white ethnic populations, such as the Irish immigrants, assimilated to their new land with ease and with minor discrimination from the dominant population.[70] In fact, the Irish, whose numbers in America increased fantastically in the decade after the so-called potato famine that lasted between 1845 and 1849, illustrate the nature and extent of problems that white, low-income, ethnic immigrants encountered in the new nation. (The problems of the Irish were later experienced by the millions of Italian, Jewish, and Eastern European immigrants of the period from 1870 to 1924.)

With the advantage of hindsight, we can see that Ireland was a land tempting disaster in the decades before 1845. Its population consisted of millions of impoverished farmers, whose numbers had so greatly increased in the seventy years before the potato famine that it was the most densely populated nation in Europe. Many Irish peasants lived in degrading poverty, often as tenants to absentee landowners or as owners of small plots of less than five acres. This agrarian and impoverished society depended on the potato for its survival—a crop that had been introduced to Europe from South America and that provided extraordinary nourishment for its burgeoning population. Even several acres of this easily grown crop sufficed to feed a family the bulk of its diet.[71]

Though there had been periodic and small famines, no one was prepared for the widespread "potato rot" that occurred in 1845, which devastated the crop on which the nation depended. Imbued with doctrines of laissez-faire economics, the British government responded to the catastrophe with sublime confidence that the depleted food supply could be remedied merely by government purchases of corn, which could be periodically sold to keep the price of corn low enough for peasants to buy it. Moreover, the government hoped that relatively modest increases in poor law relief would tide the peasants over until the ensuing year when, it was assumed, the potato harvest would be normal.[72]

Tragically, the plant disease that devastated the harvest in 1845 continued to attack the crops during the next four years. About 750,000 persons, or nearly one-eighth of the population of the country, died of starvation or disease. Cecil Woodham-Smith notes unimaginable horrors:

> at a farm in Caheragh, County Cork, a woman and her two children were found dead and half-eaten by dogs; in a neighboring cottage five more corpses . . . were lying . . . Father John O'Sullivan . . . found a room full of dead people; a man, still living, was lying in bed with a dead wife and two dead children, while a starving cat was eating another dead infant.[73]

People who were weakened by malnutrition succumbed to mass infections like typhoid fever and dysentery in a nation with only twenty-eight hospitals. Crop failures in other parts of Europe, British hatred of the Irish, prevailing notions of limited government, British insistence on financing poor relief from taxes levied on the already impoverished Irish citizens, and punitive responses to widespread riots in the Irish countryside meant that humane policies were not used to address the emergency.

Roughly one and one-half million Irish peasants sought refuge in the United States from 1845 to 1854 in what was merely the start of a long-term migration from Ireland that counted an additional two and one-half million émigrés to the United States by 1900. (Poverty, hatred of landlords, and a desire to join relatives in America fueled a continuing emigration.) Of course, this reprieve from starvation and hardship required funds for steamship passage, which was often obtained by selling family heir-looms. Moreover, many people died in passage from various diseases with many "emaciated," "cadaverous," or "feeble" after suffering on-board hardships that were "as bad as the slave trade."[74]

Once in the new land, the Irish soon found that they encountered misfortune on a scale just short of the starvation that they had escaped. Ships were sometimes turned away by American authorities on grounds that passengers were too diseased. Anti-Catholic, anti-Irish, and anti-immigrant sentiments often fused and led to riots against the émigrés. As unskilled peasants with no capital and no knowledge of agricultural techniques needed to develop larger farms on the frontier, most of the Irish immigrants moved to large eastern and midwestern cities where they lived in appalling poverty in low-income ghettos and could perform only unskilled tasks such as cleaning stables, unloading boats, and pushing carts or, in the case of women, serving as domestics.[75] In a land with few regulations, they occupied shanty towns built by speculators where as many as nine people lived in a single room and where many of them were crowded into cellars. Cholera epidemics swept through these low income areas; indeed, one report suggests that more than half the children died in some Irish communities, making the average age of persons buried less than fifteen.[76] Other Irish became the labor force for companies and governments building railroads, roads, and canals. Still others became the labor force for coal mines.

American poorhouses, as well as jails, soon contained considerable numbers of the Irish. Irish immigrants commonly took to whiskey to forget their troubles, and booze as well as poverty led to high rates of crime. Indigenous Americans believed they were being overrun; indeed, 37,000 Irish immigrants arrived in Boston in 1847 alone in a city that had only 115,000 residents in 1845.[77]

Lest we paint too dismal a picture, some Americans did raise substantial sums of money to help the new immigrants and even to pay the passage for some of them. And like later immigrants, the Irish proved to be remarkably resilient in the new nation; often with the help of the Catholic Church as well as various Protestant denominations (for the Protestant Irish), self-help activities were developed such as mutual aid associations.

But the indigenous Americans often responded with hatred as well, as Higham notes in his discussion of "American nativism" in the period from 1860 to 1925.[78] A potent "Know-Nothing" movement developed in the 1850s that was grounded in the notion that Catholics represented a menace to American national and Protestant identity and that Catholics would dilute the pure "Anglo-Saxon" racial stock of America. This hatred of Catholics spawned the American Political Party, which elected six governors in the 1850s. Though always simmering, nativism boiled over again in the 1890s and in the period from 1905 to 1924.[79]

## The Status of Women

The doctrine of "separate spheres," that had emerged in the colonial period, obtained even greater strength in the early nineteenth century and led to the "cult of domesticity," which consigned women to household and familial functions while reserving the professions and business to males. This restriction of the economic roles of women, if anything, increased in the early nineteenth century because of the increasing importance that was attached to the role of child rearing. If children in the colonial period had often been viewed as "little adults" who were to begin full-time work at age eleven, they were increasingly viewed as requiring extended moral education and socialization within the family. Although this child rearing could have been shared equally by both parents, Americans in the early nineteenth century developed the notion that women were uniquely equipped to perform this function. If women had sometimes been perceived to be immoral temptresses in the colonial period, they were increasingly portrayed as morally superior to males—a perception that led people to believe that they could best inculcate moral character into the nation's youth.[80] Married women were urged to devote themselves to raising children and to administering their households with few rights to own or manage property, except in those cases where their husbands predeceased them. Almost no married women from the middle classes and upward worked outside their households, and even many working-class women sought to avoid external work. (Female black slaves were given no choice.) Widowed women often encountered bleak realities; as in the colonial period, husbands often left the bulk of their estates to children so that widows were left to fend for themselves, sometimes surviving by renting out rooms in their homes that were often occupied, as well, by one or more of their children, to whom the house was often willed or given. High rates of male mortality meant that 32 percent of adult women were widows in the 1850s and 61 percent of women over the age of sixty.[81]

The prohibition against labor did not extend to single women, who often worked as domestic and live-in servants and received low wages, only one day per week off, and often harsh treatment by employers. Partly because they wanted more independence, some single women found work in factories in New England, where they worked long hours at low pay—but factory jobs were not plentiful since the nation did not industrialize in a major way until after the Civil War. Women were virtually excluded from medicine, law, and the clergy though growing numbers of them became school teachers (as public education became more common) and, after the Civil War, nurses.[82]

But seeds of discontent and protest were finally sown in 1848 at a convention in Seneca Falls, New York. There, a small number of men and women issued a "Declaration of Sentiments" modeled after the Declaration of Independence. The sixty-eight women and thirty-two men who signed it declared "we hold these truths to be self-evident that all men and women are created equal" and "have the duty to throw off such government" that visits on them "a long train of abuses and usurpation..." In this remarkable and prescient document, the signers attacked the cult of domesticity and the prevalent notion that women were intellectually and legally inferior to men; they demanded suffrage, access to the professions, and legal rights such as the ability to hold property while married. The Seneca Falls Conference was followed by similar conferences, roughly one each year, between 1849 and the outbreak of the Civil War in 1861.

Historians have tried to explain why feminism arose in this period and have identified various reasons. The cult of domesticity, which obtained such sway, relegated women to so much boredom and so many restrictions in their virtual imprisonment in their homes that a vanguard of women protested. Moreover, many women became leaders in the budding abolitionist movement, which fostered women's rights in several ways. Women came to see the incongruity between the equal rights doctrines of the nation and the limited legal and social roles of women as they participated in trying to overcome slavery, which represented a similar incongruity. Moreover, many female abolitionists personally experienced discrimination *as* they participated in abolitionism, both from male abolitionists (who sought to limit them to background roles) and the public (who often objected to *any* woman speaking in public). Moreover, more women were receiving the rudiments of education in a growing number of high schools and academies for women—and Oberlin became the first college to admit women in 1837.[83]

But we should not imply that the women who subscribed to feminism in this period, such as Susan B. Anthony and Elizabeth Cady Stanton, represented the mainstream of female (or male) thought at the time. Indeed, many *avant garde* women were content to seek access to the professions and to positions in teaching *within* the old framework of separate spheres and the cult of domesticity and did not agree with "radical feminists" who sought an array of public and political reforms. (In Chapter 5, we note how male abolitionists mostly abandoned women in the wake of the Civil War when they refused to include women in constitutional amendments that were designed to give the freed slaves certain civil and legal rights.)

## Social Policy Regarding Reproduction and Sexual Orientation

Sexual mores and policies regarding birth control are particularly pivotal for women because they bear children; indeed, women in colonial society often lost their lives under the burden of multiple pregnancies in absence of effective birth control. Even when not physically harmed by pregnancies, women in the nineteenth century found themselves circumscribed by familial responsibilities when they had large families because they bore the brunt of child rearing.

Several salutary developments in the nineteenth century signaled some semblance of control over reproduction. An enormous decline in the size of families occurred during the nineteenth century; if white married couples had an average of slightly over seven children in 1800, they were bearing an average of 5.42 children by 1850 and only 4.24 children by 1880. This decline in family size was caused by many factors, including economic ones (children required larger investments to prepare them for the labor force than when they were laborers on family farms); what's more, families limited children to increase their mobility, and women limited their family size to increase their personal freedom from child rearing. Moreover, unlike people in colonial society who often viewed sex in purely utilitarian terms (to have children), many Americans by the end of the nineteenth century viewed sex as a reflection of romantic love, which was increasingly seen to be desirable. But women (and men) could not have limited families if new contraceptive techniques had not developed in the nineteenth century to supplement the old standbys of abstinence, rhythm methods, and coitus interruptus, including condoms and diaphramlike devices. Though available primarily by word of mouth and vaguely worded advertisements, these techniques probably assumed larger roles in limiting families as the century evolved.[84]

But the ability of women (and men) to control reproduction was not fostered by the development of the Comstock law, which Congress enacted in 1873; named after Anthony Comstock, its sponsor, the legislation outlawed the circulation of contraceptive information and devices through the U.S. mails because of fear that the use of contraceptives would excessively limit the growth of the American population.[85] Comstock, who worked for the U.S. Postal Service, devoted the next four decades to prosecuting purveyors of "obscenity," including physicians who openly dispensed contraceptives. (In addition, many local jurisdictions enacted obscenity laws that were used by the early twentieth century, along with the Comstock law, to prosecute feminists who sought to openly discuss contraception or to disseminate birth control devices.)

Moreover, many physicians by the late nineteenth century opposed abortion and homosexuality. Abortion had been used without stigma prior to the Civil War to limit family size even if it relied on uncertain techniques such as herbs, but physicians increasingly viewed it to be an unnatural curtailing of women's reproductive function. The term *homosexuality* did not exist in the nineteenth century, and it was not a stigmatized condition though various localities had laws against sodomy (anal sexual relations between men). Some famous men, like Walt Whitman, engaged in homosexual relations. But physicians by the end of the century had declared same-sex sexual relations to represent medical pathology in a move that presaged the stigmatizing of homosexuality and lesbianism in the twentieth century.[86]

In short, sexual matters were beginning to be subject to various public policies in the latter part of the nineteenth century in a manner that suggested that reproductive rights of women and sexual freedoms of homosexuals (and lesbians) would be controversial issues and subject to public regulations.

# THE POLITICAL ECONOMY OF POLICY IN THE EARLY REPUBLIC

Many Americans viewed the social problems of the new nation to be a pestilence that threatened its moral and social order. Social problems were generally viewed as emanating from the moral defects of citizens — and particularly immigrants in the burgeoning cities. Reformers correspondingly tried to develop institutions that could purge these defects from the mentally ill, criminals, paupers, and incorrigible youth or sought preventive strategies that included temperance and moral instruction through the Sunday School movement or the expanding network of public schools.

In short, the nation's social programs imposed rather harsh and controlling kinds of services on those citizens who needed assistance. Relatively few reformers acknowledged that structural factors, such as the nation's uncertain economy, the blighted conditions of its cities, or discrimination against its immigrants, assumed a major role in causing social problems. The lack of strong reform and political organizations that represented the policy needs of the lower class, such as were developing in England, deprived the nation of alternative perspectives.

Nor did the nation develop expansive notions of social obligation; social programs, most reformers believed, should concentrate only on provision of institutional and social services to truly destitute and ill persons rather than to a broad range of its citizens. (Public education was an important exception though even it was conceived as concentrating on moral instruction.) Most services were, moreover, to be provided by local governments and private philanthropic organizations since Americans accorded the federal government virtually no social welfare roles other than maintenance of several institutions for the deaf and a small program of pensions for veterans.[87]

In Chapter 5, we discuss how these various beliefs about social policy made the nation ill-equipped to cope with the social problems that accompanied industrialization in the wake of the Civil War. Furthermore, when coupled with widespread racism, these beliefs led to particularly harsh treatment of Native Americans, Asian Americans, Spanish-speaking persons, and African Americans.

# END NOTES

1. Robert Kudrle and Theodore Marmor, "The Development of Welfare States in North America." In Peter Flora and Arnold Heidenheimer, eds., *The Development of the Welfare State* (New Brunswick, N.J.: Transaction Books, 1981), pp. 82–83.

2. Daniel Boorstin, *The Americans: The National Experience* (New York: Random House, 1965), pp. 3–218.

3. Ira Katznelson, "Working-Class Formation and the State: Nineteenth-Century England in American

Perspective." In Peter Evans, Dietrich Rueschemeyer, and Theda Skocpol, eds., *Bringing the State Back In* (Cambridge: Cambridge University Press, 1985); Edward Pessen, *Jacksonian America: Society, Personality, and Politics* (Homewood, Ill.: Dorsey Press, 1978), pp. 150, 168–169.

4. A. Barton Hepburn, *A History of Currency in the United States* (New York: Macmillan, 1915), pp. 88–161.

5. Pessen, *Jacksonian America*, p. 85; Malcolm Rohrbough, *The Land Office Business: The Settlement and Administration of American Public Lands, 1789–1837* (New York: Oxford University Press, 1968), pp. 137–156.

6. Paul Boyer, *Urban Masses and Moral Order in America, 1820–1920* (Cambridge, Mass.: Harvard University Press, 1978), pp. 3–4; Raymond Mohl, *Poverty in New York, 1783–1825* (New York: Oxford University Press, 1971), pp. 3–13.

7. Richard Bushman, "Family Security in the Transition from Farm to City, 1750–1850," *Journal of American History*, 6 (Fall 1980), 238–256.

8. James Davis, *Frontier America, 1800–1840: A Comparative Demographic Analysis of the Frontier Process* (Glendale, Calif.: Arthur H. Clark Co., 1977), pp. 19–21; Richard Slotkin, *The Fatal Environment: The Myth of the Frontier in the Age of Industrialization, 1800–1890* (New York: Atheneum, 1985), pp. 3–47.

9. Davis, *Frontier America*, pp. 16–17; Slotkin, *The Fatal Environment*, p. 47.

10. Stephan Thernstrom, *Poverty and Progress: Social Mobility in a 19th Century City* (Cambridge, Mass.: Harvard University Press, 1964), pp. 33–57.

11. Michael Katz, Michael Doucet, and Mark Stern, *The Social Organization of Early Industrial Capitalism* (Cambridge, Mass.: Harvard University Press, 1982), pp. 242–284.

12. Rowland Berthoff, *An Unsettled People: Social Order and Disorder in American History* (New York: Harper & Row, 1971), pp. 148–161.

13. Mohl, *Poverty*, pp. 14–34; Pessen, *Jacksonian America*, pp. 55–58.

14. Eric Foner, *History of the Labor Movement in the United States*, Vol. 1 (New York: International Publishers, 1955), pp. 106–143; Mohl, *Poverty*, pp. 20–30.

15. Boyer, *Urban Masses*, p. 68.

16. Foner, *History of the Labor Movement*, Vol. 1, pp. 108–120.

17. Pessen, *Jacksonian America*, pp. 77–83.

18. Boyer, *Urban Masses*, pp. 12–21, 67–75; Thernstrom, *Poverty and Progress*, pp. 42–46, 50–56; Nathan Huggins, *Protestants Against Poverty* (Westport, Conn.: Greenwood Press, 1971), pp. 3–14.

19. Berthoff, *An Unsettled People*, pp. 288–292.

20. Boyer, *Urban Masses*, pp. 3–64; Mohl, *Poverty*, pp. 159–170.

21. Mohl, *Poverty*, pp. 141, 162, 169.

22. Michael Katz, *Poverty and Policy in American History* (New York: Academic Press, 1983), pp. 134–156.

23. Huggins, *Protestants Against Poverty*, p. 177; Mohl, *Poverty*, pp. 259–265.

24. Henry Commager, *The Empire of Reason: How Europe Imagined and America Realized the Enlightenment* (Garden City, N.Y.: Anchor Press, 1977), pp. 198–235; Daniel Sisson, *The American Revolution of 1800* (New York: Knopf, 1974), pp. 448–449.

25. Louis Hartz, *Economic Policy and Democratic Thought in Pennsylvania* (Cambridge, Mass.: Harvard University Press, 1948), pp. 309–320.

26. Carl Kaestle, *Pillars of the Republic: Common Schools and American Society, 1780–1860* (New York: Hill and Wang, 1983), pp. 136–181.

27. Robert Steamer, *The Supreme Court in Crisis: A History of Conflict* (Amherst, Mass.: University of Massachusetts Press, 1971), pp. 41–44, 61–62; Edward White, *The American Judicial Tradition: Profiles of Leading American Judges* (New York: Oxford University Press, 1976), pp. 49–61.

28. Sisson, *The American Revolution*, pp. 439–453.

29. Bray Hammond, *Banks and Politics in America from the Revolution to the Civil War* (Princeton, N.J.: Princeton University Press, 1957), pp. 451–499; Pessen, *Jacksonian America*, p. 147.

30. Pessen, *Jacksonian America*, p. 296.

31. June Axinn and Herman Levin, *Social Welfare: A History of the American Response to Need* (New York: Harper & Row, 1982), pp. 80–84.

32. Boyer, *Urban Masses*, pp. 12–21; Gerald Grob, *Mental Institutions in America, Social Policy to 1875* (New York: Free Press, 1973), p. 168.

33. Ian Tyrrell, *Sobering Up: From Temperance to Prohibition in Antebellum America, 1800–1862* (Westport, Conn.: Greenwood Press, 1979), pp. 125–131.

34. Boyer, *Urban Masses*, pp. 55–57; Huggins, *Protestants Against Poverty*, pp. 199–201.

35. Reginald Horseman, *Race and Manifest Destiny* (Cambridge, Mass.: Harvard University Press, 1981), pp. 116–138, 298–303.

36. Tyrrell, *Sobering Up*, pp. 3–13, 87–115.

37. *Ibid.*, pp. 63–67.

38. *Ibid.*, pp. 235–245.

39. *Ibid.*, pp. 290–297.

40. *Ibid.*, pp. 297–305, 319–323.

41. Grob, *Mental Institutions*, p. 89; Merril Peterson, *Portable Thomas Jefferson* (New York: Viking Press, 1975), pp. 180–181.

42. Mohl, *Poverty*, pp. 14–34.

43. Axinn and Levin, *Social Welfare*, pp. 56–57.

44. Katz, *Poverty and Policy*, pp. 90–98, 134–142, 157–165.

45. *Ibid.*, pp. 129–133, 153–156, 174–181; Mohl, *Poverty*, pp. 259–260.

46. Boyer, *Urban Masses*, pp. 34–53.

47. Huggins, *Protestants Against Poverty*, pp. 179–185.

48. Boyer, *Urban Masses*, pp. 86–94; Mohl, *Poverty*, pp. 241–258.

49. Mohl, *Poverty*, p. 247; Huggins, *Protestants Against Poverty*, pp. 111–135.

50. Joseph Hawes, *Children in Urban Society: Juvenile Delinquency in Nineteenth-Century America* (New York: Oxford University Press, 1971), pp. 20–24.

51. *Ibid.*, pp. 45–51; Robert Mennel, *Thorns and Thistles: Juvenile Delinquents in the United States,* 1825–1940 (Hanover, N.H.: University Press of New England, 1973), pp. 3–31.

52. Grob, *Mental Institutions*, pp. 103–110.

53. *Ibid.*, pp. 156–157.

54. *Ibid.*, pp. 174–220.

55. Hawes, *Children*, pp. 45–51; Mennel, *Thorns*, pp. 12–31.

56. Trattner, *Homer Folks*, pp. 76–81.

57. Mennel, *Thorns*, 32–40.

58. Joyce Appleby, *Capitalism and a New Social Order: The Republican Vision of the 1790s* (New York: New York University Press, 1984), p. 2.

59. Kaestle, *Pillars*, pp. 75–103; Michael Katz, *The Irony of Early School Reform: Educational Innovation in Mid-Nineteenth Century Massachusetts* (Cambridge, Mass.: Harvard University Press, 1968), pp. 124–160.

60. Pessen, *Jacksonian America*, p. 85.

61. *Ibid.*, pp. 156–158, 288–323.

62. *Ibid.*, pp. 104–114; Thomas Cochran, *The Age of Enterprise: A Social History of Industrial America* (New York: Harper & Row, 1961), pp. 154–180; Samuel Hayes, *The Response to Industrialization, 1885–1914* (Chicago: University of Chicago Press, 1957), pp. 17–23.

63. Katznelson, "Working-Class Formation," pp. 257–260.

64. *Ibid.*, pp. 270–278.

65. Raymond Cowherd, *Political Economists and the English Poor Laws: A Historical Study of the Influence of Classical Economics on the Formation of Social Welfare Policy* (Athens, Ohio: Ohio University Press, 1977), pp. 1–23; K. D. M. Snell, *Annals of the Laboring Poor: Social Change and Agrarian England, 1660–1900* (Cambridge: Cambridge University Press, 1985), pp. 104–112.

66. Cowherd, *Political Economists*, pp. 1–23, 70–78.

67. *Ibid.*, pp. 204–278.

68. *Ibid.*, pp. 55, 262–278.

69. Michael Barker, *Gladstone and Radicalism: The Reconstruction of Liberal Policy in Britain, 1885–1894* (New York: Harper & Row, 1975), pp. 37–40; Norman Gash, *Reaction and Reconstruction*

*in English Politics: 1832–1852* (Oxford: Clarendon Press, 1965), pp. 139-140, 149–150.

70. John Ibson, *Will the World Break Your Heart? A Historical Analysis of the Dimensions and Consequences of Irish-American Assimilation.* Doctoral dissertation. Brandeis University, 1976.

71. Cecil Woodham-Smith, *The Great Hunger: Ireland 1845–1849* (New York: Signet Books, 1962), pp. 24–30.

72. *Ibid.,* p. 86.

73. *Ibid.,* p. 177.

74. *Ibid., p. 224.*

75. Ibson, *Will the World Break Your Heart?,* p. 84.

76. Woodham-Smith, *The Great Hunger,* p. 248.

77. *Ibid.,* pp. 243–265.

78. John Higham, *Strangers in the Land: Patterns of American Nativism, 1860–1925* (New York: Atheneum, 1972).

79. *Ibid.,* pp. 3–11.

80. Barbara Harris, *Beyond Her Sphere: Women and the Professions in American History* (Westport, Conn.: Greenwood Press, 1978), pp. 40ff.

81. Katz, Doucet, and Stern, *The Social Organization,* pp. 290–92.

82. Harris, *Beyond Her Sphere,* 60ff.

83. *Ibid.,* pp. 73ff.

84. John D'Emilio and Estelle Freedman, *Intimate Matters: A History of Sexuality in America* (New York: Harper & Row, 1988), pp. 58–60.

85. *Ibid.,* p. 68.

86. *Ibid.,* pp. 121–130.

87. Walter Trattner, "The Federal Government and Social Welfare in Early Nineteenth-Century America," *Social Service Review,* 50 (June 1976), 243–253.

# CHAPTER 5

# Lost Opportunities: The Frontier, The Civil War, and Industrialization

## Selected Orienting Events in the Middle and Late Nineteenth Century

| | |
|---|---|
| **1803** | Louisiana Purchase |
| **1820** | Missouri Compromise |
| **1828** | Andrew Jackson elected for first of two terms |
| **1836** | Battle of the Alamo |
| **1838–1839** | Forced march of the Cherokees |
| **1845** | The term *manifest destiny* coined |
| **1846–1848** | Mexican-American War |
| **1848** | Treaty of Guadalupe Hidalgo; Seneca Falls Convention |
| **1859** | Charles Darwin published *On the Origin of Species by Means of Natural Selection* |
| **1860** | Abraham Lincoln elected for first of two terms |
| **1861–1865** | Civil War |
| **1863** | Emancipation Proclamation |
| **1865** | Lincoln assassinated |
| **1865–1868** | Andrew Johnson was president |
| **1865–1872** | Freedmen's Bureau in existence |
| **1865–1900** | The Gilded Age, when the United States industrialized rapidly |
| **1868** | Ulysses Grant elected for first of two terms |
| **1873–1877** | An extended recession existed |
| **1877** | President Hayes used federal troops to end national railroad strike |
| **1880–1914** | Twenty-one million immigrants arrived in the United States |
| **1882** | Chinese Exclusion Act |
| **1887** | Dawes Act |
| **1890** | U.S. Census declared frontier to have officially ended; Sherman Antitrust Act |
| **1902** | Reclamation Act of 1902 |

This chapter emphasizes three epic developments that posed enormous challenges to the new nation during the nineteenth century, namely, the rapid settlement of the frontier (which spanned the first eight decades of the century), the emergence of the Civil War in the middle of the century, and the development of an industrial system (which occurred primarily during and after the Civil War). The responses of Americans to these three events can be understood as a lost opportunity for social welfare reform.

 ## POLICY AT THE FRONTIER

The American frontier has been romanticized in countless films and books. Many white settlers, as well as speculators and railroads, were financially enriched, but many settlers could not obtain land or were bankrupted in the volatile swings of the frontier economy. The frontier was also the stage for the persecution of Native Americans, Latinos, and other minorities.

### Land Policy

Most of the unsettled lands in the early and middle nineteenth century existed in territories owned by the federal government. Federal authorities had to decide whether to give land to settlers; to allow persons to buy unlimited quantities of land; to sell or give the land to churches and other organizations; or (most radically) to distribute the land to former slaves, Native Americans, impoverished immigrants, urban dwellers, and squatters.

The basic strategy for distributing the land, which was developed by the 1780s, was to sell it in blocks at public auctions to the highest bidders, provided their bids exceeded a prescribed minimum price. This strategy seemed advisable because the vast quantities of unsettled land would, it was assumed, keep land prices relatively low, avoid large public bureaucracies that would be needed if the government distributed land directly to persons, and conform to tenets of capitalism that governed the distribution of American lands almost from the beginning of the national experience. Tens of millions of acres were sold at federal land offices between the 1790s and 1880s, when the frontier no longer existed.[1]

Far from proving equitable, however, the auctions often enriched relatively affluent Americans, speculators, and railroads. Those who could bid competitively at auctions tended to be affluent persons who had recently sold their farms in settled areas. Because the federal government wanted railroads to place their lines in territories to facilitate economic growth, they gave (or sold at minimum prices) vast tracts to them, which the railroads often sold at inflated prices to settlers. Speculators and land companies soon realized that they could manipulate the auction system; with the use of scouts and secret information from officials at federal land offices, they located valuable farm and other lands, made mutual agreements not to engage in competitive bidding, and secured large tracts at the minimum federal price, which they later sold at higher prices to settlers.[2]

It was a myth that the frontier was largely sold to farmhands, poor immigrants, or poor urban dwellers. A large class of squatters settled frontier lands without titles since they lacked funds to purchase them, and they grew several crops before moving westward to renew the process. The federal government periodically tried to help squatters and financially distressed persons. Many "preemption laws" allowed squatters to purchase their land at the federal auctions. Furthermore, federal authorities tried to allow poorer persons to buy land by successively lowering the minimum sizes of land blocks from 320 to 160 to 40 acres and by decreasing the required level of down payment. But these policies were insufficient to help many settlers or to make land ownership possible for many squatters.[3] Relatively little land was distributed to freed slaves in the wake of the Civil War, and land was not widely used for charitable institutions aside from land-grant colleges.

The problems of settlers were exacerbated by the lack of sufficient regulation of the frontier banks that financed land purchases. In the absence of sufficient federal currency, notes of local banks were used as currency, but their value fluctuated wildly in periodic recessions or when the banks had to repay the foreign creditors who often financed their operations. President Jackson's veto of the United States Bank in 1832 compounded the economic turmoil.[4]

Unchecked deception and fraud existed as well. Speculators, railroads, and steamship companies hired salesmen to promise fertile American lands to European peasants, who often relinquished their life savings only to find they had bought a plot of barren land in a remote location. Speculators hired persons to falsely claim squatting rights so that they could buy it at minimum prices. Federal land agents often gave information about choice lands to speculators for a fee—and often themselves participated freely in land speculation.[5]

## Conquered Peoples

Extensive prejudice against Native Americans during the colonial period was softened by the belief that Native Americans were lazy because they lived under the destructive influence of tribal customs. Environmental explanations of the differences between Native Americans and whites of the colonial period were increasingly supplanted by a racism in the nineteenth century that promoted vicious suppression of Native Americans and Spanish-speaking persons on the frontier. American anthropologists became convinced that white persons who came from England and Germany, whom they called Anglo-Saxons, were biologically superior to other races in terms of intelligence and industriousness and that their alleged superiority had allowed them to conquer indigenous persons, develop new technology, and establish democratic and legal institutions. Unlike many colonial theorists, who assumed that Native Americans shared common biological origins with whites, these anthropologists contended that Anglo-Saxons derived from a biological stock different from that of racial minorities.[6]

These theories of biological superiority have since been disproved by modern scientists, who have shown that all human races derived from ancestors in Africa or Asia—something that the nineteenth-century anthropologists would have found disconcerting—and that Caucasians did not possess brains any larger than those of other races.[7] Racist ideas that placed Anglo-Saxons on a biological pedestal were nonetheless widely disseminated and accepted in the nineteenth century and linked to nationalism through the concept of "manifest destiny," a term coined by a Democratic politician in 1845 to describe the belief that God had willed that Anglo-Saxons develop the North American continent as a laboratory to show the world that Americans could build a utopian society that fused capitalism, Protestantism, and democracy. Anthropologists and politicians argued that indigenous peoples who blocked the expansion of the frontier should be violently suppressed and that Anglo-Saxons should not dilute their species by marrying members of other racial groups[8] (see Figure 5.1).

The frontier had existed in the colonial period but had been circumscribed by various territorial claims of the Spanish and French; the determination of the English Crown to limit the advance of settlers on some of the lands of Native Americans (see the discussion of the Proclamation Line in Chapter 3); and the tenacity of Native American tribes, which often made an effective resistance to the advance of white settlers. With the departure of the European

**FIGURE 5.1** • *Shackled Apache Native Americans captured on the Frontier about 1880*

*Source:* Smithsonian Institution, National Anthropological Archives, Photo No. 56, 208

powers by the early nineteenth century and with huge increases in the numbers of white settlers, the balance of power at the frontier shifted toward the settlers, who moreover, continued to use their advanced weapons, their ability to play tribes off against each other, and their ability to entice or force tribal leaders to sign treaties to advantage. What's more, the unexpected acquisition in 1803 of the Louisiana Territory from the French opened up a frontier extending from the Mississippi to the Pacific, with the exception of huge Spanish territories (which became Mexican land in 1821 when Mexico obtained its

independence from Spain) on the southwestern and western parts of the continent.

Jefferson, who had negotiated the Louisiana Purchase, originally had the notion that Native Americans should live on small tracts of land in their existing territories (with remaining lands to be sold to white settlers by federal land agents) but moved toward a "removal policy" that would relocate most Native Americans who were to the west of the Mississippi to lands far from the existing frontier. The relocation policy was anathema to many Native American leaders, such as the legendary leader Tecumseh, who tried over some decades to organize an effective resistance by tribes in the Ohio Valley and the South.[9] But the push of the white settlers was inexorable; often under force of arms, tribal leaders (or those cooperative persons who were labeled leaders by white officials) ceded vast tracts to the American government. When federal officials occasionally sought to protect those lands that the Native Americans kept for themselves by these various treaties, they often had little success in restraining settlers from occupying them and from brutalizing Native Americans.

Even those Native Americans who chose to become farmers were displaced as the frontier moved westward. Many Cherokees, who farmed lands in Georgia, for example, signed treaties with federal authorities that guaranteed tribal jurisdiction over certain lands and declared their statehood independent of Georgia so as to forestall efforts to take their land. Some politicians resisted their removal and cited treaty obligations, but the Georgia legislators declared them to be merely tenants who could be evicted and removed to western territories. (Georgia invited its citizens to plunder the Cherokees and enacted legislation that made it illegal for them to testify in court against white men who took their property!) The Cherokees appealed in desperation to President Jackson, who promptly ruled that the issue was a state matter and who strongly supported congressional "removal legislation" that was enacted in 1830. The Cherokees then appealed to the U.S. Supreme Court arguing that, as a foreign power, their land claims could not be violated by Georgia. Though showing some sympathy to them, the Supreme Court ruled them to be (merely) a "domestic dependent nation" that could not claim to be a foreign power; as such, the Court argued, they lacked jurisdiction. When a subsequent Supreme Court ruling was more favorable, President Andrew Jackson merely ignored it, thus paving the way for the rounding up of the Cherokees into stockades and the forcible marching of them to the territories in an area that later became the state of Oklahoma. It is estimated that as many as 45 percent of the tribe died of starvation or disease during this forced exodus. Similar policies were used to evict other, large southern tribes such as the Chocktaws, the Chickasaws, and the Creeks while the Seminoles in Florida were pushed into swampy and undesirable lands that became their reservations.[10] Tribes in the Ohio, Indiana, and Illinois areas were similarly removed to the West, often under the guise of treaties that promised that their western lands would be kept intact for them for "perpetuity." By the end of the 1830s, then, many displaced tribes existed in territories west of the Mississippi in areas that later became Kansas, Arkansas, Oklahoma, Nebraska, and Texas.[11] Other tribes were confined to relatively small reservations in scattered locations in Florida, Minnesota, and elsewhere.

Spanish-speaking people on the Western frontier were also victims. The Louisiana Purchase gave most lands west of the Mississippi to the Americans but *not* lands held by Spain that later became part of Mexico when it obtained its independence in 1821. White settlers found the area that became Texas to be suitable for ranching and for cotton in the 1820s and 1830s. As they pushed west and were resisted by the indigenous population, episodes of violence escalated, but the region was easy to conquer because of the political instability and weakness of Mexico. When a particular battle at the Alamo in San Antonio in 1836 was publicized as the massacre of innocent white settlers by bar-

baric Mexicans, many Americans sided with the efforts of the white settlers to gain independence from Mexico and establish a territorial government, which became an American state in 1845. But the Mexican government refused to recognize this new state constructed from Mexican territory. The United States declared war on Mexico in 1846 and, in a one-sided affair, routed the Mexicans in a series of battles that terminated in the ransacking of Mexico City in 1847.[12]

The Mexicans ceded territory that is now California, Nevada, New Mexico, Utah, Nevada, parts of Colorado, Wyoming, and Arizona—and they recognized the independence of Texas. To try to protect the stranded Spanish-speaking persons in the ceded territory, they insisted on a provision in the Treaty of Guadalupe Hidalgo that required Americans to honor the civil liberties and rights of the indigenous and Spanish-speaking population. But the provision had little effect on subsequent developments since Spanish-speaking persons were told that their land titles, which existed under Mexican law, had to be converted to American titles, a policy that led to the transferral of millions of acres of land to white settlers in Texas and then other areas of the land that had been ceded by Mexico. (The indigenous persons lacked legal resources as well as access to impartial judges.) White squatters often claimed their land extralegally—and many indigenous Spanish-speaking persons were massacred by land-hungry settlers.[13] Landless, lacking resources, and denied civil rights and civil liberties, the Spanish-speaking population proved a useful source of labor for American ranchers and eventually for growers of vegetable and cotton crops. The large farming operations were made possible with the passage of the Reclamation Act in 1902, which provided federal funds to build the irrigation system that brought water from the Colorado River to California. Isolated from urban populations in labor camps that were organized by large owners and companies, the Latinos were brutally suppressed when they complained about their subsistence wages and harsh working conditions.[14]

In effect, then, the settlers had engaged in three conquests by the mid-1840s: the initial development of the frontier in the colonial period, a massive relocation of Native Americans from the formation of the republic to the late 1830s, and the acquisition from the Mexicans of much of the western and southwestern part of the continent in the 1830s and 1840s. These conquests led to the formation of the various states east of the Mississippi, as well as Texas, and paved the way for the statehoods of many southwestern states as well as California, which became a state in 1850.

But the white settlers had created a problem for themselves when they had forcibly relocated many tribes west of the Mississippi, for they occupied vast tracts of land that white settlers desired — and some of these lands also contained minerals. A fourth conquest was needed to obtain from Native Americans lands that they held under treaties with the United States in areas that later became the states of Nebraska, Kansas, Arkansas, and Oklahoma, as well as the areas ceded to the United States by Mexico, such as Colorado and California.[15] Native Americans in the Pacific Northwest also had to be wrested from the land.

This fourth conquest used many of the techniques of earlier ones, such as the signing of treaties that led to tribes ceding land in exchange for minimal cash and (again) promises that their (now smaller) reservations would be guaranteed to them for perpetuity. Native Americans' resistance to the further incursions of white settlers was softened by placing railroads through their lands, mass killing of the buffalo on which they depended for sustenance, and threats that Congress would rescind prior treaties if Native Americans failed to cede their lands by signing new treaties.[16]

But a new device was also used to obtain lands. A movement began in the 1870s to break up reservations because many public officials believed that tribal ownership of land represented an unnatural and communalistic experiment that clashed with Anglo patterns of individualistic ownership of land. The Dawes Act, which Congress enacted in 1887, proposed to give 160 acres to each head of a Native American family and conditioned their access to land on their acceptance of these individual plots of land.[17] Although some protections were initially established, the new policy meant that whites could eventually take land from the Native Americans, one by one, by using a variety of tricks. By coercing or enticing them to sell their land for minimal prices, by using devious legal techniques to obtain title to their plots, or by arguing that Native Americans had failed to claim some of their allotments, speculators and crooks were able to liquidate vast holdings of Native Americans. If five major tribes had held an area equivalent to half the size of Oklahoma, for example, their holdings were reduced from 19.5 million acres in the 1850s to slightly over 300,000 acres by 1956.[18]

## Finding Laborers

Americans on the Western frontier often needed to obtain labor to grow crops, to build public improvements such as railroads, and to serve as miners. Many white settlers in Texas imported slaves from other sections of the South to make it a major cotton-growing region. We have noted that, once dispossessed from the land, Latinos provided the major source of labor for the growing of cotton, fruit, and vegetables in California.

Moreover, about one million Asians entered America between the gold rush of 1849 and the Immigration Act of 1924 in a complex pattern representing migrations from China, Japan, Korea, the Philippines, and India. (Chinese and Japanese immigrants constituted the bulk of the migration.) Unlike conquered peoples and like European immigrants, most of the Asian immigrants came voluntarily in search of a better life, but unlike their European counterparts and like slaves and Native Americans, they possessed physiological characteristics that made it easy for the white population to identify them and often to stigmatize and segregate them.

The Asian immigration began with Chinese immigrants who came to America to find gold in the 1840s and to do manual labor for farmers, manufacturers, miners, and railroads that were extending lines from the Pacific toward the East. In 1870, the 63,000 Chinese constituted almost 10 percent of the population of California. Chinese laborers were ideally suited to these tasks; they could be paid minimal wages (especially when coercive tactics were used when they threatened strikes for higher wages) and used to depress wages of white workers, and they did not constitute a political threat since they were denied legal rights as "aliens" and as persons of color. (The California Supreme Court ruled in 1854 that Chinese people could not testify in court against whites—not even if one of their number had been murdered by a white citizen.) They were disallowed from owning mines by tax levies, could not become citizens, were required to attend segregated schools, and could not vote.[19] On various transcontinental railroad lines, teams of Chinese workers met their Irish counterparts when the lines from west and east met at points in Utah and Texas.

Rampant racism and fears by white laborers that they would lose their jobs to Chinese workers led to the enactment of the Chinese Exclusion Act of 1882, which excluded further Chinese immigrants despite their usefulness to employers. Japanese labor soon provided a low-wage substitute, particularly for white landowners who sought to grow fruit and vegetables in California—and by 1902, the 139,000 Japanese residents vastly outnumbered the roughly 70,000 Chinese residents.

Like the Chinese, the Japanese immigrants were often greeted by racist epithets, such as "Jap," and realtors often refused to sell them houses. The Japanese were attacked by white laborers and were denied citizenship and the vote. A sizable network of Japanese businesses developed, including ones (such as restaurants and boarding houses) that catered to Japanese clients. At the time when large national markets for fruits and vegetables had developed by the use of refrigerated railroad cars, the Japanese quickly became major producers of these products by ingeniously adapting techniques of irrigation used in Japan to American farms. By initially leasing or renting land, they obtained resources to purchase their own land.[20]

But the growing Japanese population soon encountered white racism. Angered by their competition, white laborers demanded that the Chinese Exclusion Act, due for renewal in 1902, include a ban on Japanese immigration. But President Theodore Roosevelt, anxious for diplomatic reasons not to antagonize Japan, opposed this policy and at one point used federal troops to protect the Japanese from race riots in San Francisco, but he relented to persuade Japan in the Gentleman's Agreement of 1907 not to allow the emigration of laborers to the United States except for family members of existing residents. (Roosevelt favored exclusion of the Japanese once he had left office.) Moreover, angered by the success of the Japanese in agriculture, California enacted legislation in 1913 to disallow Japanese immigrants from obtaining land and to restrict their leases to three years. When it was discovered they were circumventing the law by placing their land in the names of their American-born children, the California legislature further tightened the legislation so as to disallow this practice and even leasing itself. (Similar legislation was enacted in twelve other states.) The Japanese suffered another rebuff in 1922 when the Supreme Court ruled that Japanese Americans could not become citizens because they were not Caucasians as specified as a condition for citizenship in 1790 federal legislation. To make matters even worse, the Congress enacted immigration legislation in 1924 that restricted the number of foreign-born persons to be admitted each year to 2 percent of the numbers of that nationality residing in the United States in 1890—a measure clearly directed at the Japanese population, which had numbered only 2,039 persons in that year. (The Chinese were still banned from any immigration.)[21]

## Appraisal of Frontier Policy

Many persons benefited from the expansion of the frontier. One can imagine the euphoria of a descendant of a serf who managed to survive the western trek and the first penniless years on a small tract in the American Midwest. Despite abuses of the auction system of land disposal, a large class of yeoman farmers developed who participated vigorously in local politics and helped one another with practical tasks. Civic participation in territorial governments was promoted by a desire to achieve admission to the Union as a state since protection from Native Americans and access to federal funds for internal improvements hinged on statehood. A tradition of sectarian and private philanthropy developed in some frontier communities.

But speculation and greed were as much the legacy of the frontier as mutual aid. Americans came to the frontier as individualists and as persons who believed in limited government, so they fashioned local institutions that emphasized the protection of property rights rather than the development of programs and institutions that would help the disabled, sick, or poor or the indigenous persons who had been displaced by the white settlers. As with farm foreclosures of the 1920s and 1980s, the society demonstrated little compassion for persons who were bankrupted by economic forces beyond their control. When assessed in terms of the sheer speed of dispersion of the population through the countryside and the speed of clearing and cultivating or ranching the land, the American frontier was an unqualified success. When measured by the criteria of development of social institutions to meet common human needs or the distribution of lands to needy persons, however, the American frontier was a failure, particularly when the crushed lives of conquered peoples are entered into the balance.[22]

The American frontier was both a reflection of American individualism and a perpetuator or intensifier of that individualism. As stories of settlement, conquest, and success reached Americans in other sections of the country, prevailing American individualism was intensified since frontier success seemed to confirm the idea that hard work and risk taking would lead to success for anyone. If unlimited land is available as a social resource, some Americans asked, why do Americans need to develop other social resources and programs to help the needy?[23]

The frontier both reflected and probably intensified American racism as well. Native Americans and Spanish-speaking peoples who attacked white settlers as they moved across the land were portrayed as barbaric and uncivilized peoples. As a laboratory experiment that juxtaposed "advanced" with "lesser" peoples, the frontier appeared to confirm the racial and genetic superiority of Anglo-Saxons. The pangs of guilt of some white settlers were eased by their belief that their conquest would improve the general quality of the human race and the nation.

The development of farms, plantations, and mines in newly developed territories, as well as the construction of roads and railroads to reach these areas, required large amounts of labor. As southerners had done, entrepreneurs at the frontier used slaves to grow cotton and tobacco, as well as Latinos and Asians to grow crops, serve as miners, build railroads, and provide workers for emerging industries. The treatment of these laborers by their employers was often brutal—and they resided in jurisdictions that enacted harsh legislation to deprive them of their basic rights. Nor were federal authorities helpful; indeed, immigration legislation as well as various court rulings served to buttress and supplement the discrimination and racism that were rampant in local jurisdictions.

## THE CIVIL WAR AND THE FREEDMEN: AN EXERCISE IN FUTILITY

More American lives were lost during the Civil War than during World War II, when expressed as a percentage of the total population, but battlefield casualties reflect only one portion of the human toll. Millions of persons, white and black, were dislocated during and after the war, and freed slaves were cast into a society with few economic or social supports.

## Origins of the Civil War

Was the war fought to help the slaves or for other objectives? Controversy exists among historians about the war's precise causes, but research suggests that the war was caused by multiple factors, many of which had little to do with improving the condition of freed slaves.[24]

By 1830, three societies had developed within the American nation that were profoundly different from one another. Since it had poor soil and long winters, New England had relatively marginal agriculture, and many of its citizens had begun to envision their region as a center for commerce and industry. Its leading citizens demanded high tariffs to protect its fledgling industry from foreign competitors and demanded federal subsidies for its small shipping industry. The expanding Northern frontier, which extended into Ohio, Indiana, Illinois, and Missouri, became the breadbasket of the nation when its crops were increasingly transported to New England in exchange for commodities. This area sought federal funds to develop roads, canals, and railroads that were vital to trade with New England. New England and the frontier communities became closely linked since each depended on the other for goods; when a poor crop occurred on the frontier, New England had to import food, so there were fewer resources to build industry, just as a recession in New England meant that prices for agricultural produce from the frontier plummeted.

The South, which included the "Old South" (states like Virginia, the Carolinas, Alabama, and Georgia) and a Southern frontier (territories in states that are now Mississippi, Louisiana, and Texas), depended on tobacco and cotton, which were often cultivated by slaves. Cotton and tobacco, like agricultural produce of the Northern frontier, became part of the world economy with the development of worldwide shipping capabilities by New England shippers, who bought and exported southern cotton in order to finance the expansion of New England industry. The conditions of the slaves varied, but many historians believe that the American version of slavery was even more repressive than slavery in South America and the West Indies. Reduced to chattel and lacking support from church, government, and legal institutions, slaves were wholly at the mercy of their masters.

Even this cursory discussion points to sectional rivalries that precipitated the Civil War. Most Northern families, who usually knew someone who had gone to the frontier to obtain land, wanted to preserve the frontier for white settlers. But the frontier also appealed to Southerners, who wanted new lands for cotton plantations. Slavery could not easily coexist with free labor since it required supportive laws, local police, courts, and public opinion to keep the slaves in their bondage and to ensure the return of runaways. Northern settlers were not likely to cooperate in the maintenance of slavery because they came from areas dominated by small farmers and free labor who feared preemption of land by plantations. Many Northerners also viewed the institution of slavery as morally flawed.[25]

This rivalry for land was exacerbated by political realities since a delicate balance existed in the Congress among New England, the Northern frontier, and the South. New England wanted high tariffs and subsidies for ships, the frontier areas wanted public money for internal improvements and cheap land, and the South wanted low tariffs and some internal improvements. If Northern interests were successful in dominating frontier regions, they would, Southerners reasoned, control the Congress by obtaining more congressmen and senators. Northerners feared in similar fashion that Southerners could increase their ranks by adding slave states to the Union at the frontier. Both Northerners and Southerners realized that the region that controlled the Congress could also write legislation to declare the frontier to be free or slave-owning areas.[26]

Because Northerners and Southerners had realized since the early part of the nineteenth century that cohabitation of specific territories was difficult, they had avoided armed conflict by the device of partitioning the frontier into slave-owning and free territories. A series of ingenious compromises from 1787 to 1850 gave sections of the frontier to each side. By 1850, however, an atmosphere of mutual paranoia had developed. The Compromise of 1850 was achieved with considerable difficulty in this tense atmosphere and did not specifically address the needs of two new territories that were rapidly filling with settlers from both the North and South, namely, Kansas and Nebraska.

Under the terms of the Missouri Compromise of 1820, these territories should have been free, but increasing numbers of Northerners and Southerners were not in a mood to compromise. Many Southerners were convinced that the Congress did not have the right to declare that they could not bring slaves into *any* territory or state, and many Northerners believed slavery should be outlawed from the start in all territories. In this embattled atmosphere, the Congress could only decide to allow each territory to decide for itself whether it wished to be free or slave owning.

As Congress decided that it could no longer assume the role of partitioner of the frontier, the battle between the North and South was transferred from the Congress to the territories, where determined settlers from each region confronted one another. As battles were waged, dramatic stories of brutality of "the other side" popularized the conflict in both the North and South.[27] Persons from both the North and South poured into the Kansas and Nebraska territories in the 1850s. Rival territorial conventions and legislatures were convened by both slave-owning and Northern settlers and variously declared the territories to be free or slave owning. Armed conflict became commonplace as persons took the law into their own hands.

Polarization between regions was soon reflected in realignment of the major political parties. Two major political parties existed in 1850—the Whigs, who drew their support heavily from New England, and the Democrats, who had strong support in both the South and states that now comprise the Midwest. With the rapid emergence of the Republican party after the presidential election of 1856, the Republican party (to which Abraham Lincoln tied his fortunes) supplanted the Whig party and quickly became the party of the North; its leaders demanded that slavery be outlawed from the outset in all territories. Leaders of the Democratic party, which became the party of the South, argued that Congress lacked the constitutional authority to outlaw slavery in the territories or anywhere else. Many Southerners believed that they had no recourse but to secede from the Union when Lincoln was elected president in 1860. They were convinced that he would close the territories to slavery and, with control of Congress assured by Northerners, lead a legislative attack on the South—perhaps even outlawing slavery itself, as advocated by a growing number of abolitionists.[28] The South fired the first shot by attacking a federal fort in South Carolina in 1861, but the seeds of the conflict, and probably its inevitability, were sown in the conflict over the rich lands of the Western frontier.

The preceding discussion suggests that many Northerners fought the war primarily to secure land and political power for their region. A second cause of the war was nationalism. South Carolinians had threatened to secede from the Union in 1832, but they were intimidated by Andrew Jackson, who believed the Union should be preserved at all costs.[29] Southerners' contemplation of secession in the 1850s exposed them to Northern wrath that derived from nationalistic sentiment. But nationalism did not foster humanitarian proposals to help slaves; indeed, nationalism was often linked to racism as Americans contemplated extending the Anglo-Saxon race from coast to coast. A third cause of the war was the Northern desire to abolish slavery. If *any* group might have fought the war with the interests of slaves at heart, it should have been the abolitionists, who courageously endured the wrath of many Northern white audiences when they promoted their cause in the decades preceding the war.

Even the abolitionists had limited notions of the kinds of ameliorative social reforms that freed slaves would need in the wake of emancipation. Most abolitionists were constrained by the racism of the nineteenth century. On the one hand, they were attracted by the gentleness of African Americans, a virtue commonly ascribed to African Americans in this era. Abolitionists argued as well that environmental factors rather than intrinsic characteristics were responsible for the alleged laziness of African Americans. But many abolitionists were also convinced that African Americans had a savage side to their nature, could not be trusted, and were subsumed by sexual urges. Some abolitionists even believed that African Americans should not be allowed to intermarry with whites and that they should not be given the vote.[30]

Abolitionists were also limited by the moral ideology that was widely applied to the social problems of poverty, alcoholism, and crime. Many abolitionists began with the premise that most slaves were morally flawed because the plantation environment had encouraged them to be shiftless and promiscuous. To rehabilitate slaves, they urged utilization of the same set of educational and poorhouse institutions that reformers sought for impoverished immigrants in the North. But they were blinded by their ideology to the need to distribute land to freedmen, to provide them with resources to allow them to purchase their own land, or to help millions of them to migrate to Northern cities, where the new industrial order, with its vast economic opportunities, was being established.[31] Furthermore, many abolitionists pointed to the relative poverty of Northern African Americans, who were concentrated in urban areas such as New York City and Philadelphia, as evidence that African Americans needed to be subjected to a supervised moral regimen after they had obtained their freedom. Some abolitionists even believed that widespread discrimination against African Americans by Northerners—who denied them the vote in most Northern states, placed them in segregated public schools, and denied them access to public transportation and public accommodations—was caused by the poor reputation that African Americans had brought on themselves by not sufficiently improving their economic status.[32]

Persons who supported the Civil War because they genuinely wanted to help the slaves, then, rarely envisioned the need for such reforms as massive distribution of land or resources to them. Sectional rivalries, nationalism, and the moralistic ideology were the primary motivations for the war, not a desire to help freedmen by enacting sweeping economic and social reforms. It is ironic that the moral-treatment ideology, which was a simplistic approach to the social needs of poor whites, was applied to the African-American population, whose problems were so obviously linked to the oppression they had experienced both in the South and the North.

## Social Policy During the War

The primary issue to be resolved during the war was the legal status of slaves. In its infamous Dredd Scott decision in 1857, the Supreme Court had declared that slaves, as well as free

**FIGURE 5.2** • *Former slaves crossing into freed territory during the Civil War*

*Source:* Library of Congress

African Americans, were not persons and thus not entitled to constitutional protections, even when they lived in free territories. Lincoln did not immediately declare the slaves to be free because he hoped to entice Southern states to negotiate an early end to the war by allowing them to retain slaves in existing states. When he finally issued the Emancipation Proclamation in 1863, he declared all slaves to be free who were in areas still in rebellion against the Union.[33]

Social welfare issues of dislocated persons received secondary attention in the turmoil of this Civil War and were addressed improvisationally. The Union (Northern) Army was the major instrument of social welfare by virtue of its presence in the South. Vast numbers of African Americans had to be supported as they left plantations, either because the Union Army had conquered Southern territory or because slaves fled behind Union lines (see Figure 5.2). The Union Army constructed and maintained many freedmen's camps, where former slaves were placed in barracks or tents and given food and health care. These camps provided harsh surroundings; roughly 25 percent of their occupants died of disease though it must be remembered that mortality rates were similar for Union troops because of the lack of modern medical technology to stem epidemics and infection. Some of the military administrators of the camps, like most citizens of the era, believed that the freed slaves were intrinsically lazy, so they placed many of them on work details on camp fortifications or had them work under contract labor on plantations in conquered territories.[34]

Many Northern philanthropic societies sent legions of volunteers to assist refugees behind Union lines; some were nonsectarian, and others drew assistance from churches. They provided clothing, food, and medical supplies and developed some schools. Various departments of government developed programs in the South though often in isolation from one another. The War Department operated the freedmen's camps, and the Treasury Department controlled lands that had been confiscated from Confederate landowners.

The first systematic inquiry into the condition of freedmen, which was conducted in 1862 when President Lincoln appointed the American Freedmen's Inquiry Commission, recommended the establishment of a federal agency to coordinate the work of federal and private agencies and to develop new programs to meet the needs of freedmen, which could not be sufficiently addressed by private philanthropy. After extended debate in the Congress, the Bureau of Refugees, Freedmen, and Abandoned Land was established. Though the bureau was informally known as the Freedmen's Bureau, its official name emphasized refugees because many legislators did not want to show favoritism to African Americans. President Johnson opposed the bureau on the grounds that it would do more for African Americans than had been done for whites. A debate about the proper location of the agency in the federal bureaucracy nearly stalemated the legislation; abolitionists wanted it to be placed in the Treasury Department, which controlled lands that had been abandoned by or confiscated from Confederate supporters, to facilitate transfer of these lands to freedmen, but legislators placed it in the War Department when it was given jurisdiction over these lands.[35]

The Freedmen's Bureau was established in 1865 in a manner that virtually ensured that it would not be able to develop sweeping economic and social programs to help the freedmen. Its position in the War Department reflected its status as a wartime, rather than permanent, agency; indeed, it was terminated in 1872. Virtually no funding was given to the new agency since it was assumed that private philanthropy, largely from the North, could address most of the needs of freedmen. The legislation was staunchly opposed by Southerners—and some Northerners—on the grounds that it represented unconstitutional delving by federal authorities into welfare matters, which were perceived by many persons to belong to the jurisdiction of state and local governments. The Freedmen's Bureau was given authority to establish courts in the South to help African Americans obtain their freedom, to make certain that terms of contract labor between freedmen and landowners were clearly written and honored, and to distribute confiscated and abandoned land, but it lacked even a full-time director of legal affairs. Many army officials were appointed to its staff because it was located in the War Department; some of them were sensitive to the economic and social needs of freed African Americans, but others possessed punitive or racist orientations.[36]

If the Freedmen's Bureau and freedmen's camps represented superficial efforts to assist freedmen, other policy setbacks also occurred during the Civil War with ominous implications for freedmen. Freedmen desperately needed land in an agricultural society since without it they had to work as tenant farmers or sharecroppers. Legislation that established the Freedmen's Bureau promised forty acres of abandoned or confiscated land to every male refugee, but it could not be implemented unless governmental authorities identified abandoned land, took possession of it, and distributed it to the penniless freedmen. Confiscation of land ran counter, however, to American veneration of the rights of owners to private property and the belief that government had no right to interfere with it; even many abolitionists did not support land confiscation during the war. Southern landowners were able to use elaborate legal strategems, as well, to foil efforts to confiscate their property, including use of local or even federal courts to oppose rulings of courts of the Freedmen's Bureau. Relatively few African Americans were resettled on farms though the Freedmen's Bureau was able to resettle roughly 40,000 persons on their own land. The most successful efforts to redistribute land were undertaken by Generals Sherman and Grant, who unilaterally gave land to African Americans in conquered territories in Georgia and Alabama. These policies were foiled after the war, however, when President Andrew Johnson declared that African Americans occupied the lands illegally and required them to surrender their lands to prior owners.[37]

## Reconstruction

As the war neared its conclusion, Lincoln faced difficult options. He could have supported a policy to guarantee freedmen the right to vote, access to public accommodations, and access to federal courts when they were harrassed by local citizens. He also could have excluded former Confederate officials from local, state, or federal government in order to prevent restoration of racist policies. But he chose the more cautious approach of deferring to the southern states by restoring their power as quickly as possible, partly because he did not want to stiffen the resolve of the South to fight to the bitter end. He appointed military governors in each state and promised a return to civilian and southern rule, subject only to the requirement that 10 percent of the white population vote their loyalty to the Union and agree to end slavery. This passive federal role, one that allowed southern states to retain laws that prohibited African Americans from voting as well as other infringements of their civil liberties, was stoutly opposed by many abolitionists since they feared that the South

would soon return to a system of quasi-slavery where African Americans would be nominally free but would lack land, resources, and the vote. The abolitionists' arguments were not heeded by Lincoln, however, who seemed intent on restoring order in the South as soon as possible and on terms that were acceptable to established southern leaders.[38]

But there was still room for hope. Lincoln's views had changed markedly between 1860 and 1865. Lincoln had been enamored with states' rights, even when they were used to enslave African Americans, and had only reluctantly (and as a war measure) moved to emancipation, but he had been persuaded by 1865 that the federal government needed to enact federal civil rights legislation and other policies to empower and help the freedmen.[39] We shall never know what policies Lincoln would have sought, for he was assassinated and then replaced by Vice President Andrew Johnson in 1865. Johnson was an unabashed southerner who had always detested African Americans and whose dislike of the southern aristocracy became transformed into a crusade to develop a political base among white monied interests in the postwar South. His term of office, which extended from 1865 until he was replaced by General Grant in 1868, was an unmitigated disaster for freedmen. He proposed to allow southern states back into the Union with virtually no requirement that they protect civil or voting rights of African Americans. He pardoned vast numbers of Confederate officials so that they could resume political careers in the South, and he even appointed some of them as officials of the Freedmen's Bureau. He declared the courts of the bureau to be exempt from the requirement that their officials declare their loyalty to the Union. He sought to dissolve the Freedmen's Bureau when its officials advocated policies that he disliked.[40]

Southerners who had expected the worst from the North, including confiscation of land, restrictions on Confederate officials from holding political office, and requirements that they protect the civil liberties of African Americans, were astounded to discover that they had a strong ally in the White House. Johnson's policies emboldened southern white leaders to develop African-American codes, which placed restrictions on the ability of African Americans to move around the countryside, restricted their rights of assembly and free speech, and allowed whipping of them when they were discourteous or insubordinate.[41]

Southern actions and President Johnson's open support of white southern interests outraged many persons in the North, who wondered whether the Civil War had been worth the carnage if the South continued to oppress freedmen. Lincoln's assassination and Johnson's provocative policies radicalized the North. In quick succession, a number of northern states rescinded legislation that deprived African Americans of the vote and other civil liberties. Johnson and the Democratic party were resoundingly defeated in the congressional elections of 1866, which were a referendum on Johnson's southern policies since Republicans successfully argued that Johnson was a captive of the South. Northerners demanded passage of a succession of civil rights acts. The Thirteenth Amendment of the Constitution, which abolished slavery, was ratified by northern states in 1865. The Military Reconstruction Act of 1867 required southern states to include universal suffrage in their constitutions before they could be readmitted to the Union and allowed the army to serve as protector of civil rights by bypassing local courts.[42]

The Fourteenth Amendment, which was ratified in 1868, rescinded the provision in the Constitution that had counted each African American as only three-fifths a person, required that all citizens be given "equal protection" under the law, and stipulated that all persons be accorded the protection of due process. The Fifteenth Amendment, which was enacted in 1870, established universal suffrage of all adult males, though it did not exclude use of poll taxes and literacy tests, which were eventually used by southern jurisdictions to disenfranchise African Americans.[43] Civil Rights Acts were also en-

acted in 1870 and 1875 that, respectively, limited the ability of states to enforce discriminatory legislation and outlawed segregation in public facilities and schools. The Ku Klux Klan Act of 1872 declared infringements of the civil rights of persons to be a federal offense.

This federal legislation was supplemented by the ongoing presence of federal troops as well as area offices of the Freedmen's Bureau. Since the South remained an occupied society until 1877, southern whites were impeded from violating the rights of freedmen or from attacking northern liberals who had settled in the South. The Freedmen's Bureau continued to hear cases in freedmen's courts, to build schools, and to provide rations to starving or penniless freedmen though its programs reached only a small fraction of them.[44]

The southern states reeled before this onslaught of federal legislation. The Democratic party, which had dominated the South for decades, was now supplanted by a Republican party that consisted of a range of white and African-American voters. The transformed southern legislatures now contained significant numbers of African-American legislators as well as sympathetic whites who had migrated to the South during and after the war. These bodies enacted many reforms, including development of schools and mental institutions and public improvements such as roads. Taxes were raised by the Republican legislatures to rebuild southern institutions that had been devastated by war.[45]

The liberalizing of the politics of the South had been accomplished, however, only by the imposition of laws and troops on the South by the North. When southern states twice refused after the war to ratify the Fourteenth Amendment, even when the North had required this action as a precondition for the removal of northern military governors, they indicated that they preferred living under military occupation to acceding to a constitutional amendment that required equal protection of the laws to all citizens.[46] What would happen, some persons wondered, if the North lost the desire to allocate resources or troops to the South?

Even before this question could be answered, ominous signs appeared. The Ku Klux Klan, in essence an arm of the southern Democratic party, began to intimidate African Americans and northern whites. Northern troops, which numbered only 15,000 soldiers, could not curb the Klan's actions in dispersed rural areas of the South. Advocates of civil rights were dismayed by the resurgence of the Democratic party in the South in the 1860s and early 1870s since it achieved its dramatic comeback by playing on racial fears of poor whites by claiming that Republicans represented freedmen and northern settlers, who were popularly known as carpetbaggers. Democrats also argued that Republican governments in the southern states, which had raised taxes in order to pay for schools and internal improvements, were imposing "big government" on the South; why not return, they asked, to laissez-faire government and low taxes that had marked the South before the Civil War?[47]

The response of the Republican party in the South to these Democratic attacks was hardly encouraging to freedmen. A wing of the southern Republican party, which included many African-American legislators, had strongly supported civil rights and social programs to help freedmen and poor whites in the aftermath of the war, but many southern Republicans, who soon came to dominate the party, softened their advocacy of civil rights legislation and displaced the freedmen and their allies with white moderate and conservative southerners.[48]

Growing indifference to the South by northerners was also alarming to the freedmen since unrelenting pressure on the South by northern politicians was needed to avert the reemergence of African-American codes. Many abolitionists, considering their work completed when slavery was ended, turned to other causes and ceased to pressure the Republican party to continue to support civil rights measures.[49] Economic problems in the North, the disastrous recession of 1873, policies governing the rates of railroads, labor disorders, currency policy, and tariffs also distracted northerners from issues in the South. Northern imposition of civil rights legislation on the South had been partly motivated by anger at the South both for precipitating the war and for its defiant passage of African-American codes after the war, but the desire for revenge was dulled with the passing of years. The costs of maintaining the military occupation of the South made many northerners disinclined to continue it.[50]

A symbolic event occurred in 1877 that illustrated the decline of northern pressure on the South. The vote had been so close between candidates Samuel Tilden (Democrat) and Rutherford Hayes (Republican) in the presidential election of 1876 that the electoral college became stalemated. The Democrats finally agreed to support Hayes to break the stalemate, but only if he agreed to withdraw troops from the South. A fateful deal was struck that dimmed the hopes of southern African Americans, who were now left to the mercy of southern whites since the Republican party, which had spearheaded federal civil rights legislation after the war, now viewed the southern question as negotiable in the push-and-pull of the political process.[51]

Reformers lost an opportunity to improve the lot of freedmen after the Civil War. The major instrument of reform, the Freedmen's Bureau, was distressingly underfunded and had limited social welfare functions. More than 30 percent of its scant resources were devoted to educational programs for African Americans, but education could hardly suffice if African Americans had no land, resources, homes, or civil and political rights.[52] Education that was given by the Freedmen's Bureau focused on teaching African Americans moral rules since it was widely assumed that African Americans, just like low-income persons in the North, could succeed in life only if they were instructed in the tenets of honesty, religion, and thrift. The Freedmen's Bureau was initially enacted to last one year after the end of the war, but it managed to survive until 1872.

Although nearly one-fifth of African-American families owned land in 1870, most of them were tenant farmers who became mired in debt as they borrowed money from the whites for seeds, fertilizer, machines, and food. African-American landowners often had to foreclose because of their inability to repay debts or to secure loans from banks that were controlled by whites. African Americans who relocated to southern cities were subject to massive discrimination in job markets as well as to segregated housing and schools.[53]

There seemed room for optimism even as late as 1877, however. African Americans still voted in most southern jurisdictions, roughly 10 percent of school-age African Americans attended schools that had been established by the Freedmen's Bureau, and a small group of African-American landowners and small businessmen existed. These gains were offset by a continuing erosion of civil rights. Civil rights legislation and the Fourteenth Amendment were interpreted so restrictively by the Supreme Court that they afforded few protections for African Americans. The requirement that persons could not be deprived of their civil liberties without due process was ruled by the Supreme Court to apply only to discrimination against African Americans by individuals rather than by states, whose discriminatory laws (such as ones requiring poll taxes or literacy tests for voters) were thus legitimized.[54]

A new generation of political leaders in the North and South, who hardly remembered the Civil War, came to power in the late nineteenth century. They increasingly assumed that African Americans should not participate in political, social, or economic affairs. A new wave of laws, so-called Jim Crow legislation, was enacted in southern states that deprived African Americans of their basic civil rights. These laws were not rescinded until nearly a century after the Civil War.[55]

## Women, Policy, and the War

Curiously, abolitionism and the Civil War were associated with policy issues of women. Many women entered the world of politics by participating in temperance, charity, and church movements in the antebellum period though they often occupied decidedly subordinate positions in separate women's auxiliaries. The women in the abolitionist movement were more daring. Many of them defied the widespread custom of not allowing women to engage in public speaking to mixed audiences or to sign public petitions despite jeers from skeptical audiences and Congress's consideration of legislation in 1834 to disallow petitions that were signed by women. Numerous women became leaders in the abolitionist crusade.[56]

These abolitionist leaders, often with support from male abolitionists, applied the logic of emancipation to themselves and began to question traditional marriage vows that required women to pledge obedience, sexist language in the Bible and hymns, discriminatory property laws, and the condescension of males. As we discussed in Chapter 4, a small number of women and men held the first convention that was devoted to women's rights in 1848 in Seneca Falls, New York, where they issued a declaration of principles that advocated changes in property laws to allow married women to inherit their husbands' property and to keep earned wages. They also sought liberalization of divorce laws and universal suffrage.[57] These women found their hopes dashed in the wake of the Civil War, however. Having expended enormous energy to emancipate slaves, many of them hoped that they would receive the vote when it was given to freedmen with passage of the Fourteenth and Fifteenth Amendments. But male legislators, many women, and the Republican party were not willing to accept this major policy change.[58]

The women's movement focused on suffrage in the Gilded Age but divided into two factions. The American Women's Suffrage Association sought to obtain signatures on petitions that beseeched each of the state legislatures to change their constitutions to grant women the vote, whereas the National Women's Suffrage Association sought a range of reforms for women, including passage of a federal constitutional amendment to enact universal suffrage. Both groups were frustrated despite some modest gains. Most states and the Congress resisted universal suffrage because of the sexism of the era as well as the determined lobbying of the liquor industry, which was certain that women would support prohibition. The two factions of the women's movement united in 1890 into the National American Women's Suffrage Association but had scant success in obtaining suffrage reforms during the remainder of the century though some states liberalized property laws and women continued to increase their enrollments in secondary and college education.[59]

 ## SOCIAL POLICY AND INDUSTRIALIZATION

The American transition from an agricultural to an industrial society was unprecedented in its speed in world history, perhaps rivaled only by the pace of Japanese and Russian industrialization in the midtwentieth century. Only 20 percent of Americans lived in cities in 1860, and the nation ranked fourth in the world in the value of its manufactured products, but 60 percent of Americans lived in cities in 1900, and the nation ranked first in its industrial output. Indeed, the number of persons in urban areas grew from five million in 1860 to twenty-five million in 1900.[60]

### Industrialization Before the Civil War

Industrialization began prior to the Civil War, when most American nonagricultural workers were still employed in such skilled crafts as carpentry and blacksmithing or in skill-based industries, such as shoemaking. But textile, food-processing, shoemaking, and mining industries developed in New England in the 1830s and 1840s. Some textile plants located in rural areas, where they employed middle-class women who boarded on the premises, and some located in urban areas, where they employed entire families. Factory owners used large numbers of children and women even before the Civil War to minimize their labor costs, particularly in textile factories. In the absence of regulations, workers were subjected to brutish working conditions; it was common to require workers to work for more than twelve hours per day (some worked as many as fifteen hours) at abysmally low rates of pay and in unsanitary, dark, and dangerous conditions. Skilled workers who had made entire products in shops or homes before industrialization were often reduced to unskilled tenders of machines.[61]

Social problems were exacerbated by the fact that industrialization was accompanied by a turbulent economic environment. American enterprises were entwined in a world economy that was marked by frequent recessions and cutthroat competition between domestic and foreign enterprises. There had been considerable hardship in eastern cities in the colonial period, but economic hardship became even more obvious as cities grew in size and as hundreds of persons became unemployed during recessions. The magnitude and frequency of economic turmoil were exacerbated by realities encountered by entrepreneurs in the early period of industrialization. England tried to sabotage the development of industry in America by imposing tariffs on American imports, by prohibiting the export of technology to America, and by dumping commodities at artificially low prices on American markets. American industrialists, in turn, were vulnerable to bankruptcy since they accumulated enormous debts from building factories and obtaining machinery.[62]

Economic problems of factory workers were exacerbated by the absence of fall-back strategies in the growing cities of New England. Although distressed farmers could try to maintain a subsistence living through simple bartering or by producing their own food, urban dwellers often did not own land and could not, like farmers, try to sell a portion of their lands or work as laborers for other farmers in order to survive hard times. Since their families were intact, members of farm families could pool their resources, but these strategies could not be pursued as easily in cities, where workers were often separated from their families.[63]

## Industrialization During the Gilded Age

A truly dramatic acceleration of the process of industrialization occurred for several reasons during the Gilded Age, which extended from the Civil War to the end of the nineteenth century. The growth of railroads facilitated the development of markets and allowed agricultural produce and raw materials to reach expanding urban areas. Funds that were required to build factories and purchase machinery were obtained from foreign sources as well as a rapidly growing American banking system. A cheap and plentiful labor supply was obtained through massive levels of immigration from Southern and Eastern Europe and from Russia. Americans obtained a competitive advantage over Europeans because their new plants were able to incorporate rapidly developing technology, and Americans provided a policy and tax environment that was favorable to entrepreneurs that included high tariffs, minimal safety regulations, and low taxes.[64] Finally, between 1885 and 1900, the Supreme Court restricted the right of government to regulate corporations by ruling, for example, that manufacturing did not fall under the jurisdiction of the federal government because it was not "commerce" and that government could only gingerly regulate corporations because

their rights were protected by the due process clause of the Fourteenth Amendment, which had originally been enacted to safeguard the rights of freedmen.[65] The Sherman antitrust legislation, which was enacted in 1890 to restrict corporate monopolies, was applied by the courts to union monopolies! Even the power of the federal government to collect income taxes was questioned in several rulings.[66] It is small wonder, then, that industrialization proceeded rapidly.

Along with industrialization came rapid population growth. Cities grew at phenomenal rates. Frontier towns, such as Cleveland, Detroit, Pittsburgh, and Chicago, became major industrial centers, and with this growth came increasing social and economic problems. Packs of wild dogs roamed the streets in some cities and maimed or killed children. Typhoid, cholera, and malaria epidemics were common and sometimes decimated the populations of entire cities. Dangerous work conditions led to scores of injuries and deaths. Immigrants were particularly subject to wretched housing and industrial exploitation.[67] The prewar pattern of periodic and devastating recessions continued unabated after the war. Major recessions caused unemployment rates that often exceeded 25 percent in major cities; indeed, 10 percent of the population of New York City was receiving welfare after the recession of 1873. Recessions sometimes lasted for many years, as illustrated by the devastating recession of 1873 (known as the long recession) that lasted until 1878.[68]

Perhaps more than in any other period in American history, economic inequality was the most obvious characteristic of American society. Two classes predominated, the laboring and entrepreneurial classes, because the nation had only a small middle class, consisting of 16 percent of its workers.[69] Factory owners characteristically hired labor on a daily basis at factory gates and often retained workers for only brief periods so that there was a complete turnover of labor in many plants each year. Americans of all social classes moved frequently, but transiency was particularly marked among the working class, whose members had to remain mobile to find jobs in an uncertain economy.[70]

Industrialization prior to the Civil War had been marked by the development of small industries, but massive corporations were formed in the latter part of the century that systematically drove small competitors from business. Not content to concentrate on making one product, many tycoons bought related companies, including the steel magnate Andrew Carnegie, who coupled his steel empire with railroad and mining interests, and the oil magnate John D. Rockefeller, who extended his oil empire to include railroads and refineries. Massive cartels monopolized the production of certain products, charged exorbitant prices, and conspired to bankrupt competitors.[71]

## The Failure of Regulation

Reformers obtained some policy victories during the Gilded Age, including establishment of limits on work hours of federal employees, local housing regulations, some local regulations of working conditions of women and children, establishment of the Interstate Commerce Commission, and passage of Sherman antitrust legislation. By contemporary standards, however, these policies were symbolic gestures in light of the magnitude of social needs. Many jurisdictions did not enact regulations of industry, housing, public health, or labor practices of employers. Unemployment insurance, workmen's compensation, or pensions for the elderly were hardly discussed. The Interstate Commerce Commission was not able to regulate railroads because it was not given formal powers or sufficient resources to accomplish its task.[72] The ineffectiveness of the Sherman Antitrust Act, enacted in 1890, was illustrated by the acceleration of the development of cartels after its passage.

Intolerance of poor persons increased after the disastrous depression of 1873. As the frontier closed and cities swelled with poor immigrants, many Americans, who feared that this growing class of landless persons could disrupt existing institutions, supported repression of unions and strikes as well as suppression of "foreign radicals" in the wake of the depression of 1873.[73] This harsh orientation to the urban poor and to radicals was coupled with increasingly punitive orientations toward Native Americans and freedmen, whom many Americans believed to be unreceptive to ameliorative educational and moral-uplift projects.[74]

The nation seemed to be returning to the mercantile policies that had been so evident in the colonial period. Land subsidies to railroads, high tariffs to discourage imports, subsidies to shipping industries and telegraph lines, and public funding of improvements to rivers and harbors were motivated by desire to build America's economy. Colonial mercantilism had been a "top-down" policy, where top officials and royalty engineered tariffs and subsidies to help the national economy and unemployed citizens. This "bottom-up" mercantilism of the Gilded Age emanated from political pressures of corporations, which included flagrant use of bribes and lobbying to advance their economic interests.[75]

Although no nation had developed advanced policies to assist industrial workers, to upgrade cities, and to help persons who experienced unemployment, European societies were fashioning initial social policies to mitigate harmful social and economic problems that accompanied industrialization. The English Parliament, for example, enacted factory regulations in 1833, 1844, 1847, 1853, 1867, 1874, and 1878 as well as many public health measures.[76] Germany enacted old-age pensions and unemployment insurance in the 1880s.[77] America, which had pioneered suffrage, land distribution, and public education, lagged behind other nations, however, in enacting social reforms.

Corporations and financiers took advantage of a power and policy vacuum after the Civil War. When the nation began to industrialize rapidly during and after the Civil War, agricultural interests were placed on the defensive and were fragmented. Unions would have been a logical countervailing force to business, but they were extraordinarily weak and focused on crafts and skilled trades rather than on unskilled workers in factories. Because large numbers of workers were not concentrated at specific sites prior to the Civil War, unions were organized by geographic locality and sought a basic wage for all skilled workers in that area.[78] Their modest organizing successes in various cities in the 1830s were shattered by the recession of 1833, which allowed employers to violate agreements, to fire union members, and to hire nonunion members. There were a number of strikes and riots by factory workers in specific locations, but few unions larger than specific work sites developed. American courts, which began a pattern of issuing rulings that severely limited the ability of unions to organize, often declared unions to represent unlawful conspiracies or to violate the rights of workers by coercing them to enlist.[79] Many American economists believed as well that the "unnatural" wage increases obtained by unions decreased economic growth by absorbing funds from the pool of investment capital.[80]

Suppression of unions of unskilled workers after the Civil War was blatant. Armed guards beat up strikers or intimidated union organizers. Owners of some Colorado mines forcibly placed strike leaders on a train that took them to Arizona, where they were left with a "don't return" edict! Industrialists found powerful allies in government and courts. Local politicians frequently used police and local militia to break strikes, and they were soon joined by federal officials, who used the national guard and federal troops. President Hayes mobilized federal troops in 1877 to break a national strike against the railroads.[81]

Recessions and immigration frustrated the work of union organizers by breaking their momentum. Waves of immigrants provided an inexhaustible source of cheap labor that was used by industrialists to break strikes and to depress wages. The weakness of unions in the late nineteenth century is illustrated by the strange saga of the Knights of Labor, a national organization that organized district assemblies of skilled and unskilled workers from many trades. The Knights engaged in secret rituals, often opposed unions and strikes on grounds that brotherhood would solve industrial problems, and supported the development of self-employment and cooperative schemes. Although it often supported progressive social legislation, its ideology precluded the development of effective pressure on industrialists.[82]

Corporate interests became major contributors to the Democratic and Republican parties at local and national levels and used campaign contributions to obtain antiunion legislation, defeat adverse regulations, obtain tax concessions, and get government contracts. Because of the weakness of governmental institutions and the lack of competing groups such as unions and agriculture, corporate and banking interests had dominated the political field and used their advantage to secure favorable policies.

Social reform was impeded as well by changes in popular culture. Many Americans had believed prior to the Civil War that the primary purpose in life was to lead a virtuous existence, which might lead to social mobility; most persons, it was widely believed, were destined to remain in relatively humble positions. Americans continued to emphasize moral virtues after the Civil War, but they placed far more emphasis on social mobility.[83] Pauperism had been reviled prior to the Civil War, but many Americans came to believe that poverty was itself an indication of personal failing, and affluent persons were increasingly revered as models of success who inspired Americans of humbler origins to redouble their efforts. The Calvinist ambivalence about wealth, which was both revered as a sign from God of His pleasure and feared as a corrupter of moral virtue, was increasingly transformed into unambiguous worship of wealth.

This shift in culture was reflected in the stature of Herbert Spencer, an English writer who popularized and applied to society the theories of the English naturalist Charles Darwin. Darwin, who fashioned a theory of evolution of animal and plant forms to explain how different species emerged, maintained that some genetic mutations can provide some individuals within a species with a competitive edge, which allows them and their descendants to survive more effectively than other members of the species. Some mutations can thus lead to modifications of the species as these new characteristics are perpetuated through natural selection. Spencer theorized that genes also influence how persons fare in society and argued that persons who excel in business or other endeavors, much like animals or plants that survive in nature, possess superior genetic characteristics. His logic led him to conservative political conclusions; if affluent classes possess superior genes, he asked, should not society allow their numbers to increase while adopting policies to bring reductions in the numbers of low-income persons? By propping up ne'er-do-wells, governments and social agencies were artificially and wrongly interfering with natural selection within the social order.[84]

Spencer's use of Darwinian theory repre-sented a sloppy and misguided application of biological theories to society. Poverty, mental illness, and other social ills are caused by innumerable factors, including environmental and societal ones, as is illustrated by the plight of racial minorities in the United States in the nineteenth century. No evidence has been found by contemporary scientists to suggest that groups, whether social classes or ethnic groups, possess genetic characteristics that predispose them to inferior educational and economic performance.[85] Spencer did not sufficiently acknowledge that wealth is often obtained in immoral ways or is inherited. The influence of Spencer should not be exaggerated, however. Many Americans did not read him, and others ignored those portions of his teachings that urged elimination of social programs. But his deification of affluent persons struck a responsive chord with many Americans during a period of phenomenal economic growth. The American romanticizing of yeomen farmers had been transformed to a romanticizing of affluent industrialists and businessmen within urban settings. Industrialists could not have wished for a more receptive environment!

## THE POLITICAL ECONOMY OF AMERICAN POLICY CHOICES IN THE NINETEENTH CENTURY

The frontier, the Civil War, and industrialization posed different social welfare challenges to America. Each of them benefited many persons, yet each of them created social casualties, such as displaced Native Americans and Latinos, destitute farmers, and victimized laborers (the frontier), freedmen and poor white refugees (the Civil War), and unemployed, underpaid, or disabled workers (industrialization).

Americans during the Gilded Age glamorized the successes, paid relatively little attention to the casualties, and chose not to construct policies to alleviate suffering. Regarding Native Americans and Spanish-speaking persons, the nation virtually pursued a policy of genocide, and Asian and Latino laborers were deprived of their fundamental rights and subjected to virulent racism in local communities. Freedmen were left to wander in a region that was marked by racism and were not given major assistance as they made the difficult transition from slavery to freedom. Industrialists had a free hand to exploit workers, including women and children, in dangerous working environments.

When comparing American perceptions of the three events, one is struck by the similar interpretations each of them received. Americans idealized the frontier as a place where American religion and values were defended against savages; they viewed industrialization as an American success story in which self-made men rose to prominence by dint of hard work; and they perceived the Civil War as the triumphs of morality over the greed of slaveowners and of nationalism over the renegade Southern secessionists. By idealizing the positive outcomes of each of these events, Americans more easily rationalized or denied the suffering and the predicaments that accompanied them.

Many Americans interpreted the negative outcomes of these three events in a manner that blamed their victims rather than American social institutions and values. In this interpretation, Native Americans caused their own demise by not farming land or by unleashing "unprovoked" attacks on white settlers. Their problems, settlers reasoned, surely stemmed from their savage nature rather than because the settlers took their land. Asians and Latinos were perceived to possess alien religious and cultural traditions that imperiled the culture of the white settlers and were often seen by white laborers as taking scarce jobs from them. Slaves were freed by Northerners and were given the same "fair shake" that had been extended to white immigrants, so their lack of economic success was surely due to personal shortcomings rather than to the racism of their society or the intrinsic difficulties in making a transition from slavery. It was widely believed that unemployed and underpaid persons in industrial society, like freedmen, could achieve social mobility if they worked hard, so union demands for fair pay were often viewed as the work of foreign agitators who wanted to introduce alien socialist institutions.

Moral treatment was an intervention that was predicated on the assumption that the moral character of individuals was the most potent factor in shaping their destinies, but this was an untenable assumption when applied to the victims of these events—landless, uneducated, and impoverished former slaves who were released

into a Southern society that detested them; Native Americans whose land was taken by false treaties or violence; and the urban poor who were at the mercy of exploitive employers and an unstable economy.

Few Americans could even envision a major and ongoing social-policy role for the federal government in this era. The federal civil rights legislation, the Freedmen's Bureau, and the stationing of troops in the South represented remarkable departures from the limited roles of the federal government prior to the war, but these were ultimately regarded as temporary measures. The absence of federal roles was evident, too, in the disinclination of Americans to regulate the emerging industrial order or to develop federal policies to distribute free lands to impoverished persons.

Each of the three events also unleashed powerful political forces that prevented Americans from grappling with social problems. Powerful and affluent agricultural interests, which had subjugated African Americans in the first instance, regained their former power in the South during the decades following the Civil War, established a strong southern constituency for the Democratic party, and successfully bargained in the Congress for withdrawal of northern troops and federal pressure to make them honor the civil and voting rights of freedmen. (They were aided by northern entrepreneurs who bought, sold, and profited from southern cotton and tobacco and favored the use of cheap black labor.) American land policy at the frontier empowered speculators, white settlers, and railroads, who pressured public authorities to repress Native Americans or to place them on reservations. A new and powerful class of entrepreneurs, which was created by industrialization, resisted unions as well as regulatory policies of the government.

By the end of the nineteenth century, Americans had developed a conservative consensus in which they took moralistic and punitive stances toward destitute persons, possessed a restrictive concept of social obligation, perceived social problems to be temporary rather than endemic to the social fabric, and favored limited government. Especially striking, however, was the inability of most Americans to support compensatory strategies to help populations that needed special assistance. Most Americans believed that government risked favoritism if it singled out specific groups for special assistance. No group in American history possessed such desperate needs as the freed slaves, whose economic problems stemmed so clearly from the horrors of slavery. The disinclination of Americans to use compensatory strategies in cases of obvious need during the nineteenth century represents a legacy of lost opportunity that has influenced social welfare policy to this day.

 ## END NOTES

1. Jack Sosin, *The Revolutionary Frontier, 1763–1783* (New York: Holt, Rinehart & Winston, 1967); Malcolm Rohrbough, *The Land Office Business: The Settlement and Administration of American Public Lands, 1789–1837* (New York: Oxford University Press, 1968).

2. Rohrbough, *The Land Office Business*, pp. 120–136.

3. *Ibid.,* pp. 200–220.

4. Edward Pessen, *Jacksonian America: Society, Personality, and Politics* (Homewood, Ill.: Dorsey Press, 1978), p. 147.

5. Rohrbough, *The Land Office Business,* pp. 190–199.

6. Reginald Horseman, *Race and Manifest Destiny* (Cambridge, Mass.: Harvard University Press, 1981), pp. 116–138.

7. Stephen Gould, *The Mismeasure of Man* (New York: Norton, 1981), p. 74.

8. Horseman, *Race and Manifest Destiny,* pp. 154–155, 220.

9. Angie Debo, *History of the Indians of the United States* (Norman, Okla.: University of Oklahoma Press, 1970), p. 90ff.

10. *Ibid.,* pp. 102ff.

11. Robert Berkhofer, *The White Man's Burden: Images of the American Indian from Columbus to the Present* (New York: Knopf, 1978), pp. 157–165.

12. Cary McWilliams, *North from Mexico: The Spanish-Speaking People of the United States* (New York: Greenwood Press, 1968), pp. 98–105; Richard Slotkin, *The Fatal Environment: The Myth of the Frontier in the Age of Industrialization, 1800–1890* (New York: Atheneum, 1985), pp. 161–207.

13. Rodolpho Acuna, *Occupied America: The Chicano's Struggle Toward Liberation* (San Francisco: Canfield Press, 1972), pp. 105–106.

14. McWilliams, *North from Mexico,* pp. 169–183.

15. Debo, *History of the Indians,* pp. 133ff.

16. *Ibid.,* pp. 249ff.

17. Berkhofer, *White Man's Burden,* pp. 166–175.

18. Debo, *History of the Indians,* pp. 276ff.

19. Ronald Takaki, *Strangers from a Different Shore* (Boston: Little, Brown, 1989), pp. 1–11.

20. *Ibid.,* pp. 79–131.

21. *Ibid.,* pp. 179–229.

22. James Davis, *Frontier America, 1800–1840: A Comparative Demographic Analysis of the Frontier Process* (Glendale, Calif.: Arthur H. Clark Co., 1977), pp. 15–17.

23. Slotkin, *The Fatal Environment,* pp. 47, 281.

24. Kenneth Stampp, *The Imperiled Union: Essays on the Background of the Civil War* (New York: Oxford University Press, 1980), pp. 191–245.

25. James McPherson, *Ordeal by Fire: The Civil War and Reconstruction* (New York: Knopf, 1982), pp. 42, 72.

26. Stampp, *The Imperiled Union,* p. 192.

27. McPherson, *Ordeal by Fire,* pp. 89–94, 114–117.

28. *Ibid.,* pp. 125–132.

29. Pessen, *Jacksonian America*, pp. 182–183, 318–319; Kenneth Stampp, *And the War Came: The North and the Secession Crisis* (Baton Rouge, La.: Louisiana State University Press, 1950), pp. 239–247.

30. Lawrence J. Friedman, *Gregarious Saints: Self and Community in American Abolitionism, 1830–1870* (Cambridge: Cambridge University Press, 1982), pp. 168–169; James McPherson, *The Struggle for Equality* (Princeton, N.J.: Princeton University Press, 1964), pp. 147–148.

31. Friedman, *Gregarious Saints*, pp. 169–170; McPherson, *The Struggle*, pp. 143–147.

32. Friedman, *Gregarious Saints*, pp. 172–178.

33. McPherson, *Ordeal by Fire*, pp. 278–279; John Hope Franklin, *From Slavery to Freedom* (New York: Knopf, 1974), pp. 275–280.

34. McPherson, *Ordeal by Fire*, pp. 394–396.

35. McPherson, *The Struggle*, pp. 189–191.

36. McPherson, *Ordeal by Fire*, pp. 509–511.

37. *Ibid.*, pp. 396–398, 506–509, 579–580; McPherson, *The Struggle*, pp. 407–416.

38. McPherson, *Ordeal by Fire*, pp. 391–392, 476–477.

39. McPherson, *The Struggle*, pp. 308–314.

40. McPherson, *Ordeal by Fire*, pp. 497–499, 513–533.

41. *Ibid.*, pp. 502–503.

42. *Ibid.*, pp. 466–467, 516–518, 520–523.

43. *Ibid.*, pp. 543–546, 566–567, 576–577.

44. C. Vann Woodward, *Reunion and Reaction: The Compromise of 1877 and the End of Reconstruction* (Boston: Little, Brown, 1951), pp. 12–13.

45. John Franklin, "Public Welfare in the South During the Reconstruction Era," *Social Service Review,* 44 (December 1970), 379–392; Michael Perman, *The Road to Redemption: Southern Politics, 1869–1879* (Chapel Hill, N.C.: University of North Carolina Press, 1984), pp. 22–25.

46. McPherson, *The Struggle*, pp. 341–366.

47. Perman, *The Road to Redemption*, pp. 149–178.

48. *Ibid.*, pp. 50–56.

49. Friedman, *Gregarious Saints*, pp. 264–280.

50. McPherson, *Ordeal by Fire*, pp. 593–600.

51. *Ibid.*, pp. 600–604.

52. McPherson, *The Struggle*, pp. 256–259, 386–397, 407–412.

53. Franklin, *From Slavery*, pp. 324–338.

54. Robert Steamer, *The Supreme Court in Crisis: A History of Conflict* (Amherst, Mass.: University of Massachusetts Press, 1971), pp. 119–127.

55. C. Vann Woodward, *The Strange Career of Jim Crow* (New York: Oxford University Press, 1957).

56. Eleanor Flexner, *Century of Struggle: The Women's Rights Movement in the United States* (Cambridge, Mass.: Harvard University Press, 1975), pp. 44–45.

57. *Ibid.*, pp. 71–77.

58. *Ibid.*, pp. 145–154.

59. Nancy Woloch, *Women and the American Experience* (New York: Knopf, 1984), p. 195.

60. Paul Boyer, *Urban Masses and the Moral Order in America, 1820-1920* (Cambridge, Mass.: Harvard University Press, 1978), p. 123; Eric Foner, *History of the Labor Movement in the United States,* Vol. 1 (New York: International Publishers, 1955), p. 58; Edward Kirkland, "Urban Growth and Industrial Development." In Allen Wakstein, ed., *The Urbanization of America* (Boston: Houghton Mifflin, 1970), p. 212.

61. David Brody, *Workers in Industrial America: Essays on the Twentieth-Century Struggle* (New York: Oxford University Press, 1980), pp. 3–9.

62. Foner, *History of the Labor Movement,* Vol. 1, pp. 51–53.

63. Richard Bushman, "Family Security in the Transition from Farm to City, 1750–1850," *Journal of Family History,* 6 (Fall 1980), 238–256.

64. Thomas Cochran, *The Age of Enterprise: A Social History of Industrial America* (New York: Harper & Row, 1961), pp. 129–153.

65. Edward White, *The American Judicial Tradition: Profiles of Leading American Judges* (New York: Oxford University Press, 1976), pp. 86, 100–105.

66. Steamer, *The Supreme Court*, pp. 143–149.

67. Boyer, *Urban Masses*, pp. 123–131.

68. Foner, *History of the Labor Movement,* Vol. 1, pp. 439–474; Herbert Gutman, "The Failure of the Movement by the Unemployed for Public Works in 1873," *Political Science Quarterly,* 80 (June 1975), 254–277.

69. Michael Katz, Michael Doucet, and Mark Stern, *The Social Organization of Early Industrial Capitalism* (Cambridge, Mass.: Harvard University Press, 1982), pp. 14–63.

70. *Ibid.,* pp. 102–130.

71. Cochran, *The Age of Enterprise,* pp. 129–153, 181–210.

72. Stephan Skowronek, *Building a New American State: The Expansion of National Administrative Capacities, 1877–1920* (Cambridge: Cambridge University Press, 1982), pp. 150–160.

73. Gutman, "The Failure"; Slotkin, *The Fatal Environment,* pp. 477–498.

74. Slotkin, *The Fatal Environment,* pp. 496–498.

75. Cochran, *The Age of Enterprise,* pp. 154–180.

76. Derek Fraser, *The Evolution of the British Welfare State: A History of Social Policy Since the Industrial Revolution* (New York: Barnes & Noble, 1973), pp. 1–22.

77. Deltev Zollner, "Germany." In Peter Kohler and Hans Zacher, eds., *The Evolution of Social Insurance, 1881–1981* (New York: St. Martins Press, 1981), pp. 4–33.

78. Foner, *History of the Labor Movement,* Vol. 1, pp. 101–113.

79. *Ibid.* pp. 77–81.

80. Sidney Fine, *Laissez-Faire and the General Welfare State: A Study of Conflict in America, 1865–1901* (Ann Arbor, Mich.: University of Michigan Press, 1956), pp. 52–64.

81. Foner, *The Great Labor Uprising,* pp. 39–49, 74–75.

82. Leon Fink, *Workingmen's Democracy: The Knights of Labor and American Politics* (Urbana, Ill.: University of Illinois Press, 1983), pp. 3–17; Foner, *History of the Labor Movement,* Vol. 2, pp. 47–92.

83. Carl Kaestle, *Pillars of the Republic: Common Schools and American Society, 1780–1860* (New York: Hill and Wang, 1983), pp. 36–39, 92.

84. Richard Hofstadter, *Social Darwinism in American Thought* (Boston: Beacon Press, 1955), pp. 41–50.

85. Gould, *The Mismeasure of Man,* p. 74.

# CHAPTER 6

# Social Reform in the Progressive Era

## Selected Orienting Events in the Progressive Era

| | |
|---|---|
| **1882** | Chinese Exclusion Act passed by Congress |
| **1886** | Formation of the AFL with Samuel Gompers as president |
| **1889** | Jane Addams established Hull House |
| **1890s** | Agricultural protest occurred in the Populist movement |
| **1890** | Establishment of the National American Women's Suffrage Association |
| **1893–1897** | Depression of 1893 caused severe unemployment |
| **1896** | The Supreme Court legitimized separate facilities for African Americans in its *Plessy* v. *Ferguson* decision |
| **1899** | Legislation establishing juvenile courts enacted in Illinois and Colorado |
| **1901–1908** | Presidency of Theodore Roosevelt |
| **1904** | National Committee on Child Labor organized |
| **1905** | Formation of International Workers of the World (IWW) |
| **1909** | Initiation of the Pittsburgh Survey by Paul Kellogg; White House Conference on Care of Dependent Children |
| **1909–1912** | Presidency of William Howard Taft |
| **1911** | Fire at the Triangle Company in New York City |
| **1911–1920** | Most states enacted mothers' pension legislation, and many states enacted workmen's compensation |
| **1912** | Unsuccessful Bull Moose campaign by Theodore Roosevelt and the Progressive party; Children's Bureau established |
| **1913–1920** | Presidency of Woodrow Wilson |
| **1914–1918** | World War I (United States entered it in 1917) |
| **1916** | Margaret Sanger opened first birth control clinic in New York City; passage of child labor legislation by Congress |
| **1918** | Supreme Court overruled federal child labor legislation |
| **1920** | Nineteenth Amendment to the Constitution granted suffrage to women |
| **1921** | Enactment of Sheppard-Towner legislation |
| **1924** | Enactment of Immigration Act of 1924 |

Quiescence was shattered in the 1890s when a rural reform movement known as Populism mobilized farmers of the Midwest and South to protest low agricultural prices, high interest rates, excessive charges of graineries and railroads, and profiteering of food processors. As they lashed out against bankers, Wall Street, and corporations, they obtained a variety of regulatory measures in local and state jurisdictions and developed cooperative storage facilities. Their reform momentum died as quickly as it had started, however, when farm prices improved, limits were placed on rates of railroads, and cooperatives were developed. Since Populism was a rural movement, however, its impact on urban reform was negligible.[1]

Urban reform had to await the turn of the century when a reform movement known as progressivism developed. It was not a focused reform movement but embraced a variety of antimonopoly, city beautification, civil service,

governmental, and social reforms. Progressives advocated prohibition, laws to outlaw prostitution, and efforts to limit immigration, along with policies to limit child labor, correct unsafe working conditions, and obtain unemployment insurance.

The number of reform projects that were included within the Progressive movement makes it difficult to establish a profile of the typical progressive reformer. Many of them were middle-class Americans who were bewildered by the emergence of massive corporations, big-city bosses, and large numbers of immigrants, yet many affluent Americans, political machines, and trade unions supported various progressive reforms. Progressivism was not dominated by members of the Democratic or Republican party. Despite its amorphous nature, progressivism was the first sustained reform movement in the United States that addressed a variety of urban issues.

 ## REALITIES IN INDUSTRIAL SOCIETY

Immigrants bore the brunt of the negative consequences of industrialization in the northern and midwestern cities of the North. Roughly twenty-one million of the total population of ninety-two million Americans in 1911 were immigrants who had come to America between 1880 and 1914 (see Figure 6.1). Major American cities consisted of separate settlements, each with its own churches, political machines, and newspapers. Forty percent of the populations of the twelve largest cities consisted of immigrants, and another 20 percent of them were second-generation descendants; 60 percent of the American industrial labor force was foreign born.[2] The immigrants came from many European nations and possessed distinctive cultures. Most Italian immigrants were rural peasants who had been forced to leave villages by an agricultural depression, rising taxes and rents,

and competition from factories that mass produced products that they had made in their homes and shops. Husbands or unmarried men often emigrated in hopes of returning to Italy with resources gained in America, but they often ultimately decided to pay the transportation costs of relatives and families. (In 1908, after a bad recession, as many Italians returned to Italy as entered America.) Russian Jews, by contrast, were mostly artisans and small merchants whose earnings had been eroded by competition with industrial products and who suffered appalling persecution. Entire Jewish families emigrated, usually with little desire to return. Both Italians and Jews were wooed by steamship companies, whose salesmen promised prosperity for the price of a ticket. But word of mouth was the primary recruiter as preceding immigrants revealed that American life, though harsh in the industrial

**FIGURE 6.1** • *Immigrants arriving in crowded quarters to the United States around the early part of the twentieth century*

*Source:* Library of Congress

cities, was better than conditions in their homelands. As they streamed in torrents along roads to seaports, they were often robbed by bandits, only to then endure the epidemics of the steamship passage.[3]

Many immigrants were shocked to find themselves in dark and crowded tenements in eastern and midwestern cities, which differed from the outdoor living of their native villages. A typical apartment contained two or three rooms with a large tub in the kitchen where people bathed and with no inside toilets. They moved frequently in response to job markets, to find less exploitive landlords, or to escape eviction.

The immigrants brought their customs with them, which differed markedly from American practices. Families often arranged marriages of the daughters. Strict discipline was used with children and adolescents, who often remained with their families until they married. Although

fathers had ultimate authority, mothers collected paychecks of all working members, purchased household goods, and parceled out sums to each family member. The immigrants shopped in crowded outdoor markets or from ever-present peddlers who sold produce on the streets. Their low wages were depleted by the substantial sums they paid to insurance and funeral-benefit companies as well as to relatives in Europe. Since they often feared hospitals, which they associated with death, they resorted to folk medicine and midwives instead.[4]

Social workers and schools often pressured them to adopt American child-rearing practices, medical practices, diet, and clothing and viewed their outdoor markets with distaste since they believed them to be unsanitary. When the children of immigrants quickly adopted American customs, conflict erupted within immigrant families, which often pressured children to accept arranged marriages, not to Americanize their names, to date only with chaperones present, and to speak their own dialect.[5]

Americans unfortunately did not realize that many of the immigrants' values and customs were viable alternatives to the American emphasis on individualism. An ethic of mutual assistance was deeply rooted in the immigrants' culture; they were extraordinarily generous to one another, exchanged job information, formed many ethnic associations, exchanged resources during hard times, and supported political leaders who pledged to help their groups with jobs and food. Social workers often believed that immigrant parents were excessively authoritarian, but each family constituted a small welfare state in which children's earnings were joined with other family assets and family members cooperated during hard times.[6] The American disdain of the immigrants' diet, which emphasized potatoes or pasta, was equally misdirected, for it allowed them to survive with minimal resources.

Life in these immigrant communities was often abysmal. Food poisoning was commonplace in the absence of public health regulations and modern refrigeration. Medications, which were sold on street corners and pharmacies, were touted as cure-alls for many conditions but often contained toxic substances or had no medicinal value. Residents often feared devastating fires. Hastily constructed wooden tenements that often contained hundreds of families became potential incinerators in the absence of housing codes. In some cases, sections of cities burned, as in the case of Chicago in 1871 and San Francisco in the wake of the earthquake of 1906. In the fire at the Triangle Company in New York City in 1911, 146 girls and women were killed, many of them impaled on iron fences after they leaped from a ten-story building with no fire escapes. This catastrophe mobilized pressure for fire and occupational safety regulations. High levels of crime existed in American cities. Street gangs from different ethnic enclaves preyed on one another. Public safety was endangered since there were few lights in cit-

ies until the development of effective municipal lighting systems in the late nineteenth century and during the progressive era. White-collar crime was also legion as corporate lobbyists bribed public officials to obtain lucrative trolley, street-building, and lighting contracts.

Many jurisdictions placed curbs on the hours of labor by the turn of this century, but poor enforcement meant that six-day weeks and twelve-hour workdays were commonplace. Many Americans believed that employers had the right to override these statutes by having workers sign "voluntary agreements" to work long hours. Immigrants received abysmal wages. Though $15 per week was needed for survival by families in Pittsburgh in 1909, two-thirds of immigrants earned less than $12.50, and half of them earned less than $10. Barely half the workers in American industry could survive on one paycheck.[7]

Many workers were even more concerned about the dangerous working conditions than about low pay. Industrialization required the use of labor-saving machinery, but these machines lacked safety devices. Roughly 35,000 Americans were killed and 536,000 injured *each* year during the progressive era—or roughly the same number of Americans in each year who were killed or injured during the entire Vietnam conflict of the 1960s. Specific industries were particularly hazardous; 328 railroad workers were killed each month in this era, and 46 deaths and 528 injuries occurred in just one steel plant in South Chicago in 1906.[8] American rates of industrial accidents were far greater than rates that existed in European nations, where factory regulations had been enacted and enforced.[9] American workers were not likely to collect funds from their employers when they sued them after industrial accidents since corporate attorneys were frequently able to delay litigation or use a variety of legal tactics to place the blame for accidents on the worker. Workers collected in only 15 percent of disability lawsuits in those cases where employers were proven to be negligent.[10]

Employers were unsympathetic to union organizing. Many of them believed that their work forces, much like their equipment and plants, were their personal property, and they feared that wage increases could bankrupt them in the wild and unpredictable economic climate of this period. Lockouts, violence, and private police forces were commonly used to intimidate strikers as well. The courts and local authorities frequently interceded to help employers. Trade unions grew from 447,000 persons in 1897 to more than two million persons in 1904, but they were usually relatively weak.[11]

Periodic recessions were devastating to workers. Thirty percent of the labor force was unemployed in many jurisdictions in the depression of 1893, which lasted until 1897 and was a grim forerunner of the Great Depression of the 1930s. Unemployment was not buffered by insurance, food stamps, and other programs that contemporary Americans take for granted. Unemployed persons, who often had no savings, were frequently evicted from their homes and had to obtain meager benefits from breadlines or poor-houses. Social conditions can be summarized with the word *insecurity*, particularly for persons in the lower third of the economic ladder. Few policies or programs existed to protect persons from disease, poverty, discrimination, disability, crime, fires, and poor living conditions. It often seemed to citizens of humble means that social predators endangered them at every juncture, whether employers who overworked them, businesses who sold them dangerous foods or medicines, or slum landlords who exacted exorbitant rents.

Families were splintered by these adverse economic conditions. When destitute women with young children approached public authorities, they were often told that they could receive assistance only if their children were placed in foster homes or with adoptive agencies since officials assumed that their own households were unwholesome; they also wanted to avoid the costs of institutionalizing children.[12] Children were often pressured by parents to take jobs at an early age. Families were often divided as their individual members went to different cities to find work.

## THE GENESIS OF REFORM

It seemed unlikely in 1900 that Americans would develop a major reform movement to address many of these social problems because of Social Darwinism, the political power of corporations, and national preoccupation with upward mobility. Political institutions seemed impervious to reform. Most state legislators met for a few months in alternate years and devoted themselves to housekeeping matters. Government was dominated at all levels by use of patronage to obtain nomination to political office, to secure electoral victories, and to obtain governmental employment. Political machines prevailed in many cities and used the lure of jobs in local municipal services, as well as ethnic loyalty, to secure the support of ward and precinct workers who delivered votes in elections for incumbents. The Democratic and Republican parties delivered nominations to local, congressional, and presidential elections to persons who were connected to machines or who could bring corporate donations to the party. In an era dominated by parties and lobbyists, presidents and governors were relatively weak figures who tended not to initiate legislation but to acquiesce in decisions that were fashioned in smoke-filled rooms.[13]

It seemed that government could not implement social programs or enforce regulations, even if they could be developed. In the absence of a modern civil service, except in some federal positions, patronage rather than competitive exams was used to fill most positions. Many bureaucrats could be bribed or intimidated by party officials. Perhaps the most damaging weakness of government, however, was its paltry size since Americans were unwilling to levy sufficient taxes to fund government institutions at any level.

Patterns of party support frustrated efforts to develop social reform. Voting patterns were dictated by complicated sectional and ethnic traditions so that neither Democrats nor Republicans focused on the needs of the working class. Democrats were the dominant party in the South, Republicans had considerable strength in New England, and the two parties divided the votes in the Midwest and West. Various ethnic groups supported one of the two major parties on the basis of local tradition rather than for their positions on social issues.[14]

## Catalytic Events

The depression of 1893, which lingered through 1896, had a decisive effect on the nation. It triggered widespread discontent with the Democrats and President Grover Cleveland, who had the misfortune to be in office. His inactivity and economic policies were believed by many persons to have caused and sustained the depression, so many voters changed their allegiance to the Republican party.[15] (With the exception of Woodrow Wilson, who held the presidency from 1913 to 1920, Republicans dominated national politics until the Great Depression of 1929, when the political balance swung back to the Democrats.)

The depression of 1893 also brought widespread disenchantment with corporate tycoons since these heros of virtue, hard work, and success had not been able to usher in unlimited prosperity as the script of the Gilded Age had dictated. Their willingness to fire workers, to shut down plants, and to use violent means of suppressing labor strikes during the depression tarnished their reputations. Many Americans read about blatant efforts of industrialists to garner special treatment for themselves and their corporations by bribing public officials or by threatening to relocate to other jurisdictions that promised more favorable tax concessions. Outlandish efforts to bribe politicians and to finance their campaigns were publicized. Flamboyant lifestyles of corporate executives, once considered a just reward for hard work, were resented by many Americans when more than a quarter of adult males were unemployed in many areas.[16]

Some Americans began to wonder whether the fantastic growth of American industry was an unlimited blessing. Industrialization had seemed at first to be a kind of new economic frontier that, like the Western frontier, could lead to unlimited opportunities for millions of Americans. But small entrepreneurs were increasingly driven from business by the ruthless tactics of corporate entrepreneurs who managed to aggregate vast economic empires. The sheer size of corporations alarmed many Americans, who wondered if their size gave them such power that they could no longer be regulated. The reputation of industrialists suffered as lurid stories about their victimization of hapless workers, women and children among them, were publicized. When stories of adulterated food, unsafe medicines, and other defective products emerged, many Americans believed that corporate executives had to be restrained by enactment of regulations.[17] Social reform thrives when "culprits" are perceived to exist because they inflame the passions of the public and inspire efforts to regulate them. As tycoons were lowered from their pedestals, they increasingly were the subject of proposals to limit their power to victimize labor, to curtail the size of their companies, and to limit their ability to bribe politicians.

## Intellectual Ferment and Public Opinion

The nation has often gone through policy swings when primary emphasis was given either to environmental or to personal factors. During conservative periods, such as the Gilded Age, the 1920s, the 1950s, and the 1980s, personal and moral problems received a good deal of attention. Relatively more emphasis was given to environmental factors in reform periods such as the progressive era, the 1930s, and the 1960s.[18] Historians do not know why these tidal swings in public opinion occur, but many Americans believed by the turn of the twentieth century that environmental factors, such as overcrowding, tenements, and poor working conditions, thwarted the healthy development of Americans. Many Progressives also feared that political machines, large corporations, and widespread corruption threatened democratic institutions. Environmentalism was critical to the development of a reform movement because, by focusing attention on a variety of social conditions that were believed to cause social ills, it increased public support of social reform to modify those conditions.

A set of conventional views had deterred reform in the Gilded Age, including the beliefs that the American Constitution was sacrosanct and should be interpreted literally and that the meaning of life derived from work, competition, and upward mobility.[19] By the late nineteenth century, however, dissent became acceptable as many Americans questioned these verities. Social Darwinists had argued that life should be devoted to competition, but many persons countered that cooperation and creativity were higher values. Ministers who were known as "social gospellers" argued that the gospel required people to help the downtrodden.[20] Social workers like Jane Addams and philosophers like John Dewey believed that people were intrinsically cooperative and became competitive only as they were exposed to environmental cues and models—including an American culture that emphasized winning at all costs. Addams extolled a "cooperative ideal" when she contended that government should try to instill a spirit of cooperation in its citizens, whether through example (such as by developing social programs) or through education. Regulations

and social programs represented, she argued, expressions of altruism rather than unwarranted interference in the private affairs of industrialists and citizens.[21]

Addams and other reformers wondered how the competitive and materialistic values of Americans could be transformed. Unlike European radicals and socialists, who romanticized the working class and believed its victory over bourgeois interests would transform society, Addams idealized a succession of groups at different points in her career. She variously hoped that immigrants would infuse American society with their simple peasant and altruistic virtues, that the creativity and playful virtues of youth would be emulated by others, and that women would transform American society by asserting values of nurturance that stemmed from their family roles.[22] Although each group proved unequal to her high expectations, she seemed never to become disillusioned.

Many theorists also contended that economic affairs, when left to their own devices, created unacceptable levels of social distress. Economic theorists had commonly contended in the nineteenth century that when government exacted taxes or unions increased wages or governments regulated hours and working conditions, the natural balance of supply and demand was disrupted. Economic theorists like Richard Ely contended, by contrast, that unregulated economic affairs led to concentration of power in the hands of elites, who consigned workers to poverty and who diverted their wealth into nonproductive ventures such as speculation and corporate takeovers.[23]

A phalanx of theorists questioned provisions of the American Constitution and the American legal system. The founding fathers constructed a Constitution, some argued, that adequately addressed the needs of an agricultural republic but that was inadequate for an industrial society, which required government to assume an active role in economic and social affairs.[24] Many Progressives argued as well that the Supreme Court ought not to have the right to overrule progressive social legislation and proposed legislation to circumscribe its powers.[25]

Many Americans also began to question whether America was a model society that should be emulated by the rest of the world. The nation *had* led the way in opening opportunities to citizens by enacting universal suffrage, land ownership, and education, but it had lagged in providing security to its citizens. As reformers, including social workers like Jane Addams and Grace Abbott, traveled extensively in Europe, they discovered various social programs and regulations that offered supports for workers and families.[26]

Jane Addams and other reformers obtained extraordinary popularity in the progressive era, as reflected by public opinion polls, where she was voted the most exemplary American.[27] Politicians of both parties who espoused various reforms were elected in large numbers to local, state, and national legislatures. As Progressives opened up the political process by allowing voters to place issues on the ballot (so-called initiatives), many reform measures were enacted even when legislators showed scant interest in them. The sheer number of reforms that were enacted in cities and states attests to the popularity of reform during this period.

Some historians have used concepts from social psychology to explain why middle-class Americans became more interested in reform in certain periods. Hofstadter, for example, argued that middle-class Americans supported reform because they feared that corporations and political machines threatened their economic and social roles. It seems unlikely, however, that a single motivation explains this swing in public opinion.[28] Different persons and groups probably supported reform for different reasons. Many Americans supported reforms because they encountered some of the social ills that were the subject of agitation in this period. They read about the corruption of officials whom they had elected, trembled when epidemics struck their cities, read about or saw the flaunting of power by corporate executives, or ate food or

consumed drugs that led to illness.[29] Religion should not be ignored as a motivating force for reform in the progressive era. Many middle- and upper-class Americans felt guilty about the sorry condition of the bottom third of their society and the victimization of women and children by employers. Though often prejudiced against immigrants, some Americans realized that their labor fueled the economic institutions of the nation, from which many of them derived personal benefit.[30]

Furthermore, a pragmatism propelled many Americans toward reform as they became convinced that conservative policies had not been effective. Conservatives in the progressive era, who often continued to voice the laissez-faire homilies of the Gilded Age, were on the defensive because reformers successfully argued that their policies had led to a disastrous depression, the victimization of women and children, and the rise of monopolies. The fruits of capitalism had failed to reach some of the desperately poor immigrants who crowded American cities.[31]

Popular opinion was aroused through the use of symbolism that allowed reforms to appear respectable and American rather than socialistic and foreign. Conservatives often portrayed progressive reformers as "outside agitators" or "socialists." The reformers contended that their reforms would save the American family, open up politics to the people, increase economic opportunity, or prevent poverty and crime. Many Americans believed that the family was in a state of serious decline since children and women had to work, children were separated from their mothers when they applied for assistance, and children were placed in prisons because of the lack of juvenile facilities. Since Americans also feared that their political institutions were increasingly dominated by political machines or corrupt politicians, they favored proposals, including the initiative and the civil service, to save democracy itself. Trust-busting was defended on the grounds it would enhance economic opportunity for ordinary citizens. Reform was widely perceived to address these noncontroversial goals, so it obtained wide-spread support.[32]

Many Americans in the progressive era also believed that they were rediscovering their own land. The rhetoric of the Gilded Age suggested that America was free of problems and on a path of unlimited prosperity, democracy, and territorial expansion that advanced the interests of the nation. By the turn of the century, however, reformers and journalists engaged in a frenzied search for factual evidence of social problems, such as the number of children and women exposed to dangerous working conditions, the number of children placed in adult prisons, the poisonous nature of many drugs, high rates of infant mortality among specific groups, and instances of political corruption.[33] The appetite for facts and figures was insatiable, as illustrated by an exhaustive six-volume survey of social conditions in Pittsburgh initiated by the social worker and reformer Paul Kellogg that described occupational hazards, housing, health, and many other facets of the lives of Pittsburgh residents.[34]

As social facts were discovered, they were disseminated to the public through popular and professional journals as well as newspapers. Reforming journalists, popularly known as muckrakers, dramatized their findings by highlighting the evil nature of wrongdoers and the innocence (and sheer number) of victims. Professionals and academics presented findings in more neutral terms. In either case, the general public was fascinated by the endless evidence of wrongdoing and suffering, which bolstered support for reform.

## The Specter of Social Unrest

Many progressive leaders were not preoccupied with problems of social unrest from the millions of immigrant workers who provided cheap labor for American industry because, with notable exceptions, most workers were relatively tranquil in this period despite their appalling working and living conditions.[35] Immigrants who did not speak English, who lacked citizenship, who often hoped to return to Europe, and who feared unemployment were not likely to engage in militant protest. Most women workers were not amenable to strikes because they hoped to work only for a brief period before marrying.

Still, the emergence of fringe—but vocal and radical—parties, such as the Socialist party and the International Workers of the World, represented a new phenomenon in the nation.[36] Their leaders espoused ideas that departed from the conventional political beliefs of the nation; many of them advocated political organization of the working class, supported national strikes, favored nationalizing of some industries, and favored policies like development of a national minimum wage. We note later in this chapter that they had scant success in obtaining high-level political offices except at the mayoral level; nonetheless, they constituted a political threat to many Americans particularly because of the sheer size of the unskilled labor force in industry and in the mines that they sought to organize. Indeed, many Progressives viewed themselves as moderates whose sensible and pragmatic reforms would blunt protest and maintain tranquility.

 ## REGULATORY REFORMS IN THE PROGRESSIVE ERA

The number of regulations that were enacted during the progressive era is suggested by Table 6.1, which lists the major progressive reforms that regulated the political process, banking and economic institutions, conditions of employment, food and drugs, employment of immigrants, and

**TABLE 6.1** • *Selected regulations that were enacted in the progressive era*

**Regulations of Businessmen**
Curtailing of size of trusts (federal)
Limitation of working hours of women and children (local)
Regulation of working conditions in plants (local)

**Regulations of the Food and Drug Industry**
Restrictions placed on content and labeling of food and drugs (federal and local)

**Regulations of Developers and Owners of Rental Properties**
Housing codes (local) and development of zoning to govern construction

**Regulations of Politicians**
Passage of the initiative, referendum, and recall (local)
Restrictions on lobbying and campaign contributions (local)
Limiting of patronage through passage of civil service legislation (local and federal)
Curtailment of the power of machines and bosses through establishment of nonpartisan elections and commissions (local)

**Protections for Immigrants**
Controls on persons who hire immigrants (federal and local)

**Protections for Women**
Curbs on interstate transportation of nonconsenting women to prevent kidnapping for prostitution (federal) and laws to restrict prostitution (local)

**Development of Fire Codes**
Controls on construction of industrial facilities as well as housing (local)

**Regulations of Taverns and Distilleries**
Enactment of prohibition (local)

**Regulations of Immigration**
Many proposals advanced to restrict immigration (federal)

**Regulations of Banks**
Laws regulating reserve requirements of banks (federal)

**Regulations Governing Professional Activities**
Enactment of licensing laws for medical, dental, legal, and other professional activities (local)

**Public Health Regulations**
Laws regulating disposal of sewage and garbage as well as food processing in restaurants (local)

**Working Hours of Women and Children**
Laws regulating hours and working conditions of women and children (local and federal)

**Working Hours of Federal Employees**
Federal legislation limiting the hours of work of federal employees

housing. Although most were enacted in local jurisdictions, they also gave state and federal governments new policy roles.

The regulatory emphasis of Progressives is understandable in the existing context of the few social controls that were placed on corporations and political and social institutions. Corporations could make products, establish working practices, and subject workers to dangers in the absence of public regulations. Politicians could accept bribes, hire relatives, and tamper with elections in the absence of public scrutiny. Homer Folks, a reformer in New York State, found that audits were rarely made of state insti-

tutions, that laundry and food concessions were awarded to friends of politicians, that no system of external monitoring existed, and that it was impossible to distinguish staff from residents in some institutions because they were dressed similarly. He conducted a tireless campaign to establish audit, licensing, and monitoring programs for public bureaucracies; to place staff positions under the civil service; to oust political appointees; to establish standards of sanitation; and to enforce existing laws that required children and insane persons to be removed from almshouses.[37] Similar projects were undertaken by many other reformers in other states.

Many of the regulations were obtained only after exhausting political battles. Thus, advocates of child labor laws, who formed reform organizations in each state as well as at the national level, battled those who argued that these laws violated parental rights, that immigrants needed the earnings of their children to survive, and that child labor prevented overcrowding of schools. Reformers who sought federal labor laws were told that the Constitution did not give the federal government jurisdiction in social matters.[38]

The regulatory reforms of the era were supplemented by efforts to rationalize the social services system and to develop a social work profession. The reformers viewed with horror the provision of services by amateurs and political appointees. The National Conference of Charities and Corrections sponsored conventions of administrators and staff of agencies to exchange information and provide training. The New York Charity Organization Society established an annual summer course for social workers in 1898 and was followed in 1903 by the formation of the Chicago School of Civics and Philanthropy and in 1904 by the New York School of Philanthropy and the Boston School for Social Workers. By 1919, the leaders of fifteen schools of social work had formed the

Association of Training Schools for Professional Social Work. These early social workers usually identified with private agencies since they viewed public institutions as last-resort programs for paupers, the insane, and criminals, but they increasingly departed from the moralistic ethos of social service staff of the nineteenth century (who had diagnosed persons by using such value-laden terms as "deserving" or "undeserving") by providing services based on analysis of familial, personal, and neighborhood factors that contributed to the problems of their clients. Instead of dictating to clients and offering personal models of morality, many social workers sought to develop give-and-take exchanges with clients and local interventions. Social work pioneers hoped to professionalize social programs by credentialing their staff in training programs.[39]

Conflicts existed in the progressive era between reformers such as Addams, who advocated coupling personal service with public-sector reforms, and social workers who opposed the development of public programs because they believed private agencies should dominate in the provision of outdoor relief. But this conflict had diminished by 1909, when Addams was selected as president of the National Conference of Charities and Corrections.[40]

 ## THE LIMITED SOCIAL PROGRAMS OF THE PROGRESSIVE ERA

Although many new regulations were passed into law, the few social programs that were enacted underscored the limited nature of social reform in the progressive era since none of them required the expenditure of large sums of money or the distribution of resources or services to poor persons. The main programs of the day included workmen's compensation, mothers' pensions, juvenile courts, and the Children's Bureau.

Employers, who used a variety of legal defenses to place part or all of the responsibility for work-related injuries on employees, variously argued that employees knew about dangers before they took employment, that employees were careless in their work, or that negligence of a fellow employee, rather than negligence of the employer, had caused work-related injuries. The costs and delays of litigation, which was so time-consuming that workers often died before awards were made to them, forced many workers into indebtedness and eventual use of poor-relief programs. Despite their legal successes, employers found the costs of litigation to be prohibitive as well, and ever-mounting awards to disabled workers and the costs of liability insurance increased their costs of doing business.[41]

Workmen's compensation laws, which were adopted by virtually all states by 1920, provided a partial remedy that was acceptable to many employers and to some unions. A state fund was established that received its revenues from a payroll tax levied on employers.[42] Workers who were injured were entitled to obtain an award that was established for specific kinds of injuries. Under the legislation, workers forfeited their right to sue employers.

Workers soon discovered that workmen's compensation was not a panacea. The payment schedules for specific injuries were appallingly low and, indeed, far lower than jury awards that had preceded enactment of workmen's compensation. By taking the edge off discontent, pressure to make the work place safer was eased. Unions were divided with respect to workmen's compensation; some believed this legislation was an improvement, but others believed it helped employers more than workers.[43]

Mothers frequently found themselves to be desperately poor because their employment paid such low wages that they could not support their families when their husbands died or left them. When they applied for poor relief, they were often told that they had to enter a poorhouse and give up their children to adoption or placement agencies though this destruction of families ran counter to the Progressives' desire to preserve the family and, furthermore, required local officials to incur the costs of maintaining entire families in institutions.[44] The mothers' pension movement swept the nation between 1911 and 1919, when most states developed programs. These laws represented a modest improvement since many destitute women and their children could now receive outdoor relief

without fearing the removal of their children. On fine details of eligibility, the laws were usually vague; legislation rarely indicated that women with out-of-wedlock children or women who had left their husbands could not receive mothers' pensions, but local administrators could and sometimes did exclude them from the program on the grounds they were morally undeserving. Many states allowed women to receive assistance even when their husbands were still present, but it is likely that such assistance was given reluctantly lest it reduce the work incentive of the husband. Some legislators believed that the programs should primarily help widows, a group widely perceived to be morally deserving.[45] The mothers' pension programs in the various states helped many women, but certain kinds of women were excluded, and the programs paid miserably low grants to women and their children.

Children were tried in adult courts, detained in jails for extended periods, and remanded to adult prisons in the nineteenth century despite the existence of houses of refuge and legal precedents that exempted minor children from penalties that had been established for adult offenders. In many jurisdictions, children who were less than fourteen years of age were exempted from capital punishment and from other penalties, but these exceptions could be waived in certain circumstances.[46] Many persons, including Judge Ben Lindsey in Denver and social reformers in Chicago, believed that mixing children with adult criminals was harmful to children and that confinement did not address familial, school, and other causes of delinquency. Since probation hardly existed as an option, even children who had committed minor offenses were institutionalized.[47]

Juvenile courts represented an innovative policy solution at the local level since cases of children were adjudicated in special courts where judges and staff could explore their family situations, examine a range of options including probation, and refer children to special juvenile institutions when they needed to be committed.

Since the courts were not developed in concert with a range of facilities and programs, however, judges often lacked innovative community programs to which they could refer juvenile offenders. Furthermore, funding was insufficient to hire the staff needed, courts lacked staff who could converse with children and parents in the tongues of the many immigrant groups that populated American cities, and most judges lacked training in social matters.[48]

The idea of establishing a national Children's Bureau originated in 1904 in the National Committee on Child Labor, was reaffirmed in a White House Conference on Care of Dependent Children in 1909, and was finally enacted in 1912; it received the meager budget of $25,640, compared to the $1.4 million that funded the federal Board of Animal Husbandry.[49] Conservatives relented even to this modest measure when its authority was limited to data gathering and advisory functions that precluded it from providing resources directly to children or to local units of government. Its dedicated social work staff issued many seminal reports in the succeeding years, but the bureau did not provide a frontal attack on the poverty, malnutrition, or poor health of the nation's children and often tried to avoid controversial issues, such as national child labor laws. Its greatest triumph was its enactment in 1921 of Sheppard-Towner legislation, which provided federal funds to states to provide clinics for pregnant women and young children, but even this small program was terminated in 1929 on the grounds that it violated states' rights and represented socialized medicine.[50]

Reformers believed that they had made a lasting breakthrough in 1916 when they finally obtained passage of national legislation to restrict use of child labor. Specifically, the legislation prohibited interstate commerce of products of firms that employed children who were less than fourteen years of age and mines that employed children less than sixteen years of age. Hopes of reformers were dashed when the Supreme Court nullified the legislation in 1918 on the grounds that the law fell outside the province of interstate commerce, which had been widely regarded as the only way that child labor laws could be constitutionally legitimized. Although the ruling did not frontally challenge the right of the federal government to regulate child labor, and the staff of the Children's Bureau was able to obtain measures that prevented federal contractors from using child labor during World War I, the ruling had a chilling effect on social reform at the national level.[51]

Other reforms in the progressive era included the development of an initial set of aftercare services for people who had been institutionalized in mental asylums. As late as 1905, virtually no aftercare services existed in the United States, so released mental patients had to fend for themselves with no assistance from anyone. Beginning in New York State and expanding to other states, social workers were employed by mental institutions to follow their wards on release and to give them services. Moreover, following the work of Clifford Beers, himself a former mental patient who had written about his ordeal in public institutions, nongovernmental societies for mental hygiene were established in various states, as well as the National Committee for Mental Hygiene, to pressure public authorities to improve mental hospitals and to develop programs to prevent mental illness.[52]

 ## CULTURAL AND POLICY REALITIES THAT LIMITED REFORM

Despite their skill in uncovering devious actions of corporate tycoons and exploiters of powerless populations, progressive reformers were often naive in their approach to social reform. They assumed that regulations would bring dramatic changes when, in fact, they often had negligible effect. The naivete of Progressives took two forms. First, their *legalistic bias* made them assume that laws would lead to dramatic changes in the behavior of wrongdoers though they soon learned that persons and institutions that were subject to regulations were resourceful in evading them, whether by coopting or bribing government officials or by escaping detection because regulatory agencies lacked funds and staff to adequately monitor compliance.[53]

Furthermore, their *procedural bias* led them to believe that changes in the procedures of government would make government dramatically more responsive to the needs of the people, as reflected by the passage of such laws as initiative, referendum, and recall that, respectively, allowed citizens to place legislation on the ballot, to hold popular votes on measures that had already been enacted by legislators, and to vote from office public officials who were widely believed to be corrupt or misdirected. These measures assumed the existence of an aroused citizenry who would vote for progressive legislation; as reformers soon learned, these techniques could also be used to recall liberal legislators or to place conservative measures on the ballot.[54] (It is an irony of history that conservative initiatives to cut social spending of government, such as Proposition 13 in California in 1978, were one legacy of progressive procedural reforms.)

Few persons would have argued that American society was not in desperate need of regulations to control the actions of industrialists, politicians, and landlords, but a law enforcement approach, which fostered the use of regulatory strategies, precluded the enactment of major programs that would confer resources and services *directly* to these powerless groups. Some Progressives sought unemployment insurance, health insurance, and other programs, but most of them emphasized regulations.

Progressive reformers also diminished their effectiveness by relying on local governments—whether cities, counties, or state legislatures—to take the lead in addressing the mounting social ills of the nation. Child labor, workmen's compensation, mothers' pension, and myriad other reforms were enacted locally. Notable exceptions existed, such as the Hepburn Act (which prohibited the interstate transportation of girls for prostitution), the Children's Bureau, and regulation of child labor, but federal legislation was meager in scope and amount compared to tens of thousands of regulations and proposals at local levels of government. Local reforms were needed, of course, but the nation desperately required national programs for a number of reasons. A strategy of policy localism required expenditure of vast amounts of energy in "reinventing the wheel" in each of the states and local jurisdictions. Resistance to reforms in specific localities was often heightened, moreover, by the argument of opponents that a specific local reform, such as prohibition of child labor, might make industry move to other localities where this restriction did not exist. Since most Americans and some reformers believed that social welfare issues belonged to local governments under the Constitution and by the precedent of the poor laws, efforts to secure national reforms occurred belatedly during the progressive era and were limited to modest reforms like the Children's Bureau.[55] Localism was increased by the continuing tendency of the Supreme Court to limit the power of the federal government—for example, in rulings that restricted the federal government to those functions specifically enumerated in the Constitution.[56]

Progressives also decreased their effectiveness by seeking so many different kinds of reforms. At least six overlapping reform agendas existed.[57]

1. Some Progressives who emphasized procedural reforms in government sought policies to reduce corruption, to give more power to experts in governments, and to foster greater participation by citizens in government.

2. Some Progressives sought regulation of the economic system to restrict the size of corporations or to develop federal controls over banking and currency.

3. A third agenda was spearheaded by members of such professions as medicine, nursing, law, teaching, and social work, who sought to develop licensing laws and accredited educational programs to upgrade the knowledge and skills of professionals.

4. Some Progressives sought legislation to restore morality to American life by restricting immigration, restricting gambling, ending prostitution, or limiting consumption of alcohol.

5. A fifth agenda focused on regulations to limit the ability of corporations, owners of rental housing, and others to victimize workers or the public.

6. A sixth agenda involved programs to redistribute resources to impoverished workers, destitute women, and other groups.

Many of these agendas were supported by specific Progressives; indeed, it was unusual for a reformer to focus on only a single issue.

The range of the reform agendas limited the effect of progressive reforms on social problems in several ways. As reformers devoted their energies to many causes and issues, they decreased the likelihood that they could significantly affect any one of them. Furthermore, reforms that assisted powerless and impoverished groups often received less attention than other reforms. Trust-busting, good-government reforms such as the initiative, referendum, and recall and prohibition and limitation of immigration often absorbed the attention of some reform leaders and the general public.[58]

The content of many progressive reforms was limited by the middle-class perspectives of many reformers. Middle-class citizens did not monopolize progressivism (various of the six progressive agendas were supported by trade unions, political bosses, and immigrant groups); nonetheless, they shaped the direction and content of many reforms.[59] Relatively affluent persons often had scant personal knowledge of the problems that immigrants and factory workers encountered in their daily lives. Trust-busting, city beautification, civil service, professional licensing, and other such reforms did not directly address the appalling social conditions of poor persons.[60] The importance of moral reforms during the progressive era also suggests the imprint of middle-class reformers, many of whom sought temperance, termination of gambling, elimination of prostitution, and anticrime measures.[61] Some progressive reformers were biased against immigrant groups and sought legislation to limit immigration. Reformers like Jane Addams struggled valiantly against the anti-immigration tide but were unable to prevent Congress from passing legislation, which would have become public law had it not been vetoed by Presidents Taft and Wilson.[62]

This middle-class imprint on reform can be usefully contrasted with England and other European nations in this period, where strong political parties that were dominated by factory workers and radicals had emerged. The Labor party had developed by 1912 into one of the three major parties in England and sought a variety of insurance, unemployment, and housing measures. When radicals and unions threatened a general strike of all workers in 1912, middle- and upper-class Englishmen (such as Lloyd George, who headed the Liberal party) supported national unemployment insurance and health insurance.[63] Even those Progressives who most favored social reforms were often uncomfortable with class conflict and had little sympathy for groups that advocated sweeping reforms.[64]

## ● | POLITICAL REALITIES THAT LIMITED REFORM

Neither the Republican party nor the Democratic party focused on the needs of workers, low-income persons, or powerless groups such as African Americans because voters tended to vote in the progressive era not on the basis of social class but according to local and family traditions that stemmed from ethnicity and sectionalism.[65] (To the extent that workers and low-income persons voted at all, they split their votes between the two major parties though African Americans usually voted for the Republican party because of its historic role in ending slavery.) Because party leaders lacked an incentive to concentrate on social reforms to help impoverished persons, social reformers often found it difficult to get their attention.

Reformers also had difficulty obtaining assistance from the groups that most needed social reforms — immigrants, workers, and African Americans. Political cooperation among immigrant groups was impeded by language barriers, ethnic rivalries, and residential segregation. They often distrusted middle-class reformers who proposed civil service and other reforms that seemed irrelevant to their practical needs. Reforms to decrease corruption in politics — including the political machines that represented the primary vehicle for distribution of jobs and food to immigrants — were often resented by them.[66]

Unions, which largely represented skilled crafts, were uncertain allies for social reformers. When Samuel Gompers, the leader of the American Federation of Labor (AFL), attributed the demise of the Knights of Labor in the 1880s to its diversion to extraneous political and social issues, he resolved to concentrate exclusively on wages and fringe benefits of union members and on organizing skilled or semiskilled white, native, and male workers.[67] Gompers' tactical decisions helped the AFL make gains in the early

years of this century but at the price of indifference to social reforms and to organizing unskilled, female, or minority workers. Furthermore, the trade union movement remained weak. Employers mounted a decisive counterattack by use of court suits, bloody repression, use of spies, employment of scabs, and redbaiting. The fledgling movement was fraught with internal dissension and outmoded organizing techniques. Factories had been dominated in the nineteenth century by skilled craftsmen, who possessed considerable autonomy and who worked within highly defined trades. But factories in this century were dominated by machinery, which relegated workers to tedious and unskilled work under the scrutiny of central management. Instead of organizing the workers of entire factories, unionists still tried to rally those groups of skilled workers within factories who performed specific tasks, a tactic that left many workers unorganized and that led to turf rivalry between competing craft unions within specific factories.[68] Gompers' decision to avoid political partisanship also limited labor's ability to develop political power and to obtain support for the minimum wage and collective bargaining legislation. The noninvolvement of labor in politics was illustrated when the AFL raised only $8,000 for electoral campaigns in 1908![69]

Trade unionists would have found it difficult to organize and to politically mobilize unskilled and semiskilled workers, who composed a massive constituency, even had they tried. Immigrants, who composed 60 percent of the industrial workforce in 1913, had extraordinary economic and social needs and were not likely to protest low wages, particularly when they knew they could be easily replaced by other immigrants. African-American workers, who constituted more than 10 percent of workers in northern iron and steel plants and felt beholden to foremen who had hired them in an era of intense racial discrimination, were reluctant to "make trouble." Female workers, who dominated the garment industry, often hoped to work only for a brief period before they married. The nation possessed, then, an enormous pool of relatively passive laborers who could be victimized and who feared retribution from local courts and police forces if they supported strikes.[70]

Gompers did not provide much assistance to social reformers. The AFL often opposed health insurance to workers on the grounds that it would undermine union efforts to obtain fringe benefits for workers. Many union leaders opposed the development of workmen's compensation laws on the grounds that workers could obtain larger awards from court litigation. A powerful radical movement might have pressured politicians to redistribute resources to the working class, but its power was limited. The Socialist party, which was established in 1901, managed to elect fifty-six socialist mayors, but its power resided mostly in local jurisdictions, and its elected officials were often indistinguishable from other progressive reformers. The International Workers of the World (IWW) was organized in 1905 and had 100,000 members by 1916, but it had little power in large industries since it represented only extremely poor workers in mining, lumbering, and agricultural sectors. (Most of its members lived in western states.) Eugene Debs, the fiery organizer of the IWW, succeeded in obtaining nearly one million of the nearly fifteen million votes cast in the election of 1912, but he was not a serious threat to the major political parties.[71]

Social reformers were themselves impeded by their lack of interest in partisan politics during much of the progressive era. Many of them were contemptuous of existing parties, which they believed were corrupt and not interested in promoting reforms. Since many of them believed that their strength derived from the morality of their positions buttressed by public exposure of wrongdoing and social ills in the mass media, they envisioned social reform as a nonpartisan activity to pressure leaders of both parties to support reforms.[72] Nonpartisanship allowed the Progressives to maintain their political purity, but it detracted from their need to develop a partisan reform constituency. Their efforts to obtain support from politicians in both political parties meant that they controlled neither of them. Relatively conservative persons remained in control of the caucuses and conventions of the two major parties and often dictated their policies—influenced by corporate interests, who remained the major source of campaign contributions for many political candidates.[73]

In many cases, reformers also found their energies to be depleted by the task of continually raising funds to maintain staff for their nonpartisan organizations. Thousands of reform groups and settlements were formed in local, state, and national settings; these organizations often vied with one another for philanthropic contributions, and their leaders sometimes found that they had to tame their activities to retain the support of affluent donors.[74]

 ## SOCIAL REFORMERS AND THE BULL MOOSE CAMPAIGN OF 1912

During the first decade of the twentieth century, both the Republican and Democratic parties were often dominated on specific issues by conservative politicians who insisted that social welfare roles ought not to be assumed by federal authorities; who believed that social activists were "demagogues," "socialists," and "sentimental idealists;" and who sought to focus party platforms on international, tariff, currency, national defense, and related issues.[75] Various conservatives supported specific pieces of social legislation—many of them, for example, favored the establishment of the Children's Bureau—but they often opposed specific reforms. Each party contained an "insurgent wing" that favored social legislation and other reforms, but its members were often outmaneuvered by conservatives in party nominating conventions and in legislative arenas. Corporate officials continued to assume a dominant role in American politics and often tried to influence candidates from both parties to oppose such reforms as lower tariffs; it was not until 1914 that Woodrow Wilson was able to slash tariffs and thus reduce prices of many commodities for workers and immigrants.[76]

Social reformers such as Jane Addams and Paul Kellogg experienced many policy successes in municipal and state arenas during the first decade of the twentieth century as they secured passage of mothers' pension, workmen's compensation, and juvenile court legislation. They became more confident as they became national celebrities. Many of them were frequently requested to give speeches, some of them authored popular books, and Jane Addams was called an American reform goddess!

But frustration also made many of the reformers want larger policy victories. The prodigious effort to enact legislation in many states and municipalities took its toll; why not, some asked, obtain sweeping national legislation to regulate working conditions of women and children, establish upper limits on hours of work, establish a progressive tax system, establish a minimum wage, and extend the vote to women? A few avant-garde reformers even favored passage of national health insurance, unemployment insurance, and old-age pensions.[77]

Many social reformers dreamed that a fundamental political realignment might occur to replace the existing political parties so that voters could choose between a relatively liberal party (with a constituency of intellectuals, workers, immigrants, and social reformers) and a relatively conservative party (with a constitu-

ency of businesspeople and affluent persons). The dream of realignment appeared realizable, however, as the election of 1912 approached. Theodore Roosevelt, who became president in 1901 on the assassination of William McKinley, had gingerly broached various reforms in his first term, but had veered from supporting many controversial reforms because he did not wish to alienate the conservative wing of the Republican party, which he needed to obtain the party's nomination in 1904. He became bolder during his second term, however, and on the eve of leaving office, left a lengthy reform agenda to the Vice President William Taft, which he hoped Taft would support were he elected in 1908.[78]

Roosevelt's hopes in Taft were misplaced. Taft became a captive of the conservative wing of the Republican party during his term in office from 1909 to 1912. A large and phlegmatic man, Taft believed that major social reforms were not needed. As Taft became more conservative, the charismatic and energetic Roosevelt became more liberal. As he dashed to and from his wild-game safaris in Africa, he added to his reform agenda support of national legislation to regulate child labor, a progressive income tax, and workmen's compensation. He proposed forming an industrial commission to conduct national economic planning to foster economic growth and regulate trusts so that their power and job-creation potentials could be realized. Feminists persuaded him to support a constitutional amendment to give women the vote.

As Taft became convinced that Roosevelt had been captured by social reformers, he feared Roosevelt would try to regain control of the Republican party by seeking its presidential nomination in 1912. Many reformers had maintained a nonpartisan stance prior to 1912 and had supported neither of the two major parties, but a number of them, including Jane Addams and Paul Kellogg, openly advocated supporting Roosevelt for the nomination.[79]

The stage was set for a confrontation at the Republican convention in Chicago in summer, 1912, but the hopes of social reformers were dashed when Taft and entrenched party leaders were able to secure the nomination for Taft in a series of power moves. They were further disheartened when the Democratic party nominated Woodrow Wilson, the governor of New Jersey and former college president, who favored states' rights and focused on trust-busting and lowering of tariffs. Instead of realignment, *both* parties seemed to be following a conservative course.[80]

Many social reformers believed that realignment might still occur if a new political party were established with Roosevelt as its leader. With lightning speed, reformers called a convention of the new party in Chicago and persuaded a reluctant Roosevelt to accept the presidential nomination of the Progressive party. The new party and its nominee were hardly rabid social reformers since only 25 percent of its platform, as well as his acceptance speech, was devoted to social reforms, but they were far more reformist than alternative parties and candidates. Their platform included support for social insurances, workmen's compensation, a minimum wage, women's suffrage, and a child labor law. Jane Addams became the first woman to address a major political convention when she seconded the nomination of Roosevelt. An atmosphere of religious and moral fervor existed in the convention of the new party as its members entered the campaign, but many practical problems bedeviled them. They had to secure a place on the ballot in the various states, obtain campaign funds, and develop a massive constituency in a nation that was wedded to the Democratic and Republican parties. Roosevelt doubted that he could prevail in the election of 1912, but he and others hoped they could educate the public sufficiently so that workers and liberals would support the Progressive party and it would replace the Republican party.

Wilson, who had supported some progressive reforms as governor of New Jersey, tried from the outset to portray Taft as an extremist on the right and Roosevelt as an extremist on the left. He persuaded Samuel Gompers and many other union leaders to support him by promising them that he would seek legislation to improve the legal status of organized labor. When portrayed as a left-winger by both Wilson and Taft, Roosevelt counterattacked vigorously by arguing that Taft and Wilson had outmoded and conservative ideas. He succeeded in differentiating his positions from those of Wilson by questioning Wilson's assertions that a minimum wage would depress prices, by arguing that a welfare state was needed in an industrial society, and by insisting that states' rights had to be superseded by national planning. He drew enormous and enthusiastic crowds in his campaign appearances. When the results were tallied, Roosevelt made a respectable showing but lost the election because ethnic and regional loyalties, as well as the allegiance of many immigrants to political bosses, led many Democratic voters to support Wilson. Wilson won, not because he was overwhelmingly popular—he received less than 50 percent of the popular vote—but because the Republican vote was split between Taft and Roosevelt.[81]

Many persons who had voted for Roosevelt still believed that political realignment was possible if the Progressive party could be kept intact and if it waged successful campaigns in the congressional elections of 1914 and the presidential election of 1916. The reformers hoped that Roosevelt would win in 1916, that the Republican party would die, and that conservatives would gravitate to the Democratic party. Social reformers wanted to be certain that the party maintained its reforming mission, and they succeeded in developing a national division of the party, which was directed by Jane Addams, that focused on social research and development of social policies. Twenty congressmen declared their allegiance to the party, as did a number of local officeholders.

Practical realities doomed the reformers' dreams of political realignment, however. Political experts decided that party funds should be devoted to hiring political experts and financing campaigns, so the social service department of the party was terminated to the dismay of reformers. The party was unable to raise the necessary funds to surmount problems of getting on the ballot in some jurisdictions. The most important problems for the Progressive party, however, were caused by Woodrow Wilson, who obtained the allegiance of many reformers by supporting social legislation during his presidency. Although he had argued in the campaign of 1912 that federal authorities should not enact a minimum wage or place restrictions on child labor and had lambasted the idea of a welfare state as paternalistic, he realized in the aftermath of his victory that he could significantly add to the political base of the Democratic party if he supported some of the reforms that had been proposed by the Progressive party. He even cautiously wooed social reformers like Jane Addams. He enacted child labor legislation, banking legislation, tariff reductions, and eventually women's suffrage.[82]

The fate of the Progressive party was virtually sealed by the congressional elections of 1914, when few Progressives were elected to office. Its demise was complete by the election of 1916, except in a few scattered locations. Roosevelt tried to secure the nomination from the Republican party in 1916 but was again rebuffed by party conservatives, who nominated Charles Hughes to oppose Wilson, who again successfully ran on the Democratic ticket with the assistance of many progressive reformers.

The failure of the Progressive party during and after 1912 demonstrated that social reform could not proceed beyond the limited policy successes of the progressive era unless reformers could obtain a power base by capturing a major party that had significant support from liberals, the working class, and racial minorities. The demise of the Progressive party also illustrated the precarious position of social reform in America despite the growing importance of a host of social problems in the cities. It would take a catastrophic depression in the late 1920s to galvanize workers, the poor, and minorities behind social reforms—and it would be a distant cousin of Theodore Roosevelt, Franklin Delano Roosevelt, who would finally accomplish the political realignment that the Progressives had sought.

 ## OUTGROUPS IN THE PROGRESSIVE ERA

It would be a mistake to view progressivism as a reform movement fought for, by, and in behalf of the immigrants who constituted such major portions of the urban population of the United States. Americans of this era harbored decidedly contradictory opinions about this huge population; though they freely used—and depended on—their cheap labor to fuel industrial growth, they resented, and sometimes even feared, this population for reasons of eugenics (would they dilute the Anglo-Saxon race?), social unrest (could America have a revolution if "agitators" awoke these immigrants, and did the political machines of the cities constitute a threat to democracy?), disease (did the immigrants pass diseases, such as tuberculosis, to others?), and culture (did Catholicism, Judaism, and ethnic culture threaten Protestant and American culture?). Nor were the Progressives, aside from certain reformers like many settlement workers, free from racism; indeed, no significant civil rights legislation was enacted or seriously considered in this period, and some decided setbacks occurred. Although women were often in the vanguard of social reform in the progressive era and although they were often its object (as illustrated by regulations of their working conditions and hours), they, despite some economic gains, remained shackled by traditional notions of their role in society.

## Racial Minorities

The civil rights gains of freedmen were nullified following the Civil War as southern whites regained their political power when northerners withdrew military and legislative pressure on the South and when the Supreme Court rendered federal civil rights laws useless. Republicans hoped to regain their southern constituency, but Democrats had become the dominant party of the South by 1900 and staunchly resisted federal efforts to protect or help African Americans. Most African Americans lived in rural areas as tenant farmers, whose low wages and indebtedness to plantation owners enmeshed them in grinding poverty. Increasing numbers of them moved to southern cities where, aside from a small elite group of affluent African Americans, they were unemployed or worked in low-paying and unskilled jobs or as domestic servants and lived within a segregated society. Americans had developed, in effect, a social system that approached apartheid and was maintained by Jim Crow laws, police, courts, and white racism.[83]

The situation was more favorable for African Americans in the North but only modestly so. The poverty of the South and absence of jobs led to a steady and growing movement of African Americans to the North though they constituted relatively small groups in northern cities in 1915. It was the enticement of jobs in burgeoning industries like meatpacking and steel that drew African Americans to the North, where their depressed wages were nonetheless considerably higher than the wages of southern African Americans. Residential areas occupied by African Americans were even more blighted than ones occupied by other immigrant groups, were more likely to be headquarters of organized crime and drug interests, and had virtually no health or other services. They experienced extraordinary discrimination in job markets since they were excluded from skilled trades and unions, often used as scabs to break unions, and were subject to race riots and mob violence when they competed with whites for jobs. Most northern African Americans, like their urban counterparts in the South, worked in unskilled jobs.[84]

Asian immigrants suffered similar discrimination and poverty on the West Coast. We noted in Chapter 5 that hundreds of Chinese immigrants had come to California in the late nineteenth century to work on the railroads and in the mines and were followed by Japanese immigrants over the next two decades. Many Americans feared the "yellow peril," believed Asians to be sinister and untrustworthy people, and feared they brought diseases to America. Many Japanese Americans developed the ingenious strategy of farming hillside land, and both Chinese and Japanese immigrants developed specialized niches in urban America, such as running laundries and small businesses; both groups, however, frequently encountered prejudice and adverse policies.[85] California enacted Alien Land Laws in 1913 and 1920 to prohibit land purchases and ownership by Japanese residents. Even in this period, long before World War II, many people feared that the Japanese would overrun the West Coast and even attack the United States. Many Americans urged extension of the provisions of the Chinese Exclusion Act of 1882 to the Japanese but had to content themselves with agreements with Japan, such as the Gentleman's Agreement of 1907, where the latter agreed to stop allowing laborers to migrate to the United States.

In the Southwest lived large numbers of Latinos, whose land was taken from them in the middle and late nineteenth century. Their numbers were swelled by Mexican immigrants, who were able to move freely across a relatively unrestricted border until 1924 when the U.S. Border Patrol was created.[86] These immigrants, as well as the indigenous Latino population, became the labor force for the irrigated cotton, vegetable, and fruit enterprises of the Southwest, which expanded enormously after the Reclamation Act of 1902 provided large federal funding for irrigation projects. (Ranching and meat processing continued to expand as well.) It is impossible to know precisely how many Latinos came across the 2,000-mile border, but some scholars estimate roughly 110,000 migrated from 1900 to 1920.[87] Latinos worked not only in the fields but in numerous canning and food-processing plants. They lived in barracks in remote rural areas and were subject to punitive labor policies of large landowners, who paid them little and brutally suppressed protest. Like many rural African Americans in the South, they were denied education and excluded from economic opportunities that developed in urban America. Their numbers grew dramatically in the wake of the economic dislocation of the Mexican Revolution of 1910 but diminished when the Immigration Act of 1917 imposed a literacy test and a head tax on them. When legally sanctioned immigration decreased, the number of undocumented workers, that is, workers who came into the United States illegally, increased. These residents were particularly brutalized by American growers, who played on their fears of deportation to undermine protests against their harsh working and living conditions.[88] Nor were conditions much better for those Latinos who settled in growing urban areas of the Southwest, where they became a sort of reserve labor force that was used by employers to break strikes and depress wages. Those few business ventures that were owned by Latinos were located in Spanish-speaking communities and were mostly small stores.[89]

As a strictly regional population in the Southwest (only 15 percent of them lived outside the Southwest even as late as 1930), Latinos were isolated politically and subject to local and regional groups, such as growers, who wished to subjugate them. The Mexican government frequently protested the working conditions and suppression of the Latino population to the U.S. State Department, but to no avail.[90]

The racial policies and orientations of Theodore Roosevelt and Woodrow Wilson support the contention that many progressive reformers saw no contradiction between social reform and racism. Partly because Roosevelt hoped to continue to have African-American support for the Republican party in the South, he invited Booker T. Washington, the African-American leader, to the White House for lunch during his first term. Unlike Marcus Garvey, who wanted African-American separatism and militance, Washington scorned conflict, favored accommodation by African Americans to existing policies, and urged them to use self-help to improve their lot. Even this luncheon with this accommodationist leader raised storms of protest against Roosevelt, who was widely portrayed in its wake as a radical on racial issues. Even as late as 1912, Roosevelt's foes referred to the luncheon to allege that he was a "nigger lover."[91]

Roosevelt was hardly a defender of civil rights, however. He refrained from public meetings with African Americans after the luncheon. He took no actions against Jim Crow legislation in the South, sided with white authorities in the infamous Brownsville incident in 1906 (in which African-American soldiers were executed on undocumented charges that they had raped white women), and did not contest lily-white delegations to Republican conventions from southern districts. Jane Addams vainly protested Roosevelt's acceptance of white southern delegations to the convention of the Progressive party in 1912, a party that was supposedly reformist.[92]

Like most white Americans in this era, Roosevelt held a racial ideology that extolled the virtues of the Anglo-American race to the detriment of other races, including African Americans, Asians, Latinos, and Native Americans. Racial doctrines that had fueled manifest destiny, which we discussed in Chapter 5, were still held by many white Americans, who accepted scientific evidence (later disproved), such as alleged differences in skull size and intelligence, as proof of the superiority of Anglo-Americans.[93] These ideological orientations, when coupled with Roosevelt's desire to obtain support of white southerners for the Republican party, fostered neglect of the problems of African Americans and other minorities.

Woodrow Wilson was even less sympathetic to the needs of African Americans than Roosevelt. He had been raised in the South, where he had adopted the racial orientations of affluent southerners. He was the presidential nominee of the Democratic party, which had relied on race baiting throughout the late nineteenth century to secure support of southern whites. Roosevelt had given African Americans some token posts in government, but Wilson refused even to give the ambassadorship to Liberia to an African American, openly supported segregated restroom facilities in federal departments, and condoned lynching in the South. So detestable were his policies to African Americans that most of them continued to vote Republican even though many social reformers switched their allegiance from the defunct Progressive party to Wilson in 1916.[94]

The courts reinforced prevailing attitudes. In *Plessy* v. *Ferguson* (1896), the Supreme Court condoned a state law that mandated separate facilities for African Americans on the grounds that state legislation that implies a legal distinction between two races does not destroy legal equality between them. The Court did not overturn prior rulings that federal civil rights legislation of the Reconstruction era applied only to the discriminatory acts of individuals rather than to the state and local governments.[95]

Jane Addams and a small band of social reformers were exceptions to the alliance of progressivism and racism. She supported the establishment of settlement houses in African-American communities, sought to improve schools, and urged improvement of protection of African Americans from lynching and race riots. She argued that African Americans possessed qualities of altruism and gentleness that made them superior in some respects to the dominant population. Her beliefs were not shared, however, by most policy makers in the North or the South or by most Americans.[96]

## Women and the Politics of Sex

As we discussed in Chapter 5, the issue of women's suffrage became the central reform issue of the women's movement with the formation of the National American Women's Suffrage Association in 1890. Women presented many petitions to state legislatures between 1890 and 1905 to modify their constitutions to allow women to vote, but they had scant success because of opposition of liquor interests and male legislators. Many women perceived the issue to be tangential to their economic and social needs. Some antisuffrage organizations were formed whose male and female leaders contended that women would destroy the unity of households by voting for their own interests and would fall prey to demagogues because of their "hysterical" tendencies. Moreover, the liquor interests strongly opposed suffrage on the grounds that women would support temperance.

More progress was made after 1905 because feminist leaders had developed sophisticated organizing skills and because the issue appeared less radical during a reform era in which women had assumed prominent roles. Indeed, twelve states had granted women the vote by 1916. Instead of emphasizing feminist arguments, suffragettes argued that voting women would support progressive reforms on education and family issues—an argument that was received favorably by males who, like many Americans in the nineteenth century, believed women's superior moral qualities and temperament made them best suited to attend to family matters and children. Immigrant husbands increasingly supported suffrage for women, who were providing a major source of labor for the garment industry. Militant suffragettes, who used disruptive organizing tactics, alienated some voters but dramatized the issue. A dramatic breakthrough occurred during World War I when Woodrow Wilson finally agreed to support the issue after such leaders as Carrie Chapman Catt threatened to target Democratic candidates for defeat and argued that suffrage was needed to maintain national unity during the war. The Nineteenth Amendment to the Constitution was finally enacted in 1920.[97]

Though suffrage got the most attention, other developments had equal importance to women. Major increases in female employment occurred in industrial settings as well as clerical, stenographic, and sales positions. (These occupations, as well as teaching, social work, and nursing, offered gender-segregated and low-paying positions, however.) Moreover, there was a sizable increase in the number of married women who worked; if only 14 percent of all women workers were married in 1900, more than 24 percent were married in 1910.

But economic gains ought not to be overstated. Women protective labor laws were developed to "protect" women from exertion that could endanger their reproductive functions or expose them to excessive mixing with males who might debase them morally and sexually. Abramovitz argues that these laws served to preserve "a sex-segregated labor market, the relative subordination of women to men, and the overall marginalization of women workers."[98] Women were rarely unionized and represented a relatively docile labor force despite some dramatic strikes in the garment industry, such as the Shirtwaist strike of 1909, where tens of thousands of women in New York City and Philadelphia protested unsafe working conditions and low wages.[99] If 20 percent of men were organized as measured by a national survey of fifteen occupations in 1905, only 3 percent of women belonged to unions.[100] Mothers' pensions laws, which might have been fashioned to provide major resources to widowed women or single heads of households—or to help them get day care so that they could continue to work—were primarily developed with the needs of children in mind. As in prior eras, it was assumed that women with children ought not to work, so the pensions were devised to provide just enough money so that divorced or separated women could stay at home.[101] Little organized day care existed for working women in this period.

Women continued to encounter difficulty obtaining sexual freedom, moreover. In addition to abstinence and rhythm methods, birth control techniques had come to include the use of condoms and diaphragms, but these techniques were made known to women by word of mouth and vaguely worded advertisements rather than through public family-planning clinics or even by physicians, who often opposed their use on grounds they interfered with the natural reproductive functions of women or reduced the growth of the white population. Moreover, the obscenity laws of most states prohibited public discussion of these techniques or distribution of birth control devices—and we noted in Chapter 4 that the Comstock laws, enacted in 1873, outlawed the dispensing of birth control information through the federal mails.

A birth control movement developed, headed by Margaret Sanger, but its leaders were frequently jailed under obscenity laws. Realizing the futility of changing obscenity laws, Sanger increasingly focused on obtaining the support of physicians for prescribing birth control since they could legally do so when medical needs existed. She also used the conservative argument that birth control would decrease the number of mentally ill and developmentally disabled persons in the population and would slow the rate of increase of the low-income population. These kinds of arguments increased the support of birth control by the medical profession, which often prescribed birth control by the late 1920s. Most low-income persons lacked personal physicians, however, and did not have access to birth control since public birth control clinics were still outlawed in many jurisdictions.[102]

Women were subjected in this period, as well, to medical practices that contemporary Americans can fathom only with difficulty. Many physicians assumed that women's reproductive systems were the cause of many of their physical ailments, so the practice of widespread hysterectomies began and continued in the United States for decades thereafter. (Even in the 1990s, rates of hysterectomies in the United States far exceed those of European nations, with little evidence they yield medical results that justify them.) Indeed, some physicians assumed that "women's *normal* state was to be sick."[103] Menstruation, menopause, and childbirth were viewed as essentially medical conditions that required endless medications and surgeries. As "delicate" people, women had to be shielded, moreover, from those occupations that required physical (or even mental) exertion. Women were also commonly believed to be subject to bouts of hysteria—a condition that required bed rest in darkened rooms for weeks or even months at a time, where the absence of stimuli would allow them to recover.[104]

Women had made little progress by 1930 in dispelling the cult of domesticity for married women, which had originated a century earlier. Endless materials exhorted them to use materials from child psychology and home economics to master the science of homemaking and to refrain from careers or other employment. Males objected to placing eminent women on commissions or in administrative positions, even within the emerging social work profession. Moreover, women's access to many professions, which had increased in the progressive era, eroded in subsequent decades. Once childbirth was defined as a narrowly medical condition, for example, women who lacked medical degrees were increasingly banned from the occupation of midwifery in contrast to European societies where this occupation remained intact.[105]

## Immigrants and the Closing of the Doors

We have discussed the torrent of immigration to the United States from European nations in the period from 1880 to 1920. With the frontier closed, immigrants concentrated in major cities and became a low-paid labor force for the industrial system of the United States.

As Higham suggests, Americans have oscillated between periods of confidence—when they believed their nation could absorb immigrants without threat to their culture or economy—and periods of fear—when they believed their nation could be endangered by religions and the culture of immigrants; when they feared immigrants would take their jobs; and when they feared immigrant groups contained anarchists or radicals who would bring social unrest.[106] In the first decade of the twentieth century, confidence reigned supreme with resurgence of the notion that America was a "melting pot" that could socialize and convert immigrants to the indigenous culture. Moreover, immigrant groups, such as the German-American Alliance, Irish groups, and Jewish groups, developed considerable political power as they fought efforts to limit immigration.[107]

Even in this period of confidence, however, groups such as the Immigration Restriction League devised ways of limiting the immigration to the nation, such as literacy tests. Racism that had been associated with manifest destiny in the nineteenth century, such as the belief in the need to preserve the purity of Anglo-Saxon stock from "dilution," began to resurface as the numbers of immigrants, who averaged 650,000 per year between 1907 and 1917, increasingly seemed like a threatening horde. (Immigrants of other races, such as Asians, were thought to represent a particular threat.)[108] Anti-Catholicism, always present, began to reemerge. The rise of the International Workers of the World (IWW), a radical labor group, was linked by many people to "foreign agitators." A sharp economic downturn during and after 1913 led to a growing sense that the immigrants threatened local jobs. And the immigrants of this era, like the Irish before the Civil War, were widely believed to bring with them diseases, as illustrated by a popular book of the era that stated:

> The new immigration contained a large and
> increasing number of the weak, the broken, and
> the mentally crippled of all races drawn from the

lowest stratum of the Mediterranean basin and the Balkans, together with hordes of the wretched, submerged populations of the Polish ghettoes. Our jails, insane asylums, and alms-houses are filled with human flotsam and the whole tone of American life, social, moral, and political, has been lowered and vulgarized by them.[109]

Immigration restrictionists found that their power increased each year in the years preceding World War I, but a curious combination of industrialists (who wanted the labor of immigrants) and friends of immigrants (such as the National Liberal Immigration League) held off restrictionist legislation though Congress enacted legislation in 1914 that President Wilson vetoed. World War I and its aftermath vastly increased fear of foreigners since Americans were angered by various European powers and the Russian Revolution. A "crusade for Americanization" developed during and after the war to make foreigners speak English and to identify

and prosecute "bolsheviks" in a red scare that led to the imprisonment of many foreigners. After a series of lesser measures, the Immigration Act of 1924 was enacted; it sought not only to limit overall rates of immigration but to give preference within the diminished flow to people from Northern Europe by the ingenious technique of limiting immigration to 2 percent quotas of the numbers of specific nationalities in the American population in 1890, when relatively few Japanese Americans, Italians, Eastern Europeans, or Russian Jews were in the United States. Thus restricted, the Italian immigration dropped from 42,000 to 4,000 and the Japanese immigration to 40.[110] Only Mexican immigrants escaped the restrictions, probably because their regional isolation in the Southwest made them less frightening to nativists and because southwestern agricultural, food-processing, and railroad interests wanted their cheap labor.[111]

## THE RESILIENCE OF JANE ADDAMS AND HER ALLIES

Progressive reformers such as Jane Addams tried to develop social reforms in a society where individualism and competitiveness blinded its citizens to social problems. Unlike European reformers, who had trade union support, American reformers had to raise funds from the wealthy to establish organizations for social reform. There were few social welfare precedents aside from local poorhouses and charities. Reformers had to obtain statistics about the incidence of various social problems, educate the public, fashion legislative testimony, engage in lobbying, network with reformers in other jurisdictions, and build coalitions. Despite their national popularity, they encountered extraordinary hostility from corporations, political machines, affluent citizens, conservatives, and even groups they sought to help, such as trade

unions and immigrants. When Addams courageously attacked American involvement in World War I, she was reviled as a traitor, even by many of her fellow reformers.

Middle-class progressive reformers who had not personally experienced social problems made determined efforts to live among immigrants by establishing settlement houses in eastern and midwestern cities. Hull House, the settlement house that Addams established in 1889, was staffed by resident volunteers who organized social reforms, social research, educational projects, preschool programs, arts programs, and recreational activities. World leaders, celebrated reformers, writers, and academicians from around the world joined Addams and her volunteers for stimulating discussions of social and political issues.

The persistence of the reformers was striking. Many of them began their work in the 1890s and continued to seek reforms until America entered World War I in 1917. When the nation turned toward conservatism during and after the war, many of them collapsed from exhaustion, expatriated, converted to conservatism, or turned to psychotherapy, which became a vogue in the 1920s. Some of the reformers bucked the conservative trend even during the 1920s, however. Addams continued to reside in Hull House, sought many new reforms, and correctly predicted that the United States would need to address the needs of the expanding African-American population in northern cities.

## THE EMERGENCE OF SOCIAL WORK

An important question had to be answered in the progressive era: Who was to staff those social agencies that helped immigrants, poor people, children who could not remain with their natural families, and so many other troubled souls? The answer to this question was partly resolved by 1920 when a new profession, called social work, had developed schools to train people to give these kinds of services. The social work profession developed in the course of considerable tension between different factions, each of which left an imprint on the emerging profession; these complex origins presaged much controversy about the direction of social work during the remainder of the twentieth century.

One of the factions consisted of people who wanted to develop a methodology for helping people in one-on-one transactions. (We later contrast them with people who came from settlement houses.) Recall from Chapter 4 that, even as early as the 1840s, various agencies were devised in eastern cities to systematize the giving of relief to poor people by using volunteers to interview them, determine if they were truly needy, and supervise them while they received assistance with an eye to making them independent as soon as possible. In some cases, different agencies compared their records so as to be certain that people were not receiving assistance from more than one agency.

These early attempts to make relief giving a disciplined process were enlarged in the decades after the Civil War in many jurisdictions. Local, nongovernmental agencies—called charity organization societies—developed in most cities to provide assistance to destitute people; these agencies could provide economic assistance, as well as personal services, to applicants outside the dreaded poorhouses but only if they deemed applicants to be deserving of assistance, that is, to not be freeloaders. The agencies were administered by a paid male who recruited and supervised female volunteers—usually relatively affluent, white, English-speaking women, who came to be known as friendly visitors. (With the lack of employment alternatives other than factory work or roles in teaching or nursing, women often gravitated to this work, which was widely perceived by contemporaries to be consonant with the moral qualities of women.) These women were taught to engage in a careful diagnostic and supervising process as they screened, aided, and finally discharged poor people who needed assistance. Above all, they were to avoid indiscriminate giving or letting their emotions dictate their actions; indeed, they were to turn away or refer to poorhouses those people who were not bent on achieving independence and moral improvement, both at point of intake and during the helping process if sufficient progress and motivation was not evidenced. They did detailed research on the motivations, history, and living arrangements of families as they decided whether and how to help destitute people. Moreover, they were to provide instruction to their wards, both through teaching (such as how to keep a clean house and prepare decent meals) and through personal example. As models of hard work, thrift, and morality, they could, it was hoped, inculcate these virtues in their clients. These friendly visitors probably exhibited contradictory tendencies in their work that reflected punitiveness and a desire to help. They were often punitive as they screened "undeserving" from "deserving" poor people. As white, English-speaking people, one can guess that they were often perceived by their immigrant wards to be somewhat condescending and punitive people. They were often unaware that the poverty of the immigrants stemmed not from faults of character, such as laziness, but from the lack of available work or job discrimination against immigrants. Yet they could be advocates with local police, educational, and other agencies and provided hands-on assistance by actually visiting the homes and neighborhoods of their clients.

The leaders of these various charity organization societies formed citywide associations to provide professional education to one another, to systematize their methodology for screening and assisting destitute people, and to share the records of different agencies so as to locate duplications of service to specific clients.

Some leaders of the charity societies formed quasi-public organizations at the state level to inspect state mental institutions, to collect data about pauperism and other social problems, and to try to decrease patronage and corruption in public institutions. A national organization, the National Conference of Charities, was established in 1879 after members of various state boards of charities, who had been meeting annually in the American Social Science Association, decided they needed their own organization; it convened annual conferences of leaders in this emerging field. (In 1884, it changed its name to the National Conference of Charities and Corrections.) They opened admission to this organization to people engaged in private,

nongovernmental charity in local agencies, and representatives of these organizations soon dominated the organization.[112]

In the last decades of the nineteenth century, the charity organization societies placed greater emphasis on paid staff, who gradually supplanted the volunteers. Not surprisingly, these paid staff often were women who remained in nonadministrative posts. By so doing, they were taking the first steps toward developing a profession, particularly as they articulated a helping methodology called casework, which explained the techniques charity workers should use when helping individual clients.

A second faction, which we can contrast with the charity organization societies, consisted of people who administered and worked in settlement houses. In 1889, Jane Addams established Hull House in Chicago, which she modeled on settlement work in London. Settlements sprang up in most large cities over the next fifteen years, where they provided an unusual mixture of services, including recreation, encouragement of crafts of various immigrant groups, the teaching of English, and a social-reform activity to foster various kinds of social reforms that were common in the progressive era, such as seeking enactment of housing codes, regulations to safeguard working conditions of women, and legislation to forbid the use of child labor. Although commonly identified with "social reform" by some historians, some settlement staff could be quite condescending to immigrants, such as by seeking to convert them to the eating and living styles of Americans. Or they could be preoccupied with socialization and recreation services with scant attention to social reform.

The settlement staff, however, often *were* quite different from the charity organization societies staff even though many of them also attended the annual meetings of the National Conference of Charities and Corrections. Settlement staff often were somewhat more reform oriented, more inclined to decrease the personal distance between professional staff and neighborhood residents, and less inclined to believe that "helping" could be reduced to a science.[113] Fueled by these differences, conflict between the two groups often occurred. For example, during the progressive era, many charity organization leaders opposed the development of mothers' pensions, which they argued was an unwarranted intrusion into the work of nongovernmental agencies. By contrast, Jane Addams and many other social workers who were identified with social reform militantly supported mothers' pensions.[114] (Even as late as 1932, some social workers believed that private agencies could suffice to manage the economic destitution that followed the inception of the Great Depression in 1929.)

How was a profession to be molded from these two disparate factions? Both charity workers and settlement staff realized that extended training was necessary if they were to develop a profession—and training had mostly taken the form of practical experience on the job, brief seminars, or courses in sociology, which had begun to be taught in universities in the 1890s.[115]

Wenocur and Reisch contend that the Charity Organization movement and Mary Richmond, a noteworthy theorist in the methodology of investigating and assisting individuals who had worked extensively with the Baltimore Charity Organization Society, seized the initiative with the assistance of the Russell Sage Foundation.[116] Richmond had long espoused the development of a training school to be affiliated with a university. Fledging efforts, such as a six-week summer program of the New York Charity Organization Society in 1898, whetted appetites for more ambitious projects. After they extended the training period to one year, they established the New York School of Philanthropy in 1910, when they extended the training period to two years. (This program later became the Columbia University Graduate School of Social Work.) In quick succession, other schools were established in Boston and at institutions of higher education, including Bryn Mawr, Ohio State, Indiana

University, and the University of Minnesota. Casework became the dominant focus of the curriculum of these various schools although smatterings of other subject matter were included. A school was formed by settlement leaders in Chicago in 1907, called the Chicago School of Civics and Philanthropy, which later became the School of Social Service Administration of the University of Chicago, but its existence did not fundamentally challenge the dominant role of people who wanted, essentially, to define the profession as an extension of the work of the charity societies. Though the emerging casework, as articulated by Richmond in her classic book, *Social Diagnosis*, lacked the punitive qualities of much of the work of the charity organization societies and was geared toward helping individuals with personal problems rather than toward determining whether they "deserved" monetary assistance, it still focused on one-on-one transactions. The founders of the Chicago School worried that the emphasis on casework, so entrenched in many of the early schools, would provide an excessively narrow focus for the new profession.[117]

The leaders in this early movement to develop a profession were, Wenocur and Reisch contend, constrained by economic realities. The budding profession depended, after all, on affluent philanthropists and university elites to provide resources and institutional support for the new training programs and agency services. The emphasis on personal casework was, from this vantage, an ideal choice, for it was noncontroversial compared to social reform as practiced by some settlements. Moreover, it seemed "scientific" in its emphasis on careful investigation and diagnosis compared to the mix of social-reform, recreational, and socialization services offered by settlements—and the leaders of the new profession could convincingly argue to universities, philanthropists, and the Russell Sage Foundation that this "core technology" required extended training in professional schools.[118] (To obtain public support, professions needed to convince others that, without the training they provide, consumers would be endangered—an assertion the leaders of the new profession made unabashedly as they argued that good intentions and altruism, by themselves, were insufficient to provide assistance to destitute families, disrupted families, mental patients, and other needy people.) The emphasis that the new professional leaders placed on training staff for work in nongovernmental agencies, such as an array of agencies providing charity, mental health, and medical services, was also attuned to an era that had few governmental services aside from poorhouses, mental institutions, and correctional facilities.

If we place the emerging profession in the larger context of the progressive era, we can see that its leaders were captive to the intellectual currents, as well as the political assumptions, of the period. Many of them were content to seek regulations of child labor, women's working conditions, and myriad other conditions rather than major social programs that occurred later in American history. Many of them sought reforms of government, including eradication of patronage and corruption from the administration of mental institutions and poorhouses. Many of them brought into the profession a preoccupation with investigation and diagnosis of the dispossessed and impoverished people of the era that derived from charity projects in the 1840s and later decades. Just as social reformers often stood at the periphery of progressivism, which was often preoccupied with establishment of "good government," busting of trusts, and moral issues like temperance, they often were at the periphery of the emerging profession; indeed, Mary Richmond believed that the mixture of social reform, recreation, and socialization work of settlements to be an unsuitable methodology for the new profession—and even inimical to its survival. Most of the leaders of the new profession assumed, like the leaders of the charity societies, that nongovernmental agencies would provide the focus of the work of the new profession; indeed, they looked with considerable cynicism at patronage-ridden public agencies like mental institutions and poorhouses.

It was too soon to tell, in 1920, precisely how the new profession would evolve. An emphasis on helping poor people was likely to continue since both charity society and settlement movements emphasized this population. A social-reform impulse, deriving from the influence of settlement workers, as well as efforts by some charity society people like Homer Folks, was likely to remain. But a clever prognosticator might have guessed that tensions in the profession at its inception would also remain. Might not casework, once married in succeeding decades to the just-emerging tenets of Freud (and later the tenets of so many other theorists of the psyche) lead some practitioners to want to serve the neurotic people of the middle and (even) upper classes *rather* than poor people? Might not the descendants of Jane Addams within the profession, who wished to emphasize "macro matters" such as policy, administration, organizing, and social reform, be placed in a relatively residual position in a profession whose organizing principles reflected the person-to-person transactions of the charity societies? Would not endless disputes emerge about the precise educational content of the professional schools—and even whether a masters degree in a graduate facility was necessary or whether certain tasks could be performed by people with only bachelor degrees? (We discuss in Chapter 8 and several other chapters how some of these tensions emerged over the next few decades.)

Lest we imply that social workers alone were subject to the limitations of the era, both physicians and attorneys, who tightened the educational requirements of their disciplines, made salutary advances yet made decisions that set back the course of social reform in the United States. Though the profession of medicine had existed for centuries, it did not possess a monopoly over health care in the midnineteenth century because, in the absence of knowledge of bacteria, other professions, such as herbalists, seemed as credible as physicians. With revolutionary scientific discoveries in Europe in the last four decades of the nineteenth century, which led to the development of inoculations, safer surgical techniques, and the introduction of effective medications, scourges such as cholera, syphilis, and typhoid fever were redressed—and physicians, who linked their profession to these new findings, obtained a credibility that rival professions lacked. Physicians seized the moment by organizing a grass-roots campaign that was developed by chapters of the American Medical Association to persuade state legislations to enact licensing laws that restricted surgical and pharmaceutical remedies to people who had obtained a medical degree. Like social workers, they linked their training facilities to universities and required a bachelors degree for admission to them.[119]

Who is to argue that this profession did not make salutary contributions to society as it waged war on ancient epidemics? But the medical profession also retarded social reform and, in some cases, set back the course of human rights. We have already noted that it "medicalized" many health conditions of women, such as childbirth, in a manner that made women subject to strange remedies, such as months of bed rest and an epidemic of hysterectomies. Many of them opposed the use of birth control on grounds women should not interfere with natural laws of reproduction. Moreover, we have noted that physicians were not reluctant to profess knowledge of sexual matters, such as declaring homosexual behavior to be medical pathology—a pronouncement that remained intact until the 1980s when it was finally reversed.

The American Medical Association (AMA), whose leaders had entertained the notion of government health insurance (by the various states) in the early twentieth century as they observed successful projects by the English and Germans, swung against the notion in the years before and after World War I. Indeed, they launched a campaign of invective against the proponents of health insurance, which included many progressive reformers and social workers, that was notable for its hysteria; health reformers were called "bolsheviks," "communists," and people who hoped to ruin "the doctor–patient relationship." When they coupled this invective with the investment of vast resources in a lobbying campaign in the capitols of all states that were entertaining the idea of health insurance, they established themselves as the primary lobbying group in the health field.[120] The opposition of the AMA to health insurance was so effective, particularly when many Americans were convinced that it was un-American, that it sabotaged the enactment of health insurance in the 1930s, the late 1940s, and 1970s—and nearly blocked passage of lesser measures in the 1960s such as Medicare. The AMA retarded the development of a strong public health system in the United States, as well, by arguing on successive occasions that even inoculations should be done only by private physicians.

The reactionary tendencies of the AMA were illustrated by its virulent opposition to the Sheppard-Towner bill, a modest measure initiated by social workers in 1918 that sought to improve maternal and child health facilities and services in rural areas through federal grants to state health departments. Although the legislation was enacted in 1921, its proponents had to overcome charges that it represented "state medicine." Pathetically small, it finally succumbed in 1929 largely because the medical profession "sought (successfully) to wrest control of infant and maternal health from female-run public clinics and place it, instead, in the hands of private, male physicians."[121]

Many of the opinions of legal scholars also made it difficult for the federal government to assume a leading role in social policy in this period. Recall that Progressives were interested in regulatory reforms, mostly in state and local jurisdictions. Even some of these regulations were threatened by adverse court rulings, such as the decision by Oregon courts to overturn a state law that banned employing women in factories for more than ten hours in a given day on grounds that the law violated the rights of women (under the Fourteenth Amendment of the Constitution) to freedom of contract. Although the Supreme Court upheld the statute in *Muller* v. *Oregon* in 1908 under the persuasive reasoning of attorney Louis Brandeis, who established a "sociological jurisprudence" that maintained that courts should consider the effects of legislation on the well-being of citizens rather than limiting decisions merely to considerations of the intent of the constitutional framers, the Oregon rulings that predated the decision by the Supreme Court indicated a widespread legal orientation inimical of reform. Moreover, many justices of the Supreme Court continued to believe that the Constitution did not sanction intrusion of the federal government into social matters, *except* under very limited conditions when a specified power of the federal government, such as its jurisdiction over interstate commerce, was involved. (Recall from Chapter 3 that the Constitition reserved to the states all powers not specified in it—and, aside from vague clauses like the general welfare clause, the Constitution was silent on social-policy matters.) Social reformers thus had to ponder how to justify social legislation legally so as to conform to the narrow and specific wording of the Constitution. When Congress enacted federal legislation in 1916 to outlaw the use of child labor in goods shipped in interstate commerce, the Supreme Court overturned the legislation in 1918 on grounds that it exceeded "the authority delgated to Congress over commerce." Congress gamely persisted only to find that the Supreme Court overruled a law that it enacted in 1919 to tax the profits of companies that did not obey the standards of the 1916 legislation. And it passed a constitutional amendment in 1924 to authorize federal laws for regulating the labor of youth under age eighteen only to fail to achieve approval of it by three-fourths of the states, as required for constitutional amendments.

The intransigency of the courts, and particularly the Supreme Court, enraged progressive reformers like Theodore Roosevelt. Since the Congress is given the power to organize and establish rules for the Supreme Court by the Constitution, progressive reformers proposed taking the powers of constitutional review from the Supreme Court by legislation—or increasing the size of the Court to dilute the power of its existing justices.[122] These projects were not successful though reformers were able to secure the appointment of Brandeis to the Court in 1916 over an avalanche of protests by many jurists and conservatives who alleged he would disregard the intentions of the framers of the Constitution.

With these kinds of legal disputes in the progressive era, the Supreme Court (as well as lesser courts) became key players in the unfolding of social reform in the United States. Until about 1938, as we note in ensuing chapters, the Supreme Court enormously delayed the assertion of social responsibility by the federal government by a succession of adverse rulings. Even after the Court had acceded to the notion that the federal government could establish social programs and regulations, it remained a key player in shaping the content of those decisions. (We note in later chapters how relatively liberal rulings of the 1950s and 1960s assumed enormous importance in speeding social reforms and how more conservative rulings in the 1980s and 1990s aligned the Court against social reformers on successive occasions.)

## THE POLITICAL ECONOMY OF SOCIAL POLICY IN THE PROGRESSIVE ERA

Progressives dramatically expanded social obligation to include a host of regulations as well as a limited set of social programs such as mothers'

pensions and workmen's compensation. These accomplishments may not appear dramatic or far-reaching to contemporary citizens, but they constituted remarkable innovations in a society that had previously restricted social policy to a small set of poorhouses, mental institutions, prisons, schools, and houses of refuge.

Even if they usually emphasized regulations of local and state governments, the Progressives served as precursors to the development of the modern welfare state by championing the role of government in addressing a range of social problems. Government, they believed, could serve as a force for amelioration of social needs rather than as merely a passive umpire that preserved law and order. Further, many Progressives believed that government need not merely provide funds and concessions to affluent persons and corporations but also ought to assist vulnerable populations such as women, children, immigrants, and factory workers. In a sense, then, Progressives legitimized a vision of positive and compassionate government that had not hitherto been expressed as widely or as articulately in a nation preoccupied with laissez-faire doctrines and deification of monied elites. Their enacted policies, in turn, served to educate the nation's citizens to the possibilities of governmental action as workers, renters, and consumers benefited from improvements in working conditions, housing, and public health.

Progressivism must nonetheless be viewed as a movement that made only modest social welfare innovations in a nation with extraordinary social needs in its growing cities. Regulations hardly constituted frontal assaults on poverty, low wages, or industrial accidents. Workmen's compensation and mothers' pensions were limited programs by any standards. Few Americans empathized with the social needs of African Americans, Spanish-speaking persons, and Asian Americans; indeed, many Progressives were deeply suspicious of these groups.

Many reformers realized that low income and working class Americans would need to rally behind a reform-minded president if the nation was to develop more far-reaching reforms. But it was unclear how such a reform constituency could develop as the failed campaign of the Progressive party illustrated in 1912. As we discuss in Chapters 7 and 8, it took the catastrophe of the Great Depression to push the nation to develop major federal social programs behind the leadership of a president who managed to achieve the political realignment that the Progressives had fantasized might be possible.

 **END NOTES**

1. Arthur Mann, ed., *The Progressive Era: Major Issues of Interpretation* (Hinsdale, Ill.: Dryden Press, 1975), p. 4.

2. David Brody, *Workers in Industrial America: Essays on the Twentieth-Century Struggle* (New York: Oxford University Press, 1980), p. 15.

3. For comparisons of Russian and Italian immigrants, see Elizabeth Ewen, *Immigrant Women in the Land of Dollars: Life and Culture on the Lower East Side, 1890–1925* (New York: Monthly Review Press, 1985), pp. 30–57.

4. *Ibid.*, pp. 112–113, 131.

5. *Ibid.*, pp. 76–91.

6. *Ibid.*, pp. 86–87.

7. Brody, *Workers*, p. 16.

8. James Weinstein, "It's Good for Business." In Mann, ed., *The Progressive Era*, p. 112.

9. *Ibid.*

10. *Ibid.*

11. Brody, *Workers*, p. 24.

12. Mark Leff, "Consensus for Reform: The Mothers Pension Movement in the Progressive Era." In Frank

Breul and Stephen Diner, eds., *Compassion and Responsibility: Readings in the History of Social Welfare Policy in the United States* (Chicago: University of Chicago Press, 1980), p. 245; Roy Lubove, *The Struggle for Social Security* (Cambridge, Mass.: Harvard University Press, 1968), pp. 98–99.

13. Stephan Skowronek, *Building a New American State: The Expansion of National Administrative Capacities, 1877–1920* (Cambridge: Cambridge University Press, 1982), pp. 39–42, 45–46, 165–176.

14. *Ibid.,* pp. 167–169.

15. Arthur Link and Richard McCormick, *Progressivism* (Arlington Heights, Ill.: Harlan Davidson, 1983), pp. 18–20; David Thelen, "Not Classes but Issues." In Mann, ed., *Progressive Era,* pp. 40-42.

16. *Ibid.,* pp. 42–45.

17. *Ibid.,* pp. 44–45.

18. Robert McElvaine, *The Great Depression: America, 1929–1941* (New York: New York Times Book Co., 1984), pp. 3–7.

19. Sidney Fine, *Laissez-Faire and the General Welfare State: A Study of Conflict in America, 1865–1901* (Ann Arbor, Mich.: University of Michigan Press, 1956), pp. 126–168; Robert Steamer, *The Supreme Court in Crisis: A History of Conflict* (Amherst, Mass.: University of Massachusetts Press, 1971), pp. 149–171; Edward White, *The American Judicial Tradition: Profiles of Leading American Judges* (New York: Oxford University Press, 1976), pp. 105–108.

20. Jane Addams, *Democracy and Social Ethics* (New York: Macmillan, 1902), pp. 1–70; Fine, *Laissez-Faire,* pp. 169–197.

21. Jane Addams, *Newer Ideals of Peace* (New York: Macmillan, 1907), p. 85.

22. For her books where she, respectively, idealizes youth, immigrants, and women, see *The Spirit of Youth and the City Streets* (New York: Macmillan, 1909); *Twenty Years at Hull House* (New York: Macmillan, 1961), pp. 169–185; *The Long Road of Women's Memory* (New York: Macmillan, 1917).

23. Fine, *Laissez-Faire,* pp. 198–251.

24. Charles Beard, *An Economic Interpretation of the Constitutional Convention* (New York: Free Press, 1965), pp. 152–188; Frederic Howe, *Confes-*

*sions of a Reformer* (New York: Scribner's, 1925), p. 169.

25. John Gable, *The Bull Moose Years: Theodore Roosevelt and the Progressive Party* (Port Woolington, N.Y.: Kennicat Press, 1978), pp. 11–13.

26. Lela Costin, *Two Sisters for Social Justice* (Urbana, Ill.: University of Illinois Press, 1983), pp. 31–38; Allen Davis, *American Heroine: The Life and Legend of Jane Addams* (New York: Oxford University Press, 1973), pp. 24–52.

27. Daniel Levine, *Jane Addams and the Liberal Tradition* (Madison, Wis.: State Historical Society of Wisconsin, 1971), pp. ix–x.

28. Link and McCormick, *Progressivism,* pp. 15, 19–20; Thelen, "Not Classes," pp. 40–45.

29. Thelen, "Not Classes," pp. 40–45.

30. William Allen White, *The Autobiography of William Allen White* (New York: Macmillan, 1946), p. 484.

31. Fine, *Laissez-Faire,* p. 168; Thelen, "Not Classes," pp. 40–41.

32. Joseph Castrovinci, "Prelude to Welfare Capitalism: The Role of Business in the Enactment of Workmen's Compensation Legislation in Illinois, 1905–1912," *Social Service Review,* 50 (March 1976), 277; Lynn Gordon, "Women and the Anti-Child Labor Movement in Illinois, 1890–1920," *Social Service Review,* 51 (June 1977), 314, 319. For discussion of the sheer power of the save-the-children ethos, see Michael Katz, *In the Shadow of the Poorhouse* (New York: Basic Books, 1986), pp. 113–115.

33. Richard Hofstadter, *Age of Reform: From Bryan to FDR* (New York: Knopf, 1955), pp. 185–195.

34. Clarke Chambers, *Paul U. Kellogg and the Survey: Voices for Social Welfare and Social Justice* (Minneapolis, Minn.: University of Minnesota Press, 1971), pp. 33–40.

35. Brody, *Workers,* pp. 17, 19, 21.

36. Levine, *Jane Addams,* pp. 160–164; Link and McCormick, *Progressivism,* pp. 35–36.

37. Walter Trattner, *Homer Folks: Pioneer in Social Welfare* (New York: Columbia University Press, 1968), pp. 76–84.

38. *Ibid.,* p. 95.

39. Roy Lubove, *The Professional Altruist* (Cambridge, Mass.: Harvard University Press, 1965), pp. 3–54.

40. Allen Davis, *Spearheads for Reform: The Social Settlements and the Progressive Movement, 1890–1914* (New York: Oxford University Press, 1967), p. 195.

41. Lubove, *The Struggle*, p. 52.

42. *Ibid.,* pp. 52–57.

43. Weinstein, "It's Good for Business," pp. 113–114.

44. Trattner, *Homer Folks*, pp. 114–119.

45. Leff, "Consensus," pp. 259–260.

46. Charles Larsen, *The Good Fight: The Life and Times of Ben Lindsey* (Chicago: Quadrangle Books, 1972), pp. 27–32.

47. Trattner, *Homer Folks*, pp. 85–93.

48. Lela Costin, *Child Welfare: Policies and Practice* (New York: McGraw-Hill, 1979), pp. 35–36.

49. Trattner, *Homer Folks*, p. 107.

50. Costin, *Two Sisters*, pp. 100–118; Josephine Goldmark, *The Impatient Crusader* (Urbana, Ill.: University of Illinois Press, 1953), pp. 100–104.

51. Costin, *Two Sisters*, p. 110.

52. Trattner, *From Poor Law to Welfare State*, 4th ed., pp. 175–177.

53. John Ehrenreich, *The Altruistic Imagination: A History of Social Work and Social Policy in the United States* (Ithaca, N.Y.: Cornell University Press, 1985), p. 38; Lee Kreader, "Isaac Max Rubinow: Pioneering Specialist in Social Insurance," *Social Service Review,* 50 (September 1976), 293, 296–298.

54. Hofstadter, *Age of Reform,* pp. 254–269.

55. Davis, *Spearheads,* pp. 170–193; Link and McCormick, *Progressivism,* pp. 28–34.

56. Steamer, *The Supreme Court,* pp. 149–171.

57. Link and McCormick, *Progressivism,* pp. 69–70, 72.

58. Paolo Coletta, *The Presidency of William Howard Taft* (Lawrence, Kans.: University Press of Kansas, 1973), p. 139; Davis, *American Heroine,* p. 189; Gable, *The Bull Moose Years,* pp. 90–91; Link and McCormick, *Progressivism,* pp. 69–70.

59. John Buenker, *Urban Liberalism and Progressive Reform* (New York: Scribner's, 1973), p. 43; Michael Rogin and John Shover, "From Below." In Mann, ed., *The Progressive Era,* pp. 20–30.

60. Davis, *American Heroine,* p. 189; Link and McCormick, *Progressivism,* pp. 69–70.

61. Boyer, *Urban Masses,* pp. 205–219; Davis, *American Heroine,* pp. 176–184; Link and McCormick, *Progressivism,* pp. 100–104.

62. Levine, *Jane Addams,* pp. 144–159; Link and McCormick, *Progressivism,* pp. 96–100.

63. George Dangerfield, *The Strange Death of Liberal England* (New York: H. Smith and R. Haas, 1935), pp. 214–330; H. V. Emy, *Liberals, Radicals, and Social Politics, 1892–1914* (Cambridge: Cambridge University Press, 1973), pp. 235–280.

64. Levine, *Jane Addams,* pp. 160–164; Link and McCormick, *Progressivism,* pp. 35–36.

65. Skowronek, *Building a New American State,* pp. 24–26.

66. Addams, *Twenty Years,* pp. 222–223; Hofstadter, *Age of Reform,* pp. 254–269; Levine, *Jane Addams,* p. 75.

67. Brody, *Workers,* pp. 23–30; Eric Foner, *History of the Labor Movement in the United States,* Vol. 2 (New York: International Publishers, 1955), pp. 184–188.

68. Brody, *Workers,* pp. 82–88.

69. *Ibid.,* p. 28.

70. *Ibid.,* pp. 14–21.

71. *Ibid.,* pp. 32–39.

72. Chambers, *Paul Kellogg,* p. 48; Davis, *American Heroine,* pp. 186, 193.

73. Davis, *American Heroine,* p. 194; Gable, *The Bull Moose Years,* pp. 6–7.

74. Davis, *American Heroine,* pp. 54–56, 125.

75. Gable, *The Bull Moose Years,* pp. 6–7.

76. Coletta, *The Presidency of William Howard Taft,* pp. 21–25.

77. Kraeder, "Isaac Max Rubinow," p. 293–298.

78. *Ibid.,* pp. 16–20.

79. Gable, *The Bull Moose Years,* p. 6.

80. *Ibid.,* pp. 112–113.

81. *Ibid.,* pp. 131–133.

82. Davis, *American Heroine,* p. 197.

83. John Dittmer, *Black Georgia in the Progressive Era, 1900–1920* (Urbana, Ill.: University of Illinois Press, 1977), pp. 8–22.

84. Florette Henri, *Black Migration: Movement North, 1900–1920* (Garden City, N.Y.: Doubleday, 1975), pp. 81–131.

85. Roger Daniels, *The Politics of Prejudice: The Anti-Japanese Movement in California and the Struggle for Japanese Exclusion* (Berkeley, Calif.: University of California Press, 1977), pp. 46–78; Jack Chen, *The Chinese of America: From the Beginnings to the Present* (San Francisco: Harper & Row, 1982), pp. 88–89, 99, 109–115.

86. Leobardo Estrada, F. Chris Garcia, Reynaldo Macias, and Lionel Maldonado, "Chicanos in the United States: A History of Exploitation and Resistance." In F. Chris Garcia, ed., *Latinos and the Political System* (Notre Dame, Ind.: University of Notre Dame Press, 1988), p. 41.

87. *Ibid.,* p. 41.

88. Rodolfo Acuna, *Occupied America: The Chicano's Struggle Toward Liberation* (San Francisco: Canfield Press, 1972), pp. 130–135.

89. Estrada et al., "Chicanos in the United States," p. 39.

90. *Ibid.,* p. 40.

91. Thomas Dyer, *Theodore Roosevelt and the Idea of Race* (Baton Rouge, La.: Louisiana State University Press, 1980), p. 105; Gable, *The Bull Moose Years,* p. 74; Dittmer, *Black Georgia,* pp. 108–109.

92. Gable, *The Bull Moose Years,* p. 74.

93. Dyer, *Theodore Roosevelt,* pp. 21–44.

94. Dittmer, *Black Georgia,* pp. 181, 186.

95. Steamer, *The Supreme Court,* pp. 125–126, 149–150.

96. Steven Diner, "Chicago Social Workers and Blacks in the Progressive Era," *Social Service Review,* 44 (December 1970), 231–236; Levine, *Jane Addams,* pp. 192–194.

97. Eleanor Flexner, *Century of Struggle: The Women's Rights Movement in the United States* (Cambridge, Mass.: Harvard University Press, 1975), pp. 319–337.

98. Mimi Abramovitz, *Regulating the Lives of Women: Social Welfare Policy from Colonial Times to the Present* (Boston: South End Press, 1988), p. 188.

99. *Ibid.,* pp. 248–255.

100. *Ibid.,* p. 199.

101. *Ibid.,* pp. 190–193.

102. Nancy Woloch, *Women and the American Experience* (New York: Knopf, 1984), pp. 363–380.

103. Barbara Ehrenreich and Deirdre English, *For Her Own Good: 150 Years of the Experts' Advice to Women* (New York: Anchor Books, 1979), p. 110.

104. *Ibid.,* pp. 131–133.

105. *Ibid.,* pp. 93–98.

106. John Higham, *Strangers in the Land: Patterns of American Nativism, 1860–1925* (New York: Atheneum, 1972), pp. 106–130, 158–193.

107. *Ibid.,* pp. 123–124.

108. *Ibid.,* 159.

109. Oscar Handlin, *Race and Nationality in American Life* (New York: Anchor Books, 1957), p. 97.

110. Higham, *Strangers in the Land,* p. 319.

111. Estrada et al., "Chicanos in the United States," p. 44.

112. Trattner, *From Poor Law to Welfare State,* 4th ed., pp. 213–214.

113. Stanley Wenocur and Michael Reisch, *From Charity to Enterprise: The Development of American Social Work in a Market Economy* (Urbana, Ill.: University of Illinois Press, 1989), pp. 50–52.

114. Trattner, *From Poor Law to Welfare State,* 4th ed., pp. 201–202.

115. *Ibid.,* p. 215.

116. Wenocur and Reisch, *From Charity to Enterprise,* pp. 47–60.

117. Trattner, *From Poor Law to Welfare State,* 4th ed., pp. 219–220.

118. Wenocur and Reisch, *From Charity to Enterprise,* pp. 77–78.

119. James Burrow, *Organized Medicine in the Progressive Era* (Baltimore: John Hopkins University Press, 1977), pp. 32–66; Ronald Numbers, *Almost Persuaded: American Physicians and Compulsory Health Insurance* (Baltimore: John Hopkins University Press, 1979), pp. 4–5.

120. Burrow, *Organized Medicine;* Numbers, *Almost Persuaded.*

121. Trattner, *From Poor Law to Welfare State,* 4th ed., pp. 198–200.

122. Gable, *The Bull Moose Years,* pp. 82, 93.

# CHAPTER 7

# The Early Stages of the New Deal

## Selected Orienting Events in the Early Stages of the New Deal

| | |
|---|---|
| **1921–1923** | Presidency of Warren Harding |
| **1925–1928** | Presidency of Calvin Coolidge |
| **1929** | Stock market crashes; Great Depression begins |
| **1929–1932** | Presidency of Herbert Hoover |
| **1932** | Reconstruction Finance Corporation established; Emergency Relief and Construction Act passed |
| **1933** | Civilian Conservation Corps (CCC), Agricultural Adjustment Agency (AAA), Public Works Administration (PWA), Federal Emergency Relief Administration (FERA) established; Civilian Works Administration (CWA) established by executive order; Tennessee Valley Authority (TVA) created; Emergency Farm Mortgage Act and Farm Relief Act enacted |
| **1933–1945** | Presidency of Franklin Roosevelt |
| **1934** | Securities and Exchange Commission (SEC) created; CWA terminated by Roosevelt |

Americans finally fashioned a series of social reforms during the Great Depression of the 1930s that far surpassed the local and regulatory reforms of the progressive era and brought the federal government into a position of policy prominence. Governmental institutions, the presidency, politics, and the courts were also markedly changed in this fateful decade that changed social welfare policy in the United States forever. Although ambitious by American standards, the reforms were relatively timid either by international or today's standards.

Reforms in the Great Depression can best be understood by analyzing the unfolding of reform in four periods.

1. In the *era of denial* (1929 to March 1933), Americans seemed stunned by the economic catastrophe and took little corrective action.

2. During the *period of emergency reforms* (March 1933 to January 1935), Americans supported a bewildering number of reforms but tended to believe that prosperity would soon return and that many reforms could be relatively temporary.

3. In the *era of institutionalized reform* (January 1935 to January 1937), Americans decided to make a number of reforms permanent.

4. Finally, during an *era of policy stalemate* (January 1937 to December 1941), the momentum of New Deal reform was decisively broken.

## THE DECADE OF THE 1920s

The progressive reform momentum was shattered when Americans focused on war preparations, the war effort, and postwar diplomacy, including an ill-fated League of Nations, but it is simplistic to blame the war and its aftermath for the demise of the progressive reform movement because Americans have moved between reform and conservatism in pendulumlike fashion since (at least) the Civil War. Some progressive reformers obtained social reforms during World War I. The Children's Bureau, for example, obtained federal directives that required federal contractors not to use child labor, even after the Supreme Court had ruled in 1916 that federal child labor legislation was unconstitutional.[1]

The decade of the 1920s, like the 1950s and the 1980s, was a period when many Americans believed that private enterprise, left unfettered by government, would bring unlimited prosperity. The nation was presided over by three Republican presidents, Warren Harding, Calvin Coolidge, and Herbert Hoover, who strenuously resisted the efforts to develop social reforms that were put forth by a small cadre of social reformers.[2] Harding stated his philosophy succinctly when he said, "What we want in America is less govenment in business and more business in government."

A second American industrial revolution occurred during the 1920s. Steel, mining, and railroad industries had developed during the first revolution; consumer products, such as cars, radios, and refrigerators, and the electrification of homes and industries provided the focus of the second one. A vast demand of unmet consumer needs existed in the United States since only one in ten urban homes was electrified in 1920, only one in one hundred households possessed radios, and only one in three families had cars. Consumer appetites for new products were whetted by the rise of a large advertising industry.[3]

A "trickle-down" economic philosophy became the dominant ethos of the decade. Officials believed that economic assistance to affluent persons and industry stimulated investments that could bring jobs to poor and working-class Americans. The low tariffs of the prewar era were supplanted by protective tariffs for American industry; federal taxes, which had been increased to pay off the national debt in the wake of World War I, were quartered in size as new tax laws reduced taxes on individuals and corporations; and many regulations that had been enacted in the progressive era were relaxed, not implemented, or struck down by various courts.[4] Policies that empowered industry and affluent persons were supplemented by vigorous suppression of organized labor. Companies sought to obtain the goodwill of employees by stock-sharing schemes, providing fringe benefits, and starting company unions that ostensibly gave workers a mechanism for negotiating for higher benefits and wages. When unions tried to organize, their leaders were often intimidated or fired—and strikes led to unabashed use of scabs, local police, the national guard, and injunctions from courts that were usually favorable to management.[5]

Social reformers were placed on the defensive during the 1920s. Some were branded as radicals, communists, or traitors. African Americans continued to live under oppressive Jim Crow laws in the South, encountered race riots and residential segregation in the North, and found it difficult to find jobs in many of the industries that were now producing consumer goods in the second industrial revolution. Although African Americans became sizable groups in many northern cities, most of them continued to work for white planters in the South.[6] Latinos and Asian Americans continued to experience rampant prejudice and adverse policies in the West and Southwest.[7] Women, who experienced new sexual freedoms in the era of the flapper, found that their voting privileges did not lead to major policy reforms to give them access to more remunerative work or to many professions.[8]

Americans were intrigued by social change and often tended to glamorize technology and science, but they were also fearful of new ideas, as was illustrated by the famous Scopes trial in 1925, when a school teacher was (unsuccessfully) prosecuted for teaching the theory of evolution in a Tennessee school. Prohibition, which was enacted in the form of the Eighteenth Amendment to the Constitution in 1919, was supported by many Protestants, who insisted that local and federal officials strictly enforce the legislation.[9] Many Americans supported stringent reductions of immigration, whether on racial grounds or because they believed the nation could no longer absorb immigrants. The Immigration Act of 1924 was blatantly racist since its aims were to maintain the "racial preponderance (of) the basic strain of our people." A limit of 150,000 people was placed on immigration each year, with quotas for each

nationality in proportion to its size in the existing population. This policy was intended to reduce the proportion of Southern and Eastern European immigration. A complete prohibition was placed on Japanese immigration.[10]

Contrasting with these conservative reforms seeking to restore traditional American values was a new interest in exploring sexual liberation and the psyche. Sigmund Freud was not taken seriously in his native Europe, but his theories— even if not immediately used by many social work practitioners—swept America much like those of Herbert Spencer in the Gilded Age.[11]

The profession of social work grew rapidly during the 1920s. Twenty-five graduate schools existed by 1929, several professional associations had developed, and three journals disseminated information. Casework emerged as the central skill during the decade; its practitioners outnumbered other kinds of social workers by a threefold margin. Mary Richmond's classic treatise during the progressive era had emphasized familial, neighborhood, and societal realities, but in the 1920s, some caseworkers became excited about the personality, so much so that they risked ignoring environmental realities as well as the need for social reforms. They tended to work in private agencies and were often relatively contemptuous of public agencies, which they wanted to restrict to aiding paupers and persons with chronic and severe mental conditions.[12] A variety of reformers still proposed reforms such as social insurances, but they were decidedly on the fringes of American society.

Surface impressions of prosperity were misleading in the 1920s because unemployment ranged from 5 to 13 percent, and agriculture was in a state of depression throughout the decade. Although the upper third of the populace conspicuously consumed consumer products, the lowest third often found that they were unemployed or that they lived near or below poverty in a society that had few governmental income-transfer programs.[13]

Controversy exists about the precise causes of the Great Depression in 1929.[14] Arguments of those theorists who contend that insufficient capital existed to allow industry and affluent persons to expand the nation's industry are contradicted by the aforementioned trickle-down policies, which placed vast sums of money in the coffers of affluent persons and corporations. Other theorists argue convincingly that the Depression occurred because American consumers lacked sufficient resources to purchase consumer goods. Some economists implicate excessive speculation and protective tariffs. Whatever its precise cause, the Great Depression of 1929, like the depression of 1893, put an immediate and decisive halt to prosperity; suggested that trickle-down policies were not a panacea; and alerted Americans to the realities of poverty, unemployment, and economic injustice.

## THE PERIOD OF DENIAL: 1929–1932

The immediate reality of massive unemployment, depressed stock prices, lost fortunes, bankrupt companies, and deflated prices was obvious to everyone in 1929, including Herbert Hoover, the incumbent president. Americans had experienced many economic downturns in their history, however, so most persons assumed that economic growth would resume.

Herbert Hoover at first seemed ideally suited to solve the nation's problems. A civil engineer who had orchestrated a massive food relief program for starving Europeans after World War I, he prided himself on a problem-solving style in which political considerations were given little role. He believed, like most Americans, that modest tinkering with the economic system would bring the nation from its economic doldrums. In accordance with trickle-down economics, he favored passage of the Reconstruction Finance Corporation (RFC), which processed $2 billion for loans to corporations and banks as well as various projects to encourage bankers and corporations to maintain or expand their economic activity. To appease critics, and because he did not believe in major governmental programs, however, Hoover implemented these policies in a restrictive manner; he insisted, for example, that corporations and banks prove that they were on the verge of bankruptcy before providing them with loans under the RFC.[15]

Hoover also believed that private agencies, principally the Red Cross and family service agencies, could address the needs of unemployed and poverty-stricken Americans without governmental assistance. He shared Franklin Pierce's ideology, which had been enunciated in the Pierce veto of nearly a century earlier, that welfare issues belonged to local government and to private philanthropy. Some historians have emphasized progressive elements of Hoover's ideology, but the preponderance of evidence suggests that he was an inflexible conservative who adhered to Social Darwinism and who equated federal social programs with socialism.[16]

Hoover's measures did not address the mounting economic needs of local governments, which were moving toward bankruptcy as their welfare expenditures increased. Pressure from the Congress to help local governments finally led to passage of the Emergency Relief and Construction Act in 1932, which authorized federal loans to local governments that could prove they had become bankrupt, but some Americans began to wonder whether more drastic measures were needed as the Depression worsened. A small group of liberal politicians in the House and the Senate proposed measures that seemed radical to many Americans, such as federal funding of major public works projects, development of federally funded employment offices, federal funding of unemployment and old-age insurance, the development of dams, and reforestation projects to create jobs and economic growth in rural areas.[17] Senators Robert Wagner of New York, Robert La Follette of Wisconsin, and Edward Costigan of Colorado led this small cadre of reformers. They drew from some proposals that had been fashioned in the 1920s by the American Association of Old Age Security, a reform group headed by Isaac Rubinow, who introduced to the United States concepts of social insurance that had been pioneered in Europe.[18] Even relatively conservative big-city bosses, such as Mayor James Curley of Boston, urged job creation and public works programs that went beyond the timid measures of Hoover.[19]

Hoover became more conservative, however, as the nation gradually moved toward more liberal ideas. An inflexible man who was isolated from and insensitive to political realities, he resorted to budget-balancing and various monetary solutions to complement his pathetically inadequate programs. He bitterly attacked liberals who, he believed, advocated socialistic measures that would compound the nation's economic problems.[20]

The nation's confidence in business—and in Hoover—began to waver by 1930. Hoover had won a sweeping victory in 1928, but the Republican party suffered such major losses in the congressional elections of 1930 that its congressional majority was reduced to a narrow margin. Most Democrats were as confused by the situation as Hoover, however, since they, too, tended to favor budget-cutting, tax reduction, and trickle-down economics to cope with the Depression. Though

many social workers supported Roosevelt, Jane Addams and some other reformers voted for Hoover in the pivotal election of 1932.[21]

Franklin Delano Roosevelt was not a liberal in the presidential campaign of 1932; he expressed more sympathy for the unemployed than Hoover, and talked vaguely of reforestation schemes, but he advocated a balanced budget and conservative fiscal policies and even derided Hoover for spending too much federal money. But Roosevelt and the Democrats won a sweeping victory in 1932 because Americans wanted to give the Democrats a chance to address the nation's problems. Although few persons believed that Roosevelt favored policies that were strikingly different from those of Hoover, some persons who knew him believed that his policies would prove more liberal than his rhetoric. As assistant secretary of the navy in World War I, he had participated in the mobilization of national resources by the federal government. As governor of New York State between 1928 and 1932, he oversaw the operations of the state's Labor Department, which administered a variety of regulations pertaining to child labor and work safety, and the Temporary Emergency Relief Administration (TERA), a modest program that provided state funds to local units of government for outdoor relief to the unemployed. He knew many social workers, including Frances Perkins, who headed the Labor Department, and Harry Hopkins, who had worked in private philanthropic agencies and directed the TERA. He was married, moreover, to a remarkable woman, Eleanor, who had been immersed in a range of social reforms during the 1920s.[22]

## THE ERA OF EMERGENCY REFORMS: 1933–1934

When Franklin Roosevelt won his decisive victory in November 1932, it was unclear what he would do with his mandate. Policy drift was no longer possible because the banking system was

threatened with collapse due to insufficient funds to cover withdrawals of panic-stricken depositors. Local governments encountered staggering welfare burdens since from 20 to 60 percent of Americans were unemployed in many cities and neighborhoods. Millions of Americans, many of them youths whose parents could no longer support them, roamed the nation, obtained beans, coffee, and floor space from local police, and were told to move on the next day. Economic inequality, which had always been severe, became even more obvious at a time when unskilled and uneducated persons and racial minorities were massively unemployed. Farmers, who were suffering catastrophic losses in a worldwide depression of prices of agricultural produce, foreclosed their farms in huge numbers; many fled an extraordinary drought that had developed in Oklahoma and adjacent states.[23]

American business was in disarray. Prices of products decreased as demand for them plummeted and as exports were slashed owing to the depressed economies of European nations. Consumer demand decreased further when employers reduced their work forces. Businesses went bankrupt as they slashed their prices in a desperate effort to retain customers. The suicide rate of investors, bankers, and company executives rose sharply.[24] Unions, which had made slow but certain progress in the late 1920s, went into virtual collapse since workers were so desperate for jobs that they feared to contest wage-cutting policies of employers.

Roosevelt had several difficult options.

1. He had to decide whether to focus on the victims of economic distress, such as unemployed and hungry persons, or to seek a range of reforms to improve the economic system.
2. When addressing the problems of destitute persons, he had to decide what combination of funds, goods, and jobs to provide them.
3. He had to decide whether to define the situation as an emergency or as a set of conditions that required permanent programs.
4. He had to decide whether to give the federal government major policy roles or provide funds to state and local governments so that they could address social and economic problems within their boundaries.

A variety of forces pushed Roosevelt and his advisors toward limited, localistic, and temporary reforms, but other forces prompted him to consider ongoing federal programs. The actual reforms that were enacted in 1933 and 1934 can be understood only in the context of this set of contradictory forces.

## Forces That Promoted Major Reforms

Roosevelt's sweeping personal victory in 1932 was the largest plurality a president had received since 1864 and provided him with a power base during the remainder of the decade. The development of a relatively liberal political party, which many progressive reformers had sought in 1912, was partially realized when Roosevelt obtained the votes of an unprecedented proportion of working-class voters who wanted government to take an active stance in addressing unemployment and poverty. (Republicans, by contrast, obtained most of their support from middle- and upper-class voters.) This realignment of parties by the social class of their supporters, which continued throughout the 1930s, was crucial to the development of social reforms in the Roosevelt Administration and in succeeding decades.[25]

Roosevelt's extraordinary power derived not only from support of the working class but also from a sizable portion of the middle class, to whom Roosevelt appealed because he exuded confidence, because they no longer believed that Republicans could solve the economic problems of the nation, and because many of them had been directly affected by the economic Depression.[26] As the progressive era had demonstrated, considerable reform sentiment must develop within the American middle class before a reform era can develop so as to offset opposition from corporations, affluent persons, conservatives, and middle-class persons who oppose reforms.

**FIGURE 7.1** • *Victims of the dust bowl of the 1930s*

*Source:* Library of Congress

The strongest pressure for reform derived, however, from the magnitude of human suffering that existed during the 1930s (see Figure 7.1). Persons of all social classes were devastated by economic suffering and resorted to desperate and improvisational survival strategies. Some persons moved into tents in the countryside during the summer; three or more families shared apartments; groups of single women shared apartments and lived from the wages of a single worker; persons tried to grow produce in gardens; and teenagers roamed the countryside when their families could not support them. Lorena Hickok, a woman reporter who was commissioned by Eleanor Roosevelt to tour the country in a car, wrote daily letters to her in which she documented the suffering of members of all social classes.[27] White-collar Americans feared foreclosure or evictions, had to pawn family possessions, feared their neighbors would discover they were on relief, and shunned wearing clothes that were made in the sewing rooms of relief programs. Malnutrition and starvation were widely reported; in some cases, thousands of children were placed in summer camps to give them adequate food. Medical care was lacking for members of all classes since many physicians and hospitals refused service to destitute persons. Many persons lacked funds, even when on welfare, to heat or light their homes or to purchase clothing. Foreclosures, evictions, layoffs, family disruption, and suicides were commonplace. When touring major American cities in 1932, Harry Hopkins observed that the hundreds of thousands of Americans who lined the streets to watch FDR's procession did not protest, yell, or applaud but stood in stunned silence.[28] This widespread suffering persisted throughout the decade despite periodic upturns in the economy. Even when the economy improved slightly, vast numbers of persons could not find employment. When Congress impatiently imposed a rule in 1939 that persons could receive no more than eighteen months of work relief, investigators found that more than two-thirds of recipients had to return to work relief because they could not find jobs.[29]

The disarray of Republicans and conservatives also helped Roosevelt following his overwhelming defeat of Hoover.[30] Business interests, which had traditionally provided considerable support for conservative politicians, were discredited by the economic collapse since their speculation and greed were widely perceived as one cause of the economic downturn. The catastrophe of the Depression shook the nation to its foundations and caused such widespread and extended suffering that the nation craved a leader who would provide leadership, even if he broached policies that would have been unthinkable several years earlier.

Roosevelt and his aides were often in disarray themselves, but they came into his first administration with relatively well-developed ideas and many areas of consensus.[31] Above all, they wanted to use the resources and power of the federal government to intervene in economic and social affairs since they believed that purposeful action could solve problems. They simultaneously rejected Adam Smith's laissez-faire economics and John Locke's restricted definition of government, which had provided the buttress for conservative philosophy in America through the Hoover administration. Roosevelt and his inner circle of advisors, the so-called brains trust, did not know the precise solutions, but they rea-

soned that interventions could be devised in trial-and-error fashion until something worked. Old verities had not worked to solve the economic malaise. Roosevelt had an open field, and he chose to seize the moment by proposing legislation and programs that transformed the nation and, in the process, created an American welfare state that endured even the conservative administration of Ronald Reagan fifty years later.

## Forces That Limited Roosevelt's Initial Policy Initiatives

Roosevelt realized that conservatives were a potential threat to social reforms. The conservative National Economic League had fought even the limited reforms of the Hoover administration. Although many businessmen supported specific pieces of New Deal legislation, they tended to be suspicious of Roosevelt both for his rhetoric—he often singled out the wealthy, bankers, and speculators for criticism—and for his policies, such as tax measures that raised corporate and individual taxes. The U.S. Chamber of Commerce stoutly resisted reforms in local and national arenas.[32]

Roosevelt encountered formidable political opposition from both political parties throughout the decade. The leadership of the Democratic party had been coopted by corporate interests during the 1920s to the extent that it favored high tariffs, limited assistance to poor persons, and a small federal bureaucracy. Roosevelt's victory over Newton Baker in the Democratic convention in 1932 was a decisive blow to this traditional leadership, but it maintained a strong—and hostile—presence in the party and often opposed Roosevelt's initiatives.[33]

Most churches in the early 1930s were profoundly conservative. Clergy in Boston from most faiths, for example, opposed federal and state programs to help the poor in the early part of the decade.[34] Many leaders of the Catholic Church became staunch defenders of the New Deal, but its bishops nonetheless opposed regulation of child labor, which they believed interfered with the privacy of the family.[35] Even though more than half the American population lived in cities during the 1930s, local, state, and national legislatures were dominated by rural legislators who were often insensitive to the needs of urban residents.[36]

Labor leaders often did not focus on advocacy of social reforms during the New Deal because they were preoccupied with obtaining the right to organize. At the start of the decade, fewer than three million American workers were organized (or two million fewer workers than in 1920), and most of them were skilled workers in various craft unions of the AFL. Considerable unrest developed among assembly-line workers and miners in the early 1930s behind the leadership of men such as John L. Lewis, who headed the United Mine Workers. But the AFL eyed these unskilled workers nervously since they were unlikely candidates for skilled electrical, carpentry, and other unions. Prompted by worker unrest, and sensing that the New Deal provided workers with a less hostile environment than prior administrations, Lewis impatiently prodded the AFL to allocate resources to unions of unskilled workers. He formed the Congress of Industrial Organizations (CIO) in 1936, which finally provided a home for steel, auto, mining, and other unions. But the bloody strikes and the sheer effort of organizing these unions meant that Lewis and others devoted limited effort to securing broader social reforms for American workers. Indeed, roughly one-half the strikes during the New Deal were held to obtain the right to form a union rather than to secure higher wages.[37]

Union leaders such as Lewis focused on traditional union issues because they lacked the socialist and radical tradition that was common within English and European labor movements.[38] Union support for reform during the New Deal also decreased because of their belated growth; much of their membership gains occurred relatively late in the decade, when employers finally tolerated them because they wanted to decrease strikes to preserve their profits from the upturn in the economy and from munitions contracts. (Massive increases in union membership also occurred during World War II, when the government supported collective bargaining to allay labor unrest.) Labor had become, by 1936, the major single contributor to the campaigns of Roosevelt, but labor was an uncertain ally with respect to some New Deal legislation and was hampered by internal dissension.[39]

Indeed, the American Federation of Labor (AFL) maintained a relatively conservative posture throughout the decade. It sometimes argued that government work programs represented forced labor but then fought opportunistically to obtain jobs in government programs for its own union members. It rarely initiated policy ideas and even feared the development of governmental policies that might facilitate organizing of unskilled workers by rival unions in automobile, steel, and other plants.[40]

The specter of adverse rulings by the Supreme Court hung over the New Deal from the outset. The Court had declared federal child labor legislation to be unconstitutional in 1916 on the grounds it was only remotely connected to the interstate commerce powers of the federal government. Four of the justices, known as the four horsemen, consistently opposed federal social legislation on the grounds it was not an enumerated power in the Constitution, and they were able to overrule social legislation when joined by two moderate justices. (Only three relatively liberal justices were on the Court.)[41]

Americans also lacked fiscal and governmental institutions to implement sweeping reforms. The federal income tax was initiated in 1913, but taxes had been drastically cut during the 1920s and only modestly increased by the Federal Revenue Act of 1932; most Americans paid no income tax at all, even after this legislation. The government financed social welfare programs by running deficits in its budget, but many Americans, including some of Roosevelt's advisors, believed that deficits exacerbated the economic problems of the nation.[42] A federal civil service system was in place, but federal bureaucracies were relatively small in 1932 and riddled with patronage and corruption. When Frances Perkins was appointed secretary of labor, for example, she found that many of its top officials were receiving payoffs for obtaining immigration papers and visas for political supporters and that they hoped she would come to her office but rarely so that they could continue to receive these payoffs.[43] Local governmental institutions were even more archaic. Public welfare offices, for example, were often staffed by cronies of local politicians, welfare funds often found their way into the pockets of politicians, and punitive policies, such as publicizing names of recipients, were used in some jurisdictions.[44]

The inadequacy of bureaucratic institutions was matched by legislatures at national and local levels as well as by the institution of the presidency. Many state legislatures met only every two years and busied themselves primarily with pork barrel and patronage matters. The Congress was saddled with a seniority system that rewarded older, southern, and conservative legislators, who chaired key committees. Committees generally lacked staffs to help them analyze legislation and develop positions. Patronage was frequently entangled with policy; when legislators or presidents broached policy recommendations, it was often assumed that their major motivation was to secure patronage for loyal supporters.[45] The institution of the presidency was unequipped to develop policy. The presidency had become a symbolic post during the 1920s, when presidents satisfied themselves with budget-balancing and patronage functions. Roosevelt dramatically changed the presidency during his first year from a symbolic institution to a policy-initiating institution when he presented a full legislative package to the Congress.[46]

Pressure for domestic reforms was also decreased by the absence of a well-developed radical movement in the United States. Strong union, socialist, and radical movements had obtained national unemployment programs in England during the 1920s though they demonstrated less strength and militance in the 1930s. Since some politicians in England feared that class conflict could lead to revolution, they were reluctant to rescind the extremely liberal unemployment and welfare benefits that had been enacted in the 1920s.[47] Dramatic strikes should not obscure the fact, however, that American workers were stunned by the Depression and, in the main, were politically quiet from 1929 to 1934. Only a small fraction of workers participated in the sitdown strikes of 1937. When a challenge from the left did develop in 1934 and 1935 (which we discuss subsequently), it was not well organized and focused only on the personal agendas of charismatic leaders.[48]

Local organizations of unemployed persons spontaneously sprung up in many localities, but their national impact was diminished by their lack of national cohesion and by their emphasis on obtaining higher benefits from existing work and relief programs.[49] Local agricultural protest movements flourished but also focused on improving benefits of existing programs as well as policies to stem the tide of foreclosures. Interest groups, which assumed far greater prominence in the United States than in European societies, where class-oriented organizations were dominant, lacked understanding of the range of programs that constituted the New Deal legislative strategy.[50] Each of them, such as labor, agriculture, and business, emphasized policies to help its members. In this welter of specific groups, a philosophy that defined and embraced public obligation for the nation's citizens seemed strangely absent.[51] Alliances never formed between groups that represented urban workers and distressed persons in rural areas; indeed, many farmers turned against the New Deal in the late 1930s because they resented its emphasis on urban reforms.[52]

Reform momentum was impeded as well by the conservative policies of a number of Roosevelt's advisors and by dissension among them. The inner circle of advisors included budget-conscious persons, such as Henry Morgenthau (secretary of the treasury) and Lewis

Douglas (director of the Bureau of the Budget), who sought to reduce social spending and often contended with Harry Hopkins, who favored increasing social spending, even when it required massive deficits. Some advisors, such as Frances Perkins, sought federal policies that ceded major policy roles to the states, in contrast to advisors like Harry Hopkins, who tended to favor federal policy roles. Louis Brandeis, the attorney general, believed that a trust-busting strategy should be used, whereas Senator Robert Wagner believed trust-busting hurt economic growth. Roosevelt often received contradictory advice and was himself confused about various issues, such as the merits of deficit spending.[53]

Roosevelt was not a radical. His defenders argued that he conceded to many compromises in his legislation because he had no political choice in light of conservative political pressures, but his critics contended that he was often too cautious, even when he had firm control of the Congress. He did not favor the ongoing assumption by the federal government of major welfare programs; he liked social insurance programs that were funded by payroll deductions rather than from general revenues, and he often acceded to advisors who advocated cuts in social programs in order to decrease federal deficits.[54]

## Emergency Relief

Roosevelt created a variety of programs that propelled the federal government for the first time into the social welfare arena. These programs provided relief, jobs, and food to destitute Americans.

Many states and localities were verging on bankruptcy in 1932 because of mounting welfare costs and diminished revenues. Roosevelt's solution was the Federal Emergency Relief Administration (FERA), an emergency program to provide funds to states for persons who needed financial assistance. It was virtually a carbon copy of the Temporary Emergency Relief Administration (TERA) that Roosevelt had developed in New York, though on a larger scale.[55]

The legislation did not give a carte blanche to state and local governments. Hopkins was a man of strong convictions who realized that poor-law traditions in states and localities were often punitive, particularly to persons capable of working—the very group that now comprised the bulk of the population that needed welfare. He was also incensed by the orientations of many private agencies, which insisted that intensive casework screening and services had to be given destitute persons as a condition of relief. Hopkins did not hold the widespread belief that the poor should receive in-kind relief or food vouchers in order to stop them from using the funds for alcohol, tobacco, and other luxuries; if wealthy persons can drink martinis, he asked, why not allow poor persons to drink beer? Hopkins also realized that firm federal administration of relief giving would be needed if corruption and patronage were to be avoided. He did not want intensive casework to be used with recipients, but he wanted trained social workers to be hired in supervisory positions so as to enhance the professionalism of welfare services and provide services to those who needed them.[56]

The subsequent legislation, which evolved in the course of consultations between Hopkins, Perkins, Senator Robert Wagner, and Roosevelt, contained provisions to minimize these various dangers. It required each state to designate a state commission that was separate from the existing welfare apparatus both to underscore the temporary nature of the federal assistance and to establish new agencies that would not be punitive. The state commissions were required to establish offices in the various counties and to establish uniform eligibility processes to be used throughout the state. Federal officials had veto power over high-level appointments to guard against patronage appointments and required the use of social workers in key supervisory positions. The legislation gave federal authorities the right to federalize FERA programs in states where irregularities existed, such as corruption or excessive patronage. It authorized $500 million in federal aid to destitute persons, of which half was given to states in a one-to-three match; the other $250 million was used as grants to states that could prove they lacked funds. FERA was technically supposed to provide welfare payments only for unemployed persons, but many states gave funds to the working poor as well since so many of them were unable to survive on their low wages. Its major thrust was to help states and localities with costs of sustaining unemployed persons, but the FERA also funded and ran camps for transients, helped college students with loans, funded cooperatives among farmers, and purchased more than four million acres of land for resale to tenant farmers.[57]

The FERA was a startling departure from prior American welfare traditions. It represented the first major federal welfare program in the nation's history. Though innovative, it also had conservative features. It was not intended to be ongoing legislation since Roosevelt was convinced that public welfare rightly belonged to states and local jurisdictions. He hoped, as well, that the Depression would run its course. The legislation did not require local units of government to give recipients a minimum level of benefits since such a requirement would have been widely interpreted as undue interference with local prerogatives. Many recipients were returned to local, and often punitive, welfare agencies when the FERA was terminated in 1935. Although federal authorities expected local government to use FERA funds to supplement their existing welfare expenditures, many of them cut their local funding so that welfare recipients scarcely benefited from the infusion of new federal money.[58] Even with the infusion of federal money, federal and local welfare spending was marked by uncertainty. Foodless holidays were declared when funds ran out. Many citizens resisted enacting state bond issues to raise funds to meet the local matching share, so federal funding was sometimes terminated for brief periods. Many local areas continued to emphasize in-kind rather than cash assistance despite the conviction of Hopkins that in-kind assistance was demeaning.[59]

FERA administrators must nonetheless be credited with putting this massive program in place with remarkable speed and efficiency. The country was divided into five regions, whose federal administrators worked closely with directors of state emergency relief organizations to be certain that federal guidelines were followed. They were often greeted with hostility by local and state officials, who resented federal intrusion and who sought to maintain practices of patronage and punitiveness. The regional and federal administrators were not afraid to persevere to correct local abuses, as was illustrated when they federalized FERA operations in six states because of irregularities.[60]

Hopkins and Roosevelt realized that the FERA did not provide work to unemployed persons and, in some cases, discouraged work when its recipients were afraid to leave FERA rolls to take jobs. Many recipients feared that they would not be recertified for welfare if their companies went bankrupt or slashed wages below the level of the FERA grants, which were barely sufficient for subsistence. Some persons even feared that the program was encouraging employers to reduce wages by allowing states to provide FERA funds to working, but impoverished, persons. Hopkins shared these various criticisms of the program when he argued in the summer of 1933 that the FERA dole was holding back large numbers of persons who could and wished to work.[61]

An obvious solution to these problems was to create a public works program. Aubrey Williams, an assistant to Hopkins, proposed to use FERA funds to create public works, to be administered through county offices of the FERA in the various states, with its work projects developed by local FERA staff in consultation with local governmental officials. Roosevelt, who also disliked the use of doles for the able-bodied poor, quickly concurred with Williams's scheme by creating through executive order the Civilian Works Administration (CWA) as part of the FERA. Another job-creation program, the Public Works Administration (PWA), favored technically complex projects, such as airports, dams, flood control projects, and military installations—projects that required so much technical planning that few of them had been initiated by the fall of 1933.[62]

CWA funds came from the FERA budget as well as from surplus funds that were commandeered from the PWA program. Between November 1933 and January 1934, 190,000 work projects were initiated that employed sixteen million Americans, a remarkable feat by any standard, even though the CWA still did not reach many unemployed persons. The program was funded by a federal–local matching formula in which the federal government paid most of the direct costs of the program.

Most work projects were proposed by local officials, who submitted tens of thousands of ideas, not only because they wanted to help the unemployed but also because an enormous backlog of road repair and other public needs existed in bankrupted local jurisdictions. The projects were approved by local officials and state FERA officials, except for those projects that were initiated by federal staff and approved in the Washington headquarters of the FERA. Eight percent of CWA funds were used for road-related construction projects, but a wide variety of local improvement projects were undertaken, including recataloging books in public libraries, constructing retaining walls, digging drainage ditches, and cleaning local parks.[63]

Many practical eligibility and reimbursement details had to be quickly solved to allow these projects to be implemented. Hopkins angered many unemployed persons who were not on FERA rolls when he decided to require that 50 percent of the enrollees come from FERA relief rolls, but he remained adamant because he felt welfare recipients should receive priority. (He also feared that unions, which saw the program as a chance to obtain employment for unemployed union workers, would dominate the recruitment process and insist that virtually all jobs go to their members, to the detriment of FERA recipients.) State employment offices certified that CWA workers were unemployed and had tried to find jobs in the private sector. Reimbursement levels were established in Washington; workers in jobs that were classified as unskilled received far less pay than skilled workers, and adjustments were made to reflect regional wage and cost-of-living levels. Hopkins succeeded in maintaining most of the job slots for unskilled persons so that the program would not be monopolized by skilled workers. The wage levels for the CWA were hardly munificent; indeed, workers with relatively large families often had to supplement their CWA paychecks with FERA assistance in order to survive.

Roosevelt also had to contend both with fears of the Republicans that the CWA would be used for patronage purposes by his administration and with Democratic officials who wanted to reward party members with jobs. He decided not to place supervisorial positions under the civil service to appease the Democrats who desired patronage; instead, he insisted that the federal FERA staff carefully screen the thousands of applicants for project supervisor positions to delete persons who lacked requisite skills, even when they were nominees of Democrats. Given the size of the operation (it involved 190,000 separate projects) and the speed of its implementation, it is remarkable that only 240 charges of serious irregularity were ever proved.[64]

The CWA was a bold initiative that gave new social welfare roles to the federal government. It was a massive program, even by today's standards, but was nonetheless an emergency measure that gave minimal benefits to destitute persons and reimbursed unskilled labor at significantly lower levels than skilled labor.

Roosevelt had promised even before he was elected to enact a scheme that would address unemployment among the nation's youth by devising conservation projects in national and state parks. No reform measure was more popular during the New Deal than the Civilian Conservation Corps (CCC), which was enacted in 1933 and provided assistance to 2.5 million young men. Its popularity stemmed from its assistance to youth; from its conservation projects, which were often located in districts of conservative legislators who might normally have opposed the program; and from its reduction of welfare rolls.

Eligibility was restricted to males between the ages of eighteen and twenty-five who were currently on welfare rolls though widespread protest against this restrictive eligibility policy led officials by 1937 to allow any unemployed youth to apply. To spread CCC benefits to as many youths as possible, Roosevelt tried to limit enrollees to one year's residence but then allowed youths to extend their stay for another year because of their difficulty finding jobs in the private economy. Recruits were paid as little as one dollar a day and required to send half their wages to their parents. The army and the Department of Interior were given joint roles in administering the CCC; the former administered the camps under a strict regimen that was supervised by sergeants, and the latter planned and supervised the work projects in the national and state forests to which the youths were sent each day in small work groups.

It is difficult to capture in prose the meaning of the CCC to unemployed youths. The unemployment rate among youths was often double the rate of adults, so many young persons would have been consigned to welfare for years had the CCC not existed. Youths were often transported great distances from midwestern and eastern cities to parks in the West in an extraordinary and broadening experience. It was implemented with remarkable speed; by the summer of 1933, 300,000 youths were placed in camps—a number that rose to 500,000 by 1934. But critics also existed. Some persons feared that the CCC was militarizing America's youth by placing them in regimented settings under the control of the army. Some critics noted that the CCC did not prepare the youths for jobs after they had left the CCC since it did not provide technical skills, emphasize remedial education, or offer employment counseling. It was not large enough to meet the needs of the vast numbers of youth who

needed jobs during the Great Depression. African-American youths were placed in segregated camps, and the program did not address the needs of destitute women.[65]

Many internal improvements were needed in the nation—whether to address such natural disasters as floods and droughts or to build airports, roads, bridges, and military installations. Work on these various projects, Roosevelt contended, served both the public interest and the needs of unemployed Americans. Accordingly, he developed the Public Works Administration (PWA) in 1933. Because large-scale projects can easily become enmeshed in corruption and patronage, Roosevelt appointed as its director Harold Ickes, a stern and perfectionist man, who insisted on the highest technical standards. His administrative style and philosophy contrasted with those of Harry Hopkins. Ickes believed that the hurriedly arranged projects of the CWA did not provide lasting economic benefit to the nation. Hopkins often persuaded Roosevelt that unemployed workers needed immediate work and that complex projects, which required considerable skilled labor, were irrelevant to the needs of many unskilled workers. Ickes was furious when Hopkins was able, repeatedly, to raid PWA funds for the CWA and its successor, the Works Progress Administration (WPA).[66]

Ickes used an identical—and lengthy—review process for each project that made extensive use of engineers and other experts so that he could convince legislators that projects were funded on their merits. Care was exercised in assembling a skilled work force, project managers, and contractors who could build a project to precise specifications. Because he distrusted corporations for placing profits ahead of the public interest, he contracted projects to the private sector with reluctance and monitored them carefully.

The PWA represented the first massive peacetime involvement by the federal government in complex public projects. Incredible numbers of bridges, airports, dams, and school buildings had been constructed by 1937 by the PWA. The program was bedeviled, however, by many problems. Roosevelt often reduced funding of the PWA on the grounds that projects were immediately needed to meet the employment needs of millions of Americans. The PWA often became embroiled in politics and troublesome lawsuits as political and community rivals developed alternative projects or even alternative versions of the same project. The PWA required local units of government to contribute a large share of the cost of specific projects, but a good many of them had to be canceled when local funds were not forthcoming. Finally, many Americans questioned whether the federal government was competing with private business and thus exceeding its proper role.[67]

Only twenty-three states had developed employment offices prior to 1933 to help unemployed workers find jobs. When federal assistance was given to states to develop employment offices with the passage of the Wagner-Peyser Act of 1933, each state developed a network of state employment offices, which were used extensively to recruit and screen persons for work in the CWA, CCC, and PWA as well as to help unemployed workers find jobs.[68]

The federal government developed a range of food programs in the Great Depression even though Hopkins and others preferred cash assistance to in-kind assistance. A food stamp program for federal workers who could show evidence of need was developed, as was a massive surplus commodities program that distributed agricultural produce to the nation's poor.[69]

## Reform of the Economic System

The FERA, CWA, CCC, and PWA rescued persons for brief periods from economic misery, but they did not directly address the collapse of the economic system itself, which had created economic misery in the first place. Since the trickle-down theories of Herbert Hoover had not

worked, Roosevelt proposed a combination of fiscal, monetary, regulatory, and market-support strategies. Indeed, Rosen argues that these economic policies were more valued by Roosevelt than his welfare and jobs programs.[70]

Hoover had feared federal deficits, but Roosevelt drastically increased social spending even though it led to unprecedented peacetime deficits. Federal taxes had been raised somewhat by 1933, but federal revenues were still wholly insufficient to cover the mounting costs of New Deal programs. The federal deficits were nonetheless modest by wartime standards or by those of the Reagan and Bush administrations of the 1980s and 1990s. Indeed, Roosevelt did not understand that even more drastic increases in social spending could have been a potent economic weapon against the Depression.[71] Since many conservatives as well as some of Roosevelt's advisors viewed these modest deficits with horror, Roosevelt was under constant pressure to slash social spending. (Theories of the English economist John Maynard Keynes, which provided a rationale for incurring large deficits during recessions and depressions, were not widely publicized or accepted in the United States until 1936.)[72]

Many banks had insufficient reserves during the 1920s to provide a margin of safety if large numbers of depositors decided to withdraw their funds or to cover bad loans and investments. The Federal Deposit Insurance Corporation, established in 1933, provided federal insurance to cover deposits when banks became insolvent. Restrictions were also placed on stock market transactions when the Securities and Exchange Commission (SEC) was established in 1934 to forestall undue speculation by investors and stockbrokers. These banking measures established confidence in economic institutions and prevented speculative abuses that had precipitated the stock market crash of 1929. Today, Americans take many of these policies for granted, but they represented an unprecedented expansion of the role of the federal government in economic affairs.[73]

Roosevelt's most difficult problem was to devise strategies for arresting the vicious circle of bankruptcies, price slashing, curtailment of production, and decreased spending power that contributed to the Depression. When confronted with unsold merchandise, businesses often slashed prices to increase their sales, but decreased prices led to lower profit margins, which, in turn, required reduction in work forces or in wages. As unemployment thus increased, consumers possessed fewer resources to purchase goods and services.

Roosevelt addressed this vicious circle with passage of the National Industrial Recovery Act of 1933, which established the National Recovery Administration (NRA). Business leaders in various economic sectors, such as the steel, coal, and mining industries, were convened to agree on prices that they would charge for products in their sectors so as to arrest the destructive slashing of prices and the erosion of profit margins. To curtail slashing of wages, they were required, as well, to establish common wage levels for specific kinds of workers though with regional variations to account for differences in the cost of living. Production quotas were devised for each company to decrease the dumping of products on slack markets.[74]

Critics feared that businesses would use this participatory process to make excessive profits by establishing self-serving policies—whether excessively low wages, high prices, or low levels of production to drive up prices. Some persons claimed the NRA was unconstitutional because it allowed businesses to use monopolistic practices, such as price and wage fixing, that were forbidden by the Sherman Antitrust Act.

Roosevelt tried to develop safeguards to forestall these abuses while still obtaining the benefits of regulation of prices, wages, and production. Business leaders had to agree to establish prices that were fair, to refrain from using child labor, to allow workers to join unions, to honor specified minimum working conditions, to exclude women from dangerous occupations, and to include union representatives in industrywide negotia-

tions. Roosevelt tried, in effect, to use the NRA not only to establish a process to stabilize prices and wages but also to advance indirectly the cause of social reform by abolishing child labor and legitimizing unions.[75]

Its goals were ambitious, and the NRA was hampered by many problems. Many liberals who argued that the NRA put "foxes in charge of the henhouse" found their fears realized when some NRA negotiations led to price increases and cuts in production that decreased employment while adding to the burdens of consumers. Employers who honored the minimum wage requirements of the NRA often worked their employees to exhaustion to recoup wage increases, whereas others resorted to a policy of labor turnover to reduce their labor costs and decrease labor unrest. Many employers by 1934 ignored provisions of the NRA when they became convinced that it was unconstitutional.[76] Many businesses found ways of harming labor as well. Since the provisions that allowed workers to organize unions were exceedingly vague, many companies formed company unions to thwart the establishment of independent unions and then told the NRA that their workers were already organized. General Hugh Johnson, the director of the NRA, took an aggressive stance in opposing efforts to form longshoreman's unions in California and even urged the use of federal troops to repress some legitimate unions on the grounds that their organizers were communists. Southern firms often succeeded in keeping wages for jobs that were held by African Americans at extremely low levels by contending that regional wages were lower than in the North.[77]

The NRA was terminated in 1935 when it was declared unconstitutional by the Supreme Court because it provided an unconstitutional delegation of power to nongovernmental entities, but its demise had been widely predicted because it had not been effective. An elaborate bureaucracy was required to arrange and oversee negotiations in thousands of industries because price and labor codes were established in virtually every industry, including, for example, firms that made fishhooks. Considerable noncompliance existed because federal administrators could not monitor its innumerable codes. The National Labor Board, which was established to monitor the provisions protecting workers who sought unions, could not effectively help many workers because it was understaffed and had limited powers.

The problem of depressed prices existed in rural areas as well, where millions of farmers were verging on bankruptcy. To address this agricultural depression, Roosevelt established the Agricultural Adjustment Agency (AAA). It convened producers of the same crop to negotiate the amounts of acreage they would grow and then reimbursed farmers for *not* planting some of their land. Curtailment of production would, planners hoped, raise prices enough to allow farmers to remain solvent and to decrease the numbers of evictions of tenant farmers and sharecroppers, who constituted the poorest and most vulnerable groups within agriculture. Funds to finance the AAA were obtained by levying a tax on food processors.[78]

As with the NRA, however, large producers often used the AAA to advance their own financial interests since they often established production policies that were favorable to themselves but harmful to small farmers and took their poorest land from production to avoid having to reduce their overall production. Many producers pocketed their growing profits and evicted tenant farmers and sharecroppers.

The AAA developed safeguards to forestall abuse of tenant farmers by landowners, but evictions continued because it lacked the staff to monitor landowners. The AAA required landowners to pass on to tenants a specified percentage of the monies they obtained from the government for taking acreage from production, but they often ignored this provision or gave sharecroppers a lower percentage of their funds. An association of tenant farmers and sharecroppers, the Southern Tenant Farmers Association, was formed in 1934 to try to stop evictions, but

grass-roots advocacy was difficult for this dispersed and impoverished group that included many low-income African Americans.[79]

Roosevelt tried to provide assistance to millions of farmers and homeowners who were threatened with foreclosure. Farm mortgages were directly purchased and refinanced by the government when the Emergency Farm Mortgage Act and the Farm Relief Act were enacted in 1933. As to homeowners, the Roosevelt administration decided to take an indirect role; rather than helping homeowners directly, the National Housing Act of 1934 established the Federal Home Administration (FHA) to insure mortgages and home improvement loans so that banks could refinance them at lower rates of interest.[80]

Why not, some persons asked, use the power of the federal government to orchestrate the economic development of entire regions since vast river systems in the United States, including the Mississippi and Missouri rivers, could be made to yield power if dams, generators, and transmission lines were constructed? The most prominent legislative advocate of regional development schemes was George Norris, a progressive Republican senator from Nebraska, who had made river development his major interest and who worked closely with Roosevelt to secure its passage.

The first project, the Tennessee Valley Authority (TVA), was established in 1933 and governed by a commission that was established to oversee development of a network of dams and generating plants. The TVA sold electricity to power cooperatives and local towns, manufactured and sold fertilizer, reforested vast amounts of land, and built flood-control projects. It was partially responsible for the economic rebirth of a vast section of America with minimal cost to the government owing to proceeds from the sale of power and fertilizer. Private power companies, which often charged excessive fees for their power, protested vigorously that the federal government was competing unfairly with them and used many legal and political strategies to sabotage the TVA, such as trying to place allies on the commission that established policy for the TVA. Defenders of the TVA were able to institutional-ize the experiment, however, even if they were unable to obtain extension of their bold design to the Missouri and other large river systems.[81]

## EMERGENCY OR PERMANENT PROGRAMS?

The federal social programs evolved as much from necessity as philosophy; since the nation's citizens and its local and state governments tee-tered on the brink of bankruptcy, Americans *had* to take ameliorative action, but no philoso-phy of socialism, which extolled major govern-mental roles as well as redistribution of re-sources from the rich to the poor, had strong roots in the United States. Would Americans, then, institutionalize their social reforms of 1933 and 1934 or dismantle them at the first opportunity?

Events of early 1934 were not encouraging to many social reformers. Roosevelt, under severe pressure to cut spending in order to reduce deficits, terminated the CWA in 1934 despite protests from many reformers.[82] He slowed the momentum of social programs for political rea-sons as well. Although he had won a sweeping victory in 1932, as well as control of both houses of Congress, he feared a conservative resurgence in congressional elections in Novem-ber 1934 since many persons were grumbling about welfare cheaters and loafers in the FERA, CWA, and PWA. Business and conservative interests, which had been on the defensive and in disarray in 1933 and early 1934, had also begun to develop a political counteroffensive. More-over, Roosevelt had his own doubts about the advisability of retaining a strong federal role in public welfare since he had always favored giving local governments the responsibility for welfare problems. He had developed the FERA because states were verging on bankruptcy in 1932, but he did not want to institutionalize it, and he did not want the federal government to assume a permanent job-creation role. He continued to hope that the economic Depression would lift so that the sheer size of federal programs could be diminished though advisors like Hopkins feared that the government would have to continue to fund public works indefinitely.[83]

Americans tend to believe that social prob-lems are abnormal or unusual phenomena that can be solved by the development of specific policies. This optimistic and problem-solving orientation is illustrated by the prolific efforts of nineteenth-century reformers to end pauperism, mental illness, crime, and alcoholism, as well as by the regulations that some Progressives believed would eliminate exploitation by corpo-rations, politicians, landlords, and drug compa-nies. Some New Deal reformers hoped as well that a frantic round of reforms would restore prosperity and eliminate poverty and unemploy-ment. Alas, none of these reformers—and none who have succeeded them—has been able to make American society into the problem-free utopia that Jefferson had desired at the inception of the republic.

Perhaps it is sensible to create and sustain many social programs that help suffering and poor citizens while we continue to try (as best we can) to develop solutions. Europeans in the Middle Ages perceived social problems as en-demic to the social fabric; though such fatalism may sometimes impede efforts to prevent or solve problems, it also promotes ongoing pro-grams to address societal needs. The American impatience with existing policies, which con-tributes to volatile and confusing shifts in policy that sometimes leave victims stranded, stems in part from a naive expectation that a problem-free society can be created.

## THE POLITICAL ECONOMY OF SOCIAL POLICY IN THE NEW DEAL

The years 1933 and 1934 could easily be selected as the most decisive years in the emergence of the modern American welfare state. The nature of social obligation was broadened to include farmers, the unemployed, destitute teenagers, homeowners, inhabitants of large river basins, and transient persons. Government officials undertook projects not only to help destitute persons but also to develop public works, a host of fiscal and monetary interventions, and efforts to stabilize wages and prices. Furthermore, when the federal government became the prime funder and organizer of these various undertakings, the tradition of relying on local welfare programs was decisively shattered, even if federal authorities asked the states to be collaborators with them in funding and implementing the new programs.

Many Americans began to change their notions about some of the five moral issues we discussed in Chapter 1 as they viewed the new policy developments of Roosevelt's first two years in office. Policies and ideas that had hitherto been taboo or restricted to a few avant-garde reformers were now both permissible and operational. Federal authorities could develop national programs with speed and efficiency—and those programs were widely perceived to be the difference between life and death for millions of destitute Americans. Once the new policies were in place, there was no turning back to the restrictive welfare traditions of the nineteenth century precisely because many Americans saw that the new policies, though imperfect, were preferable to traditional policies that now seemed mean-minded and anachronistic.

## END NOTES

1. Lela Costin, *Two Sisters for Social Justice* (Urbana, Ill.: University of Illinois Press, 1984), pp. 11–116.

2. William Leuchtenberg, *Perils of Prosperity, 1914–1932* (Chicago: University of Chicago Press, 1958). Some reformers remained active, as discussed by Clarke Chambers in *Seedtime of Reform: American Social Service and Social Action, 1918–1933* (Minneapolis, Minn.: University of Minnesota Press, 1963).

3. Leuchtenberg, *Perils,* pp. 179, 186.

4. *Ibid.,* p. 98.

5. David Brody, *Workers in Industrial America: Essays on the Twentieth-Century Struggle* (New York: Oxford University Press, 1980), pp. 48–78.

6. John Kirby, *Black Americans in the Roosevelt Era: Liberalism and Race* (Knoxville, Tenn.: University of Tennessee Press, 1980), p. 3; Raymond Wolters, *Negroes and the Great Depression: The Problem of Economic Recovery* (Westport, Conn.: Greenwood Press, 1970), p. 7.

7. Cary McWilliams, *North from Mexico: The Spanish-Speaking People of the United States* (New York: Greenwood Press, 1968), pp. 215–226.

8. Nancy Woloch, *Women and the American Experience* (New York: Knopf, 1984), pp. 382–388.

9. Leuchtenberg, *Perils,* pp. 204–224.

10. Maldwyn Jones, *American Immigration* (Chicago: University of Chicago Press, 1960), pp. 270–281.

11. Leuchtenberg, *Perils,* pp. 163–188; Roy Lubove, *The Professional Altruist* (Cambridge, Mass.: Harvard University Press, 1965), pp. 85–89.

12. Lubove, *The Professional Altruist,* pp. 124–156; John Ehrenreich, *The Altruistic Imagination: A His-*

tory of Social Work and Social Policy in the United States (Ithaca, N.Y.: Cornell University Press, 1985), pp. 43–77.

13. John Galbraith, *The Great Crash, 1929* (Boston: Houghton Mifflin, 1957), pp. 180–183.

14. Robert McElvaine, *The Great Depression: America, 1929–1941* (New York: New York Times Book Co., 1984), pp. 25–50.

15. William Bremer, *Depression Winters: New York Social Workers and the New Deal* (Philadelphia: Temple University Press, 1984), pp. 88–100; Charles Trout, *Boston, the Great Depression, and the New Deal* (New York: Oxford University Press, 1977), pp. 90–92.

16. Eliot Rosen, *Hoover, Roosevelt, and the Brains Trust: From Depression to New Deal* (New York: Columbia University Press, 1977), pp. 39–65.

17. Chambers, *Seedtime of Reform,* pp. 185–207; Joseph Huthmacher, *Senator Robert F. Wagner and the Rise of Urban Liberalism* (New York: Atheneum, 1968), pp. 71–102.

18. Chambers, *Seedtime of Reform,* pp. 217–218; Lee Kraeder, "Isaac Max Rubinow: Pioneering Specialist in Social Insurance," *Social Service Review,* 50 (September 1976), 293–298.

19. Trout, *Boston,* pp. 62–63, 97–100.

20. McElvaine, *The Great Depression,* pp. 69–71.

21. Allen Davis, *The Life and Legend of Jane Addams* (New York: Oxford University Press, 1973), pp. 287–288.

22. Bremer, *Depression Winters,* pp. 101–113.

23. William Leuchtenberg, *Franklin Roosevelt and the New Deal: 1932–1940* (New York: Harper & Row, 1963), pp. 1–3, 18–31; Trout, *Boston,* pp. 71–93.

24. Trout, *Boston,* pp. 56–72.

25. Eric Schattschneider, *The Semisovereign People* (New York: Holt, Rinehart & Winston, 1960), pp. 86–89.

26. McElvaine, *The Great Depression,* pp. 6–7.

27. Richard Lowitt and Maurine Beasley, eds., *One Third of a Nation* (Urbana, Ill.: University of Illinois Press, 1981).

28. Leuchtenberg, *Franklin Roosevelt,* p. 1.

29. Arthur MacMahon, John Millett, and Gladys Ogden, *The Administration of Federal Work Relief* (Chicago: Public Administration Service, 1941), pp. 183–184, 334–341.

30. James Patterson, *Congressional Conservatism and the New Deal* (Lexington, Ky.: University of Kentucky Press, 1967), pp. 4–7.

31. Rosen, *Hoover,* pp. 303–328.

32. Patterson, *Congressional Conservatism,* pp. 13–31.

33. Rosen, *Hoover,* pp. 308–314.

34. Trout, *Boston,* p. xi.

35. George Flynn, *American Catholics and the Roosevelt Presidency, 1932–1936* (Lexington, Ky.: University of Kentucky Press, 1968).

36. Ronald A. Mulder, *The Insurgent Progressives in the United States Senate and the New Deal* (New York: Garland, 1979), pp. 12–13; Patterson, *Congressional Conservatism,* pp. 154–155, 160–161.

37. Brody, *Workers,* pp. 82–105.

38. *Ibid.,* pp. 166–172.

39. *Ibid.,* pp. 107–116.

40. Lowitt and Beasley, *One-Third of a Nation,* p. 213; Trout, *Boston,* pp. 208–209.

41. Edward White, *The American Judicial Tradition: Profiles of Leading American Judges* (New York: Oxford University Press, 1976), pp. 178–199.

42. Henry Adams, *Harry Hopkins* (New York: Putnam, 1977), pp. 60–62; Bremer, *Depression Winters,* pp. 135–136.

43. George Martin, *Madam Secretary: Frances Perkins* (Boston: Houghton Mifflin, 1976), pp. 245–247; Lillian Mohr, *Frances Perkins* (Croton-on-Hudson, N.Y.: North River Press, 1979), pp. 131–133.

44. John Salmond, *A Southern Rebel: The Life and Times of Aubrey Willis Williams, 1890–1965* (Chapel Hill, N.C.: University of North Carolina Press, 1983), pp. 45–56.

45. Patterson, *Congressional Conservatism,* pp. 32–76.

46. Leuchtenberg, *Franklin Roosevelt,* pp. 326–328.

47. G. D. H. Cole and Raymond Postgate, *The British Common People, 1746–1946* (New York: Knopf, 1939), pp. 587–614.

48. Brody, *Workers,* pp. 120–129.

49. Lowitt and Beasley, *One-Third of a Nation,* pp. 5–6, 12–13, 31–32.

50. *Ibid.,* pp. 70–71, 78–82, 94–95.

51. Leuchtenberg, *Franklin Roosevelt,* pp. 87–89.

52. Margaret Weir and Theda Skocpol, "State Structures and the Possibility of 'Keynesian' Responses to the Great Depression in Sweden, Britain, and the United States." In Peter Evans, Dietrich Rueschemeyer, and Theda Skocpol, eds., *Bringing the State Back In* (Cambridge: Cambridge University Press, 1985), p. 145.

53. Leuchtenberg, *Franklin Roosevelt,* pp. 145–149, 256; Martin, *Madam Secretary,* pp. 258–260; Salmond, *A Southern Rebel,* pp. 68–70.

54. Bremer, *Depression Winters,* pp. 134–141, 155–157, 165, 167–170; Martin, *Madam Secretary,* pp. 258–259; McElvaine, *The Great Depression,* pp. 250–263.

55. Bremer, *Depression Winters,* p. 129.

56. Adams, *Harry Hopkins,* pp. 52–53, 71–72.

57. Josephine Brown, *Public Relief, 1929–1939* (New York: Holt, 1940), pp. 146–159, 171–190, 218–298.

58. Trout, *Boston,* pp. 148–149.

59. Lowitt and Beasley, *One-Third of a Nation,* p. 46.

60. Salmond, *A Southern Rebel,* pp. 45–56.

61. Harry Hopkins, *Spending to Save* (New York: Harper & Row, 1936), pp. 108–110.

62. Salmond, *A Southern Rebel,* pp. 55–56.

63. *Ibid.,* pp. 57–63.

64. *Ibid.,* p. 59.

65. John Salmond, *The Civilian Conservation Corps, 1933–1942* (Durham, N.C.: Duke University Press, 1967).

66. Adams, *Harry Hopkins,* pp. 57–58, 82–88.

67. Richard Lowitt, *George W. Norris: The Triumph of a Progressive, 1933–1944* (Urbana, Ill.: University of Illinois Press, 1981), pp. 95–109.

68. Martin, *Madam Secretary,* pp. 296–298; Mohr, *Frances Perkins,* p. 141.

69. Gilbert Steiner, *State of Welfare* (Washington, D.C.: Brookings Institution, 1971), pp. 198–199.

70. Rosen, *Hoover,* p. 59.

71. Susan Lee and Peter Passell, *A New Economic View of American History* (New York: Norton, 1979), pp. 383–387.

72. Dean May, *From New Deal to New Economics: The American Liberal Response to the Recession of 1937* (New York: Garland, 1981), pp. 160–161.

73. Leuchtenberg, *Franklin Roosevelt,* pp. 38–39, 42–46.

74. Wolters, *Negroes,* pp. 83–90.

75. *Ibid.,* pp. 83–90.

76. Lowitt and Beasley, *One-Third of a Nation,* pp. 341–346, 356.

77. Mohr, *Frances Perkins,* pp. 163–170; Wolters, *Negroes,* pp. 169–192.

78. Wolters, *Negroes,* pp. 3–38.

79. *Ibid.,* pp. 21–77.

80. Leuchtenberg, *Franklin Roosevelt,* p. 52.

81. Lowitt, *George W. Norris,* pp. 16–25, 110–125.

82. Bremer, *Depression Winters,* pp. 134–136.

83. Adams, *Harry Hopkins,* p. 61; Leuchtenberg, *Franklin Roosevelt,* pp. 91–94.

# CHAPTER 8

# Institutionalizing the New Deal

## Selected Orienting Events
## in the Middle and Latter Stages of the New Deal

| | |
|---|---|
| **1934** | Committee on Economic Security established by Roosevelt |
| **1935** | FERA terminated; Social Security Act passed with its constituent programs of Aid to Dependent Children (ADC), Old-Age Assistance (OAA), Aid to the Blind (AB), unemployment insurance, Social Security, child welfare, and public health programs |
| **1935** | Supreme Court declares the AAA and NRA to be unconstitutional; Senator Huey Long assassinated; Works Progress Administration (WPA) established |
| **1936** | Father Coughlin and Francis Townsend support the Union party; Congress of Industrial Organizations (CIO) established; Wagner Act passed establishing the National Labor Relations Board |
| **1936** | Roosevelt wins landslide victory for his second term |
| **1937** | Deep recession ends nation's economic recovery; Wagner-Steagall Housing Act passed |
| **1938** | Fair Employment Practices Act enacted |
| **1939** | Federal Security Agency established |
| **Early 1940s** | CCC, WPA, and NYA are terminated |
| **1940** | Roosevelt elected to third term |
| **1941** | America enters World War II; Executive Order 8802 prohibits discrimination in war industry |
| **1942** | Some 110,000 persons of Japanese ancestry evacuated to relocation centers |
| **1945** | Roosevelt dies and is succeeded by Harry Truman |

## THE SECOND NEW DEAL

The period from November 1934 to November 1936 has been called the second New Deal since new reforms were established that supplemented or replaced earlier reforms, but this term unduly emphasizes discontinuity in New Deal reforms. Indeed, because Roosevelt, Perkins, Moley, and others had supported from the outset many policies that were enacted during this period, including old-age pensions, unemployment insurance, and higher taxes on wealthy persons, it is more accurate to portray New Deal policies in this period as a logical sequel to reforms in the preceding two years. The early reforms were admittedly improvisational and focused on rescuing bankrupt local governments and righting the economy. Reforms in the second period represented Roosevelt's efforts to decide which ongoing welfare functions the federal government should assume and what its relationship toward organized labor should be.[1]

### Liberal Forces and the Second New Deal

When Roosevelt won a smashing victory in the congressional elections of November 1934, Harry Hopkins and other social reformers believed they could finally prevail over both Republicans and budget-balancers within the Democratic party. Hopkins said to fellow reformers:

> Boys, this is our hour. We've got to get everything we want—a works program, social security, wages and hours (regulation), everything—now or never. Put your minds to work in developing a complete ticket to provide security for all the folks of this country up and down and across the board.[2]

Hopkins proposed the End Poverty in America (EPIA) plan, which included an ongoing federal jobs program, a massive low-cost housing program, a set of insurance programs, establishment of large manufacturing centers, and new rural programs to help poor farmers acquire land and equipment.[3]

Liberals were joined by various persons and groups who wanted Roosevelt to regain reform momentum. Huey Long, the charismatic and demagogic senator from Louisiana, pressured Roosevelt to place heavy taxes on incomes and estates of millionaires, to greatly expand federal works programs, and to pay a higher wage to workers in public works projects. He believed that the NRA and the AAA were little more than agencies that protected the interests of large industrialists and landowners. He criticized the low wages of the CWA and attacked the budget-cutting inclinations of Roosevelt. As a militant defender of small farmers and small businessmen, he believed that their economic opportunities remained limited, resented affluent elites, and often disliked the large bureaucracies of the New Deal.[4]

Another liberal supporter, Father Charles Coughlin, a popular Jesuit priest from Detroit, attracted a massive audience to his national radio show when he proposed a variety of federal regulations of the banking system and monetary reforms. His initial support for Roosevelt turned to opposition when FDR failed to support his economic measures.[5] Other reformers concentrated on single issues. Francis Townsend, a dentist in Long Beach, California, proposed and popularized a scheme to pay a monthly pension of $200 per month to all American citizens over the age of sixty on the condition that they pledge to spend it within thirty days and agree to give up all other income. It was to be financed from a federal sales tax. He hoped the scheme would simultaneously relieve grinding poverty among the elderly and revive the economy by requiring them to spend their monthly pensions before the end of each month. He obtained twenty million signatures on a petition by 1936.[6]

Representative Lundeen of Minnesota proposed a scheme of unemployment insurance in 1934 to pay unemployment compensation from the general revenues of the nation to all unemployed persons as long as they were unemployed through no fault of their own. (Unemployed workers were to receive benefits equal to prevailing wages, and persons with part-time work were to have their wages supplemented to bring them up to the prevailing standard.) The scheme was to be administered by worker and farmer organizations.[7]

A bipartisan cadre of liberals often voted together on public housing legislation, legislation protecting the rights of unions, antilynching (of African Americans) legislation, and fair labor standards. Indeed, Senator Wagner, a leading figure in this liberal bloc, pressured the administration to be more daring in its reform strategy by initiating reform measures without the approval of FDR.[8]

Roosevelt experienced mounting pressure from social reformers and social workers. An influential contingent of social workers from New York State had assumed a particularly important role in supporting reforms during the early years of the New Deal when they offered suggestions and assumed key positions within the administration. (Hopkins and Perkins were merely the most visible members of this community.)[9] Many of them had become disenchanted with the New Deal by 1934, however, since they resented the termination of the CWA, the opportunistic exploitation of the NRA by many businessmen, and the low levels of relief of the FERA and the CWA. Their anger mounted during 1935, when they believed Roosevelt hoped to disband federal assistance to many unemployed persons and destitute families. A radical contingent of the profession, led by Mary Van Kleeck, urged social workers to become radical critics of the New Deal rather than be coopted by Roosevelt.[10]

Reformist pressure also came from the burgeoning unions that represented unskilled workers. These workers and their organizers had been radicalized by the inhuman labor practices of the corporations, high rates of unemployment among unskilled workers, and the bloody suppression of strikes in automobile and steel plants and in coal mines. Such union leaders as Walter Reuther in the auto industry and John L. Lewis in mining developed growing constituencies and power. Although they had supported the establishment of the NRA because of its protections for unions, they wondered why the Roosevelt administration seemed content with the vague and poorly enforced provisions of the NRA to protect collective bargaining.[11]

The Southern Tenant Farmers Association (STFA) was formed to protect millions of agricultural laborers who found their lot even worse after passage of the AAA three years into the New Deal. A pathetically small number of African-American sharecroppers were helped by the FERA and the Resettlement Administration to obtain their own land, but most of them remained enmeshed in poverty and heavily indebted to landowners, who charged them excessive prices for seed, fertilizer, and food. The STFA asked the administration to stop the wave of evictions of tenant farmers (which occurred as landowners curbed production to reap payments from the AAA) and to help many landless persons obtain their own farms.[12]

Although workers, liberals, and African Americans were often critical of Roosevelt, they nonetheless perceived him as clearly superior to the Republican leaders, who became even more conservative and opposed to reform after the 1934 election. This support from the left emboldened Roosevelt to initiate and support reforms, not only because he wanted to keep their support but because it was conceivable that a popular rival could emerge to the left of FDR. A poll in 1935 suggested that Huey Long would receive six million votes if he were to run for president in 1936.[13] Father Coughlin and Townsend supported the Union Party in 1936, which frontally attacked Roosevelt as being too conservative and sought to defeat both the Democrats and Republicans in the elections of 1936. Rivalry among figures and groups on the left, the assassination of Huey Long in 1935, and the sheer popularity and tactical brilliance of Roosevelt doomed the political aspirations of many of these liberal leaders, but they pushed Roosevelt to consider policies that he might otherwise have neglected.[14]

## Conservative Pressures on Roosevelt

Though conservatives never loved Roosevelt, they sometimes tolerated him because of the economic straits of the nation. A conservative coalition consisting of Republicans, Southern Democrats, and some political moderates had developed considerable cohesion within the Congress by 1935, however, and rallied opposition to FDR's policies. Southern Democrats, who held many committee chairs in the House and Senate and who had traditionally possessed a good deal of power in the Democratic party, felt that their party had been taken over by liberal northerners and by urban reformers such as Senator Wagner. Their anger mounted when they were not consulted by Roosevelt on many policy issues. Business interests, which had often supported Democratic candidates, increasingly gave their allegiance and money to Republicans when confronted with tax legislation that proposed to markedly increase the taxes of affluent persons and corporations. Roosevelt's electoral successes drove the Republican party to increasingly militant opposition to the New Deal because they realized that their party might remain a minority party for decades if they could not arrest Roosevelt's political momentum.[15]

Roosevelt's political problems were compounded by the increasing opposition of a group of thirteen Republican senators, called the insurgent progressives, who were ideological descendants of the progressive era. They had provided vital support to New Deal programs during Roosevelt's first term and had championed agricultural reforms, the TVA, antimonopoly policies, and higher taxes on the wealthy, but they disliked large federal bureaucracies, feared Roosevelt had too much power, wished to preserve strong policy roles for states, and feared

the use of social programs for political patronage. They increasingly resented the deployment of a major portion of New Deal resources to urban areas and workers. Their distrust of Roosevelt and his policies reached paranoid proportions by 1936, when they were convinced that he sought to establish a dynasty beholden to urban interests. Their anger mounted in 1937 when Roosevelt attacked the Supreme Court and did not publicly rebuke the disruptive tactics of automobile workers. Furthermore, they had come to detest the size of the federal government. Their distrust of Roosevelt, which was reciprocated when he no longer consulted them, was reflected in their negative votes on many pieces of legislation and in their increasing cooperation with Southern Democrats and Republicans.[16]

Many middle-class Americans became less enamored with Roosevelt's policies by late 1935. Since many of them believed that individuals were personally responsible for their unemployment, they resented federal work and relief programs, which they believed sapped the initiative of recipients. They increasingly questioned Roosevelt's economic policies since the nation remained mired in the Depression. Considerable animus developed toward Harry Hopkins, who was perceived to be a welfare czar and who was widely believed to reward Democrats with jobs in the federal bureaucracy. Many Americans resented the burgeoning of the federal bureaucracies, which had become highly visible during the implementation of hundreds of New Deal programs. They also disliked the brains trust, academicians, and theorists whose ideas had not solved the nation's economic malaise.[17]

The Supreme Court gave legal sanction to the conservatives in 1935 when it declared the AAA and the NRA to be unconstitutional; indeed, the Court made twelve adverse rulings against the New Deal between January 1935 and June 1936 that rested on an assortment of constitutional objections. Roosevelt wondered whether virtually all major New Deal programs might be rescinded by the Court.[18]

# LEGISLATION IN THE SECOND NEW DEAL

When considered in tandem, then, these conservative pressures led Roosevelt to abandon certain reforms, to support some of them belatedly, and to dilute or compromise others. At the same time, the liberal pressures pushed FDR to sustain his reform momentum. This bewildering combination of liberal and conservative pressure contributed to confusing patterns of deletions, continuations, and additions to New Deal programs as well as to compromises in new legislation. Some programs of the first New Deal were discontinued—whether because Roosevelt had misgivings about them (the CWA and the FERA) or because they were declared unconstitutional (the AAA and NRA)—but others, such as the CCC and PWA, continued. Major new programs were created in the second New Deal, including the Social Security Act, the National Labor Relations Board (NLRB), the Works Progress Administration (WPA), and the National Youth Administration (NYA), but their form and size often reflected compromises with conservatives. Still other pieces of legislation were proposed but not enacted, such as antilynching, tax, and public-housing legislation.

## The Social Security Act

The Social Security Act, which is the Magna Carta of the American welfare state, contained many programs to address a variety of social problems. Roosevelt wanted to decide, once and for all, which relief functions would be maintained by federal and local governments. Second, he wanted to prevent economic destitution by developing social insurances to address the economic needs of unemployed and elderly persons. Finally, he wanted to develop some permanent and ongoing programs to constitute his legacy to the nation. Roosevelt had many policy interests, but he wanted a single piece of legislation to encapsulate them since he realized that

some relatively controversial measures, such as unemployment insurance, would not pass if they were not contained within a larger piece of legislation that contained more popular programs, such as old-age pensions and welfare assistance for older persons. He reasoned as well that the Supreme Court would find it more difficult to attack specific programs if they were part of multifaceted legislation.

To plan this legislation, Roosevelt appointed a Committee on Economic Security in June 1934 that was chaired by Frances Perkins and included the secretary of the treasury, the attorney general, the secretary of agriculture, and the administrator of the FERA. A large advisory committee and a technical committee were also formed. The committee accomplished its complex task with remarkable speed and was able, after marathon sessions during the Christmas holidays, to issue its final report on January 15, 1935. The legislation passed overwhelmingly in the Congress and was signed into law by Roosevelt in August 1935. The Social Security Act contained two social insurance programs, three relief programs, and other smaller programs.[19]

Social insurances, principally unemployment insurance and old-age pensions (Social Security), were attractive to Roosevelt for several reasons. They were self-funding programs since their benefits were financed from payroll taxes that were levied on employers and employees. Roosevelt favored use of the payroll tax so that future generations would not have to fund these programs from general revenues—and he liked both insurance programs because he believed they would reduce the size of welfare rolls as many older persons and unemployed workers were lifted above a threshold of poverty by their benefits. He also knew that insurances were politically acceptable to many Americans because they represented earned benefits rather than welfare payments.[20] Roosevelt initially showed little interest in Social Security because he was preoccupied with the needs of unemployed workers, but he vigorously declared his support of it when critical stories appeared in the press in 1934.[21]

Despite the political popularity of these programs, Roosevelt believed he needed to make concessions to conservatives to ensure their passage. Over the protests of some liberals, he supported a regressive system of payroll taxes that levied stiffer taxes on low-income wage earners than on more affluent persons, and he refused to contribute general revenues to Social Security. (Liberals believed the use of general revenues would have been more equitable and would have allowed major increases in the size of benefits.) Some liberals also opposed his decision, which was supported by southern agricultural interests, not to cover farm and domestic workers.[22]

Although Roosevelt made concessions to conservatives, he also made policy choices that defied them. Some persons believed that participation in Social Security should be voluntary, but FDR insisted on mandatory participation. Frances Perkins, a believer in states' rights, initially favored allowing each state to keep its own Social Security fund, but FDR rejected this policy when it was reckoned that movement of workers between states would make it unworkable.[23]

Originally conceived as a measure to provide pensions of retired workers, Social Security was broadened in 1939 to include family members of the worker. Arthur Altmeyer, chair of the Social Security Board, explained that "this system, formerly a plan to provide old-age annuities for individual wage earners, has become a broad system of family insurance, which protects not only the wage earner but his wife and children, and if they are dependent on him, his aged parents."[24] Social Security was amended to include benefits to the wives, widows, and children of retirees—a salutary step even if it was grounded on a patriarchal notion of the family where the male breadwinners could now help their wives who, it was widely assumed, would not work.[25]

Senator Wagner and other liberals had introduced various versions of a federal unemployment insurance program since 1933, but much controversy existed about how best to proceed. Should funds collected by a payroll tax on employers be kept in a central pool in Washington or in each of the states? Should central funds exist, or should separate accounts be maintained for each industry? Should the federal government assume the lead in administering the funds, devising the level and duration of unemployment benefits, and levying taxes? Should participation in the scheme by employers be mandatory or voluntary?

The ensuing unemployment insurance program that was placed in the Social Security Act represented an ingenious compromise to these policy alternatives. A payroll tax was levied on employers by states; though participation was technically voluntary, participating employers were given generous federal tax credits to offset most of their payroll taxes. States collected the payroll taxes, but they gave the revenues to the federal government, which maintained a central fund for each state that was then used to pay unemployment benefits to workers. The federal government paid the costs to the states of administering their programs. Although this plan sounds complicated, it was a rather simple scheme to allow most of the costs of unemployment insurance to be borne by the federal government while lending the appearance that participation by employers was voluntary.[26] Each state enacted its own unemployment insurance law, which determined benefit levels and duration. Many liberal critics contended that the legislation penalized states with high levels of unemployment since their funds would be more severely burdened than states with low levels of unemployment. Others feared that conservative states might choose to pay low benefits to unemployed persons. Why, some liberal critics asked, should workers have to be unemployed for four weeks before obtaining benefits? Many liberals favored federal contributions to the program to enable it to pay higher benefits and for longer periods. They feared that many workers would be forced onto welfare rolls when not able to survive on the meager assistance that was limited to roughly fourteen weeks in many states. Many liberals were unhappy that Roosevelt capitulated to special interests when he excluded domestics, cannery workers, and farm laborers from coverage. They were nonetheless delighted that FDR supported the concept of unemployment insurance and that he did not capitulate to those who wanted each state to have its separate unemployment program.[27]

The Federal Emergency Relief Administration was supported by many liberals because it gave relief to a broad range of needy Americans, including families, single persons, older persons, and nonworking and working poor persons. Many liberals were furious when it became apparent that Roosevelt decided to scuttle the FERA and replace it with federal relief programs to only three groups of destitute persons—elderly persons (Old-Age Assistance, or OAA), children in families with one caretaker (Aid to Dependent Children, or ADC), and blind persons (Aid to the Blind, or AB).[28] All other destitute persons, including single nonelderly persons and families with two parents, were returned to local or general assistance welfare programs, which were entirely funded by state and local resources. Many of these poor relief agencies were punitive in their orientations and racist in their administration of policy.

These three programs followed a similar format. States received matching or formula funds from the federal government. Under OAA, for example, the federal government paid one-half of local grants for each eligible person as long as local grants did not exceed $30 per month. (The federal government paid only one-third of ADC grants.) Federal authorities insisted that a state agency be designated to implement the programs, that uniform standards of eligibility be established within each state to preclude specific counties from developing relatively punitive policies, and that fair hearings be established so that aggrieved recipients could appeal eligibility decisions.[29]

Liberal critics were pleased that Roosevelt had developed some permanent programs, but they were displeased that many persons were shunted to local welfare programs. They contended that the legislation mistakenly gave states the power to establish eligibility standards and levels of benefits. Would not southern and relatively conservative states, they asked, make their programs so restrictive that they would deny assistance to vast numbers of poor persons and minority persons? Since federal authorities were given no power over personnel decisions of the states and were not required to use social workers in supervisory positions, critics wondered if patronage would dominate personnel decisions of local agencies.[30] Some liberals were also unhappy that the ADC program restricted assistance to families with a single parent or that the welfare grants to these families included funds only for the children and not for the parent. The policy limiting the grants to children was not amended until 1950, when the name of the program was changed to Aid to Families with Dependent Children (AFDC). Even this restrictive program was more liberal than a version that was advocated by some social workers, who wanted relief to be given only to those children who were found, on casework investigation, to reside in "suitable homes," on the grounds that so many destitute mothers provided improper care.[31] As many persons had predicted, eligibility standards and grant levels were far more restrictive in southern and rural states than in industrial states in succeeding decades, and southerners kept benefits low to force many African-American women and their children to labor in cotton and tobacco fields, where they were paid miserable wages.[32]

Limited as they were, OAA, ADC, and AB were the first permanent and major federal relief programs. Many persons believed in 1935 that they would be extremely small programs; Social Security benefits, it was thought, would allow elderly persons to escape the OAA program; ADC did not attract much attention since most people thought it would be a federal–state version

**TABLE 8.1** • *Summary of the major provisions of the Social Security Act*

---

*TITLE I: GRANTS TO STATES FOR OLD-AGE ASSISTANCE*

---

| | |
|---|---|
| *Nature of Grants* | Secretary of treasury pays to each state 50 percent of the sums expended in a year for assistance to people over age sixty-five who are not inmates of public institutions and not including that portion of payments that exceed $30 per month. (Five percent of the federal payments are used to administer the programs by the states.) |
| *Requirements That States Must Meet* | Each state must:<br>Have a state plan for old-age assistance that is in effect in all political subdivisions of the state and that is mandatory on them<br>Pay for the nonfederal share of the costs of assistance<br>Designate a single state agency to administer the plan (or supervise the plan if local jurisdictions administer part of it)<br>Establish an opportunity for a fair hearing before the state agency for anyone who is denied assistance<br>Provide for method of selecting personnel and administering the grants that are found by the Social Security Board to be necessary for the efficient operation of the plan<br>Provide to the Social Security Board such information and data that it requests<br>Pay to the United States one-half of the net amount collected by any state (or its subdivisions) from the estate of any recipient of old-age assistance |
| *Requirements That the Social Security Board Cannot Impose on the States* | An age requirement of more than sixty-five years<br>Any residence requirement that excludes any resident of a state who has resided therein five years during the nine years immediately preceding application and who has resided therein continuously for one year immediately preceding the application |

---

*TITLE II: FEDERAL OLD-AGE BENEFITS*

---

| | |
|---|---|
| *Establishing the Trust Fund* | An account is created in the U.S. Treasury, known as the Old-Age Reserve Account, to which the funds are appropriated for each fiscal year an amount sufficient to provide for the payments under this title to retired persons |
| *Definition of Eligibility* | People who are at least sixty-five years of age who have received after December 31, 1936, and before reaching age sixty-five a total amount of wages not less than $2,000. Ineligible persons include:<br>Agricultural laborers<br>Domestic servants<br>Casual labor not in the course of the employer's trade or business<br>Service performed as an officer or member of the crew of a vessel documented under the laws of the United States or of any foreign country<br>Service performed in the employment of the United States government<br>Service performed in the employment of state governments or political subdivisions thereof<br>Service performed in the employment of not-for-profit agencies |

**TABLE 8.1** • *continued*

---

*TITLE II: FEDERAL OLD-AGE BENEFITS continued*

---

| | |
|---|---|
| *Amounts of Benefits* | If total wages after December 31, 1936, and before he reached sixty-five are not more than $3,000, the old-age benefit shall be at a monthly rate of one-half of 1 percent of such total wages |
| | If these total wages are more than $3,000, the monthly rate will be one-half of 1 percent of the first $3,000 plus one-twelfth of 1 percent of total wages that exceed $3,000 and do not exceed $45,000 |
| | But in no case shall the monthly rate exceed $85 |
| | If someone dies before reaching sixty-five, there shall be paid to his estate an amount equal to 3.5 percent of the total wages determined by the Board to have been paid to him with respect to employment after December 31, 1936 |

*TITLE III: GRANTS TO STATES FOR UNEMPLOYMENT COMPENSATION ADMINISTRATION*

---

The federal government authorized to be appropriated funds to help states administer their unemployment compensation laws (Title IX discusses the actual unemployment program) provided that the state provides fair and efficient methods of implementing the program, including fair hearings. (If a state agency denies benefits unfairly, the Board can stop making further payments to that state.)

The Social Security Board, on collecting funds in the unemployment fund of each state, will give it to the secretary of the treasury who will place it in the Unemployment Trust Fund.

Each state agency administering the program pays its benefits from funds from the Unemployment Trust Fund that are forwarded to it by federal authorities.

*TITLE IV: GRANTS TO STATES FOR AID TO DEPENDENT CHILDREN*

---

| | |
|---|---|
| *Nature of Grants* | States make payments of needy dependent children with the federal government paying to each state an amount equal to one-third of the total of the sums expended in a given quarter, but not counting the amount of grants that exceed $18 per month with respect to one dependent child (in a family) and $12 per month with respect to each additional dependent child. |
| *Eligibility* | The term *dependent child* means a child under age sixteen deprived of parental support by reason of death, continued absence from the home, or physical or mental incapacity of a parent—and the child must be living with his father, mother, grandfather, grandmother, brother, sister, stepfather, stepmother, stepbrother, stepsister, uncle, or aunt in a place of residence maintained by one or more of such relatives as his or their own home. |
| *Requirements That States Must Meet* | See requirements under Title I, which are similar to ones for ADC, though states cannot deny aid to any child who has resided in the state for one year immediately preceding the application or who was born within the state within one year of the application if its mother has resided in the state for one year immediately preceding the birth. |

(continued)

**TABLE 8.1** • *continued*

---

### TITLE V: GRANTS TO STATES FOR MATERNAL AND CHILD WELFARE

---

There are five parts to Title V:

| | |
|---|---|
| *Part 1* | Provides funds to be paid to the states to enable them to extend and improve services for promoting the health of mothers and children, especially in rural areas and in areas suffering from severe economic distress. (States must have plans for the services funded by the part approved by the chief of the Children's Bureau. (The state plan must include state contributions to the services and administration or supervision of the spending by the state's health agency.) |
| *Part 2* | Provides federal funds for helping each state extend and improve services for locating crippled children and providing them with medical, surgical, corrective, and other services and care, particularly in rural areas and areas with severe economic distress. State plans must be approved by the chief of the Children's Bureau. |
| *Part 3* | Provides funds for the purpose of enabling the Children's Bureau to cooperate with state public-welfare agencies to establish, extend, and strengthen public welfare services, called child-welfare services, for the protection and care of homeless, dependent, and neglected children, and children in danger of becoming delinquent. |
| *Part 4* | Provides funds to the states to allow them to extend and strengthen their programs of vocational rehabilitation of the physically disabled—and to allow them to continue to carry out legislation enacted in 1920 to provide vocational rehabilitation to persons disabled in industry or otherwise to help them return to employment. |
| *Part 5* | Provides funds for the maintenance of the Children's Bureau. |

---

### TITLE X: GRANTS TO STATES FOR AID TO THE BLIND

---

| | |
|---|---|
| Nature of the Grant | The federal government pays one-half of the funds expended by a state for aid to blind persons but not counting expenditures exceeding $30 a month—and 5 percent of the federal funds are to be used to administer the program. Blind people cannot be inmates of public institutions to receive assistance under this title. |
| *Requirements That States Must Meet* | Similar requirements exist as those noted in Title I. |

---

of mothers' pension programs; and AB applied only to a relatively small disabled population.[33] Had they guessed the future size of OAA and ADC rolls or realized that Aid to the Blind would be expanded in the 1950s and subsequent decades to include mentally and physically disabled persons, many conservatives, and possibly Roosevelt himself, might have tried to relegate these groups to local relief programs.

Reformers were able to obtain provisions in the Social Security Act that provided grants to localities for child welfare and maternal health programs (Title V) and public health programs (Title VI). The amounts of money involved were small; $1.5 million was authorized for the child welfare funds, but the money was allowed to be used only for the administrative costs of state agencies. These small grant programs nonetheless represented grudging acceptance of the notion that local governments needed federal assistance in providing a range of social welfare services. Not until the 1960s were federal programs enacted to fund a range of mental health, health, and other services.

The Social Security Act created programs that would have been unthinkable five years earlier. (See Table 8.1 for a summary of its major provisions.) It committed the federal government to permanent funding of an assortment of programs. However, many concessions were made to Southern Democrats and other conservatives in the specific programs, and many programs were missing from the legislation altogether. Roosevelt had contemplated including national health programs in the act, but he changed his mind because he feared that opposition from the American Medical Association and conservatives could imperil its passage. A public works program was not placed within the Social Security Act because of the controversy it would have generated.[34]

## Labor and Public Works Legislation

The National Labor Board that was established under the NRA had mediated conflicts between thousands of employers and employees. Senator Wagner proposed legislation that more clearly defined specific procedures to be followed when employees wanted to initiate a union and proposed establishment of an independent board to enforce the rights of union organizers. He fervently believed that such legislation would not only eliminate conflict but bring economic recovery by increasing consumer purchasing power through wage increases that would follow the growth of unions.[35] He proposed allowing employees to circulate petitions to their fellow workers if they wanted an election to choose a collective bargaining agent and requiring secret elections, to be monitored by a National Labor Relations Board (NLRB), if more than 50 percent of them requested it. Employers would have to officially recognize any collective bargaining agent that subsequently received support from a majority of employees, could not fire or intimidate organizers, and could not claim that a company union sufficed when workers wanted to hold elections.

Roosevelt demurred from supporting Senator Wagner's legislation when he introduced it in 1934 because he wanted the pace of union organizing to proceed gradually to avoid political backlash from business and the general public. He also wanted to place the NLRB within the Department of Labor rather than establishing it as an independent agency so that Frances Perkins could administer it. When the NRA was declared unconstitutional in May 1935, however, he supported Wagner's legislation, which had already been enacted in the Senate.[36] Despite strong opposition from business, the Wagner Act was enacted in 1936. It was partly responsible for an upsurge of union membership, which increased from 3.3 million workers in 1935 to 14 million workers in 1945, but its role should not be exaggerated since many employers ignored it, many companies finally capitulated to unions because they feared strikes would decrease their profits, and the government vigorously enforced collective bargaining during World War II to avert work stoppages.[37]

Soon after he terminated the CWA in early 1934, Roosevelt decided to develop a new work program to consolidate existing federal jobs programs into one piece of legislation. The legislation, entitled the Emergency Relief Appropriation Act, was enacted in 1935. He required most of its funds to go directly to wages rather than to administrative overhead and to be spent quickly rather than held back for long-term projects. He mandated socially useful projects to be allocated to areas in relation to the number of workers who were on welfare rolls.[38]

The intense rivalry that had existed between Ickes and Hopkins in 1933 continued following passage of the legislation. Both men wanted to head this new consolidated agency and sought Roosevelt's support. Roosevelt favored Hopkins, but he had to move gingerly so as not to alienate Ickes, congressional conservatives who disliked Hopkins, or congressmen who wanted to exercise patronage in the new massive jobs agency. (Congress insisted that appointments of all persons earning more than $5,000 be subject to the consent of the Senate.)

Roosevelt developed regulations that allowed the work programs to avoid undue patronage and placed them under Hopkins' control. He made himself the nominal head of the agency in order to curtail efforts by senators to place political friends in key jobs. He placed Ickes in charge of a large decision-making committee that had the official power to decide which work projects to fund, but he placed Hopkins in charge of a division that was empowered to recommend small work projects and to veto other project applications. As mayors, governors, and other local officials initiated thousands of modest street, library, and public improvement projects, Hopkins forwarded them to the decision-making committees, which *had* to fund them to meet Roosevelt's guideline that work funds be spent immediately. Hopkins used his veto power to defeat many of Ickes's large and complex projects on the grounds they competed with the private sector or insufficient skilled labor existed to implement them. When the frustrated Ickes obtained a ruling that all projects of more than $25,000 should be given to the PWA rather than to Hopkins's division, Hopkins merely divided the larger projects into bundles of smaller ones.[39]

The programs of Hopkins's division, named the Works Progress Administration (WPA),

dominated Roosevelt's public works strategy. Fourteen billion dollars were allocated to it between 1935 and 1940, when 7.8 million persons received work relief. The WPA completed a remarkable array of projects and assumed a major role in disaster relief work, including floods, droughts, and hurricanes. Millions of Americans obtained some semblance of dignity as they worked on these projects. The WPA inherited the local, state, and federal staff of the FERA, which was phased out following passage of the Social Security Act. Approval of projects was ultimately made in Washington, but district or state branches of the WPA initiated and approved projects in consultation with local and state officials. Various administrative arrangements were established; some projects were completely supervised by local officials, and others by WPA staff. Local units of government were usually required to contribute some 20 percent of a project's costs through provision of in-kind costs.[40]

The WPA was criticized from both the left and the right. Conservatives believed that it provided make-work jobs to persons who sought public jobs rather than work in the private sector and that it competed with the private sector. Hopkins's tireless advocacy of the program and his troubleshooting to deal with periodic crises in the field proved enough, however, to offset conservative criticism. Organized labor demanded that the WPA establish wages to correspond to prevailing wages, but Roosevelt preferred a so-called security wage that was pitched between relief benefits and prevailing wages. Critics questioned Roosevelt's policy to restrict the WPA to persons who were already on welfare rolls since this policy penalized many destitute persons who had avoided welfare. (Roughly 85 percent of WPA enrollees came from welfare rolls.) Other critics objected to the discrepancy between the wages of unskilled and skilled workers since the former received half the wages of the latter. To distribute WPA jobs broadly, only one member of a family was allowed to participate, but the policy often meant that women and adolescents could not receive work relief since administrators often gave jobs to male heads of household. The WPA did not provide training to its workers or match workers to jobs so that they could increase their employment prospects while holding WPA jobs. It did not enjoy good working relationships with public welfare and employment offices, which lacked the staff to make sufficient referrals to it.[41] The WPA was never funded at levels to help more than two-thirds of eligible persons, and Roosevelt declined to institutionalize it by placing it within the Social Security Act since some of his advisors did not want temporary programs placed within the act.[42] Both Congress and the president seemed to fear that a declaration of a permanent works program implied an admis-sion to voters that they had failed to correct the nation's economic problems, so the program struggled along with an uncertain future.[43]

At the insistence of Eleanor Roosevelt, who was a determined advocate for youth, the National Youth Administration (NYA) was established within the WPA with Aubrey Williams as its director. A broad range of programs was established, including college aid for impoverished students, aid for high school students, public jobs in recreation centers and municipal services, and camps for rural youth to provide them with trade skills. Six hundred thousand youths, many of them in extreme poverty, were aided by the NYA in 1936 and 1937 even though NYA wages were only one-third the level of prevailing wages.[44]

## THE ERA OF STALEMATE: 1936–1941

Roosevelt won a resounding victory in 1936 when the liberal coalition of intellectuals, workers, Jews, and racial minorities coalesced to provide the bulwark of his support. Eighty percent of the working class voted for him, compared to only 42 percent of affluent persons. He was, moreover, successful in retaining the support of the conservative South, which had traditionally voted Democratic. After Roosevelt's smashing presidential victory in November 1936, everyone was asking where the New Deal would go next. Hopkins, Senator Wagner, and others believed that Roosevelt had received a mandate to continue New Deal reforms to obtain public-housing programs, federal regulation of child labor and working conditions, an expansion of the WPA, and antilynching legislation.[45] Other advisors believed the victory represented only a personal mandate and urged him merely to consolidate his gains in a quiet second term. Although he often sought liberal reforms, Roosevelt's reform momentum halted in this era of stalemate.

Roosevelt's policies during this period manifested the same curious mixture of liberalism and conservatism that had marked his policies in other phases of the New Deal. He wanted to sustain his reform momentum since he had become increasingly irritated by business, banking, and industrial elites who had attacked New Deal programs and the proposed tax legislation that required them to pay higher taxes. He used class-oriented language in the election of 1936 when he attacked the selfishness and conservativeness of business elites. He was furious at Southern Democrats, who had increasingly allied themselves with Republicans to attack New Deal programs. Furthermore, he feared that his legislation would be dismantled by the Supreme Court, which had declared both the NRA and the AAA to be unconstitutional in 1935 and 1936, respectively. When the economic resurgence of 1935 and 1936 ended with a recession in 1937 that increased national unemployment rates to 17 percent, he realized that deficit spending would be needed to stimulate economic growth.[46]

However, Roosevelt was cautious about expanding New Deal reforms, and he even made drastic cuts in some programs. Because he continued to listen to advisors who believed that the economic resurgence of 1935 and 1936 could be maintained only if federal deficits were reduced, he slashed funding for many New Deal programs over the objections of liberals.[47] As he watched Hitler's antics in Germany in the mid-1930s and became convinced that America would have to rearm, he became increasingly worried about antagonizing conservatives whose support would be needed for rearmament.

With the realignment of political parties by social class in the 1930s, many middle-class persons joined working-class voters to give Roosevelt smashing victories in 1932, 1934, and 1936. However, many of them began to hedge their reform interests because the economic ills of the nation continued and the unprecedented expansion of government bureaucracy led many of them to wonder if Roosevelt was leading Americans toward socialism. The anger of many Americans often focused not on Roosevelt, however, who retained his personal popularity thoughout the decade, but on some of his advisors and programs. Hopkins was widely perceived to want unlimited personal power. Perkins was perceived to be soft on militant labor unions and to be a charity-minded social worker who blindly supported new programs. Many persons resented the intellectuals who formed Roosevelt's brains trust.[48] Some middle-class Americans also became alarmed by labor organizations, such as the Congress of Industrial Organizations (CIO), which they feared would gain inordinate power. The use of disruptive tactics by labor in the sitdown strikes of 1937, when workers occupied automobile plants, was profoundly disturbing to many middle-class citizens, who believed these disruptive techniques exceeded the bounds of fair play.[49] Middle-class defections from Roosevelt were not sudden, but the Republican party was gradually augmented in the late 1930s and early 1940s by middle-class

voters; indeed, Roosevelt's electoral majority was reduced to 53 percent of voters by 1944.

These growing doubts about New Deal reforms among the middle class were supplemented by widespread opposition to Roosevelt's attempts to pack the Supreme Court and to purge the Democratic party in 1937. Many liberals had been furious at the Court for its adverse rulings and had developed various legislative proposals for neutralizing it, such as requiring a two-thirds vote of the justices to declare legislation unconstitutional. (Congress has the constitutional power to determine the size and voting procedures of the Court.) Had Roosevelt not acted, Congress might have enacted legislation to limit the Court since 150 such measures were introduced in Congress in 1937.[50]

Roosevelt remained silent on the issue until 1937, when he introduced a legislative proposal to allow the president to appoint a new justice every time a justice failed to retire within six months of his seventieth birthday. Perkins advised him not to introduce this proposal because the Court appeared to be wavering in its attacks on New Deal programs and was widely regarded as sacrosanct.[51] When Roosevelt persisted, he ran into a storm of political protest in which he was charged with upsetting the constitutional balance of powers, seeking unlimited personal power, and trying to establish a fascist dictatorship.[52]

Roosevelt was unable to purge the Democratic party of dissident Southern Democrats, whose conservative opposition was magnified by their fears that Roosevelt would support civil rights measures. Enraged by these defections, he targeted several southern politicians for political attack by traveling to their districts to campaign for their rivals, but he suffered a humiliating defeat when each of the politicians was reelected.[53]

Roosevelt's political effectiveness in the early and middle 1930s depended in part on his image of political invincibility. He had obtained so many legislative and electoral victories that many opponents believed it to be fruitless to oppose his policies and feared that he might deny them patronage or personal support in their campaigns. His Supreme Court and political defeats in 1936 and 1937 tarnished his image of invincibility, however, and emboldened members of the conservative coalition, as well as some moderate Democrats, to question his policies.[54]

Roosevelt was accused of fascist tactics when he attacked the Court and tried to purge his party, but he was one of a relatively small number of Americans who became alarmed by Hitler's rise to power in the early 1930s. He first tried to work indirectly to alert Europeans to the impending danger and to offer them economic assistance because he knew that many Americans, including many liberals, favored isolationism. As his espousal of rearmament became more obvious, isolationists in both parties attacked his domestic policies, which also languished as he devoted more time to foreign policy. Roosevelt's preoccupation with foreign affairs was illustrated when he appointed Hopkins to be secretary of commerce in 1938 to develop rapport with top American industrialists, whose support and technical knowledge was needed during rearmament.

It was during the war itself that social reform was particularly attacked. Many Americans demanded slashes in nonessential government programs because the war effort required federal deficits that dwarfed the deficits of the 1930s. Indeed, the war provided a splendid opportunity for the conservative coalition, whose members were determined to rescind many New Deal programs. As one historian noted, "Republicans viewed the war as a struggle for supremacy at home and abroad. . . . At home, the enemy was reform. . . . The war provided an opportunity to dismantle the New Deal [with] reestablishment of the traditional American system of unfettered private enterprise at the end of the war."[55] Roosevelt hoped to maintain his New Deal programs for the duration of the war so that a new round of reform activity could occur when it had ended, but he was unable to stop conservatives from terminating the CCC, NYA, PWA, and WPA partly because he had to mute his defense of these programs to retain the support of conservatives for his international policies. It is difficult to fault his decision to give precedence to international affairs in light of the barbarism of Nazi Germany, but liberals watched nervously as prized programs were eliminated.

## POLICIES DURING THE ERA OF STALEMATE

Roosevelt was able to obtain some major policy reforms after 1936 despite the loss of his reform momentum. The funding of the WPA, CCC, and NYA, particularly after the recession of 1937, was increased. Perhaps his signal accomplishment, however, was passage of the Fair Employment Practices Act of 1938. Fair working conditions and minimum wages had been established for each industry under the NRA, but many industries returned to sweatshop conditions when the Supreme Court declared the NRA to be unconstitutional. With assistance from Perkins, Roosevelt supported legislation that established minimum wages and maximum hours, but he had to make concessions to conservatives to secure its passage. Farm labor was excluded from the legislation to appease southern and western agricultural interests. Wage-and-hour standards were phased in gradually so that the minimum wage rose from 25 cents per hour to 40 cents per hour in seven years. The maximum length of a work week diminished from forty-four hours per week to forty hours per week in three years.[56] Even this legislation aroused considerable controversy. Southern Democrats feared it would elevate the wages of poor African Americans, even when agricultural laborers were excluded from it. The AFL opposed it because they feared the minimum wage might establish a ceiling on wages and would decrease the motivation of workers to join unions. Some persons objected to placing its administration in the Department of Labor because they believed Perkins favored unions.[57]

Roosevelt was able in 1937 to obtain passage of the Wagner-Steagall Housing Act, which established the United States Housing Authority to provide low-interest loans to local authorities to build public housing.[58] The Roosevelt administration expended considerable energy in implementing the many programs of the Social Security Act. Federal regulations and policies to govern OAA, ADC, AB, and unemployment insurance programs were issued. States were monitored to be certain that uniform standards of eligibility were used, that names of recipients were not published, and that political criteria were not used in eligibility decisions. Federal officials pressured states to develop their ADC and OAA programs rapidly; nonetheless, some states had barely started their programs by 1940. Federal authorities occasionally threatened to cut off federal funds to those states that were remiss in administering their programs.[59]

Roosevelt realized by 1937 that he also needed to simplify the organization of federal programs since social welfare programs were scattered in the Departments of Interior, Treasury, Labor, and Agriculture as well as in independent programs and commissions. No department existed that focused on social welfare issues, and no cabinet-level secretary existed to coordinate the planning and implementation of social programs. He appointed a committee that recommended the establishment of a Department of Public Works and a Department of Welfare, whose directors would sit in his cabinet. The plan was defeated in the Congress in 1938 because many legislators feared that it had been masterminded by Hopkins to enhance his personal power, to increase Roosevelt's political patronage, and to increase the power of the federal government. The plan was also attacked by advocates of existing programs, such as the CCC, who feared they would lose power if they were transferred to the new agency.[60] Roosevelt reluctantly retreated to a more modest proposal to create a subcabinet agency known as the Federal Security Agency (FSA) and a Federal Works Agency under the Reorganization Act of 1939. The FSA contained the CCC, the NYA, the Public Health Service, the U.S. Employment Service, and the Social Security Board, whereas the WPA and the PWA were placed in the Federal Works Agency. This legislation was enacted, but not until 1953 was the Department of Health, Education, and Welfare finally created to house the nation's social programs.

Despite these various policy gains, Roosevelt suffered many policy losses during the waning years of the New Deal. A program to provide a large revolving federal fund to finance public works was defeated. Roosevelt declined to support health legislation and a redistributive tax act because he knew they would be defeated. When the national debt limit was periodically raised by Congress as the nation rearmed, conservatives demanded and often obtained major cuts in social spending. Roosevelt failed in his bids in 1937 and 1939 to have the CCC made a permanent program since conservatives did not want to establish the principle that ongoing federal programs were needed for the nation's youth. An ambitious proposal to develop programs like the TVA in seven other river basins was defeated.[61]

## OUTGROUPS IN THE NEW DEAL

Attention was focused on the problems of unemployment and relief since millions of Americans were economically devastated by the Great Depression. But the nation's minority groups, including women, bore a disproportionate share of the economic suffering and sometimes wondered whether the New Deal spoke to their broader needs as well as their economic deprivation. In some cases, the economic plight of whites heightened animosities between the dominant population and minority groups, both during the Depression and during World War II.

### African Americans

As the New Deal began, discrimination against African Americans continued unabated in both the North and the South. Because Jim Crow laws remained in force throughout the South, African Americans were disenfranchised, forced to live in segregated neighborhoods, required to sit at the rear of buses, and placed in separate schools. Bad as these violations of civil rights were, they were overshadowed by many instances of violence against African Americans. The Ku Klux Klan, long a presence in the South, had a resurgence in the 1920s and struck terror in the hearts of African Americans who saw an epidemic of lynchings where African Americans were often hanged.

Hard times increased racism, which sometimes took the form of race riots and lynchings, because many whites feared that African Americans would take employment from them. When faced with layoff decisions, many employers fired African Americans to retain white employees, sometimes in response to agitation by white citizens. As had been common before the 1930s, African-American workers were denied membership in many unions and were used as scabs by employers to break strikes. Southern whites were furious, too, that African Americans received far higher wages under the WPA than they had received in the fields—and feared that the New Deal programs would dramatically upset the political and economic structure of the South by dramatically improving the economic condition of African Americans.[62]

African Americans desperately needed federal civil rights legislation that would rescind Jim Crow laws and outlaw discrimination against African Americans by unions and employers as well as job and service programs that channeled resources and employment to their population. But Roosevelt, during most of the New Deal, refused even to support legislation that would make lynching a federal crime; he finally gave it (only) verbal support late in the 1930s. Nor did he support legislation to eliminate the use of the poll tax, which was widely used in the South to disenfranchise African Americans, or legislation to counter segregation in housing markets despite urging by African Americans and Senator Wagner.[63]

Why this seeming indifference by Roosevelt to civil rights? He knew that Southern Democrats would become determined opponents of his domestic legislation if he supported civil rights legislation, particularly if they voted with Republicans in the so-called conservative coalition. (This potential threat became a real one, as we have already noted, in 1937 and succeeding years when the conservative coalition militantly attacked many of Roosevelt's initiatives.)[64] Indeed, even before 1937, Roosevelt had to make key concessions in unemployment, Social Security, public welfare, NRA, and fair labor and standards legislation to obtain the support of southerners.[65] The development of civil rights legislation was also impeded by the widespread belief that discrimination against African Americans would diminish as they improved their economic condition.

Roosevelt and his aides were also disinclined to support civil rights legislation since they believed that African Americans were discriminated against since they were poor *rather than* because they were African American—a belief that led them to believe that New Deal programs like the WPA, which gave jobs to African Americans, would end discrimination more effectively than civil rights legislation. This perspective was tragically naive. Racism exists as a force that is independent of social class, as is illustrated by discrimination against affluent and well-educated African Americans in job and housing markets. Moreover, as we have already noted, some whites became even more hostile to African Americans because they were viewed as competing with them for jobs and even WPA positions. And the disposition of some whites to lynch African Americans was hardly linked to their precise economic status, as the epidemic of lynchings throughout the 1930s illustrated.

If many New Dealers were disinclined to support federal civil rights legislation, they were also reluctant to develop programs that specifically provided African-American populations with resources and jobs. A policy of requiring quotas for African Americans in specific New Deal programs was opposed because it, like the creation of special programs for African Americans, was perceived to represent reverse discrimination.[66] Without such special treatment, however, it was doubtful that African Americans could overcome the economic and social chasm that existed between themselves and the white population.

African Americans nonetheless obtained notable policy concessions. Since it was obvious that many local officials and project-review committees would exclude African Americans from eligibility in the FERA and CWA programs in 1933, African American advisors were appointed by Hopkins, Williams, Perkins, and Ickes to monitor implementation of programs and to work in tandem with investigators to detect flagrant cases of discrimination.[67] Considerable success was obtained in enrolling African Americans; 10 percent of CCC enrollees and more than 15 percent of WPA workers were African American.[68] The PWA and NYA were particularly innovative; the PWA established a quota system that required its private contractors to reach specific goals in their hiring practices, and the NYA was the only major New Deal agency that established special programs that were restricted to African-American enrollees.[69] The inclusion of millions of African Americans in New Deal programs represented a major policy feat in a nation that had often refrained from allowing many African Americans access to local relief programs.

Discrimination nonetheless existed within New Deal programs. Except for a few camps in New England, the CCC was segregated since Roosevelt feared racial conflict within integrated camps as well as political opposition from southerners. (Ugly incidents occurred in a number of camps before they were segregated.) African-American enrollees were not transported to CCC camps in other states because of opposition by whites and fear for their safety.[70] Housing built by the PWA was often segregated.[71] Many New Deal programs, such as programs to help farmers refinance their mortgages or obtain loans, could not be used by African Americans since most of them were tenant farmers. The NRA often allowed southern industrialists to establish wage codes that froze existing and inequitable wages for African-American workers.[72] Payments to landowners under the AAA to reward them for withdrawing acreage from production were often not passed on to African-American tenant farmers and sharecroppers despite legislation that required such transfers.

Curiously, African Americans gained a major victory during World War II when reformers asked why African Americans should sacrifice their lives in the war if units of the army were segregated, if African-American workers in war industries had to live in segregated housing, and if African Americans encountered discrimination in wartime industries. Many whites, including some liberals, exhorted African

Americans not to raise these issues during the war in order not to divide the nation, but A. Phillip Randolph, the fiery African-American director of the Brotherhood of Sleeping Car Porters and Maids, was so incensed by the prevalence of job discrimination against African Americans, even in war industries desperate for labor, that he advocated a massive march on Washington to force Roosevelt to sign federal legislation that would ensure the fair employment of African Americans in the defense industry. So as not to disrupt the war effort, Roosevelt finally relented in 1941 by signing Executive Order 8802 to prohibit discrimination in employment in the defense industry on the basis of race, creed, or national origin on the condition that plans for the march be abandoned. (Executive Order 8802 also established the Committee on Fair Employment Practices to monitor the private sector though the committee was given such scant funding that it could not assertively investigate many complaints of discrimination.)

Since Randolph was unable to persuade Roosevelt to sign an order to desegregate the armed forces, the war was fought with segregated battalions until President Truman finally desegregated the armed forces at the end of the war.[73] Hundreds of thousands of African Americans who returned from the military at the end of the war encountered extraordinary prejudice in both the North and the South. Moreover, the African Americans who had migrated to cities during the war constituted a growing underclass with limited economic prospects.

The New Deal, then, cannot be given a positive assessment regarding civil rights. A huge chasm existed between white and African-American populations in this era, as suggested by public opinion polls. Poll data indicated in 1939, for example, that 69 percent of whites thought African Americans were less intelligent and that most whites endorsed segregated restaurants, neighborhoods, and schools (99, 97, and 98 percent of southerners and 62, 82, and 58 percent of northerners).[74]

An African-American social worker ominously predicted in the 1930s that provision of welfare benefits to African Americans without civil rights and jobs legislation risked perpetuating their inferior economic and social status—a fear repeated three decades later by Jesse Jackson, a former aide to Martin Luther King, Jr., when he observed a massive population of destitute African Americans whose survival hinged on receipt of a variety of welfare benefits but who encountered bleak job prospects, poor educational programs, and minimal programs for job training.[75]

## Women

The achievement of suffrage did not lead to policy gains for women, who found themselves unable to vote as a bloc or to agree on policy issues. Some women, such as Eleanor Roosevelt, favored passage of protective legislation that shielded women from dangerous or physically taxing occupations; other women, who believed that protective legislation would merely close certain jobs to women, supported an equal rights amendment to the Constitution to grant women legal equality.[76]

Eleanor Roosevelt became a determined advocate for women during the early years of the New Deal. Because the CCC camps were statutorily limited to males, she persuaded her husband to establish forty-five camps for 8,500 women under the FERA. Working closely with Molly Dewson, director of the women's division of the Democratic party, she secured the appointment of many women to high-level posts in the FERA, the WPA, and other agencies.[77] Almost no women obtained work relief in the CWA, but 15 percent of WPA recruits were women. The Wagner Act helped spur organizing of women; between 1930 and 1940, for example, the International Ladies Garment Workers Union tripled its membership to 800,000 persons.

Many women, about 20 percent, lost their jobs during the Depression, but others found their employment to be more secure than males since they tended not to work in heavy industry and were employed in gender-segregated occupations that were relatively immune from the Depression. Because of the vast numbers of clerks and secretaries, the percentage of women in the federal work force rose from 14 percent in 1929 to 19 percent in 1939 — or twice the rate of increase of male employment.[78]

Women also made major strides in obtaining sexual freedom. The "flapper" of the 1920s partially escaped Victorian moral codes. A majority of married and middle-class women used birth control during the 1930s by obtaining information from their physicians. Many poor persons lacked access to birth control information, however, since birth control clinics were still illegal in many areas under the obscenity laws that had hampered Margaret Sanger two decades earlier.[79]

Economic and social gains of women in the New Deal should not obscure continuing discrimination against them. It was widely assumed that married women should relinquish their positions to allow the employment of unemployed males; indeed, some women lost federal jobs after federal legislation in 1932 (which was not rescinded until 1937) stipulated that husbands and wives could not both hold federal positions. Administrators in the CWA and the WPA often assumed that husbands should receive priority in work relief programs. NRA labor codes often established lower wages for women than for men in identical positions. Widows did not receive Social Security benefits of their deceased husbands until 1939, and even this was conditioned on a woman's living with her husband at the time of his death.[80] Social Security was also expanded in 1939 to give modest benefits to the wives of retired workers, so long, that is, as she had been his wife for at least five years and living with him at the time of the application. (Divorced women and remarried women had to forfeit these benefits for widows and wives, respectively.) Because Social Security benefits were tied to levels of wages, female

retirees, who usually came from low-wage occupations, received lower benefits than males. Many women who worked as domestics or in agricultural labor were not included in Social Security at all.[81] Unemployment insurance also discriminated against women by requiring applicants to have a recent and extended employment record, thus disqualifying entrants to the labor force who had been unemployed *before* obtaining an extended employment record — a common problem for women who reentered the labor force after an absence. Many women were also denied benefits because they refused a "suitable job" that was a distance away or that required they work during hours of the day that made it incongruent with their family responsibilities.[82] Nor were benefits paid for pregnancy or maternal (or paternal) leave — an omission that remains in place in the early 1990s. The ADC program provided *no* benefits until 1950 to the heads of households, just the children — and federal authorities provided a smaller share of the funding of ADC than OAA. ADC unfairly limited grants to single heads of households even though many impoverished women were married or single. Many trade unions not only excluded women from their leadership but often negotiated contracts that gave them lower pay than men — and leadership of the AFL demanded that women who were married leave their jobs so as to make available more employment for males.[83]

Since the cult of domesticity, which had dominated American family life for a century, remained intact, many married women who worked encountered hostility from their husbands and peers, even when they limited their horizons to gender-segregated and low-paying jobs. Moreover, psychologists, psychoanalysts, and physicians, such as Dr. Gesell and Dr. Spock, defined the role of the mother (*not* the father) as an all-encompassing one that was dictated by "the needs" of their children. "Love" between mother and child was the magic and necessary ingredient to be provided in "a perfectly nourishing environment" with mothers avoiding "outside commitments so as not to 'miss' a fascinating stage of development" so that mother and child "could enjoy each other, fulfilling one another's needs perfectly, instinctively, as if Nature in her infinite wisdom has created them (to be) two happily matched consumers consuming each other."[84] Thus defined as supermom, women were truly confined to their homes through much of their married lives.

## Latinos

Spanish-speaking persons constituted the majority of field workers in the irrigated farms of the Southwest by 1930. Despite some successes, violent suppression of agricultural unions, as well as redbaiting, led to the demise of pioneering unions. Since farm workers were not covered under the Wagner Act of 1936, they did not have collective bargaining rights that were enforced by the federal government; thus, employers could fire those persons who they felt might try to organize the workers. In remote farming areas, the workers lacked access to lawyers or advocates. Even the few unions that had developed ended with the onset of World War II, when many organizers and workers were drafted or migrated to cities. As we have already noted, farm workers did not receive Social Security benefits or unemployment insurance.

When thousands of unemployed Latinos sought welfare in the 1930s, local welfare officials demanded massive "repatriations" (forced evacuations) of them to Mexico. Roughly 400,000 Latinos were forced to leave the country between 1929 and 1934. Many of them, with $14.70 in their pockets from the U.S. government, were indiscriminately placed on trains to Mexico City despite the devastating impact on families and communities.

When faced with the need to produce huge quantities of food during World War II, the federal government initiated the bracero program through a bilateral agreement with Mexico in 1942. In return for ensuring a minimum wage and guaranteeing their just treatment, the Mexi-can government, which wanted to alleviate domestic unemployment, allowed a specified number of Mexicans to enter the country to meet labor shortages on American farms. Extended annually until 1964, the program brought a total of five million Mexican laborers to the United States. In addition, many undocumented workers continued to flow into the United States during this period. But not bound by *any* agreements with the Mexican government regarding these workers, agribusiness and those mining companies and other employers that hired them were able to treat them virtually as they wished.

Despite efforts by the Mexican government to secure rights for braceros, abuses were legion, such as poor wages, lack of housing, and lack of health care — and unions were no more successful during and after World War II than in the 1930s.

As in the instance of African Americans, considerable racial animosity developed during World War II in urban areas where sizable Latino populations had settled. In Los Angeles, for example, white sailors on shore leave frequently attacked Latino youth who wore suits made of long coats with padded shoulders, which led to the so-called zoot-suit riots. Police brutality against Latinos was rampant in Los Angeles with mass roundups and incarcerations.[85] World War II led to a vast increase in the urbanizing of Latinos, who worked in munitions factories, ship building, and other industries, but like African-American workers of the period, they lived in segregated areas that had been abandoned by white populations that fled to areas with better housing and more amenities.

## Asian Americans

The migration of Asians to the United States was effectively curbed with the Immigration Act of 1924, which limited annual immigration from specific countries to a percentage of the numbers of them that were in the United States in 1890, long before many Asians had migrated.

(Chinese migration was banned altogether by the Chinese Exclusion Act of 1882.) Though not allowed to own land in many areas by state legislation, Asian residents had shown extraordinary ability to remain in farming by leasing land or by finding cooperative Americans who placed the land in their own names while allowing the Asians to continue to farm it. Moreover, a thriving network of small businesses had developed in Chinese-American and Japanese-American communities, even if these businesses had often developed because Asian Americans were denied access to land by the legislation that disallowed them from owning it. The "Nisei" (second-generation Japanese Americans that had succeeded the "Issei," or first generation), who had become citizens by virtue of being born in the United States, placed extraordinary emphasis on education, which was seen as a way of overcoming the barriers imposed by discrimination. Truly caught between American and Japanese culture, the Nisei nonetheless sought, with their parents' blessing, to master English, to aspire to college, and to use their educational achievement to obtain jobs that had been denied their parents.[86]

But a strong undercurrent of racism existed toward this outgroup. As Takaki relates, a young Japanese man from Hawaii was shocked by the intensity of anti-Japanese racism; on hearing he was Japanese, a barber drove him out of his shop "as if he were driving away a cat or a dog."[87] People even spit on Japanese persons whom they encountered on the street. First-generation Asian Americans were denied citizenship on the grounds they were non-Caucasian aliens—and then denied access to relief programs during the Great Depression on the grounds they were not citizens! Nor were the Nisei able to escape discrimination, even with their college degrees. As the Depression hit, most Nisei were unable to find jobs for which they had been trained; virtually no jobs were open to them in engineering, manufacturing, business, or even secondary teaching. Trapped in family businesses, almost no Nisei worked for white employers even as late

as 1940.[88] Chinese Americans worked largely in restaurants and laundries since they were not allowed to work in other occupations.

Recall that many West-Coast Americans had feared an invasion from Japan even at the start of the century—and this "yellow peril" had led many people to demand an immediate cessation of all immigration from Japan. Pearl Harbor brought an immediate fear that Japanese Americans would conspire with Japanese agents during and after an invasion by the Japanese. Separated from other Asian Americans, who frantically tried to show they were not of Japanese ancestry, and targets of violence and hatred, Japanese Americans fearfully waited to see what would happen.

Immediate demands for the internment of Japanese Americans came to be widely featured in the press. Roosevelt had received confidential reports before and soon after Pearl Harbor that the Japanese Americans did not constitute a threat to national security. If an American general in Hawaii resisted all pressures to intern the Japanese Americans, General John DeWitt of the Western Defense Command became a zealous persecutor of them and conducted many search-and-seizure operations to find hidden transmitters. A chorus of rumors emerged in the press urging that Japanese Americans were conspiring with Japanese agents and that they might cooperate with the Japanese during a feared invasion. White farmers, who had resented the success of Japanese-American farmers, demanded their evacuation, partly to obtain their land.

Although Roosevelt was urged by his attorney general not to evacuate them and although it was obvious that their civil rights would be infringed on if they were rounded up and confined without due process, Roosevelt and other advisors were determined to proceed— and often used blatantly racist language in their private conversations.[89] Executive Order 9066, though not mentioning Japanese Americans, empowered the secretary of war to develop "military areas" to confine whoever he thought

**FIGURE 8.1** • *A tagged Japanese-American child awaiting relocation to an internment camp*

*Source:* Library of Congress

was a security risk. When there were rumors that Italian Americans and German Americans might be apprehended, widespread protests erupted, but no such protests emerged with respect to Japanese Americans. About 120,000 of them were rounded up and taken to internment camps located in remote rural areas with no due process and no hearings. Moreover, since they were able to take only what they could carry, they were forced to sell their houses and belongings within a matter of days, often accepting nominal amounts.

The Japanese Americans were given numbers that they wore on tags from the point of evacuation onward, housed in assembly centers, shipped to remote internment camps with no idea where they were going, and greeted by barbed wire and guard towers in the camps (see Figure 8.1). Curiously, the American authorities, who had incarcerated them as security risks, soon sought to persuade draft-age youth to volunteer for the armed services but only after they agreed to sign loyalty oaths; partly to protest the internment, many of them did not agree to volunteer—and draft protests broke out in 1944 when the military tried to conscript them. Nonetheless, 33,000 Nisei served in World War II, many with distinction.

Evacuation orders had been rescinded before the end of the war, and some of those internees who agreed to sign loyalty oaths were allowed to settle in cities not on the West Coast, such as Denver and Chicago. But the damage had been done to several generations of Japanese Americans, who even in the 1990s, had not been recompensed for lost property and deprivation of rights.

This incident, some might think, is relatively trivial since it involved a unique situation, but it was (and is) widely perceived by Asian Americans as an illustration of the effects of widespread racism on American social policy. Leaders who had implemented dozens of humane policies were nonetheless able to take extraordinary actions that were fueled by racism and with scant protests from liberals. Roosevelt, shortly before his death, admitted confidentially that he had erred in signing the executive order to intern Japanese Americans.

To critics of the New Deal, the episode was a tragic capstone to a social program that had a poor record on civil rights, not just for Asian Americans but for other minority groups and women as well. The American government did, however, finally rescind its ban on Chinese immigration in 1943—over sixty years after its original passage. America could not justify Chinese exclusion without endangering her alliance with the Chinese so that ban was lifted if only for utilitarian rather than moral reasons.[90]

## SOCIAL WORKERS IN THE NEW DEAL

By the end of the 1920s, social work had consolidated its position with the development of many schools that were largely associated with universities. An explosion of demand for social work occurred as, freed from the old preoccupation with relief giving, the profession attended to a host of problems, including family disruption, medical problems, child pathology, school problems, outpatient services to persons released from mental institutions. The old charity organization society agencies, some 200 nationwide, developed the American Association for Organizing Charity, where they officially changed their mission from relief giving to "family casework." Federated fund raising, which relied heavily on donations from corporations and their employees, provided a huge influx of funds for the social agencies. In 1921, the new profession developed a mass-membership professional organization, the American Association of Social Workers, even if most of its early members lacked professional training. The future looked promising for this new profession that had developed a core technology (social casework), a network of social agencies, sources of funding (the federations), and many schools.[91]

Social casework, though emphasizing diagnosis and "scientific work," still bore some resemblance to the older charity work because it emphasized the person-in-the-environment. Both in diagnosis and interventions, caseworkers were to examine environmental factors that shaped the problems of their clients and help them cope with situational realities. But a new contender appeared in the 1920s, psychiatric social work, which drew heavily on the work of Freud and his disciples, as illustrated by the works of Virginia Robinson and others that were markedly different from older works by Mary Richmond.[92] Psychiatric social work did not dominate the profession in many schools and agencies, but it was a highly visible wing of

social work and had a particularly strong hold on certain schools, such as Smith College and the University of Pennsylvania, and certain kinds of agencies, such as child guidance agencies and psychiatric hospitals. Some proponents of social casework feared that this new contender, which emphasized intrapsychic matters and family relationships, could sever social work from its person-in-the-environment emphasis as well as its work with relatively impoverished populations.

Social workers were not usually involved in social reform projects or in public agencies during the 1920s. Even many of the old settlements, though still existing, lost their reformist qualities as well as their visible leadership within the profession. Social workers were not highly visible in partisan politics although they supported specific candidates whom they believed were interested in certain social issues.

Many social work leaders took an intense interest in the national presidential campaign of 1928, however, even if they were divided on the merits of Al Smith, who had been receptive to social workers during his tenure as governor of New York State, and Herbert Hoover, who had pursued humanitarian work after World War I in Europe and shown interest in unemployment issues during the 1920s.[93] A sizable number of social workers continued to believe that social work should remain separate from partisan politics altogether.

Thus divided, the profession was as unready for the political upheaval of the Great Depression as many other citizens were. Many leaders maintained, as did Hoover, that private agencies would suffice to manage the economic destitution that occurred in 1929 and 1930. They were in for a rude shock, however, when they found that private agencies, like the Red Cross, lacked the funds to manage the throngs of destitute people. Indeed, vast numbers of social agencies, one-third of them in New York City alone, went bankrupt because of the rising caseloads and the drop-off in private philanthropy. Increasing numbers of social workers realized by 1930 that strong governmental action was needed, even if many of them still did not see the Democratic party as the necessary instrument of reform. (Jane Addams voted for Hoover, not Franklin Roosevelt, in 1932.)[94] By 1932, however, many social work leaders had come to dislike Hoover for his disinclination to take bold action to help unemployed people.

Curiously, the Great Depression and World War II actually benefited the social work profession. If most social workers had been employed in private agencies in the 1920s, thousands of jobs opened up in the 1930s in the myriad New Deal agencies. The number of people in social work positions increased from 40,000 in 1930 to 70,000 in 1940.[95] A cohesive community of leaders existed in New York City during the 1920s that became acquainted with Eleanor Roosevelt and Harry Hopkins and assumed leadership and consultative roles to Franklin Roosevelt during his governorship of New York State. Many of these social workers assumed influential positions in the New Deal, supported the FERA, the NRA, and the CWA, and often sought to professionalize programs of the New Deal by insisting on prominent roles for social workers in them.[96] Indeed, Hopkins supported many training programs for social workers. When the Social Security Board was established following the enactment of the Social Security Act, social workers received key appointments in it, as well as its Bureau of Public Assistance, which supervised ADC and the other welfare programs.

Social casework proved to be adaptable to these new public agencies, which sought to screen, refer, and give brief assistance to the many destitute people who used the New Deal programs. At the same time, the psychiatric wing of the profession continued to ply its trade in various private agencies, which continued to exist in the 1930s.

Although there was a good deal of growth in social work positions, many of them were filled by untrained people. Paid relatively low salaries and acutely aware that the New Deal programs provided only meager benefits to desperately poor people, these large numbers of staff developed lively protest movements—to seek both better pay for themselves and greater benefits for their clients.[97] Mary Van Kleeck and the publication *Social Work Today* made fiery denunciations of the New Deal, which many believed was captive to corporate interests. The so-called rank-and-file movement of nonprofessional public employees of New Deal programs developed unions of public employees, supported sweeping social reforms, and often joined with or helped to organize poor persons as well as their own clients. By 1937, however, their protest had dissipated, perhaps because many of them had become part of the establishment and civil service protections had been extended to them.[98]

Social work also grew in World War II. Social workers were hired by the Red Cross and other agencies that helped soldiers. Private agencies worked with relocated workers, day care, and other social issues on the home front.[99]

At various points during the 1930s and 1940s, social workers wrestled with the question of how selectively the profession should define its boundaries. One faction wanted the profession to markedly increase its membership to include legions of untrained people who worked in public programs—and in the 1940s, to include people with only baccalaureate degrees. They believed that the power of the profession would increase as it broadened its boundaries and that it could increase the quality and prestige of many social work positions by including their incumbents in the profession. Another faction wanted membership in the profession restricted to graduates of graduate-degree programs so as to keep the caliber of professional work at a high level and maintain the prestige of the profession. The two factions often clashed, but for the moment, the selective faction was victorious.[100]

As in the progressive era, the leadership of the social work profession reflected orientations of the broader period. Most of the leadership was sympathetic to Roosevelt even if sometimes embittered by actions like his termination of the CWA and some of the conservative features of the Social Security Act. Virtually all social workers were converted in the 1930s to the need for government to fund and deliver a host of services, thus ending forever the curious hold that nongovernmental agencies had on social welfare. Perhaps we can say that social work became a part of the broad coalition that Roosevelt had fashioned in the New Deal to the extent that the profession was viewed as "liberal" in succeeding decades as well. When Richard Nixon and other conservatives cast about for "enemies" some decades later, they unhesitatingly so depicted social workers—perhaps, some social workers thought, a sign that the reformist traditions of the profession remained at least somewhat intact.

Yet some social workers supported relatively backward-looking policies during the New Deal, such as those who wanted to restrict ADC grants to those families that caseworkers judged to provide "suitable homes"—a policy that would have given social workers a strange veto over the intake process in public welfare.[101] And some social workers remained safely outside the turmoil of the New Deal in child guidance and other agencies with a psychiatric focus.

On the left, a small faction sided with decidedly radical protest in the 1930s, including the Communist party, the rank-and-file movement, and the Socialist party. They often argued that social work had been coopted by Roosevelt to participate in inadequate social programs and that, by doing so, it was blunting significant social change that could occur only by aligning the profession with grass-roots dissent.

This discussion of social work in the 1920s and 1930s suggests that a lively discussion and much controversy existed within the profession over issues like to what extent should the profession engage in social action rather than only provide counseling, to what extent should the profession have relatively broad or narrow membership, and to what extent should the profession ally itself politically with liberal forces? We can see certain "central tendencies" in the developments of the 1920s and 1930s, such as the dominance of casework, the decision by most social workers to support relatively liberal social policies but not radical reforms, and the opting for a relatively restrictive membership policy. But these central tendencies ought not to obscure conflict within a profession that, in some respects, was a microcosm of the society that enveloped it.

## ASSESSMENT OF NEW DEAL POLICIES

When viewed from the perspective of the progressive era, the New Deal represents a striking departure from traditional American policies on two counts. Unlike progressive reformers, who focused on state and local reforms, Roosevelt created a *national* welfare state that superseded local programs. He also created social programs rather than focusing on a regulatory strategy, as was illustrated by the first major social programs in the United States that distributed jobs (the CWA, WPA, CCC, and PWA) and resources (the FERA and the Social Security Act) to destitute and elderly Americans. By going beyond the legalistic approach of Progressives, Roosevelt drastically altered the scope of the American welfare state.

It is easy to criticize the New Deal from the vantage of contemporary society; New Deal reforms did not include the range of civil rights, medical, housing, food stamp, and other programs that were developed in subsequent reform eras, and they often were diluted by compromises with conservatives. Roosevelt nonetheless accomplished his reforms in a society where virtually no national social programs had existed and in the face of profound social, legal, and political opposition. In venturing into new policy territory, he often stumbled and changed directions, but he developed precedent-shattering policies that helped millions of citizens survive an economic catastrophe. He opportunistically changed policies as political realities changed, but he was remarkably consistent in his basic policy goals. He was a firm believer in capitalism, but he sought regulatory, tax, and social welfare policies to mitigate economic uncertainty and the suffering that accompanied it. He opposed ideology, whether socialism or unfettered capitalism, and preferred instead to seek practical reform policies in the political context that he encountered. Frances Perkins wrote on a piece of paper in 1932 a series of six reforms that she favored; by 1940, only health insurance had not been enacted.[102]

Roosevelt's social welfare innovations were matched by political accomplishments that prevented conservatives from dismantling his social reforms after World War II. He created the modern Democratic party, which, for all its faults, embraced a relatively liberal constituency. Voting preferences in the nation were associated for the first time with social class and with political ideology; African Americans, workers, Jews, and intellectuals tended to support the Democratic party, whereas affluent Americans tended to vote Republican. The numerical size of this liberal constituency made it difficult for Republicans to rescind the New Deal—unless they could persuade large numbers of working- and middle-class voters that social reform was not in their best interest. This did not happen in a major way until the administration of Ronald Reagan in the 1980s.

Still, viewed from the vantage of today's society and compared to programs of other industrialized nations, New Deal reforms were timid.

The social reform agenda of the 1960s and 1970s was largely fashioned to address social problems that were not included within New Deal reforms—federal medical programs, national civil rights legislation, federal assistance for mentally ill persons, programs to help the disabled, educational programs for the poor, nutritional programs for the poor, and job-training programs. The New Deal did not redistribute resources from affluent to less affluent persons. The nation had entered the 1930s with wide economic differentials between the social classes. The various New Deal programs often helped less affluent persons survive their immediate destitution, and Roosevelt did obtain some tax reforms, but the federal tax system was not so fundamentally reformed as to alter existing economic inequality. The realignment of the political parties was not accompanied by an economic or social revolution that redressed inequalities between classes or races.

As a consummate politician, Roosevelt was sometimes overcautious in supporting social reforms. He did not aggressively support union organizing, did not try to institutionalize a public works program, delegated many social welfare functions to states and localities when the Social Security Act was enacted, and often resorted to budget cutting even when it led to widespread suffering. Moreover, he did not seize the opportunity to mobilize a liberal party as aggressively as he might have; he was too enamored with coalition politics, except when he ineffectually tried to purge Southern Democrats. Roosevelt did not grasp the political uses of the labor movement until late in the decade.[103]

Roosevelt and Perkins, particularly when prodded by conservatives, gave states considerable discretion in setting eligibility and program standards in many of the New Deal programs, even when this policy allowed conservative and southern states to impose punitive and racist standards. Workers in America were more heavily taxed than affluent persons by the payroll taxes of the Social Security program, and they received only short-term and relatively miserly unemployment benefits. Destitute Americans who did not fit the restrictive eligibility requirements of OAA, ADC, and AB were forced to receive welfare assistance from relatively punitive local programs.

Where do we place the blame for these various shortcomings in New Deal policy? To some extent, Roosevelt reflected the hesitations and biases of American society. America entered the decade with no tradition of federal leadership in social welfare, so the first programs were often greeted with suspicion and uncertain funding. So preoccupied were reformers with establishing the precedent of federal programs that they often could not seek their enlargement or had to make compromises to conservatives in both parties to establish them.[104] Since many of Roosevelt's advisors, as well as a large contingent of liberals in the Congress, had their ideological roots in the progressive era when emphasis was placed on local reforms, they were suspicious of developing a large federal bureaucracy or permanent federal programs.[105] Many Americans disliked programs that assisted urban dwellers and workers though most Americans lived in cities. Work relief programs were controversial in a society that assumed industrious persons could

find work or that believed government should not interfere with the private sector. Deficit spending was also unpopular.

Roosevelt was able to obtain the relatively timid policies of the New Deal only because the economic Depression, which brought unprecedented suffering, created a political climate throughout the decade that fostered the development of social reforms. Roosevelt lacked strong and certain allies on the left whom he could rely on for consistent support. Charismatic but eccentric leaders such as Father Coughlin and Huey Long were as adept at demagoguery as they were at supporting reforms. The CIO proved a more certain ally, but the AFL was lukewarm about the Fair Employment Practices Act and opportunistically used programs like the WPA to secure jobs for its own members.

It is ironic, in retrospect, that President Ronald Reagan attacked Roosevelt's New Deal in the 1980s as America's venture into socialism. It was hardly socialism; it was a tentative foundation for a welfare state that would provide minimal public benefits to some poor people and the elderly. The nation's social and economic inequalities as well as its racist and sexist policies remained intact.

## END NOTES

1. Eliot Rosen, *Hoover, Roosevelt, and the Brainstrust: From Depression to New Deal* (New York: Columbia University Press, 1977), pp. 115–119.

2. Henry Adams, *Harry Hopkins* (New York: Putnam, 1977), p. 71.

3. *Ibid.,* pp. 71–72.

4. Alan Brinkley, *Voices of Protest: Huey Long, Father Coughlin, and the Great Depression* (New York: Random House, 1982), pp. 8-81.

5. *Ibid.,* pp. 82–142.

6. Abraham Holtzman, *The Townsend Movement: A Political Study* (New York: Octagon Books, 1975).

7. Paul Douglas, *Social Security in the United States: An Analysis and Appraisal of the Federal Social Security Act* (New York: McGraw-Hill, 1939), pp. 74–83.

8. Ronald A. Mulder, *The Insurgent Progressives in the United States Senate and the New Deal, 1933–1939* (New York: Garland, 1979), p. 73.

9. William Bremer, *Depression Winters: New York Social Workers and the New Deal* (Philadelphia: Temple University Press, 1984), pp. 126–132.

10. *Ibid.,* pp. 158–163; John Ehrenreich, *The Altruistic Imagination: A History of Social Work and Social Policy in the United States* (Ithaca, N.Y.: Cornell University Press, 1985), pp. 102–108.

11. Melvyn Dubofsky and Warren Van Tine, *John L. Lewis* (New York: New York Times Book Co., 1977), pp. 203–221.

12. Raymond Wolters, *Negroes and the Great Depression: The Problem of Economic Recovery* (Westport, Conn.: Greenwood, 1970), pp. 39–55.

13. Brinkley, *Voices of Protest,* pp. 207–208.

14. *Ibid.,* p. 255.

15. James Patterson, *Congressional Conservatism and the New Deal* (Lexington, Ky.: University of Kentucky Press, 1967), pp. 50–76.

16. Mulder, *The Insurgent Progressives,* pp. 292–308.

17. Robert McElvaine, *The Great Depression: America, 1929–1941* (New York: New York Times Book Co., 1984), pp. 281–282; Richard Polenberg, *Reorganizing Roosevelt's Government: Controversy over Executive Reorganization, 1936–1939* (Cambridge, Mass.: Harvard University Press, 1966); Charles Trout, *Boston, the Great Depression, and the New Deal* (New York: Oxford University Press, 1977), pp. 310–312.

18. Robert Steamer, *The Supreme Court in Crisis: A History of Conflict* (Amherst, Mass.: University of Massachusetts Press, 1971), p. 199.

19. George Martin, *Madam Secretary: Frances Perkins* (Boston: Houghton Mifflin, 1976), pp. 341–356; Lillian Mohr, *Frances Perkins* (Croton-on-Hudson, N.Y.: North River Press, 1979), pp. 203–206; Edwin Witte, *The Development of the Social Security Act* (Madison, Wis.: University of Wisconsin Press, 1962), pp. 1–111.

20. Bremer, *Depression Winters,* p. 151; Martin, *Madam Secretary,* p. 345.

21. Mohr, *Frances Perkins,* p. 205.

22. Douglas, *Social Security,* pp. 62–68; Martin, *Madam Secretary,* p. 351.

23. Martin, *Madam Secretary,* p. 348.

24. Quoted in Mimi Abramovitz, *Regulating the Lives of Women* (Boston: South End Press, 1988), p. 253.

25. *Ibid.,* p. 254.

26. Douglas, *Social Security,* pp. 28–54, 129–150.

27. Bremer, *Depression Winters,* pp. 150–155; Clarke Chambers, *Paul U. Kellogg and the Survey: Voices for Social Welfare and Social Justice* (Minneapolis, Minn.: University of Minnesota Press, 1971), pp. 156–157.

28. Josephine Brown, *Public Relief, 1929–1939* (New York: Holt, Rinehart & Winston, 1940), pp. 303–312; Bremer, *Depression Winters,* pp. 166–167.

29. Douglas, *Social Security,* pp. 151–157, 185–196, 203–205.

30. Brown, *Public Relief,* pp. 303–306, 308, 312.

31. Winifred Bell, *Aid to Dependent Children* (New York: Columbia University Press, 1965), pp. 29–30.

32. Frances Piven and Richard Cloward, *Regulating the Poor: The Functions of Public Welfare* (New York: Pantheon Books, 1971), pp. 123–145; Bell, *Aid to Dependent Children,* pp. 41–46, 76–110.

33. Gilbert Steiner, *Social Insecurity: The Politics of Welfare* (Chicago: Rand McNally, 1966), pp. 18–26.

34. Chambers, *Paul U. Kellogg,* p. 157; Douglas, *Social Security,* p. 68; Martin, *Madam Secretary,* p. 347.

35. Joseph Huthmacher, *Senator Robert F. Wagner and the Rise of Urban Liberalism* (New York: Atheneum, 1968), pp. 190–191.

36. Martin, *Madam Secretary,* pp. 381–383.

37. David Brody, *Workers in Industrial America: Essays on the Twentieth-Century Struggle* (New York: Oxford University Press, 1980), pp. 110–112.

38. Adams, *Harry Hopkins,* pp. 72–73.

39. *Ibid.,* pp. 73–88.

40. Arthur MacMahon, John Millett, and Gladys Ogden, *The Administration of Federal Work Relief* (Chicago: Public Administration Service, 1941), pp. 313–314.

41. Bremer, *Depression Winters,* pp. 137–141.

42. MacMahon, Millett, and Ogden, *The Administration,* pp. 26–27.

43. *Ibid.,* p. 390.

44. John Salmond, *A Southern Rebel: The Life and Times of Aubrey Willis Williams, 1890–1965* (Chapel

Hill, N.C.: University of North Carolina Press, 1983), pp. 121–140.

45. McElvaine, *The Great Depression,* p. 281.

46. *Ibid.,* pp. 283, 299.

47. *Ibid.,* pp. 299–300.

48. Martin, *Madam Secretary,* pp. 323–324, 399–419; Polenberg, *Reorganizing Roosevelt's Government,* pp. 55–78.

49. Martin, *Madam Secretary,* pp. 399–406.

50. Steamer, *The Supreme Court,* p. 209.

51. Martin, *Madam Secretary,* pp. 387–390.

52. Mulder, *The Insurgent Progressives,* pp. 165–213.

53. *Ibid.,* pp. 272–274; Patterson, *Congressional Conservatism,* pp. 277–287.

54. Patterson, *Congressional Conservatism,* p. 127.

55. Richard Chapman, *Contours of Public Policy, 1939–1945* (New Haven, Conn.: Yale University Doctoral Dissertation, 1976), p. 262.

56. Martin, *Madam Secretary,* pp. 391–395.

57. *Ibid.;* Mulder, *The Insurgent Progressives,* pp. 224–227; Patterson, *Congressional Conservatism,* pp. 149–154.

58. Huthmacher, *Senator Robert F. Wagner,* pp. 224–228.

59. Charles McKinley and Robert Frase, *Launching Social Security: A Capture-and-Record Account* (Madison, Wis.: University of Wisconsin Press, 1970).

60. Barry Karl, *Executive Reorganization and Reform in the New Deal* (Cambridge, Mass.: Harvard University Press, 1963); Polenberg, *Reorganizing Roosevelt's Government.*

61. Chapman, *Contours,* pp. 1–80.

62. John Kirby, *Black Americans in the Roosevelt Era: Liberalism and Race* (Knoxville, Tenn.: University of Tennessee Press, 1980), pp. 97, 101–102, 141–142.

63. *Ibid.,* pp. 34–35; Huthmacher, *Senator Robert F. Wagner,* pp. 171–173, 242.

64. Patterson, *Congressional Conservatism,* pp. 98–99.

65. Kirby, *Black Americans,* pp. 30–34, 57–62, 82–83.

66. *Ibid.,* pp. 32, 61, 73–74; Salmond, *A Southern Rebel,* pp. 126-127.

67. Kirby, *Black Americans,* pp. 19–26, 37–47, 51–53, 58–59, 106-151.

68. *Ibid.,* p. 142; John Salmond, *The Civilian Conservation Corps, 1933–1942* (Durham, N.C.: Duke University Press, 1967), p. 101; Wolters, *Negroes,* pp. 203–209.

69. Salmond, *A Southern Rebel,* pp. 126–127; Wolters, *Negroes,* pp. 196–206.

70. Salmond, *The Civilian Conservation Corps,* pp. 91–94.

71. Kirby, *Black Americans,* p. 34.

72. Wolters, *Negroes,* pp. 98–102.

73. John Hope Franklin, *From Slavery to Freedom* (New York: Knopf, 1974), pp. 559–563.

74. Gerald Jaynes and Robin Williams, eds., *A Common Destiny: Blacks and American Society* (Washington, D.C.: National Academy Press, 1989), pp. 59–60.

75. Kirby, *Black Americans,* pp. 142–145.

76. Nancy Woloch, *Women and the American Experience* (New York: Knopf, 1984), p. 424.

77. Susan Ware, "Women and the New Deal." In Harvard Sitcoff, ed., *Fifty Years Later: The New Deal Evaluated* (Philadelphia: Temple University Press, 1985), p. 120.

78. *Ibid.*

79. Woloch, *Women,* p. 443.

80. Abramovitz, *Regulating the Lives of Women,* p. 261.

81. *Ibid.,* pp. 254–255, 292.

82. *Ibid.,* p. 293.

83. Ware, "Women and the New Deal," pp. 121, 124; Abramovitz, *Regulating the Lives of Women,* p. 224.

84. Barbara Ehrenreich and Deirdre English, *For Her Own Good* (New York: Doubleday, 1978), pp. 221.

85. Leobardo Estrada, F. Chris Garcia, Reynaldo Macias, and Lionel Maldonado, "Chicanos in the United States: A History of Exploitation and Resis-

tance." In F. Chris Garcia, ed., *Latinos and the Political System* (Notre Dame, Ind.: University of Notre Dame Press, 1988), pp. 50–51.

86. Ronald Takaki, *Strangers from a Different Shore* (Boston: Little, Brown, 1989), p. 217ff.

87. *Ibid.,* p. 179.

88. *Ibid.,* p. 219.

89. *Ibid.,* pp. 390–391.

90. *Ibid.,* p. 378.

91. Stanley Wenocur and Michael Reisch, *From Charity to Enterprise: The Development of American Social Work in a Market Economy* (Urbana, Ill.: University of Illinois Press, 1989), pp. 115–135.

92. Virginia Robinson, *A Changing Psychology in Social Case Work* (Chapel Hill, N.C.: University of North Carolina Press, 1930).

93. Bremer, *Depression Winters,* pp. 16–24.

94. *Ibid.,* pp. 34–37, 46–53.

95. Wenocur and Reisch, *From Charity to Enterprise,* p. 213.

96. Bremer, *Depression Winters,* pp. 126–132.

97. Wenocur and Reisch, *From Charity to Enterprise,* pp. 182–207.

98. Bremer, *Depression Winters,* pp. 159–165.

99. Leslie Leighninger, *Social Work: Search for Identity* (New York: Greenwood Press, 1987), pp. 103–124.

100. *Ibid.,* pp. 125–150.

101. Bell, *Aid to Dependent Children,* pp. 29–30.

102. Ware, "Women and the New Deal," p. 119.

103. Brody, *Workers,* pp. 138–146.

104. Margaret Weir and Theda Skocpol, "State Structures and the Possibilities for 'Keynesian' Responses to the Great Depression in Sweden, Britain, and the United States." In Peter Evans, Dietrich Rueschemeyer, and Theda Skocpol, eds., *Bringing the State Back In* (Cambridge: Cambridge University Press, 1985), pp. 132–137.

105. Mulder, *The Insurgent Progressives,* pp. 1–34.

CHAPTER 9

# The Era of Federal Social Services in the New Frontier and Great Society

## Selected Orienting Events in the Era of Federal Services

| | |
|---|---|
| 1945–1952 | Presidency of Harry Truman |
| 1946 | Full Employment Act |
| 1950–1953 | Korean War |
| 1950s–1960s | Massive migration of African Americans from the South to the North |
| 1953 | Department of Health, Education, and Welfare established |
| 1953–1960 | Presidency of Dwight Eisenhower |
| 1955 | Bus boycott in Birmingham initiates civil rights movement |
| 1960 | John Kennedy wins presidential election |
| 1961 | Passage of Manpower Development and Training Act (MDTA) |
| 1961–1963 | Escalating pattern of racial violence and protest in the South |
| 1962 | Michael Harrington publishes *The Other America* |
| 1963 | President Kennedy delivers nation's first presidential address on civil rights; passage of Mental Retardation and Community Mental Health Centers Construction Act |
| 1963 | John Kennedy assassinated; succeeded by Lyndon Johnson |
| 1964 | Economic Opportunity Act, Food Stamps Act, and Civil Rights Act enacted |
| 1964 | Johnson wins a landslide victory over Goldwater in presidential election |
| 1965 | Medicare, Medicaid, Elementary and Secondary Education Act, Civil Rights Act, and Older Americans Act enacted |
| mid–late 1960s | Cesar Chavez organizes farm workers |
| 1966 | National Organization for Women formed |
| 1967 | Welfare amendments establish work incentives and work programs for AFDC recipients |
| 1968 | Martin Luther King assassinated |
| 1968 | Johnson decides not to seek Democratic nomination for another term |
| 1969 | Stonewall Inn riot initiates gay rights movement |

President Franklin Roosevelt hoped that a new reform era would begin after World War II ended in August 1945, but many conservatives believed they could dismantle New Deal reforms. Social reform did not enjoy a resurgence in the Truman presidency (1945–1952) for a variety of reasons. Moreover, a stalemate ensued in the Eisenhower presidency (1953–1960) when the remaining New Deal programs survived but were not sup-plemented by many new reforms. A new era of reforms occurred during the 1960s, however; this period of reform began tentatively during the administration of John Kennedy (1961–1963), but it gained momentum in the first three years of the presidency of Lyndon Johnson (1963–1966) before dissipating in his final two years as the nation became mired in the Vietnam War.

## WORLD WAR II, THE POSTWAR ERA, AND THE 1950s

Liberals watched with dismay during World War II as many of the major social programs of the New Deal were dismantled by 1943, including the WPA, the CCC, the PWA, and the NYA. Some of them were astonished that Franklin Roosevelt failed to make a greater effort to save the programs, but the programs were probably doomed because of the precipitous near ending of unemployment during the war (these programs had focused on providing jobs to the unemployed), because the war gave conservatives more power (they could threaten not to cooperate with Roosevelt's foreign policy if he insisted on continuing these programs), and because the huge wartime deficit made it difficult to justify spending that was not essential to the war effort.[1] All the programs within the Social Security Act survived the war, however.

Liberals and conservatives sought to position themselves during the war for the postwar period. Intent on not letting liberals seize the postwar agenda, the conservatives ended funding for the National Resources Planning Board (NRPB), which Roosevelt had established and staffed with liberals to conduct planning for the postwar period and which issued reports before its demise that recommended the creation of many social programs after the war to avert an expected resumption of the Great Depression.[2] Indeed, conservatives in Congress established several planning bodies of their own for the postwar period that, predictably, recommended no major increases in social spending after the war.

The enormousness of World War II, which required a total mobilization of the domestic economy and huge, unprecedented deficits, distracted attention from the domestic social agenda. Instead of social reform, major domestic issues during the war involved the extent and nature of rationing, the extent wages and prices should be controlled (and at what levels), and the extent civilian goods should be produced during a wartime economy that focused on military production.

### The Failure of Social Reform in the Truman Era

Even with the ending of the NRPB, some highly placed liberals within the administration sought to obtain reform in the immediate aftermath of the war. They tried to get Roosevelt's ear during the war and just before his death in March 1945 and then to obtain Truman's approval before the defeat of Japan in August 1945. Following some of the earlier recommendations of the NRPB, these officials developed an intriguing and simple idea to achieve postwar social reform by indirection. Since it was commonly assumed that a recession (or worse) would occur when military spending decreased after the war, why not commit the federal government to obtaining "full employment" and mandate spending on an array of social programs, such as health insurance, housing, and expanded Social Security, as the economic means to this goal? Social spending would thus be *required* to keep the economy in full employment. And why not establish in the White House a planning council of economists who would orchestrate this liberal scenario and help the incumbent president, as well, issue an annual economic report? After many meetings among themselves, with cooperation from some liberal congressmen and support from Truman, the legislation eventually was enacted as the Full Employment Act of 1946, which established a national full-employment goal and the Council of Economic Advisors in the White House.[3]

But the legislation hardly resulted in a renewal of social reforms. Conservatives were able to dilute its language so that the government was not *required* to increase social spending when unemployment became severe. Moreover, to the surprise of many economists, no depression ensued in the wake of World War II since (among other factors) Americans had amassed enormous savings during the war in the form of war bonds that they rushed to use to buy consumer goods that had been denied them during the Great Depression and the war. Fueled by such spending and by huge exports to other nations whose economies had been devastated by the war, a postwar economic boom occurred. As this boom occurred, conservatives sought to *reduce* government spending to avert inflation — hardly the scenario that the framers of the Full Employment Act had envisioned![4]

Reform never "took off" after the war for other reasons as well. Recall that a conservative coalition of Republicans and Southern Democrats had become relatively cohesive in 1937 and had fought many of Roosevelt's initiatives (or at least sought to dilute or modify them). When the Republicans won a resounding victory in the national elections of 1946, sufficient to control both houses of Congress, they were able to de-

velop an antispending crusade that was aided by their ability to cut federal taxes so that Truman *had* to refrain from increasing social spending in order not to incur a deficit in the federal budget. (Like most Americans of this era, Truman was strongly against deficits, so people who did not want more social spending could achieve this goal by cutting taxes.)[5]

Nor were Americans enamored with social reform in this period, partly because they were preoccupied with enjoying the first extended period of relative affluence that they had enjoyed since 1929 when the Great Depression began. Imbued with savings from the war period and enticed by an array of appliances and cars, many Americans were oblivious to the needs of impoverished people in the cities and rural areas — or to the needs of African Americans who still lived under the tyrannies of poverty and Jim Crow laws.

Social reform was also impeded by international developments. When World War II ended, idealists hoped that a period of international stability, orchestrated by the United Nations, which was formed in the waning years of the war, would ensue. International events of the postwar period seemed sufficiently auspicious that funds devoted to military purposes declined almost to prewar levels.

But international stability soon began to unravel as an increasingly tense relationship between the United States and Russia developed. The Russian dictator, Joseph Stalin, was convinced that Roosevelt had agreed to allow him to dominate Eastern Europe in the wake of the war in return for the vast sacrificing of soldiers and citizens by the Russians on the eastern front during the war. Thus emboldened and wanting to build a buffer between his nation and the hated Germans who had invaded Russia on several occasions, Stalin quickly asserted control over Poland, Czechoslovakia, East Germany, and other East European nations. Moreover, civil conflict in Greece and Turkey led Americans to believe these nations could be taken over by the Russians. Believing the Russians might even want to extend their empire to Western Europe, Truman developed the so-called Marshall Plan to provide American economic assistance to Western Europe in order to make it more difficult for the Russians to develop discontent and insurrections there. Although Truman refrained from increasing the military budget, the huge expenditures for the Marshall Plan meant that no funds existed to initiate major increases in social spending, particularly when (as already noted) conservatives had cut the level of American taxes. Moreover, Truman, like Roosevelt in World War II, gave only symbolic, verbal support to social reform in the period 1947 to 1949 because he needed the support of the conservative coalition if his foreign-policy objectives, such as the Marshall Plan, were to be approved.[6]

But the *real* diversion of resources and presidential effort to military spending and international affairs—indeed the cold war itself—commenced in 1950. For several years, some top officials, such as Dean Acheson and Paul Nitze of the State Department, had believed that the United States had to dramatically increase its defense spending to counter a perceived Communist threat around the world. But they were worried that a budget-conscious Congress and president would refuse. Shortly after sending Truman a secret report detailing the need for a larger military, North Korea attacked South Korea—and Truman decided to use the invasion as a pretext not only for obtaining funds for that war but also for a massive, and ongoing, increase in American military spending.[7] American military spending rose from about $10 billion annually to $40 billion annually, with the budget escalating to considerably higher levels during the Korean and Vietnam wars. In constant dollar terms, after correcting for inflation, the military budget remained at the same extraordinary level for the next forty-two years, leading to a military budget of roughly $300 billion in 1991.

Why, you may wonder, discuss the *military* budget in a book on social welfare policy? To some extent, any budgets represent competition between spending priorities. When Americans chose to spend close to 75 percent of their national budgets in the 1950s on military spending, they could *not* spend these sums on alternative programs. Moreover, since high military spending was coupled with low federal tax rates (compared to international standards), funds available for social spending were considerably restricted. Though military spending as a percentage of the gross national product gradually declined over the next forty years because the American economy grew so rapidly, it continued to absorb much of the federal budget. Indeed, even as late as 1975, military spending when added to military-related items (such as interest on the national debt that largely derived from former wars, the Atomic Energy Commission, and the National Aeronautics and Space Administration) constituted roughly three-quarters of the national budget.

When reading other parts of this chapter, as well as ensuing chapters, then, you should bear in mind that social spending was constrained by military (and military-related) spending. Moreover, the cold war consumed a large portion of the energies of presidents as well as congressional leaders during its forty-odd years, probably to the detriment of attention to domestic matters.

Social reform in the Truman era was retarded, as well, by racial animosities by the white population toward African Americans and by the lack of political organization by the African-American community. There had been race riots during World War II in urban areas such as Detroit since the white population was angered by a large African-American migration to seek wartime jobs. Considerable racial tension remained in northern cities after the war. Moreover, southern legislators, who sometimes teamed with Republicans and some northern whites, obtained the termination of the Fair Employment Practices Commission at the end of the war, resisted Truman's efforts to revive it, and blocked other civil rights legislation. Truman made progress in desegregating the armed services but only after the war was over and in the face of outright defiance by some generals.[8]

Social reformers were often on the defensive in the postwar period as well as the 1950s because of the dynamics of the cold war. Because many cold-war warriors became obsessed with subversion of government and American society by communists, they demanded the firing of civil servants and the prosecuting of ordinary citizens who were "leftists" or "radicals"—or who had had prior membership in the Communist party. Rooting subversive people from government was a major campaign theme even in 1946, but it crescendoed into a veritable witchhunt by the early 1950s when federal officials developed lists of subversive civil servants, who were often terminated with no due process. The campaign met its ugly culmination in the Senate investigating hearings of Joseph McCarthy in the early 1950s, when McCarthy, who had already subjected many citizens to public interrogation, sought to obtain the dismissal of high-level officers of the army. When McCarthy was finally discredited and censured by the Senate, the witchhunt subsided, but the whole process had led to widespread public suspicions of social reformers who were often tainted with the label radical.

## Eisenhower and the Conservative Decade of the 1950s

Elected as a hero from World War II and as a candidate who promised to end the unpopular war in Korea, Eisenhower was a president who had had virtually no experience in domestic, nonmilitary matters.

Eisenhower's philosophy was relatively simple and quite conservative. He wanted to keep taxes to a minimum so that government did not interfere with the private economy. He had no interest in expanding social spending aside from small programs here and there. He was willing to make truly massive government commitments

to infrastructure improvements through the establishment of the interstate highway system and the St. Lawrence seaway largely because he perceived these measures to serve important military functions by facilitating the transportation of troops and military hardware in the event of a world war. (He had marveled at the German's sophisticated transportation system during World War II.)[9]

Perhaps even more than Truman, Eisenhower was obsessed with diplomatic and military maneuvering associated with the cold war. Flanked by the Dulles brothers (John Foster Dulles at the State Department and Allen Dulles at the Central Intelligence Agency), Eisenhower presided over numerous international crises abroad and innumerable debates within his administration about the size and composition of the American military forces. Fearing that the Russians wanted to bankrupt the United States by tricking it into spending excessively on its military, Eisenhower constantly sought to cut military spending, but the costly technological advances of the 1950s, such as the development of missiles and advanced aircraft, as well as the belief that America should devote huge forces to the defense of Europe, meant the large military budgets that Truman had initiated at the outset of the Korean War remained intact. Moreover, members of both political parties came to see military contracts as important sources of political gain in their districts, so the Congress often balked when Eisenhower broached various cuts in military spending. It was ironic that Eisenhower, a former war hero, made an eloquent argument against the "military–industrial complex" in his valedictory speech as he left the presidency in 1960, noting that every dollar spent on guns is a dollar not spent on humanitarian programs.[10]

Though conservative, Eisenhower made a deal with the Democrats and their leadership, such as Lyndon Johnson, who controlled the Congress during much of his tenure. In return for support for most of his foreign policy initiatives, Eisenhower agreed not to make an assault on those social programs that had survived the New Deal. Eisenhower realized that the American people, many of whom still vividly remembered the hardships of the Great Depression, wanted those New Deal programs that had survived World War II retained. Social Security continued to develop new benefits in the 1950s to make it a family program that provided benefits to the disabled, wives, widows, dependent children, and survivors. When the Russians launched Sputnik into orbit, Eisenhower supported the National Defense Education Act, which provided federal funds for science and math training in the schools. But Eisenhower can hardly be called a reformist president even if he did not seek, like Ronald Reagan in the

1980s, to undo social programs that had already been enacted.

Eisenhower's record on race relations was not progressive. Partly because of his numerous links with southern governors and friends, he believed that the federal government should leave racial matters to the states. He did not, correspondingly, assume leadership with respect to lynchings, Jim Crow laws, or the denial of suffrage to southern African Americans. When the Courts finally ordered the city of Little Rock to allow African-American children to attend its schools, he sent federal troops to enforce the order only when escalating violence, including danger to the lives of the African-American children, forced his hand.[11]

 ## THE TURN TOWARD REFORM

Many persons wondered whether the policy quiescence of the 1950s would continue after the presidential election of 1960, which pitted Richard Nixon against John Kennedy, a relatively unknown Democrat who had served in the House (1947–1952) and had been elected to the Senate in 1952. Neither man projected a reform image; indeed, the campaign focused on the first televised presidential debates, in which the two men promised to pursue anti-Communist policies. Only after a key primary in West Virginia, where Kennedy was pitted against Hubert Humphrey, a liberal reformer, did Kennedy make social reform a prominent part of this campaign; he promised to help the elderly with their medical bills, to develop programs to help poverty-stricken persons in Appalachia and inner cities, and "to get the country moving again." But his belated support of social reform, and his past indifference to reform when he had been a U.S. Senator, made many liberals somewhat leery of him, including Eleanor Roosevelt, who gave her support to him only late in the campaign.[12]

A strange combination of affluence and poverty coexisted as the nation entered the decade of the 1960s. The postwar prosperity during the 1950s occurred for several reasons. With the economies of Japan and Europe devastated by World War II, America was uniquely positioned to become the major economic power in the world and to dominate world trade. Lacking economic competitors, American industry could both export at will and dominate domestic markets.[13] Economic growth was buoyed by rising wages as well as funds that circulated in the economy from burgeoning Social Security and other social programs. A partnership was fashioned between government, the housing industry, and the automobile industry that fueled the economic growth; the federal government provided cheap housing loans to veterans and other homeowners and underwrote a large share of the costs of a massive expansion of the nation's roads, which in turn, promoted a housing boom in the suburbs and production of large numbers of automobiles. The federal government contributed indirectly to economic growth through its tax policies as well, by allowing Americans to deduct interest payments on home mortgages and loans.[14]

Serious social problems existed, however. The most obvious problems existed in the South and Southwest, where millions of African Americans, Spanish-speaking Americans, and Native Americans experienced appalling poverty as well as violation of fundamental rights. Although they had traditionally resided in rural areas, increasing numbers of them had settled in urban areas in the South and Southwest, where they encountered overt discrimination that precluded them from voting, using public facilities and transportation, and living in white neighborhoods. But there were signs even in the mid-1950s that southern African Americans would demand a new Reconstruction; leaders of African-American churches, who had often been resigned to the oppression of their people, began to discuss strategies for attacking racist policies. The urbanization of southern African Americans allowed them to be more easily organized to protest rampant discrimination.[15]

The seeds of massive African-American discontent were also sown in the North in the 1940s and the 1950s by a massive migration of African Americans from the South. African Americans fled the South for many reasons, whether to join friends who had already migrated to the North, to obtain jobs, or to escape oppression in the South. Ninety percent of the 4.5 million African Americans who migrated to the North and West between 1940 and 1970 settled in the large cities of six states: California, New York, Pennsylvania, Ohio, Michigan, and Illinois.[16] They were ghettoized in densely populated and segregated urban areas, denied housing in white areas, limited to unskilled jobs, denied membership in unions, placed within segregated and inferior school systems, disenfranchised, and subjected to police brutality.

Despite its prosperity, America was marked by extreme economic inequality in 1960; the average income of persons in the most affluent one-fifth of the population was roughly nine times the average income of those in the poorest one-fifth of the population.[17] Poverty existed in low-income areas in cities and in rural areas such as Appalachia, where housing, infant mortality, health, and income standards were similar to those in many third-world nations. Even with Social Security, unemployment insurance, and AFDC, persons in 1960 had few safety-net supports. AFDC was administered arbitrarily in many jurisdictions, with flagrant violations of the rights of persons who sought assistance.[18] Southern states paid scandalously low benefits. No subsidized nutrition program existed, which led many persons, including those who received miserly AFDC payments, to suffer malnutrition; indeed, surveys in Mississippi even as late as 1967 suggested that many children were malnourished.[19] Since the federal government had developed no major medical programs, poor persons had to rely on underfunded county and municipal hospitals. Virtually no special clinics existed at a neighborhood level for pregnant women or infants, for family planning, or for other special populations.

Since government health insurance programs did not exist, millions of elderly persons found that they could not afford medical bills when they lost private medical insurance coverage that had been increasingly provided as a fringe benefit by employers in the postwar era. Social Security pensions, which were received by millions of elderly persons, had helped ease their economic burdens, but about one-third of them lived below poverty levels even in 1967.[20]

Women had first entered the labor force in large numbers during World War II as replacements for male workers who had joined the military, but many of them were terminated when veterans returned. Millions of women remained in the labor force, however, in clerical, checkout, sales, nursing, and teaching occupations, but they were usually consigned to low-paying jobs and rarely given assistance with their daycare needs.[21]

Blue-collar workers were often employed in hazardous working conditions in chemical, plastics, pesticide, and assembly-line plants that were not subject to adequate safety regulations. Despite major gains in unionizing workers, many blue-collar workers lacked private health insurance, were forced to rely on charity medicine in public hospitals when they became seriously ill, and were buffeted by three recessions in the 1950s.

Mentally ill, developmentally disabled, and physically disabled persons encountered desperate problems. Since statutes did not exist in most jurisdictions that placed limits on involuntary commitments of mentally ill persons to institutions, many unjustified admissions were made. Many persons with severe mental disorders had to be admitted to hospitals since few community programs existed for them. Their rights were rarely safeguarded within institutions, where many of them remained for decades with little or no treatment. Mental institutions, as well as a growing number of poorly monitored nursing homes, also served as repositories for older persons, who had virtually no access to community-based services.[22] The plight of developmentally disabled children and families was equally desperate since public schools often shunned this population, few community-based services existed, and parents often had no recourse to institutionalizing their children.[23] Physically handicapped persons were provided with virtually no supportive assistance other than disability assistance and inadequate health services in county and municipal hospitals.[24]

Homosexuality was widely perceived to be a mental problem rather than a lifestyle preference. Since most states had statutes that defined the sexual practices of homosexuals to be crimes, homosexuals usually tried to disguise their sexual orientation to escape criminal sanctions, insensitive services from mental health professions, or discrimination by employers.[25] Some gay persons were involuntarily committed to mental institutions by relatives who believed them to be mentally ill because of their sexual preferences. Scores of gay persons were fired from the federal civil service, the State Department, and the armed forces in the 1950s. Quite apart from inadequate laws and social programs, widespread public discrimination existed against many kinds of minorities in 1960, including racial minorities, disabled people, and homosexuals.[26]

## DOMESTIC POLICY DURING THE KENNEDY PRESIDENCY

The lethargy of the 1950s was broken by the election in 1960 of John Kennedy, the youngest president in American history. He remains a controversial figure. Some historians and biographers portray him as a socially minded leader whose legislation was defeated because he confronted a relatively conservative Congress and public. Had he not been assassinated, they argue, he would have been reelected in 1964, would have obtained a sweeping electoral victory, and would have secured enactment of many social reforms.[27] His detractors present a less flattering portrait; they contend that he was relatively conservative in his political orientations, possessed a limited reform vision, adopted

reform causes only when he encountered strong political pressure, and enmeshed the nation in the Vietnam conflict.[28] A true portrayal probably lies between these polar accounts.

Kennedy had limited understanding of poverty and racism because he was raised in a wealthy Boston family and attended private schools. He rarely assumed leadership roles on domestic issues while a congressman and senator in the postwar era though he dutifully voted Democratic positions on many issues. His orientations toward social reform were reflected in his ambivalence about Franklin Roosevelt. His father, a wealthy businessman, had had a conflicted relationship with Roosevelt that ended in his resignation from a high-level position in Roosevelt's administration.[29] Kennedy regarded New Deal reforms, which provided economic resources and jobs to the poor, as outmoded in an affluent era when problems of poverty involved (he believed) intergenerational pockets of poverty in inner cities and rural areas. Kennedy was a problem-solving pragmatist whose advisors were adept at using economics and management tools to analyze complex problems. But social reform requires moral outrage—and it was the absence of a gut response to social problems that alienated many liberals from Kennedy in the late 1950s and that led some of them to only belatedly support his presidential bid in 1960.[30]

Like many other persons of the era, Kennedy accepted both cultural and structural explanations for the existence of poverty. Economic improvement of poor persons was impeded, he believed, by a culture of poverty that made them oriented toward the present, unable to defer gratification, and unwilling to perceive the utility of education. Structuralists believed that automation and technology consigned unskilled and poorly educated persons to unemployment or dead-end jobs. In either case, remedies focused on changing the poor themselves, whether by providing them with different orientations or by giving them training or education.[31]

These approaches to poverty were based on questionable assumptions. Research suggests that, though structural unemployment exists, most low-income workers are able to find work but are subject to brief periods of unemployment because they work in seasonal occupations or for firms that are particularly subject to economic cycles. Perhaps more important than structural factors are overt and covert forms of discrimination that relegate racial minorities and women to low-paying unskilled and semiskilled occupations and to adverse hiring and promotion decisions, particularly during recessions.[32]

The belief that the poor possessed a distinctive and dysfunctional culture was also questioned by many critics. Perspectives of poor persons often change when they receive work, which suggests that "basic orientations" are often adaptations to immediate situational realities. Certain attributes, such as present-orientedness, may be functional for populations that have little hope of saving money from low-paying jobs. Some critics questioned the methodology of middle-class social scientists, whose conclusions about the different culture of the poor sometimes derived from biased research instruments. Others noted that many of the characteristics attributed to the poor by social scientists in the 1960s were identical to stereotypes of paupers—as well as Irish Americans and other ethnic groups—that had been pervasive in the nineteenth century, when many Americans concluded that they were lazy and unmotivated. In both the nineteenth century and the 1960s, many Americans condescendingly believed that poor persons would be magically transformed if they were personally exposed to middle- or upper-class persons who could teach them to be industrious.[33]

The various explanations of poverty and unemployment that were commonly advanced in the early 1960s led to a preoccupation with policies to change the victims of poverty by providing them with services and training to the neglect of policies to redistribute resources and jobs to them. Scant attention was given to public works, tax incentives to employers to hire certain kinds of workers, affirmative action, the development of a national welfare system, or redistributive tax reform.[34] From the vantage of the poor, services, education, and job training may eventually help some persons escape poverty, but they do not help them with immediate economic needs or necessarily improve their economic condition relative to other citizens.

In Kennedy's defense, he encountered a difficult political situation in 1960. He did not receive a reform mandate from the voters when they narrowly chose him over Richard Nixon in 1960, and most Americans did not give priority, in public opinion polls of the early 1960s, to addressing issues of poverty or racial discrimination. Kennedy's political problems were magnified by divisions within the Democratic party; conservative Southern Democrats, whose support he desperately needed to defeat Republican opposition, stoutly resisted domestic reforms, whereas a group of liberal Northern Democrats, including Senator Hubert Humphrey, insisted that Kennedy develop a range of social reforms, such as the development of executive orders and legislation to protect the rights of southern African Americans. Caught in this political crossfire, Kennedy tried, with marginal success, to walk a political tightrope between the two factions. Many southern conservatives believed he was a liberal reformer who might even vigorously seek a second Reconstruction, and northern liberals often believed that he was overconcerned with appeasing Southern Democrats.[35]

Kennedy's precarious political position was exacerbated by his political style. Unlike many politicians, who pride themselves on attention to legislative details, Kennedy was widely perceived by congressmen to have been a relatively lazy legislator who missed key votes and was remiss in his legislative homework. Many powerful and senior legislators also believed Kennedy had succeeded to the presidency before his rightful time and resented his disinclination to consult with them unless he absolutely needed their votes. Some politicians believed that he prematurely and fatalistically discounted his chances to win key votes. Witty, articulate, and adept at using television to advantage, Kennedy was an entertaining president who had limited ability to convince powerful politicians to support his legislation.[36]

## Poverty and Civil Rights: Toward Reform

Kennedy grew up in a family tradition of Irish, big-city, machine politics. His grandfather had been a prominent Boston politician who had developed his power base by assiduously helping citizens obtain jobs and resources. His father was quite conservative and antisemitic; nonetheless, he was active in Democratic politics and

held the directorship of the Security and Exchange Commission during the New Deal.

Kennedy did not actively seek a leadership position on domestic issues, but he usually voted liberal positions on social issues in the Congress in the 1950s and consistently supported legislation that would help unions, which constituted a major portion of his political base. He was sensitized to problems of mental and developmental disability by a sister who was developmentally disabled. He possessed an activist philosophy that made him eager to tackle new problems, and he was supremely confident that any problem could be solved, even complex ones like poverty. He possessed an expansive conception of the presidency, which he believed should provide assertive leadership.[37]

Kennedy can best be described in the late 1950s as a potential liberal because his background made him receptive to social reform but reluctant to give it precedence over foreign affairs. He was pushed leftward during the Democratic presidential primaries in 1960 when he ran against Hubert Humphrey, who successfully invoked the reform tradition of Franklin Roosevelt and, in the process, portrayed Kennedy as indifferent to social issues. When Kennedy appealed to the Roosevelt tradition to try to obtain votes of miners and other working-class voters as the candidates moved toward a pivotal primary in West Virginia, he won a crucial victory that gave him momentum that extended to other primaries and eventually the presidential nomination of his party. He realized, too, that he would have to actively pursue social reform if he wanted to keep the allegiance of the liberal wing of the Democratic party, a group that finally, if reluctantly, supported his bid for the party's nomination.[38]

Slow but decided shifts in public opinion facilitated Kennedy's movement toward social reform. Poverty and other social issues were rarely discussed in the 1950s in public or private arenas; indeed, a bibliography of academic writings on the subject of poverty in 1960 totaled two pages![39] When Michael Harrington published *The Other America* in 1962, a book that discussed problems of the "invisible poor" in rural and urban settings, he was surprised to discover that it became a bestseller.[40] Academics, too, discovered the poor, as reflected by a rapidly expanding literature on the subject in the early 1960s. As the progressive and New Deal eras had demonstrated, social reform is possible in America when sizable numbers of middle-class Americans empathize with disadvantaged persons.

It was the civil rights movement, however, that decisively pushed Kennedy and the nation toward social reform. It began quietly in the South in 1955 when a young African-American minister, Martin Luther King, Jr., organized a boycott of buses in Birmingham to protest the policy that required African Americans to sit at the back of them. African Americans won a decisive victory when this policy was rescinded, but only after a lengthy period of tense confrontation that included sporadic acts of violence against African Americans. The bus boycott initiated a long sequence of protests that successively challenged segregation in interstate transportation, lunch counters, train stations, public swimming pools, public schools, and colleges. Involvement in these issues led, in turn, to protests against literacy tests and poll taxes that disqualified African Americans from voting in the South. Many Americans in the North began to realize that a tangled web of racist policies existed in the South that trapped African Americans at virtually every step. The nation became further sensitized to southern injustices as nonviolent protests of civil rights demonstrators were repeatedly countered by violence, unfair rulings by southern courts, intimidation, and murder.[41]

A particular murder in the summer of 1955—the killing of Emmett Till, an African-American child from Chicago who was visiting relatives in Mississippi—brought the civil rights struggle of the South to the attention of northern African Americans as well as the mass media.[42] Till had been warned by his mother to be meek when dealing with southern whites; she said, "if you have to get on your knees and bow when a white person goes past, do it willingly."[43] But Till, who had not been reared in the South, bragged to several southern boys outside a grocery store, that he had a white girlfriend up North. When one of them dared him to talk to the white female storekeeper, Till got some candy and told her, "Bye, Baby," as he was leaving. A girl who had heard about the incident predicted that "When that lady's husband come back, there is going to be trouble." As Juan Williams relates, three days later, after midnight on a Saturday, the white woman's husband and his brother-in-law came to get that "boy who has done the talkin."[44] They dragged Till from the country cabin, tortured him, murdered him, and dumped his body in a river—later saying they *had* to kill him because he refused to repent or beg for mercy. When his mother saw the mutilated body, she insisted on an open-casket funeral—and, indeed, a picture of the body, published in an African-American magazine, so shocked Chicagoans that thousands attended the funeral. The subsequent trial of the accused white slayers was equally sensational as an African-American man testified against them in open court—something that rarely happened in the South because of its risks. Other African Americans testified. When the all-white jury exonerated the defendants, mass rallies of African Americans occurred throughout the North. Although justice was never done in this case, Emmett Till became a martyr, and the civil rights struggle became a national movement. Ominously, however, white southerners reacted with rage at the audacity of the African Americans who had testified against the men and at the northern sympathy for Till, so it was clear that "the old South" would not relent quickly.

The civil rights movement, like widespread unemployment in the Great Depression and child labor in the progressive era, provided an obvious and ongoing symbol that sensitized Americans to the needs of disadvantaged persons and forced political leaders to propose policy remedies. Like the protracted unemployment of the 1930s, the vicious cycle of protest and repression would not disappear or yield to superficial remedies. Kennedy, who sought a neutral position between Southern Democrats and liberal reformers, was forced by public opinion to propose civil rights legislation in 1963, but only after he had taken a relatively passive course in 1961 and 1962.

When a pattern of escalating protest and violence in the South had taken hold in 1960 and 1961, Kennedy and his brother Robert, who was attorney general, encountered a predicament. Kennedy needed the votes of Southern Democrats if the rest of his domestic and foreign policies were to be enacted, but he also needed the support of liberal Democrats who were urging him to support federal civil rights legislation or, at the very least, to issue executive orders that forbade job discrimination in federally funded projects.

Kennedy tried for several years to follow a middle course.[45] He gave African Americans and liberals a symbolic victory when he created a presidential task force that was headed by Vice President Lyndon Johnson, but it made little progress in addressing discrimination against African Americans in employment. Though Robert Kennedy used federal marshals and FBI agents to protect demonstrators in the South, he avoided use of federal troops, even in the face of rapidly mounting violence, and insisted, moreover, that southern jurisdictions could protect demonstrators despite the obvious hostility of many local southern police chiefs to them. Kennedy refused to issue executive orders to outlaw discrimination or to develop federal civil rights legislation since both he and his brother were convinced that Reconstruction had failed because civil rights policies had been imposed on the South by the north.[46] They also naively hoped that civil rights legislation could be enacted by southern states as more African Americans became enfranchised. Kennedy's middle course was successful in 1961 and much of 1962. Southerners believed that Robert Kennedy had not used federal marshals except as a last resort, and most African Americans believed that the Kennedy brothers protected them from white extremists.

Some policy successes were obtained, even as violence escalated. When the Interstate Commerce Commission issued directives to desegregate bus and train stations, they complied and were supported by local southern police departments. But events soon made African Americans, liberals, and many northerners realize that aggressive federal intervention was needed. Robert Kennedy had hoped that the civil rights protesters would focus on voting rights rather than on desegregation of public facilities and schools because he thought registration of African Americans would be less likely to arouse a violent response and would eventually liberalize southern politics.[47] When the Student Nonviolent Coordinating Committee (SNCC) brought thousands of white students to work alongside African Americans in registering voters in 1962 and 1963, however, activists were greeted with threats, intimidation, and physical violence. Many southern authorities assumed a passive role, overlooked violence, or jailed activists. The mass media were filled with accounts of southern atrocities, but northern opinion was most aroused, African Americans ruefully noted, when white students or activists were murdered in voter registration drives.[48] Resistance by high-level southern politicians to federal court orders to desegregate universities further angered northerners.

As violence increased, liberals introduced a series of civil rights bills in the Congress and demanded support from Kennedy. Despite protests by some of his top advisors, Kennedy finally decided to propose his own civil rights legislation in 1963, which prohibited job discrimination on the basis of race and gender as well as discrimination in the registration of voters.[49] To make the legislation acceptable to moderates in both parties, he diluted voting provisions. In June 1963, he gave a televised address to endorse the legislation, which was, sadly, the first presidential address in the nation's history devoted to civil rights issues. When Senator

Everett Dirksen and other Republicans decided to join Northern Democrats, the legislation appeared destined for passage, but the ill-fated Kennedy could not claim credit for it because of his tragic death.

## The Course of Reform: Failures and Successes

Kennedy promised in the campaign of 1960 that he would support aid to education and medical insurance for the elderly, but both his medical and educational proposals became enmeshed in ideological controversy. Although European nations had developed national health insurance schemes, many Americans believed that governmental financing of medical care would threaten the doctor–patient relationship system and was, moreover, un-American. The American Medical Association led the opposition to *any* major federal programs, including public funding of inoculations, and was aided by disputes among legislators about financing and program details. Some legislators wanted to fund medical assistance to the elderly from Social Security payroll deductions, but others wanted to use a separate payroll tax or general revenues. Some legislators favored voluntary participation, and others wanted to make participation mandatory. Various legislative proposals went nowhere though some progress had been made in congressional deliberations by the summer of 1963.[50]

As the nation's first Catholic president, Kennedy did not want to appear to favor parochial schools. When he excluded religious and private schools from receiving any funds under his education bill, however, he encountered the wrath of the Catholic Church, which insisted that parochial schools receive funds as well. When he made some concessions to them, Catholic leaders as well as leaders of other denominations became emboldened to demand even more funds for their schools, to the chagrin of legislators who wanted to preserve strict separation of church and state. Passage seemed hopeless.[51]

Some economists believed that periodic recessions, pockets of unemployment, and low rates of economic growth were caused by inadequate pools of investment capital. Guided by economist Walter Heller, Kennedy proposed to increase depreciation allowances for businesses and to allow a tax credit for investments. These policies, which were enacted in 1962, were overshadowed by another proposal to drastically reduce the rates of taxes paid by businesses and wealthy persons. The bill encountered substantial opposition from conservatives, who feared that the tax cut could lead to government deficits. When Kennedy died, the legislation had passed the House, but it was not enacted until 1964. Judged in purely economic terms, Kennedy's tax measures probably spurred investment and economic growth, but from the vantage of the poor and the working class, the policies contributed to economic inequality in the nation and detracted attention from the need to accomplish reforms of the tax code to eliminate deductions and loopholes of affluent taxpayers.[52] Moreover, as we later note, they diminished funds available for social programs when the Vietnam War absorbed increasing resources in following years in the Johnson administration.

Kennedy believed that many unemployed persons could not find work because they lacked necessary skills, so he proposed and obtained passage of the Manpower Development and Training Act of 1962 (MDTA); 600,000 workers had completed technical training by 1968, but the program was plagued by problems.[53] A high dropout rate existed, workers were sometimes given skills that were not needed in local job markets, and limited relocation assistance was rendered. Some critics contend that job-training programs allow one group of trained workers to displace nontrained workers if new jobs are not simultaneously created.[54] MDTA nonetheless represented the nation's first major job-training program. (The work relief programs of the New Deal had not focused on training.)

Kennedy sought and obtained major increases in the minimum wage, partly at the behest of unions, which strongly supported the measure because they hoped it would deter movement of companies to the nonunionized and low-wage South.[55] Its supporters contended that it provided a wage floor for those workers, such as unskilled African-American workers, who were severely underpaid compared to other workers, but some economists believe that it fostered unemployment by stimulating employers to decrease the size of their labor forces.[56]

Kennedy established the Area Redevelopment Agency in 1961 to increase employment in depressed rural areas like Appalachia by providing loans and subsidies to local businesses and by improving their transportation systems.[57] Critics contend that the program created few jobs because its subsidies were too low or were targeted to tourism and other businesses that employed relatively few persons. The program was marred by political favoritism and corruption, so it was terminated in 1965.[58]

The concerns of a number of mental health experts about the absence of community-based care for persons who had been released from mental hospitals led to the establishment of a commission by Congress in 1955. Their report, *Action for Mental Health,* which was issued in 1961, recommended federal funding of community-based services. Kennedy secured the enactment of the Community Mental Health Centers Act of 1963, which provided federal funding for the construction of mental health centers that offered a range of outpatient and preventive services. The act was quickly amended to provide funds for staff as well. Because appropriations for the legislation never met the expectations of its framers, it did not address all the community needs of mental patients, who often lived in substandard board-and-care and skid-row housing.[59] It nonetheless led to the establishment of a national network of centers that provided outpatient services to millions of Americans.

Many Americans were alarmed by the marked expansion of AFDC rolls in the early 1960s. A "services strategy" was formulated in 1962, wherein the federal government provided a 75 percent match to the states to encourage local welfare departments to provide social services to AFDC recipients. It was, at best, a naive proposal. Many factors caused the growth in AFDC rolls, including migration of poor African Americans to urban areas in the North and the South, the absence of jobs for unskilled female workers, and the absence of day care. Furthermore, since rates of desertion by fathers are associated with social class, they are unlikely to decline unless jobs and resources are provided to low-income families. The continuing rise in AFDC rolls with the services strategy was inevitable, and it provided conservatives with the opportunity to propose punitive policies later in the decade.[60]

In rejecting New Deal programs to help the needy as outmoded, Kennedy missed an opportunity to develop a variety of tax, income, and nutritional programs to reduce poverty. Moreover, since he was convinced the nation needed the capability to fight guerilla wars on three continents at the same time to counter Communist insurgency, he launched the fastest buildup of the military during peacetime in American history and introduced military advisors into South Vietnam.[61]

Kennedy deserves praise, however, for shattering the conservative complacency that characterized the 1950s. He came to office with no mandate to enact major reforms and inherited a Congress in which Republicans and Southern Democrats possessed a majority. Although unable to secure passage of most of his major social legislation, he established a policy agenda for his successor; civil rights legislation, the War on Poverty, food stamps, Medicare, federal aid to public schools, and tax reforms were Kennedy initiatives that were enacted, though in modified form, by Lyndon Johnson after Kennedy was assassinated in November 1963.

## KENNEDY AND JOHNSON: A STUDY IN CONTRAST

A novelist could not have fashioned a more unusual plot. The articulate and well-educated Kennedy, fearing lack of support from pivotal southern delegates at the 1960 Democratic convention, chose the southern, crude, and politically astute Johnson to be his vice-president over the strenuous objections of Robert Kennedy. Political pundits saw it as a brilliant move to obtain support of Southern Democrats. Who could have predicted that most of Kennedy's social legislation would eventually be enacted by Johnson or that Johnson would carry the Vietnam policy that Kennedy had begun to its tragic conclusion?

Johnson excelled in political maneuvering. His grandfather and father had been involved in a strange mixture of populist and conservative Texas politics. His mother, an aristocratic figure who was unfulfilled in her marriage to an alcoholic Texan, urged him to rise above his humble origins. As early as college, when he was active in campus politics, Johnson displayed an uncanny ability to decipher the existing balance of political forces and to develop issues that could propel him into leadership roles. After a brief stint as a teacher, he became an aide to a congressman, secured an appointment as regional director in Texas of a major New Deal program, and successfully ran for Congress.[62] On his second attempt, in 1948, Johnson was elected to the United States Senate, where he quickly became a protégé of Senator Richard Russell, a powerful legislator.

By helping Russell with laborious details and serving as his confidante, Johnson cleverly positioned himself to run for the position of Senate minority leader, to which he was elected in 1953. He became an expert in the intricacies of parliamentary procedures, honed his interpersonal and persuasive skills, and augmented his power by vesting in the majority leader the power to make committee assignments.[63] He had

presidential ambitions but was not well known outside Texas and the Senate. Realizing that he could not advance beyond his position as majority leader, he accepted Kennedy's invitation to be vice president in 1960. He was deeply frustrated by 1963, however, because he was seldom consulted by Kennedy or his ivy-league staff. One can only imagine how he felt when he learned, in a Dallas hospital, that Kennedy was dead and that he would soon be the nation's next president.

Johnson achieved legislative successes that were matched only by Franklin Roosevelt; major federal resources were allocated for the first time for public schools, medical insurance for the elderly, subsidies for health care of the poor, legal aid for the poor, job training for impoverished teenagers, enforcement of civil rights for African Americans, nutritional programs, preschool programs, community development projects, health care for migrant labor, and medical services for pregnant women and for children. Whereas Franklin Roosevelt had succeeded in developing federal income and insurance programs for economic security, Johnson extended federal programs into myriad areas that had fallen outside the province of federal policy. His legislative successes can be explained by a combination of facilitating factors.

Kennedy bequeathed to Johnson many pieces of legislation that had made varying degrees of progress through the legislative process. Kennedy thus provided Johnson with an instant agenda that facilitated his legislative tasks.[64] He was aided, moreover, by sustained pressure from civil rights groups—violent reprisals against civil rights demonstrators, as well as continuing protests, inflamed public opinion in the North, which became more sympathetic not only to African Americans but to the plight of poor persons.

Nor should we ignore the fact that Johnson had genuine compassion for the poor and people with other problems. It is always difficult to determine motivation when examining the actions of politicians; this was particularly so with Johnson, who possessed much political ambition and was obsessed with personal failure. Did he so invest himself in seeking legislation to obtain a high reputation, or did he genuinely seek to help people with problems? No doubt Johnson, like most politicians, had mixed motives, but one of his closest aides, Joseph Califano, argues persuasively that Johnson often had noble motives that derived from his populist origins.[65] In any event, Johnson was *driven* to seek social reforms, spent incalculable hours writing legislation, and repeatedly invested himself to the point of exhaustion to achieving its enactment.

Johnson used his political skills to advantage. He immediately wrapped himself in the mantle of Kennedy by promising to enact his legislative measures and by keeping his top staff. By portraying himself as a humble successor to Kennedy, who would devote himself tirelessly to the fulfillment of the slain leader's unfulfilled aspirations, he endeared himself to the American people as well as legislators. He summoned to the White House virtually every legislator, lobbyist, interest-group leader, and citizen who could advance the progress of Kennedy's pending legislation. He obtained detailed information about their policy opinions, specific legislative objectives that they desired, and their willingness to compromise on key points. He assembled, in effect, a massive team to develop a legislative program to support his domestic measures.[66]

Johnson was a welcome change to congressional leadership since he discussed specific pieces of legislation with them before legislation was introduced to Congress. He was adept, as well, at giving legislators credit for specific pieces of legislation during the legislative process and in signing ceremonies. The chasm between the White House and Congress, which had sabotaged Kennedy's legislation, was bridged.

Johnson maintained political support from a broad spectrum of legislators and interest groups.[67] Many liberals, including Robert Kennedy, feared that Johnson would develop conservative policies since he was a southerner, but Johnson dashed these fears when he declared his allegiance to Kennedy's entire legislative package, including civil rights. Indeed, his decisive commitment to civil rights, which he made almost immediately after succeeding to the presidency, was a remarkably bold move that signaled to southerners, as it did to northern liberals, that he would be a reform-minded president. Yet he was also adept at giving concessions to southerners, as reflected by provisions in many pieces of legislation that gave southern states a disproportionate amount of program funds by weighting their distribution to poorer states. (Southern states had the lowest per capita incomes in the United States.) He carefully cultivated support from both unions and business; he supported increases in the minimum wage, favored by unions, and he vigorously sought passage of Kennedy's tax cuts for businesses and individuals. His ability to appeal to both conservative and liberal audiences was illustrated by his support for both budget-cutting and social reform. He prided himself on fiscal conservatism when he sometimes proposed cuts in the federal budget that exceeded those desired by House Republicans or when he blocked efforts by liberals to drastically expand funding for the War on Poverty, the food stamp program, or the AFDC program. Yet he supported passage of a staggering number of social reforms and would brag, much as a fisherman who has had a good day, about the sheer number of programs that he had enacted.[68]

Johnson was a master of the arts of timing, negotiation, and compromise. Since he knew that momentum was crucial, he carefully introduced his legislation each year in a planned sequence, beginning with the easiest and ending with the more difficult measures. He made skillful compromises in legislation to defuse opposition yet astutely avoided an image of softness by refusing to back down when he believed that vital principles were at stake or that compromises would make him appear overtimid. He rewarded politicians with patronage and resources for their districts, not for votes on specific issues, which would have led them to expect rewards every time they supported measures, but for a pattern of support over an extended period. He had an uncanny ability to make slight changes in the wording of legislation to mollify objections of legislators or interest groups—but his compromises would be limited only to those changes that were necessary for passage.[69]

Johnson, who feared that his skein of successes would terminate when his political honeymoon had ended, received extraordinary assistance from the Republicans when they nominated Barry Goldwater in 1964 to be their presidential candidate. The conservative Goldwater presented an easy target for Johnson when

he violated the unspoken rule in American politics to place legacies of the New Deal, such as Social Security and the Tennessee Valley Authority, above partisan politics. Since Goldwater both espoused foreign intervention against Communist regimes and hinted that he might consider use of tactical nuclear weapons in such struggles, Johnson portrayed himself as a man of peace, a claim that was not perceived to be hypocritical since he had not yet committed thousands of troops to Vietnam.[70] Enough liberal and moderate Democrats were elected in the landslide victory of 1964 that Johnson's legislative program could not be scuttled by the conservative coalition of Republicans and Southern Democrats. He proceeded to use this mandate to enact Kennedy's pending legislation, as well as many proposals that his numerous task forces developed, using a general theme of reform called The Great Society.

 ## JOHNSON'S SOCIAL WELFARE LEGACY

### Civil Rights Legislation

Johnson refused to compromise with southerners in 1964 when they tried to dilute civil rights legislation that had been drafted by the Kennedy administration. The Civil Rights Act of 1964 was a historic measure that marked the first time since Reconstruction that the federal government assumed a major role in protecting voting rights of southern African Americans. The act required the desegregation of public facilities and prohibited discrimination in hiring practices of firms and institutions that received federal contracts. The U.S. attorney general was also given the right to file suits to desegregate schools.

The immediate effects of this legislation were diminished because litigation was often required to bring compliance, but it led to a civil rights revolution for southern African Americans within six months. Public accommodations and public transportation were desegregated by

1965. The attorney general initiated suits against local school districts that discriminated against minorities and supported an ever-tightening series of guidelines that successively required them to use one set of facilities for all students. It was an extraordinary set of achievements by any standard. Southern whites found they were unable to persuade the Supreme Court to overrule federal civil rights powers, as had occurred during Reconstruction. The Department of Justice, often headed by officials who questioned various aspects of civil rights legislation, did not attack its central provisions.[71]

The measure was flawed in important respects, however. It outlawed the use of poll taxes and literacy tests, but a tedious and case-by-case enforcement process was needed that allowed many jurisdictions to continue discriminatory practices. Johnson did not aggressively implement Title VII of the act, which outlawed discrimination in employment, as reflected by his failure to give the Department of Labor a significant role in monitoring federal contracts for discrimination. Title VII established an Equal Employment Opportunity Commission (EEOC) to monitor discrimination in employment, but it did not receive the power to initiate suits until 1972. Furthermore, Johnson decided for political reasons not to aggressively attack de facto segregation of northern schools.[72]

Johnson had not planned to introduce additional civil rights legislation in 1965, but he changed his mind when confronted with massive civil rights protests in the South that were directed at continuing and widespread denial of suffrage to African Americans. To allow faster legal action than had been possible in case-by-case litigation, the Civil Rights Act of 1965 gave the federal government the right to presume discrimination in any state or its subdivisions where less than 50 percent of minorities voted in federal elections and in areas that used literacy or other screening tests. In such areas, federal authorities were allowed to directly administer elections. These policies were remarkably successful in terminating the last vestiges of overt discrimination in the registering of voters.[73]

## Earl Warren and the Supreme Court

The Supreme Court, under the leadership of Chief Justice Earl Warren between 1953 and 1969, provided its own impetus to the advancement of civil rights and civil liberties. Warren had been governor of California and an important Republican politician, who had, moreover, taken a number of conservative positions in California; indeed, he had even assumed a key role in incarcerating Japanese Americans in World War II when serving as the state's attorney general. Eisenhower, looking for a prominent Republican and owing a political debt to Warren, felt he would be an ideal conservative justice when he appointed him to be chief justice in 1953. But Eisenhower had misread his man; Warren believed, above all, in the doctrine of

fairness—a doctrine that led him to preside over a Court that in sixteen years made a series of liberal rulings that radically transformed American jurisprudence. (Years later, Eisenhower believed the appointment of Warren was his biggest political error and was not on speaking terms with Warren in the closing years of his presidency—and some conservatives were so enraged by decisions of the Warren Court that they repeatedly sought to bring pressure to have him impeached.)[74]

The precedent-shaking nature of the Warren Court began almost at the outset with the historic *Brown* v. *Board of Education* ruling in 1954. Reverend Oliver Brown of Topeka, Kansas, had brought suit against his city's board of education because he was angry that his child had to take a bus to the other side of town when a school reserved for whites was much closer. Thurgood Marshall of the NAACP argued that segregation had such harmful psychological effects on minorities that the mere fact of segregation meant inferior education. He and other civil rights attorneys had been impressed by some experiments of the African-American social scientist Kenneth Clark. In tests with African-American children in the North, Clark found that, when asked to identify a doll that most resembled themselves (by color), many African-American children refused to answer or would cry and run out of the room. When the same test was given to African-American children in the South, Clark found a different, but equally disturbing, result; the children would often point to the brown doll and say, matter-of-factly, "That's a nigger. I'm a nigger," thus accepting as given their subordinate status.[75] Although some of the civil rights lawyers did not want to use this "soft" evidence, others, such as Marshall, prevailed since they felt the Court would not hold segregated facilities to be a violation of the equal protection clause of the Fourteenth Amendment to the Constitution without it. By contrast, the attorney representing the board of education contended that no definitive proof had been shown that segregated students fare worse in life *because* of their segregation. Were the court to rule in Marshall's behalf, it would repudiate more than fifty years of tradition stemming from the *Plessy* v. *Ferguson* decision of 1896, which had upheld the separate-but-equal doctrine. At stake was the very structure of education in many jurisdictions, which established so-called dual school systems, one for white students and the other for African-American students—and possibly, further down the judicial road, the structure of northern education, which had dual systems based not on law but on the combination of neighborhood schools and residential segregation, meaning that the schools of vast numbers of minority children were segregated. Warren, who was appointed chief justice after the deliberations on the *Brown* case had been underway for many months, decided he wanted a unanimous ruling and finally got one that upheld the logic of the NAACP and that found the psychological testimony, which derived from Clark's work, to be key.[76]

Other rulings, some almost as controversial, followed in rapid succession, such as ones that forced localities to reapportion voting districts to protect voting rights of minorities, to respect the rights of apprehended criminal suspects, to protect the rights of persons with radical beliefs, to give procedural protections to persons on death row, to enhance the power of the press, to strike down state laws that outlawed interracial sexual relations and marriage, to require the provision of public defenders to impoverished defendants, and to overturn laws that prohibited the sale of contraceptives. The cumulative effects of these and other rulings was enormous. Many conservatives, who were infuriated by these rulings, sought to develop a grass-roots campaign to impeach Warren and hoped that, one day, conservative presidents would make appointments that would turn the Court into a conservative institution. (As we note later, they succeeded in this objective during the 1980s.)

We can say, then, that the Supreme Court was an important part of the social reforms of the 1960s under the tutelage of Earl Warren.

Though the Court is not a legislative body, its decisions had profound effects on the policies of local institutions that, in turn, affected the lives of minorities and poor people.

## Medicare and Medicaid

An ingenious compromise was fashioned by the administration and Wilbur Mills, powerful chairman of the House Ways and Means Committee, that facilitated passage of Medicare and Medicaid programs in 1965 as Titles XVIII and XIX of the Social Security Act. Medicare received widespread attention because of the political clout of elderly persons and the extensive discussion of their needs in preceding years. Kennedy's desire to obtain health insurance had been frustrated by controversy about details of the program, but Mills and Johnson developed a strategy that incorporated facets of the proposals of members of both parties.[77] The program was divided into two parts. Participation in Part A, which funded selected hospital services of elderly persons, was mandatory and financed by a payroll tax on workers and employers. Participation was voluntary in Part B, which financed services of physicians and was funded by a combination of monthly premiums on elderly persons and funds from the general revenues of the federal government.

Medicare was a godsend to many elderly persons who lacked funds to pay for their medical bills without selling their personal possessions. By making eligibility automatic on payment of payroll taxes and premiums, elderly persons received assistance without the stigma of a means test. Elderly persons did not have to visit local welfare departments but obtained eligibility through Social Security offices. Medical researchers have attempted to evaluate the effect of Medicare on the health and health practices of elderly persons, but conflicting findings and methodological issues have made evaluation difficult. Since most elderly persons participate in it, for example, it is difficult to assess whether they would have been more or less healthy without it. The program appears to have increased health care utilization of physicians and hospitals by poor persons, who had often refrained from seeking medical care except for emergency conditions. Had the Medicare program not existed, it is likely that many more elderly persons would have become insolvent and forced on welfare rolls, but the program also diminished the amount of free medical care that had been donated to impoverished elderly persons prior to passage of Medicare.[78]

Medicare can be criticized on several grounds. Since it subsidized acute health care services, it provided only a limited buffer against medical insolvency and did not help persons with chronic or long-term conditions. It reimbursed only a maximum of sixty days in the hospital, covered only one-hundred days of convalescent care, and did not reimburse out-of-hospital nursing home care. These restrictive policies meant that many elderly persons who exhausted their scanty Medicare benefits suffered the indignity of depleting their savings and assets to become eligible for Medicaid, which is a means-tested program.[79]

At the insistence of the American Medical Association, physicians were allowed to charge higher rates for Medicare than the maximum fees authorities would reimburse, so elderly persons had to contribute their own resources. Studies reveal that these costs, plus various other out-of-pocket costs for covered and uncovered services, meant that elderly persons in 1986 financed nearly the same percentage of their total medical costs as before the passage of Medicare.[80] Out-of-pocket medical costs of elderly persons would have risen even further without the assistance of Medicare, however, because of increasing use of expensive medical technologies and sharp increases in the real cost of medical services.

Medicare contributed to medical inflation by reimbursing providers at prevailing rates so that they had no incentive to decrease their charges or to curtail unnecessary surgeries.[81] By confining itself to financing existing curative services in line with the disease model of medicine, Medicare did not promote innovative alternatives to nursing home care, failed to foster preventive services for elderly persons, and did not provide outreach services to the frail elderly.[82] In short, Medicare funded conventional services for a population that needed innovative programs, and it covered only a small fraction of their medical needs.

State, county, and municipal officials had funded medical services to poor persons for decades but with considerable assistance from those physicians who donated free services. Their costs had steadily increased, and many poor persons delayed treatment because of the inaccessibility of their services. The Medicaid program was enacted in 1965 to address the medical needs of welfare recipients as well as so-called medically indigent persons, who, though not destitute, could not pay their medical bills.

Unlike Medicare, which vested financing, administration, and policy roles in the federal government, Medicaid was a matching grant program, like AFDC, in which federal authorities paid a substantial share of the medical services but ceded to the states major administrative and policy roles. States had to provide some basic services, such as outpatient and emergency care, had to enroll AFDC recipients, and were allowed to decide which (if any) additional services they wanted to provide and to devise eligibility criteria. As in the AFDC program, conservative and poor states covered fewer services and had more restrictive eligibility criteria than other states.[83]

Many legislators erroneously assumed that Medicaid would be a small program that would focus on the medical needs of AFDC recipients. Governors of New York and California, who had already been pressured to devise health insurance programs, believed that they could use the relatively generous federal match of the Medicaid program to develop free health services for their blue-collar citizens as well; indeed, at one point, 40 percent of the population in New York State was eligible for its Medicaid program. As congressional legislators observed the mounting federal costs of the Medicaid program and realized that a disproportionate share of federal funds went to a few liberal states, they enacted policies in 1967 that restricted Medicaid coverage in all states to persons who earned no more than 133 percent of a state's AFDC standard by 1970.[84]

It is difficult to gauge the precise effects of Medicaid on poor persons. Their use of outpatient services increased dramatically, and rural residents similarly increased their use of all medical services. Although Medicaid funding led many physicians and hospitals to discontinue their donations of free or low-cost services to poor persons, the total number of services available to the poor increased.[85] Medicaid can nonetheless be criticized on similar grounds as Medicare. It encouraged inflation by infusing massive resources into the medical system with few cost controls. It did not encourage development of innovative outreach and preventive services to poor persons, who often distrusted medical authorities or postponed treatment until illnesses had become severe. Few poor persons mainstreamed into the medical system used by middle-class Americans since regular medical providers resented the restrictive levels of reimbursement that many states established. Many poor persons were served by "Medicaid mills," where physicians reaped large profits from high-volume services. Two systems of care continued after the passage of Medicaid. Middle-class Americans used nonprofit or for-profit hospitals. Low-income and medically indigent persons used public hospitals, inner-city clinics, and foreign-born or foreign-trained doctors who often lacked operating privileges in local hospitals.[86]

Another program to aid the elderly, the Older Americans Act (OAA), passed Congress in 1965. It authorized under Title III the development of a national network of Area Agencies on Aging (AAAs) to coordinate services for the elderly.[87] OAA has subsidized many kinds of services since its inception, including nutritional

programs, services for the homebound frail elderly, and training programs. Critics contend that AAAs, which were supposed to be vigorous advocates, have often been preoccupied with delivering services to the elderly.[88]

## Aid to Education

Proposals to extend federal aid to public schools had foundered on constitutional and political issues that were associated with the relationship between church and state, but Johnson fashioned a clever compromise that eventually led to passage of the Elementary and Secondary Education Act of 1965 (ESEA).[89] It provided federal assistance to public schools with relatively high concentrations of low-income children, and it allowed private schools to share books and other materials that had been purchased by public schools.

Sharp differentials in educational spending at the local level between affluent and poor neighborhoods persisted even after ESEA was enacted. Its provision of relatively unrestricted funds to schools led many of them to use the funds to underwrite their regular expenses rather than to upgrade the instruction of low-income students; indeed, some jurisdictions even reduced their level of educational spending after they received ESEA funds.[90] Gaps in educational achievement between middle- and upper-income students and low-income students continue to defy solution. Are the gaps due to poor facilities, poor instruction, or familial background? Do low-income children often discontinue school because they believe it will not lead to jobs? What combination of outreach, instructional, facility, and other changes are needed to help low-income students improve their educational performance?[91]

Johnson also developed a range of educational subsidies for low-income persons who sought junior college and college education.[92] Despite the shortcomings of ESEA and other legislation, striking educational gains were made by African Americans in the 1960s at both secondary and college levels.[93]

## The War on Poverty, Welfare Reforms, and Food Stamps

When Kennedy realized in early 1963 that his domestic policy was stumbling, he commissioned top aides to develop an antipoverty program, but they had only begun assembling lists of job-training and youth-employment schemes when he died. The so-called War on Poverty was developed after his death and consisted of a collection of job-training, youth-employment, and medical services that various government departments had failed to enact during the Kennedy administration.[94] Specifically, the legislation included the Job Corps to provide impoverished youth with job training in urban and rural residential centers, the Neighborhood Youth Corps to provide teenagers with employment in local agencies, a legal aid program to provide free legal assistance to the poor, and medical clinics in low-income areas. The measure also included a "community action program" that established local community action agencies (CAAs) to coordinate local programs for the poor and to fund and operate various programs. (The popular Head Start program for preschool children was funded from community action funds.)

The community action program soon became the most controversial part of the Office of Economic Opportunity. One group of officials believed the CAAs would concentrate on planning and coordinating functions in poverty areas. Another group, which included Richard Boone and David Hackett, believed that existing programs and agencies were unresponsive to poor persons and wanted the CAAs to be forceful advocates for poor persons. To increase this likelihood, they placed in the legislation the requirement that the CAAs promote the "maximum feasible participation of the poor" in their governing boards.[95] Virtually no legislators noticed this phrase, but it was widely used by community activists in succeeding years to insist that community elections be used to give poor persons the right to choose community representatives for the CAA boards.

Johnson and Shriver wanted OEO programs implemented as rapidly as possible because they realized that demonstrable results were needed to make the programs appealing to a wide spectrum of legislators, but the speedy implementation of dozens of different programs, as well as the administratively complex CAAs, led to widespread charges of corruption, patronage, and inefficiency.[96] In the early planning of OEO, administration officials hoped to focus on demonstration programs in a limited number of cities, but Johnson insisted on broader coverage to enhance the visibility and impact of OEO. OEO was plagued, moreover, with incessant charges and countercharges as well as by local confusion about the objectives of the ambiguous CAAs.

Critics have questioned a number of the provisions of OEO. It was not wise to suggest that a War on Poverty could be declared, waged, and won with a collection of small programs that were supplemented by an ambiguous advocacy program. It is impossible to wage even a limited action against poverty if no income or resources are given to the poor, but OEO provided only personal and community services. When Sargeant Shriver, the energetic OEO director, sought to include public works within OEO, he received a chilly reception from Johnson, who believed that services, training, and coordination could somehow end poverty without income transfers or creation of new jobs.[97] Policy expectations were established that could not be fulfilled, and political opponents criticized the limited effectiveness of OEO in reducing poverty and demanded its curtailment or elimination.

It also is not politically feasible for governments to directly subsidize local protest organizations, even if the concept appears attractive at first glance. Governmental officials who are the targets of such protests will attack the advocacy program as unwarranted federal intrusion into local affairs, particularly when they include powerful mayors who constitute a significant part of the political constituency of the Democratic party. One can imagine the delight of Republicans, who were desperately seeking issues to slow the momentum of the Johnson legislative avalanche, when local Democratic officials, such as Mayor Richard Daley of Chicago, attacked the CAAs.

OEO cannot be dismissed as a disaster, however. Many of its programs were highly innovative and, though transferred from OEO to other agencies in subsequent years, continue to exist. OEO initiated a large legal aid program to the poor that represented them against landlords, local merchants, and unresponsive government agencies.[98] Neighborhood health centers, which markedly improved the health of many low-income persons, were established, as were nutritional and health programs for youth.[99] As top officials in OEO increasingly questioned the merit of advocacy by CAAs, they earmarked their funds for service programs such as Head Start, a popular preschool program that combined recreational, educational, and health programs in summer as well as during the school year. The effectiveness of Head Start in raising scores of low-income children on various tests has been questioned, but some studies suggest that it had long-term and beneficial effects on the educational performance of its enrollees.[100]

Resentment against AFDC recipients was relatively muted in the 1950s, but it mounted during the 1960s. The growth of AFDC increased dramatically as uprooted persons fled rural areas, found bleak job prospects in urban areas, and were emboldened by civil rights protests to seek their rights. Increasing numbers of women joined AFDC rolls by the late 1960s because receipt of AFDC entitled them to receive Medicaid, food stamps, day care, and work-related incentive payments.

It was not only the growing size of AFDC that spirited mounting resentment against AFDC women but also changing orientations toward work. Despite increases in the number of working women during the 1950s, many persons believed in the early 1960s that women should remain at home with their children. This sentiment decreased markedly during the 1960s, however, as more women of all social classes joined the labor force. Along with this trend came increasing demands that female welfare recipients obtain employment instead of welfare.[101]

The Johnson administration had a number of options as they encountered conservative opposition to AFDC. They could have capitulated to conservatives and accepted a variety of punitive strategies to force AFDC women off the rolls; they could have insisted that AFDC women should not be compelled to work; or they could have devised programs to make it possible for AFDC women to work. Most of the women wanted to work, but the last-mentioned course would have required careful planning since AFDC women averaged only an eighth-grade education, often suffered discrimination in labor markets, required expensive day-care programs, sometimes possessed physical or mental problems, and often could not find employment. But the Johnson administration never chose a consistent strategy. Some conservatives wanted to force AFDC women to work so that they could supply cheap labor to southern farmers. Northern liberals, who had become supporters of welfare rights, opposed compulsory assignment to jobs for women with young children, insisted that jobs pay at least the minimum wage, and demanded that the level of AFDC grants be raised.[102] The administration did not believe it could oppose conservatives since they had considerable strength in the Congress, and Johnson was unsympathetic to welfare recipients, whom he believed often sought benefits rather than employment.[103]

The resulting policy of the administration, which was reflected in the welfare amendments of 1967, was a confusing mixture of incompatible policies that ultimately satisfied no one. Some punitive policies were adopted, including a work requirement for all women who did not have children younger than six years of age, at prevailing rather than minimum wages. A federal freeze on funds for AFDC was enacted but, for technical and political reasons, never implemented. Liberals were delighted to obtain a series of exemptions in the law that allowed welfare women to escape the work requirement if they were ill or if work was "inimical" to the welfare of the family. They also obtained a work incentive provision that allowed many working women to continue to augment their wages with welfare payments by allowing them to retain the first $30 and one-third of remaining earnings. Women who obtained relatively high-paying jobs lost their eligibility, but this policy led to large increases in the welfare rolls because it allowed many women in low-paying jobs to retain their welfare eligibility. Some liberals also liked provisions that established the Work Incentive Program (WIN), which funded training programs and day care.

The 1967 amendments represented, then, a confused policy. Liberals were victorious, on balance, since few women were forced to take jobs due to exemptions and the rolls increased rapidly in the wake of work incentive provisions. Their victory came at a high price, however. Their insistence that women should not be forced to work blinded them to the reality that most AFDC women wanted to work though for decent wages. Instead of focusing on methods of outmaneuvering conservatives to dilute the work requirement, they could have tried more diligently to develop millions of public service jobs or subsidized jobs in private industry to be accompanied by good day-care programs. They would have encountered formidable opposition from conservatives because the costs of day-care, training, and job creation would have far

exceeded the cost of merely providing AFDC grants or the cost of the WIN programs, which provided superficial training and inadequate day-care services. Still, had the administration developed an effective and humanistic work strategy that had actually reduced the size of AFDC rolls, they might have outflanked conservatives and taken the AFDC issue from them.

The Food Stamps Program was enacted in 1964 in the wake of a series of pilot feeding programs during the Kennedy administration. Policy makers realized that distribution of surplus food to the poor was cumbersome and required recipients to travel to centralized storage sites. A system was devised for providing food stamps or coupons to families that purchased them at a sum considerably less than their retail value at those stores that would accept them. Families on welfare were automatically eligible, but many poor families not on welfare could also be certified by local welfare departments. Localities were given the option of participating in the program, with the Department of Agriculture paying the entire cost. Successive amendments in 1968, 1971, 1973, and 1978 dramatically expanded funding for the program, established national eligibility standards, made the program mandatory in all states, and developed methods to allow recipients to receive coupons without having to make cash payments. The Food Stamps Program was a landmark achievement because it gave to millions of impoverished families the resources to purchase food in quantities not possible with meager welfare checks.

## THE OVEREXTENDED PRESIDENT AND THE LOSS OF CREDIBILITY

The extraordinary legislative successes of Johnson on the domestic front were unprecedented in American history when measured by their sheer numbers: His successes in 1964 carried into 1965, when he obtained passage of 84 of the 87 measures that he submitted to Congress, and

into 1966, when 97 of 113 measures were enacted.[104] Nor did he obtain these successes by waving a magic wand; he invested enormous amounts of time in the legislative process.

But even in 1965, Johnson had decided to embark on a high-risk gamble. Kennedy had bequeathed to him an uncertain legacy in Vietnam, where he had committed large numbers of military "advisors" to help the South Vietnamese ward off insurrections from the Vietcong, a Communist group that sought to wrest power through guerrilla warfare from the corruption-ridden and conservative dictatorial government of South Vietnam. Johnson went through an extended period of discussion of Vietnam with his top aides during 1964 and early 1965 to decide whether he should commit large numbers of American troops to the area. The details of these talks fall beyond our purpose here, but the ultimate decision does not, because the committing of hundreds of thousands of troops to South Vietnam by the end of 1965 had profound consequences for Johnson's social policies.[105]

To understand the complex relations between Johnson's foreign policy and his domestic policy, we need to return to our discussion of the sheer size of American military spending *before* Johnson committed troops to Vietnam *and* a fateful decision that was made in 1964 to drastically lower the American income taxes. Recall that Truman had committed the nation to extraordinary levels of ongoing military spending in 1950 so that most of the American federal budget went for military purposes. Kennedy bequeathed to Johnson this cold war budget and had even added significantly to it because he believed that the United States needed the capability to fight two and one-half wars simultaneously, that is, a war against Russia (probably in Europe), a war against China, and a war in a third-world country such as Vietnam.[106]

As a true believer in the threat of Communist insurrection around the world, Johnson accepted this large military commitment with alacrity. But Johnson *also* accepted another legacy from Kennedy and his economic advisors, who were convinced that American economic growth would suffer if the nation did not pump more money into the economy. They advised that government had to pump more money into the economy either by raising the federal budget or by lowering federal income

taxes to stimulate more consumer spending. Since conservatives were unlikely to allow more spending, Kennedy's aides recommended large tax cuts, which Johnson obtained from the Congress in 1964 during the first year of his presidency.[107]

Johnson committed himself to ambitious domestic reforms, then, in an environment of economic scarcity occasioned by military spending and tax cuts—and this budgetary scarcity was increased, as well, by his decision to send large numbers of troops to Vietnam in 1965. A "normal" politician might have decided, in these circumstances, to reconsider either his tax policies or his domestic policies or his decision to send troops to Vietnam in order not to strain the budget excessively *or* to anger the Congress, which might wonder how he could engage in multiple endeavors that so stressed the federal budget. Johnson was committed, however, to *each* of these policies; he wanted to save the world from Communism by decisively defeating the Vietcong and he wanted to be the greatest reform president in American history.[108] Moreover, he knew that if he asked the Congress to raise taxes to pay for the war and his social reforms, the conservatives in Congress from both parties would demand, as their price, that he cut "nonessential" social spending, much as they had forced Franklin Roosevelt in World War II to terminate the WPA, CCC, and NYA.[109]

To extricate himself from this situation, Johnson engaged in activities that can only be called devious and manipulative. To minimize the strain on the federal budget and the size of the deficit, he sold huge amounts of American assets, such as stockpiled metals like aluminum and copper that the government had accumulated in case of war.[110] He made the true costs of Vietnam appear somewhat smaller by taking a lot of manpower and equipment that had been devoted to defending Europe and transferring them to Vietnam. He constructed his military budget on the premise that the war would be over by June 1966—hardly a realistic scenario that (falsely) made it look as though Vietnam spending would be relatively small.[111] Although enacting vast numbers of social programs, he often devoted little money to each of them so as to diminish their fiscal impact. For example, the much-publicized War on Poverty never received more than $2 billion.

These various tactics, in turn, angered political groups on whom Johnson depended. Conservatives of both parties, already angered by the numbers of social reforms that Johnson proposed, accused him of hiding the true costs of the war—a charge that antiwar factions, who saw the war as diverting funds from social reforms, readily supported. Social reformers looked nervously at his Vietnam policy as they wondered if it would curtail Johnson's domestic agenda and as they slowly realized that, unlike other wars, it was disproportionately fought by troops drawn from African-American and Latino communities.

 ## THE BELEAGUERED PRESIDENT: 1967–1968

Johnson managed to maintain his political balance in his high-wire balancing act through much of 1966. He refused to diminish his commitment to all-out war in Vietnam despite discouraging reports from the battlefields that indicated that the enemy was not likely to yield and that mounting numbers of Americans would lose their lives or be maimed. He refused to diminish his commitment to domestic reforms as he obtained passage of dozens of new social programs even though they were often funded meagerly. And he refused to push Congress to raise taxes for fear of igniting pressure by conservatives to reduce social spending.

By early 1967, however, even the politically agile Johnson was increasingly caught in his complex web. Indeed, Johnson got caught in the vortex of conflicting political factions that for different reasons became disenchanted with his leadership. Conservatives in Congress more assertively attacked Johnson's credibility, accusing him of submitting deceptive budgets and suggesting he should cut social spending. Public opinion polls suggested that the widespread sympathy of middle- and working-class Americans for the plight of low-income Americans and African Americans that had existed in 1964 and 1965 had waned by 1968.[112] Once African Americans had obtained civil rights legislation that decreased discrimination in the South, they sought reforms to address poverty, housing discrimination, education, and other problems in the North. Northern whites, who had often supported efforts to reduce discrimination in the South, were enraged when *they* became the targets of protest. Indeed, Martin Luther King, Jr., observed that he had never seen more hatred than he experienced in open housing marches in white Chicago suburbs in 1967.[113] When the Department of Justice attacked de jure segregation in the South, many northern whites applauded, not realizing that the de facto segregation in their school districts would soon become the focus of reform.

Many whites responded negatively, as well, to the increasingly militant tactics of African Americans, women, Latinos, and Native Americans.[114] King, who remained an influential leader until his assassination in 1968, found it increasingly difficult to persuade a new breed of African-American leaders that nonviolence represented an inviolable principle rather than a tactic. Stokely Carmichael coined the term *black power* on a civil rights march in 1966 and graphically portrayed the trend among many African Americans toward separatism, development of African-American economic institutions, and violent protest.[115] This militance seemed to many white Americans to be reflected in the large number of urban riots and disturbances that

**FIGURE 9.1** • *President Lyndon Johnson meets with African-American and congressional leaders in the wake of race riots in Detroit in July 1967*

*Source:* Library of Congress

occurred in northern cities as well as some southern cities between 1965 and 1968; 239 civil disturbances erupted with 8,133 persons killed and 49,604 persons arrested (see Figure 9.1).[116]

Northern whites were also angered by the development of policies that implicated them in the civil rights struggles. Many northern whites supported the efforts to attack the overt racism of southern officials and institutions but opposed policies to desegregate northern schools by the use of busing, viewed affirmative action with skepticism, and believed the Warren Court had been too kind to criminal offenders. Scandals in the War on Poverty, which were seized on by Republicans and conservatives, gave the impression that domestic policies were not well conceived.

The uneasiness of white Americans, whose support is critical to the course of social reform, was compounded by economic problems in the nation. It was widely assumed when Johnson proclaimed the War on Poverty in 1964 that economic growth would allow the condition of all social classes to improve simultaneously, but increasing rates of inflation and deficits led some Americans to believe that social spending was incompatible with economic growth. Inflation and other economic concerns had replaced social concerns in public opinion polls by 1968.

Johnson's popularity with liberals and social reformers also began to wane. Although many liberals had remained silent on Vietnam in 1966 and even early 1967, the silence was decisively broken in August 1967, when the *New York Times* called the war a "bottomless pit" and urged Johnson to curtail the American commitment to it.[117] Moreover, some liberals even became disenchanted with Johnson's domestic policy despite the torrent of reforms that were enacted. They noticed that many of the reforms were not well funded. Some of them were angered by periodic cuts in social spending that Johnson made to appease the charges by conservatives that he was "fiscally irresponsible." All viewed the unfolding debacle in Vietnam, where body bags were coming back to the United States by the thousands and where Johnson had engaged in a bombing campaign against a third-world country that was unprecedented in military history. Johnson had escalated the Vietnam conflict from a few military advisors and spies in 1964 to more than 540,000 troops in 1968. The resulting military defeat had a staggering cost in lives and resources. By the conclusion of American involvement in the grisly affair in 1973, more than 55,000 Americans had been killed and 304,000 Americans had been injured. The U.S. Senate estimates that 1.4 million South Vietnamese were killed and wounded, another 850,000 enemy soldiers were killed, and 10.3 million refugees were created. Americans expended more than $135 billion on the war.[118]

Johnson believed that the fall of South Vietnam would lead to Communist victories in other nations in Southeast Asia, and he assumed that the non-Communist regimes in South Vietnam possessed relatively broad support despite their corruption, insensitivity to land reform, and domination by conservative elites. Johnson reasoned that the U.S. Air Force, with napalm, helicopters, and B-52 bombers, could prevail over poorly supplied and sparsely clad Asians, that air strikes would demoralize the North Vietnamese, and that the enemy would accept his promises to provide them with billions of dollars on the cessation of hostilities. But Johnson underestimated the resolve of the North Vietnamese, who were deeply committed to a long-term conflict that they had already waged for decades.[119]

The war had both indirect and direct effects on social policy. It created an atmosphere that was not conducive to the continuation of social reform since it focused attention on foreign affairs. It splintered the coalition that had supported civil rights and other reforms since many African Americans, liberals, youths, intellectuals, and clergy opposed it.[120] The increasingly militant demonstrations against the war antagonized some moderate whites who supported the war effort. The war also led to reductions in levels of funding for social programs.

The war eroded Johnson's credibility. Many Americans remembered bitterly that Johnson had run in 1964 as a peace candidate against Goldwater. His deception in hiding the true costs of the war and his habit of overstating American military gains made many Americans distrust him.[121] Much as Franklin Roosevelt had squandered his landslide electoral victory of 1936 by attempting to pack the Supreme Court, Johnson lost his political momentum when he committed the nation to the war.[122]

Some liberals were also infuriated in 1968 when Johnson orchestrated a tax increase to pay for the war, which he realized only by promising conservatives that he would call for substantial cuts in social spending. He had long promised that the nation could have both "guns and butter," but he seemed now to acknowledge that Vietnam would lead to significant cuts in butter.

Caught in conflicting forces, Johnson tried to conciliate each side by making concessions. He relented to tax increases and cuts in social spending, as well as continuing commitment to the war, in order to assuage conservatives. He continued to propose social reforms in order to keep the support of liberals—and generally chose to avoid coercive policies in the wakes of the urban riots. Indeed, following the Detroit and Newark riots, he established, in 1967, the

National Advisory Committee on Civil Disorders, often called the (Otto) Kerner Commission after its chairperson, to investigate the causes of riots. His concessions to one side of the increasingly polarized political debates, however, often served to antagonize the other side.

By the spring of 1968, Johnson's ratings in public opinion polls had sunk to such low levels that many pundits began to wonder if he could win reelection in 1968. His hand was forced when Eugene McCarthy, a relatively unknown senator running on an antiwar plank, almost defeated him in the New Hampshire primary. Stung by this near defeat, Johnson withdrew from the presidential race in hopes that he could orchestrate a peace settlement in Vietnam.

When Richard Nixon defeated Vice President Hubert Humphrey, the Democratic candidate in November, The Great Society came to an official close. But actually The Great Society had come to a close in the rice paddies of Vietnam long before the election results were tallied.

Johnson left the presidency a tormented man. His international policies had led to uncertain outcomes and a loss of popularity. In the last year of his presidency, he toyed with initiating some new and massive reforms, such as a child health program, but he decided not to introduce them because of their certain defeat. Almost all Great Society reforms had been enacted in two years, 1964 and 1965 — a period that seemed light-years removed from the troubled final years of Johnson's presidency.

## OUTGROUPS IN THE 1960s

Since we have discussed policy reforms with respect to African Americans throughout the preceding part of this chapter, we devote the remaining part to other outgroups.

The civil rights struggles of African Americans captured the attention of the nation during much of the decade extending from 1955 — when Rosa Parks refused to move to the back of the bus just before the bus boycott in Montgomery — through most of the 1960s. It was an epic struggle with drama, violence, defeats, and victories. This struggle especially captivated *other* outgroups who experienced various forms of discrimination, including women, Latinos, gays and lesbians, Asian Americans, and Native Americans. Each of these groups, in turn, developed reformist leaders and engaged in various forms of protest. Indeed, the momentum of their mobilizing carried protest well into the 1970s before reform ebbed somewhat in the 1980s.

### Women

Things were never the same once "Rosie the Riveter" entered the work force, by the millions, in the production plants of World War II. She was supposed to return to her domestic roles when the war ended — and 3.25 million women were pushed from or persuaded to leave industrial jobs after World War II. But the genie was out of the bottle because, having tasted economic roles, a dramatic upturn in female employment occurred after the war and during the 1950s. By 1952, more women were employed than at the height of World War II, and the trend continued upward during the next four decades.[123] But women were not made to feel good about their work; indeed, the mass media and many theorists implied or stated that working women risked harming their children or losing their femininity.[124]

Following World War II, an effort to secure an Equal Rights Amendment (ERA) to the Constitution assumed center stage among female activists. A host of distinguished women, Margaret Sanger, Pearl Buck, and Katharine Hepburn among them, supported the amendment and formed a coalition of organizations under the Women's Joint Legislative Committee. Advocates hoped the ERA would sweep aside many laws in states that still limited the rights of women to own and sell property, to make contracts, to control bequests, and to exercise parental authority. But other female leaders opposed the amendment on the grounds that women *needed* special protections, such as protective labor legislation, and that these might be erased by the amendment. Its fate was sealed, however, when it passed the Senate but failed to obtain the necessary two-thirds vote.[125] Other women sought legislation to guarantee equal pay for equal work for women in private employment, but many legislators opposed it on the grounds that higher female wages might entice many women to abdicate their parenting role by seeking work.

But women who sought new challenges discovered innumerable barriers in the early 1960s. Relatively few women obtained access to training in male-dominated professions like law, medicine, and business or to work in the building trades, so they were usually limited to gender-segregated jobs in clerical, sales, unskilled manufacturing, teaching, nursing, and social work. Women were widely perceived to be fragile—they were not even allowed to run long distances in track—so "protective laws" kept them from arduous work. A sort of biologic conspiracy existed as well; required to be absent from the labor force for extended periods, often at least until their children had reached high school, they could not easily reenter it and, if they did, could not easily "catch up to" male workers who had been working continuously. Women had to contend, as well, with opposition from their husbands and lack of sympathy from

their children, who often had expectations that women should do the bulk of household chores. Moreover, since the nation had virtually no governmentally subsidized child care in the early 1960s, working women had to pay for day care from their, usually low, paychecks.

As the 1960s began, some female activists hoped that President Kennedy would be sympathetic, but they obtained scant sympathy from him initially. Under pressure, President Kennedy appointed Esther Peterson to be director of the Womens Bureau in the Department of Labor, where she mobilized a campaign for enactment of equal pay legislation, which had foundered after World War II. Congress enacted an Equal Pay Act in 1963, but this legislation left out large groups of women, including domestics and farm workers, and did not speak to discrimination that blocked women from certain kinds of jobs and promotions.[126] (Because of a gender-segregated work place for many women, the subject of equal pay was moot.) Moreover, Kennedy established a Commission on the Status of Women in 1961 to review existing policies in employment, social insurance, tax, labor, and social-services areas and to issue a report. The commission recommended against an Equal Rights Amendment to the Constitution on grounds that women could bring suit under existing constitutional provisions such as the equal protection clause of the Fourteenth Amendment. The commission made many constructive suggestions, such as decreasing sex discrimination in the civil service by pay and promotion and recommending more high-level presidential appointees. (Kennedy had already issued an executive order in 1961 requiring private employers with federal contracts not to discriminate on the basis of race *or* gender.) It also recommended broadening access of women to education but did not push entry of women into fields dominated by males. The commission, however, did not attack the fundamental sex-role structure of American society or the prevailing notion that women should be the primary child rearers, nor did it seek basic changes in Social Security, which discriminated against single women who were not dependants or widows.[127]

American women needed a theorist akin to Simone de Beauvoir, the French feminist who had so articulately analyzed the constraints placed on women in modern society. They found this theorist in Betty Friedan, whose classic book, *The Feminine Mystique,* was published in 1963.[128] Friedan dissected the malaise of suburban women who, "as she made the beds, shopped for groceries, matched slipcover material, ate peanut butter sandwiches with her children, chauffeured Cub Scouts and Brownies . . . was afraid to ask even of herself—'Is this all?'"[129] Friedan contended that a mystique of feminine fulfillment had developed in which the American housewife achieved a kind of happiness as housewife and mother that no women had ever obtained in prior eras. If she lacked this happiness, Friedan contended, she was taught to blame herself, that is, to look inward for neurotic tendencies, "penis envy," or other personal failings. Isolated in her suburban "concentration camp," women had no chance to explore options or seek new challenges.[130] Her book ended with a ringing plea for "a new life plan for women," where emancipated from past myths, women would "see through the delusions of the feminine mystique" to develop their own careers that would fully challenge them.[131]

The accession of Lyndon Johnson showed promising early results when he appointed many more females to high-policy posts than had Kennedy, but Johnson was indifferent to the inclusion, in Title VII of the Civil Rights Act of 1964, of a ban on sex discrimination. A number of legislators opposed this provision on grounds that it could threaten protective labor legislation for women, such as laws regulating the hours and conditions of women's work. Some powerful southern legislators supported it for the wrong reasons; they hoped that the addition of the controversial provision would kill the entire Civil Rights Act, which they opposed. But

eleven of the twelve female legislators in the House of Representatives spoke eloquently for the measure by insisting that women deserved the same protections as racial minorities who were included in Title VII.[132] When the ban and the legislation were passed by the Senate, women had finally been included in major civil rights legislation, unlike their unfortunate exclusion in the wake of the Civil War about one century earlier—but the inclusion did not stem from militant support for it by the administration. Nor did the Equal Opportunities Commission, established to investigate discrimination in employment by Title VII, focus on sex discrimination since it was so preoccupied with race discrimination. As Harrison notes, some of the EEOC commissioners and staff did not even perceive the sex-discrimination provisions of the Civil Rights Act to be legitimate, but merely something some conservatives had placed in it to obtain its defeat.[133]

Some advances were made through legal rulings such as the ruling by the Supreme Court in *Giswold* v. *Connecticut* in 1965 where it declared a law to be illegal that made the use of contraceptives a crime, but the ruling left intact the ban on abortions in many states and did not speak to the absence of family planning clinics in many jurisdictions. Other court rulings abolished certain residency requirements, midnight raids, and "man-in-the-house" rules that various states had devised to cut AFDC welfare rolls.

Although these early policy successes represented important gains, they were also token measures or inadequately implemented. Recognizing that women needed to develop political clout, Betty Friedan and other women formed the National Organization for Women (NOW) in 1966 to seek federal action on women's employment issues, such as tighter bans on sex discrimination by federal contractors, the full deductibility of day-care expenses, and more enforcement powers for the EEOC. Most significant, NOW from the outset questioned the long-standing assumption that females should primarily be the child rearers and their husbands the breadwinners.[134]

NOW assertively sought to pressure Johnson to include women in the executive order that he had issued in September 1965 that required affirmative action programs to ensure equal opportunity for all races. By October 1967, they had succeeded, thus paving the way for affirmative action programs by local and state governments, federal contractors, and the federal government—and establishing the precedent that the term *sex* would appear whenever the phrase "race, creed, color, or national origin" appeared.[135] NOW also initiated another bid for an Equal Rights Amendment and secured widespread support for the measure from many candidates.

As important as these political developments, women had begun to develop consciousness-raising groups where issues like sexual abuse, harassment on the job, rape, women's health, abortion, and job discrimination became topics of conversation rather than taboo subjects. However uneven and inadequate, these issues would become important policy issues over the next several decades.

By the end of the Johnson presidency, then, important gains had occurred for women, but in retrospect, they were only token advances. Though women had made huge gains in obtaining higher education, had received one-third of all the master's degrees granted in the United States by 1968, and represented 58 percent of the labor force, the economic position of white women relative to white men had declined during the decades after World War II. Full-time female workers earned, on average, only 58.2 percent of the income of men in 1969, down from 63.3 percent in 1956.[136]

Critics of the feminist movement in the 1960s note that it often did not speak to the needs of African-American or low-income women. African-American women, who had often had to work, were less worried about the feminine mystique and more worried about the lack of economic opportunity and decent wages for themselves and for African-American males.

## Gays and Lesbians

The extent of prejudice against gays in the early 1950s is best revealed by a quote from Senator Kenneth Wherry (R., Neb.), who asserted that he wished to "harry every last pervert from the federal government services" on grounds that "homosexuals in government are a moral and security issue . . . the lack of emotional stability which if found in most sex perverts, and the weakness of their moral fiber, makes them susceptible to the blandishments of foreign espionage agents."[137] This virulent prejudice must be placed in the context of longstanding harassment, incarceration, and discrimination against gays and lesbians that stemmed from a combination of religious ideas that equated sexual deviance with sin, psychiatric and medical thought that saw it as mental or physical pathology, and criminology that sometimes perceived it as criminal behavior. (Sodomy and other homosexual acts were widely punishable as crimes.) Many people with homosexual or lesbian orientations came to think of themselves as diseased owing to the lack of public discussion and understanding of their lifestyle.

World War II brought more attention to homosexuality, not only because the army made strenuous efforts to screen homosexuals from service but also because so many homosexuals escaped its net. For the first time, gay people discovered that many others shared their sexual orientations—and same-sex associations were surprisingly common and open in barracks, dance halls, and combat zones. And the Women's Army Corps became, in the words of D'Emilio, the "quintessential lesbian institution."[138]

Gay soldiers formed gay communities in New York, San Francisco, Los Angeles, and other major cities following the war, and institutions, such as gay bars, become widespread. Sexual behavior became more openly discussed in the conservative 1950s, as reflected by the widely read Kinsey report that discussed taboo topics like masturbation. And Kinsey found that nearly 50 percent of males admitted erotic responses to their own sex, even if only 4 percent admitted they were exclusively homosexual.[139]

But gay life in the 1950s remained constricted by societal laws and prejudices. Witch hunts against communists in government often included homosexuals and lesbians. Eisenhower, in an executive order aimed at dismissing loyalty risks from government, explicitly listed "sexual perversion" and proceeded to remove homosexuals from government at the rate of forty per month in the first sixteen months after the order; many job seekers were denied employment when they were thought to be homosexual.[140] Moreover, 2,000 persons per year were removed from the military in the early 1950s—a number that rose by another 50 percent by the early 1960s. State and local governments screened their 12.5 million employees with similar zeal and also found homosexuality as a suitable grounds for dismissal.[141]

Gays and lesbians were also subject to arrests by local police forces and vice squads, who frequented gay bars, restrooms, lesbian bars, and even personal residences. D'Emilio estimates that there were more than 1,000 arrests per year in the District of Columbia in the early 1950s.[142] Gay bashing was common, as well, from local gangs and petty criminals.

There were beginnings toward the development of organizations and leadership in the gay and lesbian community in the 1950s, but they lacked a mass membership and had little success in changing social policies. A major problem among gays and lesbians was publicly revealing their sexual orientations for fear of reprisal from law authorities or recrimination from landlords or employers. Moreover, many gays and lesbians had internalized homophobia.[143]

A less oppressive social climate began to develop in the 1960s, which, in turn, promoted the development of activism among gays and lesbians. A succession of court rulings had gradually limited the ability of local and federal governments to censor or prohibit "obscene literature," so publications by gay and lesbian writers and groups could circulate more freely. As with so many other policies, the Warren Court led the way, culminating in the ruling in 1967 (*Redrup* v. *New York*) that maintained that "a book cannot be proscribed unless it is found to be *utterly* without redeeming social value" even though the book is "patently offensive." In the more permissive climate of the 1960s, mass-based magazines like *Playboy* were circulated — an unthinkable development in the 1950s. Howard Becker and other sociologists wrote on deviance from a relativistic perspective where they avoided making moral judgments about forms of behavior like homosexuality and urged an end to criminal penalties as well as exclusion from the armed forces. Lawyers began to develop suits against statutes that prohibited sodomy on grounds they violated personal liberty, and some local chapters of the American Civil Liberties Union (ACLU) became interested in pursuing discriminatory actions such as exclusion of homosexuals from the civil service. Court decisions in a few states had legitimized the right of gays and lesbians to assemble in local bars. Some homosexuals drew hope from movements in Europe that sought to decriminalize sex acts among consenting adults.[144] Some courageous clergy declared that the sexual orientations of homosexuals and lesbians were legitimate, not sinful, lifestyle choices. And some city governments, such as the Civil Service Commission of New York City, began to relax the restrictions against the hiring of gays and lesbians. Even mental health and health professionals began to reexamine traditional perspectives, and a committee established by the National Institute of Mental Health in 1967, though not declaring homosexuality to be "normal," urged tolerance of such persons.[145]

By 1967, the accommodationist and gradualist perspectives of leaders of various civil rights, feminist, and student groups had begun to be supplanted by more radical perspectives, such as leaders who espoused black power in the civil rights movement. It was in this context that a pivotal development in New York City ignited the gay liberation movement in 1969. Some police officers and detectives raided the Stonewall Inn, a gay bar in Greenwich Village. When the officers took the bartender, the Stonewall's bouncer, and three drag queens, a riot broke out, which spread into the Village and continued through the next night. For the first time, the gay and lesbian movements attracted a mass membership and developed a political agenda to modify myriad policies as well as to change diagnostic categories of the American Psychiatric Association. Moreover, they made "coming out" a key organizing strategy, hoping to persuade millions of gay and lesbian people to publicly announce their sexual orientations despite possible reprisals.[146] Early successes, such as the decision of the American Psychiatric Association in 1973 not to declare gay and lesbian people to be mentally ill, buoyed the spirits of the organizers. But their work had barely begun for the prejudices of American history hung heavy over a nation that was only starting to rethink traditional stereotypes.

## Latinos, Native Americans, and Asian Americans

Like African Americans, Latinos entered the 1960s as a population that was centered both in rural areas, such as on the farms and ranches of the Southwest and farms of the upper Midwest, and in rapidly growing urban areas, such as in the Southwest and in midwestern cities like Chicago and Kansas City. Moreover, a huge influx of Puerto Ricans occurred in the 1950s in East-Coast cities, particularly New York City, where between 850,000 and 1.2 million of them resided by 1970.[147] Puerto Ricans often came to the United States for economic reasons because they had been displaced by the expansion of large American sugar and coffee corporations and because factories and service industries in New York wanted and solicited cheap labor. As

with prior immigrant groups, many of them hoped to return to their homeland after they had improved their economic condition—but in the end, most remained. Moreover, a substantial population of Cuban Americans settled in the United States, particularly in South Florida, in the wake of the Cuban Revolution of 1959 that brought Fidel Castro to power.

The so-called Chicano movement signaled the beginning of militant organizing projects that centered on Mexican Americans and undocumented workers and was led by a series of charismatic leaders, including Reies Lopex Tijerina, who sought to restore lost Spanish and Mexican land grants in New Mexico, and Corky Gonzales, who organized grass-roots groups in Denver. It was Cesar Chavez, however, who captured national attention when he developed the United Farm Workers Organizing Committee to empower the Mexican agricultural laborers. Recall that the Wagner Act of 1936, which established procedures that gave federal protections to persons who sought to organize unions, did not apply to farm workers, so organizers could be summarily fired or intimidated when employers believed them to be "making trouble." After building a cadre of leaders, Chavez organized a march on Sacramento, the capital of California, in 1966 to dramatize the plight of farm workers. A flurry of organizing activities ensued that solicited support by well-publicized national boycotts of crops like grapes and lettuce to pressure agribusiness to recognize the right of their workers to organize. Simultaneously, Chavez pressured politicians in California to enact legislation that would provide for the state the kinds of protections that the Wagner Act afforded other workers. The extent of activism of the Latino community was illustrated by voter registration drives, pressure on the EEOC to assertively investigate job discrimination against Latinos, the development of the Mexican American Legal Defense and Education Fund (a counterpart in the Latino community to the NAACP), pressure that led to an extension of the provisions of the Voting Rights Act of 1965 to Latinos, and the development of various coordinating councils to link the work of many advocacy groups.[148]

The organizing of Puerto Rican protests against poor working conditions and wages, as well as atrocious living conditions, was frustrated by the extent that Puerto Ricans retained their personal ties to their homeland; large numbers of them moved back and forth in a manner that undermined the cohesion of their communities.[149] Unlike the farm workers, who had a relatively identifiable "enemy" in agribusiness and African Americans who could attack Jim Crow laws, urban Puerto Ricans were enmeshed in the constellation of factors that perpetuate urban poverty.

Native Americans had been placed on reservations during the nineteenth century after they had been evicted from their ancestral lands. These reservations were frequently assigned to one tribe, with the government agreeing to supply certain commodities or services (such as a school) in return for the ceding of ancestral lands to the U.S. government by the tribe. The early reservation experience was difficult for Native Americans; the reservations were too small to allow them to hunt and be self-sufficient, so they had to rely on assistance from government agents and missionary groups. As we discussed in Chapter 5, the federal government decided in 1887 through the Dawes Act, soon after establishing the reservations, to break up tribes by individualizing their landholdings, making them American citizens, and providing them with a government school system so as to socialize them to American ways. The chief instruments of this Americanizing strategy were the agents of the Bureau of Indian Affairs.[150] Congress conferred citizenship on all Native Americans in 1924.

But the Americanizing strategy did not work because the indigenous culture of the Native Americans made them resist it. Rather than assimilating to American culture, many Native Americans lost their land to speculators and crooks or chose to lease it to others to farm. Still

living on or near reservations, many Native Americans became dependent on government rations. The Indian agent and his staff were empowered by the Snyder Act in 1921 to help Native Americans with a range of education, welfare, health, agricultural, and other functions and to provide technical assistance to Indian policy and Indian judges.

By the 1920s and 1930s, government policy again reversed itself to emphasize preservation of reservations and culture. Indeed, the Indian Reorganization Act of 1934 promoted the establishment of tribal organizations, economies, and government as well as the purchase of additional lands for the reservations. This desire to help Native Americans become self-sufficient stemmed partly from their economic desperation in the Great Depression. By the 1940s and 1950s, the pendulum swung again as federal legislators and officials sought to diminish federal responsibilities in (once again) an assimilationist strategy. Various "termination acts" in the 1950s and early 1960s ended federal responsibility for various tribes, who had to turn to state governments for economic and other assistance.

The pendulum swung back toward federal responsibility and tribal authority in the 1960s and 1970s. The War on Poverty placed considerable emphasis on supporting the culture of Native Americans as well as their indigenous communities and tribal functions. Some of the reservations that had been terminated in the 1950s were restored to federal authority. Many of the programs of The Great Society channeled funds to the reservations for housing assistance, education, and economic development. The Bureau of Indian Affairs, which had often sought to enforce American customs on Native Americans, became an advocate for Native Americans "in the same manner as the Department of Agriculture is pro-farmer and the Department of Labor, pro-labor."[151] Both Presidents Johnson and Nixon strongly opposed the termination policy, sought to develop Native American participation in their governance, and favored continuation of federal technical and economic assistance to tribes. Indeed, the Indian Self-Determination and Education Assistance Act as well as other legislation in the 1970s sought to give tribes the authority to decide whether to assume responsibility for administering federal programs of the Interior Department or the Department of Health, Education, and Welfare.

Nor were Native Americans quiescent politically during the turbulence of the 1960s. Indigenous groups demanded compensation for lands that were taken from Native Americans illegally, strived for protections for minerals and timber on reservations, and sought to challenge stereotypical portrayals of Native Americans in films. Like African Americans and Latinos, they engaged in direct action, such as the occupation of Alcatraz, an abandoned federal prison on an island in San Francisco Bay, to dramatize their demands.

As with other racial minorities, a significant number of Native Americans moved to urban areas where they often resided in deteriorated communities and in poverty. Caught between two cultures, and rather than assimilating to the extent that many other minority groups did, Native Americans often had difficulty establishing their personal and collective identities. When the colonists arrived in the seventeenth century, there were roughly ten million Native Americans, but by 1970 their numbers had dwindled to some 827,000 though many of them had become absorbed into the general population.[152]

Asian Americans in Hawaii and California made important gains in achieving their civil rights in the wake of World War II and in the 1950s. Disenfranchised before World War II, Asian plantation laborers were registered in a massive drive by the International Longshoreman's and Warehousemen's Union during the war and secured an act by the Hawaii legislature that was akin to the Wagner Act. Sugar workers were able to unionize in a multiracial union that included Filipino, Japanese, and Portuguese

laborers. Californian Japanese Americans were able to obtain from the Supreme Court a ruling that California's laws, which prohibited a non-citizen alien from conveying his or her land to a citizen child, were unconstitutional. The California Supreme Court ruled in 1948 that laws that prohibited people of different races from having sexual contact (antimiscegenation laws) were unconstitutional. California voters decisively defeated an initiative in 1946 that was placed on the ballot to reaffirm the alien land law. In 1956, Japanese Americans placed on the ballot an initiative to overturn the alien land laws altogether and won. In 1952, the federal government finally terminated provisions of the 1790 naturalization law that refused citizenship to non-caucasions partly because of lobbying by Japanese Americans.[153]

But immigration limitations on Asians continued despite token concessions to various nationalities following World War II. The blatantly racist immigration policies of the United States, which gave larger annual quotas to European nations than to Asian nations, finally led to the Immigration Act of 1965. This act abolished the national-origins quotas and allowed annual admissions of 170,000 immigrants from the Eastern Hemisphere and 120,000 from the Western Hemisphere, not including immediate family members. As Takaki notes, "the new law represented a sharp ideological departure from the traditional view of America as a homogeneous white society."[154] Indeed, a second wave of Asian immigrants ensued during the next thirty years that brought a massive increase in the Asian population; significant Japanese, Chinese, and Filipino populations were supplemented by Vietnamese, Korean, Asian Indian, Laotian, and Cambodian groups, as we discuss in Chapter 11.

## The Ghettoization of Racial Minorities

By the end of the 1960s, a pattern of the urban ghettoization of racial minorities in American cities had become well pronounced, but it was to become even more marked over the next two decades. As Latinos and African Americans entered American cities, they tended to reside in segregated communities that had often been abandoned by other ethnic groups that fled to suburban areas. New York City provides an example; by 1970, whites composed 63.3 percent of its population, whereas African Americans and Latinos, respectively, composed 19.2 and 15.2 percent of its population. By 1990, the white population had declined to 41.3 percent of the city's population, whereas African-American and Latino populations had, respectively, risen to 27.7 and 23.7 percent of its population.[155] (Similar statistics existed for other major American cities.)

Of course, Irish, Italian, Jewish, and other ethnic enclaves had traditionally existed in American cities, but their plight was enviable compared to that of the racial minorities. Their upward mobility—that is, their ability to afford more expensive housing in better communities and the suburbs—was enhanced by the fact that their immigration occurred just as the United States was industrializing, so they obtained a foothold from the outset in the growing American economy even if they often began with poorly paid positions. By the time Latinos and African Americans reached the cities in massive numbers in the 1950s and succeeding decades, they found it more difficult to penetrate an economic structure dominated by the whites who had preceded them. Moreover, white immigrants had not ghettoized *by race* in a society that encircled them, with vast middle-class populations in suburbs where jobs had increasingly located. Denied education in rural areas before they left for the cities, these minority groups were probably less prepared to use education as the vehicle of upward mobility, as had the Jews, Asian Americans, and white-ethnic populations of prior eras. Moreover, the inner-city schools often lacked staff that could relate to African-American and Latino youth, and the classrooms were usually overcrowded.

The ghettoization of urban minorities was coupled, moreover, with selective outmigration from their communities of those members who *were* upwardly mobile, leaving a vast sea of destitute people who often lacked the role models, indigenous businesses, vibrant churches, and community cohesiveness that other white-ethnic groups had enjoyed.

## SOCIAL WORK IN THE 1960s

Social work emerged from the Great Depression with a determination to upgrade the profession by making a bachelor's degree mandatory for admission to graduate programs and by making all graduate programs last for two years. Casework remained the dominant technology of the profession with macro practice occupying a decidedly secondary niche. Moreover, social workers in many states wanted to establish state-enforced standards and tests to register or certify those social workers who met or passed them; that is, they wanted to establish lists of social workers who could then receive priority over nontrained workers in filling government and agency positions. The profession was trying, in effect, to distinguish its members from the legions of untrained staff who worked in government and nongovernment agencies.[156] Some people wondered if the profession risked being too elitist by requiring extended graduate training, but advocates of the master's degree insisted that it was required to improve standards and to obtain competence in casework.

The National Council on Social Work Education was established in 1946—and renamed the Council on Social Work Education (CSWE) in 1952—to launch a study of social work education that would clarify relationships between undergraduate and graduate education. It concluded that graduate education was needed for professional practice with undergraduate education providing only a preprofessional base. However, undergraduate education remained even though its status paled next to graduate programs; in 1951, 400 schools taught undergraduate courses in social work.[157] The National Association of Social Workers (NASW) was formed in 1955 from seven separate social work associations with a membership of roughly 18,000 members and with new members limited to people with two years of graduate study.

An important question remained: To what extent would this profession be committed to social action and social justice, as implied by early founders like Jane Addams and the rank-and-file movement of the 1930s? Would casework, with its emphasis on individual counseling, both draw into social work only those students whose perspectives were narrowed to individual remedies and socialize some of them to view social action as extraneous to professional work? Developments in the 1950s did not augur well for those who wanted a social-action perspective to be prominent in the profession. The macro side of the profession, such as community organization and administration, remained ill defined. Social policy offerings were uneven in schools of social work and often emphasized historical materials rather than also providing students with tools to engage in advocacy for the poor or other populations. A prominent set of educators infused casework with so much psychiatric content that it became irrelevant to those working-class and poor persons unable or unwilling to participate in extended intrapsychic explorations. Still, a movement to have a "generalist" curriculum began to give social work students a breadth of content to include many modalities rather than narrowly defined casework training.

The profession was influenced by the turbulence of the 1960s. Even in the late 1950s, an exhaustive study of social work education recommended that community organization and

administration join casework and group work as fully recognized interventions in social work, even if policy was still relegated to largely theoretical, philosophical, and historical roles. The advocacy of the War on Poverty infused life into the macro disciplines in social work; many scores of students joined these branches in the growing numbers of schools that offered concentrations in them.[158] The NASW engaged in extensive lobbying and advocacy in the 1960s, unlike the 1950s, when it maintained a lower profile.[159] Further, many theorists sought to redefine casework to make it more relevant to the poor and different ethnic minorities; ecological perspectives and case advocacy become more prominent in the writings of various theorists.[160] Social work, which remained the dominant profession in many nongovernmental social agencies, retained, moreover, its foothold in public agencies in the 1960s where its members were much involved in mental health, child welfare, and public welfare agencies. Thus enriching its mission and buoyed by the expansion of the welfare state, social work seemed positioned to provide much of the staff for a range of agencies and functions while retaining a reformist mission.

But the profession was hardly free from controversy. Some people believed it to be too conservative, as protests by students in various schools of social work in the 1960s and by activists at national conferences attested. (Many of them wanted more assertive roles by social workers in challenging existing programs and policies.)[161] Though somewhat broadened, questions remained about the dominance of casework in social work. A decision by the NASW in 1969 to give regular membership to holders of bachelor's degrees from those undergraduate programs that met CSWE criteria was controversial within the profession; its advocates insisted that it would give NASW more political clout by vastly enlarging its membership, but its detractors insisted that it would lower standards and decrease the prestige, and thus the power, of the social work profession by "diluting" its membership.[162]

## ASSESSMENT OF THE GREAT SOCIETY

Johnson possessed genuine sympathy for impoverished persons, yet he was no more disposed than Kennedy to expand income maintenance, public works, unemployment, or Social Security programs.[163] Because he encountered fortuitous times and possessed formidable legislative skills, he was able to enact a torrent of social legislation. But critics contend that this highly ambitious man, who wanted to enact more programs than Franklin Roosevelt, became seduced by his legislative successes and equated quantity with quality.[164] So obsessed was he with enacting measures that he gave insufficient attention to their implementation. Passage of innumerable bills became even more problematic when coupled with Johnson's budgetary frugality, which stemmed from his dislike of big spenders and from his diversion of national resources to the Vietnam conflict.[165] The War on Poverty never received more than $2 billion in any fiscal year even though it was the centerpiece of his domestic strategy.

The Great Society represented a curious paradox; though it was a period of unprecedented social reform, social spending did not increase markedly during The Great Society, when expressed as a percentage of total federal spending, partly because Johnson did not commit major funds to many of his initiatives and programs like Medicare had not become fully established.[166] The economic position of poor persons and racial minorities improved markedly, but these improvements probably stemmed primarily from the economic growth of the period. Johnson nonetheless vastly broadened the policy roles of the federal government to include federal funding of programs in medical, nutritional, preschool, educational, legal, civil rights, and gerontologic areas. Roosevelt established the foundations of the American welfare state, and Johnson dramatically expanded its scope in a remarkably brief period.

## THE POLITICAL ECONOMY OF REFORM IN THE 1960s

Social reforms occurred at a dizzying pace in the 1960s but for reasons quite different from why reforms occurred during the New Deal. Unlike the 1930s, the United States experienced economic growth in the 1960s, so reform did not stem from the economic malaise of the general public. A number of factors must be viewed in tandem as they stimulated reform. A pent-up demand for reform existed because few new social programs had been established since the onset of World War II owing to the conservative hold on Congress in the Truman administration, the conservatism of Eisenhower, the inability of Kennedy to obtain passage of his domestic mea-

sures, and the diversion of funds and presidential attention to the crises of the cold war.

We can speculate that Kennedy reinstilled a sense of idealism in certain segments of the population, even if he had few reforms enacted by the time of his death. American public opinion was profoundly influenced, moreover, by the civil rights movement, which daily brought to the American public an unending series of atrocities in the South as civil rights activists dramatically challenged a range of discriminatory laws and practices.

Nor can we underestimate the efforts of Lyndon Johnson, who seized the moment to turn the assassination into a series of legislative victories even in 1964. The landslide victory of Johnson in 1964, moreover, gave the Democrats such commanding majorities in both houses of Congress that Johnson could use his formidable skills to fashion a torrent of legislative successes. Pressure from the civil rights movement, as well as its emulation by groups such as women, the disabled, gays and lesbians, and other minorities, kept pressure on decision makers not to relent. And the riots in the cities were a constant and grim reminder that America had a large population of destitute citizens whose plight had not been frontally addressed by the civil rights legislation.

As might be expected in a nation that had created a sizable welfare state so late in its history, substantial opposition to the rate of growth of federal roles in social welfare began to appear by 1966. Racial animosity, dislike of big government, antipathy to the poor, and dislike of radicals and social reformers, which had been somewhat muted from 1964 to 1966, reappeared. The Vietnam War probably accelerated and intensified polarization between persons favoring and opposing social reforms because they tended to take divergent positions on the war.

The Great Society was, then, a significant reform movement, but like the New Deal, it occurred in a society that was reluctant to develop an embracing welfare state. As the nation headed toward the 1970s, reformers wondered if the set of programs would endure or be swept away in a new and conservative era. As with the programs of the Social Security Act, time would show that many of the creations of The Great Society would be surprisingly resilient in coming decades. By the same token, the size and nature of the American welfare state would prove to be highly controversial in the ensuing decades.

## END NOTES

1. Joseph Lash, *Eleanor and Franklin* (New York: W.W. Norton, 1971), pp. 597 ff.

2. Richard Chapman, "Contours of Public Policy, 1939–1945" Unpublished dissertation (New Haven, Conn.: Yale University, 1976), pp. 300 ff.

3. Stephen Bailey, *Congress Makes a Law* (New York: Columbia University Press, 1950), pp. 220–234.

4. Mary Hinchey, "The Frustration of the New Deal Revival: 1944–1946," Unpublished dissertation (Columbia, Mo.: University of Missouri, 1965).

5. James Savage, *Balanced Budgets and American Politics* (Ithaca, N.Y.: Cornell University Press, 1988), pp. 161–175.

6. See, for example, discussion of Barton Bernstein, "The Ambiguous Legacy: The Truman Administration and Civil Rights." In Barton Bernstein, ed., *Politics and Policies of the Truman Administration* (Chicago: Quadrangle Books, 1970), pp. 269–314.

7. Paul Nitze, *From Hiroshima to Glasnost: At the Center of Decision* (New York: Grove Weidenfeld, 1989).

8. Bernstein, "The Ambiguous Legacy," pp. 269–314.

9. Richard Davies, *Age of Asphalt: The Automobile, the Freeway, and the Condition of Metropolitan America* (Philadelphia: J.B. Lippincott, 1975).

10. Herbert Parmet, *Eisenhower and the American Crusades* (New York: Macmillan, 1972), pp. 570–572.

11. Stephen Ambrose, *Eisenhower, the President,* Vol. II (New York: Simon & Schuster, 1984), pp. 411–435.

12. William Leuchtenberg, *In the Shadow of FDR: From Harry Truman to Ronald Reagan* (Ithaca, N.Y.: Cornell University Press, 1983), pp. 78–84; Allen Matusow, *The Unraveling of America: A History of Liberalism in the 1960's* (New York: Harper & Row, 1984), pp. 15–17.

13. Charles Hulton, "The Legacy of Reaganomics." In John Palmer and Isabel Sawhill, eds., *The Legacy of Reaganomics* (Washington, D.C.: Urban Institute, 1984), p. 7.

14. Geoffrey Hodgson, *America in Our Time* (Garden City, N.Y.: Doubleday, 1976), p. 51.

15. *Ibid.*, pp. 54–64, 184–189.

16. *Ibid.*, pp. 58–60.

17. Paul Taubman, *Income Distribution and Redistribution* (Reading, Mass.: Addison-Wesley, 1978), p. 15.

18. Winifred Bell, *Aid to Dependent Children* (New York: Columbia University Press, 1965), pp. 93–110; Frances Piven and Richard Cloward, *Regulating the Poor: The Functions of Public Welfare* (New York: Pantheon, 1971), pp. 123–177.

19. Gilbert Steiner, *State of Welfare* (Washington, D.C.: Brookings Institution, 1971), pp. 226–227.

20. Peter Gottschalk and Sheldon Danziger, "Macroeconomic Conditions, Income Transfers, and the Trend in Poverty." In D. Lee Bawden, ed., *The Social Contract Revisited: Aims and Outcomes of President Reagan's Social Welfare Policy* (Washington, D.C.: Urban Institute, 1984), p. 191.

21. William Chafe, *The American Woman: Her Changing Social, Economic, and Political Roles* (New York: Oxford University Press, 1972), pp. 174–195.

22. Bernard Bloom, *Community Mental Health* (Monterey, Calif.: Brooks/Cole, 1977), pp. 11–20.

23. Peter Tyor and Leland Bell, *Caring for the Retarded in America: A History* (Westport, Conn.: Greenwood Press, 1984), pp. 123–145.

24. The number of handicapped persons is discussed by Frank Bowe in *Rehabilitating America: Toward Independence for Disabled and Elderly People* (New York: Harper & Row, 1980), pp. 24–54.

25. Jonathan Katz, *Gay American History: Lesbians and Gay Men in the U.S.A.* (New York: Harper Colophon Books, 1976), pp. 432, 596.

26. Hodgson, *America in Our Time*, p. 45.

27. See Theodore Sorenson, *Kennedy* (New York: Harper & Row, 1965); Arthur Schlesinger, Jr., *A Thousand Days: John F. Kennedy in the White House* (Boston: Houghton Mifflin, 1965); William Manchester, *Portrait of a President* (Boston: Little, Brown, 1962).

28. Henry Fairlie, *The Kennedy Promise* (Garden City, N.Y.: Doubleday, 1973); Victor Lasky, *J.F.K., the Man and the Myth* (New York: Macmillan, 1963); Richard Walton, *Cold War and Counterrevolution: The Foreign Policy of John F. Kennedy* (New York: Viking Press, 1972).

29. Leuchtenberg, *In the Shadow of FDR*, pp. 76–84.

30. *Ibid.*, p. 77; Matusow, *The Unraveling of America*, p. 14.

31. Henry Aaron, *Politics and the Professors* (Washington, D.C.: Brookings Institution, 1981), pp. 17–25; James Patterson, *America's Struggle Against Poverty* (Cambridge, Mass.: Harvard University Press, 1981), pp. 115–125.

32. Aaron, *Politics and the Professors*, pp. 35–49, 220–225.

33. William Ryan, *Blaming the Victim* (New York: Pantheon, 1971), pp. 112–135.

34. Vincent Burke, *Nixon's Good Deed: Welfare Reform* (New York: Columbia University Press, 1974), p. 36; Hodgson, *America in Our Time*, pp. 82–98.

35. Tom Wicker, *JFK and LBJ: The Influence of Personality upon Politics* (New York: Morrow, 1968), pp. 85–87.

36. *Ibid.*, pp. 90–92.

37. *Ibid.*, pp. 25–28; Hodgson, *America in Our Time*, pp. 99–110.

38. Leuchtenberg, *In the Shadow of FDR*, pp. 85–88.

39. Aaron, *Politics and the Professors*, p. 17.

40. Michael Harrington, *The Other America: Poverty in the United States* (New York: Macmillan, 1962).

41. Matusow, *The Unraveling of America*, pp. 60–96.

42. Juan Williams, *Eyes on the Prize: America's Civil Rights Years, 1954–1965* (New York: Viking, 1987), pp. 39–61.

43. *Ibid.*, p. 41.

44. *Ibid.*, pp. 39–61.

45. Matusow, *The Unraveling of America,* pp. 62–63.

46. Carl Brauer, *John F. Kennedy and the Second Reconstruction* (New York: Columbia University Press, 1977), pp. 16–17, 204.

47. *Ibid.,* pp. 112–113.

48. Matusow, *The Unraveling of America,* p. 348.

49. *Ibid.,* pp. 90–91; Brauer, *John F. Kennedy,* pp. 265–268.

50. Theodore Marmor, *The Politics of Medicare* (Chicago: Aldine Books, 1975), pp. 39–53.

51. Wicker, *JFK and LBJ,* pp. 132–146.

52. Hodgson, *America in Our Time,* pp. 247–248.

53. Matusow, *The Unraveling of America,* pp. 104–105; James Sundquist, *Politics and Policy: The Eisenhower, Kennedy and Johnson Years* (Washington, D.C.: Brookings Institution, 1968), pp. 85–91.

54. Matusow, *The Unraveling of America,* p. 105.

55. *Ibid.,* p. 100.

56. See James Singer, "A Subminimum Wage—Jobs for Youths or a Break for Their Employers?" *National Journal* (January 24, 1981), 146–148.

57. Sundquist, *Politics and Policy,* pp. 97–105.

58. Matusow, *The Unraveling of America,* pp. 100–102.

59. Bloom, *Community Mental Health,* pp. 19–25.

60. Steiner, *State of Welfare,* pp. 35–40.

61. David Halberstam, *The Best and the Brightest* (New York: Random House, 1972), pp. 154–301.

62. Robert Caro, *The Years of Lyndon Johnson* (New York: Knopf, 1982); Doris Kearns, *Lyndon Johnson and the American Dream* (New York: Harper & Row, 1976), pp. 19–96.

63. Kearns, *Lyndon Johnson,* pp. 103–106.

64. *Ibid.,* p. 179; Wicker, *JFK and LBJ,* pp. 161–163.

65. Joseph Califano, *The Triumph and Tragedy of Lyndon Johnson: The White House Years* (New York: Simon & Schuster, 1991), pp. 106–121.

66. Wicker, *JFK and LBJ,* pp. 163–169; Kearns, *Lyndon Johnson,* pp. 170–176.

67. Kearns, *Lyndon Johnson,* pp. 190, 224–227; Wicker, *JFK and LBJ,* pp. 209–211.

68. Vaughn Bornet, *The Presidency of Lyndon B. Johnson* (Lawrence, Kans.: University of Kansas, 1983), pp. 134, 225, 333, 343; Patterson, *America's Struggle,* p. 141; Wicker, *JFK and LBJ,* pp. 177–178.

69. Kearns, *Lyndon Johnson,* pp. 190, 224–227.

70. Wicker, *JFK and LBJ,* pp. 212–235.

71. Sundquist, *Politics and Policy,* pp. 259–271.

72. Matusow, *The Unraveling of America,* pp. 203–213.

73. *Ibid.,* pp. 180–187.

74. Ambrose, *Eisenhower, the President,* Vol. II, p. 425.

75. Williams, *Eyes on the Prize,* pp. 23, 32.

76. *Ibid.,* p. 23.

77. Paul Starr, *The Social Transformation of American Medicine* (New York: Basic Books, 1984), pp. 369–370.

78. *Ibid.,* pp. 97–103, 373; Frank Thompson, *Health Policy and the Bureaucracy: Politics and Implementation* (Cambridge, Mass.: M.I.T. Press, 1981), pp. 180–185.

79. Nancy Eustis, Jay Greenberg, and Sharon Patten, *Long-Term Care for Older Persons: A Policy Perspective* (Monterey, Calif.: Brooks/Cole, 1984), pp. 135–137.

80. *Ibid.,* pp. 133–135.

81. Starr, *The Social Transformation,* pp. 375–378.

82. Many legislative proposals have been considered to develop innovative outreach and community projects. See Eustis, Greenberg, and Patten, *Long-Term Care,* pp. 189–192.

83. Rosemary Stevens, *Welfare Medicine in America: The Case of Medicaid* (New York: Free Press, 1974), pp. 51–71.

84. *Ibid.,* p. 131.

85. Karen Davis and Cathy Schoen, *Health and the War on Poverty: A Ten-Year Appraisal* (Washington, D.C.: Brookings Institution, 1978), pp. 62–67; Thompson, *Health Policy,* pp. 148–153.

86. Davis and Schoen, *Health and the War on Poverty,* pp. 67–91; Dorothy Kupcha, "Medicaid: In or Out of the Mainstream?" *California Journal,* 10 (May 1979), 181–183.

87. Donald Gelfand and Jody Olsen, *The Aging Network: Programs and Services* (New York: Springer, 1980), pp. 9–16.

88. William Lammers, *Public Policy and the Aging* (Washington, D.C.: Congressional Quarterly Press, 1983), pp. 180–183.

89. Sundquist, *Politics and Policy,* pp. 210–215.

90. Matusow, *The Unraveling of America,* pp. 223–226.

91. Aaron, *Politics and the Professors,* pp. 70–92.

92. Bornet, *The Presidency of Lyndon Johnson,* pp. 223–224.

93. *Ibid.,* pp. 224–227.

94. Sundquist, *Politics and Policy,* pp. 134–150.

95. Daniel Moynihan, *Maximum Feasible Misunderstanding: Community Action in the War on Poverty* (New York: Free Press, 1969), pp. 79–100.

96. Matusow, *The Unraveling of America,* pp. 243–265.

97. Burke, *Nixon's Good Deed,* pp. 18, 23–24.

98. Matusow, *The Unraveling of America,* pp. 266–267.

99. Davis and Schoen, *Health and the War on Poverty,* pp. 133–134, 177–189.

100. Matusow, *The Unraveling of America,* p. 266.

101. Bruce Jansson, *The History and Politics of Selected Children's Programs and Related Legislation in the Context of Four Models of Political Behavior,* Doctoral dissertation (Chicago: University of Chicago, 1975), pp. 145–146, 160–161.

102. Steiner, *State of Welfare,* pp. 40–50.

103. Burke, *Nixon's Good Deed,* pp. 22–24, 35–41.

104. Califano, *Triumph and Tragedy of Lyndon Johnson,* p. 149.

105. See William Gibbons, *The U.S. Government and the Vietnam War: Executive and Legislative Roles and Relationships,* Part III (Princeton, N.J.: Princeton University Press, 1990).

106. Michael Boll, *National Security Planning: Roosevelt Through Reagan* (Lexington, Ky.: University of Kentucky Press, 1988).

107. See oral histories by Walter Heller at the Lyndon Johnson Presidential Library.

108. Califano, *Triumph and Tragedy of Lyndon Johnson,* pp. 106–121.

109. *Ibid.,* pp. 94–97.

110. *Ibid.,* pp. 97–98.

111. *Ibid.,* p. 111.

112. Matusow, *The Unraveling of America,* pp. 204–206.

113. *Ibid.,* p. 205.

114. *Ibid.,* pp. 422–426; Hodgson, *America in Our Time,* pp. 368–383.

115. Matusow, *The Unraveling of America,* pp. 345–360.

116. Leuchtenberg, *A Troubled Feast,* p. 173.

117. Califano, *Triumph and Tragedy of Lyndon Johnson,* p. 248.

118. Gloria Emerson, *Winners and Losers* (New York: Random House, 1976), p. 357; Guenter Lewy, *America in Vietnam* (New York: Oxford University Press, 1978), p. 445; Alan Millette, ed., *A Short History of the Vietnam Conflict* (Bloomington, Ind.: University of Indiana, 1978), p. 131.

119. Kearns, *Lyndon Johnson,* pp. 251–275; Wicker, *JFK and LBJ,* pp. 252–253.

120. Matusow, *The Unraveling of America,* pp. 376–394.

121. Kearns, *Lyndon Johnson,* pp. 302–304.

122. Leuchtenberg, *In the Shadow of FDR,* pp. 147–150.

123. Susan Faludi, *Backlash: The Undeclared War Against American Women* (New York: Crown Publishers, 1991), p. 56.

124. *Ibid.,* p. 57.

125. Cynthia Harrison, *On Account of Sex: The Politics of Women's Issues, 1945–1968* (Berkeley: University of California Press, 1988), pp. 3–23.

126. *Ibid.,* pp. 89–105.

127. *Ibid.*, pp. 139–156.

128. Betty Friedan, *The Feminine Mystique* (New York: W.W. Norton, 1963).

129. *Ibid.*, p. 15.

130. *Ibid.*, p. 282.

131. *Ibid.*, pp. 338–378.

132. Harrison, *On Account of Sex*, pp. 176–180.

133. *Ibid.*, pp. 187–191.

134. *Ibid.*, p. 200.

135. *Ibid.*, pp. 201–202.

136. *Ibid.*, p. 171.

137. Jonathan Katz, *Gay American History*, p. 99.

138. John D'Emilio, *Sexual Politics, Sexual Communities: The Making of a Homosexual Minority in the United States, 1940–1970* (Chicago: University of Chicago Press, 1983).

139. *Ibid.*, p. 35.

140. *Ibid.*, p. 44.

141. *Ibid.*, p. 46.

142. *Ibid.*, p. 49.

143. *Ibid.*, pp. 124–125.

144. *Ibid.*, pp. 129–148.

145. *Ibid.*, p. 217.

146. *Ibid.*, p. 235.

147. James Jennings, "The Puerto Rican Community: Its Political Background." In F. Chris Garcia, ed., *Latinos and the Political System* (Notre Dame, Ind.: University of Notre Dame Press, 1988), p. 65.

148. Juan Gomez Quinones, *Chicano Politics* (Albuquerque, N.M.: University of New Mexico Press, 1990), pp. 101–153.

149. Jennings, "The Puerto Rican Community," p. 75.

150. Theodore Taylor, *The Bureau of Indian Affairs* (Boulder, Colo.: Westview Press, 1984), pp. 18–19.

151. *Ibid.*, p. 25.

152. *Ibid.*, p. 27.

153. Ronald Takaki, *Strangers from a Different Shore* (Boston: Little, Brown, 1989), pp. 406–420.

154. *Ibid.*, p. 419.

155. Angelo Falcon, "Black and Latino Politics in New York City: Race and Ethnicity in a Changing Urban Context." In Garcia, ed., *Latinos and the Political System*, pp. 172–173.

156. Stanley Wenocur and Michael Reisch, *From Charity to Enterprise: The Development of American Social Work in a Market Economy* (Urbana, Ill.: University of Illinois Press, 1989), pp. 211–213.

157. *Ibid.*, pp. 252–255.

158. Jack Rothman, "Macro Social Work in a Tightening Economy," *Social Work,* 24 (May 1980), 274–282.

159. Leslie Leighninger, *Social Work: Search for Identity* (New York: Greenwood Press, 1987), p. 217.

160. Bruce Jansson, *Social Welfare Policy: From Theory to Practice* (Belmont, Calif.: Wadsworth, 1990), pp. 8–11.

161. Leighninger, *Social Work: Search for Identity*, p. 217.

162. *Ibid.*, pp. 214–215.

163. Burke, *Nixon's Good Deed*, pp. 20, 22–24, 36–39.

164. Lawrence O'Brien, *No Final Victories: A Life in Politics from John F. Kennedy to Watergate* (Garden City, N.Y.: Doubleday, 1974), pp. 196–197.

165. Kearns, *Lyndon Johnson*, pp. 282–284.

166. Jack Meyer, "Budget Cuts in the Reagan Administration: A Question of Fairness." In Bawden, ed., *The Social Contract Revisited*, p. 36.

# CHAPTER 10

# The Paradoxical Era: 1968–1980

## Selected Orienting Events in the Paradoxical Era

| | |
|---|---|
| **1968** | Richard Nixon wins narrow presidential victory over Hubert Humphrey |
| **1969** | Nixon proposes Family Assistance Plan |
| **1970** | Family Planning and Population Research Act enacted; Occupational Safety and Health Act (OSHA) enacted |
| **1971** | National eligibility standards established for food stamp program |
| **1972** | Earned income tax credit (EITC) established for poor wage-earners; Local Fiscal Assistance Act establishes general revenue sharing; Social Security benefits indexed to rise with inflation; Supplementary Security Income (SSI) program established |
| **1972** | Nixon wins landslide victory over George McGovern |
| **1973** | Comprehensive Employment and Training Act (CETA) enacted; Food Stamp Program federalized and made mandatory; Rehabilitation Act passed |
| **1973** | Supreme Court issues *Roe* v. *Wade* decision legalizing abortion |
| **1974** | Juvenile Justice and Delinquency Prevention Act enacted; Title XX (social services) added to Social Security Act |
| **1974** | Nixon resigns presidency under threat of impeachment owing to the Watergate scandal and is succeeded by Gerald Ford |
| **1975** | Education for All Handicapped Children Act passed |
| **1976** | Jimmy Carter defeats Gerald Ford for the presidency |
| **1977** | Carter introduces welfare reform plan, which is later defeated |
| **1978** | Report of President's Commission on Mental Health issued |
| **1979** | Carter introduces unsuccessful national health insurance plan; Office of Education separated from Department of Health, Education, and Welfare (HEW), which became Department of Health and Human Services (DHHS) |
| **1980** | Adoption Assistance and Child Welfare Act enacted; Mental Health Systems Act passed |

Presidents Richard Nixon (1968–1974), Gerald Ford (1974–1976), and Jimmy Carter (1976–1980) were relatively conservative presidents who had little outward interest in major social reforms. Yet social spending rose dramatically during this ostensibly conservative period. Indeed, few people realize that the first term of Nixon's presidency (1968–1972) ranks as a major period of social reform. Sar Levitan, a noted policy commentator, argued that "the greatest extensions of the modern welfare system were enacted under the conservative Presidency of Richard Nixon with bipartisan congressional support, dwarfing in size and scope the initiatives of Lyndon Johnson's Great Society."[1] Although Levitan seems to forget that many of Nixon's reforms consisted of simply expanding programs he inherited from The Great Society, such as the Food Stamps Program, he, like Tom Wicker, a biographer of Nixon, correctly notes that many social reforms and considerable increases in social spending occurred in the Nixon years.[2] Nixon was also extremely conservative in much of his rhetoric and turned sharply to the right in 1972. This was a transitional era with conflicting tendencies that served to bridge the reformist period of The Great Society with the conservative presidency of Ronald Reagan in the 1980s.

## RICHARD NIXON: POLITICAL OPPORTUNIST

Richard Nixon achieved early successes in House and Senate races in the late 1940s and early 1950s by alleging that his opponents had left-wing tendencies and by spearheading congressional investigations of Alger Hiss, a State Department official who was accused and ultimately convicted of spying for Russia. These tactics earned him the suspicion of liberals, but they brought him sufficient public support that Dwight Eisenhower chose him to be his running mate in his presidential campaigns of 1952 and 1956. Nixon obtained the Republican nomination for the presidency in 1960, but he narrowly lost to John Kennedy. After losing a bid for a seat in the Senate in 1962 in California, he retired from politics, only to resurface as the Republican presidential candidate in 1968 against Hubert Humphrey, whom he subsequently defeated by a thin margin.

Liberal critics of Nixon had long accused him of willingness to use redbaiting and other dubious tactics to secure power, but his opportunism also led him to support liberal domestic policies when he believed they would enhance his political career. These calculations sometimes led him to support moderate positions during the 1950s, when Republicans understood that frontal attacks on New Deal programs, such as Social Security, were unpopular.[3]

Nixon correctly perceived that a power vacuum existed in the Republican party in the wake of the Democratic landslide victory over Goldwater in 1964. By assuming the role of mediator and statesman within the leaderless and demoralized party and by aggressively campaigning for Republicans of all persuasions in succeeding years, he successfully positioned himself for the presidential bid in 1968.[4] Nixon obtained the nomination for the presidency in 1968 because he convinced each segment of the Republican party, including liberal, moderate, and conservative wings, that he represented them.[5]

His election campaign in 1968 did not suggest that he would soon initiate or support a series of domestic reforms. Sensing that the Democratic contender, Hubert Humphrey, was vulnerable among working- and middle-class voters because he was identified with the Vietnam conflict and with black-power and other reform groups, Nixon avoided major social issues, promised peace with honor, and pledged he would be tough on the issue of crime. He appealed to southerners by promising to terminate federal efforts to desegregate schools and by giving Senator Strom Thurmond, a conservative southerner, a prominent role in selecting the law-and-order theme of his campaign. He chose Spiro Agnew as his vice president in an obvious effort to appeal to white backlash sentiment and repeatedly attacked alleged social-reform excesses of The Great Society.[6]

Nixon's conservative rhetoric in the campaign of 1968 was not a good predictor of his subsequent policy choices, particularly in the first three years of his presidency before he made a decided turn to the right. His motivation for supporting various social reforms defies easy analysis because he was an enigmatic man to whom Churchill's characterization of Russia ("a riddle wrapped in a mystery inside an enigma") might aptly apply. Wicker contends that Nixon was not devoid of sympathy for the poor because of his own experience with poverty during his childhood though he also notes that Nixon's choices were dictated by political concerns, such as his desire to increase the base of the Republican party.[7] Indeed, other writers place considerable stock in the "Disraeli thesis"—that is, that Nixon's reading of English history led him to want to be an American conservative who, much like the English conservative prime minister of the nineteenth century, would pull into his political party new working-class constituents who would like his reforms.[8] Indeed, many theorists believe that he was intrigued by the arguments of Kevin Phillips, a Republican theorist who maintained that a new majority for the Republican party could be built by attracting into it large numbers of working-class voters, Catholics, members of white ethnic groups, and residents of the sunbelt.[9] Yet other commentators suggest

that much of his behavior derived from a perverse pleasure in upstaging or surprising the Democrats.[10] Another intriguing theory is that Nixon supported social reform mainly to retain the support of liberals in both political parties for his foreign policies, including his Vietnam policy, which came under attack by liberal legislators.[11] If this was indeed the case, it represented an interesting reversal from Franklin Roosevelt and Lyndon Johnson, both of whom had to *cut* social spending to placate congressional (conservative) foes. Nixon also knew that Democrats, who controlled both houses of Congress, would push him to support many liberal measures. Doubtless, Nixon was often driven by some combination of these motivations, but the "bottom line" was that he supported or agreed to an array of social reforms.

But Nixon's use of a reform strategy to broaden his political constituency was undertaken with ambivalence, both for ideological and political reasons. Nixon was not instinctively a liberal, even if he was willing to espouse liberal causes for political reasons. He despised many liberal Republican senators, such as Charles Percy of Illinois. Many of his advisors, as well as broad sections of his party, were conservative and unlikely to support liberal policies. An "inner circle of ambivalence" thus existed in the White House in Nixon's first term and led to contradictory policies. And this ambivalence turned by 1972 to outright opposition to many social policies and to a determination to cut social spending, even by "impounding" funds that Congress had already appropriated for specific programs.[12]

## NIXON'S STRATEGY: FLOATING COALITIONS AND OUTBIDDING

As reformer, Nixon both initiated social legislation and responded positively to congressional initiatives. When Nixon supported social reforms,

he used a "floating coalition" and "political outbidding." The *floating coalition strategy* depended on fashioning a coalition, whose composition varied from issue to issue, which included the support of some liberal Republicans, some moderate Republicans who were loyal to the president, and some Democratic liberals and moderates who placed their ideology before their party—that is, a bipartisan coalition comprising moderates and liberals who could oppose conservatives.[13] In the *political outbidding strategy,* he endorsed social reforms that were initiated by Democrats but offered expansive amendments to them—or accepted them with little change—so that he could obtain partial credit for their passage.[14] It was a strange spectacle to many political observers since no Republican president since Theodore Roosevelt had sought to enact numerous domestic reforms, much less to try to beat the Democrats at their own reform game.

The use of floating coalitions and outbidding by a Republican president represented bold strategies but ones that could be successful only in a particular kind of political environment. First, he had to want to expand the political base of his party and had to believe, as well, that blue-collar and white ethnic voters desired social reforms. Second, he had to believe that he could develop social reforms that were different enough from Democratic reforms that he could persuade members of his own party that he was not merely copying the kinds of Democratic reforms that Republicans had opposed since the New Deal. Where Lyndon Johnson had sought programs that emphasized social and medical services, community participation of the poor, and expanded roles for the federal government, Nixon sought reforms that provided jobs and income, expanded policy roles of local governments, and used private market mechanisms rather than direct government provision.[15] He believed that these kinds of social reforms were sufficiently superior to the Democrats' reforms that many Republicans would support them and that they would endear him to blue-collar voters, local officials, and the business community. To underscore the distinctiveness of Republican reforms, Nixon unleashed scathing attacks on the reforms of The Great Society, which he depicted as undisciplined and ineffective programs that enriched bureaucrats and social workers.[16]

Third, Nixon had to believe that increased domestic spending would not jeopardize the nation's economic growth by causing deficits or by drawing capital from investments. He believed that economic surpluses would exist following the Vietnam conflict that would be sufficient to fund new programs, and he favored the use of increased social spending to bring about economic recovery during and after a sharp recession in 1970.[17] Finally, he needed to have a significant number of liberal advisors to provide him with reform ideas and to fend off conservative advisors who were beholden to the conservative wing of the Republican party though, in keeping with his policy ambivalence in his first term, he also appointed many conservative advisors.[18] He named the relatively liberal Robert Finch as his secretary of the Department of Health, Education, and Welfare and, when Finch suffered a nervous breakdown, replaced him with Elliot Richardson. He appointed Daniel Moynihan, a moderate Democrat who was critical of The Great Society but favored income, job, and other reforms, to be the director of his Urban Affairs Council.

## FROM STRATEGY TO POLICY

Reforms that were enacted by Nixon during his first term (1968–1972) included the Supplementary Security Income (SSI) program, major revisions in the Food Stamp Program, indexing of the Social Security program, revenue sharing, the consolidation of social services in Title XX to the Social Security Act, addition of a family planning program to the Public Health Act, assorted health legislation, development of affirmative action policies, establishment of the Occupational Safety and Health Administration (OSHA), and policies that led to desegregation of virtually all southern schools. These policy enactments, which would have represented a remarkable achievement even for a Democratic president, were supplemented by two major proposals that were not enacted: a proposal to reform welfare programs (the Family Assistance Program, or FAP) and a proposal for national health insurance. In Nixon's second term (1972–1973), the Comprehensive Employment and Training Act (CETA), the Community Development Block Grant Program, the Rehabilitation Act of 1973, and the Child Abuse Prevention Act of 1973 were enacted.

## Welfare Policy

Virtually no one was satisfied with the AFDC program; liberals believed it limited assistance to families with single parents in many states and disliked its low eligibility levels and often paltry grants, and conservatives believed it encouraged substantial numbers of AFDC women not to work and included too many working mothers who had retained their eligibility owing to the work incentive provisions of 1967.[19] Nixon had several options when faced with this cross-fire from liberals and conservatives. He could have sought merely incremental and liberalizing reforms to increase the levels of benefits in low-benefit states, as suggested by a task force headed by Richard Nathan, or he could have favored incremental and conservative reforms, such as those suggested by economist Arthur Burns, to strengthen the work requirement and to create public service jobs.

At the urging of Daniel Moynihan, however, Nixon decided to seek a comprehensive reform of the nation's welfare system, partly because his advisors feared that the Democrats would preempt the issue by announcing their own reform

measure from a commission that had been appointed by Johnson.[20] Moynihan convinced Nixon that his plan offered a lasting policy solution to a vexing problem because it focused on provision of income, work incentives, and public service jobs. At a critical juncture, Moynihan told Nixon that the new program would allow termination of scores of social workers, whom Nixon detested and associated with Democratic reforms, and would extend benefits to many blue-collar and white ethnic voters since intact families and working (but poor) persons were both eligible.[21]

Democrats and Republicans alike were astonished when President Nixon announced in August 1969 that he wanted to revamp the nation's welfare programs by establishing a Family Assistance Plan (FAP) to replace the AFDC and AFDC-U programs with a program that would provide federal assistance to all families who fell beneath a federally prescribed minimum income. (AFDC-U had given states the option in 1961 to offer AFDC assistance to families with unemployed fathers, but fewer than half of them had exercised this option.) FAP provided for all intact families a nationwide guaranteed income that was higher than prevailing welfare standards in many southern states. It had even more generous work incentives than the 1967 provisions, proposed creation of large numbers of public service jobs for welfare recipients, and contained a large day-care program. In one policy stroke, then, FAP proposed to repeal the AFDC program and replace it with a national program. It did not constitute truly massive redistribution of resources to the poor, however, since it would have provided only $4.5 billion in additional federal outlays.[22]

FAP soon became enmeshed in the same cross-fire between liberals and conservatives that had plagued the AFDC program. Since Nixon feared it would be defeated by a combination of Republican and Democratic conservatives, he stressed that FAP contained a strong work incentive and work requirement. The legislation breezed through the House because of the diligent help of Wilbur Mills, chairman of the Ways and Means Committee, but it encountered opposition from conservative Republicans and Democrats in the Senate Finance Committee, who succeeded in demonstrating that thousands of FAP recipients would lose eligibility for Medicaid, public housing, and food stamps as their welfare benefits and earnings catapulted them above eligibility levels of these programs. Loss of these benefits would, they argued, severely jeopardize recipients' incentives to work.[23] Many liberal senators also attacked FAP because trade unions, which supported the minimum wage, objected to provisions that required federal authorities to pay only the prevailing wages in local jurisdictions. The National Welfare Rights Organization (NWRO), the grass-roots protest movement of welfare recipients, contended that the national minimum benefit should be significantly increased and objected to work requirements in the legislation. Most members of NWRO, who resided in northern cities of high-benefit states, would have obtained little direct benefit from FAP, which emphasized improvement of benefits in low-benefit states in the South. NWRO leaders sought amendments to increase benefit levels, weaken the work requirement, expand day-care provisions, and raise wage levels in public service jobs.[24]

Despite this sniping from both conservatives and liberals, FAP came surprisingly close to passage because of numerous amendments that the administration made to appease both factions though it finally lost a decisive vote in the Senate in 1970. When the legislation was reintroduced by the administration in 1971 with minor changes, it was caught in an even more furious exchange between liberals and conservatives and was finally defeated in 1972.[25]

An important policy reform was nonetheless achieved. An obscure provision was attached to the welfare reform measure in 1971 that proposed to federalize the adult welfare programs of Old Age Assistance, Aid to the Blind, and Aid to the Disabled by creating the Supplementary Security Income (SSI) program.[26] SSI proposed

to federalize these adult programs, just as FAP had proposed to federalize AFDC, but older and disabled persons were not associated with the long tradition of controversy that had beset AFDC women, who were variously accused of malingering, seeking welfare funds to have more kids, and leading immoral lives. SSI also benefited from a massive constituency of older persons that was represented by powerful organizations in Washington, in contrast to the absence of a constituency for FAP. (Some legislators whose votes were crucial to passage of FAP noted that they did not receive a single letter from constituents about it during 1971.)

The federal government assumed responsibility for most of the welfare costs for these adult recipients under SSI. Since SSI was administered by the Social Security Administration and its local offices, the stigma of obtaining assistance for welfare was decreased for elderly citizens, who no longer received their welfare from public welfare offices. The legislation rescued older persons from the often punitive federal–state Old-Age Assistance Program, assisted hundreds of thousands of deinstitutionalized mentally ill persons, and provided funds for many physically handicapped persons, including Vietnam vets. The development of SSI led to a massive increase in enrollments from 3.1 million persons in 1970 to 4.1 million persons in 1980.[27]

SSI nonetheless had serious flaws. Elderly and disabled persons were allowed to keep their homes and could not have their estates attached, but they were not entitled to use food stamps. Grants were hardly munificent. Additionally, elderly persons who lived in states that did not supplement the federal minimum benefits received lower benefits than elderly persons in more generous states. The early federal guidelines that defined mental and physical disability were vague; Presidents Carter and Reagan instituted guidelines and procedures that led to disallowing of grants to tens of thousands of persons with serious mental and physical handicaps.[28]

Democrats had initiated and received political credit for the Food Stamp Program when it was enacted in 1964. They continued their leadership when George McGovern, the liberal Democratic senator, held hearings during the late 1960s on issues of nutrition and hunger in the United States.[29] He contended that the Food Stamp Program addressed the nutritional needs of only a small fraction of hungry Americans. Furthermore, conservatives had shown that the eligibility criteria of food stamps did not mesh with the criteria of FAP. Nixon believed that he could both solve the technical problems of food stamps and regain the initiative from the Democrats in the nutrition arena by federalizing food stamps, establishing national eligibility standards, making participation in the program mandatory for all states, and developing a revised benefit schedule to allow families with no earned income, as well as larger families, to receive additional benefits. By securing these bold changes, Nixon transformed food stamps from a welfare program to a program that was used by large numbers of working but poor persons.[30] These liberal reforms were enacted in 1970 and 1973 and dramatically increased the size of the program; federal expenditures for it increased from 10.4 million enrollees in 1970 to 19.4 million enrollees in 1980.[31] A broad constituency of protest groups, liberals, agricultural interests, and conservative politicians from rural areas supported these reforms.

## Social Security

Congress had periodically revised Social Security benefits upward to compensate for their erosion by inflation in a ritual that was used by members of both parties to garner support from elderly constituents. But members of both parties saw a need to adjust benefits automatically and annually for inflation to ensure that benefit levels did not lag behind inflation. Nixon proposed a small benefit increase in Social Security and indexing in 1972, but Democratic Congressman Wilbur Mills, who had presidential aspirations and realized that Democrats would benefit in the elections of 1972 if they could

claim to have championed the needs of elderly persons, proposed indexing as well as a 20 percent increase in benefits![32] Such liberal increases would normally have required major increases in payroll taxes, but Mills refrained from proposing them to avoid the political outcry that would ensue and because actuaries for the Social Security Administration, who had developed new predictive economic models based on overoptimistic assumptions, maintained that the trust fund would remain solvent even with massive increases in benefits. Nixon decided to support Mills's proposals so as to obtain partial credit for them and compensate for the defeat of FAP, which had deprived his administration of credit for a major social reform.[33]

Everyone realized that indexing would increase benefits, but virtually no one predicted that the onset of double-digit inflation in ensuing years would lead to extraordinary increases in Social Security benefits—or that the technical formulas that were used to compute benefit increases would allow these increases even to exceed rates of inflation.[34] The old system of incremental and periodic benefit increases had been replaced by an automatic system that led to rapid increases in benefits without associated increases in payroll taxes. Furthermore, the ratio of benefit receivers to employed workers increased, so the fund was further depleted. Benefit outlays of the Social Security program increased from $68.2 billion in 1970 to $135 billion in 1980.[35]

As with FAP and SSI, outbidding between the two parties, as well as Nixon's desire to expand the base of the Republican party, led a conservative president to support massive increases in social spending. The declining proportion of wage-earners to retirees, as well as Nixon's failure to raise the level of the payroll tax, ensured the emergence of a funding crisis for Social Security that had to be addressed by subsequent presidents. But the Social Security increases were a major reason the percentage of elderly persons who lived beneath poverty lines decreased from 29.5 to 15 percent between 1967 and 1979 and to less than 5 percent when the value of in-kind benefits, such as medical care, was included.

## Revenue Sharing and Social Services

Since many Republicans believed that the New Deal and The Great Society had concentrated excessive power in the federal bureaucracy, Nixon proposed to give federal funds directly to local units of government with few strings attached so that local officials could decide how they wished to use them. Nixon also had more sinister motivations for this policy. He had become increasingly paranoid about the federal bureaucracy in his first three years of office and was convinced that federal bureaucrats, in liaison with sympathetic legislators and supportive (liberal) interest groups, had wrested power from him. By giving funds directly to the local and state units of government, he could "bypass" the federal bureaucracy and even, to some extent, the Congress, which no longer would be able to develop specific programs. (Congress would merely allocate funds that would be given to local governments to use, more or less, as they pleased.)[36]

The Local Fiscal Assistance Act of 1972, so-called general revenue sharing, was enacted in 1972 and gave funds to local governments to use for their operating expenses. Nixon also proposed six block grants to allow authorities to provide resources to local governments in broad areas such as housing and job training. This "special revenue sharing" would, he argued, eventually replace many of the existing federal programs, which were encumbered, he believed, by excessive federal rules, guidelines, and regulations.[37] Why not, Nixon asked, simultaneously terminate some existing programs and give local governments relatively unrestricted funds to spend on broad program areas? He had little success in obtaining special revenue sharing, however, because many congressmen did not want to relinquish their control of federal pro-

grams and feared that some states would no longer fund programs for relatively powerless groups of poor and minority persons who benefited from existing federal programs. Nixon obtained passage of only two special revenue-sharing programs, the Comprehensive Employment and Training Act of 1973 (CETA) and the Community Development Block Grant portion of the Housing and Community Development Act of 1974 (CDBG).

General and special revenue sharing were suited to Nixon's political strategy, for they represented a brand of social reform that was different from traditional Democratic programs. Some advisors of Lyndon Johnson, notably economist Walter Heller, had themselves urged passage of revenue sharing, but Johnson had demurred in favor of traditional categorical programs.[38] The policy field was thus open to Nixon, and he seized the opportunity to enact his version of reform to curry the favor of state and local officials who liked revenue sharing because it augmented their funds. The federal government paid roughly $6 billion a year between 1973 and 1980 to local governments in general revenue sharing and, in so doing, substantially eased their fiscal problems during the 1970s.[39] Critics noted, however, that local authorities often did not use these resources to help disadvantaged citizens—CDBG funds were used in one city to build a municipal golf course!

Job-training programs had proliferated in confusing fashion during the 1960s, so Nixon proposed to consolidate them in the Comprehensive Employment and Training Act (CETA). An administrative mechanism was devised that vested considerable power in state and local organizations, known as prime sponsors, which issued contracts with public agencies and industry to provide jobs and job training. CETA subsidized hundreds of thousands of public service jobs under Title VI in both public and nonprofit agencies—jobs that were not means tested since applicants had merely to demonstrate that they were unemployed. Incredibly, a Republican president had proposed and obtained enactment of a proposal that was reminiscent of the public works programs of the 1930s.[40]

As we discussed in Chapter 9, Congress gave states 75 percent matching funds in 1962 to provide social services to existing or potential recipients of AFDC. Although some states seemed unaware of the legislation or used the money only for traditional services, such as home visits to AFDC recipients, discerning policy analysts in various states, including California, Oregon, Pennsylvania, and Washington, realized that they could use these funds to develop a range of programs. Furthermore, when a federal administrator who prized expansiveness replaced a cost-conscious one, the use of the funds increased dramatically since some state officials used the funds for drug, mental health, public education, and even highway construction programs.[41] The Nixon administration sought to place a ceiling on the runaway program in 1972. To protect the program and to counter HEW regulations that limited its services to current recipients and applicants of welfare programs, the Congress created Title XX of the Social Security Act with funds to be allocated to states according to a formula and to be used, with broad latitude by each state, to enhance self-support of individuals, family care or self-care, community-based care, and institutional care. The legislation was enacted in 1974.[42] States usually chose relatively traditional services, such as day care and various other services that were provided by established agencies. To impose discipline on the program, a ceiling of $2.5 billion was established for annual expenditures—a figure that remained relatively constant in succeeding years. Title XX represented the first time the federal government had officially committed itself to funding a variety of social services to persons who were usually near or under the poverty line. It illustrated as well the reformist nature of Nixon's first term since Nixon, who despised services and social workers, did not veto legislation that covered services for existing and potential welfare recipients in a block grant.

## Civil Rights

Nixon's strange mixture of conservative rhetoric and liberal deeds was nowhere more conspicuous than in civil rights. Nixon had won five southern states in the presidential election of 1968 and hoped to increase his southern gains in 1972, but he feared that George Wallace would again try to sweep the South by supporting racist policies. Thus, Nixon did not support desegregation of southern schools in 1969 and 1970. He fired a liberal attorney in the Justice Department who favored cutting federal funds from segregated districts and supported a proposed constitutional amendment to prohibit busing. Nixon often used rhetoric that relied on code words, like "the silent majority of law abiding citizens," to distance himself from racial minorities and to appeal to racial animosities in the broader population.

Yet some commentators believe that Nixon's policies on racial issues constitute a strength of his administration.[43] When federal courts insisted that intentional segregation had to be terminated, Nixon finally relented and empowered George Shultz, his secretary of labor, to organize a series of southern committees that succeeded in securing voluntary desegregation of southern schools. When the number of African-American students in segregated southern schools was reduced from 68 percent in 1968 to 8 percent in 1972, the cycle of reform in the South that had begun with the Civil Rights Acts of 1964 and 1965 was completed.[44] Nixon's successes in the South were not matched by similar efforts in the North, however, since he chose not to use busing to combat de facto segregation.

Between 1971 and 1974, Congress and the administration enacted a variety of laws and administrative measures that prohibited sex discrimination in training programs and employment. HEW instituted legal action to force colleges to end discrimination against women, just as the Supreme Court struck down various local laws that discriminated against women.

**FIGURE 10.1** • *Women take to the streets*

*Source:* Library of Congress

The Justice Department brought suit against such corporations as American Telephone and Telegraph that led to large awards to women who had been denied promotions. Women made extraordinary gains in obtaining training and membership in the professions and business.[45] Nixon approved the Equal Employment Opportunity Act of 1972 that gave the Equal Employment Opportunity Commission the power to use court rulings to enforce its orders. His administration included women in affirmative action orders that were sent to contractors of the federal government[46] (see Figure 10.1).

Moreover, the Nixon administration developed the so-called Philadelphia Plan, which required building contractors that obtained federal contracts to institute affirmative action for minorities—a policy stoutly opposed by trade unions. This plan was subsequently extended to all federal contractors as well as to state and local employees such as local police and fire departments. (These policies led to extraordinary increases in employment of minorities and women in public agencies.)[47]

The Rehabilitation Act of 1973 was a historic measure to accord physically disabled persons protections from discrimination; section 504 states that "no otherwise qualified handicapped individual . . . shall . . . be excluded from participating in, be denied the benefits of, or be subjected to discrimination under any program of activity receiving federal assistance." This legislation, as well as associated lawsuits, led to massive efforts to make buildings, public transportation, and jobs available to handicapped persons.[48] Funds were appropriated to help disabled students be mainstreamed in public schools under the Education for All Handicapped Act of 1975.[49]

## Health Policy and Other Legislation

Various health and family measures were enacted during Nixon's administration. Medicare was revised in 1973 to extend coverage to nonelderly persons with kidney disease. The Health Maintenance Act of 1973 provided seed money to promote establishment of medical organizations that are funded by annual payments from enrollees rather than from traditional fee-for-service payments.[50] The Family Planning Services and Population Act of 1970 had helped 4 million low-income women obtain family-planning services by 1980, including 1.3

million teenagers.[51] The Juvenile Justice and Delinquency Act of 1974 provided resources to local juvenile diversion projects to help runaways and truants who had heretofore been stigmatized by court and juvenile detention services.[52] The Child Abuse Prevention Act of 1974 provided research funds to be disseminated to universities and pilot projects to develop effective interventions.[53]

The Occupational Safety and Health Act of 1970 was landmark legislation that propelled the federal government into oversight of safety standards in American industry in an era when toxic chemicals and new technology demanded new protections. The Department of Labor was charged with devising standards and establishing local agencies to implement inspection.[54]

Finally, legislation establishing an earned income tax credit was enacted in 1973 that gave workers who earned less than $4,000 a tax credit (a payment) equivalent to 10 percent of their earnings. Though modest, it was the first legislation to use the tax system as a vehicle for giving resources to the poor.

## NIXON'S TURN FROM REFORM TO CONSERVATISM

Social reform flourished in the first three years of Nixon's first term: Spending for poverty programs had increased by $27 billion in the Kennedy and Johnson administrations (in 1986 dollars), but it increased by $54 billion in the Nixon and Ford administrations.[55] When confronted with a deep recession, trade deficits, and inflation, Nixon even imposed wage and price controls in 1971.[56] But during this liberal period, Nixon's rhetoric remained staunchly conservative, even as he supported reform measures; he regularly lambasted programs of The Great Society, "big spenders," and liberalism and remained silent on subjects of civil rights and race relations. He repeatedly attacked service programs that were staffed by social workers,

child development staff, psychologists, psychiatrists, and community activists. He believed that these programs were ineffective, coddled the poor, and represented a misguided Democratic approach to social reform. He sought major reductions in federal funding of neighborhood health centers, community action programs, and community mental health centers.[57] Head Start was saved from massive cuts only because of its extraordinary political popularity.

Nixon's antipathy to service programs was illustrated by his veto of child development legislation in 1971. Since the Head Start program had stimulated interest in expanding funding for preschool, day-care, regional planning, and advocacy services for children and since some experts were convinced that many families were endangered by high rates of dissolution and the increasing rates of employment of mothers, legislation was initiated in committees of the House and the Senate to provide a variety of free or low-cost services to American families.

It was uncertain whether Nixon would support this legislation though his secretary of HEW, Elliot Richardson, appeared to support it when he insisted in 1971 that the legislation be amended to make it more acceptable to the administration. But Nixon vetoed it with conservative language that reflected the right wing of the Republican party. He charged that the legislation would destroy the institution of the family, which should be retained "in its rightful position as the keystone of our civilization . . . (and) would commit the vast moral authority to (institutional) child rearing as against the family-centered approach." It was a devastating blow to reformers, who were unable to obtain similar legislation in succeeding years.[58]

A changing political climate shaped Nixon's decision by summer 1972, and even more obviously by fall 1973, to disavow new social legislation. It had been reasonable to assume in 1968, after The Great Society, that blue-collar and white ethnic Americans could be wooed by social initiatives like FAP, SSI, national health insurance, and the indexing of Social Security. Partly because of the conservative rhetoric of Nixon and Agnew, however, many white ethnic, blue-collar, and middle-class persons had become preoccupied by 1972 with issues of crime, inflation, and government spending and had become resentful of African Americans, who were, they believed, receiving unwarranted or disproportionate benefits from federal programs. The term *white backlash* was frequently used to characterize the resentments of these citizens.[59]

Many white Americans had also become alarmed by tactics and language of leaders of various reform groups that had emerged in the late 1960s.[60] Many African Americans espoused black separatism and black power; Native Americans and Spanish-speaking persons developed protests against local and federal officials, schools, and universities; feminists espoused women's liberation; disabled persons demanded reforms to decrease job discrimination and to make buildings and public transportation accessible to them; and gays and lesbians pressured politicians and employers to redress existing discriminatory practices. The militance of these groups stemmed in considerable measure from disillusionment with The Great Society. African Americans realized that the civil rights gains of the 1960s, which had largely addressed legal and overt discrimination in the South, had not slowed the ghettoization of African Americans or the expansion of an African-American underclass, whose members had limited education and high unemployment and often depended on AFDC, food stamps, and other social programs. Leaders of African-American, feminist, Latino, Native-American, homosexual, and disabled groups believed that their members suffered from feelings of inferiority that stemmed from living in a society that overtly or covertly discriminated against them. African Americans urged one another to develop pride in their race and heritage; women advocated feminist education to develop solidarity; and leaders of the gay and lesbian communities urged their members to declare their sexual orientations publicly. Efforts to mobilize these populations alienated many Americans, who resented the separatism and the challenge to dominant policies that this language implied.

Nixon and Agnew were not interested in a sympathetic interpretation of the mobilization of these various groups. They quickly perceived its political uses for themselves.[61] Why not, they reasoned, condemn the rhetoric and tactics of these groups in order to polarize working- and middle-class persons against activists and reformers? Why not try to identify the Democratic party with these groups—and themselves with "the silent majority of law-abiding citizens"? Their resolve was strengthened by public opinion polls that indicated that many Americans believed that crime and inflation were major issues in America and that civil rights, social spending, and social reform efforts had proceeded too rapidly. These sentiments were linked to the growing economic distress of stagflation, the simultaneous appearance of high unemployment and inflation.[62] Economic stagnation made some blue-collar Americans fear that African Americans, women, and others might take jobs from them, and inflation contributed to their malaise by reducing the real income of many families and by making it difficult to obtain credit as interest rates soared. Furthermore, many Americans believed that the nation had to cut its social spending to decrease the rate of inflation, which had emerged by 1968 as a major problem.[63] Nixon's conservative strategy of polarizing Americans against reformers was facilitated as well by developments within the Democratic party. Democrats made a concerted effort following the 1968 election to increase participation by African Americans, women, and others in party councils at the expense of the power of incumbent politicians and powerful brokers, such as Richard Daley, the mayor of Chicago. These reforms had the unintended effect, however, of enhancing Nixon's political fortunes since he could argue that the Democratic party had been taken over by special interests. When the party reforms allowed a particularly liberal senator (George McGovern) to obtain the Democratic nomination for the presidency in 1972, Nixon portrayed him as an extremist who was beholden to these interests.[64]

Nixon's conservative policies were promoted, as well, by Republican conservatives, who believed they represented the mainstream of the party. Conservative advisors, such as the economist Arthur Burns and Martin Anderson, had been outflanked by liberal advisors, such as

Robert Finch, Daniel Moynihan, and Elliot Richardson, but a definite thinning in the ranks of liberal advisors occurred as Nixon's first term progressed. Indeed, by 1972, the conservative John Ehrlichman emerged as his leading advisor on domestic matters.[65]

Soon after his reelection in 1972, Nixon began a personal war against liberals that was motivated by his political decision to move toward the right, to fight inflation with budget cuts, and to discipline federal civil servants who he believed colluded with special interests and congressional aides of liberal legislators to resist the implementation of conservative policies. Nixon manipulated the civil service system to place into office conservative persons of dubious merit, impounded funds that had already been appropriated by Congress for social programs, proposed major decreases in the funds of most major programs, and demanded a major reduction of the federal work force. Because many members of Congress and the federal bureaucracy were embittered by these tactics, an atmosphere of suspicion and polarization developed in the Capitol.[66]

Nixon's effectiveness in waging this war against liberalism was stymied, however, by the Justice Department's and the Congress's investigation of the coverup of the burglary of the Democratic campaign headquarters in the Watergate Hotel in 1972 by the Republican National Committee. Inquiries, which began with investigations of the burglars, soon implicated presidential aides, cabinet officials, and Nixon himself. The Congress was on the verge of impeachment proceedings when Nixon resigned from office in August 1974 and was succeeded by Vice President Gerald Ford.

## THE BRIEF REIGN OF GERALD FORD

Ford was a political conservative who had spent years in the Congress criticizing programs of The Great Society. He was, moreover, an unimaginative man who was unable to initiate legislation even when urged by his advisors. As did Nixon, he became even more conservative as his term progressed. Nelson Rockefeller, his vice president, pressured him to support urban development reforms, to expand health care, and to support other policy reforms, but his power, as well as that of other liberal Republicans, was soon eclipsed in internal power struggles within the administration.[67] Ford's major policy became the presidential veto, which he used with remarkable frequency to stymie legislation and spending increases that were proposed by the Congress.

Because of Democratic majorities in both houses, Congress was able to override a number of vetoes and to increase funding for school lunches, education, and health care programs. Ford finally realized that increases in social spend-ing were needed to counter the deep recession of 1975 though Congress had to override his veto to establish a public works program to help the unemployed. His term can best be characterized as a continuing stalemate between conservatives and liberals over the size of social spending.[68]

Little social legislation was enacted during Ford's tenure. The Education for All Handicapped Children Act was passed in 1975, which provided federal subsidies to schools to enable them to mainstream physically and mentally handicapped children into regular classes. Although it allowed many handicapped children to escape special institutions, it was so inadequately funded in succeeding years that its effect was much diminished.[69]

 ## THE EMERGENCE OF JIMMY CARTER

A journalist who had covered five prior presidential campaigns wrote that he had never experienced more pervasive suspicion of government among the electorate than in 1976.[70] Jimmy Carter, an astute southern politician who had recently terminated his tenure as governor of Georgia, decided in 1972 to mount a campaign to secure the Democratic nomination for the presidency in 1976, but he was relatively unknown in other sections of the nation and had virtually no links to trade unions, powerful incumbent politicians, or other groups that usually helped Democratic aspirants. His relative obscurity became an asset, however, in the post-Watergate political climate of 1976. When he lambasted the federal bureaucracy, red tape, and undue centralization of authority in the nation, he did not seem to be hypocritical because he had not participated in their development.[71]

Carter's outsider status enabled him to develop a strategy to appeal to a cross-section of political opinion. His attacks on the political establishment appealed to some populist liberals. To obtain support from conservatives, he emphasized moral values, his religiosity as a "born again" Baptist, his southernness, his dislike of big-spending liberals, and his support of major increases in defense spending. Moderates liked his cultivation of big business, his internationalism, and his emphasis on making the federal government less corrupt and more efficient. Most moderates and conservatives liked his anti-government rhetoric. Carter told all groups that he was an efficient problem solver who would not succumb to ordinary politics when making decisions.[72]

Carter obtained the Democratic nomination by developing grass-roots organizations in primary states before other Democratic candidates. He also ran a clever race against Gerald Ford, who was tainted by his prior association with the discredited Nixon, whom he had pardoned to exempt him from prosecution for Watergate. Ford's membership in the Washington establishment and the recession of 1975 were also liabilities. Carter won the election by a slim margin when he carried the South and key midwestern states.

Even the most astute president would have found it difficult to govern in 1976, however, since congressional legislators were determined to insist on full participation in the legislative process after Watergate and to demonstrate their resentment of Carter's repeated criticisms of Congress. Many legislators had also developed specific programs that they wanted to enact after many programs had been vetoed by Nixon and Ford.[73] Carter encountered a bleak economic situation as well since he inherited a massive deficit from Ford, high rates of inflation, and increasing levels of social spending. Inflation became a national crisis when Middle Eastern countries decided to stop shipments of oil to the United States in reprisal for American assistance to Israel; when gasoline prices rose from 37 cents per gallon in 1970 to $1.60 in 1977, double-digit inflation became a reality.

Carter was ill-equipped to contend with these harsh political and economic realities. As an aloof "engineer without deep philosophic roots," he did not enjoy the give-and-take of the political process. He liked to tackle problems in the isolation of the White House.[74] His condescending attitude toward legislators infuriated them, as did his disinclination to consult them. Carter surrounded himself, moreover, with untested advisors from Georgia who did not communicate with legislators. Tip O'Neill, the Democratic majority leader in the House, had not even met Hamilton Jordan, Carter's chief advisor, several years after Carter's election. Carter failed to develop alliances with groups and legislators who would normally have assisted a Democratic president—union leaders distrusted him because he opposed increases in the minimum wage; Catholics and Jews were antagonized by his flaunting of his Protestant fundamentalism; big-city mayors believed that he did not understand urban problems; and social reformers believed him to be indifferent to the needs of the poor.[75] Carter was unable, moreover, to intelligently schedule his domestic measures. Since Carter disdained partial or incremental approaches in favor of comprehensive solutions, Congress was overwhelmed by his rapid-fire delivery to them of comprehensive energy, welfare, government reorganization, and health measures.[76]

## Carter's Domestic Legislation

Unlike Roosevelt, Truman, and Johnson, Carter was not much interested in domestic legislation. His priorities were reorganization of the federal bureaucracy, the Middle East, renegotiation of the Panama Canal Treaty, and energy policy. He did not like measures that required major increases in social spending because he favored reductions in federal spending.[77] Critics contend, as well, that he was suspicious of welfare recipients, alcoholics, and drug addicts because he believed large numbers of them fraudulently used government programs.[78] He enacted relatively little social legislation because of his political style and intrinsic conservatism as well as the difficult political and economic environment that he encountered.

Carter supported national health insurance in his campaign of 1976, but he took no action on this measure after his election until Senator Edward Kennedy, brother of the late President Kennedy, accused him of reneging on his campaign promise. Fearing that Kennedy would oppose him for the presidential nomination in 1980 and that he might use this issue, Carter belatedly introduced his own version of health insurance in 1979, which combined an insurance plan for employees, to be financed by payroll deductions, and a government-funded scheme for nonworkers.[79] Kennedy's scheme favored government controls, government financing, and government regulation of health care. Neither Carter's nor Kennedy's scheme was politically feasible in the climate of 1979, however, when double-digit inflation and large deficits made politicians unwilling to increase government spending.

Carter introduced a comprehensive scheme for welfare reform in 1977 that, like Nixon's a few years earlier, became caught in a cross-fire between liberals and conservatives. Carter's scheme was imaginative and more ambitious than FAP since he proposed to consolidate AFDC, food stamps, and SSI to provide a national minimum income for families, individuals, and elderly persons. He also proposed to develop a three-tiered benefit system in which able-bodied but nonworking persons received the lowest benefits, persons who were exempted from work (disabled persons and women with preschool children) received middle-level benefits, and the working poor received the highest benefits (when their benefits were added to their earned income). He proposed creation of 1.4 million public service jobs for recipients.[80]

Controversy was so heated and focused on so many issues that Joseph Califano, secretary of the Department of Health and Human Services from 1977 to 1979, declared welfare reform to be the Middle East of domestic politics.[81] Conservatives wanted to exempt only women with children under the age of six from the work requirement, whereas many liberals wanted to exempt women with children under the age of fourteen. Conservatives insisted that persons holding public service jobs receive prevailing wages, whereas liberals wanted them to be paid the federal minimum wage. Some defenders of food stamps and SSI objected to their merger into the larger welfare reform program. Persons quibbled about the relative size of the minimum benefits for nonworking recipients and the monies to be spent on work incentives for the employed poor. Many conservatives feared that extension of governmental benefits to working persons would pauperize them.[82]

Not surprisingly, then, welfare reform was defeated in the Senate in 1978. Califano concluded in 1981 that comprehensive reform of the American welfare system was probably not politically feasible; attention should focus instead on incremental improvements as well as on experiments to test controversial policies.[83] This pessimistic appraisal seemed applicable to national health insurance as well, which seemed as politically elusive as welfare reform.

Millions of Americans had suffered the trauma of unemployment during the 1970s despite the existence of CETA; many were unemployed for brief periods, but its toll on their physical and mental health was consider-able. Racial minorities and teenage populations bore a particularly heavy burden since more than 30 percent of them were unemployed in many areas. Senator Hubert Humphrey and Congressman Augustus Hawkins introduced legislation in 1974 to improve the situation by requiring the creation of federal public service jobs at any time when the national unemployment rate exceeded 3 percent.[84] The legislation was strongly opposed by the Ford administration on the grounds that it was not feasible to create this many jobs, that federal jobs would draw persons away from the private sector, that the cost of the measure was prohibitive, and that public sector jobs would make many persons dependent on government.[85] Humphrey and Hawkins reintroduced their legislation in 1976, after Carter had been elected, in hopes that strong support by the administration would facilitate its passage, but Carter did not aggressively fight efforts by conservatives to amend the legislation. Carter supported the Full Employment and Balanced Growth Act, but it was a diluted and meaningless version that was finally enacted in 1978.[86]

Carter's political conservatism led him to provide uncertain support to a variety of measures to help children. His legislation to provide comprehensive services to families headed by teenagers was enacted but was hardly funded since the administration did not decisively promote it.[87] He did not support expanded federal funding of child care since it would have required major new federal expenditures.[88] Carter vacillated on legislation to extend federal subsidies to local centers that helped battered women; strong opposition from conservatives who insisted that social workers exaggerated the extent of the problem defeated the legislation in 1980.[89]

Carter was nonetheless able to obtain passage of legislation that sought to rescue children from long-term stays in the foster care system, where hundreds of thousands of them were poorly cared for and shuffled between numerous placements. Although AFDC paid the costs of court-ordered foster care placements, the federal government had traditionally left the funding and planning of adoption and foster care services to local public and private agencies. (Minority children, as well as older children and those with serious physical and mental disabilities, were particularly unlikely to be adopted or returned to their natural homes.) Under the Adoption Assistance and Child Welfare Act of 1980, federal authorities encouraged local child welfare agencies to obtain adoptions for many of these children by providing subsidies to families that adopted children and by requiring states to maintain status reports on all children in foster care so that they could be expeditiously placed into adoption or returned to their natural homes within specified time limits. The legislation also expanded federal assistance to states for foster care.[90]

Carter was also able to expand Medicaid programs to screen and treat low-income children and to help pregnant women.[91] The federal government had required local authorities to screen low-income children under the Medicaid legislation in 1965, but compliance had been inadequate, and screened children were often not helped with treatment, even when serious problems were found.

Carter seemed more intent on consolidating existing civil rights laws than adding new protections because he wanted to retain the support of southerners, who had been indispensable to his victory in 1976. He was sufficiently indifferent to issues of affirmative action that he supported a white plaintiff, Allan Bakke, when he sued a public medical school of the University of California on the grounds it had given preference to minorities with lesser qualifications in its admission policies. After Joseph Califano, the secretary of HEW, persuaded the administration to oppose Bakke, the Justice Department provided testimony that eventually influenced the Supreme Court to uphold the principle of affirmative action while disallowing the use of numerical quotas.[92]

The rights of disabled persons were enhanced during the Carter administration though only after extensive pressure from certain interest groups. The Architectural and Transportation Compliance Board, established in 1973, issued regulations in 1980 that required extensive modifications in federal buildings.[93]

Rosalyn Carter, the wife of the president, made mental health her major domestic issue and assumed an important role in establishing a Presidential Commission on Mental Health, which issued a four-volume report in 1978 that analyzed many program, policy, and financing issues in the mental health system. The report cited the lack of insurance coverage for outpatient services, inadequate community services for persons with chronic and severe mental problems in community settings, and the lack of services for elderly and adolescent populations.[94] Its findings did not lead to major reforms, however, for the legislation that came from it did not provide centers with funds to implement to the populations the new services that were required by the Mental Health Systems Act of 1980.

An important policy debate occurred in the administration as it confronted a financing crisis in the Social Security program. Califano, who believed that Social Security should provide a safety net for those elderly persons who were poor while providing lower benefits to affluent persons, proposed taxing the benefits of affluent elderly persons so that proceeds from the tax could be used to bail out the trust fund. But some of the founders of the Social Security program, such as Wilbur Cohen, believed that benefits should continue to bear a strong relationship to the amount of payroll taxes that persons had paid into the system; since affluent persons had usually paid higher taxes, they should, Cohen argued, receive higher benefits than other persons. They feared that Califano's proposal would encourage the transformation of Social Security into a welfare rather than a universal program.[95] Califano lost this battle, but his recommendation was approved during Ronald Reagan's first term when it became obvious that even the major increases in the payroll taxes that Carter had engineered were insufficient to preserve the solvency of the trust fund.[96]

The SSI program grew at a fantastic pace during the mid-1970s because thousands of persons with mental and physical disabilities were using it. Carter resolved to slow its rate of increase by restricting benefits to the level of wages that recipients had received before their disability and by allowing them to retain their Medicaid benefits. He also pressured administrative judges, who were hired by the government to decide whether persons were entitled to SSI, to make fewer favorable decisions. Although there had been abuse of the program, the new policy had its own dangers, for it deprived some severely disabled persons of needed benefits.[97]

The Department of Health, Education, and Welfare grew rapidly during the 1960s and 1970s, but staff morale plummeted following successive cuts in personnel and heavier workloads. They needed leadership from a president who would empathize with their problems, reduce pointless regulations, and troubleshoot work and logistical problems.[98] Carter was often as paranoid as Nixon about federal bureaucrats. Nonetheless, Carter placed Medicare and Medicaid under a single office known as the Health Care and Finance Administration, eliminated many unnecessary regulations, and established a department for tracking and assessing programs and policies and budgetary controls. Finally, in a controversial move that was partly inspired by Carter's desire to repay the National Education Association for its assistance in the 1976 election, the Office of Education was separated from HEW, which was renamed the Department of Health and Human Services (DHHS).[99]

Carter had decided by 1978 to effect massive cuts in social programs as part of his desperate effort to diminish double-digit inflation and to provide resources for substantial increases for military spending. Budget cuts of the last two years of Carter's administration can be seen as the beginning of a long and conservative assault on social spending that subsequently extended through the presidency of Ronald Reagan.[100]

To the chagrin of feminists, Carter was militantly against abortion and supported a constitutional amendment to overrule the *Roe* v. *Wade* decision of the Supreme Court, which had declared in 1973 that state laws that prohibited abortions during the first trimester were unconstitutional. When a constitutional amendment proved to be politically impractical, Carter supported legislation that was eventually enacted to prohibit use of federal Medicaid funds for abortions.[101] The legislation allowed the use of Medicaid funds for abortions in selected medical circumstances, but these circumstances were defined so narrowly that low-income women could obtain abortions with Medicaid funds only if their lives were endangered by childbirth or within seventy-two hours of a rape or incest.[102] Since the number of federally financed abortions declined from 275,000 in 1976 to 1,250 in 1978, most abortions for low-income women were financed by local government and charitable institutions. Unlike more affluent women, some poor women were driven to "black market" (and frequently dangerous) abortions or delivered unwanted children because of the difficulty of obtaining abortions from local institutions.[103]

## Carter's Fall from Political Grace

Only two years after his election, Carter had the worst popularity rating of any president in recent American history at a comparable point in his presidency. It sank even further by 1979 in the wake of soaring prices of oil, continuing stagflation, a Congress that wanted to assert its independence, and widespread public disenchantment with government.[104]

Carter was nonetheless able to obtain the Democratic nomination for the presidency in 1980 despite a vigorous challenge by Senator Edward Kennedy. But Carter faced another outsider who used many of the same antiestablishment tactics that Carter himself had used in 1976. This time, however, Carter was the insider, and Ronald Reagan, his Republican opponent, the outsider. Carter was dealt a final misfortune when he was unable to free a group of hostages who were captured by a band of terrorists when they overran the American embassy in Iran. Reagan defeated Carter easily in the 1980 election and began a new era of conservative policies that attacked the liberal reforms of the preceding fifty years.

## THE HIDDEN SOCIAL SPENDING REVOLUTION OF THE 1970s

The policy changes that were made in the 1970s constitute a hidden social spending revolution in American social policy. Nondefense spending went from 8.1 percent of the gross national product in 1961 to 11.3 percent in 1971 and 15.6 percent in 1981. About two-thirds of this domestic budget consisted of social insurance and means-tested social programs. Total federal social spending rose from $67 billion in 1960 to $158 billion in 1970 (in 1980 dollars) and $314 billion in 1980.[105] Many social programs grew tremendously in their total cost during the 1970s, as Table 10.1 illustrates.[106]

For the first time in American history, a relatively sophisticated safety net of social programs existed for persons who lacked resources, whether because they were old, unemployed, ill, or poor. Many persons used only a single program from the potpourri of social programs. A man who became unemployed during the recession of 1976 might use only unemployment benefits because he considered use of food stamps or Medicaid programs to be unnecessary or stigmatizing or because his net income made him ineligible for them. Other families used only the Food Stamps Program, and still others

**TABLE 10.1** • *Increases in outlays for specific programs (in billions of constant dollars) during the 1970s*

|  | 1970 | | 1980 | |
|---|---|---|---|---|
|  | *Federal* | *Total* | *Federal* | *Total* |
| Food Stamps | $ 2.0 | $ 2.0 | $ 10.0 | $ 10.0 |
| SSI | – | 4.1 | 7.0 | 8.6 |
| Unemployment Insurance | 7.7 | 7.7 | 18.5 | 18.5 |
| Medicaid | 5.8 | 10.9 | 15.3 | 25.4 |
| Medicare | 15.2 | 15.2 | 38.3 | 38.3 |
| AFDC | 5.1 | 9.2 | 8.8 | 13.9 |
| CETA and MDTA | 2.4 | 2.4 | 3.6 | 3.6 |
| Social Security* | 68.2 | 68.2 | 134.8 | 134.8 |
| Housing Assistance | 2.8 | 2.8 | 4.9 | 4.9 |
| Total | 109.2 | 122.5 | 241.4 | 258.0 |

* *Expenditures include federal costs as well as expenditures from funds generated by payroll taxes.*

received Medicaid. The range of different cash-transfer, in-kind, and services programs allowed families to select specific programs that improved their quality of life at a specific point in time.[107]

Many other consumers used combinations of programs. A single woman with several preschool or school-age children might receive AFDC, obtain food stamps, receive health services that were reimbursed by Medicaid, and live in publicly subsidized housing. An elderly family might use Medicare, SSI, and Social Security benefits. A young adult who had received a kidney transplant could receive SSI as well as medical services from Medicare. An unemployed person could receive unemployment insurance, job training from CETA, food stamps, and Medicaid. The availability of combinations of programs was crucial to many individuals and families since single programs often did not suffice. Combinations of programs were most crucial for large families, whose members needed a range of services and resources.[108]

Many persons who needed relatively short-term assistance used such programs as unemployment insurance, food stamps, and Medicaid for brief periods of unemployment, illness, or poverty. Other persons needed assistance for longer periods. Of all the recipients of the nation's welfare programs, about 50 percent used them for less than three years, about 33 percent used them from three years to seven years, and about 12 percent used them for eight or more years.[109] Impoverished women with children were likely to use AFDC, food stamps, and Medicaid. Unemployed males tended to use unemployment insurance and food stamps. The elderly used SSI, Social Security, Medicare, and Medicaid. Disabled persons used SSI and Social Security disability benefits. (The Social Security program had become far more than a pension program for the elderly by the 1970s since its benefits often subsidized surviving family members when a parent died and helped pay for the education of surviving children.)[110] The programs were not used only by low-income per-

sons; indeed, roughly three of every four dollars of social welfare benefits (whether cash, in-kind benefits, or services) were delivered in programs that were not means tested, such as Medicare, Social Security, and unemployment insurance.[111] Government loan programs for college students were greatly expanded in the 1970s and were used extensively by middle- and even upper-income families. Countless people found their quality of life improved by receipt of cash, in-kind benefits, or services from one or more of the social programs.

Evidence also suggests that extraordinary progress was made during the 1970s in reducing the incidence of poverty as measured by the percentage of the population that fell under official poverty lines. By this measure, the poverty rate declined from 14.2 percent of the population in 1967 to 11.1 percent of the population in 1979. When in-kind transfers, such as food stamps and Medicaid, are also included, the poverty rate declined to 6.4 percent in 1979 — an extraordinary accomplishment though 15 percent of African Americans, 12 percent of Latinos, and 18 percent of female-headed households still remained in poverty.[112]

The achievement of reductions in poverty during the 1970s was even more impressive than gains during the 1960s since the reductions in poverty during the 1960s were facilitated by the Vietnam conflict and the economic activity that accompanied it. By contrast, expenditures for the military declined from 8 percent of the GNP in 1966 to 5.5 percent of the GNP in 1981.[113] The reduction in poverty was obtained in the 1970s even when the economy was plagued by problems of stagflation, an economic condition that did not exist during the 1960s. The striking successes in reducing poverty in the 1970s can be attributed in considerable measure to the effects of expansion of cash and in-kind social programs. The average value of payments, benefits, and services to families and individuals was $1,252 in 1970 (in 1980 dollars), but it reached $1,896 in 1980.[114] Progress in reducing poverty was thus obtained only because social programs were more comprehensive than during any other period in American history.

The progress in improving the material status of Americans was accompanied by a revolution in human rights. Regulations and litigation of the Equal Employment Opportunity Commission (EEOC) were supplemented by many court rulings that bolstered the rights of minorities and women in job markets and in college admissions. The rights of physically and mentally handicapped persons were advanced by important court decisions, by legislation, and by government regulations that significantly decreased the extent they were warehoused in custodial institutions or not allowed access to public facilities. Although the embattled homosexual community encountered grass-roots movements to deny them teaching positions, they were able to defeat key local initiatives to deny them teaching positions.

 ## WHY WAS THE SPENDING REVOLUTION HIDDEN?

When conservatives attacked social spending and the welfare state during the 1980s, secure in the knowledge that one of their own (Ronald Reagan) was in the White House, they focused their attacks on the New Deal and Great Society reforms. But they ought to have attacked Richard Nixon and his presidential successors during the paradoxical era of the 1970s as well, for their reforms led to startling increases in social spending that rivaled earlier periods of reform. Many different factors combined to hide the extent of reforms of the 1970s. The political rhetoric of Nixon was often conservative, in contrast to Roosevelt's denunciation of "monied interests" and Johnson's expressed sympathy for poverty-stricken persons. Each of the three presidents in the 1970s began their administrations with relatively liberal emphases but ended their terms as determined conservatives, which made them appear to focus on reductions rather than increases in social spending. Nixon was far more conservative in his second term than in his first, Ford more conservative in 1976 than in 1975, and Carter more conservative after 1978 than in his first two years.[115] Each president was forced to abandon reform measures by their southern constituencies, high inflation and deficits, and public indifference to reform.

The nature of the reforms of the 1970s also obscured their reality. Whereas Democrats had typically sought new programs, some of Nixon's reforms were simply procedural and administrative changes in existing programs, such as indexing of Social Security, federalizing of food stamps, and SSI. Nixon's reforms often had a conservative appearance because they deemphasized the role of the federal government; both CETA and revenue sharing allocated funds to localities. Such appearances are deceiving, however, because CETA and revenue sharing were substantial additions to the American welfare state, as Ronald Reagan realized a few years later when he succeeded in virtually eliminating them. Nixon's reforms were disguised as well by the fact that they lacked a dramatic name like the New Deal.

Finally, where the New Deal and Great Society reforms resulted from the successful mobilizing of a liberal coalition of unions, intellectuals, Jews, blue-collar voters, racial minorities, and other interest groups against conservatives, passage of reforms in the 1970s often resulted from a more complex and less dramatic political process in which members of both parties sought partial credit for reforms.

## OUTGROUPS IN THE 1970s

### Changes in Tactics and Organization

There were important changes in the tactics and organization of groups representing women, racial minorities, and gays and lesbians in the 1970s. Relatively radical leadership had emerged in various outgroups in the middle and late 1960s who placed considerable stock in nonviolent marches and demonstrations, building pride of members, and recruiting mass membership. In some groups, older leaders were being supplanted by new leaders, such as Martin Luther King, Jr. just before his assassination in 1968 by Malcolm X and Stokely Carmichael, both advocates of black power.

By the mid-1970s, this first wave of activists was succeeded by a second wave, whether because the earlier groups and leaders had become burned out, been subjected to intimidation by federal officials such as the FBI, or become discouraged by intragroup dissension between radicals and those more inclined to accept incremental changes in existing policies.[116] It had also become clear by the mid-1970s that each of the outgroups faced dauntingly complicated problems in obtaining legislative and legal advances for their groups that could not easily be addressed by direct action. They needed to work on a number of fronts simultaneously, obtain expert legal advice, surmount honest differences within their groups about how best to proceed, and possess "staying power" as complex legislation and lawsuits were processed and litigated. Indeed, each movement became splintered into various groups that worked on specific issues that supplemented the older general-purpose groups such as the National Association for the Advancement of Colored People and the National Organization for Women.

The women's movement illustrates the transformation of the organizing of the outgroups in the 1970s. Women found they had to work on multiple fronts that included efforts to redress job discrimination, reform laws on rape in the various states, develop funding for shelters for battered women, seek resources for child care, obtain legislation allowing maternal (and paternal) leaves for pregnant women and for parents of newly born children, secure equal pay for comparable work, increase child-support payments from divorced or absent fathers, increase training and assistance to "displaced homemakers," obtain enactment of an Equal Rights Amendment, develop lawsuits to force promotions and hiring of women when they encounter discrimination, contest court rulings that threatened affirmative action, and seek legislation to ban sexual harassment in places of work. Various specific organizations were developed to deal with each of these issues, with loose connections between them and the National Organization for Women.[117]

The women's movement also illustrates how different groups had to try to overcome internal dissent *within* their movement. African-American women and other women of color sometimes contended that the leadership of the established groups was insensitive to their needs; thus, some African-American women thought that more attention should be devoted to the needs of poor women and that the views of some radical feminists who attacked the institution of marriage did not reflect the interest of the African-American community in supporting African-American males within their marriages.[118] Old controversies resurfaced, such as those between women who favored protectionist legislation and women who favored strict equality for women and men. If protectionists wanted legislation that gave *women* maternal leaves, custody rights, alimony, and child support, other women wanted legislation that gave men and women complete equality under the law, that is, that gave men and women equal rights to child support, alimony, support payments, and leaves.[119] Conflict between straight and lesbian women developed in various women's organizations about how much emphasis the women's movement should place on battling against discrimination encountered by lesbian women.

## The Mobilization of New Sets of Outgroups

We discussed African Americans, Asian Americans, Latinos, Native Americans, and women in Chapter 9, but the members of other outgroups also developed leadership and organizations in the late 1960s. Many policies that affected older persons were developed in the 1960s and early 1970s, including Medicare, the Older Americans Act, Supplementary Security Income (SSI), and indexing of Social Security benefits.[120] A "gray lobby" was energized by rapid growth in the membership of the American Association of Retired Persons (AARP), the National Council of Senior Citizens (NCSC), the Gray Panthers, and many other groups.[121] Indeed, by the 1980s, AARP used its vast resources to mobilize support for those legislators who were sympathetic to positions of older persons.

With their numbers tragically increased by the Vietnam War as well as automobile accidents, a robust movement for disabled persons developed in the late 1960s. Various groups had long represented disabled veterans, blind persons, deaf persons, the developmentally disabled, and people with specific diseases such as cerebral palsy, but none of them focused on the civil rights of disabled persons, and each was dominated by providers of specific services to these groups. Some programs, such as the federal vocational rehabilitation program, had long provided services to persons with physical disabilities, but the emerging interest in extending the rights of disabled persons was first reflected in the enactment in 1968 of the Architectural

Barriers Act that promoted modification of federal facilities. In the 1960s and early 1970s, various local groups with an interest in civil rights developed, such as the Center for Independent Living in Berkeley, California. Disabled persons came to be concerned about discrimination against them in work places and the numbers of physical impediments (such as the absence of ramps and elevators) that made their access to transportation and facilities problematic. But there was little networking among members of different subgroups of the disabled population until 1972 when President Nixon vetoed the Rehabilitation Act, at which time an array of persons demonstrated in favor of the legislation at the annual conference of the President's Committee on Employment of the Handicapped. The disability movement "took off" after 1973 when the American Coalition of Citizens with Disabilities (ACCD) sought to pressure the Nixon, Ford, and Carter administrations to put resources, legal advocacy, and commitment behind the civil rights provisions of the Rehabilitation Act of 1973, whose section 504 prohibited discrimination against the disabled.[122]

Americans had lagged behind Europeans in developing child care and children's allowances, but little pressure was placed on federal politicians prior to the mid-1960s except by small professional organizations such as the Child Welfare League of America. A White House Conference on Children was held about every ten years, but it tended to be a symbolic event. The establishment of the Head Start Program in 1964 provided a dramatic breakthrough for children, even if it was poorly funded. The veto by President Nixon of child development legislation in 1971 provided impetus for the development of the Children's Defense Fund in 1973 by Marian Wright Edelman—the most assertive advocate for children in Washington, D.C. during the next two decades—and various coalitions of professional groups that banded together to seek passage of measures like the Adoption Assistance and Child Welfare Act of 1980. Various child advocacy groups developed, as well, in local and state jurisdictions. Unlike advocacy for groups with mass memberships, such as AARP, advocates for children had to depend on the goodwill and interest of groups, such as the National Organization for Women, that often gave relatively little attention to the needs of children.[123]

## The 1970s as a Revolution in Rights

Although civil rights are commonly associated with the pivotal Civil Rights Acts of 1964 and 1965, the "rights revolution" reached its zenith in the mid-1970s. Often affiliated with the kinds of advocacy groups we have discussed, as well as within the Justice Department itself, attorneys who had received their training in the civil rights movement of the 1960s developed a vast quantity of litigation for the various outgroups. As one example, in *O'Connor* v. *Donaldson*, the Supreme Court ruled that mental patients who are placed in mental institutions have a right to treatment and cannot simply be warehoused, as was so often done. Other rulings extended protections to immigrants who were placed in detention camps, to homosexuals, to the disabled, to the indigent, to developmentally disabled persons, to persons in jail, and to prisoners on death row. The courts forced the Justice Department to outlaw segregated school systems in the South and forced busing of school children in the North. Against corporations such as AT&T, women won class-action lawsuits that required backpayments of huge sums of money to women who had been unfairly denied promotions or who had encountered wage discrimination — not to mention rulings such as *Roe* v. *Wade* that disallowed state laws that prohibited abortion during the first trimester. The building trades, which had historically excluded racial minorities and women from apprenticeship programs and jobs, were the subject of Court judgments that forced them to train minorities and women.

Litigation promoted by the Age Discrimination Act of 1967 and the Rehabilitation Act of 1973 required some employers to hire or retain elderly persons and disabled persons.[124] Advocates found a generally receptive response from the Supreme Court even after Earl Warren had retired in 1969 as chief justice and been replaced by Warren Burger, who remained chief justice until 1986.

This explosion of litigation and rulings was supplemented by the growth in size of government regulatory bodies, such as the Equal Employment Opportunities Commission, whose budget grew from $3.25 million in 1966 to $111.4 million in 1979. Court rulings and regulatory pressure had a marked impact on the decisions of colleges, corporations, and public agencies like fire and police departments. For example, the percentage of African-American police officers in Atlanta increased from 10 to 29.9 percent between 1968 and 1975.[125]

## The Beginnings of Backlash

Each of the outgroups obtained policy successes in the 1970s and 1980s, but each of them also encountered a significant backlash from movements and conservatives that opposed social change. In the case of women, Phyllis Schlafly became an outspoken critic of the Equal Rights Amendment (ERA) as well as several other policy measures that feminists sought. Schlafly wanted to preserve traditional sex roles and was convinced that the ERA would force women to take jobs in order to provide half the family's income, end laws that gave mothers custody of children, and cause them to lose the right to obtain alimony.[126] Her opposition was joined by many conservatives during the 1970s and 1980s to myriad policies that feminists sought.

Many Republicans, hopeful of gaining votes from low- and moderate-income whites who believed they were losing jobs to minorities, mounted a vigorous attack on affirmative action as well as busing. Leaders of the building trades often chose to disregard federal regulations until forced to act by litigation or federal regulators.

Disabled persons encountered the wrath of many colleges and some employers who were reluctant to expend scarce funds to make buildings accessible and jobs available to handicapped persons. They orchestrated a sit-down strike at one point in the office of the secretary of health, education, and welfare to force the drafting of regulations to implement the Rehabilitation Act of 1973.[127]

Gays and lesbians encountered an antigay backlash that was orchestrated by the New Right. Gay rights ordinances were repealed in 1977 and 1978 in Dade County, Florida, Saint Paul, Minnesota, Wichita, Kansas, and Eugene, Oregon. A California legislator mounted a campaign in the late 1970s to place on the ballot an initiative to prohibit gays and lesbians from teaching in public schools. Harvey Milk, a gay member of the board of supervisors in San Francisco, was assassinated in 1978, along with the city's mayor, who supported gay and lesbian issues.[128]

 ## THE POLITICAL ECONOMY OF SOCIAL POLICY IN THE 1970s

We have emphasized the hidden nature of social reforms in the 1970s, but we can also discern in this paradoxical era the harbingers of a more conservative time. Though Nixon often supported, even initiated, social reforms, he used rhetoric in his public utterances, as well as during his private conferences with advisors, that reflected racism and antisemitism. If he supported the Family Assistance Plan, he also led highly publicized efforts to attack welfare fraud. If he sometimes supported policies for women and other groups, he also knew that the FBI often had agents or informers in various dissident groups. His brooding presence symbolizes the contradictions of the 1970s, where he alternated between conservative rhetoric and support of social initiatives in his first term only to swing decisively toward conservativeness in his second term. We have noted that Presidents Ford and Carter were often very conservative in their domestic policies, even when they supported various reforms. Full-fledged conservative movements against "excesses" of reform emerged in the form of backlash against feminism, affirmative action, social spending, and taxes so that

activists from the women's movement, the gay and lesbian movement, and racial-minority groups felt increasingly on the defensive.

It had seemed, with the end of the Vietnam War, that major and ongoing reductions in military spending would occur. Sharp reductions *did* occur and were used to fund increases in social spending during the decade, but some Americans became convinced by the mid-1970s that the Soviet Union, which had dramatically increased the number and power of its missiles, threatened to overtake the American lead in military weapons. Angered by several arms control treaties, which they believed made undue concessions to the Russians, these Americans led a crusade to dramatically increase military spending—a plea that fell on the receptive ears of Ronald Reagan, who made increases in military spending a major pledge in his campaign of 1980.[129]

Historians sometimes err by characterizing historical eras as liberal *or* conservative. The decade of the 1970s was a peculiar mixture of these two tendencies. Major policy reforms took place but in the context of a nation with an emerging conservative movement that came to view even Richard Nixon as too liberal. Conservatives confidently awaited the returns of the 1980 presidential election, and they were not disappointed by the results.

 # END NOTES

1. Sar Levitan and Clifford Johnson, *Beyond the Safety Net: Reviving the Promise of Opportunity in America* (Cambridge, Mass.: Ballinger, 1984), p. 2.

2. Tom Wicker, *One of Us: Richard Nixon and the American Dream* (New York: Randon House, 1991), pp. 484–541.

3. James Reichley, *Conservatives in an Age of Change: The Nixon and Ford Administrations* (Washington, D.C.: Brookings Institution, 1981), pp. 48–52.

4. Jules Witcover, *The Resurrection of Richard Nixon* (New York: Putnam, 1970), pp. 104–225.

5. *Ibid.,* pp. 57–58.

6. *Ibid.,* pp. 361–379.

7. Tom Wicker, *One of Us,* pp. 410–413.

8. Elliot Richardson, "The Paradox," In Kenneth Thompson, ed., *The Nixon Presidency* (New York: University Press of America, 1987), pp. 53ff.

9. Rowland Evans and Robert Novak, *Nixon in the White House* (New York: Random House, 1971), pp. 42–43, 108, 117–118, 211–214; William Leuchtenberg, *In the Shadow of FDR: From Harry Truman to Ronald Reagan* (Ithaca, N.Y.: Cornell University Press, 1983), pp. 168–169; Reichley, *Conservatives in an Age of Change,* pp. 58–70.

10. Hugh Graham, *The Civil Rights Era: Origins and Development of National Policy, 1960–1972* (New York: Oxford University Press, 1990), p. 322.

11. Leonard Garment, "Richard Nixon." In Thompson, ed., *The Nixon Presidency,* pp. 99ff.

12. Richard Nathan, *The Plot that Failed: Nixon and the Administrative Presidency* (New York: John Wiley & Sons, 1975), pp. 37–56.

13. Reichley, *Conservatives in an Age of Change,* pp. 79–87.

14. Bruce Jansson, *The History and Politics of Selected Children's Programs and Related Legislation in the Context of Four Models of Political Behavior,* Doctoral dissertation (Chicago: University of Chicago, 1975), pp. 54–55.

15. Reichley, *Conservatives in an Age of Change,* pp. 56, 72, 154–156.

16. Sar Levitan and Robert Taggart, *The Promise of Greatness* (Cambridge, Mass.: Harvard University Press, 1976), pp. 24–28.

17. Reichley, *Conservatives in an Age of Change,* pp. 219–224.

18. *Ibid.,* pp. 59–64, 68–72; Evans and Novak, *Nixon,* pp. 37–74.

19. Daniel Moynihan, *The Politics of a Guaranteed Income* (New York: Random House, 1973), pp. 352–396.

20. *Ibid.,* pp. 192–226; Reichley, *Conservatives in an Age of Change,* pp. 138–142.

21. Vincent Burke, *Nixon's Good Deed: Welfare Reform* (New York: Columbia University Press, 1974), p. 67.

22. W. Joseph Heffernan, *Introduction to Social Welfare Policy* (Itasca, Ill.: Peacock, 1979), pp. 241–250.

23. Moynihan, *The Politics of a Guaranteed Income,* pp. 458–483.

24. *Ibid.,* pp. 439–452.

25. Burke, *Nixon's Good Deed,* pp. 177–187.

26. *Ibid.,* pp. 198–204.

27. Timothy Smeeding, "Is the Safety Net Still Intact?" In D. Lee Bawden, ed., *The Social Contract Revisited: Aims and Outcomes of President Reagan's Social Welfare Policy* (Washington, D.C.: Urban Institute, 1984), pp. 75, 78.

28. Linda Demkovitch, "Administration About-Face on Disability Could Be a Blessing in Disguise," *National Journal,* 16 (April 28, 1984), 823–825; Donald Chambers, "Policy Weaknesses and Political Opportunities," *Social Service Review,* 1 (March 1985), 1–17.

29. Nicholas Kotz, *Let Them Eat Promises* (Garden City, N.Y.: Doubleday, 1971), pp. 206–213.

30. Levitan and Taggart, *The Promise of Greatness,* p. 67; Moynihan, *The Politics of a Guaranteed Income,* pp. 493–494.

31. Smeeding, "Is the Safety Net Still Intact?" p. 78.

32. Martha Derthick, *Policymaking for Social Security* (Washington, D.C.: Brookings Institution, 1979), pp. 345–368.

33. *Ibid.,* pp. 358–362.

34. Craig Roberts, *The Supply-Side Revolution: An Insider's Account of Policy-Making in Washington* (Cambridge, Mass.: Harvard University Press, 1984), pp. 260–261.

35. Peter Gottschalk and Sheldon Danziger, "Macroeconomic Conditions, Income Transfers, and the Trend in Poverty." In Bawden, ed., *The Social Contract Revisited,* p. 191.

36. Nathan, *The Plot that Failed,* pp. 37–56.

37. Robert Magill, *Social Policy in American Society* (New York: Human Sciences Press, 1984), pp. 127–128; Reichley, *Conservatives in an Age of Change,* pp. 156–159.

38. Reichley, *Conservatives in an Age of Change,* p. 155.

39. George Hale and Marian Palley, *The Politics of Federal Grants* (Washington, D.C.: Congressional Quarterly Press, 1981), pp. 111–113.

40. Walter Williams, *Government by Agency: Lessons from the Social Program Grants-in-Aid Experience* (New York: Academic Press, 1980), pp. 42–43.

41. Martha Derthick, *Uncontrollable Spending for Social Services Grants* (Washington, D.C.: Brookings Institution, 1975), pp. 29–34.

42. Congressional Quarterly Service, Inc., *Congressional Quarterly Almanac,* Vol. XXIX (Washington, D.C., 1973), p. 575.

43. Wicker, *One of Us,* pp. 484–507, 522–523; Graham, *The Civil Rights Era,* pp. 475–476.

44. Reichley, *Conservatives in an Age of Change,* pp. 188–189.

45. Levitan and Taggart, *The Promise of Greatness,* pp. 150–155; Nancy Woloch, *Women and the American Experience* (New York: Knopf, 1984), pp. 524–526.

46. Graham, *The Civil Rights Era,* pp. 393–449.

47. *Ibid.,* pp. 322–345.

48. Frank Bowe, *Rehabilitating America: Toward Independence for Disabled and Elderly People* (New York: Harper & Row, 1980), pp. 59–91.

49. Joseph Califano, *Governing America* (New York: Simon & Schuster, 1981), pp. 314–315.

50. Paul Starr, *The Social Transformation of American Medicine* (New York: Basic Books, 1984), pp. 396–401, 402–403.

51. Gilbert Steiner, *The Futility of Family Policy* (Washington, D.C.: Brookings Institution, 1981), pp. 49–50.

52. Lela Costin, *Child Welfare: Policies and Practice* (New York: McGraw-Hill, 1979), p. 49.

53. Bruce Jansson, *Theory and Practice of Social Welfare Policy* (Belmont, Calif.: Wadsworth, 1984), p. 335.

54. Frank Thompson, *Health Policy and the Bureaucracy: Politics and Implementation* (Cambridge, Mass.: M.I.T. Press, 1981), pp. 217–251.

55. David Stockman, *The Triumph of Politics* (New York: Harper & Row, 1986), p. 410.

56. Reichley, *Conservatives in an Age of Change,* pp. 219–221.

57. For example, funding pressures on neighborhood health centers are discussed by Isabel Marcus in *Dollars for Reform* (Lexington, Mass.: D.C. Heath, 1981), pp. 89–115.

58. Jansson, *The History and Politics,* pp. 233–309; Gilbert Steiner, *The Children's Cause* (Washington, D.C.: Brookings Institution, 1976), pp. 90–117.

59. Geoffrey Hodgson, *America in Our Time* (Garden City, N.Y.: Doubleday, 1976), pp. 412–428; Kevin Phillips, *The Emerging Republican Majority* (New Rochelle, N.Y.: Arlington House, 1969), pp. 168–175, 182–184, 321–330.

60. Hodgson, *America in Our Time,* pp. 401–411.

61. Reichley, *Conservatives in an Age of Change,* pp. 54–55; Tom Wicker, "Introduction." In John Osborne, *The Nixon Watch* (New York: Live-right, 1970), pp. viii–x.

62. Hodgson, *America in Our Time,* pp. 425–428, 455.

63. Reichley, *Conservatives in an Age of Change,* pp. 208–209.

64. Hodgson, *America in Our Time,* p. 366.

65. Reichley, *Conservatives in an Age of Change,* pp. 232–233, 239–242.

66. *Ibid.,* pp. 234–237, 242–247.

67. *Ibid.,* pp. 307–311.

68. *Ibid.,* pp. 322–325.

69. Bowe, *Rehabilitating America,* pp. 102–107, 130; Peter Tyor and Leland Bell, *Caring for the Retarded in America: A History* (Westport, Conn.: Greenwood, 1984), p. 150.

70. Haynes Johnson, *In the Absence of Power* (New York: Viking Press, 1980), p. 114.

71. Robert Shogan, *Promises to Keep: Carter's First Hundred Days* (New York: Thomas Crowell, 1977), pp. 22–28.

72. *Ibid.,* pp. 28–48.

73. Johnson, *In the Absence of Power,* pp. 38–48.

74. *Ibid.,* p. 295.

75. *Ibid.,* pp. 101, 154–168.

76. *Ibid.,* pp. 163–164; Shogan, *Promises to Keep,* p. 199.

77. Califano, *Governing America,* p. 334; Johnson, *In the Absence of Power,* p. 217.

78. Shogan, *Promises to Keep,* p. 189.

79. Califano, *Governing America,* pp. 96–117.

80. Heffernan, *Introduction to Social Welfare Policy,* pp. 259–266.

81. Califano, *Governing America,* p. 321.

82. *Ibid.,* pp. 320–366.

83. *Ibid.,* pp. 364–367.

84. Reichley, *Conservatives in an Age of Change,* pp. 397–399.

85. *Ibid.*

86. Congressional Quarterly Service, Inc., *Congressional Quarterly Almanac,* Vol. XXXIV (Washington, D.C., 1978), pp. 272–279.

87. Steiner, *The Futility of Family Policy,* pp. 85–88.

88. *Ibid.,* pp. 93–94.

89. *Ibid.,* pp. 163–173.

90. *Ibid.,* pp. 144–155.

91. Karen Davis and Cathy Schoen, *Health and the War on Poverty: A Ten-Year Appraisal* (Washington, D.C.: Brookings Institution, 1978), p. 86.

92. Califano, *Governing America,* pp. 231–243.

93. *Ibid.,* pp. 258–262, 314–315; Timothy Clark, "Here's One Midnight Regulation That Slipped Through Reagan's Net," *National Journal,* 13 (February 7, 1981), 221–224.

94. U.S. President's Commission on Mental Health, *Report to the President* (Washington, D.C.: Government Printing Office, 1978).

95. Jansson, *Theory and Practice of Social Welfare Policy,* pp. 445–446.

96. Califano, *Governing America,* pp. 388–396.

97. *Ibid.,* pp. 384–386.

98. Johnson, *In the Absence of Power,* pp. 49–81.

99. *Ibid.,* p. 293.

100. Meyer, "Budget Cuts in the Reagan Administration." In Bawden, ed., *The Social Contract Revisited,* p. 36.

101. Califano, *Governing America,* p. 67; Johnson, *In the Absence of Power,* pp. 299–300.

102. Califano, *Governing America,* pp. 82–86.

103. *Ibid.*

104. Johnson, *In the Absence of Power,* pp. 277–317.

105. Meyer, "Budget Cuts in the Reagan Administration," p. 35; Gregory Mills and John Palmer, "The Federal Budget in Flux." In Gregory Mills and John Palmer, eds., *Federal Budget Policy in the 1980s* (Washington, D.C.: Urban Institute, 1984), p. 14; Stockman, *The Triumph of Politics,* p. 411.

106. Table 10.1 from Smeeding, "Is the Safety Net Still Intact?" p. 75.

107. Levitan and Taggart, *The Promise of Greatness,* pp. 70–74.

108. *Ibid.,* pp. 72–73.

109. Blanche Bernstein, "Welfare Dependency." In Bawden, ed., *The Social Contract Revisited,* pp. 129–130.

110. Martha Derthick, *Policymaking for Social Security,* pp. 254–270.

111. Meyer, "Budget Cuts in the Reagan Administration," p. 38.

112. Gottschalk and Danziger, "Macroeconomic Conditions," p. 191.

113. Mills and Palmer, "The Federal Budget in Flux," p. 14.

114. Gottschalk and Danziger, "Macroeconomic Conditions," pp. 188–189.

115. Evans and Novak, *Nixon,* pp. 227–228; Reichley, *Conservatives in an Age of Change,* p. 314; Califano, *Governing America,* pp. 402–448.

116. Flora Davis, *Moving the Mountain: The Women's Movement in America Since 1960* (New York: Simon & Schuster, 1991), pp. 137–138.

117. *Ibid.,* pp. 137–154.

118. *Ibid.,* pp. 362–367.

119. *Ibid.,* pp. 305–307.

120. C. L. Estes, *The Aging Enterprise* (San Francisco: Jossey-Bass, 1979).

121. H. J. Pratt, *The Gray Lobby* (Chicago: University of Chicago Press, 1976).

122. Richard Scotch, *From Good Will to Civil Rights* (Philadelphia: Temple University Press, 1984), pp. 34–59, 82–120.

123. Susan Tolchin and Martin Tolchin, *Clout: Women's Power and Politics* (New York: Coward, McCann, and Geoghegan, 1974), p. 230.

124. Thomas Edsall, *Chain Reaction: The Impact of Race Rights, and Taxes on American Politics* (New York: W. W. Norton, 1991), pp. 107–115.

125. Edsall, *Chain Reaction,* p. 117.

126. Donald Mathews and Jane Sherron De Hart, *Sex, Gender, and the Politics of ERA* (New York: Oxford University Press, 1990), pp. 154–165.

127. Scotch, *From Good Will,* pp. 111–120.

128. John D'Emilio, "Gay Politics and Community in San Francisco Since World War II." In Martin Duberman, Martha Vicinus, and George Chauncey, *Hidden From History: Reclaiming the Gay and Lesbian Past* (New York: Meridian Books, 1990), pp. 468–473.

129. Michael Boll, *National Security Planning: Roosevelt Through Reagan* (Lexington, Ky.: University of Kentucky Press, 1988), pp. 188–197.

# CHAPTER 11

# The Conservative Counterrevolution in the Era of Reagan and Bush

## Selected Orienting Events in the Counterrevolution

| | |
|---|---|
| **1978** | Tax revolt initiated by passage of Proposition 13 in California |
| **1980** | Ronald Reagan wins landslide victory over Jimmy Carter |
| **1981** | Omnibus Budget Reconciliation Act (OBRA) makes deep cuts in social programs and establishes seven block grants; Economic Recovery Tax Act of 1981 (ERTA) sharply reduces personal and corporate taxes; Presidential Task Force on Regulatory Relief established; Executive Order mandates review of regulations by the Office of Management and Budget |
| **1981–1983** | Nation's deepest recession since the 1930s |
| **1982** | Job Training Partnership Act (JTPA) enacted; Tax Equity and Fiscal Responsibility Act (TEFRA) raises corporate taxes and cuts social programs |
| **1983** | Diagnostic-related groups (DRGs) introduced by DHHS to finance Medicare's hospital fees; Social Security amendments increase retirement age, reduce some benefits, and subject pensions of some retirees to taxes |
| **1984** | Reagan wins landslide victory over Walter Mondale |
| **1985** | Balanced Budget and Emergency Deficit Control Act (Gramm-Rudman-Hollings) enacted |
| **1986** | Tax reform reduces highest tax rate and eliminates many deductions |
| **1987** | Enactment of Stewart B. McKinney Homeless Assistance Act |
| **1988** | Enactment of Family Support Act |
| **1988** | Election of George Bush |
| **1990** | Enactment of Americans with Disabilities Act and the Child Care and Development Block Grant program |
| **1991** | Enactment of Civil Rights Act |
| **1992** | Los Angeles riots |

## THE ASCENDANCY OF CONSERVATISM

Conservatism was the political mainstream of the nation in the Gilded Age, the 1920s, and the 1950s, when localism, limited federal social welfare roles, and unfettered capitalism prevailed, but it gave way to liberal policies during the Great Depression and the early 1960s.[1] The minority status of conservatives was illustrated by the landslide defeat in 1964 of Barry Goldwater by Lyndon Johnson, who accused Goldwater of attacking Social Security, TVA, and other legacies of the New Deal. The Goldwater defeat was swiftly followed by Lyndon Johnson's legislative successes in 1965 and 1966, so it seemed as if conservatism had run its course in national politics.

Between 1966 and 1980, however, a number of developments led to a remarkable resurgence of conservatism that culminated in the election of Ronald Reagan. The standard of living of the American working and middle classes had improved markedly during the 1950s and 1960s despite occasional recessions and sharp inflation in the early 1950s. Most people believed that government officials, armed with Keynesian economic theory, could continue this rosy scenario by adjusting government spending downward (to reduce inflation) or upward (to reduce unemployment). The American economy was widely perceived to be an expanding pie that would benefit all segments of the population.[2]

The simultaneous appearance of inflation and unemployment in the 1970s rudely upset this economic utopia. Many middle-class Americans found their earnings sharply eroded by inflation and by higher taxes as inflation pushed them into higher federal tax brackets.[3] Many local units of government increased their taxes to pay the local share of the costs of federal programs and to fund higher costs of local and municipal services.

This concern about taxes led to grass-roots movements to reduce tax rates at the local level. Howard Jarvis's movement in California for Proposition 13 in 1978, which drastically reduced local property taxes, was followed by tax revolts in many other states. Liberal legislators watched these local tax revolts with trepidation, for they realized they could eventually stimulate protests against the federal tax system that funded federal social programs.[4] Concern about federal deficits also undermined social reform in the 1970s since many Americans wondered if social spending had to be cut sharply to reduce deficits.[5]

The hopes of conservatives were buoyed by the declining strength of the Democratic party. Richard Nixon carried five southern states in 1968, a Republican achievement that had not been matched since Reconstruction. The liberal flank of the Democratic party began to weaken as blue-collar workers became increasingly uneasy about social reform and preoccupied with their own economic problems. White backlash led to widespread opposition to affirmative action and social programs, which were widely perceived to disproportionately benefit women, African Americans, and other racial minorities. Many Jewish voters opposed the use of quotas since this policy had often been used to exclude them from admission to colleges and the professions.[6]

Feminists and African-American activists were increasingly viewed with suspicion in a nation that resisted affirmative action. "Big-spending liberals" were often perceived to be an anachronism in a society that experienced large deficits.[7] Trade unions, which had provided electoral and campaign support for the Democrats, were weakened as the economy shifted from manufacturing to service industries, as new jobs were increasingly located in the non-unionized South, and as many industries moved to foreign nations to reduce their labor costs. The ill-fated presidencies of Lyndon Johnson and Jimmy Carter, as well as the assassinations of John and Robert Kennedy, also weakened the Democratic party.

Americans had lived through a long period of social reform that had extended from 1960 through the 1970s. They had demonstrated in prior eras that they could tolerate social reforms for limited periods, so it was not surprising that the pendulum swung toward conservativism. Conservatives found the public to be more receptive to their arguments that social programs had not solved poverty and other social problems and that social spending was incompatible with economic growth.

The movement of persons and jobs to the Sunbelt during the 1950s, 1960s, and 1970s, which led nearly 40 million Americans to leave the Northeast and the Midwest, depleted traditional bastions of Democratic strength and greatly increased the voting populations of conservatives. When placed in this new environment —and removed from trade unions, big-city mayors, and incumbent liberal politicians—these voters, who tended to be relatively conservative and middle class, often became more politically conservative. The movement of populations to the Sunbelt was accompanied by the continuing development of suburbs that were far more conservative in their voting preferences than urban areas since their populations had little stake in the social programs of urban residents.[8]

The traditional strength of the Democratic party was also undermined by the maturing of the large war-baby generation, who were born from 1946 to the late 1950s. These Americans had not lived through the Great Depression and, in the case of suburban residents, had little or no contact with racial minorities. They were often preoccupied with materialism and with personal survival in labor markets that were increasingly crowded with young job seekers from their generation.[9]

When taken in tandem, these various demographic and social trends placed the Democratic party in jeopardy, particularly as Republicans developed marketing and campaign tactics to reach sunbelt, suburban, service-oriented, and youthful citizens. No sudden erosion in the strength of the Democratic party occurred, particularly in local elections, but its power in senatorial and presidential elections had diminished significantly by the early 1980s.

The Republican party in its national legislative strategies was adept at using these various developments in the 1970s to wrest from the Democratic party two specific groups of voters: northern white, Catholic voters and southern white, lower and lower-middle class voters. Knowing that many of these voters believed that The Great Society had disproportionately assisted racial minorities and that their rising taxes were caused by this expansion of the welfare state, Republican strategists sought (often successfully) to associate the Democrats with welfare programs, urban riots, high taxes, busing, and affirmative action—and to identify their own party with "the silent majority of law-abiding citizens." Using advanced marketing techniques, they addressed literature to these two groups of voters and succeeded in persuading many of them to vote for Republican candidates in presidential races. When added to their traditional suburban and relatively affluent constituency, these new voters gave the Republicans a decided advantage, particularly in the presidential elections of 1968, 1972, 1980, 1984, and 1988.[10]

## The Legitimization of Conservatism

Liberal reformers had dominated political dialogue from the New Deal through the presidency of Lyndon Johnson.[11] A cadre of conservative thinkers, such as sociologist Robert Nisbet, had promulgated theories during the 1950s and early 1960s about the merits of limiting policy roles of the federal government and about the need to establish the family, neighborhoods, and local government as buffers between citizens and government. Other theorists, such as Richard Weaver, had established libertarian positions, which emphasized development of policies that maximized freedom by abolishing most government regulations and minimizing taxes. But conservative theorists of the 1950s were relatively isolated from the political process and even distrustful of the general public, which, they believed, was easily manipulated by liberals and the mass media.[12]

The defeat of Goldwater in 1964 made conservatives realize that they needed to participate in the political process to gain power and that they had to use aggressive advertising and outreach to convince the American public to elect conservative legislators.[13] Nixon and his allies used the term *silent majority* in 1968 to describe their belief that most Americans favored localism, elimination of government regulations, and reductions in social spending.

In a departure from the abstract conservative philosophy of the 1950s, a number of theorists began to analyze public policy and to offer recommendations that stemmed from their conservative ideology. Milton Friedman, the conservative economist from the University of Chicago who published *Capitalism and Freedom* in 1962, discussed a series of policies to radically reduce the regulatory power of government; he denounced public housing programs, licensing of professionals, traditional welfare programs, and a host of other liberal policies.[14] A critique of existing urban renewal programs was advanced by Martin Anderson in *The Federal Bulldozer* in 1964 when he argued that private housing markets more effectively met consumer needs than government urban renewal and housing programs.[15] Conservatives had established think tanks by the end of the 1960s, such as the American Enterprise Institute and the Heritage Foundation, to compete with such liberal organizations as the Brookings Institution and the Urban Institute. William Buckley initiated a national television show, "Firing Line," which he used as a forum to present conservative views, and developed *The National Review,* a conservative journal that supplemented viewpoints in *The Public Interest, Commentary,* and other conservative publications.

The chastening effect of the Goldwater defeat also made conservatives more willing to participate in political campaigns. Some of them, such as Kevin Phillips, developed theories about how conservatives could wrest political power from the Democrats by appealing to blue-collar, white ethnic, and sunbelt voters. Presidents Nixon and Ford did not appoint many conservative theorists to top positions since they preferred businesspeople and attorneys, but conservative economists such as Alan Greenspan and William Simon received top positions. The respectability of conservative points of view was further enhanced by criticisms of the Democratic party and reforms of The Great Society by prominent intellectuals, such as Nathan Glazer and Daniel Moynihan, who pointedly attacked social programs, community action programs, affirmative action, and liberalism.[16]

The constituency of conservatism expanded considerably in the late 1970s, when it obtained a large grass-roots following within fundamentalist religious groups, particularly the Southern Baptist Church. Outraged that the Internal Revenue Service did not allow segregated private schools to have tax exemptions, white parents, who had removed their children to these private schools to escape integrated public schools, as well as curriculum they believed to represent "secular humanism," swung toward the Republicans, who promised to help rescind the IRS ruling.[17] The New Religious–Political Right (NRPR) was formed as an umbrella group that contained many independent congregations, individual members, and groups like the Moral Majority. It contained ninety constituent organizations by 1980, extending from the national Pro-Life Political Action Committee to the Interfaith Committee Against Blasphemy.[18] Jerry Falwell, an outspoken Baptist preacher, quickly became the leader of the Moral Majority, a grassroots pressure group that favored the abolition of abortion, censorship of literature to limit pornography, and policies to allow prayer in schools and that lent its support to many political conservatives who advocated sharp reductions in social spending. The various member groups of the NRPR engaged in educational programs, which were funded by tax-deductible contributions, that involved distribution of millions of items of literature through the mails, churches, and personal contacts. Some of them also engaged in extensive political activities that included lobbying and contributions to political campaigns.[19]

## Ronald Reagan as Catalyst

A conducive climate existed for the emergence of a conservative movement by the late 1970s, and it found a catalyst in Ronald Reagan, a former movie actor turned politician. Reagan came from a family in Illinois that had suffered some poverty and turmoil because Reagan's father was an alcoholic; it seems likely that Reagan's dislike of welfare recipients and impoverished persons stemmed in part from the trauma his family encountered as it sought to remain independent despite his father's erratic behavior.[20]

Reagan was a devoted follower of Franklin Roosevelt in the 1930s, but during his postwar acting career, he became convinced that government regulations had unfairly forced a movie company with which he was associated to divest its holdings in a chain of cinema theaters. He increasingly resented the high taxes that he had to pay as his income increased from his movie career. His distrust of communists, which was to assume paranoid proportions in succeeding decades, increased as he observed the growth of power of communists and radicals in an actors' union. He devoted himself to his movie career during the late 1940s, where he chose parts that mirrored his personal philosophy, such as the part of the Notre Dame football coach Knute Rockne, a self-made man who preached the virtues of hard work and morality. Reagan remained a Democrat until 1962, but he had gradually moved to the right during the 1950s, when he developed a national reputation as a public speaker for conservative audiences.[21]

Reagan idealized self-made men who obtained upward mobility through traditional virtues of hard work, persistence, and risk taking. He realized that some Americans encountered hard times, but he was convinced that private philanthropy and the assistance of family and friends were usually sufficient remedies. Since he discounted the importance of racism and discrimination, he believed that African Americans, Latinos, and Native Americans could emulate the successes of white citizens.[22] The economy worked best, he believed, when government assumed virtually no role in regulating it and did not tax its citizens beyond the minimal amount needed to fund defense spending and keeping a police force. He regarded the nineteenth century as the golden era of American history, when individualism, localism, risk taking, and free enterprise dominated the nation. His political hero was Calvin Coolidge, who articulated a conservative philosophy and made deep and successive cuts in federal taxes during the 1920s.[23] Although Reagan admired Franklin Roosevelt's political skills and decisive leadership, he considered Roosevelt a villain who had introduced alien and destructive policies, including the development of the federal bureaucracy, federal regulations, handouts or doles to millions of Americans, and heavy federal taxes. Roosevelt had systematically destroyed the vision of the founding fathers, he thought, and developed massive welfare and public works programs to gain a political constituency for the Democratic party. Reagan was critical of liberal rulings of the Supreme Court in the 1950s and 1960s under Chief Justice Earl Warren since he believed liberal justices had ignored the intentions of the framers of the Constitution when they limited the powers of the police. Reagan did not support federal civil rights legislation in the 1960s since he believed that states could protect the civil rights of their citizens.[24]

His political philosophy can be criticized on many counts. The nostalgic view of American history that eulogized generations of self-made men overlooked the systematic oppression of racial minorities and women. Since his "frontier philosophy" accorded women primarily domestic functions, he did not appoint many women to policy positions during his terms as governor of California and as president.[25] He did not fully realize that many persons who led salutary lives often encountered hard times. Roosevelt's New Deal, far from consisting of a radical departure, provided a minimal set of subsistence supports for such persons. Reagan's obsession with self-sufficiency precluded him from understanding the plight of millions of working but poor Americans who cannot support their families. He did not favor social welfare programs to aid poor persons because he believed that economic inequality provided incentives for the poor to improve their economic conditions.[26]

Other troubling characteristics of Reagan appeared even as he was governor, only to resurface during his presidency. Lou Cannon, a reporter who followed him over decades and interviewed him more than forty times, believes that Reagan's childhood experiences with an alcoholic father led him frequently to live in a fantasy world of movies, Western heros, and war heros that made him inattentive to details and unable to grasp the consequences of some of his decisions, such as irresponsible fiscal policies that led to huge deficits.[27] He was so obsessed with the three themes of lowering taxes, increasing America's defenses, and cutting social spending that he was not interested in other issues.[28]

## Reagan's Emergence as a National Hero

Persons with Reagan's ideology were widely viewed to be extremist in the 1960s, even by many Republicans, but Reagan began to shed the label of extremism by winning successive victories for the governorship of California in 1966 and 1970 in a state with large numbers of liberal, trade union, and minority voters. Although his policies were decidedly conservative, Reagan often displayed political pragmatism. While criticizing intellectuals, he substantially increased the budget of the state university as well as state assistance to public schools; while criticizing

social spending, he allowed significant increases to occur in the state's budget; while criticizing taxes, he increased the state's taxes by $1 billion; and while criticizing sexual permissiveness and abortion, he supported policies that allowed large state funding of abortions. Even as governor, however, these pragmatic accommodations were accompanied by harsh and uncompromising attitudes toward impoverished people as reflected by slashes in the budgets of selected public welfare, mental health, and child welfare programs. His open opposition to the federal Civil Rights Acts of 1964 and 1965 was followed by indifference to civil rights as governor. Reagan also initiated a punitive workfare program that forced some recipients into low-paying and menial jobs. He appointed conservative "law and order" justices and continued the rhetoric that extolled conservative values.[29] Moreover, he exhibited a penchant for fiscal irresponsibility as governor by making such large tax cuts that he later had to increase taxes to reduce the budget deficit.[30]

Reagan was persuaded by conservatives to run against Gerald Ford for the Republican nomination for the presidency in 1976, but his poor showing in the primaries suggested that he was still regarded as a political maverick. Conservatives, who were unhappy with the politically moderate Ford, tried to persuade Reagan to start a new conservative party both during and after the 1976 race, but he refused because he realized that it would ruin his chances to enter the mainstream of the Republican party.[31] He decided to pursue the presidency in 1980 in the aftermath of his defeat for the nomination in 1976, but like Nixon before him, he realized that traditional Republican negativism would not suffice to attract a broad range of voters.

## Supply-Side Economics: A Positive Way to Be Negative

It was during this period of drift that Reagan and his aides chanced on a theory known as supply-side economics, which became a major theme of his candidacy.[32] Keynesian economics, which had dominated economic thinking in the United States since the late 1930s, emphasized the use of government spending and changes in interest rates to offset recessions and inflation; spending was increased and interest rates were decreased in recessions, and converse policies were used to combat inflation. Even Republican presidents, such as Eisenhower, Nixon, and Ford, had used its tenets to guide their economic policies. But Keynesian economics was increasingly under attack by the mid-1970s because it seemed inadequate to solve stagflation. Milton Friedman added new doubts when he suggested that monetary policy—increases or decreases in the supply of money—could powerfully influence the economy. When the government increased the money supply too rapidly, he argued, the nation experienced rapid growth with ensuing inflation, whereas severe reductions in the supply of money often caused recessions.

In this welter of economic theories, economist Arthur Laffer, whose ideas were popularized by journalist Jude Wanniski, argued that Keynesian economics had neglected the importance of the supply of capital to economic growth because of their preoccupation with consumer demand, interest rates, and government spending. They reasoned that economic growth requires steady increases in investment, but investment can occur only if sufficient amounts of capital are accumulated by wealthy persons and corporations and invested in job-creating businesses. But affluent persons are unlikely to invest their excess money in such businesses, Laffer argued, if their money is subject to high marginal rates of taxation that reduce their profits from investments; in such circumstances, Laffer contended, affluent persons buy expensive cars, antiques, and other luxuries rather than placing their funds in income-producing investments. No amount of consumer demand, they concluded, can cause economic growth if a shortage of investment capital exists.[33] Some Republican politicians, including Congressman Jack Kemp,

accepted the logic of supply-side economics and vigorously promoted tax reduction.

Quite apart from its technical merits, supply-side theory appealed to Reagan and his advisors on political grounds since it purported to offer a solution to stagflation by simultaneously addressing problems of inflation and unemployment.[34] Increases in pools of investment capital would, they argued, increase employment by creating jobs while inflation would decrease as entrepreneurs invested in technology and new machinery that made workers more productive. Supply-side economics also provided justification for major reductions in taxes, which are usually popular with the electorate and with conservatives. But would not tax cuts exacerbate the nation's mounting deficits, which had approached $50 billion by the mid-1970s? Not so, countered the supply-siders, since increases in investments that stem from lower tax rates would promote economic activity that would increase government revenues, even with reductions in taxes.[35]

Supply-side economics also provided a convenient way to appeal to the traditional Republican constituency as well as to blue-collar voters. Supply-side theorists were most interested in tax reductions for affluent persons, but it was relatively easy to accompany tax reductions for these persons with some reductions for blue-collar and middle-class persons by proposing reductions in each of the various federal tax brackets.[36] In short, Reagan hoped to achieve Nixon's dream of enlarging the base of the Republican party, not by the development of social programs but by his economic policy.[37]

Ronald Reagan was not alone in his advocacy of supply-side economics since the concepts had obtained sufficient appeal by 1978 that tax-cut proposals nearly passed both houses of Congress with bipartisan support.[38] But Reagan was the only presidential contender in either party who strongly supported the theory; indeed, George Bush, who ran against Reagan in the Republican primaries of 1980, labeled Reagan's policies as "voo-doo economics."[39] Supply-side economics, then, provided a positive way to be negative. Reagan could demand tax cuts (a negative policy) in order to promote economic growth, reductions in both unemployment and inflation, reductions of the federal deficit, and increases in the income of Americans of all social classes (positive policies).

Since supply-side economists were convinced that economic growth would follow tax cuts, they did not believe that major cuts in government spending were required to curtail deficits. Reagan coupled supply-side economics, however, with his traditional demands that social spending be radically reduced and that many government regulations be rescinded. Reagan's demands for reductions in the role of the federal government might have been dismissed earlier in the decade as Republican negativism, but they struck a sympathetic chord with many Americans in the political climate of the late 1970s, when Americans were distrustful of federal bureaucrats and Congress.[40] Moreover, many white Americans were convinced their taxes rose during the 1970s because of increases in spending for social programs that they believed were used primarily by racial minorities.

## The Campaign of 1980: Two Styles

Reagan obtained the nomination of the Republican party in 1980, but Carter, his opponent, enjoyed a substantial lead in polls in early September, scored heavily when he attacked Reagan as trigger-happy, and used his presidential access to the media to advantage.[41] The political climate of 1980 was very different from that of 1964, however, and Reagan was far more politically adept than Goldwater. His political success stemmed from his ability to adapt his political message to the mood of voters in 1980 with considerable aid from media and political consultants. Carter's response to the economic ills of

the nation was to cut social spending, but Reagan coupled this response with his supply-side version of sweeping tax cuts. Carter projected an image of policy vacillation, but Reagan consistently presented his conservative philosophy and advocacy of rearmament. Reagan's rugged appearance made him appealing to those male voters who believed Carter to be soft. (Carter was more appealing to female voters but not sufficiently to offset Reagan's lead with male voters.) Carter's campaign promises to specific interest groups, such as the National Education Association, made him seem beholden to them, but Reagan claimed to be speaking for the entire nation. Carter emphasized the difficulties in righting the economy, but Reagan exuded an optimism that was similar to Roosevelt's optimism in 1932.

Reagan was aided by public opinion that strongly favored conservatism. After the trauma of Vietnam, Watergate, stagflation, and hostages in Iran, many Americans wanted a respite with a president who could make the world seem simpler than it was, who could unite the nation behind patriotism and national values, and who seemed to stand for moral values. Reagan appealed to the restiveness of many white Americans with the pace of reform of the preceding two decades and their opposition to affirmative action, quotas, and busing. He made extraordinary promises that appealed to those Americans who sought easy answers to stagflation, including a prediction that he could cut taxes, increase defense spending, *and* balance the budget![42] He played on the racial and social fears of white voters by stressing opposition to busing, affirmative action, quotas, and welfare; indeed, he loved to recount the story of a "welfare queen" who had enriched herself through welfare fraud.[43] Reagan won a landslide victory in which he obtained a large majority of the male vote, carried the entire southern and western regions of the nation, and wrested large numbers of blue-collar votes from the Democratic party.[44]

## THE REAGAN POLICY BLITZKRIEG

As the conservative equivalent of Roosevelt's achievements during his first one-hundred days in office, Reagan achieved during his first eight months of his presidency major budget cuts, tax cuts, elimination of many regulations, reductions in the policy roles of the federal government, and massive increases in military spending. A number of conditions allowed Reagan to move quickly and successfully on his conservative agenda. The Democrats were thoroughly demoralized by the size of Reagan's victory in 1980. They feared that his victory might presage further gains by Reagan during upcoming elections, when he might establish a permanent shift of blue-collar and white ethnic populations to the Republican party.[45] Thus intimidated by Reagan, the Democrats were also in disarray as they planned their political strategy. Some of them wanted their party to militantly oppose Reagan's policies by reasserting liberal principles, but others feared that opposition would allow Reagan to accuse them of resisting the will of the people. Other Democrats hoped to offer budget and tax alternatives to Reagan's positions to allow the Democratic party to obtain partial credit for conservative policies.[46] They encountered serious practical and leadership problems as well. Since the Republicans had obtained a numerical superiority in the Senate in 1980, they possessed a crucial bastion in the Congress as long as they remained united. The Democratic party maintained a majority in the House, but it was a slim majority of thirty-eight seats that could be overcome if there were defections to the Republicans from conservative Southern Democrats, whose constituencies often favored Reagan's policies. The Democrats lacked effective leadership to develop their policy strategy since Tip O'Neill, the majority leader in the House, was widely perceived to lack skills in initiating policies and had awarded

crucial committee and party positions to conservative Democrats following an internal party struggle in 1980.[47]

Reagan and his aides plotted a brilliant strategy to capitalize on the weakness of the Democrats and the desperate economic situation. Their tactics included militance, centralization, surprise, preparedness, cooptation of conservative Southern Democrats, and preemption of federal revenues through tax cuts and increase in military spending.

The term *militance* is usually applied to the strategy of radicals, but it usefully describes the risk-taking orientation of Reagan and his top advisors, who wanted drastic reductions in social programs and regulations.[48] Reagan knew that he could not instantly eradicate most of the welfare state because of political support for many social programs, but he hoped to reduce government spending from 23 to 19 percent of the GNP by 1984 and to hold government spending increases to 7 percent per year, which was far below the 16 percent increases in the last years of the Carter administration. Cuts in social spending were particularly needed because of projected massive increases in military spending, which Reagan wanted to increase by 160 percent over the current dollar defense budget during the next six years—rising from \$142 billion in 1980 to \$368 billion by 1986. Reagan's inner circle of advisors quickly decided that they could be successful only if they created a climate in which virtually every program and governmental unit were asked to sacrifice for the common good and where opposition to cuts in particular programs was viewed as sabotaging efforts to reduce deficits and restore economic growth.[49] They wanted recalcitrant congressmen to realize that they risked opposition from Reagan in upcoming elections, particularly in those districts in the South and West where Reagan had run more strongly than incumbents. They even hoped to persuade some Southern Democrats to become Republicans in return for choice committee assignments and other political concessions.[50]

Although Reagan was committed to seeking budget cuts, he was equally interested in tax cuts, both to instill economic growth and to reduce federal revenues that might otherwise be used to fund social programs.[51] In a sense, then, Reagan was using the tax cuts to force budget cuts. Since he knew that tax cuts were politically popular in the constituencies of most congressmen, whereas budget cuts were more problematic in that legislators risked angering specific constituencies when they cut social programs, he hoped to force Congress to make deep cuts in social programs by exacerbating the deficit problem by cutting government taxes (and revenues). It was an ingenious strategy of linking tax cuts, budget cuts, and deficits to achieve his conservative objectives.[52] Indeed, David Stockman, the budget director, revealed to Senator Daniel Moynihan in 1985 that Reagan had told him in 1981 that Reagan *wanted* a huge deficit in order to force Congress to cut costly social spending.[53]

Many Democrats were acutely aware of Reagan's strategy but encountered a political predicament. Realizing that it would be difficult in the conservative political atmosphere of 1980 to oppose *both* tax and budget cuts, many liberal Democrats decided to support budget cuts and oppose tax cuts. They regarded the latter as particularly pernicious since they diminished revenues that were needed to fund social programs.[54] They reasoned, then, that cooperation with large budget cuts would make it appear as if they were not obstructionists, so they could then oppose the tax cuts. Their strategy backfired, however, because they did not realize that the tax cuts were so popular with their colleagues and with the electorate that the Congress would enact them despite massive budget cuts.

Military expenditures had increased in absolute terms during most of the 1970s, but the per-

centage of federal military spending had decreased from 49 percent of the federal budget in 1960 to 21 percent in 1980. President Carter had initiated increases in military spending, but Reagan sought drastic increases that were unprecedented during peacetime. Indeed, his advisors wanted to expend $1.46 trillion on defense in the next five years—a sum so large that even hawkish David Stockman believed it would make a massive federal deficit inevitable.[55] These incredible increases in defense spending, like the proposed tax cuts, were highly popular with an American public that had become convinced that Americans dealt with the Soviet Union from a position of weakness. As Congress realized that Reagan would obtain major increases in defense spending, it recognized that cuts in social programs were needed to restrain budget deficits. The issue of guns versus butter, which had surfaced during the Vietnam conflict, reemerged, but many Americans now believed that guns needed to take precedence. Like the tax cuts, the increase in defense spending was a threat to social spending because it diminished resources that could be invested in social programs.

Reagan soon realized, however, that his budget cuts would be endangered if he attacked social programs with powerful constituencies, such as Social Security, Medicare, Head Start, SSI, disability payments for veterans, summer jobs programs, and lunch programs for low-income schools. In addition to declaring these programs immune from cuts, Reagan cleverly argued that he was not cutting aggregate social spending in absolute terms but was merely cutting the rate of increase in social spending. He announced as well that he would preserve a safety net of basic programs for destitute and ill Americans so that none of them would lose welfare protections.[56] These arguments, he hoped, would make him appear compassionate, even as he proposed massive cuts in many social programs.

Reagan's decision to focus on means-tested programs rather than so-called entitlement programs like Medicare and Social Security had profound—and disastrous—consequences for many impoverished Americans. Entitlements constituted 41 percent of the nation's spending in 1980; indeed, Social Security alone constituted almost 33 percent of the nation's domestic budget. Reagan was therefore forced to take all the $50 billion in proposed cuts from those programs that specifically gave services and resources to poor persons.[57] His argument that he was only slowing the rate of increase of aggregate social spending was technically correct, but it disguised the fact that many specific programs that assisted poor persons were eliminated or severely slashed. The real value of AFDC benefits had eroded during the late 1970s, for example, but Reagan proposed decreasing the federal share even further. He proposed massive cuts in food stamps and Medicaid as well as in nutritional, mental health, and public health programs.[58]

To offset efforts by lobbyists and defenders of specific programs who would try to mobilize opposition to his cuts, Reagan relied heavily on David Stockman and Edwin Meese to develop and implement a centralized strategy.[59] The youthful Stockman, formerly a conservative member of the House, had detailed knowledge of government programs and finance, which he had developed when he fashioned Republican budget alternatives to Carter's budgets in the late 1970s. Impressed by Stockman's knowledge, Reagan appointed him director of the Office of Management and Budget (OMB), the agency that develops the president's budget. Meese, a conservative attorney who had been Reagan's attorney general in California, was given the authority to control domestic policy decisions within the White House as well as the flow of paper to Reagan. He was joined by James Baker, a clever negotiator who orchestrated policy compromises with Congress, and Michael Deaver, an expert in public relations.

Reagan, Stockman, Deaver, and Meese realized that their objective of securing cuts in social programs could not be accomplished if they gave the opposition time to organize, if they allowed recently appointed cabinet officials to advocate increased funds for their departments, or if they gave opponents of specific cuts the opportunity to join forces with opponents of other cuts. To obtain their support, Stockman, Meese, and Baker held a series of briefings with recently appointed cabinet officials, where they announced plans for major cuts in programs of their departments and urged them to be team players. Richard Schweiker, the newly appointed secretary of the Department of Health and Human Services, conceded to most of the proposed cuts in social programs, not only because of the pressure that was placed on him but also because he had converted to conservatism after a relatively liberal voting record as a senator.[60]

Stockman quickly conducted extensive consultations with many congressmen, as well, where he informed them of proposed cuts and sought their ideas for further cuts. He compiled in a large black book the growing list of proposed cuts, which quickly totaled $50 billion, a staggering and unprecedented sum. No one was allowed access to this book, which was stored in a safe in his office, but the repeated leaks of proposed cuts kept the opposition off guard and strengthened the impression that everyone would have to sacrifice. A siege atmosphere existed, where it seemed unpatriotic to oppose cuts in specific programs.[61]

The Democrats threatened to defeat Reagan's policies because they possessed a majority in the House, but Reagan remedied this situation by cultivating the support of conservative Southern Democrats who favored his tax, military, and budget-cutting policies. These renegade Southern Democrats, who were called boll weevils, repeatedly gave Reagan a majority of votes in the House when their votes were combined with Republican supporters. Their support of his policies was obtained by consulting with them and by giving some of them, such as Phillip Gramm of Texas, important roles as sponsors and designers of legislation. When House Democrats learned that boll weevils might defect to Reagan, they were under even more pressure to capitulate to Reagan's policies since they knew they could be outvoted by the Reagan coalition of Republicans and boll weevils.[62]

## The Triumph of Conservatism

Reagan's strategy led to three major victories for conservatives in the summer of 1981: Budget cuts were achieved through passage of the Omnibus Budget Reconciliation Act (OBRA) in July, tax cuts were enacted in August, and increases in defense spending were made final in the fall.

It is difficult under ordinary conditions for a president to control the budgetary process since numerous congressional committees can override his budgetary suggestions in the lengthy budgeting process. We do not provide a detailed account of the budgetary maneuvering in the spring, summer, and fall of 1981 because its complex and technical details fall beyond the purview of our discussion. Suffice it to say that David Stockman became the orchestrator of administration policy as he literally "camped out" in the Congress, arranged coalitions of Republicans and boll weevils, outmaneuvered liberal Democrats, and made extensive use of Reagan's popularity and the mass media to obtain enactment of OBRA, tax cuts, and increases in defense spending.

OBRA made deep cuts in social programs and eliminated fifty-seven social programs by folding them into seven block grants, entitled social services; community services; alcohol, drug abuse, and mental health services; maternal and child health services; community development services; primary health services; and preventive health services.[63] Creating block grants allowed Reagan to cut social spending for those programs within the block grants since the funds allocated to the grants were considerably less than had been allocated to the individual programs.

Reagan achieved another victory in August when the largest tax cut since the end of World War II was enacted. It made substantial reductions in taxes of individuals and made even larger cuts in the taxes of many corporations. It markedly increased economic inequality by granting larger tax cuts to affluent persons than to middle- and working-class Americans—and coincided with sharp cuts in social programs for the poor. The boll weevils and Republicans were joined by many Democrats who had initially planned to contest the tax cuts but who feared retaliation from voters.[64]

Reagan also succeeded in obtaining the huge increases in defense spending that he had so fervently sought. With the defense increases in place, Reagan had obtained the counterrevolution that he had espoused since the early 1950s —tax cuts, social-spending reductions, and defense increases.

When characterizing the nature of Reagan's policy successes in 1981, it is important to reiterate that, though he cut the funding associated with many programs that help low-income persons, he chose not to include in his cuts big-ticket social programs with large middle-class constituencies, such as Medicare and Social Security. In subsequent years of his presidency, he similarly chose to exclude these programs from his cuts. Indeed, one commentator calls Reagan the "guns *and* butter president" rather than the "guns versus butter president" because aggregate social spending continued to rise as well as defense spending.[65] He chose to make this strategic concession partly because his aides had calculated that Congress, including many Democrats, would not accede to his increased spending on military programs if he also sought to cut these middle-class programs.

## OBRA, Tax Reductions, and Deregulation

A host of conservative policies were contained within the complex tangle of the OBRA legislation, which recommended budget cuts that totaled $40 billion for 1982 and an additional $50 billion by 1984. First, some programs were terminated—for example, CETA, the public service program for unemployed workers. Second, deep cuts were made in many means-tested programs. The extent of cuts in these programs that were used by low-income persons was deeply disturbing to many liberals — and Reagan relentlessly sought to cut these programs in succeeding years as well. All told, Reagan managed during his administration to cut AFDC by 17.4 percent, cutting 400,000 persons from the rolls. One million persons lost eligibility for food stamps when it suffered cuts of 14.3 percent. The Social Services Block Grant, which provided an array of services to poor people, was cut by 23.5 percent.[66] The cuts in the housing programs of the Department of Housing and Urban Development reduced funding for low- and moderate-income housing from $33.5 billion in 1981 to $14 billion in 1987, or a cut of 57 percent.[67]

Third, indirect methods of cutting expenditures were enacted in OBRA. Since Reagan believed that social programs should address only the needs of truly needy persons, he hoped to reduce the number of able-bodied persons who received welfare and other benefits.[68] His solution was to lower the eligibility levels for food stamps, state AFDC programs, and unemployment insurance. He also eliminated work-incentive payments in the AFDC program so that many working women could no longer receive welfare benefits, even if they were beneath official poverty lines. AFDC rolls were cut dramatically by this policy, but it was ironic that an administration that wanted to encourage, even require, work for welfare recipients had provided a disincentive to work by forcing many women working in low-wage jobs to return to welfare rolls.[69]

If OBRA dramatically reduced benefits and services directed at low-income persons, Reagan's tax legislation increased the gap between poor- and moderate-income persons and relatively affluent persons. The Economic Recovery Tax Act that passed the Congress in August 1981 provided for 20 percent cuts in the income taxes of most Americans, spread over three years, and a major reduction in corporate taxes.[70] But these cuts were highly inequitable. Between 1981 and 1985, for example, the combined tax rates for the lowest one-fifth of the population went from 8.4 to 10.6 percent (or $137 in additional taxes per payer), whereas the tax rate of persons in the top one-fifth declined from 27.3 to 24 percent (or tax reductions of $2,531 per payer). These tax increases were even more onerous on poor persons because their *pretax* income declined during the decade as so many of them worked in low-paid service jobs rather than in unionized, industrial jobs.[71] The tax legislation was also a decisive blow to the principle of progressive taxation that liberals had traditionally championed because it gave larger tax breaks to rich people than to poor people. Further, tax credits that were given in 1973 to low-income persons who earned less than $5,600 were not indexed; their value had been seriously eroded by the inflation of the 1970s.[72]

Reagan issued an executive order in 1981 that gave OMB the duty of reviewing government regulations to delete those that were not demonstrated to be cost effective, and a cabinet-level Task Force on Regulatory Relief, chaired by Vice President George Bush, was established. The number of federal regulations was reduced from 90,000 to 76,000 between 1980 and 1984. To the consternation of some liberals, the administration drastically reduced regulations of the EEOC, OSHA, and many categorical programs so that key civil rights and other provisions were deleted.[73] Reagan severely curtailed the effectiveness of OSHA, the EEOC, and the Department of Labor's Office of Contract Compliance Programs. He cut their staffs, delegated many monitoring functions to states, sought to enforce affirmative action only when proof had been first obtained of discrimination by employers, and limited affirmative action monitoring to very large corporations. Reagan appointed officials who did not favor affirmative action to the top echelons of these regulatory agencies, such as Clarence Thomas to head the EEOC. Moreover, he appointed Clarence Pendleton to direct the Civil Rights Commission; Pendleton used his position to fight the principle of affirmative action.[74]

## Reagan's Loss of Momentum

It seemed in September 1981 that the Reagan counterrevolution would continue unabated for years to come, but he did not achieve striking policy successes during the remainder of his first term for a number of reasons. A split developed within the administration between two factions.[75] One group, headed by David Stockman and James Baker, feared that the federal deficit would continue to grow uncontrollably unless taxes were increased, further cuts were made in social spending, and reductions were made in defense spending. Another group, which included supply-side economists, were adamantly against tax increases, which they feared would jeopardize economic growth. They believed that sufficient economic growth would be generated by the 1981 tax cuts to produce additional tax revenues to ease the federal deficit. Some of them were so confident in this prediction that they did not believe further deep cuts in social programs were needed.

Stockman had embraced tax reduction policies uneasily during the early and middle 1980s because he feared massive increases in the federal deficit, but he advocated delaying or reducing tax reductions in the summer of 1981.[76] In interviews with a journalist friend during the summer and fall of 1981, which were published in an article in December 1981, he admitted that top officials in the administration had tinkered with economic models to make it appear as if federal deficits would not be exacerbated by the tax cuts, and he alleged that some officials in the administration had used supply-side theory as a convenient rationale for giving huge tax concessions to affluent persons and corporations.[77] Supply-siders were also furious with Stockman and Baker for not protesting the tight-money policy of the Federal Reserve Board, which had been devised by its chairman to drive down the

extraordinary inflation that plagued the nation since they feared that this policy would create a recession that would discredit supply-side policies. Some of them even believed that Stockman wanted a recession to discredit them.[78]

Both sides in this titanic struggle within the administration were convinced of the rightness of their cause and attributed evil intentions to opponents. Reagan resisted pleas by Stockman and Baker to increase taxes, to the delight of supply-siders. When he finally assented by spring 1982 to a large tax increase known as the Tax Equity and Responsibility Act (TEFRA), which took away some of the massive tax concessions that had been given to corporations in 1981, some supply-side officials left the administration.[79] Rumors circulated of dissension among Meese, Deaver, and Baker. Meanwhile, many persons increasingly wondered whether anyone was in charge at the White House because Reagan appeared to lack understanding of policy issues.[80]

Reagan's momentum was slowed as well by a deep recession, which began in 1981 and extended into 1983. Unemployment rose to double-digit figures and was particularly harmful to racial minorities, teenagers, and women. It contributed to growing doubts about the administration's economic policies, and contributed as well to the growing federal deficit since government tax revenues decreased as economic activity slackened.[81] By the end of fiscal year 1984, the cumulative deficits in the Reagan administration had surpassed the cumulative deficits of all preceding American presidents; indeed, some commentators feared the United States would be reduced to the status of many third-world nations, such as Mexico and Brazil, which found their economic growth impeded by the size of interest payments on their national debts.

The recession made many persons more aware of the plight of poor persons, who suffered from unemployment and the cuts in means-tested social programs. National media ran extended stories about increases in rates of poverty in the nation, the growing inequality between rich and poor Americans, and pockets of unemployment that existed in places like Youngstown and Cleveland, Ohio, where basic industries such as steel had closed plants in response to foreign competition.[82] Congress became restive, as well, because of the lack of equity in administration policies. Reagan had declared virtually all the entitlement programs off bounds for cuts, but he proposed further cuts of means-tested programs for the poor. His tax policies had led to windfall gains for many corporations and affluent persons. The charge that Reagan lacked compassion appeared to be gathering strength in 1982 and 1983 because of the cumulative effects of his budget-cutting and tax policies, as well as his fiscal and monetary policy, which had contributed to the recession.[83]

Many congressmen also believed they had been manipulated by the White House and by Stockman during budget and tax deliberations in 1981. Should the director of the Office of Management and Budget, they asked, personally orchestrate budget objectives and goals of the Congress? Some congressmen believed that they had been betrayed by the White House; although Stockman had implied in 1981 that the OBRA cuts would suffice, he proposed further deep cuts in late 1981 and in succeeding years. Was it fair for Reagan, some asked, to indirectly force the Congress to make cuts in social programs by reducing government revenues both by slashing taxes and by dramatically increasing military spending? Not a few congressmen resented Reagan's frequent use of television and radio to urge the public to pressure Congress to enact his policies.[84]

Whereas many Democrats had capitulated to Reagan's blitzkrieg in 1981, they were more willing to resist Reagan's policies during the remainder of his first term. Since the recession made their constituents more concerned about unemployment than about inflation, it was easier for them to resist Reagan's cuts. Reagan found it more difficult to outvote regular Democrats with a coalition of boll weevils and Republicans when the Democrats gained a number of House seats in congressional elections of 1982. Indeed, some liberal Republicans, known as gypsy moths, sided with Democrats against many spending cuts. Though still in disarray, the Democrats held their ground against further cuts in hopes that they could defeat Reagan in 1984.

## Social Security, Job Training, and Medicare Policies

Reagan's policy successes during the remainder of his first term were negligible though he was able to obtain additional cuts in social programs, made major changes in the Social Security program and Medicare, and created his own job-training legislation.

Stockman had hoped from the outset to include Social Security and Medicare in the budget cuts since they constituted a large portion of domestic spending. When he became further concerned about deficits, Stockman pushed the president to rescind the minimum Social Security benefit that was given to persons, such as elderly nuns, who had not paid into the trust fund during their working years. Stockman also sought to institute a penalty for persons who sought early retirement benefits. A storm of political protest greeted these proposals when the president made them public. Democrats accused him of reneging on his pledge to exempt the Social Security program from budget cuts, and many Republicans dissociated themselves from policies that they believed could be politically disastrous. The proposals were defeated by a vote of 96 to 0 by the Senate in 1981.[85]

Reagan and most legislators realized, however, that changes had to be made in Social Security since benefit outlays continued to exceed revenues from payroll deductions despite sharp increases in payroll taxes that had been made by President Carter. To deflect controversy from himself, Reagan appointed a blue-ribbon task force that recommended that the option to take

Social Security benefits at age 62 be rescinded and that benefits be delayed until persons reached age 68. It also recommended that a substantial portion of the Social Security benefits of retired persons whose earnings exceeded $20,000, whether from work or investments, be taxed, with ensuing revenues to be returned to the trust fund. To decrease the size of reductions in general benefits, many politicians supported the taxation of benefits of affluent persons, a policy that partially offset the regressive nature of Social Security payroll taxes.[86] The recommendations received bipartisan support and were enacted in 1983.

Reagan also encountered a funding emergency in Part A of the Medicare program, whose benefit outlays for hospital bills had increased faster than payroll tax revenues. Federal Medicare expenditures had increased from $15.2 billion in 1970 to $38.3 billion in 1980 because of the aging of the population, the increasing use of technology, and the failure of government authorities to prevent doctors and hospitals from charging excessive fees and providing unnecessary treatments.[87] Reagan's advisors developed an indirect method of restraining costs of Medicare. To place pressure on hospitals to discharge patients as soon as possible and to prevent them from charging excessive fees, federal Medicare authorities established national levels of payment for 467 specific diagnoses or "diagnostic-related groups" (DRGs). Thus, federal authorities paid hospitals an established fee for all patients who were admitted for appendectomies, no matter how long they remained in the hospital or whether they developed complications. The policy led to some decrease in health expenditures by 1986, but critics argued that this reimbursement approach created additional problems. Would not many hospitals try to discharge patients prematurely—or serve only those patients who were not likely to develop complications? Would not affluent persons purchase insurance to finance supplemental services so that, once again, public policy would create a two-tiered system of health care? The formula

also appeared to favor the growing network of for-profit hospitals that primarily served those middle- and upper-class clientele who are least likely to experience medical complications.[88]

Federal authorities also wanted to contain the increasing costs of Medicaid, whose combined federal and state funding had increased from $10.9 billion in 1970 to $25.4 billion in 1980. They cut the federal share of Medicaid funding in the OBRA legislation and offered incentives to states to reduce the rates of growth of Medicaid. They encouraged states to offer Medicaid contracts only to those hospitals and clinics that offered low bids so that Medicaid patients found that they could use even fewer providers than were previously available.[89]

The health care system was characterized in 1986 by increasing competition and turmoil. Some easing of the rate of price increases for medical care had occurred by the middle of the decade, but basic flaws in American medicine, such as its excessive use of technology and absence of preventive care, were still not addressed by the American medical system.[90] Critics lamented continuing inequities in American medicine. Roughly thirty million Americans lacked any health insurance or eligibility to the means-tested Medicaid program or access to the age-tested Medicare programs. Millions of Medicaid patients could obtain treatment only in inner-city clinics, where physicians were often foreign-born and lacked privileges in area hospitals.[91]

Federal authorities had not developed adequate policies to help elderly patients with chronic health-care problems. Medicare was intended to help elderly persons with acute conditions, so many elderly persons soon exhausted it (and their private insurance) and had to deplete their assets to obtain eligibility for the means-tested Medicaid program, which covered ongoing costs of convalescent homes, nursing homes, and home health care. Medicaid authorities had, in turn, developed confusing and poorly monitored policies in federal and state arenas to regulate nursing home care and to fund community-based care of frail and elderly persons. Medicare and Medicaid authorities, as well as private insurance companies, had commissioned a series of experiments in the 1980s to test various community-based methods of helping frail elderly persons, but no comprehensive national policy had been developed by the late 1980s.[92] Perhaps the most serious health problem of the 1980s was the emergence of the Acquired Immune Deficiency Syndrome (AIDS), which we discuss in more detail later.[93]

Reagan was determined to terminate the CETA program because he believed its subsidy of tens of thousands of public service jobs in public and not-for-profit agencies interfered with private job markets. After slashing its funds, Reagan finally abolished it in favor of his own program, the Job Training Partnership Act (JTPA), enacted in 1982. The federal government gave funds with relatively few restrictions to states, which in turn, funded local private industry councils (PICS). PICS, made up of business, agency, and government officials, awarded contracts to job placement agencies and to local industries, which received a fee for each person that they placed with private business. Critics contended, however, that the training and reimbursement policies of JTPA made it irrelevant to the needs of many low-income persons since placement agencies often were reimbursed only for successful placements. The failure of JTPA to provide training and day-care subsidies to placement agencies, businesses, or trainees made it impossible for many women and low-income persons to use the program.[94]

Reagan had folded fifty-seven categorical programs in 1981 into seven block grants. In 1982, he proposed to reduce the federal role in social welfare much futher by offering to undertake complete federal financing and administration of Medicaid if the states carried full costs and responsibility for AFDC, food stamps, and forty-three other programs. To attract the support of governors, he offered to cede to local units a limited amount of federal gasoline and cigarette excise taxes. The proposed swap was defeated, however, for several reasons. Although Reagan claimed that he did not want to short-change local units of government, astute analysts computed that the scheme would lead local units of government to suffer large net losses in revenue. As in the case of the block grants in OBRA, Reagan could not resist the impulse to couple defederalization with budget cuts. Officials in industrialized states in the Midwest and New England, which had particularly high expenses for welfare, believed that their states would benefit from defederalization far less than sunbelt states because they lacked oil, coal, and gas production, as well as the high rates of economic growth, to provide them with sufficient resources to address social needs.[95] Many state officials were disinclined to support the scheme because they were angered by the turmoil that earlier Reagan administration cuts had caused in their budgets. Reductions in federal funding of social programs had meant that local authorities had to assume additional expenses at the very time when popular tax revolts had led to sharp reductions in local taxes. Few federal legislators desired to carry defederalization further since they derived political support from federal programs.

Indeed, it can be argued that the Reagan years reduced *both* federal and state budgets to chaos. The huge deficits at the federal level meant that congressional officials devoted more time to the budget process than to other, more pressing domestic issues. Moreover, the deficits placed extraordinary pressure on programs for low-income persons, as we have noted. The budgets of many states rose sharply in the 1980s as states sought to address "a wave of family dissolution, homelessness, AIDS, drug and crack babies" as well as costs on immigration from abroad, increased costs of prisons, remarkable increases in costs of Medicaid and AFDC, and a doubling of spending on education by states—all during a decade when federal aid went from $110 billion in 1978, in inflation-adjusted dollars, to $88 billion in 1982 and only back up to $96 billion by 1990 (see Figure 11.1). Indeed, when AFDC and portions of the Medicaid program

**FIGURE 11.1** • *Homelessness became a major national problem in the 1980s*

*Source:* Library of Congress

are not considered, federal aid to the states fell by one-third during the 1980s.[96] Under the pressure of these escalating social costs and when coupled with federal cuts, many local jurisdictions had serious budget deficits.

## Moral Reforms

The Moral Majority had hoped that Reagan would take strong action to stop abortions, to attack pornography, to allow prayer in the public schools, and to provide tax concessions for tuition payments for children in private schools, but their confidence in him was premature. Reagan knew that these issues, like temperance in the nineteenth century and in the 1920s, were divisive. The demand for tax concessions for the tuition costs of private schools was widely viewed as public underwriting of educational segregation. Many women opposed the development of a constitutional amendment to override the 1973 Supreme Court decision that had declared state laws prohibiting abortion during the first trimester to be unconstitutional. Many persons in both parties opposed federal legislation or a constitutional amendment to allow school prayer in schools, and civil libertarians stoutly resisted federal laws to outlaw pornography. Reagan feared that personal identification with these divisive issues would jeopardize his other budget-cutting, tax, and deregulatory legislation.[97] Correspondingly, he voiced support for moral reforms but did not invest time or resources in them.

Meese became Reagan's emissary to leaders of the Moral Majority and tried to placate them.

Disappointed by Reagan's inaction, the Moral Majority nevertheless had notable victories. The Congress continued to disallow use of Medicaid funds for abortion and cut funds for family planning, which the Moral Majority believed fostered promiscuity. The Justice Department advocated supportive rulings from the courts with respect to pornography, school prayer, and other cases though it received few favorable rulings. A Presidential Commission on Pornography requested national censorship of magazines like *Playboy* in 1986. The Supreme Court upheld a Georgia statute that declared oral sex between consenting adults to be illegal.

The Moral Majority and its allies also developed expertise in targeting liberal legislators in election campaigns. They supported conservative opponents with vast media, advertising, mailing, and door-to-door campaigns that sought to tarnish the reputations of liberal candidates, who were variously called murderers (of fetuses), supporters of pornography, and atheists. Participation by the Moral Majority and its allies in campaigns often allowed conservative candidates to take the high road by not personally engaging in these tactics while nonetheless encouraging character assassination by the moral crusaders. These tactics contributed to the defeat of a number of liberal legislators who were in close races.[98]

But the nation was hardly embracing the tenets of the Moral Majority. Courts often ruled against them in school prayer, pornography, and abortion cases. Their tactics in political campaigns sometimes caused a sympathy vote for liberal candidates. Many persons wondered whether a secular and urban society would truly accept the ideas of persons who, like temperance crusaders in earlier periods, sought to impose their moral standards on others.[99]

 ## STALEMATE AND SCANDAL

### The Election of 1984

Reagan relished the opportunity to face Walter Mondale, the front-runner among Democratic contenders in 1984, since Mondale could easily be associated with the unpopular Carter and with unions and liberalism. After some vacillation, Reagan's resolve to run again was strengthened by improvement in the nation's economy following the recession of 1983.[100]

The election campaign in 1984 was a rerun of the 1980 campaign. When many major Democratic candidates opposed one another in the presidential primaries, the unity of the Democratic party was dissolved. Mondale obtained early endorsements from major trade unions as well as from professional groups, but his lead was severely challenged by Senator Gary Hart, who made Mondale appear politically vulnerable by winning decisive victories in key primaries. The Democratic party was deeply split.

Some Democrats, such as civil rights groups, many trade unions, intellectuals, and some mayors, continued to embrace federal social welfare programs and civil rights. Mondale felt most at home with this group, but even here he found his support contested by the African-American civil rights activist Jesse Jackson, who ran a determined campaign that mobilized unprecedented numbers of African-American voters. Other Democrats, such as Hart, were neoliberals who disdained major increases in social spending but favored federal incentives to industries to promote America's ability to compete with the Japanese.[101] Hart's support came mainly from young professionals, who had little knowledge of social reform movements in either the Great Depression or The Great Society.[102]

Mondale finally won the nomination of the divided Democratic party, but he did not overcome Reagan's lead in the polls. In a major victory for feminists, Mondale chose Geraldine

Ferraro as the vice-presidential candidate, but her family finances became a major campaign issue that slowed Mondale's momentum. Mondale tried to make the mounting budget deficit a campaign issue—he actually proposed major increases in federal taxes—but the issue was too abstract for most voters, who did not believe the deficits slowed economic growth and did not like his remedy of increased taxes. As front-runner, Reagan avoided substantive issues during most of the campaign and focused instead on his leadership and personal skills as well as his success in restoring economic growth. As in 1980, he targeted white voters and used code words like affirmative action and quotas to mobilize them against the Democrats. By holding his own during his second televised debate with Mondale, he deflected the charge that he was too old to be president. He won another landslide victory though the Democrats maintained their numbers in Congress.

## Reagan's Second Term

Unlike his victory in 1980, when Reagan made tax and budget reduction central themes, he won a personal victory in 1984 that did not constitute a mandate for specific policies. The American people, who tended to place themselves to the left of Reagan in public opinion polls, liked him as a person, believed him to be a decisive leader, and favored his buildup of the military but did not elect him to continue his assault on the welfare state. His mandateless victory, then, did not give him the momentum that he needed to expand his conservative policies of the first term.

The politics of his second term can best be described as a stalemate. As in this first term, Reagan tried to use the specter of the federal deficit to increase pressure on the Congress to reduce social spending. He proposed yet another series of massive increases in defense spending with his Strategic Defense Initiative (SDI), a space-based, laser-guided antimissile system for which appropriate technology had not yet been developed. Reagan proposed to spend $1 trillion on this venture over a decade, and the program quickly became a priority of defense spending. Congressional legislators balked at his proposals to cut domestic spending, however, and even made some modest increases in some programs. Entitlements remained out of bounds for cuts though Reagan tried indirectly to cut them by proposing major increases in consumer fees for services subsidized by Medicare.

In this stalemated atmosphere, an unlikely coalition in Congress enacted legislation to address the unprecedented federal deficits, which had continued to increase. The Balanced Budget and Emergency Deficit Control Act, commonly known as the Gramm-Rudman-Hollings Act, was enacted by Congress in 1985. Many congressmen were furious that Reagan proposed neither tax increases nor cuts in military spending to alleviate the deficit, so they assented to a measure that required across-the-board cuts in domestic and military programs if the budget did not meet specified spending reductions in coming years that would eventually lead to a balanced budget. But this measure hardly solved the deficit problem since it implied that *spending* rather than the combination of inadequate *revenues* (from taxes) and large military budgets was the basic problem. It was this combination of tax cuts and increases in military spending that had, in 1981, led to the budget deficits, but few politicians wanted to propose tax increases even though American tax rates had plummeted far lower than any Western industrialized nation. Sharp decreases in military spending were proposed by a few legislators, but most politicians were hesitant to cut the defense budget when it funded projects in their constituencies. Many commentators doubted that Congress would actually bring the budget into balance even with the enactment of Gramm-Rudman-Hollings.

Tax reform became a central issue in Reagan's second term and eclipsed deficit reduction in congressional deliberations. It was finally enacted in 1986 after complicated political maneuvering. It achieved the laudable goal of simplifying federal taxes by decreasing the number of tax brackets and loopholes, vastly increased corporate taxes, and took roughly six million low-wage earners from the tax rolls. But it also repudiated the liberal belief that the federal tax system should be progressive since it reduced the top tax bracket of affluent Americans to a modest 33 percent, which was not much higher than taxes paid by middle- and working-class Americans. The tax reforms did not generate considerably more revenues than the old tax system, so the federal deficit was not reduced, and insufficient federal revenues existed to fund social programs.[103]

Social reformers could nonetheless count several modest victories during Reagan's second term. The denial of disability payments to disabled persons under the SSI program, which had often been arbitrary and unwarranted during Reagan's first term, was challenged by several court rulings and resulted in restoration of benefits in thousands of cases. The Department of Health and Human Services was forced to concede that many persons with mental disabilities, such as schizophrenia, could not work and required ongoing assistance from the federal government.[104] The Family Support Act of 1988 provided training funds, as well as child care funds, for projects by various states to help AFDC recipients enter the labor force though many critics doubted if the program was sufficiently robust to make much difference. Perhaps most important, Congress managed to fend off Reagan's continuing demands for further cuts in many social programs, even if funding for programs that helped poor people had not recovered from cuts earlier in the decade.

## PASSING THE TORCH: FROM REAGAN TO BUSH

It was, some commentators have argued, the last campaign of the cold war when George Bush, who had been Reagan's vice president, battled Michael Dukakis for the presidency in 1988.[105] Both candidates believed that the party that could attract blue-collar and white voters to its side would win the election. It was the quintessential public-relations campaign, with both candidates guided by advertising and marketing experts who fashioned their television advertisements.

Both candidates tried to depict themselves as tough on crime, as patriotic, and as believers in a strong defense. Bush sought to depict Dukakis as soft on crime by use of an advertisement that argued that he had inadvisedly released an African-American prisoner (Willie Horton) from jail. He accused Dukakis of being "liberal," a charge that in the conservative era of the 1980s seemed akin to the stigma attached to "communism" in the early 1950s! Dukakis, in turn,

argued he would battle crime and drugs—and even resorted to riding in a tank to show that he would maintain a strong defense establishment. Social issues, such as poverty, homelessness, and AIDS, were hardly discussed during most of the campaign as the candidates emphasized their credentials with respect to crime, patriotism, and defense.

When it finally became clear that Bush was leading in the public opinion polls, Dukakis belatedly decided to develop more traditional Democratic themes, such as social reform, but his newly found liberalism came too late to have a decided effect. Nor was the American public, which had been lulled to complacency by the Reagan administration, in a mood for fundamental changes in domestic or international arenas. George Bush was elected by an overwhelming majority, but the Democrats retained control of both houses of Congress.

It was unclear when Bush took office how he

would use his victory because, unlike Reagan in 1980, he had not developed a clear agenda. It soon became clear, however, that Bush essentially continued the central themes of the Reagan administration of large military spending and resistance to increases in taxes. As former head of the Central Intelligence Agency and ambassador to China and to the United Nations, Bush was preoccupied with foreign policy during most of his first term — so domestic issues received extraordinarily scant attention from Bush despite campaign pledges to be the education president, the environmental president, and the president who would resolve the widespread usage of drugs by Americans. Even in the wake of the dissolution of the Soviet empire from 1990 onward, Bush was loath to markedly reduce funds for the American military establishment, which continued to absorb about $300 billion a year. Moreover, Bush was constrained by a campaign pledge not to raise new taxes. Although Bush was not harshly against social spending, like Reagan, and although he assented to increases in social spending far greater than had occurred in the Reagan years, he was largely passive on domestic matters and freely used his veto to stymie an array of measures that were proposed by Democrats.[106]

Caught in this fiscal bind, preoccupied with foreign affairs, and possessing a conservative ideology that was strongly enforced by John Sununu, his chief of staff until mid-1991, Bush offered few social initiatives that were backed up with funding. The Bush administration, which also encountered a Democratic Congress, was marked by the same curious combination of policies as the Reagan administration: deficits, massive defense budgets, and absence of dramatic social reform initiatives yet maintenance of almost all the existing programs of the American welfare state.

## SOCIAL POLICIES OF THE BUSH ADMINISTRATION

### Social Spending and the Politics of the Budget

As had been true during much of the Reagan administration, the fate of social policy was considerably shaped during the annual budget process when Congress and the executive branch determined what fraction of the budget to allocate to defense and social spending sectors. Recall that Reagan's strategy to markedly reduce federal social spending by massively increasing the federal deficit (by lowering taxes and increasing defense spending) had been only partially successful since overall social spending had increased though many programs for poor people had found their funding decreased. Congressmen who favored retention of the American welfare state were, in effect, able to obtain their preferences in the heated budget negotiations of the period while Reagan was able to retain his tax and military preferences.[107]

This budgetary stalemate continued into the Bush administration. No less than Reagan, Bush was committed to the notion that the United States should maintain a worldwide military presence and large conventional and strategic forces. Like Reagan, he was committed to not raising taxes, as illustrated by his often-repeated pledge in 1988: "Read my lips, no new taxes." Unlike Reagan, however, Bush was less able to counter increases in domestic spending because the Democrats controlled both houses of Congress and because he lacked some of Reagan's ideological fervor against federal programs. So the budget stalemate continued with its huge deficits, but social spending rose at a much higher rate than in the Reagan administration.[108]

Social reformers were hardly satisfied, however, with these gains in social spending, particularly in the wake of international developments in Eastern Europe and the Soviet Union. In the wake of concessions made to them by Soviet leader Mikhail Gorbachev, and with the assertion of their rights, Eastern European states obtained greater independence from the Soviet Union. Moreover, the Soviet Union rapidly disintegrated, leading to a historic decision by leaders of its many republics to dissolve it in 1991.

Some social reformers perceived this thawing of the cold war as a remarkable, unprecedented opportunity to recast the federal budget. Why not, they had increasingly argued by early 1990, declare a "peace dividend" to transfer as much as $150 billion annually from the military budget to the domestic-spending budget? Why not pull American troops from Europe and Asia, dramatically reduce American nuclear forces, and increasingly rely on multinational forces and the United Nations to keep the peace?[109]

A budgetary battle ensued in 1990 that rivaled the ferocity and duration of the budget battle of 1981, when Reagan had obtained the tax cuts, spending reductions, and military increases at the inception of his presidency. Many legislators wanted to markedly decrease military spending and increase social spending, but the Bush administration was adamantly opposed to reducing military spending. Some legislators who wanted to reduce the budget deficit pushed to increase federal taxes, but Bush was under great pressure from conservatives to remain true to his pledge in 1988 not to raise taxes.

In a complex and extended set of negotiations between the Congress and the administration, which culminated in a budget summit of 1990, an uneasy compromise was fashioned that gave something to everyone but that avoided fundamental changes in the American federal budget. Under pressure to reduce the deficit, Bush conceded to some new taxes. The current military and domestic-spending shares of the budget were preserved, but the overall budget

was to be reduced incrementally in coming years by placing caps or limits on the aggregate social-spending and military sectors of the budget.[110] To prevent "raiding" of the military budget by social reformers, the agreement stipulated that reductions in defense spending could *not* be used to increase social spending. In effect, the agreement was a standoff to delay reconsideration of budget priorities until 1993—conveniently after the next presidential elections, when it was widely predicted that "all hell would break loose" when members of both parties would battle to shape the new configuration of the federal budget. Would the military budget be severely cut, and if so, would the savings be used for social programs or merely to reduce the vast deficit or even to fund new tax cuts?

Many social reformers were dismayed by the budget agreement of 1990. It made an immediate peace dividend impossible since it disallowed using reductions in defense spending for social spending. It required legislators to take funds from existing social programs whenever they proposed new social programs. Moreover, the budget agreement was quickly succeeded in early 1991 by the war with Iraq, a conflict that quieted (for the moment) discussion of a peace dividend.

But it was clear that the budget settlement of 1990 was merely the first salvo in budget controversies that would extend through the 1990s and that would profoundly shape the course of the American welfare state. Nor were these budget debates likely to be amicable. The conservative wing of the Republican party, which had been bolstered and emboldened during the Reagan era, was so infuriated when Bush agreed to a modest increase in taxes in 1990 that they pressured him in 1992 to apologize for his decision and to pledge never again to raise taxes. Having worshipped Reagan, the right wing of the Republican party remained distrustful of Bush and pressured him to veto civil rights and other social reform measures and to resist efforts by liberals to "raid" the defense budget.[111] The Pentagon, the vast network of military contractors who existed in the districts of every federal politician, and politicians who retained a cold-war definition of America's international role would likely resist major cuts in defense spending. Social reformers would find it difficult to obtain new initiatives as long as the deficit remained and since many Americans believed in the veracity of contentions of conservatives that "you can't solve problems by throwing money at them" or "the federal government is the cause, not the solution, of problems."

## Domestic Reforms

Few social reform initiatives were enacted from 1989 through 1992 because of budget deficits, the conservatism of Bush and his aides, and the preoccupation of the president with international affairs. We discuss several civil rights initiatives and child care legislation in the ensuing discussion of outgroups in the era of Reagan and Bush.

We can characterize Bush's policies in the areas of education, antidrug programs, and welfare as expressing "lofty goals" but committing few resources and little presidential attention.[112] Regarding substance abuse, for example, Bush committed new funds to interdiction of drugs from abroad but failed to emphasize treatment or prevention programs. His education policy emphasized procedural reforms, such as development of national tests and proposals to test voucher systems, but little direct assistance to local schools that often labored under severe shortages of resources.

Bush seemed oblivious of many other domestic issues. His plan for reform of the national health system, unveiled in 1992, proposed to use tax deductions and credits to help low-income persons purchase private health insurance, but the suggested levels of these tax concessions were far beneath the likely health needs of low- and moderate-income Americans. He took little interest in the homeless population and took few steps to address the housing needs of millions of low-income Americans who often could not obtain decent housing or had to pay 50 percent or more of their modest income for it.[113] Nor did Bush attend to the problem of poverty despite the increasing economic inequality that had developed in the United States during the 1980s.

Events in May 1992 reminded Americans that life remained brutish in American inner cities despite the development of various social programs in the decades after the riots in many cities during the 1960s. An African American by the name of Rodney King had been viciously beaten by Los Angeles policemen in the spring of 1991, but unlike many other instances of police brutality, the incident was recorded by a bystander on videotape. Most Americans—and virtually all African Americans—saw the tape on national television, which depicted eighty seconds of merciless beating of King by a group of policemen. After King brought charges against the policemen, an extended trial took place in spring 1992. Most Americans were astonished to hear that a verdict of "not guilty" was rendered by an all-white jury, but African Americans in Los Angeles reacted with a fury that led to three days of burning and looting of many business establishments in Los Angeles and its environs. (Some Latinos participated in the riots as well.)

Caught by surprise, the Bush administration initially blamed the riots on the social programs of The Great Society, but when it became clear that this simplistic assertion was not widely accepted, engaged in complex negotiations with the Congress to develop a program to provide various job-training, housing, recreation, and other programs for the inner cities and for Los Angeles that would cost several billion dollars.

Many critics of the emerging legislation suggested that it was grossly inadequate. Led by the mayors of many major cities, for example, about 150,000 people marched on the nation's Capitol on May 17, 1992, to demand massive increases in federal aid to the cities and for social programs to provide health, housing, and job-training programs for inner-city residents. They argued that spending for the military increased by $579 billion during the 1980s while federal funds to cities and states were cut by $78 billion.

As the first term of the Bush administration neared conclusion, the Los Angeles riots raised important questions about the likely response of white, suburban Americans, who constituted a majority of the nation's voters. Separated from racial minorities of the inner cities, would they be happy with law-and-order strategies and symbolic remedies, particularly in light of long-standing efforts by politicians—and particularly the Republican party—to polarize white voters from racial minorities? Or would they realize that their own well-being, as the burning of some shopping malls in suburban areas in the Los Angeles riots grimly suggested, hinged on efforts to bring inner-city residents into the economic mainstream of American society? The early response of politicians of both parties was not encouraging, but this dramatic indicator of social distress in American cities had the potential of invigorating a debate about national priorities during a period when international tensions had markedly decreased.

## OUTGROUPS IN THE ERA OF REAGAN AND BUSH

Members of many outgroups were dismayed when Ronald Reagan became president in 1980 because they knew that the conservative movement possessed policy preferences that could jeopardize gains that they had made in the preceding two decades. The twin leaders of the conservative movement, Ronald Reagan and Barry Goldwater, had, after all, both strongly opposed the enactment of the Civil Rights Acts of 1964 and 1965 on grounds that states should be charged with such matters. Conservatives tended to oppose programs that sought to equalize conditions between groups in the population, such as between racial minorities and Caucasians, on grounds that they represented "reverse discrimination."

Members of outgroups feared, as well, that Reagan (and then Bush) would pack the Supreme Court, as well as lower federal courts, with appointees who would overrule many of the decisions of the Warren and Burger Courts that had supported civil rights, affirmative action, the right to choose abortions, and desegregation. Conservatives tended to take a "strict constructionist" approach to constitutional interpretation that required rulings to adhere to those preferences of the writers of the Constitution—hardly a hopeful doctrine when, as we noted in Chapter 3, the founders had legitimized slavery in many places in the Constitution and many contemporary social problems, such as abortion and affirmative action, were not widely recognized in colonial society. Conservatives often opposed the assertion of *group* rights and needs through class action suits on the basis of patterns of discrimination, thus restricting legal recourse only to instances when *individuals* could prove specific discriminatory actions had been taken against themselves by persons who *intended* to harm them. (Enormous gains in eradicating discrimination against women and racial minorities in employment had been obtained in the 1960s and 1970s through such class action suits.)[114]

Members of the various outgroups realized, even before his election, that Reagan would seek to diminish the size and roles of regulatory agencies such as the Equal Employment Opportunity Commission. Since these agencies enforced civil rights and related statutes, efforts to weaken them would jeopardize effective implementation of those statutes that survived court tests in the Reagan administrations.

And members of outgroups were acutely aware that the conservative movement had been in the forefront of efforts in the 1970s to oppose policies to further extend their rights. Conservatives had variously opposed the Equal Rights Amendment, local ordinances that gave gays and lesbians protections against discrimination in jobs, affirmative action, efforts to desegregate schools, and many other policies.[115]

Nor were they sanguine about the fate of many of the social programs that were particularly important to impoverished Americans, who constituted a large proportion of the African-American, Latino, and Native-American populations. Conservative politicians had sought throughout the 1970s to identify programs like AFDC, food stamps, public housing, and public employment with racial minorities in an effort to capitalize (and enflame) resentments from white citizens, so it was widely expected that an assault would be launched against these programs.

As if all these fears were not enough, many members of outgroups were aware that Reagan's likely tax and economic policies would be harmful to persons in lower economic strata. Supply-side economics, which was akin to the "trickle-down economics" of the 1920s, would give huge tax concessions to affluent persons while not necessarily lowering the taxes of poorer citizens. Strategies to induce economic growth in the economy would not likely include "bottom-up" approaches such as investing in the nation's infrastructure and schools or in training programs for its workers.

## Predictions Come True

The Reagan and Bush years constitute the largest redistribution of resources and rights *upward* in the nation's history. Though the welfare state remained intact and specific programs within it grew considerably from 1980 through 1992, the actual economic position of poor persons worsened owing to a deterioration of wages, *and* reductions in social benefits and services, *and* increases in taxes. The poor, as well as

many persons just above them on the economic ladder, were poorer not only in absolute dollars, when their economic resources are adjusted for inflation, but also compared to more affluent persons. Moreover, the hard-won gains of rights during the 1960s and 1970s, such as protections against job-related discrimination and the right to abortions, were in jeopardy because of the appointment of conservative justices to the Supreme Court and to lower courts.[116]

All the fears of members of outgroups were realized during the Reagan period, particularly during his first term when the Republicans controlled the Senate and often could muster a conservative majority in the House. Although Bush presented a more accommodating posture, his court appointments, as well as many of his policies, did not represent a fundamental departure from the politics of Reagan despite the ire of conservatives who were furious that Bush had made even modest tax increases and had signed a specific piece of civil rights legislation.

## Racial Minorities and the Poor

A good deal of evidence had appeared by 1992, assembled by an array of authors and studies, that showed that the economic position of the lowest quintile of citizens had eroded considerably during the tenure of Presidents Reagan and Bush.[117] The data implicated three factors.

1. With the loss of American industrial and unionized jobs during the 1970s and 1980s, increasing numbers of Americans found an erosion in the real value of their paychecks. Moreover, many companies cut their fringe benefits, such as health benefits, during these two decades—though many enterprises that employed people in the lowest quintile had never provided health benefits or provided only residual benefits.

2. The cuts in social benefits and services of the American welfare state, particularly ones targeted to poor persons, contributed

to their economic decline. We have already discussed extensive cuts in AFDC, food stamps, and public-housing programs. Moreover, poor persons had to pay higher fees in Medicaid, Medicare, and other social programs.

3. Although some concessions were made in certain tax provisions, such as a tax credit extended by the federal government to some working but poor persons, the overall tax rates of poor and working persons increased when payroll taxes for Social Security and Medicare are added to increases in the regular income tax.

This deterioration of the economic status of poor persons was matched by a deterioration of the economic status of persons in the second-lowest quintile.[118] As the two lowest quintiles suffered these losses, the two upper quintiles, and particularly the uppermost one, experienced economic gains. Indeed, 60 percent of the economic gains of the decade of the 1980s accrued to the top 1 percent of the population, that is, to persons earning more than $350,000 a year.[119] Viewed in this light, the Reagan and Bush years represented an economic counterrevolution that some persons feared could convert the United States to an economic structure increasingly akin to some third-world nations that had vast disparities between rich and poor persons, with a relatively small middle class—indeed, a social structure similar to the Gilded Age, which we discussed in Chapter 5.

Economic data do not fully describe the poor quality of life of many residents of inner-city neighborhoods where low-income African Americans, Latinos, and Native Americans lived. A full discussion of the predicaments of the low-income African-American population, as well as possible solutions, had not developed in the 1970s and 1980s; conservatives, who blamed the poor for causing their own demise, dominated policy discussions.[120]

However one assesses the causes of their poverty and whether or not one uses the term *under-class* to refer to them, indisputable evidence suggests that the problems of inner-city African-Americans, as well as Latinos and Native Americans, have become a major, national problem. We noted earlier in this chapter how pent-up frustrations of inner-city residents were manifested in the Los Angeles riots of May 1992. These segregated populations have extraordinary rates of poverty, drug usage, poor health, poor educational attainment, unemployment, homicides, and gang violence. Large numbers of low-income males are killed in violent encounters or are incarcerated. And the rates of single-headed families in these inner-city populations have markedly increased over the last twenty-five years.

As Peterson suggests, different theories exist to explain the social and economic problems of these segregated populations. Some persons contend that the welfare state has been inadequately developed so that it does not sufficiently help inner-city residents with economic, health, social-service, educational, and job-training remedies. Other people implicate cultural factors that prompt behaviors such as teenage pregnancy. Conservatives maintain that welfare and other programs provide "perverse incentives." Still others argue that the loss of industrial, unionized, and well-paying jobs in international competition has deprived relatively unskilled persons of employment or consigned them to service jobs that pay only the minimum wage.[121] The Reagan and Bush administrations, as well as presidential candidates in 1980, 1984, and 1988, displayed scant interest in these inner-city problems. Although the Los Angles riots of May 1992 suggested the need for sweeping social reforms to bring inner-city minorities into the economic mainstream, the palliatives that congressional leaders and the Bush administration discussed in the wake of the riots provided little assurance that most Americans wanted decisive action. And the huge federal deficits, as well as budget deficits in most states and major cities, meant that immediate funds were not available in a nation that was disinclined either to raise its taxes or to dramatically cut its defense spending.

Public opinion remained indifferent to a population that was largely unseen by the white, suburban populations who refrained from setting foot in these inner-city areas.

With the enactment of the Immigration Law of 1965 and succeeding legislation such as the 1975 Indochina Migration and Refugee Assistance Act and the 1980 Refugee Act, a large influx of immigrants came to the United States between 1965 and 1991 from Central America and Mexico and from Asian nations such as Vietnam, China, Laos, Thailand, India, Cambodia, South Korea, and the Philippines—whether to join relatives, escape political persecution, or seek better conditions. The influx was so large that the Asian-American population grew from one million in 1965 to five million in 1985; almost four times as many Asians entered the nation in this period as did between 1849 and 1965.[122] Though these immigrants settled disproportionately on the West Coast, large enclaves of them existed throughout the nation.

As might be expected with such a diverse population, generalizations about them are fraught with danger. Some of them were highly educated professionals and persons with sophisticated technical skills. Others gravitated to businesses. Refugees from Vietnam and Central America and the Caribbean, including boat people, represented diverse social backgrounds.

Even some entrants who possessed advanced skills found the adjustment difficult because of their inability to speak English, job discrimination, and social discrimination. About half those Vietnamese refugees who reside in California were on public assistance in 1990.[123] Some of the refugees suffered from mental trauma that stemmed from harrowing experiences in refugee camps and war zones. As with immigrants of preceding eras, tensions often developed between first-generation immigrants and their children, who quickly learned English and the mores of the dominant culture.

Advocates for refugees from political persecution from countries like El Salvador fought a determined battle to stop their deportation, whether through the courts, through hearings of the Immigration Service, or by offering them sanctuary in churches and homes.

The Civil Rights Act of 1991 was enacted after two years of negotiations between the Congress and the White House. The impetus for the legislation derived from a series of nine rulings by the conservative Supreme Court that called into question the principle of affirmative action as well as limited the ability of persons to seek remedies to alleged bias in the work place. In its decision in 1989 in *Wards Cove Packing Co.* v. *Atonio,* for example, the Court held that the burden of proof resided with an employee who held that a company's practices had an adverse impact on racial minorities, women, or other minorities; she or he had to prove that the practices did not serve a legitimate business purpose. The antidiscrimination provisions of the legislation applied both to governmental and private places of employment and reaffirmed the ability of employees to bring "disparate impact lawsuits" under Title VII of the Civil Rights Act of 1964, that is, lawsuits alleging that specific hiring or promotion decisions adversely affected women, racial minorities, or other minorities. The legislation also allowed workers to seek monetary damages in cases of alleged intentional discrimination.

## Gays and Lesbians

Having made some gains in obtaining their rights in the 1970s, the gay population was wholly unprepared for the worst medical catastrophe of modern times, the AIDS epidemic. Epidemiologists believe a gay airline steward, Gaetan Dugas, became infected and passed a mysterious disease that attacked the immune system to numerous sex partners in the early 1980s to trigger the American AIDS epidemic. Researchers at the National Centers for Disease Control perceived by spring 1982 that an epidemic had developed that had already killed 119 persons, but they did not know the cause of the disease and had not even assigned a name to it. But they had determined that it was concentrated in the gay, male population. When the virus that caused the disease was finally identified in early 1984 (officially designated the Human Immunodeficiency Virus, or HIV, in 1986), the horrific nature of the epidemic became clear. Transmitted by an exchange of fluids during sexual relations and with its early concentration in gay males, the disease threatened to become a sort of biologic genocide visited on an unsuspecting population.

Frantic efforts by the gay community to mobilize action to arrest the epidemic ensued. Edward Brandt, the assistant secretary for Health, who asked in early 1984 for the modest sum of $55 million to be spent on research to develop a blood test, a vaccine, and a cure, encountered indifference from the Reagan administration. The American Life Lobby, a conservative group, claimed that Brandt's plea to make AIDS a top priority of the Health Service was "an outrageous legitimization of a lifestyle repugnant to the vast majority of Americans."[124]

Researchers soon discovered by mid-1984 that the disease was also transmitted through blood transfusions, from intravenous use of drugs, by prostitutes, and by bisexuals to their spouses. Since drug usage with nonsterilized needles was disproportionately located in inner cities, the disease spread rapidly to African-American and Latino addicts.

Americans are prone to surges of interest in and indifference to specific social problems. Although the mass media had published many articles on the disease in 1983, coverage soon diminished despite the mounting deaths. The Reagan administration requested only $51 million for 1985—and many conservatives demanded that the confidentiality of blood testing for AIDS be compromised by reporting cases to public health departments despite widespread fears that this policy would lead to boycotts of the tests since victims of AIDS encountered virulent prejudice and discrimination in housing and

on jobs, as well as from insurance companies. Though congressional pressure pushed funding to $96 million in 1985, the Reagan administration sought to *reduce* the funding to $85.5 million in the ensuing year despite a prediction by government researchers that the epidemic could kill up to 50,000 persons (or the same number of fatalities as occurred during the Vietnam War) within a few years.[125] The gay community developed a massive education and self-help campaign to help victims of AIDS and to promote safe sex to prevent it, but they received scant assistance from the federal government. African-American and Latino communities proved less able to develop self-help campaigns partly because homosexuality was a stigmatized condition. The failure of governmental authorities to develop a determined preventive program in inner-city areas, thus consigning thousands of persons to death, was a national disgrace.

When it became known that Rock Hudson had AIDS in mid-1985 and with the development of a report by C. Everett Koop, the Surgeon General, in October 1986, government action increased markedly. But increases in funding were still sufficiently modest that gays, lesbians, and their allies repeatedly demonstrated in Washington, including a march of 600,000 persons in 1987. Widespread prejudice against the disease continued unabated as suggested by the failure to enact antidiscrimination laws in many states, opposition to providing addicts with sterilized needles, the decisions by many physicians not to treat persons who were HIV-positive, and continuing calls for mandatory reporting of persons who tested HIV-positive. Nor did President Bush demonstrate active interest in the issue.

As the epidemic neared the end of its first decade in the United States, the death toll exceeded 138,000 persons and was making rapid advances in heterosexual populations, particularly among intravenous drug users. (About one million persons were HIV-positive in May 1992.) The nation's disinclination to provide sex education and condoms to its youth had, moreover,

**FIGURE 11.2** • *A member of the AIDS activist group, Act Up, confronts Jerry Brown, a presidential candidate in 1992*

*Source: The New York Times*

slowed effective preventive programs. Although the public schools of New York City decided in 1991 to distribute condoms to high school students, most other school districts were not as enlightened. Nor did Americans develop public service announcements, such as were widely used in European countries, to promote safe sex. Activists hoped that the announcement by Magic Johnson in late 1991 that he was HIV-positive might finally force a massive prevention program (see Figure 11.2).

Though often preoccupied with AIDS, gay and lesbian activists also worked on many other fronts. They sought legislation in various states to outlaw job discrimination in the civil service, military, police and fire departments, and private markets; to outlaw housing discrimination; to allow same-sex couples to obtain access to Social Security, and job-related fringe benefits; to obtain the right to adopt children; to obtain custody and visitation rights; and to overturn antisodomy laws in twenty-six states.[126]

## From Disabled to ''Differently Abled'' Persons

Buoyed by the Rehabilitation Act of 1973, a robust movement of persons with disabilities evolved and mobilized behind an "independent living centers" movement. Wishing to shed traditional images of helplessness, some advocates favored the term *differently abled* to describe persons with handicapping conditions. A national network of local organizations received federal funding to provide an array of outreach, educational, and advocacy services with the intent of freeing persons from dependence on medical institutions and, when possible, use of government payments for nonworking disabled persons, whether under the means-tested SSI program or Social Security disability insurance (SSDI) for persons disabled on the job. With the use of technology and advocacy, they succeeded in increasing the employment of persons with chronic physical, developmental, and mental problems. Vast progress was made in making many public facilities accessible by way of ramps, elevators, and other aids and in obtaining special programs to help persons with conditions like dyslexia in educational programs. Even with these improvements, many persons with chronic conditions remained mired in poverty or lacked access to the latest technology. Equally important, persons with chronic problems often needed personal assistants to help them with chores, transportation, and other matters, but government programs, which largely focused on giving funds for survival needs, rarely provided these aids. Indeed, persons with chronic problems often encountered a dilemma: If they worked, their benefits were often taken from them, but their wages were so low that they could not survive without their benefits. Many disabled persons thus returned to their SSI or SSDI benefits rather than remaining in the work force.

Advocates obtained enactment of the Americans with Disabilities Act of 1990, which barred discrimination in the work place, housing, and public accommodations. (It provided far more detailed language than the Rehabilitation Act of 1973.) Though representing progress, activists feared that the government would confine itself to policing the rights of the differently abled rather than funding an array of services, such as personal aides, that they needed to become full-fledged members of society.[127]

## Women

As Faludi notes, a curious paradox emerged in the 1980s: The women's liberation movement was widely blamed for depriving women of their feminism, their traditional rights to custody and alimony, and their special protections from hazardous work—in effect, for being too militant and thus jeopardizing traditional rights—yet women remained underpaid, denied access to many kinds of jobs, subject to a "glass ceiling," and greatly underrepresented in political offices.[128] Unlike other nations, moreover, the United States lacked a family leave program, and more than 99 percent of American employers do not provide child care. Family planning services for the poor remained poorly funded, and the *Roe* v. *Wade* decision seemed vulnerable to new court rulings. The Anita Hill incident, where an African-American female law professor alleged that Clarence Thomas, an African-American nominee to the Supreme Court, had sexually harassed her when she had worked for him in the EEOC, radicalized many women who were offended that an all-male group of senators questioned Thomas in a weak and fumbling way.[129]

Women encountered major political opposition in the 1980s from conservatives. Far from insisting that males should assume larger roles in parenting, some spokespersons for the New Right openly advocated turning the clock back to 1954 with respect to women working, abortion rights, and women's rights. They fought the Equal Rights Amendment and even introduced the Family Protection Act in Congress in 1981, which sought to "eliminate federal laws supporting equal education, forbid 'intermingling of the sexes in any sport or other school-related activities'; require marriage and motherhood to be taught as the proper career for girls; deny federal funding to any school using textbooks portraying women in nontraditional roles . . . and ban federally funded legal aid for any woman seeking abortion counseling or a divorce.'[130]

Considerable backsliding occurred in the decade, such as reduced judicial appointments and fewer women in top policy positions. The Supreme Court narrowed women's rights in the *Webster* v. *Reproductive Health Services* decision in 1989 that allowed Missouri to make major new restrictions on abortion, the *Rust* v. *Sullivan* decision in 1991 that upheld regulations of the Reagan administration that prohibited federally funded clinics from counseling pregnant women about abortion, and various rulings attacking affirmative action and quotas. The labor force became even more gender segregated. In 1986, women earned on average 64 cents to every dollar earned by male workers, the same ratio that had existed thirty-one years earlier, in 1955. Efforts by the EEOC to vigorously litigate cases against large corporations that excluded women from entire categories of workers, such as exclusion of women from high-paying commission sales jobs, ebbed.

The crusade by the New Right against abortions illustrates the temper of the 1980s. Anti-abortion groups burned or bombed seventy-seven family planning clinics between 1977 and 1989. Eighty-five percent of counties in the nation did not provide abortion services by 1987, requiring many women to cross county or state boundaries. Medicaid funding had not been available for abortions since the mid-1970s, and only twelve states continued to fund abortions, requiring women to obtain funding from a small number of private agencies or from private insurance or personal funds. Muzzled by regulations, health providers that received federal funds could not even discuss reproductive alternatives with women—and sex-education classes funded by the Adolescent Family Life Act with-

held all information on abortion and birth control from students.[131]

The Democrats did not vigorously attack the Republicans' indifference to women's issues despite extensive alienation of women from the Republican party. Intimidated by the conservatives, they often reflected the antifemale bias of the decade, as did Michael Dukakis, when as the Democratic contender in 1988, he chose to be silent on women's issues.[132]

Women's groups and their allies were able to obtain child-care legislation in 1990 that channeled some funds to the states to fund child-care programs. A Family and Medical Leave Coalition of labor, senior citizens, and women's groups was able to move a family leave bill, which allowed men and women paid leave from work before and after the birth of a child, through the Senate in 1991 but failed to surmount conservative opposition that it represented an unfair obligation for corporations even though the policy had already been enacted in many industrialized nations.[133]

## Children

The well-being of children depends on the economic and social condition of their parents as well as on the kinds of health, educational, and social-service programs that society provides them. The score card was not impressive on either count. After declining in the 1960s and remaining stable in the 1970s, the rates of poverty among children and youth rose rapidly in the early 1980s to roughly 25 percent and then stabilized at these high rates for the rest of the decade. If roughly 15 percent of white children were poor in 1989, about 44 percent of African-American children and 36 percent of Latino children were poor. Falling earnings, low levels of AFDC and food stamps, and poor child-support enforcement contributed to this high rate.

The poverty of growing numbers of children was linked, as well, to the growth in the percentage of families that had only a single head of household. The term *feminization of poverty* was coined to describe the extent of poverty in female-headed households. If only 23 percent of all poor families were headed by women in 1959, this figure had risen to 52 percent by 1989. About 51 percent of children in families headed by a woman were poor in 1989 compared to only 10 percent in two-parent families. Such families had high rates of poverty because females tend to be in lower-paying work and single heads can draw on only a single source of wage income.[134] Ozawa asserts that more women had become single heads of household because of increasing rates of teenage pregnancy and increasing rates of divorce.[135]

The poverty of many children was coupled with inadequate policies to deal with an array of other problems that they encountered. Roughly 300,000 cocaine-addicted babies were born each year, and drug-treatment and prevention programs had failed to reach many teenagers who used drugs. Between 1965 and 1988, the arrest rate for violent crimes by 18-year-old males more than doubled, with rates particularly high in the lower economic class of both racial-minority and white populations. Homicides accounted for almost half of all deaths among young males. As Kozol documents in his book, *Savage Inequities*, the schools of poor children were overcrowded, lacked instructional aides, and often had worse teachers than more affluent districts.[136]

There were many indications that the child welfare system could not cope with the sheer number of children who were reported to be neglected or abused by their caregivers. In the wake of the enactment of the Adoption Assistance and Child Welfare Act of 1980, which gave funds to the states to hire more child welfare staff and required them to develop a "permanency plan" for all children removed from their natural homes, the numbers of children in foster care was almost halved in five years. But the number zoomed upward by 29 percent to about 360,000 children by 1991—and was predicted to exceed 500,000 children by the year 2000. Though

staff were added in many jurisdictions, acute shortages developed because of a 147 percent increase in reports of abused and neglected children between 1979 and 1989, for an astonishing total of 2.4 million reported cases in 1989.[137]

Children's advocates nonetheless gained a number of incremental policy victories in the 1980s and seemed on the verge of some additional ones in 1992. By securing more funding for the Education for All Handicapped Act of 1975, millions of disabled children were mainstreamed into the regular public schools. The Medicaid program was amended to include a program that gave one million low-income children preventive checkups. Despite its inadequate funding and implementation, the Adoption Assistance and Child Welfare Act led to better foster care for many children as well as higher rates of adoption and reunification with their natural families. Advocates succeeded in 1991 in getting Congress to agree to the principle that they would expand the Head Start Program to cover all children in coming years. Incremental increases had been obtained in the Earned Income Tax Credit in the 1980s—a means-tested program that gave to qualifying families a tax rebate—and Congress agreed to raise the credit so that the benefit would rise another 70 percent by 1994. (A family earning less than $10,730 could claim a tax refund of almost $1,000 in 1990.)

With passage of the Child Care and Development Block Grant in 1990, children's advocates finally obtained the first major, national child-care program since World War II. It channeled funds through the states for child-care services, administration, and staff training; though inadequately funded, it established a precedent that child care belonged within the purview of the federal government.

The AFDC program had been a highly controversial one since the mid-1960s when many citizens became alarmed at its rate of growth. But the benefits of this program, supposedly to help destitute heads of households and their children, had eroded during the 1970s and 1980s so that the grants of the median state were only 45 percent of the official poverty line in 1990, or only $367 a month for a family of three. Even when supplemented by food stamps and Medicaid, these resources were insufficient to meet the bare-bone needs of many families. When the Family Support Act of 1988 was enacted, people hoped that its job-training and child-care funds would allow many AFDC women to enter the labor market, but the act fell far short of its potential owing to inadequate funding at federal and state levels and the harsh realities of labor markets for relatively unskilled female workers who often could obtain only minimum-wage jobs that rendered them even poorer than had they remained on AFDC.

Incremental gains in addressing some social problems during the decade, then, were often offset by the rapid growth of other social problems, such as cocaine-addicted babies and huge increases in reported cases of child abuse and neglect, that current programs could not adequately address. A number of Americans urged the United States to emulate programs in Europe and Canada, such as parental leave, expanded child care, and children's allowances.[138]

## Aging Americans

Aging Americans appeared at first glance to have improved their condition in the 1970s and 1980s. Rates of poverty had plummeted in this population from 35 to 12.8 percent between 1959 and 1989. With the enactment of Medicare and the Older Americans Act in 1965, and with the enactment of SSI and the indexing of Social Security in the early 1970s, older people obtained medical services, social services, and resources that represented major innovations. Indeed, many commentators noted that a huge portion of the federal budget was devoted to older persons, including the 29.4 percent of the federal budget (or $341.4 billion) that was devoted to just two programs in 1990, Medicare and Social Security. Unlike poor Americans, elderly persons largely avoided the budget cuts of

the 1980s because Reagan (and then Bush) feared antagonizing this politically powerful group.[139]

But elderly persons had many serious problems of their own. Because consumer fees associated with Medicare were so high and so many services were not covered, elderly persons paid roughly 50 percent of their medical costs. Moreover, they paid upward of 50 percent of home health costs and long-term care costs since Medicare offered scant coverage to these services because of its focus on short-term and hospital-based care. Many older citizens had to divest themselves of their savings when they encountered catastrophic health conditions in order to be able to obtain medical funds from the means-tested Medicaid program.[140] Despite some day-treatment and other services for victims of Alzheimer's disease, which had become the fourth greatest killer of older persons by 1992, many older persons and their families were ravaged by the disease, both financially and in terms of scarce services.

As if these problems were not enough, older persons also encountered a strong movement in the 1980s that sought to cut social spending on older persons. Some persons, such as former Governor Richard Lamm of Colorado, argued that many funds spent on older Americans should be diverted to children since society would reap economic gains by making younger people more productive. Daniel Callahan, a prominent moral philosopher, contended that the United States should refuse heroic and expensive health remedies to all persons over the age of eighty, such as disallowing stays in intensive care units, so as to permit these funds to be spent on younger people. Others argued that lobby groups representing older persons, such as the American Association of Retired Persons, possessed such power that older citizens were able unfairly to obtain a disproportionate share of the public purse. In an era of deficits in federal and state budgets, many legislators feared making home health care and long-term care more available because of its likely costs.[141]

# The Homeless

Many social problems of the 1980s and 1990s cannot be described by referring to a single outgroup since persons affected by them came from several outgroups as well as the general population. Consider homelessness. As the 1980s began, most Americans would likely have associated homelessness with relatively small areas of cities, often known as skid row, where alcoholic persons resided. A public opinion poll in 1991 found that 54 percent of Americans reported they saw homeless people in their communities or on their way to work—and the Urban Institute estimated in 1987 that about 600,000 persons were homeless in the United States, including persons in shelters, using soup kitchens, and on the streets. Homeless people are a diverse population. When examining characteristics of homeless people in cities of more than 100,000, the Urban Institute concluded that about one-fifth of them had a history of mental hospitalization; about 15 percent are children; about 81 percent are male; about one-third had been patients in a detoxification, alcohol treatment, or drug treatment program; and about 29 percent of single men had served time in prison. These homeless people had an average monthly income of $135, or less than one-third of the federal poverty level, and half of them had not had a steady job in more than two years. Persons had been homeless for a median of ten months.[142]

The response of the federal and state governments to this problem in the Reagan and Bush administrations was half-hearted, at best. Most vexing to advocates for the homeless was the presidents' disinclination to publicly discuss the issue or for Democratic candidates in 1984 and 1988 to demand ameliorative policies. Congress enacted the Stewart B. McKinney Homeless Assistance Act of 1987, but it focused its resources on the construction costs for shelters and was burdened with bureaucratic delays in giving states funds. States and localities devoted considerable funds to the problem by the late 1980s and were particularly effective in meeting the emergency needs of those homeless people who used their shelters. But outreach programs to homeless people who avoided organized services and shelters, transitional programs to help homeless people obtain housing and jobs, and preventive programs to help people from becoming homeless were poorly articulated in most jurisdictions. Nor did most jurisdictions provide case management services to homeless persons, even in shelters. Absent high-level leadership from federal or state authorities, voluntary agencies, including missions, churches, neighborhood coalitions, and social agencies, often took the lead in providing services.[143]

As Rossi notes, it is easy when discussing the homeless to ignore the simple fact that "the essential and defining symptom of homelessness is lack of access to conventional housing." The stocks of inexpensive housing were depleted in the 1980s by rising rents, conversion of many apartments to condominiums, and the continuing destruction of low-income housing for urban renewal (particularly buildings with apartments for single persons).[144] We have already noted how the Reagan administration virtually ended many programs of the Department of Housing and Urban Development. Nor can we ignore the effects of deinstitutionalizing of the nation's mental hospitals from the early 1960s onward that, when coupled with stricter rules for involuntary commitments, placed hundreds of thousands of mental patients on the streets without adequate services. And the ranks of the homeless included increasing numbers of individuals and families who could not afford housing because of the loss of industrialized, unionized employment in the United States in the 1980s.

# The Erosion of Rights

A prime objective of Ronald Reagan and George Bush was to transform the federal judiciary into an instrument of conservative ideology. They succeeded to an extent unrivaled in modern times. With the appointment of Justice Clarence

Thomas in late 1991, the number of "liberals" on the Supreme Court had been reduced to two justices (Blackmun and Stevens). Under the leadership of William Rehnquist, who succeeded Warren Burger in 1986, the Court seemed poised to stress conservative goals in the 1990–1991 session when it overturned a number of precedents and contemplated "shattering the Warren and Burger legacies . . . in the areas of abortion, separation of church and state, affirmative action, and free speech."[145] Moreover, Reagan and Bush had appointed by 1992 more than half of all the 828 federal appeals and court judges in the United States—judges who had usually been given "ideological litmus tests" to be certain they would support conservative positions on controversial issues.[146]

It was too soon to tell precisely what directions the Supreme Court would take, but advocates for women and racial minorities feared a rollback in many policies that had been sanctioned by the Warren or Burger Court or by Congress in specific legislation. Advocates realized that they would need to secure new legislation to offset adverse rulings by the Court; thus, gay activists, chagrined that the Supreme Court upheld in 1986 a Georgia statute that declared sodomy to be illegal, responded by pressuring state legislatures to overturn similar statutes. Advocates for the disabled enacted the Americans with Disabilities Act in 1990 after the Court had declined to cover handicapped people under existing civil rights statutes. Civil rights advocates were able to obtain the enactment of the Civil Rights Act of 1991 that overturned ten prior Court decisions that had restricted the rights of employees to sue against bias and to obtain money damages in the case of harassment based on sex, religion, or disability.[147]

The ideological divergence between Congress and the Supreme Court suggested that Congress would be revisiting issues during the next decades that they *thought* they had resolved before the Court declared various of their statutes to be unconstitutional. In effect, the rulings of the Supreme Court would often provide a major portion of the legislative agenda of the Congress—a frustrating and time-consuming process that was reminiscent of the conservative Court in the era of Franklin Roosevelt that finally led Roosevelt to try to "pack" the Court with liberal justices. An interesting example of the Court's rulings occurred in March 1992 when, by a 7 to 2 vote, the Court ruled that federal judges cannot force states to improve their care of abused and neglected children under the 1980 Adoption Assistance and Child Care Act on grounds that the legislation did not specifically say that persons can sue in federal court. Outraged by this ruling, children's advocates faced the task of amending the legislation in Congress.[148]

## THE SOCIAL WORK PROFESSION

The profession of social work proved remarkably resilient during the decades after The Great Society despite the conservative attack on the kinds of social programs that employed social workers. Schools of social work at the graduate level held their own during this period, as did undergraduate programs. Membership of the National Association of Social Workers (NASW) exceeded 100,000 persons by the mid-1980s, with roughly nine-tenths of them having a master of social work—and more than 200,000 persons in the work force had either a bachelor or master of social work. About 40 percent of NASW members were employed in not-for-profit agencies, 45 percent in public agencies (mostly at state, county, or local levels), and the balance in for-profit agencies. Large numbers of social workers were employed in health, mental health, and child-and-family sectors. Though most social workers held direct-service positions, many of them held administrative posts, and some worked in community-organizing and policy-making positions as well.

The profession had successes and failures in political battles to preserve its access to jobs. On the positive side, the profession succeeded in obtaining licensing in many states, which in turn, often led to the inclusion of social work in reimbursement by private insurance companies and Medicare. A number of public positions in agencies like child welfare, however, were "declassified" in the 1970s and 1980s in particular jurisdictions —that is, a requirement of local authorities was removed that a social work degree was necessary to hold specific kinds of jobs. But a number of public agencies actively recruited trained social workers by the early 1990s in fields such as protective services for abused children, and many positions in the large not-for-profit sector required a social work degree or even a social work license. The inexorable expansion of some social problems and the development of new ones, such as AIDS, substance abuse, homelessness, and Alzheimer's disease, created new openings for a field whose technologies could easily be adapted to an array of social needs.

Perhaps the most controversial issue concerned the role of private practice in the profession. Although most social workers were salaried, many of them had private practices on the side, and many of them aspired to full-time private practice for its monetary rewards and the autonomy it offered. Critics feared that these private practitioners could draw the profession from its role in serving relatively poor persons and in serving as an advocate for powerless groups.[149] Indeed, some private practitioners sought to avoid the title "social worker" for titles like "psychotherapist" though "clinical social worker" was also used.

It was too soon to tell precisely what effects the emergence of private practice would have on the profession. On the one hand, private practice, particularly as it avoided the title of "social work" and sought to disengage the profession from agency practice and powerless groups, *was* a threat to the reformist mission of the profession. Private practice, however, did not appear to have fundamentally changed the field by the early 1990s; indeed, its impact seemed less inhibitive of a broad-based mission for the field than psychiatric social work in the 1950s, when the profession seemed more congruent with the conservatism of that era than the conservatism of the 1980s. Nor was it even clear that most persons who aspired to private practice rejected the mission of the profession since more than a few of them wished to avoid the stifling work requirements of some social agencies, particularly public ones where workloads had often become excessive.[150]

We cannot use the positions of NASW as the only measure, but they suggest that social work had not veered to the right in the 1970s and 1980s. NASW in the 1980s, in its conferences, policy positions, and newsletter, frequently attacked the conservative positions of the Reagan and Bush administrations, assertively sought national health insurance and an array of social reforms, and actively participated in coalitions with advocacy groups such as the Children's Defense Fund. In 1975, it established a political action arm, called PACE, that backed candidates who supported social reforms. Official policies that NASW's delegate assembly adopted over a period of twenty years suggest the field took an array of progressive, even radical, positions on subjects as diverse as AIDS, economic policy, long-term care, and the rights of children.[151]

Nor does an examination of the work of theorists in social work suggest that the profession veered to the right in the 1980s. An ecological perspective that required social workers to examine human functioning in a broad context that included environmental and policy issues remained intact. Many theorists emphasized "diversity," that is, making social work services relevant to a range of oppressed populations, including African Americans, Latinos, Native Americans, women, gays, lesbians, and the poor. Macro practitioners often remained on the fringes in many schools, but they maintained a determined existence and were strongly represented in national conferences of the Council on Social Work Education.[152]

By the same token, social work could hardly be called a radical presence in a society with enormous unmet needs. *All* professions are influenced by "conservatizing forces" such as funding from government and business elites; referrals from other professionals; and recruits who come from white, middle, and upper

classes. As Wenocur and Reisch established when discussing its origins, social work is no exception—and Rothman makes a similar point about the profession in the contemporary period.[153] But social work remained *relatively* more reformist than other professions such as law, medicine, and business, whose members tend to be more conservative than social workers and whose professional associations did not usually take controversial positions on current issues.[154] Social work should not be placed on a pedestal, but it should not be accused of forsaking its reformist heritage, either.

## THE POLITICAL ECONOMY OF REFORM IN THE ERA OF REAGAN AND BUSH

The Reagan and Bush era was the first major era of conservatism since the 1950s. The ascendancy to power of these presidents required a shift in the votes of white Americans, particularly northern white Catholics and southern whites in lower and moderate income brackets during presidential elections. Skillfully using rhetoric that flamed racial animosities and social tensions, Reagan and Bush cultivated these white voters and secured their support in pivotal elections. They appealed, as well, to Americans who wanted political and social stability after the numerous traumas of the 1960s and 1970s, such as Vietnam, Watergate, and stagflation.

Compared to many other nations, America developed a welfare state belatedly. Even the spending increases of the 1960s and 1970s left Americans behind many industrialized nations in levels of governmental social spending when expressed as a percentage of the gross national product, and these belated welfare achievements did not obviate a host of serious problems.

The Reagan administration sought to arrest social welfare spending just as programs established in the 1960s and 1970s had begun to address a variety of needs of social problems.

Reagan led a conservative counterrevolution that substantially reduced domestic spending, massively increased military spending, and drastically reduced the policy roles of the federal government. Conservatives were only partially successful in obtaining their policy goals, however, because many legislators and citizens did not share their conservative goals and the Democrats controlled the House of Representatives throughout the Reagan and Bush years and the Senate from 1986 onward.

Some historians are likely to criticize the self-serving and inequitable nature of many of Reagan's policies. Far from cutting all social programs, the administration cut primarily those used by low-income Americans. Tax cuts in 1981 enriched affluent Americans and corporations far more than other Americans; the tax reform of 1986 drastically reduced the official tax rates of affluent Americans. The defense industry reaped unprecedented peacetime profits, even without considering the trillion-dollar SDI initiative. Affirmative action policies were attacked by the president, the Justice Department, and the director of the Civil Rights Commission. By increasing deficit spending, Reagan was asking future generations to fund his defense and tax-reduction policies. The administration hoped to foster conservative policies long after the 1980s by devising tax, deficit, and defense policies that would create a shortage of resources for social spending.

Crippled by international scandals in Iran and Nicaragua in late 1987, and reduced to lame-duck status, Reagan had lost political momentum by the midpoint of his second term. Democrats once again controlled both houses of Congress after the 1986 elections.

Although President George Bush was more responsive to some social problems than Reagan, and although his rhetoric was often more diplomatic, his policies did not fundamentally differ from those of his predecessor. Partly because the Democrats had larger majorities in the House and Senate under Bush than Reagan, Bush *had* to accept larger spending increases in many social programs.

Political uncertainties appeared by 1992, however, that suggested that conservative hege-mony might one day end. Many Americans had descended from the middle class to lesser economic status as unionized jobs were replaced (if at all) by lesser paying service jobs. The easing of the cold war made it harder for conservatives to use patriotism to rally their constituency by invoking the threat of Communism. Members of the various outgroups had reasons for wanting more liberal administrations as they fought adverse court rulings and cuts in various programs.

Many persons wondered, however, whether the nation could find resources (in light of its budget deficits) and the will to attack festering social problems that it encountered as it moved toward the twenty-first century. Problems such as lack of medical insurance, homelessness, AIDS, growing economic inequality, poor schools, poverty among racial minorities in inner cities, family violence, the feminization of poverty, and gang warfare cried out for solutions and creative programs, but burdened systems of human services were inadequate to these tasks.

 **END NOTES**

1. George Nash, *The Conservative Intellectual Movement in America Since 1945* (New York: Basic Books, 1976), pp. 253–295.

2. Geoffrey Hodgson, *America in Our Time* (Garden City, N.Y.: Doubleday, 1976), pp. 473–478.

3. Craig Roberts, *The Supply-Side Revolution: An Insider's Account of Policy-Making in Washington* (Cambridge, Mass.: Harvard University Press, 1984), p. 18.

4. Robert Kuttner, *Revolt of the Haves: Tax Rebellions and Hard Times* (New York: Simon & Schuster, 1980), pp. 349–350.

5. James Reichley, *Conservatives in an Age of Change: The Nixon and Ford Administrations* (Washington, D.C.: Brookings Institution, 1981), pp. 387–390.

6. Pete Hamill, "The Revolt of the White Lower-Middle Class." In Louise Howe, ed., *The White Majority: Between Poverty and Affluence* (New York: Random House, 1970), pp. 10–22.

7. T. R. Reid, "Kennedy." In David Broder et al., ed., *The Pursuit of the Presidency, 1980* (Washington, D.C.: Berkeley Books, 1980), pp. 68, 77; Martin Schram, "Carter." In Broder, ed., *The Pursuit,* p. 116.

8. Kevin Phillips, *Post-Conservative America: People, Politics, and Ideology in a Time of Crisis* (New York: Vintage Books, 1983), pp. 53–63.

9. Susan Littwin, *The Postponed Generation: Why America's Grown-Up Kids Are Growing Up Later* (New York: Morrow, 1986), pp. 18–25, 191–213.

10. William Leuchtenberg, *In the Shadow of FDR: From Harry Truman to Ronald Reagan* (Ithaca, N.Y.: Cornell University Press, 1983), pp. 1–160.

11. Thomas Edsall, *Chain Reaction: The Impact of Race, Rights, and Taxes on American Politics* (New York: W.W. Norton, 1991), pp. ix–7, 174.

12. Nash, *The Conservative Intellectual Movement,* pp. 36–56.

13. *Ibid.,* pp. 291–295.

14. Milton Friedman, *Capitalism and Freedom* (Chicago: University of Chicago Press, 1962).

15. Martin Anderson, *The Federal Bulldozer: A Critical Analysis of Urban Renewal, 1949–1962* (Cambridge, Mass.: M.I.T. Press, 1964).

16. Peter Steinfels, *The Neoconservatives: The Men Who Are Changing America's Politics* (New York: Simon & Schuster, 1979), pp. 45–46, 108–160.

17. Edsall, *Chain Reaction,* p. 131.

18. Phillips, *Post-Conservative America,* pp. 180–192.

19. Samuel Hill and Dennis Owen, *The New Religious Political Right in America* (Nashville, Tenn.: Abingdon, 1982), pp. 51–76.

20. Robert Dallek, *Ronald Reagan: The Politics of Symbolism* (Cambridge, Mass.: Harvard University Press, 1984), pp. 13–18.

21. Lou Cannon, *Reagan* (New York: Putnam's, 1982), pp. 91–97.

22. *Ibid.,* pp. 147–165.

23. Laurence Barrett, *Gambling with History: Reagan in the White House* (New York: Penguin Books, 1983), pp. 44–63; Rowland Evans and Robert Novak, *The Reagan Revolution* (New York: Dutton, 1981), pp. 91–95.

24. Dallek, *Ronald Reagan,* p. 34.

25. Barrett, *Gambling with History,* pp. 426–427.

26. See the views of a top aide, Martin Anderson, in *Welfare: The Political Economy of Welfare Reform in the United States* (Palo Alto, Calif.: Hoover Institution, 1978), pp. 87–132.

27. Lou Cannon, *President Reagan: The Role of A Lifetime* (New York: Simon & Schuster, 1991), pp. 206–231.

28. Haynes Johnson, *Sleepwalking Through History: America in the Reagan Years* (New York: W.W. Norton, 1991), pp. 65–76.

29. Cannon, *Reagan,* pp. 176–184.

30. Johnson, *Sleepwalking Through History,* p. 87.

31. *Ibid.,* p. 197.

32. Evans and Novak, *The Reagan Revolution,* pp. 84–111.

33. Roberts, *The Supply-Side Revolution,* pp. 24–25.

34. Barrett, *Gambling with History,* p. 236.

35. Evans and Novak, *The Reagan Revolution,* pp. 95–96.

36. Roberts, *The Supply-Side Revolution,* pp. 12–13.

37. William Greider, "Republicans." In Broder, ed., *The Pursuit,* pp. 163, 168–169.

38. Roberts, *The Supply-Side Revolution,* pp. 69–88.

39. Cannon, *Reagan,* p. 325.

40. David Stockman, *The Triumph of Politics* (New York: Harper & Row, 1986), pp. 56–57.

41. Cannon, *Reagan,* pp. 273–278.

42. Johnson, *Sleepwalking Through History,* p. 131.

43. Edsall, *Chain Reaction,* p. 206.

44. Broder, ed., *The Pursuit,* p. 341.

45. Richard Cohen, "They're Still a Majority," *National Journal,* 13 (January 31, 1981), 189–191.

46. *Ibid.*

47. Barrett, *Gambling with History,* pp. 146–147.

48. Stockman, *The Triumph of Politics,* pp. 8–9, 11.

49. Timothy Clark, "Want to Know Where the Budget Ax Will Fall? Read Stockman's Big Black Book," *National Journal,* 13 (February 14, 1981), 274–281.

50. "Party Switchers," *National Journal,* 13 (June 20, 1981), 1095.

51. Robert Samuelson, "Reagan's Bet," *National Journal,* 13 (February 21, 1981), 301–307.

52. Evans and Novak, *The Reagan Revolution,* pp. 109–110.

53. *The New York Times* (July 11), 1985), part A, p. 14.

54. *Ibid.,* pp. 109–110.

55. Stockman, *The Triumph of Politics,* pp. 269–298.

56. *Ibid.,* p. 92; Barrett, *Gambling with History,* pp. 144–145.

57. Jack Meyer, "Budget Cuts in the Reagan Administration: A Question of Fairness." In D. Lee Bawden, ed., *The Social Contract Revisited* (Washington, D.C.: Urban Institute, 1984), pp. 33–68.

58. Clark, "Want to Know Where the Budget Ax Will Fall?" pp. 274–281.

59. Barrett, *Gambling with History,* pp. 94–106, 187–198.

60. *Ibid.,* p. 71.

61. Clark, "Want to Know Where the Budget Ax Will Fall?" pp. 274–281.

62. Timothy Clark et al., "Congress Works a Minor Revolution—Making Cuts To Meet Its Budget Goals," *National Journal,* 13 (June 20, 1981), 1114–1115.

63. Richard Cohen, "For Spending Cuts, Only the Beginning," *National Journal,* 13 (August 8, 1981), 1414.

64. Barrett, *Gambling with History,* pp. 164–170.

65. Cannon, *President Reagan,* p. 279.

66. Edsall, *Chain Reaction,* p. 192.

67. Johnson, *Sleepwalking Through History,* p. 181.

68. Anderson, *Welfare,* pp. 43–58.

69. Blanche Bernstein, "Welfare Dependency." In Bawden, ed., *The Social Contract Revisited,* p. 138.

70. Robert Samuelson, "For the Economy, Unanswered Questions," *National Journal,* 13 (August 8, 1981), 1407.

71. Edsall, *Chain Reaction,* pp. 159–161.

72. W. Joseph Heffernan, *Introduction to Social Welfare Policy* (Itasca, Ill.: Peacock, 1979), pp. 179–180.

73. Murray Weidenbaum, "Regulatory Reform." In George Eads and Michael Fix, eds., *The Reagan Regulatory Strategy* (Washington, D.C.: Urban Institute, 1984), pp. 15–41.

74. Timothy Clark, "Affirmative Action May Fall Victim to Reagan's Regulatory Reform Drive," *National Journal,* 13 (August 11, 1981), 1248–1252.

75. Roberts, *The Supply-Side Revolution,* pp. 226–245; Stockman, *The Triumph of Politics,* pp. 320–323.

76. Roberts, *The Supply-Side Revolution,* pp. 165–179.

77. William Greider, "The Education of David Stockman," *Atlantic Monthly,* 248 (December 1981), 27–54.

78. *Ibid.,* pp. 197–212.

79. Barrett, *Gambling with History,* p. 139.

80. Alexander Haig, *Caveat: Realism, Reagan, and Foreign Policy* (New York: Macmillan, 1984), pp. 303–316.

81. Charles Stone and Isabel Sawhill, *Economic Policy in the Reagan Years* (Washington, D.C.: Urban Institute, 1984), pp. 22–25.

82. "Reagan's Polarized America," *Newsweek* (April 5, 1982), 20–28.

83. Barrett, *Gambling with History,* pp. 401–402.

84. *Ibid.,* pp. 348–349.

85. Stockman, *The Triumph of Politics,* pp. 192–193.

86. Timothy Clark, "Social Security Ball in Your Court, Greenspan Panel Tells Reagan, O'Neill," *National Journal,* 14 (November 20, 1982), 1889–1991.

87. Paul Starr, *The Social Transformation of American Medicine* (New York: Basic Books, 1984), pp. 383–388.

88. Linda Demkovitch, "Hospitals That Provide for the Poor Are Reeling from Uncompensated Costs," *National Journal,* 16 (November 24, 1984), 2245–2249.

89. *Ibid.*

90. Joseph Califano, *America's Health Care Revolution: Who Lives? Who Dies? Who Pays?* (New York: Random House, 1986), pp. 11–36, 58–68.

91. Dorothy Kupcha, "Medicaid: In or Out of the Mainstream," *National Journal,* 10 (May 1979), 181–183.

92. Nancy Eustis, Jay Greenberg, and Sharon Patten, *Long-Term Care for Older Persons: A Policy Perspective* (Monterey, Calif.: Brooks/Cole, 1984), pp. 1–7.

93. Marlene Cimons, "AIDS Shock Wave Due To Sweep U.S.," *Los Angeles Times* (December 7, 1986), 1, 35.

94. Richard Corrigan, "Private Sector on the Spot as It Prepares To Take Over Job Training," *National Journal,* 15 (April 30, 1983), 894–897.

95. Bruce Jansson, *Theory and Practice of Social Welfare Policy: Analysis, Processes, and Current Issues* (Belmont, Calif.: Wadsworth, 1984), pp. 133–134.

96. Neil Pierce, "The Myth of the Spendthrift States," *National Journal* (August 3, 1991), 1941.

97. Barrett, *Gambling with History*, p. 61.

98. Hill and Owen, *The New Religious Political Right*, pp. 72–76.

99. Peter Goldman and Tony Full, *The Quest for the Presidency, 1984* (New York: Bantam Books, 1985), pp. 35–36.

100. TRB, "Neoliberals, Paleoliberals," *New Republic* (April 9, 1984), 6, 41.

101. Goldman and Full, *The Quest for the Presidency*, pp. 48–58.

102. *Ibid.*, pp. 368–374.

103. Jeffrey Birnbaum and Alan Murray, *Showdown at Gucchi Gulch* (New York: Vintage Books, 1988), pp. 284–291.

104. Donald Chambers, "Policy Weaknesses and Political Opportunities," *Social Service Review*, 59:1 (March 1985), 1–17.

105. Sidney Blumenthal, *Pledging Allegiance: The Last Campaign of the Cold War* (New York: Harper-Collins, 1990).

106. Burt Solomon, "Grading Bush," *National Journal* (July 8, 1991), 1331–1335.

107. Cannon, *President Reagan*, p. 279.

108. See, for example, the series of articles on the peace dividend in *The New York Times* in 1991, such as its editorial on May 9, 1990, part A, p. 30.

109. Barbara Sinclair, "Governing Unheroically (and Sometimes Unappetizingly): Bush and the 101st Congress." In Colin Campbell and Bert Rockman, *The Bush Presidency: First Assessments* (Chatham, N.J.: Chatham House Publishers, 1991), pp. 174–181.

110. *Ibid.*, pp. 174–181.

111. Bert Rockman, "Leadership Style of George Bush." In Campbell and Rockman, *The Bush Presidency*, p. 7.

112. Paul Quirk, "Domestic Policy: Divided Government and Cooperative Presidential Leadership." In Campbell and Rockman, *The Bush Presidency*, p. 82.

113. Solomon, "Grading Bush," p. 1335.

114. Edsall, *Chain Reaction*, p. 186.

115. *Ibid.*, pp. 99–115.

116. *Ibid.*, pp. 192–197, 215–255.

117. See, for example, U.S. House Ways and Means Committee, *The 1990 Green Book* (Washington, D.C.: Government Printing Office, June 5, 1990), pp. 1106–1107; Kevin Phillips, *Rich and Poor: Wealth and the American Electorate in the Reagan Aftermath* (New York: Random House, 1990), pp. 8–25, 74–91; Edsall, *Chain Reaction*, pp. 160–161.

118. Phillips, *Rich and Poor*, pp. 8–25, 74–91.

119. *New York Times*, March, 15, 1992, p. 1.

120. William Wilson, "Cycles of Deprivation and the Underclass Debate," *Social Service Review*, 59 (December 1985), 541–559.

121. Paul Peterson, "The Poverty Paradox." In Christopher Jencks and Paul Peterson, *The Urban Underclass* (Washington, D.C.: Brookings Institution, 1990), pp. 9–16.

122. Ronald Takaki, *Strangers from a Different Shore* (Boston: Little, Brown, 1989), p. 420.

123. Sucheng Chen, *Asian Americans: An Interpretive History* (Boston: Twayne Publishers, 1991), p. 170.

124. Randy Shilts, *And the Band Played On* (New York: St. Martins Press, 1987), p. 456.

125. *Ibid.*, p. 525.

126. *San Francisco Examiner* (June 5, 1989), 12.

127. Julie Kosterlitz, "Enablement," *National Journal* (August 31, 1991), 2093.

128. Susan Faludi, *Backlash: The Undeclared War Against American Women* (New York: Crown Publishers, 1991), pp. 59–72.

129. *Ibid.*, pp. xiii–xxiii.

130. *Ibid.*, p. 236.

131. *Ibid.*, pp. 412–421.

132. *Ibid.*, pp. 273–275.

133. Richard Cohen, "Family Leave Fight Perplexes Advocates," *National Journal* (November 23, 1991), 2878.

134. Children's Defense Fund, *State of America's Children* (Washington, D.C., 1991), pp. 24–25.

135. Martha Ozawa, "Introduction: An Overview." In Martha Ozawa, ed., *Women's Life Cycle and Economic Security* (New York: Greenwood Press, 1989), pp. 2–8.

136. Jonathan Kozol, *Savage Inequities* (New York: Crown Publishers, 1991).

137. Children's Defense Fund, *State of America's Children*, p. 122.

138. Sheila Kamerman and Alfred Kahn, "Social Policy and Children in the United States and Europe." In John Palmer, Timothy Smeeding, and Barbara Torrey, eds., *The Vulnerable* (Washington, D.C.: Urban Institute Press, 1988), pp. 351–380.

139. Robert Binstock, "The Politics and Economics of Aging and Diversity." In Scott Bass, Elizabeth Kutza, and Fernando Torres-Gil, eds., *Diversity in Aging: Challenges Facing Planners and Policy Makers in the 1990s* (Glenview, Ill.: Scott, Foresman, 1990), pp. 73–77.

140. Jack Meyer and Marilyn Moon, "Health Care Spending on Children and the Elderly." In Palmer, Smeeding, and Torrey, eds., *The Vulnerable*, p. 180.

141. Binstock, "Politics and Economics of Aging," pp. 77–82.

142. Martha Burt and Barbara Cohen, *America's Homeless: Numbers, Characteristics, and Programs that Serve Them* (Washington, D.C.: Urban Institute Press, 1989), pp. 2–4, 27–31.

143. *Ibid.*, pp. 141–161.

144. Peter Rossi, *Down and Out in America: The Origins of Homelessness* (Chicago: University of Chicago Press, 1989), pp. 181–184.

145. Joan Biskupic, *The Supreme Court Yearbook, 1990–1991* (Washington, D.C.: Congressional Quarterly, Inc., 1992), p. 10.

146. W. John Moore, "Righting the Courts," *National Journal* (January 25, 1992), 200.

147. W. John Moore, "In Whose Court?" *National Journal* (October 5, 1991), 2397.

148. Linda Greenhouse, "Justices Bar Using Civil Rights Suits to Enforce U.S. Child Welfare Law," *New York Times* (March 26, 1992), A15.

149. Harry Specht, "Social Work and the Popular Psychotherapies," *Social Service Review* 64 (September 1990), 345–357.

150. Amy Butler, "The Attractiveness of Private Practice," *Journal of Social Work Education* (Winter 1992), 47–60.

151. *Social Work Speaks: NASW Policy Statements, 2nd ed.* (Silver Spring, Md.: National Association of Social Workers, 1991).

152. Bruce Jansson, *Social Welfare Policy: From Theory to Practice* (Belmont, Calif.: Wadsworth, 1990), pp. 8–11.

153. Stanley Wenocur and Michael Reisch, *From Charity to Enterprise: The Development of American Social Work in a Market Economy* (Urbana, Ill.: University of Illinois Press, 1989), pp. 6–18; Gerald Rothman, *Philanthropists, Therapists, and Activists* (Cambridge, Mass.: Schenkman Publishing Co., 1985), pp. 155–161.

154. See the discussion of the American Medical Association throughout Paul Starr, *The Social Transformation of American Medicine* (New York: Basic Books, 1984).

# CHAPTER 12

# The Political Economy of the American Welfare State

The American welfare state can be called reluctant for many reasons.[1] When defining "reluctance," we can distinguish between levels of social spending, the amounts that Americans pay out-of-pocket when they seek social and medical programs, the late development of American social welfare institutions compared to those of many other nations, and the volatility of the American welfare state.

Americans allocate a smaller share of the nation's gross national product for social welfare than many European societies. Stockman estimates that Americans spend roughly 23 percent of the gross national product on domestic spending when local, state, and federal expenditures are aggregated and when federal national security and debt-servicing charges are not considered. (This figure includes local educational expenditures and a variety of state and federal programs.) By contrast, the Japanese spend 30 percent, the British and West Germans spend about 40 percent, and the Swedes spend roughly 50 percent of their gross national products for comparable programs.[2]

These relatively low expenditures by the Americans are linked, in turn, to the relatively low tax rates of the United States.[3] Although considerable taxes are collected by local units of government in the United States, the combined yield is far less than many other European democracies. If we also consider that Americans have budgeted larger shares of their national income to military spending during the cold war, we can understand why American social spending lags behind many other nations.[4]

Furthermore, the American welfare state developed belatedly compared to many European nations. Many of the reforms of the American Social Security Act and The Great Society were enacted decades earlier in European nations. Germany and Britain had versions of national health programs by the early part of this century, for example, and full-fledged national health insurance by 1950. Various health insurance, public works, day-care, and job-training programs that exist in European nations have yet to be enacted in the United States.

American welfare programs are subject to more uncertainty than the relatively stable welfare programs of European nations.[5] Public works programs of the New Deal, the National Youth Administration, many programs of the War on Poverty, and various housing programs have been terminated. Fluctuations in the funding of programs have been common; thus, various programs in the New Deal received drastic cuts, the funding of many of the programs of The Great Society were cut in the late 1960s, and mental health centers and a variety of means-tested programs for the poor received deep cuts in the administrations of Richard Nixon and Ronald Reagan.[6] Liberal reformers have often found their legislative successes attacked in subsequent conservative periods, such as the 1920s, the 1950s, and the 1980s. Flux has occurred in European nations, as well, such as during the 1980s when many of them had conservative regimes of their own, but the volatility of their programs has probably been less marked.

Many American consumers pay relatively large shares of their personal income for social, medical, and educational services—a trend that has sharply increased in the 1980s and 1990s—and local and federal governments have increased fees and payment-shares for many public programs. Elderly persons, for example, pay a large share of medical costs under Medicare because of various fees associated with the program, and many of them must deplete their savings altogether when they develop chronic or catastrophic health care problems. Many mothers continue to fund a large share of day-care costs because of the lack of adequate funding or eligibility. We are not suggesting that consumers ought not to shoulder some share of the cost of the services they use, but Americans risk placing a sizable burden on many low-income, moderate-income, and middle-income citizens.

Finally, the American welfare state is reluctant in its failure to provide universal access to certain foundation programs that many Europeans take for granted. These programs include basic medical benefits for all citizens, economic benefits (such as children's allowances) for all families, day-care programs, and housing programs. By not providing these basic benefits, Americans exact much hardship on those citizens who are relatively poor because they cannot count on certain necessities of life. The case of AIDS provides an excellent example. In European nations, victims of AIDS can count on basic medical benefits throughout the duration of their disease, but American victims of this disease, lacking a national health policy, often experience uncertainty whether they can receive medical care after they have exhausted their private insurance benefits. Similarly, low-income (or moderate-income) women, not able to count on universal day care, must encounter uncertainties and make difficult choices that European women do not often deal with.

We do not mean to imply that the American welfare state lacks *any* redeeming qualities. Partly because Americans have emphasized rights in their Constitution and because outgroups have invested enormous energy in obtaining their rights, Americans have often obtained legislation that conveys rights to certain groups of citizens. The disabled provide an excellent example; though Germany often provides its disabled citizens with better services, it has not developed legislation that accords them protections against job discrimination. Nor should we ignore the salutary benefits of volunteers, not-for-profit agencies, self-help groups, and private philanthropy, all of which are less developed in European nations. Critics of the American welfare state can assert, however, that these distinctively American emphases could easily be retained were the American welfare state made more generous.

 ## WHY A RELUCTANT WELFARE STATE?

Various societal, political, and cultural factors have made the American welfare state a reluctant one, such as the absence of a feudal tradition, the immigrant origins of the nation, the existence of a pervasive social welfare mythology, the absence of a powerful radical tradition, the power of conservatives, the effects of racism and prejudice, the diversion of resources to the military, and the preoccupation with moral crusades like temperance. The small size of the American welfare state, its belated development, and its fragmented nature have also contributed to the rise of a reluctant welfare state.

## Absence of Feudalism in an Immigrant Society

As Appleby notes, no political consensus existed in colonial America even though most colonial leaders favored a relatively limited central government that had few social welfare roles.[7] The founding fathers fervently wanted a democratic republic, yet many of them were fearful of the common people, who they believed could be enticed to support demagogues. Punitive orientations toward poor persons coexisted with a desire to help them by regulating the price of bread and the level of wages, by providing legal protections to indentured servants, and by developing poor-law institutions. Conflicting orientations were reflected in the political battle between Thomas Jefferson and Alexander Hamilton during the 1790s. Hamilton favored strong centralized government institutions that implemented a national policy of mercantilism, whereas Jefferson favored a weak federal government, a predominant political role for the states, and an unregulated capitalist economy that conformed to the tenets of Adam Smith.

This tangle of conflicting tendencies was replaced by a near consensus by 1800 when Jefferson's forces routed the Federalists in national elections. The ideology of Adam Smith and John Locke, who favored limited government, became the ascendant ideology of the nation. The distrust of the common people, so evident in the work of the framers of the Constitution, disappeared as a democracy of "the common people" was idealized. The ambiguous ideology of the nation with respect to poor persons was transformed into the moral treatment and relatively punitive doctrines of the nineteenth century.

Such social problems as pauperism, alcoholism, and mental illness were widely believed to be caused by defects of moral character that could be addressed by enveloping persons in the structured regimens of institutions, by providing them with personal and moral models in communities, and by deterring them from seeking assistance in the first instance by developing punitive programs.

In his classic discussion of American political culture, Louis Hartz contended that the absence of competing perspectives in the New World stemmed from the nation's history.[8] If the United States had had a monarchy like England, large national bureaucracies that had superintended mercantilistic policies, centralized financial institutions, a Parliament that had developed many powers, the Anglican Church, a powerful class of aristocrats that wanted to keep many of their traditional prerogatives, and (particularly by the nineteenth century) strong organizations and movements that represented the interests of working-class persons, Jefferson's political ideas would have been vigorously contested by many other persons, social classes, and institutions.[9] Had these traditions and institutions been present in the United States, powerful interests would have supported a strong federal government to develop a national economic policy, a national poor-relief strategy, distribution of frontier lands to impoverished persons in the cities and in the South, and vigorous regulation of the emerging industrial order to protect the nation's workers. Since the new nation had none of these traditions and institutions, Jefferson's ideology evolved into an American consensus in support of weak governmental institutions that was not seriously challenged until the early twentieth century with the rise of the Progressive movement.

Remember that the early immigrants in the colonies were not representative of European society but reflected a segment of it that was particularly critical of feudalism, the state church, and strong government. American colonists were therefore particularly receptive to the ideas of European theorists who wished to dramatically modify European government and religious institutions. These freedom-enhancing and individualism-enhancing ideas developed extraordinary strength in a frontier society with no competing traditions. New generations of citizens, as well as the children of the endless waves of immigration, became socialized to these ideas—and often came to equate them with the identity of the emerging nation, which they frequently contrasted to the moribund institutions and culture of Europe.[10]

Some immigrants who came to the nation in the nineteenth century had beliefs that were strikingly different from the American consensus, such as Jewish immigrants from Eastern Europe and Russia who had radical or socialist beliefs. These dissenters engaged in strikes and political protest but often found themselves to be labeled as representing alien and un-American beliefs.[11] Separated from growing constituencies of radical workers and intellectuals in Europe, these immigrants had limited impact on the politics of a nation that worshipped capitalism and limited government.

Hartz's analysis has profound implications for social welfare policy. Social welfare institutions cannot develop in the absence of strong governments that possess fiscal resources, civil servants, and policy mandates, but American political ideology extolled weak government. A national strategy to address poverty, mental illness, and other such problems requires a strong national government, but American political philosophy emphasized the rights of states to implement policies not specifically enumerated in the Constitution. Social programs cannot be developed without resources, but the nation did not develop a lasting national income tax until 1913. Large social programs cannot be addressed without public programs, but many Americans, even in the colonial period, assumed that private philanthropy could suffice for many social problems. Regulations and social programs are needed to address many social problems that emanate from the uncertainties and

dangers that exist in capitalistic and industrial economies, such as unemployment, work accidents, low wages, and victimizing of children and women, but American political ideology idealized unregulated capitalism.

The failure to develop national social programs to help impoverished persons and workers in the nineteenth century was partly caused by the absence of a feudal tradition in the New World. Residents of the small villages of feudal society shared communitarian values; the villagers worked their strips in their common fields together, grazed their livestock in common pastures, obtained wood from shared woodlands, developed village policies, and elected members to negotiate with noblemen. Security and predictability were emphasized in legal traditions that guaranteed descendants of serfs the right to farm lands of noblemen in return for services. Mutual obligation was stressed; serfs received certain rights and protections from noblemen and monarchs in return for labor and service. In the New World, however, these cohesive villages were replaced by dispersed farms, whose owners were preoccupied with their individual economic goals. Sharing of food, reliance on traditional rents and prices, and security of land tenure were overshadowed by speculation, mobility, and risk taking. Religion became a quest for salvation through a rigorous regimen of worship and morality. This individualism inhibited the development of collective social welfare institutions since it reflected the belief that persons should forge their personal destinies with scant assistance from society. Far from being embedded in a tradition that emphasized mutual obligation and security, social welfare was often perceived in the New World as a residual activity for deviant persons who lacked the work ethic. The colonists were not uncaring or selfish persons, but sharing and security were accorded less importance in America than in the villages of England.

As feudalism unraveled in Europe over several centuries, the values of security and sharing, as well as distrust of capitalism, persisted and were transferred from villages to the nation. The descendants of the serfs, who had increasingly located in cities, believed that local and national governments owed them protections and resources, much as noblemen and monarchs had owed them in the feudal period. Aided by middle-class radicals and socialists, powerful working-class organizations developed and demanded various kinds of public protections and programs. Recent analysis of the role of poorhouses in the South of England suggests that they were sometimes accorded extraordinary roles in the eighteenth century; they provided a range of income, food, clothing, and work benefits to large numbers of citizens who believed they possessed a right to them—as surely as serfs in preceding centuries had believed that noblemen owed them assistance during famines and use of the land.[12] Vast numbers of persons used benefits of some of the poorhouses even though other poorhouses were doubtless administered in more punitive fashion. Although they were also used punitively to cart people back to points of origin, laws of settlement in the South of England in the eighteenth century were widely used to entitle citizens to poor-law benefits after they had lived in a jurisdiction for one year rather than to force them to return to their places of origin before the year had expired.[13]

Unlike the United States, however, no consensus existed in England about poor-relief policy in the nineteenth century. Proponents of relatively generous poor-relief policy were vigorously opposed by persons who favored punitive policies, opposed intervention by government in the economic order, and resisted the passage of factory regulations.[14] Indeed, opponents of expansive social and economic roles for poorhouses were able to secure the enactment of national policies in 1834 to establish a national network of punitive poorhouses.[15] This policy was strongly resisted by working-class organizations, however, and was only partially implemented. The proponents of expansion of the welfare state represented a powerful tradition

within England, even when they had to contend with more punitive perspectives in the eighteenth and nineteenth centuries—and their power remained intact and became wedded to the emerging Labor party in the early part of the twentieth century. Partly because of these reform traditions, the English had created many social programs by the early twentieth century, including a national health program that helped workers.

Because the United States lacked feudal traditions, a different scenario unfolded in America. The earliest settlers in the New World brought many communal traditions to their colonies in Virginia and Massachusetts, but these traditions rapidly eroded in a society that lacked feudal villages, common fields, and shared expectations. Unlimited land invited settlers to farm in dispersed locations. Practices that were initially taboo in Europe, such as raising prices and speculation, were quickly accepted in the New World. More research is needed on American poorhouses, but it seems as though they did not assume the importance that they obtained in eighteenth-century England, either in the range of benefits that they provided or in the number of citizens who used them. This was partly due to the absence of resources to fund them in the New World and to the lack of traditions of mutual obligation that were so pronounced in England. Benjamin Franklin reflected a widespread suspicion of poor relief when he noted that he "sometimes doubted whether the laws peculiar to England, which compel the rich to maintain the poor, have not given the latter a dependence, that very much lessens the care of providing against the wants of old age."[16]

## Outgroups and the American Welfare State

European societies are more homogeneous than the United States since they have not experienced waves of immigration. Nor do most of them have racial-minority populations of a size that rivals the combined populations of African-

American, Latino, Asian-American, and Native-American groups.

We can speculate that the importance of ethnic and racial-minority outgroups has contributed to the relatively slow growth of the American welfare state in several ways. Because of the persistence of racism and prejudice, ethnic and racial-minority outgroups often provided convenient scapegoats for the broader population, which often believed that unemployment, crime, and other social ills were concentrated within them rather than distributed throughout the population. Irish Americans, Italian Americans, Russian Jews, African Americans, Asian Americans, and Latinos were each stigmatized at various points in American history. If the broader population believed these groups to possess social ills, it felt less need to develop overarching welfare institutions for the general population.

The various outgroups did not provide effective opposition to the policies of the broader society until relatively recently in American history. It was not until the 1960s, for example, that African-American, Latino, gay, and feminist outgroups developed mass-member organizations that effectively challenged existing policies though women had rallied successfully to obtain suffrage earlier in the century and many leaders had courageously sought policy changes at specific points in American history. In eras when the federal government was relatively weak, outgroups found it hard to develop policy changes in conservative state and local legislatures that were often dominated by agricultural and business interests. The sheer extent of prejudice against them often made their members turn inward to develop self-help projects, such as the small businesses of Asian Americans and American Jews.

When the mobilization of the outgroups accelerated in the 1960s and early 1970s, insurgent leaders were able to place considerable pressure on legislators and high officials. But social reform that is organized by specific outgroups is probably less able to obtain policy changes than social reform that is organized by social class, which was more common in European nations under the aegis of Labor, Socialist, and Communist parties. In one sense, social reform in the United States was balkanized or fragmented into the efforts of different outgroups that often found it difficult to make common cause. Indeed, animosity sometimes developed between the different groups, such as tensions between African Americans and women in the decades after the 1960s over scarce jobs, between African Americans and Latinos in the Southwest, and between straight women and lesbians in the feminist movement.

Outgroups often emphasized, as well, the obtaining of *rights* for their members rather than social programs. Civil rights activists in the 1950s and early 1960s sought to erase Jim Crow laws; Asian Americans fought to eradicate laws that limited their rights to own land earlier in the century; and feminists sought to eradicate discrimination against themselves in education, employment, and medical settings. We do not mean to criticize this emphasis on the securing of rights since each of the outgroups experienced profound prejudice and discriminatory policies, but the securing of rights, however necessary, may have detracted from efforts to obtain national health insurance, day care, more munificent job-training programs, and other social programs.

## Absence of a Powerful Radical Tradition

The working class has the most to gain from the development of pension, welfare, work inspection, factory regulation, and other social programs because its members are most subject to economic uncertainty, poverty, and victimization by employers. Welfare states are therefore likely to grow most rapidly in those nations where the working class is organized to demand the enactment of social programs and regulations and where radical ideology, such as socialism, promotes class struggle as well as expansion of the welfare state. Indeed, radical ideology served two functions in European societies. First, it emphasized the need to develop programs and policies to assist the working class. Second, it emphasized common or collective needs of the society that extended beyond the working class to the entire society. Both functions enhanced the expansion of the welfare state; its proponents demanded both the enactment of proposals that would specifically help the working class and the enactment of programs, such as public health and old-age pensions, that assisted the entire population.

Americans have not lacked for social protest or radical thinkers. Utopian theorists favored the development of communal villages in the nineteenth century, legions of radical workers engaged in strikes and violence in the nineteenth and twentieth centuries, and radical parties (such as the International Workers of the World, the Socialist party, and the Communist party) were present in the progressive and New Deal eras. Compared to European societies, however, working-class protest and radical ideologies were weak.[17]

The weakness of radical dissenting political ideology in the United States can also be traced to the absence of a feudal tradition in the United States. Medieval society consisted of a hierarchy of classes extending from serfs upward to noblemen. As this society unraveled over centuries, these various groups retained a strong sense of identity, even as capitalism and industrialization advanced in the eighteenth and nineteenth centuries. Many English workers, who were the descendants of serfs and who believed they had certain rights that stemmed from their common status in society and from their work, were angered when industrialists victimized them and when society offered them few protections.

The development of protest was enhanced, as well, by the recognition of many persons of the realities of class conflict. Industrialists, whose power was further augmented when many of them intermarried with descendants of the landed aristocracy, were perceived to be a powerful group whose leadership often opposed proposals to regulate them or to tax them. In this embattled context, then, the cohesiveness of the working class was increased, and its leaders developed ideologies, such as socialism, that urged the development of class consciousness and an expansive welfare state.

The United States possessed its own version of an aristocracy, as well as industrialists and financiers who exerted extraordinary power in the nineteenth century and particularly in the Gilded Age, but many Americans subscribed to the fiction that they had created a society that was dominated by "the common man." The nation thus defined wealthy persons as common people who had achieved their status by dint of hard work. Thus democratized, the American wealthy elite were to be emulated rather than to be defined as a social class that had to be opposed by the working class. In the absence of perceived class conflict, the American working class did not develop cohesion. Furthermore, males in the American working class obtained the right to vote early in the nation's history, unlike European workers, who often could not vote until well into the nineteenth century. The ability to vote gave American workers an illusory sense of power since it was widely assumed that common people controlled the nation's political institutions. The remarkable resources of industrialists in the Gilded Age, however, allowed them to frequently finance campaigns of politicians or even to bribe them, so the power of American workers was often symbolic at best.

The power of the American working class has often been diminished, as well, by the successive waves of immigration to the nation and migration to northern cities. Immigrant groups spoke different languages and established their own communities and political organizations. Conflict sometimes erupted between them as their members competed for jobs and local political offices. The identification of many American workers with their social class has also been weakened by their aspirations to join the middle class. Just as indentured servants and immigrants aspired to own their own land or to start new businesses in the colonial period, so many working-class persons aspired to obtain gold, land, or wealth through hard work and luck in the nineteenth century. More recently, many blue-collar workers have aspired to and gained the trappings of suburban life, complete with two cars and home ownership. Even though upward mobility is not greater in the United States than in many European nations, Americans often believe that it is.

Radical organizers can be powerful only if they can convince substantial numbers of workers to subscribe to their leadership and doctrines, but American trade unions provided scant assistance to radicals. American labor leaders encountered such formidable obstacles in establishing trade unions in the Gilded Age that Samuel Gompers, the leader of the American Federation of Labor, determined that power for unions could be obtained in American society by focusing on specific wage and benefit issues, by avoiding partisan entanglements, and by avoiding controversial policy issues. He often opposed the development of governmental programs on the grounds they made it more difficult to use the allure of fringe benefits to entice workers to join unions. While labor was supporting the Democratic party in the 1930s, its leaders focused on recruitment and organizational issues as well as on enactment of legislation to accord them the right to organize unions without fear of lockouts, injunctions, or physical violence. Thus preoccupied with practical survival issues, and lacking a radical ideology such as socialism, organized labor did not aggressively champion social issues, such as the expansion of the welfare state, although its leaders supported many specific reforms of the New Deal and The Great Society.

Many American reformers have nonetheless displayed remarkable courage, persistence, and resilience. Dorothea Dix, Jane Addams, Harry Hopkins, Hubert Humphrey, and Martin Luther King, Jr., often encountered formidable opposition, even when they sought relatively modest reforms. Unlike many European socialists, how-

ever, these reformers often focused on the needs of specific groups rather than on measures to help the entire working class. Dix emphasized the needs of the mentally ill; Addams variously focused on the needs of immigrants, children, and women; Hopkins emphasized the needs of unemployed workers; and King emphasized the needs of African Americans until the mid-1960s, when he increasingly sought to develop an encompassing poor people's movement. A welfare state that grows by virtue of successive and incremental additions for specific subgroups within the population is likely to grow more slowly than a welfare state that serves the entire working class.

This proclivity to conceptualize reforms for specific subgroups has been enhanced by the social realities of immigration, ethnicity, and race in a heterogeneous society. It is difficult to develop coalitions of disparate groups, such as African Americans, women, and Spanish-speaking persons, since these subgroups have sometimes distrusted and competed with one another. Unemployed males in the New Deal often opposed efforts by women to obtain access to work-relief programs, and African Americans in the 1970s often feared that women would gain the most from affirmative action policies. Jesse Jackson, who hoped to develop a "rainbow coalition" in the election of 1984, was mainly supported by African-American voters.

The absence of a powerful radical tradition in the United States meant that radicals were absent when political compromises were fashioned between moderate and conservative politicians at numerous points in the nation's history. When liberal politicians such as Franklin Roosevelt and John Kennedy fashioned their tax and social legislation, they were far more fearful of conservative opposition than of the influence of radicals; indeed, both Kennedy and Roosevelt realized that a coalition of Republicans and conservative Democrats could scuttle their domestic legislation. Had radicals also been part of the negotiating process, major legislation might have been more redistributive, made fewer concessions to the rights of states, and been broader in scope.[18] In the absence of class-based politics, interest groups have assumed far more importance in the United States than in Europe. Unfortunately for the nation's citizens with stigmatized social problems, the most powerful interest groups tend to represent the interests of corporations and conservatives, whose needs have been disproportionally represented in the negotiating process.

## The Power of American Conservatives

American conservatives have fought social reforms because they required increases in taxation, enlarged the federal government, interfered with local prerogatives, equalized economic and social conditions, or ran counter to the economic interests of corporations. Conservative defense of the status quo had its golden era in the United States in the nineteenth century, but its proponents possessed extraordinary power even during the liberal reform periods of the progressive, New Deal, and Great Society eras because they could meld the power of the Republican party with conservative Southern Democrats.

American conservatism provided a more devastating resistance to the development of social reforms than European conservatism. European conservatives had helped construct the strong monarchies and central governments of European nations from the sixteenth through the nineteenth centuries because they wished to facilitate national economic planning, preserve their own prerogatives, place controls and regulations on industrialists and bankers whom they sometimes regarded as rivals, or advance their paternalistic traditions in helping the downtrodden. Even when conservatives supported a central government to quell social uprisings, they enhanced its power and hence its ability to finance and administer social programs. By contrast, American conservatives obtained their ideology not from the traditions of the landed aristocracy but from theorists like John Locke

and Adam Smith. Whereas European aristocrats often used government to perpetuate their paternal status, American conservatives wanted nearly to obliterate government, except as it specifically helped corporations, facilitated economic growth, and developed a large military establishment during the cold war.

If tension often existed between the European aristocracy and industrialists, American industrialists had no serious competitors in the political corridors of local and national governments in the Gilded Age. Taxes, tariffs, and subsidies were devised to advance their interests. Their power was gradually diminished in the twentieth century as unions, reformers, and citizens demanded various regulations of them, but corporate lobbying efforts and campaign contributions have made them powerful political forces. Corporations have not always opposed expansion of the welfare state, but organizations like the U.S. Chamber of Commerce and the National Association of Manufacturers have consistently opposed proposals that would significantly increase government welfare expenditures or subvert their corporate interests.

## Social Welfare Mythology

Americans have developed a multifaceted mythology to justify their failure to develop a relatively generous welfare state. It includes the belief that social programs do more harm than good, that social problems can be easily solved, that problems can be avoided by creating equal opportunity, and that laissez-faire policies can suffice to solve social problems. We call these interrelated beliefs mythology because they are not supported by evidence.

DOING HARM BY DOING GOOD   Americans have been obsessed since the colonial period with the notion that charitable acts will bring adverse consequences. Benjamin Franklin contended that "to relieve the misfortunes of our fellow creatures is concurring with the Deity; it is godlike; but, if we provide encouragement for laziness, and support for folly, may we not be fighting against the order of God and Nature, which perhaps has appointed want and misery . . . as necessary consequences of idleness and extravagance?"[19] Leaders of the Charity Organization Society and the Sunday School movement contended in the nineteenth century that generous relief to the poor would encourage laziness; this preoccupation led the former to seek to provide every indigent person with a friendly visitor who could screen out those persons who were corrupted by relief giving. Care was taken in the New Deal to set wage levels in public works programs so low that they would not tempt persons to rely on them. Welfare reform was defeated on successive occasions in the 1970s because many persons feared it would undermine the incentive to work. Conservatives and many liberals in the 1980s fear that the existence of the African-American underclass has been caused by overgenerous welfare programs.

Concern about the deleterious effects of relief giving on poor persons has been complemented by fears that diversion of resources to charity would harm the nation's economy. Many economists opposed efforts by unions in the Gilded Age to seek higher wages on the grounds that such "artificial" increases would discourage entrepreneurs from making investments that were required to sustain economic growth. New Dealers often feared that large welfare expenditures would draw investment funds from the economy, thus diminishing the number of jobs. Following World War II, opponents of efforts to raise the minimum wage contended that the policy would lead employers to reduce the size of the labor force. Conservatives argued in the 1980s that diversion of a larger share of the nation's resources to social programs would decrease economic growth by depleting investment capital.

Fears that doing good might cause harm should not be dismissed as trivial since social welfare history is replete with altruistic projects that were unsuccessful. The Temperance movement did not convert many Americans to abstinence. Crowded and custodial mental institutions and prisons may have harmed more persons than they helped. Dramatic increases in the minimum wage can bring layoffs for some low-wage employees. Welfare reforms that raised benefit levels so that they vastly exceeded existing wages of unskilled persons have tempted some to seek welfare as a substitute for work.

Analysis of welfare history suggests, however, that Americans have often made premature judgments about the possible dangers of social reforms. Persons who leap to the judgment that altruism can be deleterious often fail to recognize that the status quo carries its own dangers. Low welfare benefits can bring economic desperation that leads to additional problems, such as stress, marital and family conflict, malnutrition, and hopelessness from economic deprivation and lack of economic opportunity. High unemployment brings a tragic toll of suicide, mental illness, and substance abuse in its wake. The kinds of dangers that are associated with punitive social programs or an absence of economic opportunity are commonly overlooked in the zeal to identify the possible dangers of social programs.

Persons who highlight the dangers of altruism often neglect, as well, to note that social programs can be ineffective not because they are intrinsically defective but because their recipients live in a hostile world. A relatively generous welfare program may encourage some recipients to decide not to work, not because they are lazy but because they can find only positions that pay low wages. Raising the minimum wage would lead to some displacement of workers because many employers currently use teenage, undocumented, transient, and other low-paid workers to artificially boost their profits. If social programs were evaluated in their social context, then, more attention would be devoted to reforming injustices in society rather than prematurely assuming that the programs themselves are faulty.

Americans often contend not only that specific social programs lead to adverse consequences but that dramatic increases in social spending would decrease economic growth by diverting funds from productive investments and undermine the work ethic. If these arguments were correct, however, we would discern an inverse relationship between economic growth and the size of welfare states, but nations with relatively large welfare states, such as Sweden and Germany, often have higher rates of economic growth than the United States.[20] The socialized health systems of many European nations are associated with lower rates of mortality and morbidity than the private American system—and are considerably less expensive to operate. Arguments against expansive welfare states sometimes reach comical proportions. Some Americans surmised, for example, that the large Swedish welfare state caused many of its citizens to commit suicide by depriving them of the need to work hard, but historians discovered that the high suicide rate in Sweden had antedated the development of its welfare state.

Americans are fond of evaluating the effectiveness of social programs and recommending that programs be terminated or reduced in size when the evaluations indicate that they are not effective. These evaluations are often based on a single criterion; thus, welfare programs are judged faulty if they induce more persons to seek welfare, the Head Start program is declared to be ineffective if it fails to raise the intelligence scores of its enrollees, and mental health programs are declared to be unsuccessful when they do not reduce commitments to state hospitals. Since most social programs have multiple objectives, however, it is fallacious to evaluate them on only one criterion. Welfare programs provide sustenance to destitute persons, for example, so the generosity of their benefits ought to be considered as well. The Head Start program provides medical, nutritional, developmental, and parent-education services, so its effectiveness should be assessed in the context of these various objectives. The mental health system receives high marks for deinstitutionalizing mentally ill persons but low marks for consigning many of

them to a lonely existence in board-and-care homes in skid-row areas.

Henry Aaron makes a provocative point when he contends that social research can often strengthen the hand of conservatives.[21] Formidable methodological and interpretive problems render large-scale evaluations of social programs problematic; indeed, researchers are trained to be skeptical about the findings of any study, even when it suggests positive outcomes. When persons insist that social reforms must await research findings that prove they will be effective or that social programs must be proved to be effective in order to be continued—a common tendency in the United States—they contribute to the opposition to social reform, even if they do so in the name of scientific research.

SOLVING PROBLEMS AND PANACEAS   The American colonists had the dream that they could create a problem-free society. The Puritans sought to purge sinfulness from society by encouraging a regimen of work and morality. Thomas Jefferson, like many other colonial leaders, hoped Americans could create a republic of yeoman farmers and could avoid the problems of class conflict, poverty, and urbanization seen in European nations. This belief in the possibility of a utopian society engendered two social welfare fallacies. First, it led many Americans to overlook harsh realities. Inequality and unemployment, as well as a relatively rigid class structure, were embedded in American society in the nineteenth century, both in the nation's cities and on the frontier, yet generations of Americans in the nineteenth century idealized the frontier as a place where anyone could prosper, saw the emerging industrial order as the source of new jobs, and believed that the nation provided unlimited opportunities to immigrants. Relatively high unemployment existed in the 1920s, yet the belief in unlimited prosperity led many of the nation's leaders to ignore danger signs that ultimately led to the Great Depression. Despite the growth of an underclass in the nation's cities and high rates of rural poverty, optimism returned in the 1950s when many Americans believed that most families would soon possess suburban homes. Although inequality and poverty remained, conservative leaders of the 1980s, armed with supply-side economics, predicted that economic growth would eliminate poverty and increase tax revenues so substantially that the massive federal deficit would disappear, even with tax cuts and massive increases in military spending. Of course, just the opposite occurred, but the conservative rhetoric inhibited the development of social programs by making Americans believe that persistent social problems did not exist.

Second, even when Americans acknowledged that serious social problems existed, they often believed that the problems could be easily solved. Jefferson believed that land ownership, education, and democratic institutions would eradicate poverty and other social ills; the moral treatment reformers of the nineteenth century assumed that character-forming institutions could eradicate poverty, mental illness, delinquency, and crime; charity organization leaders placed faith in friendly visitors and case screening; Progressives saw regulations as panaceas; framers of the Social Security Act were convinced that Social Security would eliminate poverty among the elderly; framers of the welfare service amendments of 1962 hoped to markedly decrease welfare rolls by providing many welfare families with the services of social workers; some reformers believed in the 1960s that a collection of service and community programs in the War on Poverty would eradicate poverty; and in the 1980s, supply-side economists were convinced that reductions in the nation's taxes would eliminate poverty.

This optimistic faith in simple solutions has impeded deeper analysis of the causes and persistence of social problems throughout the nation's history. Poverty is linked to structural causes, such as recessions, low wages in certain sectors of the economy, disabling mental and physical conditions, low levels of skills and education, and discrimination. Single or simple

solutions did not eliminate or mitigate poverty in the nineteenth century when breadlines formed during numerous recessions or when immigrants found themselves at the mercy of employers who paid them low wages. The government regulations of the progressive era did little to help destitute immigrant workers in the nation's cities. The Social Security program did not eradicate poverty among elderly persons even though many of its framers were convinced that it would. Successive welfare reforms of the 1960s did not reduce the welfare rolls. The War on Poverty had minimal impact on the incidence of poverty in the United States. The Reagan administration's cuts in social spending and punitive welfare policies did not substantially reduce the size of welfare rolls.

Naive optimism about the possibility that single programs can solve major social problems has fostered cynicism about the effectiveness of existing social programs. Americans have launched social programs at innumerable points in their history with fanfare. When the programs failed to eliminate the problems, persons demanded their discontinuation, only to begin another cycle of hope and disillusionment. Americans have seldom realized that simple solutions rarely suffice to remedy complex problems or that the success of single programs is even less likely when they are poorly funded or implemented. The mental institutions of the midnineteenth century became custodial institutions because they were poorly funded in subsequent decades. Regulations of housing and public health were often rendered ineffective in the progressive era because they were not monitored. The War on Poverty never received more than $2 billion in a given year.

Networks of mutually reinforcing programs are needed to address social problems. The problem of the feminization of poverty in the contemporary period could be reduced, for example, by a cluster of programs that include a children's allowance, income tax rebates and exemptions, policies that require divorced fathers to make support payments, and tax incentives to employers to encourage them to hire women who are single heads of households—but none of these remedies, by itself, would make a significant impact on the problem.[22] It is also difficult for social programs to succeed without fundamental reforms designed to improve the economic and social status of disadvantaged persons. Individuals can benefit from services, job training, and improved education, but these positive benefits can be negated when they remain in blighted neighborhoods, suffer unemployment, or experience grinding poverty.

THE MISLEADING ANALOGY OF THE FAIR FOOT-RACE  Jefferson hoped that Americans could avoid the perils of a class-structured society by giving all citizens access to the land and to education. The abundance of frontier lands, the remarkable speed of industrialization, the prosperity of many Americans, economic growth, and success stories of immigrants who achieved wealth encouraged perpetuation of Jefferson's dream and the corollary notion that an expansive welfare state was not needed in a society that had created ample opportunities for its citizens to obtain wealth.

As our discussion in preceding chapters has indicated, many citizens had an unfair advantage. For an example, let us consider the hypothetical case of descendants of an Irish immigrant family that came to this country in the 1850s and the descendants of African-American slaves. The Irish immigrant family lived in appalling conditions in Philadelphia and encountered considerable prejudice, but many members of the first two generations worked in industrial plants in Philadelphia and attended public school. By the third generation (roughly 1940), various descendants had purchased homes, obtained jobs from Irish ward bosses, and completed high school. Many descendants in the fourth generation no longer lived in Irish communities but in the suburbs, and a number of them attended colleges and entered professions. The African-American family, whose members were emancipated from slavery, lived in grinding poverty in the rural South of the postbellum years. Public education was not available to its members, who lived in shanty homes near the fields they tended as sharecroppers and field hands. For three generations, family members eked out a subsistence existence. Although some members sporadically attended segregated schools, successive generations perceived little utility in education because rural African Americans could not enter occupations where literacy was needed. Members of the three generations learned to live in their segregated conditions and saw little hope of improving their economic status. When a family migrated north to Chicago in the 1950s, it lived in a vast African-American and segregated community in a city that was dominated by white politicians, white trade unions, and businesses owned by white entrepreneurs. Unlike the descendants of the Irish immigrants, who by 1960, had accumulated wealth, education, and desirable positions in the economic order in the North, most members of the African-American family were illiterate and unskilled and faced the task of "catching up" in a society that was dominated by whites. Their race exposed them to prejudice, they lacked the support of political machines, they found it hard to get industrial positions, and the resources of African-American churches had been overwhelmed by the sheer size of the African-American population that had flooded into northern cities. Urban African Americans did not fare well in northern schools, which were generally overcrowded and staffed by white teachers.

The analogy to a fair footrace ignores the fact that many citizens begin the race with a huge disadvantage. It is useful to improve education and services to disadvantaged populations, but their responses to them are strongly conditioned by their social class and the experiences of their ancestors. Social policy that focuses on improving the education of disadvantaged citizens represents, at best, a long-term strategy that ignores that other advantaged citizens are likely, in the meantime, to continue to improve their educational status. Improvements in opportunity need to be coupled with programs that provide resources and jobs to disadvantaged groups "here and now."

BELIEFS ABOUT MARKETS AND GOVERNMENT American beliefs about markets and government have retarded the development of the welfare state. The tenets of Adam Smith, which idealized private markets by suggesting that they worked best when left to themselves, promoted opposition to factory regulations, taxes, redistribution of resources from affluent to less affluent persons, public works, and national economic planning. Many Americans have viewed the welfare state itself as interfering with private markets by diverting economic resources to non-market endeavors, such as income maintenance programs.

Ample evidence exists, however, that unregulated markets are not necessarily in the best public interest. Entrepreneurs have often victimized workers, consumers, and investors. Although many economic theorists have believed that implementation of their theories would end recessions, no one has yet succeeded. Racial minorities and women have disproportionately borne the burden of economic suffering. Unregulated private markets do not bring an equitable distribution of wealth. Government regulations, social programs, taxes on affluent persons, and economic planning are needed to offset these kinds of problems that are created by capitalism, but many Americans have naively assumed that these interventions, rather than capitalism, caused social distress and inequality. American idealizing of capitalism stems in part from the fact that the economies of the colonies were capitalistic almost from the outset. Although the colonists assumed that capitalism was a natural way to organize economic affairs, many Europeans were suspicious of it because it had been superimposed on feudal societies that distrusted usury, speculation, variable prices, and profits.

The capitalist mythology about free markets is often coupled with simplistic views of government that have emphasized its defects while ignoring its benefits. Many Americans in the colonial era believed that strong governments would subvert the freedoms of the people, absorb vast amounts of the nation's wealth, and contribute to the power of incumbents. These same fears were frequently expressed by opponents of reforms of the New Deal and The Great Society and by conservatives in the 1980s. But government programs, for all of their defects, arose to address intractable social problems that required a societal response. Red tape, inefficiency, and patronage have plagued government institutions, but these problems have been of lesser magnitude than those that would face the nation if a weak federal government still existed. Many Americans have erroneously believed, moreover, that increases in social spending necessarily bring massive increases in the size of bureaucracies. When federal authorities provide matching funds and standards while allowing local governments to implement programs, they limit the growth of federal bureaucracies.[23]

NONGOVERNMENTAL SUBSTITUTES Many immigrants, such as Jews, Japanese Americans, and peasants from Italy, brought with them rich traditions of mutual assistance. They developed civic associations, mutual aid organizations, and social welfare activities within their churches and synagogues. They hired persons from their own groups in their businesses, created agencies that specialized in services to members of their groups, and developed political organizations to obtain government jobs and contracts for their own people.[24] These immigrant traditions complemented an extensive pattern of private philanthropy that had existed since the colonial era and that led to a proliferation of private agencies and volunteer activities.

Such nongovernmental assistance should not be idealized, however. Immigrants were often forced to help one another because they encountered a hostile society that lacked adequate social programs. Some groups proved more adept than others in developing mutual aid.

This tradition of nongovernmental programs slowed the development of a welfare state in several ways. Some Americans believed that nongovernmental agencies were superior to public programs; why not, Herbert Hoover asked in 1930, avoid the perils of big government by using private agencies to provide relief? Some citizens were less likely to pressure officials to develop social programs when they were preoccupied with voluntary projects for their own groups.

The extensive practice of corporations of providing fringe benefits to their employees also delayed the development of the welfare state. Many persons hoped in the 1920s to expand fringe benefits so extensively that no public welfare state would be needed.[25] Unions were so preoccupied with negotiating fringe benefits, such as health insurance, in the 1950s and succeeding decades that they placed less emphasis on securing national health insurance. Corporate fringe benefits serve a valuable purpose, but those employees who work for large companies with sizable reserves are more likely to receive them than other employees — and all employees are likely to see them shrink during recessions. Furthermore, unemployed, retired, or part-time persons do not benefit from them.

## Moral Crusades

Although the term *crusades* may seem melodramatic, it describes the fervor of many temperance, antidrug, antiobscenity, antihomosexual, anticrime, and antiabortion projects.[26] Throughout American history, determined reformers have expended enormous effort in trying to eradicate immoral behavior, whether by prohibiting it or by engaging in public education to change public mores. These crusades have diverted attention from other kinds of social reforms and have often exacerbated discrimination against those stigmatized persons whose personal lifestyle choices were publicly condemned.

Preoccupation with changing the morality of the nation's citizens has often focused specifically on poor persons and racial and ethnic minorities. Moralists in different eras believed that poor persons possessed different norms that prompted them to be lazy, to engage in crime, or to have limited horizons — proclivities that are presumed to cause their poverty. The Sunday School movement, antipauperism projects, efforts of the Charity Organization Society, some settlement houses of the Progressive movement, and some service programs of The Great Society variously sought to provide middle-class models of behavior, to provide surveillance, to discipline, to convert, or to teach frugality and morality to the poor. This inclination to perceive paupers as amoral, shiftless, criminal, and lazy individuals has detracted from efforts to provide them with resources, jobs, education, housing, and tax concessions.

In the contemporary era, the efforts of the Moral Majority and other, kindred groups has focused on myriad lifestyle issues, such as restricting the rights of gays and lesbians, not allowing women to have abortions, obtaining prayers in public schools, fighting programs to give sex education and condoms to youth, and opposing efforts to prevent the spread of AIDS through distribution of sterilized needles (see Figure 12.1). Each of these projects, in turn, has required specific outgroups, such as women and homosexuals, to develop protracted and difficult countercampaigns. In European societies, where these kinds of moral clashes are less common, more attention can be given by reformers to securing social reforms or combating efforts to decrease social spending.

## Military Diversions

Americans have spent staggering sums on wars, extending from the Civil War through the Vietnam conflict. These wars not only absorbed funds but drew to a premature close various reform movements, such as the progressive, New Deal, and Great Society eras. The attention of the nation was diverted in each case to interna-

**FIGURE 12.1** • *"Right-to-Lifers" seek to outlaw abortions in the 1980s*

*Source:* Library of Congress

tional issues, the ranks of liberals were split into prowar and antiwar contingents, and conservatives succeeded in convincing the nation that it could not afford both guns and butter.

But it was military spending during the cold war, from 1950 until at least the early 1990s, that absorbed the largest sustained portion of the resources of the United States. Though Britain and France had significant armed forces, they were much smaller than the American forces when their budgets are examined as a percentage of gross national product—and West Germany (before reunification) and Japan spent far smaller amounts.

The cold war absorbed the nation's resources from 1950 onward at roughly $300 billion per year in constant 1992 dollars for a staggering total of some $12.6 trillion.[27] President Reagan hoped to add another trillion dollars to military spending with his Strategic Defense Initiative, in addition to regular and ongoing military expenditures that he had already increased at an unprecedented rate during peacetime, but Congress balked at this initiative when its costs became evident. While the United States was expending these resources, European nations and Japan had invested their resources instead in productive investments as well as in various social programs.

Conflicts between social and military spending had occurred at various points in American history before the Cold War. Jane Addams had fought Theodore Roosevelt's rearmament plans in the years preceding World War I, and liberals had vainly opposed efforts by conservatives to cut social spending during and after World War II. But these specific episodes of competition between military and social-spending sectors paled by comparison to the cold war when the military absorbed such consistently high amounts of resources for more than forty years.

It is true that liberals did not often contest the military budgets, whether because they believed the Communist threat to be real, because they feared being called "soft on Communism," or because they wanted defense jobs for constituents. (Thousands of corporate officials as well as the congressional liaison staff of the Pentagon constituted a formidable source of pressure on the nation's appropriations and legislative committees, who often gave precedence to military expenditures.)[28] Perhaps the most explicit competition between guns and butter occurred during the Vietnam conflict and immediately afterward, though neither liberals nor conservatives prevailed. Conservatives were able to obtain cuts in social spending as their price for accepting higher taxes to fund the war, but liberals were able to secure some major cuts in the defense budget. This skirmish between advocates of guns and butter was inconclusive, and military spending again returned to its older levels in constant dollars with the huge military buildup of the Reagan administration.

We should note, of course, that military spending, though probably reducing rates of spending on social programs, also had social welfare functions. Low-income and minority youth often enlisted because the military provided them with secure employment and training. The Veterans Administration became a massive health system for millions of poor veterans and their families. The defense industry provided economic growth and employment in many sections of the nation, and its leaders vigorously lobbied for expansion of military contracts. Such welfare functions of the military had negative consequences as well. Minority youth often found when they left the military that the skills they had acquired did not easily transfer to jobs in the civilian economy. The economies of many towns, cities, and regions became so dependent on military spending that they were vulnerable to economic hardship when the cold war eased in the 1990s.

## Classism and Racism

Prejudice against low-income persons exists in any society. Malthus and many other theorists contended in nineteenth-century England, for example, that persons in the lower class possessed brutish dispositions that disposed them to have innumerable children, to engage in crime, and to be alcoholic. Similar prejudice has existed in the United States. Benjamin Franklin argued that "it seems to be a law of nature, that the poor should be to a certain degree improvident, that there may always be some to fulfill the most servile, the most sordid, and the most ignoble offices in the community."[29] Animosity toward unemployed paupers, who were often reviled as subhuman, was extended in the Gilded Age to poor persons, who were sometimes believed to possess inferior genes. Americans have often believed that poor persons possess cultural predispositions that contribute to their economic status, even if the precise language that has been used to describe them has changed. Writers in the 1840s contended that poor persons were lazy and shiftless; social scientists in the 1960s described them as "unable to defer gratification" and "present-oriented."[30] Poor persons are often profoundly influenced by the stress and stigma that stems from their impoverishment, but theorists have often assumed that these responses are fundamental to their character and largely immutable.

Prejudice against poor persons, which has fostered the development of punitive strategies and benign neglect, has been supplemented by theories that extol the merits of economic inequality. Many European aristocrats and American leaders in the eighteenth century contended that their economic and social superiority could be safeguarded by allowing social elites to retain their leadership to prevent the rise of demagogues, who they feared could capitalize on the ignorance, emotions, and licentiousness of the common people. Many European economists argued in the nineteenth century that affluent persons possessed the resources to provide investments that ultimately led to the employment of persons in the lower class. When Benjamin Franklin wrote that "what the rich expend, the labouring poor receive in payment for their labour," he was arguing that affluence of an upper class is needed to support and sustain poor persons.[31] Many American politicians in the twentieth century, including Calvin Coolidge and Ronald Reagan, argued that the nation had to increase economic inequality so that an affluent class would have the resources to make job-creating investments that would ultimately benefit poor persons.

These prejudices and economic theories, which have deterred the development of generous social programs and other policies to decrease economic inequality, have been less influential in Europe because they have been more effectively challenged by leaders of working-class organizations and political parties. European socialists and radicals countered that affluent persons were themselves social parasites who used their resources to victimize the working class and to maintain extravagant lifestyles. American liberals, who have not been forced to articulate more radical positions because of the absence of a powerful radical political constituency, have often advocated positions that have been surprisingly similar to those of American conservatives. Thus, Franklin Roosevelt supported relatively meager unemployment benefits and regressive Social Security taxes, Presidents Kennedy and Johnson enacted tax cuts that markedly increased economic inequality, and many liberals have supported massive increases

in military spending at the expense of social programs.

Racism has often slowed the expansion of the welfare state as well. Negative stereotypes of African Americans, Spanish-speaking persons, and Native Americans have made Americans loath to enact civil rights legislation or to develop social programs to assist them. Many abolitionists believed African Americans to be intrinsically lazy. Progressive leaders such as Theodore Roosevelt and Woodrow Wilson were deeply prejudiced against minorities. Many high-level African-American advisors were appointed to New Deal programs, and millions of African Americans used various New Deal programs, but antilynching and civil rights legislation were not supported by Roosevelt. John Kennedy belatedly supported civil rights legislation, but only when the mounting pattern of violence in the South forced his hand.

Animosity in the white population toward ethnic and racial subgroups has diminished popular support for reforms. Poor white farmers were reluctant to make common cause with poor African-American farmers in the Populist movement; many white Americans distrusted immigrants in the progressive era; southern whites resented the use of social programs by African Americans in the New Deal; and many white workers opposed reforms of The Great Society because they believed they unduly assisted racial minorities. White backlash developed in competition between whites and African Americans in large cities like Chicago in the progressive era, culminating in race riots in 1919, and similar attitudes enabled George Wallace to obtain a large constituency in his bids for the presidency in the late 1960s and early 1970s.[32] Although poor and working-class whites have needed social reforms as desperately as members of racial and ethnic groups, lasting coalitions between whites and minority groups were usually unsuccessful. Whites have often believed that programs of the welfare state were used primarily by racial minorities or ethnic groups even though whites are the major participants of most programs. White Americans believed in the midnineteenth century that poorhouses were exclusively used by immigrants, just as they believed in the contemporary era that recipients of AFDC, food stamps, and other programs are largely African Americans. Because working-class citizens of European society perceive social programs of their welfare states to be *their* programs, they are more likely to support their continuation and expansion.

Prejudices against other specific groups have similarly impeded the development of the American welfare state. Sexism impeded the development of family planning, day-care, and affirmative action programs; prejudice against mental patients slowed the growth of expenditures for a range of community services, such as halfway houses; prejudice against homosexuals delayed a social response to problems of discrimination against homosexuals as well as to the AIDS catastrophe; and ageism delayed the development of humanitarian community-based alternatives to nursing homes as well as funding of policies for chronic medical conditions.

## The Structure of the Welfare State

More than in most nations, the American welfare state is vertically fragmented among the various levels of government. Local units of government fund most of the nation's educational system. Some matching grant programs are funded by national and federal authorities, some programs are funded exclusively by the federal government, and other programs are funded by private philanthropy. This vertical complexity promotes a beneficial sharing of financial responsibility by different levels of government, but it decreases pressure on politicians to increase funding of the federal welfare state by encouraging "buckpassing," that is, efforts by the various levels of government to make other jurisdictions assume the funding responsibility for specific programs. In some cases, such as Ronald Reagan's cuts in social spending, officials in one level of government can make sweeping cuts in

their spending by maintaining that other officials—or the private sector—will "pick up the slack." (These cuts were not followed by commensurate increases by other levels of government or by the private sector, to the detriment of citizens who relied on these social programs.) Each level of government thus has an incentive not to increase its funding of programs too rapidly lest other levels limit their levels of funding. The sheer complexity of funding arrangements compounds the difficulties of lobbying by supporters of social programs since they have to reach a range of governmental authorities rather than concentrating (as in most European nations) on national authorities.

## The Disinclination to Raise Taxes

Unless funded exclusively by fees from their users, social programs can exist only if revenues are raised from taxes by local, state, or federal authorities. A welfare state, then, depends on revenues for its existence and its generosity to people in need of assistance. The reluctance of the American welfare state has been linked to a long-standing American dislike of taxes. An overview of the evolution of American taxes suggests that U.S. history has been an extended Boston tea party, where taxes have often been perceived as alien even when imposed by the American government.

Americans first developed a federal income tax during the Civil War but abruptly canceled it when the war was over. Although various reformers wanted an ongoing federal income tax, the Supreme Court declared an income tax law to be unconstitutional in 1894, thus setting the stage for enactment of the Sixteenth Amendment to the Constitution in 1913.[33] Even this federal income tax did not assume truly major proportions until World War II, when the tax was finally levied on most citizens.

A detailed account of the evolution of the income tax in the decades after World War II falls beyond our discussion, but we note several important facts.

1. Americans have been sufficiently opposed to taxation that the revenue yields of combined federal, state, and local taxes have been far lower than the yields of most European nations when computed as a percentage of gross national product.

2. The total yields have been frequently depleted by dramatic cuts in income and corporate taxes; important cuts were made by the Congress in 1948 over the veto of President Harry Truman, by Presidents Kennedy and Johnson in 1961 and 1964, by President Nixon in 1969, and by President Reagan in 1981.

3. The depletion of federal revenues has been exacerbated by numerous loopholes in the tax code to benefit specific interests or groups in the population, including, for example, provisions that allow homeowners to deduct mortgage interest payments. Cuts have often been supported, as well, on grounds that they will spur economic growth by providing more capital to entrepreneurs and to affluent persons who, it is assumed, will use their additional funds to invest in jobs—a sometimes dubious assumption, as illustrated by the relatively few jobs created in the wake of the massive cuts in taxes by Reagan in 1981.

4. The relatively low levels of American taxes have placed significant pressure on budget allocations for social programs. Prior to the Reagan and Bush eras, most Americans opposed large budget deficits; since the nation was firmly committed to large military expenditures, social spending *had* to be restrained in order to keep the budget in balance, particularly because Americans were not prone to consider raising federal taxes to pay for military *and* social programs. Though tension between guns and butter was most dramatic during the Vietnam War, it has existed throughout the cold war, with cuts often made in social spending rather than in military spending.

5. Social spending rose during the Reagan and Bush eras, but its rate of increase was diminished by the huge budget deficits that President Reagan developed by lowering taxes in 1981 while increasing military spending.

6. Even with the end of the cold war, the size of the budget deficits, when coupled with the traditional American disinclination to raise taxes, has continued to place pressure on the rate of increase in social spending in the United States.

This cursory summary of salient events in recent tax history suggests that welfare historians should place more emphasis on the revenue or tax side of the welfare state. Put succinctly, the reluctance of the American tax system has contributed to the reluctance of the American welfare state.

## THE MULTIFACETED CAUSES OF RELUCTANCE

Many theorists have sought single explanations of the reluctant American welfare state. Some theorists emphasize cultural factors, such as the inclination of Americans to blame the victims of poverty for their condition.[34] Other theorists stress ideological factors by noting the absence of competing radical perspectives in American society.[35] Radical historians and theorists emphasize the sheer (and sometimes uncontested) power of American conservatives and corporate interests as they used their power to influence the development of specific policies and the outcomes of elections.[36] Other theorists, who suggest that "soft" variables, such as ideology, should be discounted, implicate economic and demographic variables.[37]

Existing theorists err by seeking oversimple explanations. Our analysis of the evolution of American policy suggests that American welfare reluctance is caused by a set of multiple interacting factors that cannot easily be disentangled. Many theorists identify a piece of the puzzle but mistake it for the whole solution. Radical historians are correct in noting that the power of conservatives and corporations was often used to defeat or to dilute social reforms and that they often possessed considerable power in a nation that lacked a powerful radical tradition. In many cases, however, conservatives and corporations did not have to assume a dominant role because the nation's culture, its powerful social welfare mythology, and the influence of racism and prejudice predisposed many politicians not to develop social programs, to redistribute wealth, or to massively expand the welfare state. Conservatism has often not been monolithic, as suggested by the division in the ranks of Republicans over social reforms that were supported by Richard Nixon. Some radical historians erroneously conclude that, because a radical left was often excluded from policy decisions, little conflict occurred in the United States over social welfare policy.[38] Limited as their policy proposals may have been when viewed from socialist perspectives, American liberal reformers had to battle as hard as their radical counterparts in Europe to obtain even limited successes in a society that was relatively hostile to reform.

Theorists who emphasize the impact of culture on the American response to social problems are correct in noting its deterrent effects on the development of the American welfare state, but they often do not capture its complexity. We suggest that a multifaceted social welfare mythology existed in the United States that consistently placed social reformers on the defensive by suggesting that reform brings more harm than good. This mythology interacted with racism, prejudice, tendencies to idealize limited government and unregulated markets, and patriotic sentiment to yield a powerful deterrent to the development of social welfare policy. Important as this multifaceted culture was, however, it is not a sufficient explanation for the reluctant welfare state because groups in Europe maintain similar beliefs. It was the absence of a powerful radical faction that gave these beliefs a peculiar importance in the United States since powerful opponents were not present to contest them.

The proponents of political or cultural explanations fail to devote enough attention to the effects of the American welfare state itself in deterring its own growth.[39] The small size of the American welfare state in the nineteenth and early twentieth centuries was both a manifestation and a cause of American reluctance to fund its welfare state. A nation with a strong mythology against welfare had to be educated to the fallacies of that mythology by actually experiencing, in their families and communities, the beneficent effects of social programs. This educational process did not seriously begin until many Americans benefited from social programs in the New Deal. Welfare states contribute to political pressures by encouraging the beneficiaries of their programs to demand expansion of existing programs, by stimulating reformers to emulate the successes of prior reformers, and by encouraging politicians to support the expansion of social programs to obtain votes. These educational and political effects of the American welfare state did not become operative in a major way until the nation developed its first set of federal programs in the New Deal, nearly 150 years after the birth of the republic.

When Americans finally developed a national welfare state, they structured it so that it did not obtain as much support as the welfare states of Europe. The eligibility of many means-tested programs was established at such low levels that blue-collar workers, who were important supporters of the expansion of European welfare states, found social programs to be irrelevant to themselves; indeed, they often believed that its programs were primarily used by racial minorities. Fewer universal programs existed in the United States. Funding and policy responsibilities were so dispersed and fragmented that it was difficult for reformers to know where to apply pressure. Moreover, there was a balkanization of social reform by the sheer number of outgroups, which often became the leading edge of reform rather than class-based, mass political parties such as the Labor, Socialist, and Communist parties of Europe.

More attention needs to be given to interactions among the various factors that impeded the development of an expansive welfare state. Thus, for example, the failure of the American working class to exert pressure on policy makers to expand the welfare state was increased by racism. Many American workers accepted various tenets of American social welfare mythology, including the belief that generous welfare programs would lead to extensive freeloading and other dire consequences. This belief was itself strengthened by racism since whites were particularly likely to believe that African Americans were susceptible to laziness. The disinclination of Americans to generously fund their programs, then, stemmed not just from separate factors but from their combined and interacting effects.

The evolution of the welfare state can be conceptualized as the links of a chain. In each historical era, political, ideological, mythological, and structural factors determined the nature of policies that were selected, rejected, or not considered. Policy choices in specific eras, as well as factors that caused Americans to choose them, provided the starting points for policy efforts in succeeding eras. The policy legacy of a specific era differed from those of preceding eras because of changes in policy, in ideology, and in the welfare state that gradually developed with the progression of time and events.

The major thrust of ideology and politics in the colonial era and in the nineteenth century discouraged the development of major social programs. When Progressives and New Dealers finally began their reform work, they existed in a society whose antireform tendencies were deeply entrenched, where conservatives believed social reforms were fundamentally wrong, and where reformers were widely perceived to represent alien, even un-American, ideas. American social reformers were consistently placed on the defensive in the twentieth century because of this legacy of preceding eras.

Even when the nation came to develop a national welfare state in the 1930s and succeeding decades, reformers had to fight a series of battles in which conservatives objected that each major proposal would establish a precedent that would further (and wrongly) expand the power of the federal government. Although the welfare state grew in fits and starts as reformers were able to win specific battles that gradually expanded the scope of the welfare state, each battle was a difficult one that required liberals to make important concessions to conservatives, such as lowering eligibility levels, giving states key policy roles, refraining from establishing national standards, and placing punitive provisions in programs. Liberals often made these compromises grudgingly, but their vision of reform was often far more limited than European reformers. Even with this uncertain and halting process of reform, liberals feared that the nation would turn against the welfare state under the leadership of conservative presidents or Congresses. And they were justified in their fears; considerable animus developed toward social spending during World War II, the 1950s, the Vietnam War, the second term of Richard Nixon, and the 1980s.

In European nations, by contrast, policy eras that preceded the twentieth century provided a legacy that was more receptive to the development of expansive welfare states. Feudalism contributed a legacy of ideas of mutual obligation, central authority, and class consciousness that shaped the response of European nations to capitalism, industrialization, and urbanization. When theorists like Malthus and Spencer articulated ideas that were antithetical to reform, they were challenged by dissenting perspectives that, by the turn of the twentieth century, were powerfully injected into political arenas by Socialist, Labor, and Social Democratic parties. Because of the presence of radicals as well as the tendency of many Europeans to stress mutual obligation, their early reforms were more far-reaching than American ones—and their reforms were enacted earlier. Their welfare states stimulated more support for their programs from the general public than in America because the programs were widely perceived to be relevant to larger portions of their populations.

A challenge for contemporary Americans consists not only in understanding the evolution and nature of the American responses (or non-responses) to social problems but in making moral judgments about them. Do we wish to evolve a welfare state that is more like those of European nations, or do we want to severely limit its size? Policy developments of the past two centuries suggest that these questions will not be resolved for generations and that reformers will encounter many obstacles along the way.

## THE POLITICAL ECONOMY OF SOCIAL POLICY

The preceding discussion suggests that American social welfare policy is deeply enmeshed in the culture, politics, and economics of the nation. Many factors have shaped the timing of the emergence of specific policies, as well as their content. Were we to try to study social welfare policy *apart* from its societal context, we would be unable to understand why Americans made certain choices and not others.

A historical perspective is useful because it enables us to examine the *changing* political economy of the nation. By placing policies in the context of specific eras, we can better understand why certain choices were made in those periods and why other policies, however meritorious, were not considered at all or were roundly defeated. Moreover, a historical approach allows us to better understand how the contemporary American welfare state represents an accumulation of policies that derive from different, preceding eras. The surviving policies

of the progressive era, the New Deal period, The Great Society, and the 1970s form a sort of collage that, when added to policy additions in the contemporary period, form the American welfare state. These traditions and precedents that stem from prior eras have, in turn, shaped our choices today because they are part of the current context of the policy-making process.

Similarly, it is not possible to understand how Americans dealt with various outgroups in their midst without placing their experiences in the broader political economy of the nation. Many policies of the welfare state stem directly from encounters between specific outgroups and the broader society in specific eras. As with the welfare state considered more broadly, each outgroup encounters policies in contemporary society that represent a series of legislative enactments and court rulings that were enacted in prior eras—and these enactments and rulings are part of the context that they encounter today.

## FROM DETERMINISM TO SOCIAL ACTION

That policies are shaped by the political economy of the nation ought not to suggest, of course, that they are *determined* by cultural,

political, and other forces. In the last analysis, people—whether legislators, advocates, presidents, courts, or government officials—make policies. Sensitized to the ways that the political economy of the American welfare state has influenced the policy choices of decision makers, people have to decide which policies are meritorious and which are not—and then try to change those policies that they dislike. As we discuss in Chapter 13, analysis of the reluctant welfare state can prompt us to engage in social reform in the contemporary period.

## END NOTES

1. The term *reluctant welfare state* was coined by Harold Wilensky and Charles Lebeaux, *Industrial Society and Social Welfare* (New York: Free Press, 1965), pp. xii–xxv.

2. David Stockman, *The Triumph of Politics* (New York: Harper & Row, 1986), p. 392.

3. Carolyn Webber and Aaron Wildavsky, *A History of Taxation and Expenditure in the Western World* (New York: Simon & Schuster, 1986), p. 522.

4. Paul Kennedy, *The Rise and Fall of the Great Powers: Economic Change and Military Conflict from 1500 to 2000* (New York: Random House, 1987), pp. 413–437.

5. The strength of sentiment in nations like Sweden against cutting social welfare programs is discussed by William Tuohy, "Sweden: A Rocky Turn for Welfare," *Los Angeles Times* (April 24, 1981), 1.

6. Gregory Mills and John Palmer, "The Federal Budget in Flux." In Gregory Mills and John Palmer, eds., *Federal Budget Policy in the 1980s* (Washington, D.C.: Urban Institute, 1984), p. 34.

7. Joyce Appleby, *Capitalism and a New Social Order: The Republican Vision of the 1790s* (New York: New York University Press, 1984), pp. 51–78.

8. Louis Hartz, *The Liberal Tradition in America* (New York: Harcourt, Brace, and World, 1955), pp. 3–32.

9. Authority was central to feudalism and contributed to the development of strong central governments in Europe. See Robert Heilbroner, "Benign Neglect in the United States," *Transaction*, 7:12 (October 1970), 61.

10. See Bernard Bailyn, *The Ideological Origins of the American Revolution* (Cambridge, Mass.: Harvard University Press, 1967), pp. 22–54.

11. The isolation of socialism from mainstream progressivism is discussed by Hartz, *The Liberal Tradition in America,* pp. 134–136.

12. K. D. M. Snell, *Annals of the Laboring Poor: Social Change and Agrarian England, 1660–1900* (Cambridge: Cambridge University Press, 1985), pp. 104–137.

13. *Ibid.,* pp. 104–137.

14. See Raymond Cowherd, *Political Economists and the English Poor Laws* (Athens, Ohio: Ohio University Press, 1977), pp. 1–23, 70–79.

15. *Ibid.,* pp. 204–278.

16. Quoted in June Axinn and Herman Levin, *Social Welfare: A History of the American Response to Need* (New York: Harper & Row, 1982), p. 29.

17. Hartz, *The Liberal Tradition in America*, pp. 134–136, 266–270.

18. This point is made by Geoffrey Hodgson, *America in Our Time* (Garden City, N.Y.: Doubleday, 1976), pp. 247, 484–490.

19. Quoted in Axinn and Levin, *Social Welfare,* p. 29.

20. Thurow, "A Look at Trickle-Down Economics," p. 106.

21. Henry Aaron, *Politics and the Professors* (Washington, D.C.: Brookings Institution, 1981), pp. 97–98, 164–167.

22. See Irvin Garfinkel, "Years of Poverty, Years of Plenty: An Essay Review," *Social Service Review,* 59:2 (June 1985), 283–304.

23. See John Chubb, "Federalism and the Bias for Centralization." In John Chubb and Paul Peterson, *The New Direction in American Politics* (Washington, D.C.: Brookings Institution, 1985), pp. 292–301.

24. For a summary of historical research on the development of mutual-aid and self-help projects, see Clarke Chambers, "Toward a Redefinition of Welfare History," *Journal of American History*, 73:2 (September 1986), 407–433.

25. See David Brody, *Workers in Industrial America: Essays on the Twentieth-Century Struggle* (New York: Oxford University Press, 1980), pp. 48–78.

26. No one captures more fully the fervor of moral crusades than Paul Boyer, *Urban Masses and Moral Order in America, 1820–1920* (Cambridge, Mass.: Harvard University Press, 1978).

27. Richard Stubbing, "The Defense Budget." In Mills and Palmer, eds., *Federal Budget Policy*, p. 83.

28. For a discussion of lobbying pressure by the Pentagon and corporations, see James Fallows, *National Defense* (New York: Random House, 1981).

29. Quoted in Axinn and Levin, *Social Welfare*, p. 30.

30. Comparisons of orientations toward the poor in the 1960s and the nineteenth century are discussed by Steven Schlossman, "The 'Culture of Poverty' in Antebellum Social Thought," *Science and Society*, 38:1 (Spring 1974), 150–166.

31. Quoted in Axinn and Levin, *Social Welfare*, p. 30.

32. Pete Hamill, "The Revolt of the White Lower-Middle Class." In Louise Howe, ed., *The White Majority: Between Poverty and Affluence* (New York: Random House, 1970), pp. 10–22.

33. Jerold Waltman, *Political Origins of the U.S. Income Tax* (Jackson, Miss.: University Press of Mississippi, 1985), pp. 102–114.

34. See Webber and Wildavsky, *A History of Taxation and Expenditure in the Western World*, pp. 560–614.

35. John Barnes and Talapady Srivenkataramana, "Ideology and the Welfare State: An Examination of Wilensky's Conclusions," *Social Service Review*, 56:2 (June 1982), 230–245.

36. Richard Cloward and Frances Piven, *Regulating the Poor: The Functions of Public Welfare* (New York: Pantheon, 1971).

37. Harold Wilensky, *The Welfare State and Equality: Structural and Ideological Roots of Public Expenditure* (Berkeley, Calif.: University of California Press, 1975), pp. 15–28, 47–49.

38. See discussion by Brody in *Workers*, p. 127.

39. This point was stimulated by the various readings in Peter Evans, Dietrich Rueschemeyer, and Theda Skocpol, eds., *Bringing the State Back In* (Cambridge: Cambridge University Press, 1985).

# CHAPTER 13

# Taking Sides

No one can pretend neutrality when reading social welfare history since it forces its readers to develop policy preferences and an understanding of the historical and social forces that underlie policy choices. Contemporary conservatives view themselves as ideological descendants of the founding fathers, nineteenth-century capitalism, and Presidents Coolidge, Hoover, Eisenhower, and Reagan. These persons favored retention of the status quo, took minimal (or no) actions to redress infringements of the rights of racial minorities, and reduced or minimally expanded the welfare state. Contemporary liberals perceive themselves as ideological descendants of Presidents Theodore and Franklin Roosevelt, Wilson, Kennedy, and Lyndon Johnson. These leaders were in the vanguard of the movement to build an American welfare state, even if their limited vision and the political opposition they encountered made it a reluctant welfare state.

This liberal tradition has been an ambiguous one. Liberals have courageously championed a variety of reforms in a society that was often insensitive to the needs of minorities and the lower class, but they have rarely embraced sweeping reforms. Thus, Progressives emphasized regulations rather than social programs; New Dealers gave states large policy roles in the ADC and other programs, even when this meant that southern and conservative states could construct extremely punitive programs; neither Progressives nor New Dealers were inclined to support major civil rights legislation; and Kennedy and Johnson were disinclined to redress economic inequality in the nation or to support major reforms of the welfare system. Liberals, like conservatives, have often espoused jingoistic policies, whether Theodore Roosevelt's Asian and Latin-American forays or Kennedy's and Johnson's preoccupation with Vietnam.

American radicals identify with union organizers of the nineteenth and twentieth centuries, legendary radical figures such as Eugene Debs and Norman Thomas, and socialists and communists of the 1930s. They often identify with grass-roots social movements, including movements to abolish imprisonment for debt and to end slavery prior to the Civil War, the International Workers of the World in the progressive era, the Southern Tenant Farmers Association, the unemployed workers movement, the industrial workers movement in the New Deal, the civil rights and welfare rights movements of the 1960s, and organizations representing homeless persons in the 1980s.[1] The American radical tradition has always occupied a tenuous political position in a society that lacked a socialist or powerful radical tradition. Few radical persons have been elected to national offices, in contrast to Europe, where many heads of state have represented labor or socialist perspectives. Leaders of radical social movements have found it difficult to sustain their movements or to obtain national cohesion, particularly when public policy enactments granted some of their demands. For example, abolitionism disappeared following the Civil War despite continuing violations of the rights of freedmen; African Americans found it difficult to sustain the civil rights movement after passage of the Civil Rights Acts of 1964 and 1965; and the national welfare rights movement found its strength eroded in the wake of administrative and court rulings that decreased the arbitrariness of welfare administrators.

## DIVERGENT POLICY POSITIONS

Citizens in societies with conflicting policies and relatively harsh traditions must at some point shape their personal values. Do they share the values of contemporary American conservatives, liberals, radicals, or socialists? Do they favor the expansion of social welfare roles of the federal government, advocate the status quo, or want reductions in existing programs? What policy positions do they advocate with respect to contemporary social problems such as homelessness and providing medical care to medically indigent and impoverished persons?

Moral philosophers and religious leaders have identified many moral principles that influence policy choices. Table 13.1 lists some of these principles. Most persons would agree that each of these moral principles represents an important guiding principle in organizing social life. Legal principles, the Bill of Rights, the due process clause of the Fourteenth Amendment, other provisions of the Constitution, religious doctrines, moral teachings, and common traditions discuss and uphold these principles.

The differences between conservatives, liberals, and radicals rest, in considerable measure, on the different relative importance or weighting they give to these moral principles. Conservatives place heaviest emphasis on the principle of freedom; they value the freedom to retain personal wealth, to conduct enterprises with minimal public regulation, and to give local units of government major policy roles. Their emphasis on societal rights, particularly those functions involving maintenance of public order and morality, sometimes leads them to favor policies that limit the personal freedoms of persons who are perceived as somehow deviant. Libertarians agree with conservatives with respect to the primacy of freedom but oppose these kinds of societal rights policies that enforce a single standard of public morality.

Liberals emphasize freedom but favor a broad range of policies to protect citizens from the vicissitudes of private markets and economic misfortune. A distinction can be drawn between those liberals who favor a relatively expansive welfare state that attempts both to equalize opportunity and to decrease economic inequality (stalwart liberals) and those liberals who emphasize the equalizing of opportunity (traditional liberals). Stalwart liberals favor relatively generous welfare programs that give liberal benefits to poor citizens, favor an income tax that accomplishes considerable economic uplifting of persons in the lowest economic strata, and favor affirmative action policies in hiring procedures and training programs. Hubert Humphrey and Robert Kennedy exemplify stalwart liberals.

**TABLE 13.1** • *Moral principles*

| | |
|---|---|
| *Autonomy* | The right to make critical decisions about one's own destiny |
| *Freedom* | The right to hold and express personal opinions and take personal actions |
| *Preservation of Life* | The right to continued existence |
| *Honesty* | The right to correct and accurate information |
| *Confidentiality* | The right to privacy |
| *Equality* | The right of individuals to receive the same services, resources, opportunities, or rights as other persons |
| *Social Justice* | The right of equal access to social resources |
| *Due Process* | The right to procedural safeguards when accused of crimes or when benefits or rights are withdrawn |
| *Beneficence* | The right to receive those treatments, services, or benefits that allow one to establish or maintain a decent standard of well-being |
| *Societal or Collective Rights* | The right of society to maintain and improve itself by safeguarding the public health and welfare, avoiding unreasonable or unnecessary expenditures, and preserving public order |

Traditional liberals, such as John Kennedy and Lyndon Johnson, emphasize educational, medical, and job-training supports for citizens but do not favor tax or welfare policies that substantially redistribute resources to poor persons. Stalwart liberals seek to temper freedom with social justice by supporting a wide range of social programs and some redistribution of resources to low-income persons. Traditional liberals are more cautious in seeking reforms that address economic inequality but favor equalizing opportunity through the expansion of educational, medical, and social services.

Many kinds of radical positions exist. Some radicals, such as socialists, believe that incremental improvements in the existing welfare state are insufficient. They favor drastic equalizing of economic conditions by heavily taxing incomes of affluent persons so that resources can be massively redistributed to less affluent classes. Many socialists advocate government ownership of segments of private industry, both to accomplish a leveling of income and to give government the power that it needs to offset the political

resources of capitalists. Militant supporters of the rights of specific groups, such as African Americans and women, emphasize major economic and social changes to allow members of their groups to markedly improve their economic and social status.

This brief discussion of conservatism, liberalism, and radicalism suggests that the three ideologies differ with respect to the five moral issues in social welfare policy that we discussed in Chapter 1: the morality of services, the nature of social obligation, preferred interventions, compensatory strategies, and the magnitude of federal policy roles. Conservatives tend to favor deterrent policies, believe that social programs should address a narrow range of social problems, emphasize personal or moral causes of social problems, dislike compensatory programs such as affirmative action, and minimize the domestic policy roles of the federal government. Radicals find efforts to restrict access to or benefits of social programs to be demeaning to their recipients, want society to address a wide range of social problems, believe that social problems are caused by environmental factors such as inequality and unemployment, seek drastic equalizing of resources between social classes, and support massive increases in the power of the federal government. Liberals can best be characterized as falling between conservatives and radicals on an ideological continuum. Many factions exist within conservative, liberal, and radical camps.[2]

## THE CASE FOR MAJOR EXPANSION OF THE WELFARE STATE

Some may wonder whether it matters that the nation's economic, social welfare, and tax policies sustain and even contribute to the worsening of economic inequality. Marked economic inequality has existed, after all, throughout the nation's history. Several factors suggest, however, that the extent of social and economic inequality in contemporary society poses particularly severe problems for the nation. A vast and demoralized group of "truly disadvantaged persons" exists in all the major cities of the nation. This underclass lacks institutional supports; teenagers and males are often unemployed at startling rates that approach 40 percent; its youth leave schools in numbers that approach 60 percent; its residents experience frightening levels of burglary, assault, and drug abuse. Although the AIDS epidemic was widely perceived to afflict primarily white homosexual males, huge numbers of its victims were African-American and Spanish-speaking drug users in inner-city areas by the late 1980s. Most of the residents of state and federal prisons are members of low-income racial minorities. The social and economic problems of this underclass have become so large and severe—and so entwined with drug, prison, health, welfare, and educational problems—that they cannot be addressed by incremental additions to the welfare state or by reliance on traditional programs.

The problems of these truly disadvantaged persons were compounded by the problems of workers who were displaced by the international economic competition of the 1970s and the 1980s. In the 1950s and 1960s, the United States enjoyed economic advantage over foreign nations whose economies were devastated in World War II. But by the mid-1970s, European nations, Japan, South Korea, and Taiwan had built entirely new industrial economies. They accomplished their economic rejuvenation by saving a large proportion of their earnings and investing the capital in new technologies. They often invested heavily in their human resources by spending large sums on health, education, and job training for citizens of all social classes. Their cities had been rebuilt following World War II and did not have vast blighted communities, like American cities. They often used the technical and financial powers of their governments to stimulate those industries and technologies that were best positioned to contribute to the growth of their economies.

The welfare states of these nations, which had initially been developed for altruistic reasons or because of the power of Labor and Socialist parties, served their nation's economic objectives by developing and sustaining an educated and healthy labor force. In contrast, the American welfare state lacked the resources and the organization to address the problems of the underclass, displaced workers, the homeless, and others. The American educational system was widely regarded to be underfunded and ineffective. American job-training and vocational-education programs were poorly funded and episodic—and often focused their resources on workers who already possessed basic skills. American corporations viewed their workers as labor commodities that could be cast aside during recessions or displaced when cheaper sources of labor could be found by relocating to third-world nations. Public works, which were needed to sustain and retrain unemployed and displaced workers, were opposed by most conservatives and many liberals.

Few signs existed that Americans had grasped the seriousness of their social and economic problems in the early 1990s. Conservatives repeated their customary positions. Instead of realizing that millions of racial minorities and displaced workers were unemployed because of structural unemployment or because they lacked requisite skills, conservatives supported punitive welfare programs, issued studies that simplistically blamed welfare programs for unemployment, and demanded a vast expansion of the capacity of the nation's prisons. Compensatory strategies, which were urgently needed to address the needs of the underclass, were resisted on the grounds they represented reverse discrimination. It was only several decisions of the Supreme Court that stopped the Reagan and Bush administrations from jettisoning them, but with the appointment of conservatives in the Reagan and Bush era, the Court often did not provide a means of buffering national policy from conservative attacks. Conservatives contended that private markets could solve the nation's economic problems, even when other nations were skillfully using national economic planning to develop their economies.

Stunned by policy reversals in the Reagan administration, preoccupied with restoring spending levels of specific programs, and championing the policy concerns of specific subgroups, American liberals did not develop sweeping social and economic strategies and massive programs to help the nation's disadvantaged and displaced workers enter the economic mainstream. Neither of the two leading Democratic candidates in the 1984 presidential election offered far-reaching proposals for social reforms. Jesse Jackson, the African-American leader, embraced a range of sweeping reforms but was widely believed to be too far to the left to have a strong chance of gaining the Democratic party's nomination. Michael Dukakis belatedly developed liberal themes in his campaign in 1988. Democrats in the 1992 election proposed a strange mixture of tax measures, such as tax cuts on capital gains or a flat tax, that sounded surprisingly like initiatives of conservatives. Or they proposed a mélange of incremental changes that hardly spoke to the magnitude of the budget deficits or the range of problems that the nation encountered.

Problems of disadvantaged and displaced workers were joined by other problems that had reached serious proportions. The health care system was in chaos. It approached 15 percent of the nation's gross national product by the mid-1990s, a sum so enormous that government, employers, unions, and insurance companies embraced efforts to cut the costs and fees of doctors and hospitals. Cost-cutting strategies showed marginal success but created other problems, such as premature discharges of many persons from hospitals and unwillingness of many hospitals to treat medically indigent persons. The two-tiered system of care for poor and nonpoor persons led to inferior or inaccessible care for many of the poor, which made them even more inclined to seek services only when their medical conditions were serious. Roughly thirty-seven million Americans lacked any health insurance or eligibility for government programs. The AIDS catastrophe highlighted the deficiencies of the health care system, such as its inability to emphasize preventive services, its lack of community-based services, and its insensitivity to terminally ill persons.

The nation was also ill prepared for the projected massive increases in the number of elderly persons. Government medical programs emphasized private hospital and nursing-home services to the detriment of community-based ones. Federal authorities were reluctant to subsidize long-term health care for elderly citizens unless they had depleted their assets to obtain eligibility to the means-tested Medicaid program. Many persons wondered whether the younger generation would be willing to fund the massive programs that would be needed by elderly Americans.

In developments reminiscent of the Great Depression, hundreds of thousands of homeless Americans lived on the streets in the 1980s. Their numbers included single persons and families that could not afford housing, deinstitutionalized mental patients, and substance abusers. Although many private agencies rose to the challenge, no national policy existed to provide them with housing, services, and employment programs. Indeed, cuts in the funding of federal housing subsidy programs and of community mental health centers exacerbated the problem.

Most observers agreed that the word *crisis* accurately described the condition of the nation's families. Millions of single parents were forced to work in low-wage jobs, were unable to afford decent housing, and were mired in poverty. Large numbers of adolescents had problems with substance abuse, teenage pregnancies, and unemployment. Problems of family violence included wife abuse, child abuse, and the abuse of elderly grandparents. Federal planners had hoped that federal subsidies to states would encourage adoptions, but they had little effect in decreasing the number of children and adolescents who rotated between foster care placements. Many women had to make agonizing choices between their family's survival needs and the need to fund good (and expensive) day-care programs for their children.

The ability to fund needed reforms was severely limited by the chaotic condition of the nation's tax and budget systems. The federal deficit reached unprecedented levels and deterred the development of new programs. Federal taxes were reduced far beneath the levels of European nations. The cuts in social spending of the Reagan administration placed severe pressure on the budgets of local and state governments at a time when their sources of revenue had been depleted by local taxpayer revolts. Foundations, corporations, and individuals were deluged by the funding requests of not-for-profit agencies, which in

turn, often could not sustain their programs because of the cuts in government funding.

Radical perspectives were needed to expand and enrich discussions of policy remedies to address these serious social problems. Liberals in the New Deal and Great Society had typically proposed federal programs that provided federal subsidies to the states to provide services and resources to persons with specific kinds of problems. The severity and complexity of the nation's problems suggested, however, that multifaceted programs were needed to address serious problems such as homelessness, AIDS, and family violence. Furthermore, many critics believed that fundamental changes were needed in the structure of the health care, foster care, and educational systems.

Poor persons are far more likely than middle- and upper-class Americans to be ill, disabled, uneducated, alcoholic, substance abusers, incarcerated in prisons, and unemployed owing to the stress, stigma, and limited opportunities that are associated with poverty. When poverty-stricken persons are in class-segregated and racially segregated neighborhoods and are subjected to discrimination, poverty poses even greater burdens for its victims. Liberals had usefully championed programs to provide remedial relief to poor citizens but had not supported major changes in the tax code to massively redistribute resources to poor persons or policies to guarantee full employment.

The need for basic changes in the social and economic conditions of many citizens provided a compelling rationale for drastically *increasing* the size of the American welfare state. Individual programs for specific needs are important, but the broader purpose of a welfare state is to provide a combination of social programs, tax policies, and economic policies. Single parents need, for example, housing, day-care, job-training, medical, service, and nutritional programs; safe neighborhoods; access to predictable job markets; and an adequate income that derives from some combination of children's allowances, wages, tax rebates, and support payments. But the notion of increasing social spending was hardly a common theme in an America that, after two decades of conservative rhetoric and deficits engineered by these conservatives, had come to see social spending as the cause of the nation's ills.

Curiously, Americans seemed not to understand that other nations had larger national budgets, as a percentage of their GNPs, and higher taxes than their nation. Moreover, far smaller shares of those higher budgets were absorbed by military spending or by the health care system, so they possessed more funds to invest in their citizens, whether in educational systems, social programs, or economic programs.

Of course, social programs are not always effective, and diligence must be taken to discover what works best and with whom. But the need to know more hardly justifies social workers with caseloads of one hundred families in child welfare units, inner-city schools with classes of fifty students, children in impoverished families, lack of preventive services for AIDS, and forcing

millions of Americans with catastrophic health conditions to "spend down" to indigency. Nor can Americans justify the existence of inner-city areas that resemble East Berlin in the wake of World War II.

We do not know how many social problems that afflict society would markedly diminish were the nation to fund an expansive welfare state that provided these kinds of programs for all its citizens. It it likely, however, that many social problems are caused or exacerbated by the harsh realities that currently confront many Americans. Ultimately, however, choices about the size of the welfare state hinge not on such calculations but on the relative weight that is given to values of social justice and equality and to competing priorities such as defense spending. Had even a small fraction of the $12.6 trillion of military expenditures between 1950 and 1992 in constant 1992 dollars been allocated to social purposes, numerous social programs could have been expanded and new ones enacted, even without major increases in federal spending.

## THE TENACITY OF SOCIAL REFORM IN AMERICAN HISTORY

In Chapter 12, we mentioned several obstacles to reform in America, such as the absence of a powerful radical tradition and a social welfare mythology that diverts attention from social problems. Social reformers who expect easy victories are likely to become disenchanted because they lack the ideological and institutional supports and traditions that assist many European reformers. Moreover, reformers are likely to live through several conservative eras when their ideas will be particularly suspect and when their energies will be devoted to defensive battles to retain existing programs and to avert spending cuts.

It is easy to dwell on the obstacles to reform and failures of reformers in the United States, but many generations have had many reform successes that, singly and together, have made their society more humane. Many contemporary Americans cannot remember and can hardly comprehend the institution of slavery, imprisonment for indebtedness, capital punishment for relatively minor crimes, poorhouses, labor practices that required many laborers to work fourteen hours a day, unsafe working conditions that killed roughly 35,000 Americans per year in the progressive era, child labor, routine denial of

**FIGURE 13.1** • *Young women demonstrating against child labor in the progressive era*

*Source:* Library of Congress

civil rights and welfare benefits to racial minorities, lynchings of large numbers of African Americans, race riots, flagrant violation of the legal rights of radicals, incarceration of persons who publicly discussed birth control, the routine firing of gays and lesbians, widespread malnutrition, and the denial of education to disabled persons. Even this partial list suggests that American reformers have had surprising successes, even if they sometimes had to work for generations to accomplish some of them.

Curiously, conservatives are more adept than liberals at identifying their historical roots, such as their affinity with many of the ideas of the founding fathers. Indeed, some conservatives equate their ideology with patriotism itself, with the obvious implication that reformers possess alien ideas. But reform is just as integral to the nation's history as conservatism (see Figure 13.1). Jane Addams exhorted Americans to define patriotism in the context of cooperative or sharing values rather than in militaristic or competitive values and to find the meaning of their society from the altruism that was so evident in immigrant communities and among women.[3] Reform ideas can sometimes be found in unlikely places. For example, Jefferson and many of the founding fathers were afraid that undue discrepancy between the incomes of affluent and impoverished citizens might cause social turmoil and demoralize persons in the lower economic strata. Dwight Eisenhower, who committed his life to a career in the military, warned of "the conjunction of an immense military establishment and a large arms industry" and urged Americans to "guard against the acquisition of unwarranted influence by the military–industrial complex."[4]

Reformers should not forget that conservative eras have been followed by liberal periods since the inception of the republic. It is worth remembering that abolitionists, Progressives, New Dealers, and liberal reformers of the 1960s had their formative experiences not during reform periods but during the conservative eras that preceded them. Many reformers had despaired that their nation would again experience reform and had been accustomed to hearing rhetoric to the effect that conservative trends would dominate the nation for decades. Conservatives in the Gilded Age, the 1920s, and the 1950s had confidently predicted that the nation would experience unending prosperity and that its citizens would gratefully pay homage to corporate and conservative officials by choosing them to lead the nation.[5] In each case, however, the nation was soon enveloped in social reform, whether because its citizens had tired of the narcissism and materialism of conservative eras; because of catastrophic events such as the Great Depression; because of popular anger against the victimizing of women, children, workers, or African Americans; or because of failures of the policy prescriptions of conservatives who advocated trickle-down economics, limited government, and unregulated markets.

We have emphasized in our analysis the materialistic and individualistic characteristics of American culture, but these qualities coexist with altruism and other moral principles. Some social scientists contend that Americans have both private and public tendencies; if materialism and personal goals prevail during conservative periods, altruism and concern about societal needs prevail during liberal periods.[6] This insight into American culture, which is confirmed historically by the rhythm of conservative and reform periods, suggests that reformers can successfully appeal to those aspects of American culture that emphasize assistance to innocent

victims, assurance of equal rights, and provision of resources to needy citizens.

Reformers should realize, too, that social reform is possible even during conservative periods. Fine and Chambers, respectively, note that reformers obtained some successes even during the Gilded Age and the 1920s.[7] Partly because many Americans remembered how New Deal programs saved them from the hardships of the Great Depression, President Eisenhower did not attack those social programs that had survived World War II, and he even made substantial additions to the Social Security Act.[8] We have noted that the decade of the 1970s was an ambivalent one that combined conservative presidents with increases in social spending that equaled those of the 1960s. Although President Reagan made devastating cuts in means-tested programs, his major policy successes occurred during the first year of his presidency. Indeed, public opinion polls suggest that he did not markedly change American policy preferences on domestic matters during his presidency and that most Americans favored retention (or even expansion) of the commitment of the federal government to existing social programs.[9] Reagan felt compelled to agree that he would preserve "safety-net" programs from cuts. When he tried to frontally attack Social Security and Medicare, he suffered stinging defeats during both his first and second terms. Indeed, David Stockman, who favored sweeping cuts in social spending, noted remorsefully in 1986 that the "Reagan Revolution" had failed.[10] Democratic candidates at local, state, and congressional levels bucked the national Republican trends not only in the 1980s but also in the 1920s and the 1950s. Both Eisenhower and Reagan had to contend with powerful Democratic contingents in both houses of Congress as well as in state and local governments that resisted cuts in social spending.

Reformers should note as well the rich traditions of reform that are associated with the many groups that have experienced discrimination in the United States. The emphasis in the late 1960s and the 1970s on the rights of women, African Americans, gays and lesbians, Latinos, and Native Americans had the salutary effect of making these groups more aware of historical reformers and the possibility of political redress for grievances. A reform heritage has arisen to challenge conservative mythology, including the resurrection of formerly obscure names of distant and courageous persons as well as infamous events and persecutions. Discovery of older reform traditions has stimulated many Americans to become involved in social reform today.

Reformers have often benefited during the nation's history from the pragmatism of the American people, who often place problem solving above ideology. Conservatives can preach free-market and limited-government ideology, but Americans are unlikely to follow their dictates if they believe that assertive interventions are needed to redress pressing problems. Theodore Roosevelt, Franklin Roosevelt, John Kennedy, and Lyndon Johnson adeptly contrasted their activist, interventionist policies with the passivity of conservative politicians.

As with reformers in preceding eras, a central challenge to reformers in the 1990s is to make expansion of the welfare state a relevant issue to many of the groups of voters who are becoming increasingly influential in the nation's politics. Elderly voters, who have traditionally voted for relatively conservative candidates, have medical and social welfare needs that are poorly addressed by existing policies. Large numbers of workers in the service sector, including clerical and sales personnel, receive limited fringe benefits and are increasingly being supplanted by temporary workers. Women have day-care problems, often receive low wages, and face discriminatory hiring and promotion policies. Latino voters in southwestern states experience problems of poverty, poor education, and substance abuse. African Americans have high unemployment rates and would benefit from a variety of educational and social welfare benefits. Reformers need to construct proposals that address the needs of these groups and

develop broad-based support for social reforms. Many young people realize that their economic prospects are bleaker than their parents'.

Reformers may despair at the difficulties of establishing coalitions of the disparate ethnic, racial, sexual, economic, and age groups that have the most to gain from expansion of the welfare state, but coalitions of reform-oriented groups have occurred at numerous points in the nation's history. We noted in Chapter 6 that immigrant, middle-class, and working-class voters supported progressive politicians. Franklin Roosevelt fashioned a coalition of blue-collar, racial-minority, intellectual, Jewish, and ethnic voters that maintained considerable cohesion during the three decades following the New Deal. Although this liberal coalition frayed during the 1970s and 1980s, it could again develop as the separate hardships of different groups lead their members to believe that reform-oriented candidates are again needed. But reformers will need to be skillful in forging coalitions in a society where racism and economic rivalry have often splintered coalition politics.

When seen in the context of American social welfare history, social reformers can obtain a greater sense of their importance and can take courage from the endurance of many social reformers. But analysis of the previous activities of reformers should also prompt reformers to seek expanded definitions of reform. More than the liberal reformers of past eras, today's reformers need to broaden their concerns to include tax policies, economic planning, and military spending since these kinds of policies have such important consequences for social welfare policy. Social welfare policy has traditionally focused on income maintenance or public welfare, child welfare, mental health, and housing policies. Although these policies are vitally important, they do not address the needs of all citizens. The failure to develop regional and national economic planning in recent decades has made it difficult to help displaced workers, to assist the underclass in entering the economic mainstream, or to channel resources to depressed areas.

Moreover, reformers should advocate policies to reduce economic inequality. The extraordinary difference between the wealth of the highest and the lowest quintiles, which stand in a ratio of ten to one, offends the principle of social justice and contributes to the economic suffering of persons in the lowest economic strata. This issue has been missing from the agendas of most reformers in preceding eras despite its importance.

Reformers should also place more emphasis on the implications of national citizenship for the welfare state. Since we derive our citizenship from the nation rather than from the states, all citizens expect national authorities to superintend defense and economic policy. But no compelling rationale exists for allocating social welfare functions to state and local agencies although conservatives are fond of saying that local governments are "more responsive" to the needs of people than the federal government. If the federal government is responsive to the needs of the people with respect to economic and defense policy, why is it less responsive with respect to welfare policy, day-care policy, or medical policy? The wide variation in the eligibility standards and benefits of many social programs in the various states violates the principles of equality and social justice.

Social reformers should not be timid about making explicit reference to the values that justify their proposals. When Harry Hopkins responded to critics who questioned his programs that relieving hunger was not debatable, he affirmed the principles of beneficence, social justice, and equality. Many Americans sympathize with the underprivileged, support equal rights, and believe that persons in similar circumstances should receive similar treatment, but they often do not perceive the relevance of these concepts to social welfare issues. We have noted that materialism is deeply rooted in American culture but that Americans are also concerned about collective needs. Previous reformers had much success by emphasizing arguments that appealed to these public values of the American people.

As social reformers expand their reform horizons, they should realize that no single blueprint can prescribe political tactics or reform objectives. Some reformers have placed themselves outside mainstream institutions and political parties, including members of various social movements, radical organizers, supporters of peace movements, advocates for oppressed groups, and members of dissident parties such as the American Socialist party. Other persons have worked within the major political parties, churches, the labor movement, civic groups like the League of Women Voters, and mainstream civil rights groups. Other persons have sought change from within governmental, educational, and social welfare agencies.

Reform-oriented persons in all these settings encounter difficult tactical and philosophical dilemmas. Radicals have to decide whether to advocate relatively militant positions or to advocate policies that are more acceptable to the general public and to the leaders of established institutions. Martin Luther King, Jr., was accused by black-power leaders of cooperating excessively with white politicians, for example, yet he had decided for both tactical and philosophical reasons to oppose separatism and the use of violence. Hubert Humphrey and George McGovern were stigmatized and scapegoated within the Democratic party at specific points in their careers, yet both of these politicians had long records of effective reform advocacy. Serious splits developed in the ranks of reformers in the New Deal when Frances Perkins and Harry Hopkins were widely reviled by radical social workers as well as by such leaders as Huey Long. Though serious differences may exist among reformers, they must not forget that their most serious foes are indifference and apathy and, of course, conservatives.

Awareness of these dilemmas, as well as the legitimacy of the choice of external and institutional vantage points, may make reformers less likely to squander their scarce resources on internecine conflict.

| ## SOCIAL WORK PROFESSIONALS AND POLICY CHOICES

The hundreds of thousands of professionals who deliver services and resources of the welfare state to consumers include physicians, nurses, psychologists, and social workers who work in a variety of public, not-for-profit, and for-profit agencies and practices. The social work profession illustrates dilemmas and choices that confront intermediaries between the welfare state and consumers. Most social workers are employed in salaried positions in nonprofit, public, or profit-oriented agencies. Because funds are rarely given without accompanying policies, regulations, and demands for accountability, social workers must interact frequently with funders, legislators, and government officials. They work with relatively controversial persons and populations—the mentally ill, poverty stricken, aging, addicted, delinquent, violent, unemployed, gay and lesbian, disabled, and racial minorities. They use helping strategies that lack the broad social acceptance of such professions as law and medicine. Lack of widespread acceptance or understanding of social work means that social workers are more subject to social policies that control, restrict, and regulate their practice. This lack of credibility leads funders and legislators to insist on careful documentation of their work, to place limits on the intensity or duration of their work with consumers, and to resist policies that stipulate advanced training to perform specific kinds of tasks.

Social workers often work with problems that are sufficiently complex that experts disagree about how best to address them. Drug addiction, alcoholism, serious mental disorders, juvenile delinquency, child abuse, and many similar problems are often caused by a variety of personal, familial, genetic, community, economic, cultural, and other factors. The sheer complexity of these problems invites controversy about how best to address them. Precisely because they are often caused by many factors, some of which the social worker may not be able to identify or address, tangible success may be difficult to achieve. Because of these difficulties that are intrinsic to their work, social workers often encounter suspicion, indifference, or hostility from funders, evaluators, taxpayers, and consumers.

Therefore, they need to develop positions on policy issues at numerous points in their work. In some cases, for example, they have conflicting allegiances that stem from their dual identification with high-level policies and with consumers. Should they heed high-level directives, even when they believe them to be misguided? They sometimes experience uncertainty that stems from an absence of articulated policy. In the instance of involuntary commitments to state institutions, for example, laws in many states specify that mental patients can be institutionalized only if they are a threat to the safety of others or to themselves. What set of actions or expressions indicates that a threat exists? Similarly, social workers must decide in child welfare agencies whether to recommend that children be removed from their natural homes in the absence of precise definitions of the level, duration, and kinds of abusive behavior that are needed to justify removal.

The intermediary position of social workers between government, society, and consumers leads to tension between obedience and reform. In the case of punitive, misdirected, or simplistic policies, they have to decide whether and when to assume professional and personal risks. When should they question policies? When should they encourage others to oppose disliked policies? When should they refuse to implement specific policies? These issues are difficult to resolve because they involve not only distant policy authorities but also colleagues and administrators in social agencies with whom they have frequent contact.

Even when they do not encounter tensions between societal policies and expectations and their own professional values, social workers must be alert to the subtle influence of societal prejudice on their own work. Perhaps a social worker believes that alcoholics should be able to control their condition, a belief that leads him or her to act in a punitive fashion toward this group. Perhaps a social worker unwittingly refers women to one set of job listings and men to other, more challenging positions. Or perhaps a social worker in the emergency room of a hospital gives more immediate and responsive treatment to children than to elderly persons. As these examples suggest, prejudices are not necessarily conscious.

Social workers have to decide whether, when, and how to support political candidates or social movements that address policy issues in the broader society. Do Democrats, Republicans, socialists, libertarians, or other political parties offer the best platforms for addressing social problems in the nation? What are the merits of specific reforms to help welfare, gay, African-American, Latino, female, and other populations? Is it appropriate to mobilize the clients or consumers of an agency to protest specific policies and, if so, under what circumstances?

Even the clinical or counseling work of social workers is enmeshed in policy considerations. Some social workers, perhaps aspiring to psychiatric status, base their counseling on Freudian and other theories that emphasize familial and intrapsychic phenomena. Counselors have to decide what causal factors undergird pathology; if they choose primarily intrapsychic ones, they risk repeating the simplistic approaches of moral-treatment reformers of the nineteenth century, who assumed that unemployment and other ills stemmed from character flaws. Counselors have to decide when "pathology" is pathology or when it represents a functional adaptation to an oppressive environment. If it is a functional adaptation, the counselor may wish not to change it. Social workers may decide in some cases to emphasize the provision of sur-vival skills to empower consumers to cope with adverse conditions, or they may act as advocates or help clients obtain assertiveness and political skills to become their own advocates.

Persons from low-income groups want and need tangible assistance, such as referrals, information, and survival strategies, but many of the nation's counselors and psychiatrists often emphasize the kind of talking therapies that have scant relevance to the economic problems of millions of Americans. Such class bias, though more subtle, is a modern version of the condescending assistance that was given to destitute persons by many volunteers in the charity organization societies of the nineteenth century.

The relevance of the five moral issues in social welfare policy to the professional practice of social workers may be illustrated by the example of the service strategy of a treatment center for victims of rape. The center is located in a major metropolitan hospital and is directed by a social worker who pioneered the development of services to victims of rape.

The staff perceives the problems of victims of rape to be complex rather than simple. Victims of rape traditionally received medical services when they were examined in emergency rooms, but this clinic also provides services to address a range of emotional, medical, legal, and social problems of rape victims. Feelings of powerlessness exacerbated recovery from the assault, so the staff assumes advocacy functions and links victims to self-help groups. The staff vigorously pursues compensatory strategies for victims of rape since they believe that victims of violent crimes need resources to help them obtain the range of services that are needed following this event. They lobbied state authorities to provide financial compensation to victims of rape. They sought funding for their center to allow them to provide sustained services to the women since they knew that the trauma often lingered for months or even years. The director has vigorously sought federal funding for homes of battered women since her interest in problems of rape led her to become an advocate for social programs for other victims of violence. She strongly disagrees with the contention of many conservatives that family services should be funded exclusively by local government or by charity.

The staff realized that some hospital personnel, police, judges, and attorneys possess punitive orientations toward victims of rape, such as the mistaken belief that victims usually cause their attacks by flirtatious behavior. They devoted considerable time to public education projects, to case advocacy, and to the securing of policy changes to diminish prejudice toward and punitive treatment of rape victims.

Perhaps more than other professions, then, social workers, whose work is affected at numerous points by policies of the welfare state and American orientations toward stigmatized groups, need to develop personal and professional positions on the five moral issues. These positions evolve into a *policy identity,* a set of explicit values and positions that shape one's selection or rejection of policy choices. A policy identity not only clarifies and unifies positions on the five moral issues but also helps social workers articulate strategies and interact with other professionals and staff within agencies and organizations. The social workers in our example had to contend with punitive positions of some hospital staff and members of the police department before reform had occurred in their policies.

The case of the rape center also suggests that a policy identity is linked to conceptions of the mission of the profession. The staff director contends that social workers should provide multifaceted services to all of their clients rather than focusing only on emotional components, including counseling, education, advocacy, environmental modification, provision of tangible assistance, referrals, self-help groups, and legal assistance. She also believes that social workers should place priority on assisting powerless and vulnerable populations that lack helpers and advocates in a society that has not been favorably disposed to them.

The preceding case example illustrates how the policy identity of the center's director influenced her choice of policies with respect to the five moral issues. But this example should not convey the misleading impression that social workers currently have, or have ever had, a consensus on the five moral issues. Indeed, professions can be conceptualized as coalitions of professionals whose members possess different skills, who advocate different kinds of policies, and who favor different models of practice. A dimension of professional practice consists of developing positions about the mission of one's profession as well as deciding whether to and how to participate in its internal politics.

The social work profession has mirrored divisions within the larger society in each historical era.[11] Since many social workers supported the moral screening and personal services of the charity organization society, they opposed efforts by Jane Addams and other reformers to establish mothers' pensions and other public programs during the progressive era. Although an accommodation was reached between the social reform and charity groups in the profession, considerable tension remained. Dissension existed within the profession about the propriety of supporting Theodore Roosevelt in the Bull Moose campaign of 1912, not only because he strongly advocated development of some national social welfare policies but also because some social workers feared that involvement in partisan politics would diminish their image as altruistic reformers. Divisions existed within the profession during the New Deal as well. Some social workers believed that Roosevelt had devised relatively conservative policies; others staunchly defended him, and a group of psychoanalytic professionals was hardly interested in the policy reforms of the decade. Similar divisions existed during the 1960s. Some social workers mobilized tenant, community, and welfare groups and participated in the civil rights movement, whereas others distantly observed the tumult of the decade from the havens of traditional agencies that provided services that were based on Freudian theories.

Internal struggles within the profession over its leadership and policies have occurred within the National Association of Social Workers, the Council of Social Work Education, agencies, and schools of social work. Professional counterparts to conservative, radical, and liberal ideologies exist. Some social workers are not interested in or even opposed to societal reforms because their models of practice give scant importance to societal factors in causing social problems. Other social workers, who believe that economic and social institutions of the nation must be reformed in order for social pathology to be reduced, want the profession to assume radical positions on social issues. A moderate group within the profession favors incremental additions to the welfare state, favors professional practice that attends to environmental and emotional aspects of pathology, and believes that social workers should assume service roles in a variety of established agencies.

The power of these various factions within the profession has varied in different periods. Not surprisingly, relatively conservative factions became more powerful during conservative eras such as the 1920s, 1950s, and 1980s. Freudian concepts and practice assumed considerable influence in the 1920s and 1950s, when many social workers emulated psychiatric models of practice. A private-practice movement gathered momentum in the 1980s; though much diversity existed in its ranks, many of its adherents favored entrepreneurial practice that emulated psychiatric practice, even if they did not fundamentally alter the curriculum of schools or the policy positions of national organizations like NASW. By contrast, relatively radical segments of the profession obtained visibility in the 1930s and 1960s, when they secured leadership positions in the profession, obtained macro additions to curriculum, and insisted that person-in-the-environment paradigms be retained.

The business of fashioning a policy identity is never completed since we encounter moral issues as citizens and professionals throughout our lives. New issues arise in different settings and eras, and positions that once seemed clear may become less clear. In some cases, our standpoints change as we are coopted into conventional ways of thinking by our position or status within the establishment or when we fear risks that accompany advocacy for powerless groups or unpopular causes.

Perhaps the personal challenge that each of us encounters is to develop core perspectives that provide guideposts for our personal and professional lives yet to remain open to divergent positions and new experiences. If so, the analysis of social welfare history becomes merely a first step in an ongoing process of moral definition.

# END NOTES

1. For a discussion of social movements, see Frances Piven and Richard Cloward, *Poor People's Movements: Why They Succeed and How They Fail* (New York: Vintage Books, 1979).

2. For a typology of conservatives, see James Reichley, *Conservatives in an Age of Change: The Nixon and Ford Administrations* (Washington, D.C.: Brookings Institution, 1981), pp. 22–41.

3. See Jane Addams, *Newer Ideals of Peace* (New York: Macmillan, 1907).

4. William Leuchtenberg, *A Troubled Feast: American Society Since 1945* (Boston: Little, Brown, 1979), pp. 27–28.

5. Sidney Fine, *Laissez-Faire and the General Welfare State: A Study of Conflict in America, 1865–1901*

(Ann Arbor: University of Michigan Press, 1956), pp. 96–125; David Brody, *Workers in Industrial America: Essays on the Twentieth-Century Struggle* (New York: Oxford University Press, 1980), pp. 48–81.

6. Herbert McClosky and John Zaller, *The American Ethos: Public Attitudes Toward Capitalism and Democracy* (Cambridge, Mass.: Harvard University Press, 1984), pp. 162, 291–292; Arthur M. Schlesinger, *The Cycles of History* (Boston: Houghton Mifflin, 1986), pp. 23–48.

7. Clarke Chambers, *Seedtime of Reform: American Social Service and Social Action, 1918–1933* (Minneapolis, Minn.: University of Minnesota Press, 1963), pp. 29–58, 153–182; Fine, *Laissez-Faire and the General Welfare State,* pp. 259–369.

8. Leuchtenberg, *A Troubled Feast,* pp. 88–91.

9. Everett Ladd, "The Reagan Phenomenon and Public Attitudes Toward Government." In Lester Salamon and Michael Lund, eds., *The Reagan Presidency and the Governing of America* (Washington, D.C.: Urban Institute, 1985), pp. 221–249.

10. David Stockman, *The Triumph of Politics: Why the Reagan Revolution Failed* (New York: Harper & Row, 1986), pp. 376–411.

11. For a discussion of the development of the profession, see Leslie Leighninger, *The Development of Social Work as a Profession, 1930–1960* (Westport, Conn.: Greenwood, 1986).

# Name Index

## A

Aaron, Henry, 240nn: 31, 32, 39; 242n91, 339n21

Abramovitz, Mimi, 146nn: 98–101; 197nn: 24, 25; 198nn: 80–82

Acuna, Rudolpho, 108n13, 146n88

Adams, Henry, 167n42, 168nn: 56, 66, 83; 196nn: 2, 3; 197nn: 38, 39

Addams, Jane, 144nn: 20–22; 145n66, 355n3

Ambrose, Stephen, 239n11, 241n74

Amussen, Susan, 35nn: 66, 70

Anderson, Martin, 312nn: 15, 26; 313n68

Appleby, Joyce, 34nn: 26, 27, 37, 44, 45, 51, 56; 35n60, 58nn: 4, 7, 15; 59n22, 60n100, 83n58, 339n7

Applewhite, Harriet, 59n55, 60n70

Axinn, June, 60n68, 83nn: 31, 43; 339nn: 16, 19; 340nn: 29, 31

## B

Bailey, Stephen, 239n3

Bailyn, Bernard, 34nn: 24, 42; 58nn: 6, 7, 12, 13; 60n93, 339n10

Barker, Michael, 83n69

Barnes, John, 340n35

Barrett, Laurence, 312nn: 23, 25, 34, 47; 313nn: 59, 60, 64, 79, 83, 84; 314n97

Bass, Scott, 315n139

Baugh, Daniel, 34nn: 22, 30, 31; 35nn: 59, 61

Bawden, D. Lee, 240n20, 269n27, 270n35, 271n100, 272n109

Baxter, Stephen, 34nn: 22, 49

Beard, Charles, 144n24

Beasley, Maurine, 167nn: 27, 40; 168nn: 49, 50, 59, 76

Bell, Leland, 240n23, 271n69

Bell, Winifred, 197nn: 31, 32; 199n101; 240n18

Bennett, Judith, 35n69

Berkhofer, Robert, 108nn: 11, 17

Bernstein, Barton, 239nn: 6, 8

Bernstein, Blanche, 272n109

Berthoff, Rowland, 82nn: 12, 19

Binstock, Robert, 315nn: 139, 141

Birnbaum, Jeffrey, 314n103

Biskupic, Joan, 315n145

Bloom, Bernard, 240n22, 241n59

Blumenthal, Sidney, 314n105

Boll, Michael, 242n106, 272n129

Boorstin, Daniel, 81n2

Bornet, Vaughn, 241n68, 242nn: 92, 93

Boswell, John, 35nn: 80, 82

Bowe, Frank, 240n24, 270n48, 271n69

Boyer, Paul, 82nn: 6, 15, 18, 20; 83nn: 32, 34, 46, 48; 109nn: 60, 67; 145n61, 340n26

Brauer, Carl, 241nn: 46, 47

Bremer, Francis, 34n43; 58nn: 1, 2, 3; 59n33

Bremer, William, 167nn: 15, 22, 42; 168nn: 54, 55, 82; 196nn: 9, 10; 197nn: 20, 27, 28, 41; 199nn: 93, 94, 96, 98

Bremner, Robert, 60nn: 65–67, 74

Breul, Frank, 143n12

Brinkley, Alan, 196nn: 4, 5; 197nn: 13, 14

Broder, David, 311n7, 312nn: 37, 44

Brody, David, 109n61, 143nn: 2, 7, 11; 144n35, 145nn: 67–71; 166n5, 167nn: 37–39, 168n48, 197n37, 340nn: 25, 38; 356n5

Brown, Josephine, 168n57, 197nn: 28, 30

Brown, Richard, 34n39, 59n29

Buenker, John, 145n59

Burke, Vincent, 240n34, 242nn: 97, 103; 243n163, 269nn: 21, 25, 26

Burrows, James, 147nn: 119, 120

Burt, Martha, 315nn: 142, 143

Bushman, Richard, 82n7, 109n63

Butler, Amy, 315n150

## C

Califano, Joseph, 241n65; 242nn: 104, 108–111, 117; 270n49, 271nn: 77, 79, 81–83, 92, 96, 97, 101–103; 313n90

Campbell, Colin, 314nn: 109, 110, 111, 112

Cannon, Lou, 312nn: 21, 22, 27, 29, 39, 41, 56; 313n65, 314n107

# Subject Index

## A

abolitionists, 79, 95, 97, 101
abortion, 230, 261, 276, 303, 304, 308
Acheson, Dean, 203
Acquired Immune Deficiency Syndrome, 1, 289, 300, 301, 302, 330, 344
Adams, Abigail, 47
Adams, John, 41
Addams, Jane
  orientations toward minorities, 133
  policy orientations of, 117, 118, 128–130, 138, 139
  popularity of, 128
  resilience of, 136–137
  role in Progressive Party, 127–130
Adoption Assistance and Child Welfare Act, 260, 266, 305, 308
adoptions, 260, 305
adoption subsidies, 260
AFDC (*see* Aid to Families with Dependent Children)
AFDC-U, 248
affirmative action, 226, 231, 252–254, 260, 268, 285, 292, 308
African Americans
  in colonial era, 44–46
  in nineteenth century, 93–101
  in progressive era, 131–133
  in New Deal, 185–187
  in 1940s and 1950s, 187, 203–206

in 1960s, 209–212, 216–218, 225–226
in 1970s, 252–254, 265–267
in 1980s and 1990s, 298–300
Age Discrimination Act, 267
Agricultural Adjustment Agency, 164, 170, 172, 186
Aid to the Blind, 175, 184, 249
Aid to Dependent Children, 175, 178, 184, 188
Aid to the Disabled, 184, 249
Aid to Families with Dependent Children
  arbitrariness of administration, 206
  as part of safety net, 262–264
  eroding benefits of, 285, 304–306
  inclusion of adult caregiver, 175
  1967 amendments to, 222, 223
  Reagan reforms of, 285, 304–306
  relationship to Medicaid, 219
  relationship to welfare reform, 248–252
  service amendments to, 213
  work incentives, 222, 223, 293
AIDS (*see* Acquired Immune Deficiency Syndrome)
Alamo, 89
alcoholism, 52, 66, 68–70
almshouses (*see* poor houses)
Altmeyer, Arthur, 174
Alzheimer's disease, 306
American Association of Retired Persons, 266, 267, 306

American Association of Social Workers, 192
American Civil Liberties Union, 232
American Coalition of Citizens with Disabilities, 266
American Enterprise Institute, 276
American Federation of Labor, 126, 127, 156, 157, 184
American Freedmen's Inquiry Commission, 97
American Medical Association, 141, 212, 219
American Psychiatric Association, 233
Americans with Disabilities Act, 303
American Revolution, 50, 51
American Sunday School Union, 71, 72
American Temperance Society, 71, 72
American Women's Suffrage Association, 101
Anderson, Martin, 256, 276
antilynching legislation, 181
antipauperism, 70–72
antisemitism, 32
apprenticeship, 41, 42
Aquinas, Thomas, 18
Architecture and Transportation Compliance Board, 260
Area Agencies on Aging, 220
Area Redevelopment Agency, 213
Asian Americans (*see also* Chinese Americans, Japanese Americans, Vietnamese immigrants)